Chevrolet Astro & GMC Safari Mini-vans Automotive Repair Manual

by Ken Freund and John H Haynes

Member of the Guild of Motoring Writers

Models covered:
Chevrolet Astro and GMC Safari mini-vans
1985 thru 1993
Does not include All-Wheel Drive information

(9X10 – 1477)

ABCDE
FGHIJ
KLM
2

Haynes Publishing Group
Sparkford Nr Yeovil
Somerset BA22 7JJ England

Haynes North America, Inc.
861 Lawrence Drive
Newbury Park
California 91320 USA

Acknowledgements

We are grateful for the help and cooperation of the General Motors Corporation for their assistance with technical information, certain illustrations and vehicle photos, and the Champion Spark Plug Company, who supplied the illustrations of various spark plug conditions.

© Haynes North America, Inc. 1988, 1990, 1991, 1993

With permission from J.H. Haynes & Co. Ltd.

A book in the **Haynes Automotive Repair Manual Series**

Printed in the USA

ISBN 1 56392 077 8

Library of Congress Catalog Card Number 93-78151

Portions of materials contained herein have been reprinted with permission of General Motors Corporation, Service Technology Group

Contents

Chevrolet Astro mini-van

About this manual

Its purpose

The purpose of this manual is to help you get the best value from your vehicle. It can do so in several ways. It can help you decide what work must be done, even if you choose to have it done by a dealer service department or a repair shop; it provides information and procedures for routine maintenance and servicing; and it offers diagnostic and repair procedures to follow when trouble occurs.

It is hoped that you will use the manual to tackle the work yourself. For many simpler jobs, doing it yourself may be quicker than arranging an appointment to get the vehicle into a shop and making the trips to leave it and pick it up. More importantly, a lot of money can be saved by avoiding the expense the shop must pass on to you to cover its labor and overhead costs. An added benefit is the sense of satisfaction and accomplishment that you feel after having done the job yourself.

Using the manual

The manual is divided into Chapters. Each Chapter is divided into numbered Sections, which are headed in bold type between horizontal lines. Each Section consists of consecutively numbered paragraphs.

At the beginning of each numbered section you will be referred to any illustrations which apply to the procedures in that section. The reference numbers used in illustration captions pinpoint the pertinent Section and the Step within that section. That is, illustration 3.2 means the illustration refers to Section 3 and Step (or paragraph) 2 within that Section.

Procedures, once described in the text, are not normally repeated. When it is necessary to refer to another Chapter, the reference will be given as Chapter and Section number i.e. Chapter 1/16). Cross references given without use of the word ''Chapter'' apply to Sections and/or paragraphs in the same Chapter. For example, ''see Section 8'' means in the same Chapter.

Reference to the left or right side of the vehicle is based on the assumption that one is sitting in the driver's seat, facing forward.

Even though extreme care has been taken during the preparation of this manual, neither the publisher nor the author can accept responsibility for any errors in, or omissions from, the information given.

NOTE

A **Note** provides information necessary to properly complete a procedure or information which will make the steps to be followed easier to understand.

CAUTION

A **Caution** indicates a special procedure or special steps which must be taken in the course of completing the procedure in which the **Caution** is found which are necessary to avoid damage to the assembly being worked on.

WARNING

A **Warning** indicates a special procedure or special steps which must be taken in the course of completing the procedure in which the **Warning** is found which are necessary to avoid injury to the person performing the procedure.

Introduction to the Chevrolet Astro and GMC Safari

Chevrolet and GMC mini-vans are conventional front engine/rear wheel drive layout.

Inline four-cylinder and V6 engines are used for power, with fuel injection available on later models.

Power from the engine is transferred to either a four or five-speed manual or a four-speed automatic transmission.

Suspension is independent at the front with A-frames and coil springs. The rear suspension on all models consists of longitudinal composite fiberglass leaf springs.

The steering box is mounted to the left of the engine and is connected to the steering arms through a series of rods with power assist available as an option.

The brakes are power assisted disc-type at the front and self-adjusting drums at the rear.

Vehicle identification numbers

Modifications are a continuing and unpublicized process in vehicle manufacturing. Since spare parts manuals and lists are compiled on a numerical basis, the individual vehicle numbers are essential to correctly identify the component required.

Vehicle Identification Number (VIN)

This very important identification number is located on a plate attached to the driver's side cowling just inside the windshield (see illustration). The VIN also appears on the Vehicle Certificate of Title and Registration. It contains information such as where and when the vehicle was manufactured, the model year and the body style.

Service parts identification label

This label is located inside the glove compartment and should always be referred to when ordering parts. The vehicle Service parts identification label contains the VIN, wheelbase, paint and special equipment and option codes (see illustration).

Engine code numbers

The engine code numbers can be found in a variety of locations, depending on engine type.

On the four-cylinder engine, the engine code number is found on a pad located on the left side of the block, to the rear of the exhaust manifold.

On the V6 engine, the code number is located on a pad at the front edge of the block, under the right cylinder head, adjacent to the water pump (see illustrations).

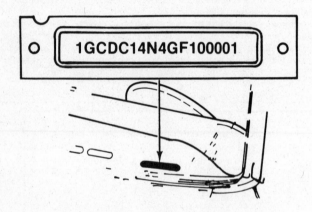

The Vehicle Identification Number (VIN) is visible on the driver's side cowling inside the windshield

The Service parts identification label is found in the glove compartment and contains information important when ordering parts

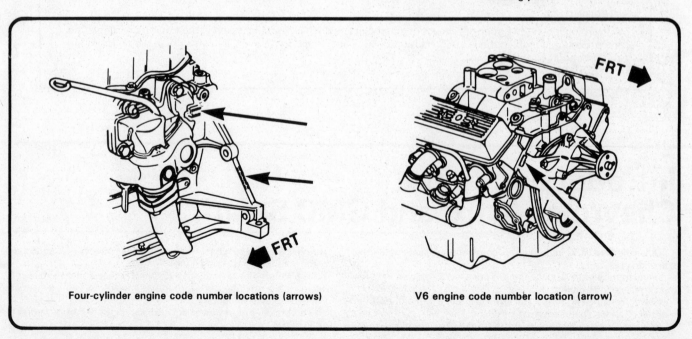

Four-cylinder engine code number locations (arrows)

V6 engine code number location (arrow)

Buying parts

Replacement parts are available from many sources, which generally fall into one of two categories – authorized dealer parts departments and independent retail auto parts stores. Our advice concerning these parts is as follows:

Retail auto parts stores: Good auto parts stores will stock frequently needed components which wear out relatively fast, such as clutch components, exhaust systems, brake parts, tune-up parts, etc. These stores often supply new or reconditioned parts on an exchange basis, which can save a considerable amount of money. Discount auto parts stores are often very good places to buy materials and parts needed for general vehicle maintenance such as oil, grease, filters, spark plugs, belts, touch-up paint, bulbs, etc. They also usually sell tools and general accessories, have convenient hours, charge lower prices and can often be found not far from home.

Authorized dealer parts department: This is the best source for parts which are unique to the vehicle and not generally available elsewhere (such as major engine parts, transmission parts, trim pieces, etc.).

Warranty information: If the vehicle is still covered under warranty, be sure that any replacement parts purchased – regardless of the source – do not invalidate the warranty!

To be sure of obtaining the correct parts, have engine and chassis numbers available and, if possible, take the old parts along for positive identification.

Maintenance techniques, tools and working facilities

Maintenance techniques

There are a number of techniques involved in maintenance and repair that will be referred to throughout this manual. Application of these techniques will enable the home mechanic to be more efficient, better organized and capable of performing the various tasks properly, which will ensure that the repair job is thorough and complete.

Fasteners

Fasteners are nuts, bolts, studs and screws used to hold two or more parts together. There are a few things to keep in mind when working with fasteners. Almost all of them use a locking device of some type, either a lockwasher, locknut, locking tab or thread adhesive. All threaded fasteners should be clean and straight, with undamaged threads and undamaged corners on the hex head where the wrench fits. Develop the habit of replacing all damaged nuts and bolts with new ones. Special locknuts with nylon or fiber inserts can only be used once. If they are removed, they lose their locking ability and must be replaced with new ones.

Rusted nuts and bolts should be treated with a penetrating fluid to ease removal and prevent breakage. Some mechanics use turpentine in a spout-type oil can, which works quite well. After applying the rust penetrant, let it work for a few minutes before trying to loosen the nut or bolt. Badly rusted fasteners may have to be chiseled or sawed off or removed with a special nut breaker, available at tool stores.

If a bolt or stud breaks off in an assembly, it can be drilled and removed with a special tool commonly available for this purpose. Most automotive machine shops can perform this task, as well as other repair procedures, such as the repair of threaded holes that have been stripped out.

Flat washers and lockwashers, when removed from an assembly, should always be replaced exactly as removed. Replace any damaged washers with new ones. Never use a lockwasher on any soft metal surface (such as aluminum), thin sheet metal or plastic.

Fastener sizes

For a number of reasons, automobile manufacturers are making wider and wider use of metric fasteners. Therefore, it is important to be able to tell the difference between standard (sometimes called U.S. or SAE) and metric hardware, since they cannot be interchanged.

All bolts, whether standard or metric, are sized according to diameter, thread pitch and length. For example, a standard 1/2 — 13 x 1 bolt is 1/2 inch in diameter, has 13 threads per inch and is 1 inch long. An M12 — 1.75 x 25 metric bolt is 12 mm in diameter, has a thread pitch of 1.75 mm (the distance between threads) and is 25 mm long. The two bolts are nearly identical, and easily confused, but they are not interchangeable.

In addition to the differences in diameter, thread pitch and length, metric and standard bolts can also be distinguished by examining the bolt heads. To begin with, the distance across the flats on a standard bolt head is measured in inches, while the same dimension on a metric bolt is sized in millimeters (the same is true for nuts). As a result, a standard wrench should not be used on a metric bolt and a metric wrench should not be used on a standard bolt. Also, most standard bolts have slashes radiating out from the center of the head to denote the grade or strength of the bolt, which is an indication of the amount of torque that can be applied to it. The greater the number of slashes, the greater the strength of the bolt. Grades 0 through 5 are commonly used on automobiles. Metric bolts have a property class (grade) number, rather than a slash, molded into their heads to indicate bolt strength. In this case, the higher the number, the stronger the bolt. Property class numbers 8.8, 9.8 and 10.9 are commonly used on automobiles.

Strength markings can also be used to distinguish standard hex nuts from metric hex nuts. Many standard nuts have dots stamped into one side, while metric nuts are marked with a number. The greater the number of dots, or the higher the number, the greater the strength of the nut.

Metric studs are also marked on their ends according to property class (grade). Larger studs are numbered (the same as metric bolts),

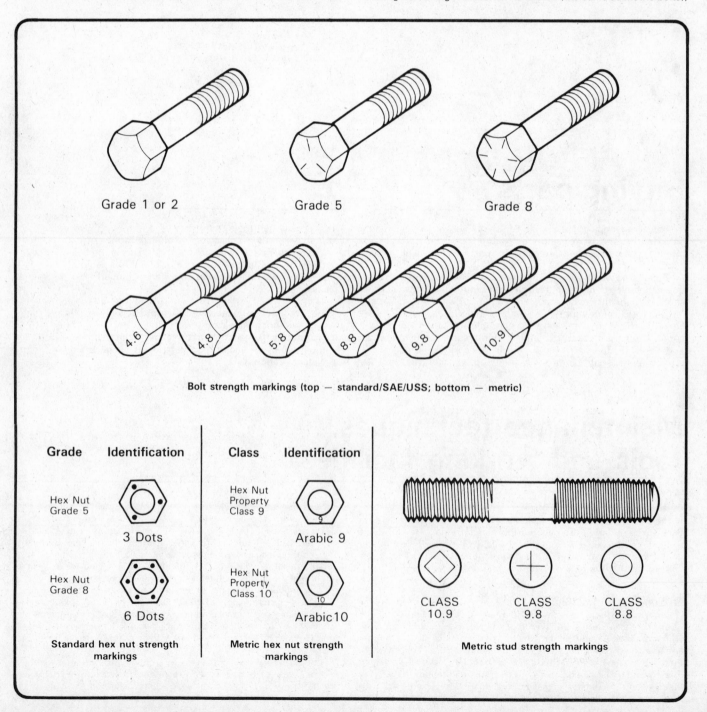

Bolt strength markings (top — standard/SAE/USS; bottom — metric)

Grade	Identification	Class	Identification
Hex Nut Grade 5	3 Dots	Hex Nut Property Class 9	Arabic 9
Hex Nut Grade 8	6 Dots	Hex Nut Property Class 10	Arabic 10

Standard hex nut strength markings

Metric hex nut strength markings

CLASS 10.9   CLASS 9.8   CLASS 8.8

Metric stud strength markings

while smaller studs carry a geometric code to denote grade.

It should be noted that many fasteners, especially Grades 0 through 2, have no distinguishing marks on them. When such is the case, the only way to determine whether it is standard or metric is to measure the thread pitch or compare it to a known fastener of the same size.

Standard fasteners are often referred to as SAE, as opposed to metric. However, it should be noted that SAE technically refers to a non-metric *fine thread* fastener only. Coarse thread non-metric fasteners are referred to as USS sizes.

Since fasteners of the same size (both standard and metric) may have different strength ratings, be sure to reinstall any bolts, studs or nuts removed from your vehicle in their original locations. Also, when replacing a fastener with a new one, make sure that the new one has a strength rating equal to or greater than the original.

Tightening sequences and procedures

Most threaded fasteners should be tightened to a specific torque value (torque is the twisting force applied to a threaded component such as a nut or bolt). Overtightening the fastener can weaken it and cause it to break, while undertightening can cause it to eventually come loose. Bolts, screws and studs, depending on the material they are made of and their thread diameters, have specific torque values, many of which are noted in the Specifications at the beginning of each Chapter. Be sure to follow the torque recommendations closely. For fasteners not assigned a specific torque, a general torque value chart is presented here as a guide. These torque values are for dry (unlubricated) fasteners threaded into steel or cast iron (not aluminum). As was previously mentioned, the size and grade of a fastener determine the amount of torque that can safely be applied to it. The figures listed here are approximate

Metric thread sizes	Ft-lb	Nm/m
M-6	6 to 9	9 to 12
M-8	14 to 21	19 to 28
M-10	28 to 40	38 to 54
M-12	50 to 71	68 to 96
M-14	80 to 140	109 to 154
Pipe thread sizes		
1/8	5 to 8	7 to 10
1/4	12 to 18	17 to 24
3/8	22 to 33	30 to 44
1/2	25 to 35	34 to 47
U.S. thread sizes		
1/4 — 20	6 to 9	9 to 12
5/16 — 18	12 to 18	17 to 24
5/16 — 24	14 to 20	19 to 27
3/8 — 16	22 to 32	30 to 43
3/8 — 24	27 to 38	37 to 51
7/16 — 14	40 to 55	55 to 74
7/16 — 20	40 to 60	55 to 81
1/2 — 13	55 to 80	75 to 108

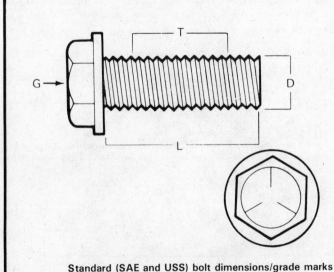

Standard (SAE and USS) bolt dimensions/grade marks

G   Grade marks (bolt strength)
L   Length (in inches)
T   Thread pitch (number of threads per inch)
D   Nominal diameter (in inches)

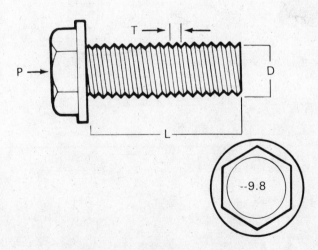

Metric bolt dimensions/grade marks

P   Property class (bolt strength)
L   Length (in millimeters)
T   Thread pitch (distance between threads in millimeters)
D   Diameter

for Grade 2 and Grade 3 fasteners. Higher grades can tolerate higher torque values.

Fasteners laid out in a pattern, such as cylinder head bolts, oil pan bolts, differential cover bolts, etc., must be loosened or tightened in sequence to avoid warping the component. This sequence will normally be shown in the appropriate Chapter. If a specific pattern is not given, the following procedures can be used to prevent warping.

Initially, the bolts or nuts should be assembled finger-tight only. Next, they should be tightened one full turn each, in a criss-cross or diagonal pattern. After each one has been tightened one full turn, return to the first one and tighten them all one-half turn, following the same pattern. Finally, tighten each of them one-quarter turn at a time until each fastener has been tightened to the proper torque. To loosen and remove the fasteners, the procedure would be reversed.

Component disassembly

Component disassembly should be done with care and purpose to help ensure that the parts go back together properly. Always keep track of the sequence in which parts are removed. Make note of special characteristics or marks on parts that can be installed more than one way, such as a grooved thrust washer on a shaft. It is a good idea to lay the disassembled parts out on a clean surface in the order that they were removed. It may also be helpful to make sketches or take instant photos of components before removal.

When removing fasteners from a component, keep track of their locations. Sometimes threading a bolt back in a part, or putting the washers and nut back on a stud, can prevent mix-ups later. If nuts and bolts cannot be returned to their original locations, they should be kept in a compartmented box or a series of small boxes. A cupcake or muffin tin is ideal for this purpose, since each cavity can hold the bolts and nuts from a particular area (i.e. oil pan bolts, valve cover bolts, engine mount bolts, etc.). A pan of this type is especially helpful when working on assemblies with very small parts, such as the carburetor, alternator, valve train or interior dash and trim pieces. The cavities can be marked with paint or tape to identify the contents.

Whenever wiring looms, harnesses or connectors are separated, it is a good idea to identify the two halves with numbered pieces of masking tape so they can be easily reconnected.

Gasket sealing surfaces

Throughout any vehicle, gaskets are used to seal the mating surfaces between two parts and keep lubricants, fluids, vacuum or pressure contained in an assembly.

Many times these gaskets are coated with a liquid or paste-type gasket sealing compound before assembly. Age, heat and pressure can sometimes cause the two parts to stick together so tightly that they are very difficult to separate. Often, the assembly can be loosened by striking it with a soft-face hammer near the mating surfaces. A regular hammer can be used if a block of wood is placed between the hammer and the part. Do not hammer on cast parts or parts that could be easily damaged. With any particularly stubborn part, always recheck to make sure that every fastener has been removed.

Avoid using a screwdriver or bar to pry apart an assembly, as they can easily mar the gasket sealing surfaces of the parts, which must remain smooth. If prying is absolutely necessary, use an old broom handle, but keep in mind that extra clean up will be necessary if the wood splinters.

After the parts are separated, the old gasket must be carefully scraped off and the gasket surfaces cleaned. Stubborn gasket material can be soaked with rust penetrant or treated with a special chemical to soften it so it can be easily scraped off. A scraper can be fashioned from a piece of copper tubing by flattening and sharpening one end. Copper is recommended because it is usually softer than the surfaces to be scraped, which reduces the chance of gouging the part. Some gaskets can be removed with a wire brush, but regardless of the method used, the mating surfaces must be left clean and smooth. If for some reason the gasket surface is gouged, then a gasket sealer thick enough to fill scratches will have to be used during reassembly of the components. For most applications, a non-drying (or semi-drying) gasket sealer should be used.

Hose removal tips

Warning: *If the vehicle is equipped with air conditioning, don't disconnect any of the A/C hoses unless the system has been depressurized by a dealer service department, repair shop or service station.*

Hose removal precautions closely parallel gasket removal precautions. Avoid scratching or gouging the surface that the hose mates against or the connection may leak. This is especially true for radiator hoses. Because of various chemical reactions, the rubber in hoses can bond itself to the metal spigot that the hose fits over. To remove a hose, first loosen the hose clamps that secure it to the spigot. Then, with slip-joint pliers, grab the hose at the clamp and rotate it around the spigot. Work it back and forth until it is completely free, then pull it off. Silicone or other lubricants will ease removal if they can be applied between the hose and the outside of the spigot. Apply the same lubricant to the inside of the hose and the outside of the spigot to simplify installation.

As a last resort (and if the hose is to be replaced with a new one anyway), the rubber can be slit with a knife and the hose peeled from the spigot. If this must be done, be careful that the metal connection is not damaged.

If a hose clamp is broken or damaged, do not reuse it. Wire-type clamps usually weaken with age, so it is a good idea to replace them with screw-type clamps whenever a hose is removed.

Tools

A selection of good tools is a basic requirement for anyone who plans to maintain and repair his or her own vehicle. For the owner who has few tools, the initial investment might seem high, but when compared to the spiraling costs of professional auto maintenance and repair, it is a wise one.

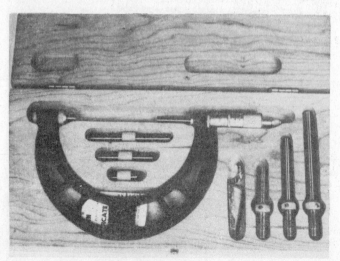

Micrometer set

Dial indicator set

Dial caliper

Hand-operated vacuum pump

Timing light

Compression gauge with spark plug hole adapter

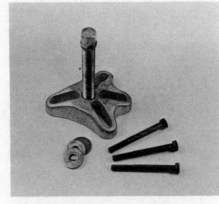

Damper/steering wheel puller

General purpose puller

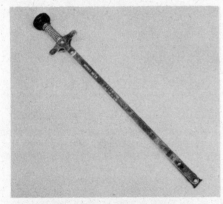

Hydraulic lifter removal tool

Valve spring compressor

Valve spring compressor

Ridge reamer

Piston ring groove cleaning tool

Ring removal/installation tool

Ring compressor

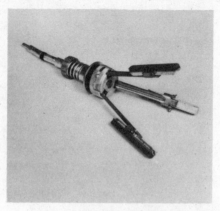

Cylinder hone

Brake hold-down spring tool

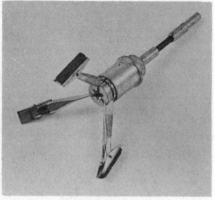

Brake cylinder hone

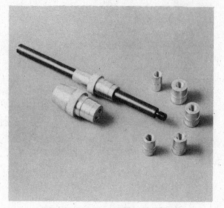

Clutch plate alignment tool

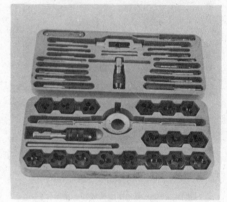

Tap and die set

To help the owner decide which tools are needed to perform the tasks detailed in this manual, the following tool lists are offered: *Maintenance and minor repair, Repair/overhaul* and *Special*.

The newcomer to practical mechanics should start off with the maintenance and minor repair tool kit, which is adequate for the simpler jobs performed on a vehicle. Then, as confidence and experience grow, the owner can tackle more difficult tasks, buying additional tools as they are needed. Eventually the basic kit will be expanded into the repair and overhaul tool set. Over a period of time, the experienced do-it-yourselfer will assemble a tool set complete enough for most repair and overhaul procedures and will add tools from the special category when it is felt that the expense is justified by the frequency of use.

Maintenance and minor repair tool kit

The tools in this list should be considered the minimum required for performance of routine maintenance, servicing and minor repair work. We recommend the purchase of combination wrenches (box-end and open-end combined in one wrench). While more expensive than open end wrenches, they offer the advantages of both types of wrench.

Combination wrench set (1/4-inch to 1 inch or 6 mm to 19 mm)
Adjustable wrench, 8 inch
Spark plug wrench with rubber insert
Spark plug gap adjusting tool
Feeler gauge set
Brake bleeder wrench
Standard screwdriver (5/16-inch x 6 inch)
Phillips screwdriver (No. 2 x 6 inch)
Combination pliers — 6 inch
Hacksaw and assortment of blades
Tire pressure gauge
Grease gun
Oil can
Fine emery cloth
Wire brush

Battery post and cable cleaning tool
Oil filter wrench
Funnel (medium size)
Safety goggles
Jackstands (2)
Drain pan

Note: *If basic tune-ups are going to be part of routine maintenance, it will be necessary to purchase a good quality stroboscopic timing light and combination tachometer/dwell meter. Although they are included in the list of special tools, it is mentioned here because they are absolutely necessary for tuning most vehicles properly.*

Repair and overhaul tool set

These tools are essential for anyone who plans to perform major repairs and are in addition to those in the maintenance and minor repair tool kit. Included is a comprehensive set of sockets which, though expensive, are invaluable because of their versatility, especially when various extensions and drives are available. We recommend the 1/2-inch drive over the 3/8-inch drive. Although the larger drive is bulky and more expensive, it has the capacity of accepting a very wide range of large sockets. Ideally, however, the mechanic should have a 3/8-inch drive set and a 1/2-inch drive set.

Socket set(s)
Reversible ratchet
Extension — 10 inch
Universal joint
Torque wrench (same size drive as sockets)
Ball peen hammer — 8 ounce
Soft-face hammer (plastic/rubber)
Standard screwdriver (1/4-inch x 6 inch)
Standard screwdriver (stubby — 5/16-inch)
Phillips screwdriver (No. 3 x 8 inch)
Phillips screwdriver (stubby — No. 2)

Pliers — vise grip
Pliers — lineman's
Pliers — needle nose
Pliers — snap-ring (internal and external)
Cold chisel — 1/2-inch
Scribe
Scraper (made from flattened copper tubing)
Centerpunch
Pin punches (1/16, 1/8, 3/16-inch)
Steel rule/straightedge — 12 inch
Allen wrench set (1/8 to 3/8-inch or 4 mm to 10 mm)
A selection of files
Wire brush (large)
Jackstands (second set)
Jack (scissor or hydraulic type)

Note: *Another tool which is often useful is an electric drill motor with a chuck capacity of 3/8-inch and a set of good quality drill bits.*

Special tools

The tools in this list include those which are not used regularly, are expensive to buy, or which need to be used in accordance with their manufacturer's instructions. Unless these tools will be used frequently, it is not very economical to purchase many of them. A consideration would be to split the cost and use between yourself and a friend or friends. In addition, most of these tools can be obtained from a tool rental shop on a temporary basis.

This list primarily contains only those tools and instruments widely available to the public, and not those special tools produced by the vehicle manufacturer for distribution to dealer service departments. Occasionally, references to the manufacturer's special tools are inluded in the text of this manual. Generally, an alternative method of doing the job without the special tool is offered. However, sometimes there is no alternative to their use. Where this is the case, and the tool cannot be purchased or borrowed, the work should be turned over to the dealer service department or an automotive repair shop.

Valve spring compressor
Piston ring groove cleaning tool
Piston ring compressor
Piston ring installation tool
Cylinder compression gauge
Cylinder ridge reamer
Cylinder surfacing hone
Cylinder bore gauge
Micrometers and/or dial calipers
Hydraulic lifter removal tool
Balljoint separator
Universal-type puller
Impact screwdriver
Dial indicator set
Stroboscopic timing light (inductive pick-up)
Hand operated vacuum/pressure pump
Tachometer/dwell meter
Universal electrical multimeter
Cable hoist
Brake spring removal and installation tools
Floor jack

Buying tools

For the do-it-yourselfer who is just starting to get involved in vehicle maintenance and repair, there are a number of options available when purchasing tools. If maintenance and minor repair is the extent of the work to be done, the purchase of individual tools is satisfactory. If,

on the other hand, extensive work is planned, it would be a good idea to purchase a modest tool set from one of the large retail chain stores. A set can usually be bought at a substantial savings over the individual tool prices, and they often come with a tool box. As additional tools are needed, add-on sets, individual tools and a larger tool box can be purchased to expand the tool selection. Building a tool set gradually allows the cost of the tools to be spread over a longer period of time and gives the mechanic the freedom to choose only those tools that will actually be used.

Tool stores will often be the only source of some of the special tools that are needed, but regardless of where tools are bought, try to avoid cheap ones, especially when buying screwdrivers and sockets, because they won't last very long. The expense involved in replacing cheap tools will eventually be greater than the initial cost of quality tools.

Care and maintenance of tools

Good tools are expensive, so it makes sense to treat them with respect. Keep them clean and in usable condition and store them properly when not in use. Always wipe off any dirt, grease or metal chips before putting them away. Never leave tools lying around in the work area. Upon completion of a job, always check closely under the hood for tools that may have been left there so they won't get lost during a test drive.

Some tools, such as screwdrivers, pliers, wrenches and sockets, can be hung on a panel mounted on the garage or workshop wall, while others should be kept in a tool box or tray. Measuring instruments, gauges, meters, etc. must be carefully stored where they cannot be damaged by weather or impact from other tools.

When tools are used with care and stored properly, they will last a very long time. Even with the best of care, though, tools will wear out if used frequently. When a tool is damaged or worn out, replace it. Subsequent jobs will be safer and more enjoyable if you do.

Working facilities

Not to be overlooked when discussing tools is the workshop. If anything more than routine maintenance is to be carried out, some sort of suitable work area is essential.

It is understood, and appreciated, that many home mechanics do not have a good workshop or garage available, and end up removing an engine or doing major repairs outside. It is recommended, however, that the overhaul or repair be completed under the cover of a roof.

A clean, flat workbench or table of comfortable working height is an absolute necessity. The workbench should be equipped with a vise that has a jaw opening of at least four inches.

As mentioned previously, some clean, dry storage space is also required for tools, as well as the lubricants, fluids, cleaning solvents, etc. which will soon become necessary.

Sometimes waste oil and fluids, drained from the engine or cooling system during normal maintenance or repairs, present a disposal problem. To avoid pouring them on the ground or into a sewage system, pour the used fluids into large containers, seal them with caps and take them to an authorized disposal site or recycling center. Plastic jugs, such as old antifreeze containers, are ideal for this purpose.

Always keep a supply of old newspapers and clean rags available. Old towels are excellent for mopping up spills. Many mechanics use rolls of paper towels for most work because they are readily available and disposable. To help keep the area under the vehicle clean, a large cardboard box can be cut open and flattened to protect the garage or shop floor.

Whenever working over a painted surface, such as when leaning over a fender to service something under the hood, always cover it with an old blanket or bedspread to protect the finish. Vinyl covered pads, made especially for this purpose, are available at auto parts stores.

Booster battery (jump) starting

Certain precautions must be observed when using a booster battery to start a vehicle.

a) Before connecting the booster battery, make sure the ignition switch is in the Off position.

b) Turn off the lights, heater and other electrical loads.

c) Your eyes should be shielded. Safety goggles are a good idea.

d) Make sure the booster battery is the same voltage as the dead one in the vehicle.

e) The two vehicles MUST NOT TOUCH each other!

f) Make sure the transmission is in Neutral (manual) or Park (automatic).

g) If the booster battery is not a maintenance-free type, remove the vent caps and lay a cloth over the vent holes.

Connect the red jumper cable to the *positive* (+) terminals of each battery.

Connect one end of the black jumper cable to the *negative* (–) terminal of the booster battery. The other end of this cable should be connected to a good ground on the vehicle to be started, such as a bolt or bracket on the engine block **(see illustration)**. Use caution to ensure that the cable will not come into contact with the fan, drivebelts or other moving parts of the engine.

Start the engine using the booster battery, then, with the engine running at idle speed, disconnect the jumper cables in the reverse order of connection.

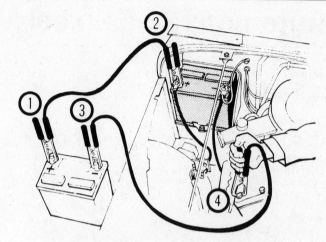

Make the booster battery cable connections in the numerical order shown (note that the negative cable of the booster battery is NOT attached to the negative terminal of the dead battery)

Jacking and towing

Jacking

The jack supplied with the vehicle should only be used for raising the vehicle when changing a tire or placing jackstands under the frame. **Warning:** *Never work under the vehicle or start the engine while this jack is being used as the only means of support.*

The vehicle should be on level ground with the wheels blocked and the transmission in Park (automatic) or Reverse (manual). If the wheel is being replaced, loosen the wheel lug nuts one-half turn and leave them in place until the wheel is raised off the ground.

Place the jack under the vehicle suspension in the indicated position **(see illustration)**. Operate the jack with a slow, smooth motion until

the wheel is raised off the ground. Remove the tire and install the spare. Tighten the lug nuts until they're snug, but wait until the vehicle is lowered to use the wrench.

Lower the vehicle, remove the jack and tighten the nuts (if loosened or removed) in a criss-cross pattern.

Towing

The manufacturer does not recommend towing with all four wheels on the ground. Towing should therefore be left to a dealer or professional towing service.

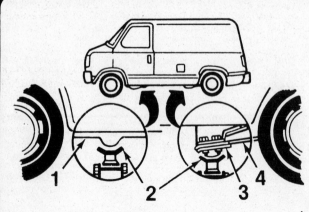

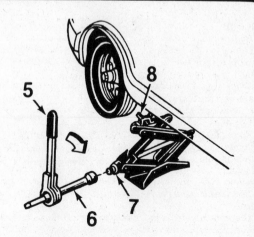

Jacking points

1 Front frame pad
2 Jack head
3 Rear spring bracket
4 Rear fiberglass spring
5 Jack ratchet handle
6 Jack extension
7 Jack hex head
8 Jack head engagement

Automotive chemicals and lubricants

A number of automotive chemicals and lubricants are available for use during vehicle maintenance and repair. They include a wide variety of products ranging from cleaning solvents and degreasers to lubricants and protective sprays for rubber, plastic and vinyl.

Cleaners

Carburetor cleaner and choke cleaner is a strong solvent for gum, varnish and carbon. Most carburetor cleaners leave a dry-type lubricant film which will not harden or gum up. Because of this film it is not recommended for use on electrical components.

Brake system cleaner is used to remove grease and brake fluid from the brake system where clean surfaces are absolutely necessary. It leaves no residue and often eliminates brake squeal caused by contaminants.

Electrical cleaner removes oxidation, corrosion and carbon deposits from electrical contacts, restoring full current flow. It can also be used to clean spark plugs, carburetor jets, voltage regulators and other parts where an oil-free surface is desired.

Demoisturants remove water and moisture from electrical components such as alternators, voltage regulators, electrical connectors and fuse blocks. It is non-conductive, non-corrosive and non-flammable.

Degreasers are heavy-duty solvents used to remove grease from the outside of the engine and from chassis components. They can be sprayed or brushed on, and, depending on the type, are rinsed off either with water or solvent.

Lubricants

Motor oil is the lubricant formulated for use in engines. It normally contains a wide variety of additives to prevent corrosion and reduce foaming and wear. Motor oil comes in various weights (viscosity ratings) from 5 to 80. The recommended weight of the oil depends on the season, temperature and the demands on the engine. Light oil is used in cold climates and under light load conditions. Heavy oil is used in hot climates and where high loads are encountered. Multi-viscosity oils are designed to have characteristics of both light and heavy oils and are available in a number of weights from 5W-20 to 20W-50.

Gear oil is designed to be used in differentials, manual transaxles and other areas where high-temperature lubrication is required.

Chassis and wheel bearing grease is a heavy grease used where increased loads and friction are encountered, such as for wheel bearings, balljoints, tie rod ends and universal joints.

High temperature wheel bearing grease is designed to withstand the extreme temperatures encountered by wheel bearings in disc brake equipped vehicles. It usually contains molybdenun disulfide (moly), which is a dry-type lubricant.

White grease is a heavy grease for metal to metal applications where water is a problem. White grease stays soft under both low and high temperatures (usually from −100°F to +190°F), and will not wash off or dilute in the presence of water.

Assembly lube is a special extreme pressure lubricant, usually containing moly, used to lubricate high-load parts such as main and rod bearings and cam lobes for initial start-up of a new engine. The assembly lube lubricates the parts without being squeezed out or washed away until the engine oiling system begins to function.

Silicone lubricants are used to protect rubber, plastic, vinyl and nylon parts.

Graphite lubricants are used where oils cannot be used due to contamination problems, such as in locks. The dry graphite will lubricate metal parts while remaining uncontaminated by dirt, water, oil or acids. It is electrically conductive and will not foul electrical contacts in locks such as the ignition switch.

Moly penetrants loosen and lubricate frozen, rusted and corroded fasteners and prevent future rusting or freezing.

Heat-sink grease is a special electrically non-conductive grease that is used for mounting HEI ignition modules where it is essential that heat be transferred away from the module.

Sealants

RTV sealant is one of the most widely used gasket compounds. Made from silicone, RTV is air curing, it seals, bonds, waterproofs, fills surface irregularities, remains flexible, doesn't shrink, is relatively easy to remove, and is used as a supplementary sealer with almost all low and medium temperature gaskets.

Anaerobic sealant is much like RTV in that it can be used either to seal gaskets or to form gaskets by itself. It remains flexible, is solvent resistant and fills surface imperfections. The difference between an anaerobic sealant and an RTV-type sealant is in the curing. RTV cures when exposed to air, while an anaerobic sealant cures only in the absence of air. This means that an anaerobic sealant cures only after the assembly of parts, sealing them together.

Thread and pipe sealant is used for sealing hydraulic and pneumatic fittings and vacuum lines. It is usually made from a teflon compound, and comes in a spray, a paint-on liquid and as a wrap-around tape.

Chemicals

Anti-seize compound prevents seizing, galling, cold welding, rust and corrosion in fasteners. High temperature anti-seize, usually made with copper and graphite lubricants, is used for exhaust system and manifold bolts.

Anaerobic locking compounds are used to keep fasteners from vibrating or working loose, and cure only after installation, in the absence of air. Medium strength locking compound is used for small nuts, bolts and screws that you expect to be removing later. High strength locking compound is for large nuts, bolts and studs which you don't intend to be removing on a regular basis.

Oil additives range from viscosity index improvers to chemical treatments that claim to reduce internal engine friction. It should be noted that most oil manufacturers caution against using additives with their oils.

Gas additives perform several functions, depending on their chemical makeup. They usually contain solvents that help dissolve gum and varnish that build up on carburetor and intake parts. They also serve to break down carbon deposits that form on the inside surfaces of the combustion chambers. Some additives contain upper cylinder lubricants for valves and piston rings, and others chemicals to remove condensation from the gas tank.

Miscellaneous

Brake fluid is specially formulated hydraulic fluid that can withstand the heat and pressure encountered in brake systems. Care must be taken that this fluid does not come in contact with painted surfaces or plastics. An opened container should always be resealed to prevent contamination by water or dirt.

Weatherstrip adhesive is used to bond weatherstripping around doors, windows and trunk lids. It is sometimes used to attach trim pieces.

Undercoating is a petroleum-based tar-like substance that is designed to protect metal surfaces on the underside of the vehicle from corrosion. It also acts as a sound-deadening agent by insulating the bottom of the vehicle.

Waxes and polishes are used to help protect painted and plated surfaces from the weather. Different types of paint may require the use of different types of wax and polish. Some polishes utilize a chemical or abrasive cleaner to help remove the top layer of oxidized (dull) paint on older vehicles. In recent years many non-wax polishes that contain a wide variety of chemicals such as polymers and silicones have been introduced. These non-wax polishes are usually easier to apply and last longer than conventional waxes and polishes.

Safety first!

Regardless of how enthusiastic you may be about getting on with the job at hand, take the time to ensure that your safety is not jeopardized. A moment's lack of attention can result in an accident, as can failure to observe certain simple safety precautions. The possibility of an accident will always exist, and the following points should not be considered a comprehensive list of all dangers. Rather, they are intended to make you aware of the risks and to encourage a safety conscious approach to all work you carry out on your vehicle.

Essential DOs and DON'Ts

DON'T rely on a jack when working under the vehicle. Always use approved jackstands to support the weight of the vehicle and place them under the recommended lift or support points.

DON'T attempt to loosen extremely tight fasteners (i.e. wheel lug nuts) while the vehicle is on a jack — it may fall.

DON'T start the engine without first making sure that the transmission is in Neutral (or Park where applicable) and the parking brake is set.

DON'T remove the radiator cap from a hot cooling system — let it cool or cover it with a cloth and release the pressure gradually.

DON'T attempt to drain the engine oil until you are sure it has cooled to the point that it will not burn you.

DON'T touch any part of the engine or exhaust system until it has cooled sufficiently to avoid burns.

DON'T siphon toxic liquids such as gasoline, antifreeze and brake fluid by mouth, or allow them to remain on your skin.

DON'T inhale brake lining dust — it is potentially hazardous (see *Asbestos* below)

DON'T allow spilled oil or grease to remain on the floor — wipe it up before someone slips on it.

DON'T use loose fitting wrenches or other tools which may slip and cause injury.

DON'T push on wrenches when loosening or tightening nuts or bolts. Always try to pull the wrench toward you. If the situation calls for pushing the wrench away, push with an open hand to avoid scraped knuckles if the wrench should slip.

DON'T attempt to lift a heavy component alone — get someone to help you.

DON'T rush or take unsafe shortcuts to finish a job.

DON'T allow children or animals in or around the vehicle while you are working on it.

DO wear eye protection when using power tools such as a drill, sander, bench grinder, etc. and when working under a vehicle.

DO keep loose clothing and long hair well out of the way of moving parts.

DO make sure that any hoist used has a safe working load rating adequate for the job.

DO get someone to check on you periodically when working alone on a vehicle.

DO carry out work in a logical sequence and make sure that everything is correctly assembled and tightened.

DO keep chemicals and fluids tightly capped and out of the reach of children and pets.

DO remember that your vehicle's safety affects that of yourself and others. If in doubt on any point, get professional advice.

Asbestos

Certain friction, insulating, sealing, and other products — such as brake linings, brake bands, clutch linings, torque converters, gaskets, etc. — contain asbestos. *Extreme care must be taken to avoid inhalation of dust from such products since it is hazardous to health*. If in doubt, assume that they *do* contain asbestos.

Fire

Remember at all times that gasoline is highly flammable. Never smoke or have any kind of open flame around when working on a vehicle. But the risk does not end there. A spark caused by an electrical short circuit, by two metal surfaces contacting each other, or even by static electricity built up in your body under certain conditions, can ignite gasoline vapors, which in a confined space are highly explosive. Do not, under any circumstances, use gasoline for cleaning parts. Use an approved safety solvent.

Always disconnect the battery ground (−) cable *at the battery* before working on any part of the fuel system or electrical system. Never risk spilling fuel on a hot engine or exhaust component.

It is strongly recommended that a fire extinguisher suitable for use on fuel and electrical fires be kept handy in the garage or workshop at all times. Never try to extinguish a fuel or electrical fire with water.

Fumes

Certain fumes are highly toxic and can quickly cause unconsciousness and even death if inhaled to any extent. Gasoline vapor falls into this category, as do the vapors from some cleaning solvents. Any draining or pouring of such volatile fluids should be done in a well ventilated area.

When using cleaning fluids and solvents, read the instructions on the container carefully. Never use materials from unmarked containers.

Never run the engine in an enclosed space, such as a garage. Exhaust fumes contain carbon monoxide, which is extremely poisonous. If you need to run the engine, always do so in the open air, or at least have the rear of the vehicle outside the work area.

If you are fortunate enough to have the use of an inspection pit, never drain or pour gasoline and never run the engine while the vehicle is over the pit. The fumes, being heavier than air, will concentrate in the pit with possibly lethal results.

The battery

Never create a spark or allow a bare light bulb near a battery. They normally give off a certain amount of hydrogen gas, which is highly explosive.

Always disconnect the battery ground (−) cable *at the battery* before working on the fuel or electrical systems.

If possible, loosen the filler caps or cover when charging the battery from an external source (this does not apply to sealed or maintenance-free batteries). Do not charge at an excessive rate or the battery may burst.

Take care when adding water to a non maintenance-free battery and when carrying a battery. The electrolyte, even when diluted, is very corrosive and should not be allowed to contact clothing or skin.

Always wear eye protection when cleaning the battery to prevent the caustic deposits from entering your eyes.

Household current

When using an electric power tool, inspection light, etc., which operates on household current, always make sure that the tool is correctly connected to its plug and that, where necessary, it is properly grounded. Do not use such items in damp conditions and, again, do not create a spark or apply excessive heat in the vicinity of fuel or fuel vapor.

Secondary ignition system voltage

A severe electric shock can result from touching certain parts of the ignition system (such as the spark plug wires) when the engine is running or being cranked, particularly if components are damp or the insulation is defective. In the case of an electronic ignition system, the secondary system voltage is much higher and could prove fatal.

Conversion factors

Length (distance)
Inches (in)	X	25.4	= Millimetres (mm)	X	0.0394 = Inches (in)
Feet (ft)	X	0.305	= Metres (m)	X	3.281 = Feet (ft)
Miles	X	1.609	= Kilometres (km)	X	0.621 = Miles

Volume (capacity)
Cubic inches (cu in; in^3)	X	16.387	= Cubic centimetres (cc; cm^3)	X	0.061 = Cubic inches (cu in; in^3)
Imperial pints (Imp pt)	X	0.568	= Litres (l)	X	1.76 = Imperial pints (Imp pt)
Imperial quarts (Imp qt)	X	1.137	= Litres (l)	X	0.88 = Imperial quarts (Imp qt)
Imperial quarts (Imp qt)	X	1.201	= US quarts (US qt)	X	0.833 = Imperial quarts (Imp qt)
US quarts (US qt)	X	0.946	= Litres (l)	X	1.057 = US quarts (US qt)
Imperial gallons (Imp gal)	X	4.546	= Litres (l)	X	0.22 = Imperial gallons (Imp gal)
Imperial gallons (Imp gal)	X	1.201	= US gallons (US gal)	X	0.833 = Imperial gallons (Imp gal)
US gallons (US gal)	X	3.785	= Litres (l)	X	0.264 = US gallons (US gal)

Mass (weight)
Ounces (oz)	X	28.35	= Grams (g)	X	0.035 = Ounces (oz)
Pounds (lb)	X	0.454	= Kilograms (kg)	X	2.205 = Pounds (lb)

Force
Ounces-force (ozf; oz)	X	0.278	= Newtons (N)	X	3.6 = Ounces-force (ozf; oz)
Pounds-force (lbf; lb)	X	4.448	= Newtons (N)	X	0.225 = Pounds-force (lbf; lb)
Newtons (N)	X	0.1	= Kilograms-force (kgf; kg)	X	9.81 = Newtons (N)

Pressure
Pounds-force per square inch (psi; lbf/in^2; lb/in^2)	X	0.070	= Kilograms-force per square centimetre (kgf/cm^2; kg/cm^2)	X	14.223 = Pounds-force per square inch (psi; lbf/in^2; lb/in^2)
Pounds-force per square inch (psi; lbf/in^2; lb/in^2)	X	0.068	= Atmospheres (atm)	X	14.696 = Pounds-force per square inch (psi; lbf/in^2; lb/in^2)
Pounds-force per square inch (psi; lbf/in^2; lb/in^2)	X	0.069	= Bars	X	14.5 = Pounds-force per square inch (psi; lbf/in^2; lb/in^2)
Pounds-force per square inch (psi; lbf/in^2; lb/in^2)	X	6.895	= Kilopascals (kPa)	X	0.145 = Pounds-force per square inch (psi; lbf/in^2; lb/in^2)
Kilopascals (kPa)	X	0.01	= Kilograms-force per square centimetre (kgf/cm^2; kg/cm^2)	X	98.1 = Kilopascals (kPa)

Torque (moment of force)
Pounds-force inches (lbf in; lb in)	X	1.152	= Kilograms-force centimetre (kgf cm; kg cm)	X	0.868 = Pounds-force inches (lbf in; lb in)
Pounds-force inches (lbf in; lb in)	X	0.113	= Newton metres (Nm)	X	8.85 = Pounds-force inches (lbf in; lb in)
Pounds-force inches (lbf in; lb in)	X	0.083	= Pounds-force feet (lbf ft; lb ft)	X	12 = Pounds-force inches (lbf in; lb in)
Pounds-force feet (lbf ft; lb ft)	X	0.138	= Kilograms-force metres (kgf m; kg m)	X	7.233 = Pounds-force feet (lbf ft; lb ft)
Pounds-force feet (lbf ft; lb ft)	X	1.356	= Newton metres (Nm)	X	0.738 = Pounds-force feet (lbf ft; lb ft)
Newton metres (Nm)	X	0.102	= Kilograms-force metres (kgf m; kg m)	X	9.804 = Newton metres (Nm)

Power
Horsepower (hp)	X	745.7	= Watts (W)	X	0.0013 = Horsepower (hp)

Velocity (speed)
Miles per hour (miles/hr; mph)	X	1.609	= Kilometres per hour (km/hr; kph)	X	0.621 = Miles per hour (miles/hr; mph)

Fuel consumption*
Miles per gallon, Imperial (mpg)	X	0.354	= Kilometres per litre (km/l)	X	2.825 = Miles per gallon, Imperial (mpg)
Miles per gallon, US (mpg)	X	0.425	= Kilometres per litre (km/l)	X	2.352 = Miles per gallon, US (mpg)

Temperature
Degrees Fahrenheit = (°C x 1.8) + 32   Degrees Celsius (Degrees Centigrade; °C) = (°F - 32) x 0.56

*It is common practice to convert from miles per gallon (mpg) to litres/100 kilometres (l/100km),
where mpg (Imperial) x l/100 km = 282 and mpg (US) x l/100 km = 235

Troubleshooting

Contents

This section provides an easy reference guide to the more common problems which may occur during the operation of your vehicle. These problems and possible causes are grouped under various components or systems, such as Engine, Cooling system, etc., and also refer to the Chapter and/or Section which deals with the problem.

Remember that successful troubleshooting is not a mysterious *black art* practiced only by professional mechanics. It's simply the result of a bit of knowledge combined with an intelligent, systematic approach to the problem. Always work by a process of elimination, starting with the simplest solution and working through to the most complex — and never overlook the obvious. Anyone can forget to fill the gas tank or leave the lights on overnight, so don't assume that you are above such oversights.

Finally, always get clear in your mind why a problem has occurred and take steps to ensure that it doesn't happen again. If the electrical system fails because of a poor connection, check all other connections in the system to make sure that they don't fail as well. If a particular fuse continues to blow, find out why - don't just go on replacing fuses. Remember, failure of a small component can often be indicative of potential failure or incorrect functioning of a more important component or system.

Engine

1   Engine will not rotate when attempting to start

1   Battery terminal connections loose or corroded. Check the cable terminals at the battery. Tighten the cable or remove corrosion as necessary.
2   Battery discharged or faulty. If the cable connections are clean and tight on the battery posts, turn the key to the On position and switch on the headlights and/or windshield wipers. If they fail to function, the battery is discharged.
3   Automatic transmission not completely engaged in Park or clutch not completely depressed.
4   Broken, loose or disconnected wiring in the starting circuit. Inspect all wiring and connectors at the battery, starter solenoid and ignition switch.
5   Starter motor pinion jammed in flywheel ring gear. If equipped with a manual transmission, place the transmission in gear and rock the vehicle to manually turn the engine. Remove the starter and inspect the pinion and flywheel at earliest convenience.
6   Starter solenoid faulty (Chapter 5).
7   Starter motor faulty (Chapter 5).
8   Ignition switch faulty (Chapter 12).

2   Engine rotates but will not start

1   Fuel tank empty.
2   Battery discharged (engine rotates slowly). Check the operation of electrical components as described in previous Section.
3   Battery terminal connections loose or corroded. See previous Section.
4   Carburetor flooded and/or fuel level in carburetor incorrect. This will usually be accompanied by a strong fuel odor from under the engine cover. Wait a few minutes, depress the accelerator pedal all the way to the floor and attempt to start the engine.
5   Choke control inoperative (Chapter 4).
6   Fuel not reaching carburetor or fuel injector(s). With the ignition switch in the Off position, remove the engine cover, remove the top plate of the air cleaner assembly and observe the top of the carburetor (manually move the choke plate back if necessary). Depress the accelerator pedal and check that fuel spurts into the carburetor. If not, check the fuel filter (Chapter 1), fuel lines and fuel pump (Chapter 4).
7   Fuel injector(s) or fuel pump faulty (fuel injected vehicles) (Chapter 4).
8   No power to fuel pump (Chapter 4).
9   Worn, faulty or incorrectly gapped spark plugs (Chapter 1)
10 Broken, loose or disconnected wiring in the starting circuit (see previous Section).
11 Distributor loose, causing ignition timing to change. Turn the distributor as necessary to start the engine, then set the ignition timing as soon as possible (Chapter 1).
12 Broken, loose or disconnected wires at the ignition coil or faulty coil (Chapter 5).

3   Starter motor operates without rotating engine

1   Starter pinion sticking. Remove the starter (Chapter 5) and inspect.
2   Starter pinion or flywheel teeth worn or broken. Remove the cover at the rear of the engine and inspect.

4   Engine hard to start when cold

1   Battery discharged or low. Check as described in Section 1.
2   Choke control inoperative or out of adjustment (Chapter 4).
3   Carburetor flooded (see Section 2).
4   Fuel supply not reaching the carburetor (see Section 2).
5   Carburetor/fuel injection system in need of overhaul (Chapter 4).
6   Distributor rotor carbon tracked and/or damaged (Chapter 1).
7   Fuel injection malfunction (Chapter 4).

5   Engine hard to start when hot

1   Air filter clogged (Chapter 1).
2   Fuel not reaching the injector(s) (see Section 2).
3   Corroded electrical leads at the battery (Chapter 1).
4   Bad engine ground (Chapter 12).
5   Starter worn (Chapter 5).
6   Corroded electrical leads at the fuel injector (Chapter 4).

6   Starter motor noisy or excessively rough in engagement

1   Pinion or flywheel gear teeth worn or broken. Remove the cover at the rear of the engine (if so equipped) and inspect.
2   Starter motor mounting bolts loose or missing.

7   Engine starts but stops immediately

1   Loose or faulty electrical connections at distributor, coil or alternator.
2   Insufficient fuel reaching the carburetor or fuel injector(s). Disconnect the fuel line. Place a container under the disconnected fuel line and observe the flow of fuel from the line. If little or none at all, check for blockage in the lines and/or replace the fuel pump (Chapter 4).
3   Vacuum leak at the gasket surfaces of the carburetor or fuel injection unit. Make sure that all mounting bolts/nuts are tightened securely and that all vacuum hoses connected to the carburetor or fuel injection unit and manifold are positioned properly and in good condition.

8   Engine lopes while idling or idles erratically

1   Vacuum leakage. Check mounting bolts/nuts at the carburetor/fuel injection unit and intake manifold for tightness. Make sure that all vacuum hoses are connected and in good condition. Use a stethoscope or a length of fuel hose held against your ear to listen for vacuum leaks while the engine is running. A hissing sound will be heard. Check the carburetor/fuel injector and intake manifold gasket surfaces.
2   Leaking EGR valve or plugged PCV valve (see Chapters 1 and 6).
3   Air filter clogged (Chapter 1).
4   Fuel pump not delivering sufficient fuel to the carburetor/fuel injector (see Section 7).
5   Carburetor out of adjustment (Chapter 4).
6   Leaking head gasket. If this is suspected, take the vehicle to a repair shop or dealer where the engine can be pressure checked.
7   Timing chain and/or gears worn (Chapter 2).
8   Camshaft lobes worn (Chapter 2).
9   Worn exhaust valve guides (four-cylinder engine). A Chevrolet Dealer Service Bulletin has been issued for this condition (no. 87-155, 6A, June, 1987). Contact your General Motors dealer for assistance.

9   Engine misses at idle speed

1   Spark plugs worn or not gapped properly (Chapter 1).
2   Faulty spark plug wires (Chapter 1).
3   Choke not operating properly (Chapter 1).

4   Sticking or faulty emissions system components (Chapter 6).
5   Clogged fuel filter and/or foreign matter in fuel. Remove the fuel filter (Chapter 1) and inspect.
6   Vacuum leaks at the intake manifold or at hose connections. Check as described in Section 8.
7   Incorrect idle speed or idle mixture (Chapter 1).
8   Incorrect ignition timing (Chapter 1).
9   Uneven or low cylinder compression. Check compression as described in Chapter 2.
10   Worn exhaust valve guides (four-cylinder engine). A Chevrolet Dealer Service Bulletin has been issued for this condition (no. 87-155, 6A, June, 1987). Contact your General Motors dealer for assistance.

10   Engine misses throughout driving speed range

1   Fuel filter clogged and/or impurities in the fuel system (Chapter 1). Also check fuel output at the carburetor/fuel injector (see Section 7).
2   Faulty or incorrectly gapped spark plugs (Chapter 1).
3   Incorrect ignition timing (Chapter 1).
4   Check for cracked distributor cap, disconnected distributor wires and damaged distributor components (Chapter 1).
5   Leaking spark plug wires (Chapter 1).
6   Faulty emissions system components (Chapter 6).
7   Low or uneven cylinder compression pressures. Remove the spark plugs and test the compression with gauge (Chapter 2).
8   Weak or faulty ignition system (Chapter 5).
9   Vacuum leaks at the carburetor/fuel injection unit or vacuum hoses (see Section 8).
10   Worn exhaust valve guides (four-cylinder engine). A Chevrolet Dealer Service Bulletin has been issued for this condition (no. 87-155, 6A, June, 1987). Contact your General Motors dealer for assistance.

11   Engine stalls

1   Idle speed incorrect (Chapter 1).
2   Fuel filter clogged and/or water and impurities in the fuel system (Chapter 1).
3   Choke improperly adjusted or sticking (Chapter 4).
4   Distributor components damp or damaged (Chapter 5).
5   Faulty emissions system components (Chapter 6).
6   Faulty or incorrectly gapped spark plugs (Chapter 1). Also check spark plug wires (Chapter 1).
7   Vacuum leak at the carburetor/fuel injection unit or vacuum hoses. Check as described in Section 8.

12   Engine lacks power

1   Incorrect ignition timing (Chapter 1).
2   Excessive play in distributor shaft. At the same time, check for worn rotor, faulty distributor cap, wires, etc. (Chapters 1 and 5).
3   Faulty or incorrectly gapped spark plugs (Chapter 1).
4   Fuel injection unit not adjusted properly or excessively worn (Chapter 4).
5   Faulty coil (Chapter 5).
6   Brakes binding (Chapter 1).
7   Automatic transmission fluid level incorrect (Chapter 1).
8   Clutch slipping (Chapter 8).
9   Fuel filter clogged and/or impurities in the fuel system (Chapter 1).
10   Emissions control system not functioning properly (Chapter 6).
11   Use of substandard fuel. Fill tank with proper octane fuel.
12   Low or uneven cylinder compression pressures. Test with compression tester, which will detect leaking valves and/or blown head gasket (Chapter 2).

13   Engine backfires

1   Emissions system not functioning properly (Chapter 6).
2   Ignition timing incorrect (Chapter 1).

3   Faulty secondary ignition system (cracked spark plug insulator, faulty plug wires, distributor cap and/or rotor) (Chapters 1 and 5).
4   Carburetor/fuel injection unit in need of adjustment or worn excessively (Chapter 4).
5   Vacuum leak at the fuel injection unit or vacuum hoses. Check as described in Section 8.
6   Valves sticking (Chapter 2).
7   Crossed plug wires (Chapter 1).

14   Pinging or knocking engine sounds during acceleration or uphill

1   Incorrect grade of fuel. Fill tank with fuel of the proper octane rating.
2   Ignition timing incorrect (Chapter 1).
3   Carburetor/fuel injection unit in need of adjustment (Chapter 4).
4   Improper spark plugs. Check plug type against Emissions Control Information label located under hood. Also check plugs and wires for damage (Chapter 1).
5   Worn or damaged distributor components (Chapter 5).
6   Faulty emissions system (Chapter 6).
7   Vacuum leak. Check as described in Section 8.
8   Blocked cylinder head coolant passages (1986 four-cylinder engine only). A General Motors recall notification has been issued for this condition. Contact your General Motors dealer concerning it.

15   Engine diesels (continues to run) after switching off

1   Idle speed too high (Chapter 1).
2   Electrical solenoid at side of carburetor not functioning properly (not all models, see Chapter 4).
3   Ignition timing incorrectly adjusted (Chapter 1).
4   Thermo-controlled air cleaner heat valve not operating properly (Chapter 1).
5   Excessive engine operating temperature. Probable causes of this are malfunctioning thermostat, clogged radiator, faulty water pump (Chapter 3).

Engine electrical system

16   Battery will not hold a charge

1   Alternator drivebelt defective or not adjusted properly (Chapter 1).
2   Electrolyte level low or battery discharged (Chapter 1).
3   Battery terminals loose or corroded (Chapter 1).
4   Alternator not charging properly (Chapter 5).
5   Loose, broken or faulty wiring in the charging circuit (Chapter 5).
6   Short in vehicle wiring causing a continual drain on battery.
7   Battery defective internally.

17   Ignition light fails to go out

1   Fault in alternator or charging circuit (Chapter 5).
2   Alternator drivebelt defective or not properly adjusted (Chapter 1).

18   Ignition light fails to come on when key is turned on

1   Warning light bulb defective (Chapter 12).
2   Alternator faulty (Chapter 5).
3   Fault in the printed circuit, dash wiring or bulb holder (Chapter 12).

19   'Check engine' light comes on

See Chapter 6

Fuel system

20 Excessive fuel consumption

1 Dirty or clogged air filter element (Chapter 1).
2 Incorrectly set ignition timing (Chapter 1).
3 Choke sticking or improperly adjusted (Chapter 1).
4 Emissions system not functioning properly (not all vehicles, see Chapter 6).
5 Carburetor idle speed and/or mixture not adjusted properly (Chapter 1).
6 Carburetor/fuel injection internal parts excessively worn or damaged (Chapter 4).
7 Low tire pressure or incorrect tire size (Chapter 1).

21 Fuel leakage and/or fuel odor

1 Leak in a fuel feed or vent line (Chapter 4).
2 Tank overfilled. Fill only to automatic shut-off.
3 Emissions system clogged or damaged (Chapter 6).
4 Vapor leaks from system lines (Chapter 4).
5 Carburetor/fuel injection internal parts excessively worn or out of adjustment (Chapter 4).

Cooling system

22 Overheating

1 Insufficient coolant in system (Chapter 1).
2 Water pump drivebelt defective or not adjusted properly (Chapter 1).
3 Radiator core blocked or radiator grille dirty and restricted (Chapter 3).
4 Thermostat faulty (Chapter 3).
5 Fan blades broken or cracked (Chapter 3).
6 Radiator cap not maintaining proper pressure. Have cap pressure tested by gas station or repair shop.
7 Ignition timing incorrect (Chapter 1).

23 Overcooling

1 Thermostat faulty (Chapter 3).
2 Inaccurate temperature gauge (Chapter 12)

24 External coolant leakage

1 Deteriorated or damaged hoses or loose clamps. Replace hoses and/or tighten clamps at hose connections (Chapter 1).
2 Water pump seals defective. If this is the case, water will drip from the weep hole in the water pump body (Chapter 3).
3 Leakage from radiator core or header tank. This will require the radiator to be professionally repaired (see Chapter 3 for removal procedures).
4 Engine drain plugs or water jacket core plugs leaking (see Chapter 2).

25 Internal coolant leakage

Note: *Internal coolant leaks can usually be detected by examining the oil. Check the dipstick and inside of the rocker arm cover(s) for water deposits and an oil consistency like that of a milkshake.*

1 Leaking cylinder head gasket. Have the cooling system pressure tested.
2 Cracked cylinder bore or cylinder head. Dismantle engine and inspect (Chapter 2).

26 Coolant loss

1 Too much coolant in system (Chapter 1).
2 Coolant boiling away due to overheating (see Section 22).
3 Internal or external leakage (see Sections 24 and 25).
4 Faulty radiator cap. Have the cap pressure tested.

27 Poor coolant circulation

1 Inoperative water pump. A quick test is to pinch the top radiator hose closed with your hand while the engine is idling, then let it loose. You should feel the surge of coolant if the pump is working properly (Chapter 3).
2 Restriction in cooling system. Drain, flush and refill the system (Chapter 1). If necessary, remove the radiator (Chapter 3) and have it reverse flushed.
3 Water pump drivebelt defective or not adjusted properly (Chapter 1).
4 Thermostat sticking (Chapter 3).

Clutch

28 Fails to release (pedal pressed to the floor — shift lever does not move freely in and out of Reverse)

1 Clutch fork off ball stud. Look under the vehicle, on the left side of transmission.
2 Clutch plate warped or damaged (Chapter 8).
3 Clutch hydraulic system low or has air in system and needs to be bled (Chapter 8).

29 Clutch slips (engine speed increases with no increase in vehicle speed)

1 Clutch plate oil soaked or lining worn. Remove clutch (Chapter 8) and inspect.
2 Clutch plate not seated. It may take 30 or 40 normal starts for a new one to seat.
3 Pressure plate worn (Chapter 8).

30 Grabbing (chattering) as clutch is engaged

1 Oil on clutch plate lining. Remove (Chapter 8) and inspect. Correct any leakage source.
2 Worn or loose engine or transmission mounts. These units move slightly when clutch is released. Inspect mounts and bolts.
3 Worn splines on clutch plate hub. Remove clutch components (Chapter 8) and inspect.
4 Warped pressure plate or flywheel. Remove clutch components and inspect.

31 Squeal or rumble with clutch fully engaged (pedal released)

1 Release bearing binding on transmission bearing retainer. Remove clutch components (Chapter 8) and check bearing. Remove any burrs or nicks, clean and relubricate before reinstallation.
2 Weak linkage return spring. Replace the spring.

32 Squeal or rumble with clutch fully disengaged (pedal depressed)

1 Worn, defective or broken release bearing (Chapter 8).
2 Worn or broken pressure plate springs (or diaphragm fingers) (Chapter 8).
3 Air in hydraulic line (Chapter 8).

33   Clutch pedal stays on floor when disengaged

1   Bind in linkage or release bearing. Inspect linkage or remove clutch components as necessary.
2   Clutch hydraulic cylinder faulty or there is air in the system.

Manual transmission

Note: *All the following references are to Chapter 7, unless noted.*

34   Noisy in Neutral with engine running

1   Input shaft bearing worn.
2   Damaged main drive gear bearing.
3   Worn countershaft bearings.
4   Worn or damaged countershaft end play shims.

35   Noisy in all gears

1   Any of the above causes, and/or:
2   Insufficient lubricant (see checking procedures in Chapter 1).

36   Noisy in one particular gear

1   Worn, damaged or chipped gear teeth for that particular gear.
2   Worn or damaged synchronizer for that particular gear.

37   Slips out of high gear

1   Transmission mounting bolts loose.
2   Shift rods not working freely.
3   Damaged mainshaft pilot bushing.
4   Dirt between transmission case and engine or misalignment of transmission.

38   Difficulty in engaging gears

1   Loose, damaged or out-of-adjustment shift linkage. Make a thorough inspection, replacing parts as necessary.
2   Air in hydraulic system (Chapter 8)

39   Oil leakage

1   Excessive amount of lubricant in transmission (see Chapter 1 for correct checking procedures). Drain lubricant as required.
2   Side cover loose or gasket damaged.
3   Rear oil seal or speedometer oil seal in need of replacement.
4   Clutch hydraulic system leaking (Chapter 8).

Automatic transmission

Note: *Due to the complexity of the automatic transmission, it is difficult for the home mechanic to properly diagnose and service this component. For problems other than the following, the vehicle should be taken to a dealer or reputable repair shop.*

40   General shift mechanism problems

1   Chapter 7 deals with checking and adjusting the shift linkage on automatic transmissions. Common problems which may be attributed to poorly adjusted linkage are:

Engine starting in gears other than Park or Neutral
Indicator on shifter pointing to a gear other than the one actually being used
Vehicle moves when in Park
2   Refer to Chapter 7 to adjust the linkage.

41   Transmission will not downshift with accelerator pedal pressed to the floor

Chapter 7 deals with adjusting the TV cable to enable the transmission to downshift properly.

42   Transmission slips, shifts rough, is noisy or has no drive in forward or reverse gears

1   There are many probable causes for the above problems, but the home mechanic should be concerned with only one possibility — fluid level.
2   Before taking the vehicle to a repair shop, check the level and condition of the fluid as described in Chapter 1. Correct fluid level as necessary or change the fluid and filter if needed. If the problem persists, have a professional diagnose the probable cause.

43   Fluid leakage

1   Automatic transmission fluid is a deep red color. Fluid leaks should not be confused with engine oil, which can easily be blown by air flow to the transmission.
2   To pinpoint a leak, first remove all built-up dirt and grime from around the transmission. Degreasing agents and/or steam cleaning will achieve this. With the underside clean, drive the vehicle at low speeds so air flow will not blow the leak far from its source. Raise the vehicle and determine where the leak is coming from. Common areas of leakage are:

a)   Pan: Tighten mounting bolts and/or replace pan gasket as necessary (see Chapters 1 and 7).
b)   Filler pipe: Replace the rubber seal where pipe enters transmission case.
c)   Transmission oil lines: Tighten connectors where lines enter transmission case and/or replace lines.
d)   Vent pipe: Transmission overfilled and/or water in fluid (see checking procedures, Chapter 1).
e)   Speedometer connector: Replace the O-ring where speedometer cable enters transmission case (Chapter 7).

Driveshaft

44   Oil leak at front of driveshaft

Defective transmission rear oil seal. See Chapter 7 for replacement procedures. While this is done, check the splined yoke for burrs or a rough condition which may be damaging the seal. Burrs can be removed with crocus cloth or a fine whetstone.

45   Knock or clunk when the transmission is under initial load (just after transmission is put into gear)

1   Loose or disconnected rear suspension components. Check all mounting bolts, nuts and bushings (Chapter 10).
2   Loose driveshaft bolts. Inspect all bolts and nuts and tighten them to the specified torque.
3   Worn or damaged universal joint bearings. Check for wear (Chapter 8).

46 Metallic grating sound consistent with vehicle speed

Pronounced wear in the universal joint bearings. Check as described in Chapter 8.

47 Vibration

Note: *Before assuming that the driveshaft is at fault, make sure the tires are perfectly balanced and perform the following test.*

1   Install a tachometer inside the vehicle to monitor engine speed as the vehicle is driven. Drive the vehicle and note the engine speed at which the vibration (roughness) is most pronounced. Now shift the transmission to a different gear and bring the engine speed to the same point.
2   If the vibration occurs at the same engine speed (rpm) regardless of which gear the transmission is in, the driveshaft is NOT at fault since the driveshaft speed varies.
3   If the vibration decreases or is eliminated when the transmission is in a different gear at the same engine speed, refer to the following probable causes.
4   Bent or dented driveshaft. Inspect and replace as necessary (Chapter 8).
5   Undercoating or built-up dirt, etc. on the driveshaft. Clean the shaft thoroughly and recheck.
6   Worn universal joint bearings. Remove and inspect (Chapter 8).
7   Driveshaft and/or companion flange out-of-balance. Check for missing weights on the shaft. Remove the driveshaft (Chapter 8) and reinstall 180° from original position, then retest. Have the driveshaft professionally balanced if the problem persists.

Axles

48 Noise

1   Road noise. No corrective procedures available.
2   Tire noise. Inspect the tires and check tire pressures (Chapter 1).
3   Rear wheel bearings loose, worn or damaged (Chapter 8).

49 Vibration

See probable causes under Driveshaft. Proceed under the guidelines listed for the driveshaft. If the problem persists, check the rear wheel bearings by raising the rear of the vehicle and spinning the wheels by hand. Listen for evidence of rough (noisy) bearings. Remove and inspect (Chapter 8).

50 Oil leakage

1   Pinion seal damaged (Chapter 8).
2   Axleshaft oil seals damaged (Chapter 8).
3   Differential inspection cover leaking. Tighten the bolts or replace the gasket as required (Chapters 1 and 8).

Brakes

Note: *Before assuming that a brake problem exists, make sure that the tires are in good condition and inflated properly (see Chapter 1), that the front end alignment is correct and that the vehicle is not loaded with weight in an unequal manner.*

51 Vehicle pulls to one side during braking

1   Defective, damaged or oil contaminated brake pads or shoes on one side. Inspect as described in Chapter 9.
2   Excessive wear of brake shoe or pad material or drum/disc on one side. Inspect and correct as necessary.

3   Loose or disconnected front suspension components. Inspect and tighten all bolts to the specified torque (Chapter 10).
4   Defective drum brake or caliper assembly. Remove the drum or caliper and inspect for a stuck piston or other damage (Chapter 9).

52 Noise (high-pitched squeal with the brakes applied)

Disc brake pads worn out. The noise comes from the wear sensor rubbing against the disc. Replace the pads with new ones immediately (Chapter 9).

53 Excessive brake pedal travel

1   Partial brake system failure. Inspect the entire system (Chapter 9) and correct as required.
2   Insufficient fluid in the master cylinder. Check (Chapter 1), add fluid and bleed the system if necessary (Chapter 9).
3   Brakes not adjusting properly. Make a series of starts and stops with the vehicle is in Reverse. If this does not correct the situation, remove the drums and inspect the self-adjusters (Chapter 9).

54 Brake pedal feels spongy when depressed

1   Air in the hydraulic lines. Bleed the brake system (Chapter 9).
2   Faulty flexible hoses. Inspect all system hoses and lines. Replace parts as necessary.
3   Master cylinder mounting bolts/nuts loose.
4   Master cylinder defective (Chapter 9).

55 Excessive effort required to stop vehicle

1   Power brake booster not operating properly (Chapter 9).
2   Excessively worn linings or pads. Inspect and replace if necessary (Chapters 1 and 9).
3   One or more caliper pistons or wheel cylinders seized or sticking. Inspect and rebuild as required (Chapter 9).
4   Brake linings or pads contaminated with oil or grease. Inspect and replace as required (Chapters 1 and 9).
5   New pads or shoes installed and not yet seated. It will take a while for the new material to seat against the drum (or rotor).

56 Pedal travels to the floor with little resistance

Little or no fluid in the master cylinder reservoir caused by leaking wheel cylinder(s), leaking caliper piston(s), loose, damaged or disconnected brake lines. Inspect the entire system and correct as necessary.

57 Brake pedal pulsates during brake application

1   Wheel bearings not adjusted properly or in need of replacement (Chapter 1).
2   Caliper not sliding properly due to improper installation or obstructions. Remove and inspect (Chapter 9).
3   Rotor or drum defective. Remove the rotor or drum (Chapter 9) and check for excessive lateral runout, out-of-round and parallelism. Have the drum or rotor resurfaced or replace it with a new one.

Suspension and steering systems

58 Vehicle pulls to one side

1   Tire pressures uneven (Chapter 1).
2   Defective tire (Chapter 1).
3   Excessive wear in suspension or steering components (Chapter 10).

4   Front end in need of alignment.
5   Front brakes dragging. Inspect the brakes as described in Chapter 9.

59   Shimmy, shake or vibration

1   Tire or wheel out-of-balance or out-of-round. Have professionally balanced.
2   Loose, worn or out-of-adjustment wheel bearings (Chapters 1 and 8).
3   Shock absorbers and/or suspension components worn or damaged (Chapter 10).

60   Excessive pitching and/or rolling around corners or during braking

1   Defective shock absorbers. Replace as a set (Chapter 10).
2   Broken or weak springs and/or suspension components. Inspect as described in Chapter 10.

61   Excessively stiff steering

1   Lack of fluid in power steering fluid reservoir (Chapter 1).
2   Incorrect tire pressures (Chapter 1).
3   Lack of lubrication at steering joints (Chapter 1).
4   Front end out of alignment.
5   See Section 63.

62   Excessive play in steering

1   Loose front wheel bearings (Chapter 1).
2   Excessive wear in suspension or steering components (Chapter 10).
3   Steering gearbox out of adjustment (Chapter 10).

63   Lack of power assistance

1   Steering pump drivebelt faulty or not adjusted properly (Chapter 1).
2   Fluid level low (Chapter 1).
3   Hoses or lines restricted. Inspect and replace parts as necessary.
4   Air in power steering system. Bleed the system (Chapter 10).

64   Excessive tire wear (not specific to one area)

1   Incorrect tire pressures (Chapter 1).
2   Tires out-of-balance. Have professionally balanced.
3   Wheels damaged. Inspect and replace as necessary.
4   Suspension or steering components excessively worn (Chapter 10).

65   Excessive tire wear on outside edge

1   Inflation pressures incorrect (Chapter 1).
2   Excessive speed in turns.
3   Front end alignment incorrect (excessive toe-in). Have professionally aligned.
4   Suspension arm bent or twisted (Chapter 10).

66   Excessive tire wear on inside edge

1   Inflation pressures incorrect (Chapter 1).
2   Front end alignment incorrect (toe-out). Have professionally aligned.
3   Loose or damaged steering components (Chapter 10).

67   Tire tread worn in one place

1   Tires out-of-balance.
2   Damaged or buckled wheel. Inspect and replace if necessary.
3   Defective tire (Chapter 1).

Chapter 1 Tune-up and routine maintenance

Contents

1

Specifications

Recommended lubricants and fluids

Engine oil type	SG, SG/CC or SG/CD
Engine oil viscosity	See accompanying chart
Automatic transmission fluid	Dexron II automatic transmission fluid (ATF)
Manual transmission lubricant	Dexron II automatic transmission fluid (ATF)
Differential lubricant	
US	SAE 80W or SAE 80W-90 GL-5 gear lubricant
Canada	SAE 80W GL-5 gear lubricant
limited slip differential (all)	Add GM limited-slip additive to the specified lubricant
Chassis grease	GM lubricant 6031 or equivalent NLGI No. 2 chassis grease

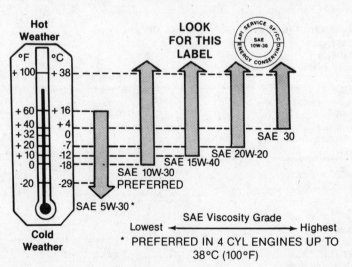

Recommended SAE viscosity grade engine oils
For best fuel economy and cold starting, select the lowest SAE viscosity grade oil for the expected temperature range.

ENGINE OIL VISCOSITY CHART

Recommended lubricants and fluids (continued)

Engine coolant	Mixture of water and ethylene glycol-base antifreeze
Brake fluid	Delco Supreme 11 or DOT-3 brake fluid
Clutch fluid	Delco Supreme 11 or DOT-3 brake fluid
Power steering fluid	GM power steering fluid or equivalent
Manual steering box lubricant	GM lubricant 4673M or equivalent
Wheel bearing grease	GM lubricant 1051344 or NLGI No. 2 moly-base wheel bearing grease

Capacities

Engine oil (with filter change, approximate)
    four-cylinder engine .... 3 qts
    V6 engine .... 5 qts
Cooling system (approximate)
    four-cylinder engine
        without rear heater .... 10 qts
        with rear heater .... 13 qts
    V6 engine
        without rear heater .... 13.5 qts
        with rear heater .... 16.5 qts
Fuel tank
    standard .... 17 gal
    optional .... 27 gal
Cooling system
    four-cylinder engine .... 10 qts
    V6 engine .... 13.5 qts
Automatic transmission .... 10 pts
Manual transmission
    4-speed .... 1.3 qts
    5-speed .... 2.2 qts

CYLINDER NUMBERS AND DISTRIBUTOR SPARK PLUG WIRE TERMINAL LOCATIONS

Cylinder location and distributor rotation

Ignition system

Ignition timing .... Refer to Vehicle Emission Control Information label in engine compartment

Spark plug type
    four-cylinder models .... AC type R43CTS-6
    V6 models .... AC type R43CTS
Spark plug gap
    four-cylinder models .... 0.060 inch
    V6 models
        through 1991 .... 0.035 inch
        1992
            with TBI (VIN Z) .... 0.035 inch
            with CPI (VIN W) .... 0.045 inch
        1993 .... 0.045 inch
Firing order
    four-cylinder engine 1-3-4-2
    V6 engine 1-6-5-4-3-2

Cylinder location and distributor rotation

General

Engine idle speed .... Refer to Vehicle Emission Control Information label in engine compartment

Radiator pressure cap rating .... 15 psi

Drivebelt tension (conventional V-belts only)

Four-cylinder engine
    alternator
        vehicles with C60 A/C compressor
            new .... 169 lbs
            used .... 90 lbs
        vehicles with C41 heater
            new .... 146 lbs
            used .... 67 lbs
    power steering pump
        new .... 146 lbs
        used .... 67 lbs
    air conditioning compressor
        new .... 169 lbs
        used .... 90 lbs

V6 engine
    alternator
        new .... 135 lbs
        used .... 67 lbs
    power steering pump
        new .... 146 lbs
        used .... 67 lbs

air conditioning compressor	
new	169 lbs
used	90 lbs
AIR pump	
new	146 lbs
used	67 lbs

Filters

	AC part no.
Oil filter type	
four-cylinder engine	AC PF47
V6 engine	AC PF51
Air filter type	
four-cylinder engine	AC 785C
V6 engine	
with TBI..	AC 773C
with CPI	AC A1163C
PCV valve	
four-cylinder engine	
1985 and 1986 models...................................	AC CV881C
1987 models.	AC CV845C
1988 models	AC CV895C
V6 engine	AC CV789C
PCV filter	
four-cylinder engine	AC FB73
V6 engine (if equipped).....................................	AC FB59
Fuel filter (EFI equipped engine only)	AC GF481

Brakes

Brake pad wear limit..	1/8 in
Brake shoe wear limit	1/16 in

Torque specifications

	Ft-lbs
Differential (axle) fill plug....................................	10 to 20
Engine oil drain plug	20
Wheel lug nuts...	90 to 100
Manual transmission check/fill plug	15 to 25
Manual transmission drain plug.............................	15 to 25
Automatic transmission oil pan bolts	10
Carburetor bolts	
long	7
short	11
Throttle body nuts	12
Carburetor-mounted fuel filter nut	18
Spark plugs	
four-cylinder engine	10 to 15
V6 engine	22

Typical V6 engine compartment component layout (viewed from the passenger compartment with the engine cover removed)

1 *Throttle Body Injection (TBI) (air cleaner assembly removed)*
2 *Distributor*
3 *EGR valve*
4 *Spark plug wires*
5 *PCV valve*

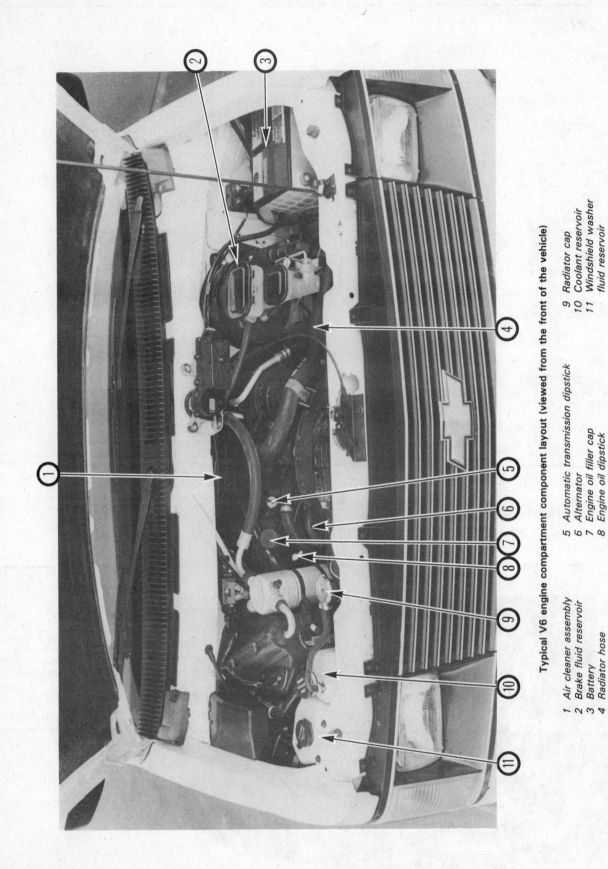

Typical V6 engine compartment component layout (viewed from the front of the vehicle)

1 Air cleaner assembly
2 Brake fluid reservoir
3 Battery
4 Radiator hose
5 Automatic transmission dipstick
6 Alternator
7 Engine oil filler cap
8 Engine oil dipstick
9 Radiator cap
10 Coolant reservoir
11 Windshield washer
    fluid reservoir

Underside view of engine/transmission (V6 engine shown)

1 Radiator hose
2 Drivebelt

3 Steering linkage grease fitting
4 Balljoint grease fitting
5 Automatic transmission pan

6 Exhaust pipe
7 Shock absorber

1

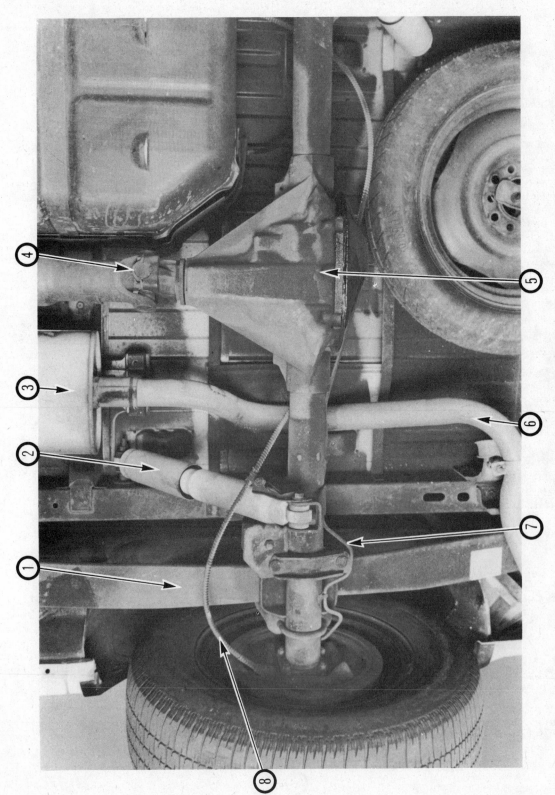

Typical rear underside component layout

1 Spring
2 Shock absorber
3 Muffler
4 Driveshaft universal joint
5 Rear axle/differential
6 Exhaust pipe
7 Brake line
8 Parking brake cable

1 GM mini-van Maintenance schedule

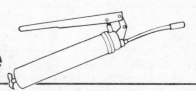

The following maintenance intervals are based on the assumption that the vehicle owner will be doing the maintenance or service work, as opposed to having a dealer service department do the work. Although the time/mileage intervals are loosely based on factory recommendations, most have been shortened to ensure, for example, that such items as lubricants and fluids are checked/changed at intervals that promote maximum engine/driveline service life. Also, subject to the preference of the individual owner interested in keeping his or her vehicle in peak condition at all times, and with the vehicle's ultimate resale in mind, many of the maintenance procedures may be performed more often than recommended in the following schedule. We encourage such owner initiative.

When the vehicle is new it should be serviced initially by a factory authorized dealer service department to protect the factory warranty. In many cases the initial maintenance check is done at no cost to the owner (check with your dealer service department for more information).

Every 250 miles or weekly, whichever comes first

Check the engine oil level (Section 4)
Check the engine coolant level (Section 4)
Check the windshield washer fluid level (Section 4)
Check the brake and clutch fluid levels (Section 4)
Check the tires and tire pressures (Section 5)

Every 3000 miles or 3 months, whichever comes first

All items listed above plus:
Check the automatic transmission fluid
    level (Section 6)
Check the power steering fluid level (Section 7)
Check and service the battery (Section 8)
Check the cooling system (Section 9)
Inspect and replace, if necessary, all underhood
    hoses (Section 10)
Inspect and replace, if necessary, the windshield
    wiper blades (Section 11)

Every 7500 miles or 12 months, whichever comes first

All items listed above plus:
Change the engine oil and filter (Section 12)*
Lubricate the chassis components (Section 13)
Inspect the suspension and steering
    components (Section 14)*
Inspect the exhaust system (Section 15)*
Check the manual transmission lubricant
    level (Section 16)*
Check the differential (rear axle) oil
    level (Section 17)*

Rotate the tires (Section 18)
Check the brakes (Section 19)*
Inspect the fuel system (Section 20)
Check the carburetor choke operation (Section 21)
Check the carburetor/throttle body mounting nut
    torque (Section 22)
Check the throttle linkage (Section 23)
Check the thermostatically-controlled air
    cleaner (Section 24)
Check the engine drivebelts (Section 25)
Check the seatbelts (Section 26)
Check the starter safety switch (Section 27)
Check the spare tire and jack (Section 28)

Every 30,000 miles or 24 months, whichever comes first

All items listed above plus:
Check and adjust, if necessary, the engine
    idle speed (Section 29)
Replace the fuel filter (Section 30)
Replace the air and PCV filters (Section 31)
Check and adjust, if necessary, the ignition
    timing (Section 32)
Change the automatic transmission
    fluid (Section 33)**
Change the manual transmission
    lubricant (Section 34)
Change the differential (rear axle) oil (Section 35)
Check and repack the front wheel
    bearings (Section 36)
Service the cooling system (drain, flush and
    refill) (Section 37)
Inspect and replace, if necessary, the PCV
    valve (Section 38)
Inspect the evaporative emissions control
    system (Section 39)
Check the EGR system (Section 40)
Replace the spark plugs (Section 41)
Inspect the spark plug wires, distributor cap
    and rotor (Sections 42 and 43)

* This item is affected by "severe" operating conditions as described below. If your vehicle is operated under severe conditions, perform all maintenance indicated with an asterisk (*) at 3000 mile/3 month intervals. Severe conditions are indicated if you mainly operate your vehicle under one or more of the following:

Operating in dusty areas
Towing a trailer
Idling for extended periods and/or low speed operation
Operating when outside temperatures remain below freezing and when most trips are less than four miles

** If operated under one or more of the following conditions, change the automatic transmission fluid every 12,000 miles:

In heavy city traffic where the outside temperature regularly reaches 90°F (32°C) or higher
In hilly or mountainous terrain
Frequent trailer pulling

2 Introduction

This Chapter is designed to help the home mechanic maintain the Chevrolet Astro/GMC Safari with the goals of maximum performance, economy, safety and reliability in mind.

Included is a master maintenance schedule (page 31), followed by procedures dealing specifically with each item on the schedule. Visual checks, adjustments, component replacement and other helpful items are included. Refer to the accompanying illustrations of the engine compartment and the underside of the vehicle for the locations of various components.

Servicing your vehicle in accordance with the mileage/time maintenance schedule and the step-by-step procedures will result in a planned maintenance program that should produce a long and reliable service life. Keep in mind that it is a comprehensive plan, so maintaining some items but not others at the specified intervals will not produce the same results.

As you service your vehicle, you will discover that many of the procedures can — and should — be grouped together because of the nature of the particular procedure you're performing or because of the close proximity of two otherwise unrelated components to one another.

For example, if the vehicle is raised for chassis lubrication, you should inspect the exhaust, suspension, steering and fuel systems while you're under the vehicle. When you're rotating the tires, it makes good sense to check the brakes since the wheels are already removed. Finally, let's suppose you have to borrow or rent a torque wrench. Even if you only need it to tighten the spark plugs, you might as well check the torque of as many critical fasteners as time allows.

The first step in this maintenance program is to prepare yourself before the actual work begins. Read through all the procedures you're planning to do, then gather up all the parts and tools needed. If it looks like you might run into problems during a particular job, seek advice from a mechanic or an experienced do-it-yourselfer.

3 Tune-up general information

The term *tune-up* is used in this manual to represent a combination of individual operations rather than one specific procedure.

If, from the time the vehicle is new, the routine maintenance schedule is followed closely and frequent checks are made of fluid levels and high wear items, as suggested throughout this manual, the engine will be kept in relatively good running condition and the need for additional work will be minimized.

More likely than not, however, there will be times when the engine is running poorly due to lack of regular maintenance. This is even more likely if a used vehicle, which has not received regular and frequent maintenance checks, is purchased. In such cases, an engine tune-up will be needed outside of the regular routine maintenance intervals.

The first step in any tune-up or diagnostic procedure to help correct a poor running engine is a cylinder compression check. A compression check (see Chapter 2 Part C) will help determine the condition of internal engine components and should be used as a guide for tune-up and repair procedures. If, for instance, a compression check indicates serious internal engine wear, a conventional tune-up will not improve the performance of the engine and would be a waste of time and money. Because of its importance, the compression check should be done by someone with the right equipment and the knowledge to use it properly.

The following procedures are those most often needed to bring a generally poor running engine back into a proper state of tune.

Minor tune-up

Check all engine related fluids (Section 4)
Clean, inspect and test the battery (Section 8)
Check and adjust the drivebelts (Section 25)
Replace the spark plugs (Section 41)
Inspect the distributor cap and rotor (Section 42)
Inspect the spark plug and coil wires (Section 42)
Check and adjust the ignition timing (Section 32)
Check the PCV valve (Section 38)
Check the air and PCV filters (Section 31)
Check the cooling system (Section 9)
Check all underhood hoses (Section 10)

Major tune-up

All items listed under Minor tune-up plus . . .
Check the EGR system (Section 40)
Check the ignition system (Chapter 5)
Check the charging system (Chapter 5)
Check the fuel system (Section 20)
Replace the air and PCV filters (Section 31)
Replace the distributor cap and rotor (Section 43)
Replace the spark plug wires (Section 42)

4 Fluid level checks

Refer to illustrations 4.4, 4.6, 4.8 and 4.19

Note: *The following are fluid level checks to be done on a 250 mile or weekly basis. Additional fluid level checks can be found in specific maintenance procedures which follow. Regardless of intervals, be alert to fluid leaks under the vehicle which would indicate a fault to be corrected immediately.*

1 Fluids are an essential part of the lubrication, cooling, brake, clutch and windshield washer systems. Because the fluids gradually become depleted and/or contaminated during normal operation of the vehicle, they must be periodically replenished. See *Recommended lubricants and fluids* at the beginning of this Chapter before adding fluid to any of the following components. **Note:** *The vehicle must be on level ground when fluid levels are checked.*

Engine oil

2 The engine oil level is checked with a dipstick that extends through a tube and into the oil pan at the bottom of the engine.

3 The oil level should be checked before the vehicle has been driven, or about 15 minutes after the engine has been shut off. If the oil is checked immediately after driving the vehicle, some of the oil will remain in the upper engine components, resulting in an inaccurate reading on the dipstick.

4 Pull the dipstick from the tube and wipe all the oil from the end with a clean rag or paper towel. Insert the clean dipstick all the way back into the tube, then pull it out again. Note the oil at the end of the dipstick. Add oil as necessary to keep the level between the ADD mark and the FULL mark on the dipstick **(see illustration)**.

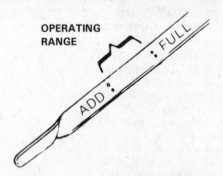

OPERATING RANGE

4.4 The engine oil level must be maintained between the marks at all times — it takes one quart of oil to raise the level from the ADD mark to the FULL mark

5 Do not overfill the engine by adding too much oil since this may result in oil fouled spark plugs, oil leaks or oil seal failures.

6 Oil is added to the engine after removing a pull off cap **(see illustration)**. An oil can spout or funnel may help to reduce spills.

7 Checking the oil level is an important preventive maintenance step. A consistently low oil level indicates oil leakage through damaged seals, defective gaskets or past worn rings or valve guides. If the oil looks milky in color or has water droplets in it, the cylinder head gasket(s) may be blown or the head(s) or block may be cracked. The engine should be checked immediately. The condition of the oil should also be checked. Whenever you check the oil level, slide your thumb and index finger up the dipstick before wiping off the oil. If you see small dirt or metal particles clinging to the dipstick, the oil should be changed (Section 12).

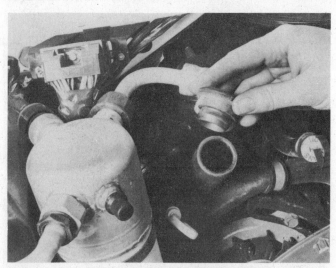

4.6   Oil is added to the engine after removing the pull-off cap from the filler tube

4.8   The engine coolant and windshield washer fluid reservoirs are located next to each other — DO NOT mix them up when adding fluids!

Engine coolant

Warning: *Do not allow antifreeze to come in contact with your skin or painted surfaces of the vehicle. Flush contaminated areas immediately with plenty of water. Don't store new coolant or leave old coolant lying around where it's accessible to children or pets — they're attracted by its sweet taste. Ingestion of even a small amount of coolant can be fatal! Wipe up garage floor and drip pan coolant spills immediately. Keep antifreeze containers covered and repair leaks in your cooling system immediately.*

8   All vehicles covered by this manual are equipped with a pressurized coolant recovery system. A white plastic coolant reservoir located in the engine compartment is connected by a hose to the radiator filler neck **(see illustration)**. If the engine overheats, coolant escapes through a valve in the radiator cap and travels through the hose into the reservoir. As the engine cools, the coolant is automatically drawn back into the cooling system to maintain the correct level.

9   The coolant level in the reservoir should be checked regularly. **Warning:** *Do not remove the radiator cap to check the coolant level when the engine is warm.* The level in the reservoir varies with the temperature of the engine. When the engine is cold, the coolant level should be at or slightly above the FULL COLD mark on the reservoir. Once the engine has warmed up, the level should be at or near the FULL HOT mark. If it isn't, allow the engine to cool, then remove the cap from the reservoir and add a 50/50 mixture of ethylene glycol-based antifreeze and water.

10   Drive the vehicle and recheck the coolant level. If only a small amount of coolant is required to bring the system up to the proper level, water can be used. However, repeated additions of water will dilute the antifreeze and water solution. In order to maintain the proper ratio of antifreeze and water, always top up the coolant level with the correct mixture. An empty plastic milk jug or bleach bottle makes an excellent container for mixing coolant. Do not use rust inhibitors or additives.

11   If the coolant level drops consistently, there may be a leak in the system. Inspect the radiator, hoses, filler cap, drain plugs and water pump (see Section 9). If no leaks are noted, have the radiator cap pressure tested by a service station.

12   If you have to remove the radiator cap, wait until the engine has cooled, then wrap a thick cloth around the cap and turn it to the first stop. If coolant or steam escapes, let the engine cool down longer, then remove the cap.

13   Check the condition of the coolant as well. It should be relatively clear. If it's brown or rust colored, the system should be drained, flushed and refilled. Even if the coolant appears to be normal, the corrosion inhibitors wear out, so it must be replaced at the specified intervals.

Windshield washer fluid

14   Fluid for the windshield washer system is located in a plastic reservoir in the engine compartment **(see illustration 4.8)**.

15   In milder climates, plain water can be used in the reservoir, but

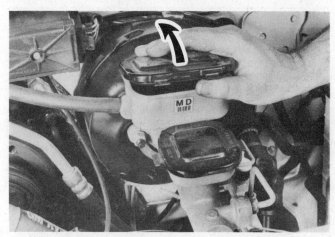

4.19   The brake fluid level is easily checked by looking through the clear reservoir — when adding fluid, grasp the tabs and rotate the cover up as shown

it should be kept no more than 2/3 full to allow for expansion if the water freezes. In colder climates, use windshield washer system antifreeze, available at any auto parts store, to lower the freezing point of the fluid. Mix the antifreeze with water in accordance with the manufacturer's directions on the container. **Caution:** *Don't use cooling system antifreeze — it will damage the vehicle's paint.*

16   To help prevent icing in cold weather, warm the windshield with the defroster before using the washer.

Battery electrolyte

17   All vehicles with which this manual is concerned are equipped with a battery which is permanently sealed (except for vent holes) and has no filler caps. Water doesn't have to be added to these batteries at any time. If a maintenance-type battery is installed, the caps on the top of the battery should be removed periodically to check for a low water level. This check is most critical during the warm summer months.

Brake and clutch fluid

18   The brake master cylinder is mounted on the front of the power booster unit in the engine compartment. The clutch cylinder used on manual transmissions is mounted adjacent to it on the firewall.

19   The fluid inside is readily visible. The level should be above the MIN marks on the reservoirs **(see illustration)**. If a low level is indicated, be sure to wipe the top of the reservoir cover with a clean rag to prevent contamination of the brake and/or clutch system before removing the cover.

20 When adding fluid, pour it carefully into the reservoir to avoid spilling it onto surrounding painted surfaces. Be sure the specified fluid is used, since mixing different types of brake fluid can cause damage to the system. See *Recommended lubricants and fluids* at the front of this Chapter or your owner's manual. **Warning:** *Brake fluid can harm your eyes and damage painted surfaces, so use extreme caution when handling or pouring it. Do not use brake fluid that has been standing open or is more than one year old. Brake fluid absorbs moisture from the air. Excess moisture can cause a dangerous loss of braking effectiveness.*

21 At this time the fluid and master cylinder can be inspected for contamination. The system should be drained and refilled if deposits, dirt particles or water droplets are seen in the fluid.

22 After filling the reservoir to the proper level, make sure the cover is on tight to prevent fluid leakage.

23 The brake fluid level in the master cylinder will drop slightly as the pads and the brake shoes at each wheel wear down during normal operation. If the master cylinder requires repeated additions to keep it at the proper level, it's an indication of leakage in the brake system, which should be corrected immediately. Check all brake lines and connections (see Section 19 for more information).

24 If, upon checking the master cylinder fluid level, you discover one or both reservoirs empty or nearly empty, the brake system should be bled (Chapter 9).

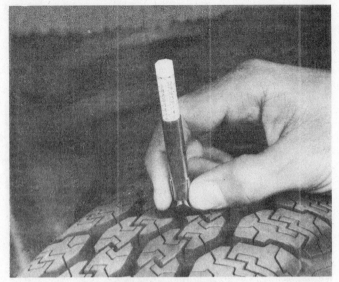

5.2   A tire tread depth indicator should be used to monitor tire wear — they are available at auto parts stores and service stations and cost very little

5   Tire and tire pressure checks

Refer to illustrations 5.2, 5.3, 5.4a, 5.4b and 5.8

1   Periodic inspection of the tires may spare you the inconvenience of being stranded with a flat tire. It can also provide you with vital information regarding possible problems in the steering and suspension systems before major damage occurs.

2   The original tires on this vehicle are equipped with 1/2-inch side bands that will appear when tread depth reaches 1/16-inch, but they don't appear until the tires are worn out. Tread wear can be monitored with a simple, inexpensive device known as a tread depth indicator **(see illustration)**.

3   Note any abnormal tread wear **(see illustration)**. Tread pattern irregularities such as cupping, flat spots and more wear on one side than the other are indications of front end alignment and/or balance prob-

lems. If any of these conditions are noted, take the vehicle to a tire shop or service station to correct the problem.

4   Look closely for cuts, punctures and embedded nails or tacks. Sometimes a tire will hold air pressure for a short time or leak down very slowly after a nail has embedded itself in the tread. If a slow leak persists, check the valve stem core to make sure it's tight **(see illustration)**. Examine the tread for an object that may have embedded itself in the tire or for a ''plug'' that may have begun to leak (radial tire punctures are repaired with a plug that's installed in a puncture). If a puncture is suspected, it can be easily verified by spraying a solution of soapy water onto the puncture area **(see illustration)**. The soapy solution will bubble if there's a leak. Unless the puncture is unusually large, a tire shop or service station can usually repair the tire.

Condition	Probable cause	Corrective action	Condition	Probable cause	Corrective action
Shoulder wear	• Underinflation (both sides wear) • Incorrect wheel camber (one side wear) • Hard cornering • Lack of rotation	• Measure and adjust pressure. • Repair or replace axle and suspension parts. • Reduce speed. • Rotate tires.	Feathered edge Toe wear	• Incorrect toe	• Adjust toe-in.
Center wear	• Overinflation • Lack of rotation	• Measure and adjust pressure. • Rotate tires.	Uneven wear	• Incorrect camber or caster • Malfunctioning suspension • Unbalanced wheel • Out-of-round brake drum • Lack of rotation	• Repair or replace axle and suspension parts. • Repair or replace suspension parts. • Balance or replace. • Turn or replace. • Rotate tires.

5.3   This chart will help you determine the condition of your tires, the probable cause(s) of abnormal wear and the corrective action necessary

5.4a   If a tire loses air on a steady basis, check the valve core first to make sure it's snug (special inexpensive wrenches are commonly available at auto parts stores)

5.4b   If the valve core is tight, raise the corner of the vehicle with the low tire and spray a soapy water solution onto the tread as the tire is turned slowly — slow leaks will cause small bubbles to appear

5   Carefully inspect the inner sidewall of each tire for evidence of brake fluid leakage. If you see any, inspect the brakes immediately.
6   Correct air pressure adds miles to the lifespan of the tires, improves mileage and enhances overall ride quality. Tire pressure cannot be accurately estimated by looking at a tire, especially if it's a radial. A tire pressure gauge is essential. Keep an accurate gauge in the vehicle. The pressure gauges attached to the nozzles of air hoses at gas stations are often inaccurate.
7   Always check tire pressure when the tires are cold. Cold, in this case, means the vehicle has not been driven over a mile in the three hours preceding a tire pressure check. A pressure rise of four to eight pounds is not uncommon once the tires are warm.
8   Unscrew the valve cap protruding from the wheel or hubcap and push the gauge firmly onto the valve stem (see illustration). Note the reading on the gauge and compare the figure to the recommended tire pressure shown on the placard on the driver's side door pillar. Be sure to reinstall the valve cap to keep dirt and moisture out of the valve stem mechanism. Check all four tires and, if necessary, add enough air to bring them up to the recommended pressure.
9   Don't forget to keep the spare tire inflated to the specified pressure (refer to your owner's manual or the tire sidewall). Note that the pressure recommended for the compact spare is higher than for the tires on the vehicle.

5.8   To extend the life of your tires, check the air pressure at least once a week with an accurate gauge (don't forget the spare!)

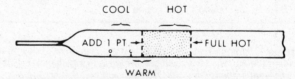

6.6   When checking the automatic transmission fluid level be sure to note the fluid temperature

---

6   Automatic transmission fluid level check

Refer to illustration 6.6

1   The automatic transmission fluid level should be carefully maintained. Low fluid level can lead to slipping or loss of drive, while overfilling can cause foaming and loss of fluid.
2   With the parking brake set, start the engine, then move the shift lever through all the gear ranges, ending in Park. The fluid level must be checked with the vehicle level and the engine running at idle. **Note:** *Incorrect fluid level readings will result if the vehicle has just been driven at high speeds for an extended period, in hot weather in city traffic, or if it has been pulling a trailer. If any of these conditions apply, wait until the fluid has cooled (about 30 minutes).*
3   With the transmission at normal operating temperature, remove the dipstick from the filler tube. The dipstick is located at the front of the engine compartment on the passenger's side.
4   Carefully touch the fluid at the end of the dipstick to determine if it is cool, warm or hot. Wipe the fluid from the dipstick with a clean rag and push it back into the filler tube until the cap seats.
5   Pull the dipstick out again and note the fluid level.

6   If the fluid felt cool, the level should be about 1/8 to 3/8-inch above the ADD mark (see illustration). If it felt warm, the level should be near the lower part of the operating range. If the fluid was hot, the level should be near the FULL HOT mark. If additional fluid is required, add it directly into the tube using a funnel. It takes about one pint to raise the level from the ADD mark to the FULL HOT mark with a hot transmission, so add the fluid a little at a time and keep checking the level until it's correct.
7   The condition of the fluid should also be checked along with the level. If the fluid at the end of the dipstick is a dark reddish-brown color, or if it smells burned, it should be changed. If you are in doubt about the condition of the fluid, purchase some new fluid and compare the two for color and smell.

7.2   The power steering fluid reservoir is located near the front of the engine below the brake master cylinder (arrow) — turn the cap _clockwise_ for removal

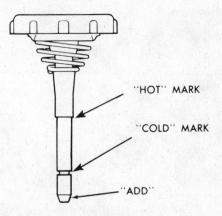

7.6   The marks on the power steering fluid dipstick indicate the safe range

7   Power steering fluid level check

Refer to illustrations 7.2 and 7.6

1   Unlike manual steering, the power steering system relies on fluid which may, over a period of time, require replenishing.
2   The fluid reservoir for the power steering pump is located on the pump body at the front of the engine (**see illustration**).
3   For the check, the front wheels should be pointed straight ahead and the engine should be off.
4   Use a clean rag to wipe off the reservoir cap and the area around the cap. This will help prevent any foreign matter from entering the reservoir during the check.
5   Twist off the cap and check the temperature of the fluid at the end of the dipstick with your finger.
6   Wipe off the fluid with a clean rag, reinsert the dipstick, then withdraw it and read the fluid level. The level should be at the HOT mark if the fluid was hot to the touch (**see illustration**). It should be at the COLD mark if the fluid was cool to the touch. Never allow the fluid level to drop below the ADD mark.
7   If additional fluid is required, pour the specified type directly into the reservoir, using a funnel to prevent spills.
8   If the reservoir requires frequent fluid additions, all power steering hoses, hose connections and the power steering pump should be carefully checked for leaks.

8   Battery check and maintenance

Refer to illustrations 8.1 and 8.6
Warning: _Certain precautions must be followed when checking and servicing the battery. Hydrogen gas, which is highly flammable, is always present in the battery cells, so keep lighted tobacco and all other open flames and sparks away from the battery. The electrolyte inside the battery is actually dilute sulfuric acid, which will cause injury if splashed on your skin or in your eyes. It will also ruin clothes and painted surfaces. When removing the battery cables, always detach the negative cable first and hook it up last!_
Caution: _If the vehicle is equipped with a Delco Loc II audio system (1992 and later models with a Compact Disc player), be sure the lockout feature is turned off before performing any procedure that requires disconnecting the battery (refer to your owner's manual for further information on this system)._

1   Battery maintenance is an important procedure which will help ensure that you are not stranded because of a dead battery. Several tools are required for this procedure (**see illustration**).
2   When checking/servicing the battery, always turn the engine and all accessories off.
3   A sealed (sometimes called maintenance-free), side-terminal battery is standard equipment on these vehicles. The cell caps cannot be re-

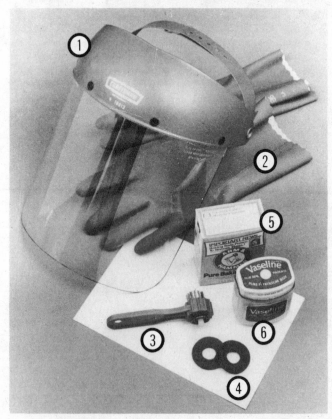

8.1   Tools and materials required for battery maintenance

1   **Face shield/safety goggles** — _When removing corrosion with a brush, the acidic particles can easily fly up into your eyes_
2   **Rubber gloves** — _Another safety item to consider when servicing the battery; remember that's acid inside the battery!_
3   **Battery terminal/ cable cleaner** — _This wire brush cleaning tool will remove all traces of corrosion from the battery and cable_
4   **Treated felt washers** — _Placing one of these on each terminal, directly under the cable end, will help prevent corrosion (be sure to get the correct type for side terminal batteries)_
5   **Baking soda** — _A solution of baking soda and water can be used to neutralize corrosion_
6   **Petroleum jelly** — _A layer of this on the battery terminal bolts will help prevent corrosion_

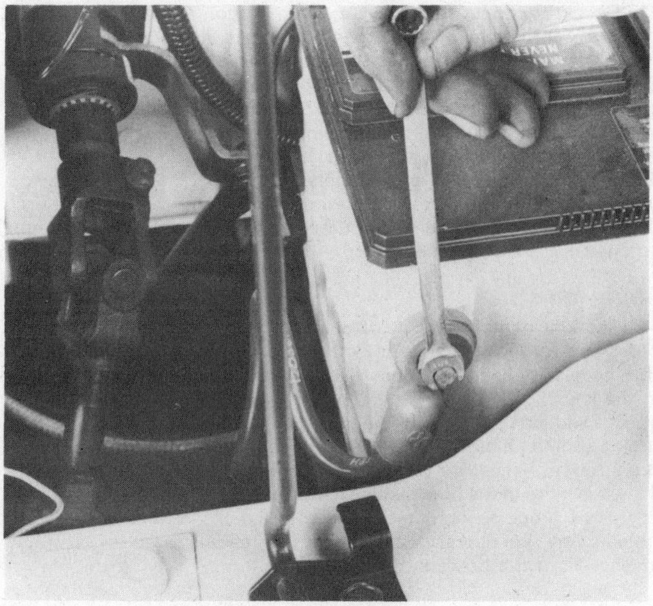

8.6 Make sure the battery terminal bolts are tight

moved, no electrolyte checks are required and water cannot be added to the cells. However, if a standard top-terminal aftermarket battery has been installed, the following maintenance procedure can be used.

4 Remove the caps and check the electrolyte level in each of the battery cells. It must be above the plates. There's usually a split-ring indicator in each cell to indicate the correct level. If the level is low, add distilled water only, then reinstall the cell caps. **Caution:** *Overfilling the cells may cause electrolyte to spill over during periods of heavy charging, causing corrosion and damage to nearby components.*

5 The external condition of the battery should be checked periodically. Look for damage such as a cracked case.

6 Check the tightness of the battery cable bolts **(see illustration)** to ensure good electrical connections. Inspect the entire length of each cable, looking for cracked or abraded insulation and frayed conductors.

7 If corrosion (visible as white, fluffy deposits) is evident, remove the cables from the terminals, clean them with a battery brush and reinstall them. Corrosion can be kept to a minimum by applying a layer of petroleum jelly or grease to the bolt threads.

8 Make sure the battery carrier is in good condition and the hold-down clamp is tight. If the battery is removed (see Chapter 5 for the removal and installation procedure), make sure that no parts remain in the bottom of the carrier when it's reinstalled. When reinstalling the hold-down clamp, don't overtighten the bolt.

9 Corrosion on the carrier, battery case and surrounding areas can be removed with a solution of water and baking soda. Apply the mixture with a small brush, let it work, then rinse it off with plenty of clean water.

10 Any metal parts of the vehicle damaged by corrosion should be coated with a zinc-based primer, then painted.

11 Additional information on the battery, charging and jump starting can be found in the front of this manual and in Chapter 5.

9 Cooling system check

Refer to illustration 9.4

1 Many major engine failures can be attributed to a faulty cooling system. If the vehicle is equipped with an automatic transmission, the cooling system also cools the transmission fluid and thus plays an important role in prolonging transmission life.

2 The cooling system should be checked with the engine cold. Do this before the vehicle is driven for the day or after it has been shut off for at least three hours.

3 Remove the radiator cap by turning it to the left until it reaches a stop. If you hear a hissing sound (indicating there is still pressure in the system), wait until this stops. Now press down on the cap with the palm of your hand and continue turning to the left until the cap

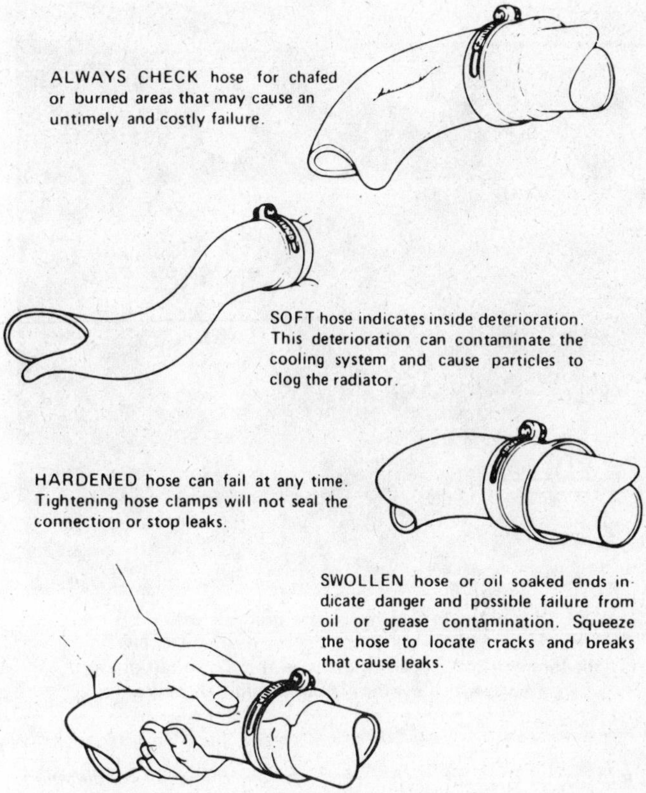

9.4 Hoses, like drivebelts, have a habit of failing at the worst possible time — to prevent the inconvenience of a blown radiator or heater hose, inspect them carefully as shown here

can be removed. Thoroughly clean the cap, inside and out, with clean water. Also clean the filler neck on the radiator. All traces of corrosion should be removed. The coolant inside the radiator should be relatively transparent. If it is rust colored, the system should be drained and re-filled (Section 37). If the coolant level is not up to the top, add additional antifreeze/coolant mixture (see Section 4).

4 Carefully check the large upper and lower radiator hoses along with the smaller diameter heater hoses which run from the engine to the firewall. On some models the heater return hose runs directly to the radiator. Inspect each hose along its entire length, replacing any hose which is cracked, swollen or shows signs of deterioration. Cracks may become more apparent if the hose is squeezed **(see illustration)**. Regardless of condition, it's a good idea to replace hoses with new ones every two years.

5 Make sure that all hose connections are tight. A leak in the cooling system will usually show up as white or rust colored deposits on the areas adjoining the leak. If wire-type clamps are used at the ends of the hoses, it may be a good idea to replace them with more secure screw-type clamps.

6 Use compressed air or a soft brush to remove bugs, leaves, etc. from the front of the radiator or air conditioning condenser. Be careful not to damage the delicate cooling fins or cut yourself on them.

7 Every other inspection, or at the first indication of cooling system problems, have the cap and system pressure tested. If you don't have a pressure tester, most gas stations and repair shops will do this for a minimal charge.

10 Underhood hose check and replacement

Refer to illustration 10.1

General

1 **Caution:** *Replacement of air conditioning hoses must be left to a dealer service department or air conditioning shop that has the equip-*

10.1 Air conditioning hoses are best identified by the metal tubes used at all bends (arrow) — DO NOT disconnect or accidently damage the air conditioning hoses as the system is under high pressure

ment to depressurize the system safely. *Never remove air conditioning components or hoses* (see illustration) *until the system has been depressurized.*

2   High temperatures in the engine compartment can cause the deterioration of the rubber and plastic hoses used for engine, accessory and emission systems operation. Periodic inspection should be made for cracks, loose clamps, material hardening and leaks. Information specific to the cooling system hoses can be found in Section 9.

3   Some, but not all, hoses are secured to the fittings with clamps. Where clamps are used, check to be sure they haven't lost their tension, allowing the hose to leak. If clamps aren't used, make sure the hose has not expanded and/or hardened where it slips over the fitting, allowing it to leak.

Vacuum hoses

4   It's quite common for vacuum hoses, especially those in the emissions system, to be color coded or identified by colored stripes molded into them. Various systems require hoses with different wall thicknesses, collapse resistance and temperature resistance. When replacing hoses, be sure the new ones are made of the same material.

5   Often the only effective way to check a hose is to remove it completely from the vehicle. If more than one hose is removed, be sure to label the hoses and fittings to ensure correct installation.

6   When checking vacuum hoses, be sure to include any plastic T-fittings in the check. Inspect the fittings for cracks and the hose where it fits over the fitting for distortion, which could cause leakage.

7   A small piece of vacuum hose (1/4-inch inside diameter) can be used as a stethoscope to detect vacuum leaks. Hold one end of the hose to your ear and probe around vacuum hoses and fittings, listening for the "hissing" sound characteristic of a vacuum leak. **Warning:** *When probing with the vacuum hose stethoscope, be very careful not to come into contact with moving engine components such as the drivebelt, cooling fan, etc.*

Fuel hose

Warning: *There are certain precautions which must be taken when inspecting or servicing fuel system components. Work in a well ventilated area and do not allow open flames (cigarettes, appliance pilot lights, etc.) or bare light bulbs near the work area. Mop up any spills immediately and do not store fuel soaked rags where they could ignite. On vehicles equipped with fuel injection, the fuel system is under pressure, so if any fuel lines are to be disconnected, the pressure in the system must be relieved first (see Chapter 4 for more information).*

8   Check all rubber fuel lines for deterioration and chafing. Check especially for cracks in areas where the hose bends and just before fittings, such as where a hose attaches to the fuel filter.

9   High quality fuel line, usually identified by the word *Fluroelastomer* printed on the hose, should be used for fuel line replacement. Never, under any circumstances, use unreinforced vacuum line, clear plastic tubing or water hose for fuel lines.

10   Spring-type clamps are commonly used on fuel lines. These clamps often lose their tension over a period of time, and can be "sprung" during removal. Replace all spring-type clamps with screw clamps whenever a hose is replaced.

Metal lines

11   Sections of metal line are often used for fuel line between the fuel pump and carburetor or fuel injection unit. Check carefully to be sure the line has not been bent or crimped and that cracks have not started in the line.

12   If a section of metal fuel line must be replaced, only seamless steel tubing should be used, since copper and aluminum tubing don't have the strength necessary to withstand normal engine vibration.

13   Check the metal brake lines where they enter the master cylinder and brake proportioning unit (if used) for cracks in the lines or loose fittings. Any sign of brake fluid leakage calls for an immediate thorough inspection of the brake system.

---

11   Wiper blade inspection and replacement

1   The windshield wiper and blade assembly should be inspected periodically for damage, loose components and cracked or worn blade elements.

2   Road film can build up on the wiper blades and affect their efficiency, so they should be washed regularly with a mild detergent solution.

3   The action of the wiping mechanism can loosen the bolts, nuts and fasteners, so they should be checked and tightened, as necessary, at the same time the wiper blades are checked.

4   If the wiper blade elements (sometimes called inserts) are cracked, worn or warped, they should be replaced with new ones.

5   Pull the wiper blade/arm assembly away from the glass.

6   Depress the blade-to-arm connector and slide the blade assembly off the wiper arm and over the retaining stud.

7   Pinch the tabs at the end, then slide the element out of the blade assembly.

8   Compare the new element with the old for length, design, etc.

9   Slide the new element into place. It will automatically lock at the correct location.

10   Reinstall the blade assembly on the arm, wet the windshield and check for proper operation.

---

12   Engine oil and filter change

Refer to illustrations 12.3, 12.9, 12.14 and 12.18

1   Frequent oil changes are the most important preventive maintenance procedures that can be done by the home mechanic. As engine oil ages, it becomes diluted and contaminated, which leads to premature engine wear.

2   Although some sources recommend oil filter changes every other oil change, we feel that the minimal cost of an oil filter and the relative ease with which it is installed dictate that a new filter be installed every time the oil is changed.

3   Gather together all necessary tools and materials before beginning this procedure (see illustration).

4   You should have plenty of clean rags and newspapers handy to mop up any spills. Access to the underside of the vehicle is greatly improved if the vehicle can be lifted on a hoist, driven onto ramps or supported by jackstands. **Warning:** *Do not work under a vehicle which is supported only by a bumper, hydraulic or scissors-type jack.*

5   If this is your first oil change, get under the vehicle and familiarize yourself with the locations of the oil drain plug and the oil filter. The engine and exhaust components will be warm during the actual work,

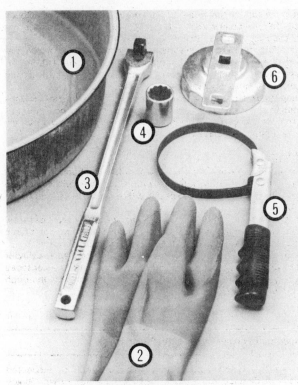

12.3 These tools are required when changing the engine oil and filter

1 **Drain pan** — *It should be fairly shallow in depth, but wide in order to prevent spills*
2 **Rubber gloves** — *When removing the drain plug and filter it is inevitable that you will get oil on your hands (the gloves will prevent burns)*
3 **Breaker bar** — *Sometimes the oil drain plug is pretty tight and a long breaker bar is needed to loosen it*
4 **Socket** — *To be used with the breaker bar or a ratchet (must be the correct size to fit the drain plug)*
5 **Filter wrench** — *This is a metal band-type wrench, which requires clearance around the filter to be effective*
6 **Filter wrench** — *This type fits on the bottom of the filter and can be turned with a ratchet or breaker bar (different size wrenches are available for different types of filters)*

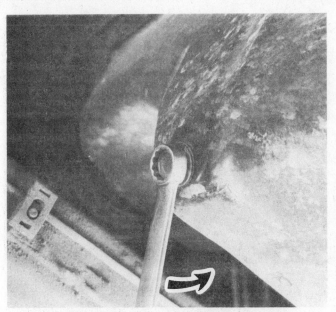

12.9 The oil drain plug is located at the bottom of the pan and should be removed with a socket or box-end wrench — DO NOT use an open-end wrench, as the corners on the bolt can be easily rounded off

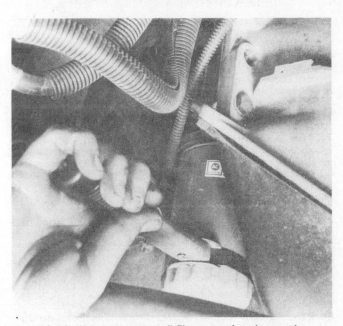

12.14 Use a strap-type oil filter wrench to loosen the filter — if access makes removal difficult, other types of filter wrenches are available

so note how they are situated to avoid touching them when working under the vehicle.

6   Warm the engine to normal operating temperature. If the new oil or any tools are needed, use this warm-up time to gather everything necessary for the job. The correct type of oil for your application can be found in *Recommended lubricants and fluids* at the beginning of this Chapter.

7   With the engine oil warm (warm engine oil will drain better and more built-up sludge will be removed with it), raise and support the vehicle. Make sure it's safely supported!

8   Move all necessary tools, rags and newspapers under the vehicle. Set the drain pan under the drain plug. Keep in mind that the oil will initially flow from the pan with some force; position the pan accordingly.

9   Being careful not to touch any of the hot exhaust components, use a wrench to remove the drain plug near the bottom of the oil pan (**see illustration**). Depending on how hot the oil is, you may want to wear gloves while unscrewing the plug the final few turns.

10   Allow the old oil to drain into the pan. It may be necessary to move the pan as the oil flow slows to a trickle.

11   After all the oil has drained, wipe off the drain plug with a clean rag. Small metal particles may cling to the plug and would immediately contaminate the new oil.

12   Clean the area around the drain plug opening and reinstall the plug.

Tighten the plug securely with the wrench. If a torque wrench is available, use it to tighten the plug.

13   Move the drain pan into position under the oil filter.

14   Use the filter wrench to loosen the oil filter (**see illustration**). Chain or metal band filter wrenches may distort the filter canister, but it doesn't matter since the filter will be discarded anyway.

15   Completely unscrew the old filter. Be careful; it's full of oil. Empty the oil inside the filter into the drain pan.

16   Compare the old filter with the new one to make sure they're the same type.

17   Use a clean rag to remove all oil, dirt and sludge from the area where the oil filter mounts to the engine. Check the old filter to make sure the rubber gasket isn't stuck to the engine. If the gasket is stuck to the engine (use a flashlight if necessary), remove it.

12.18 Lubricate the oil filter gasket with clean engine oil before installing the filter on the engine

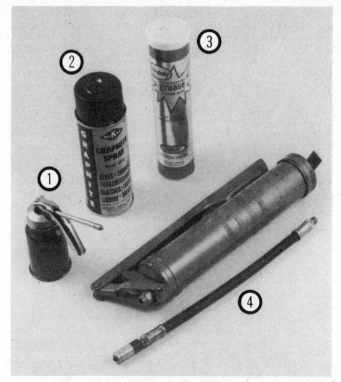

13.1 Materials required for chassis and body lubrication

1 **Engine oil** — *Light engine oil in a can like this can be used for door and hood hinges*
2 **Graphite spray** — *Used to lubricate lock cylinders*
3 **Grease** — *Grease, in a variety of types and weights, is available for use in a grease gun. Check the Specifications for your requirements*
4 **Grease gun** — *A common grease gun, shown here with a detachable hose and nozzle, is needed for chassis lubrication. After use, clean it thoroughly!*

18 Apply a light coat of clean oil to the rubber gasket on the new oil filter **(see illustration)**.
19 Attach the new filter to the engine, following the tightening directions printed on the filter canister or packing box. Most filter manufacturers recommend against using a filter wrench due to the possibility of overtightening and damage to the seal.
20 Remove all tools, rags, etc. from under the vehicle, being careful not to spill the oil in the drain pan, then lower the vehicle.
21 Move to the engine compartment and locate the oil filler cap.
22 If an oil can spout is used, push the spout into the top of the oil can and pour the fresh oil through the filler opening. A funnel may also be used.
23 Pour four quarts of fresh oil into the engine. Wait a few minutes to allow the oil to drain into the pan, then check the level on the oil dipstick (see Section 4 if necessary). If the oil level is above the ADD mark, start the engine and allow the new oil to circulate.
24 Run the engine for only about a minute and then shut it off. Immediately look under the vehicle and check for leaks at the oil pan drain plug and around the oil filter. If either is leaking, tighten with a bit more force.
25 With the new oil circulated and the filter now completely full, recheck the level on the dipstick and add more oil as necessary.
26 During the first few trips after an oil change, make it a point to check frequently for leaks and proper oil level.
27 The old oil drained from the engine cannot be reused in its present state and should be disposed of. Oil reclamation centers, auto repair shops and gas stations will normally accept the oil, which can be refined and used again. After the oil has cooled it can be drained into a suitable container (capped plastic jugs, topped bottles, milk cartons, etc.) for transport to one of these disposal sites.

13 Chassis lubrication

Refer to illustrations 13.1, 13.2 and 13.6

1 Refer to *Recommended lubricants and fluids* at the front of this Chapter to obtain the necessary grease, etc. You'll also need a grease gun **(see illustration)**. Occasionally plugs will be installed rather than grease fittings. If so, grease fittings will have to be purchased and installed.
2 Look under the vehicle and see if grease fittings or plugs are installed **(see illustration)**. If there are plugs, remove them and buy grease fittings, which will thread into the component. A dealer or auto parts

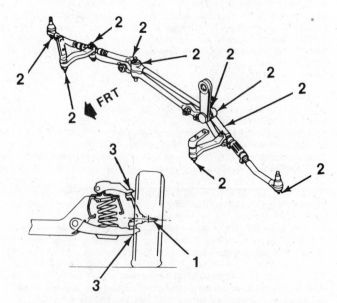

13.2 This diagram shows where the steering component grease fittings are located

1 *Wheel bearings (Section 36)*
2 *Steering linkage grease fittings*
3 *Balljoint grease fittings*

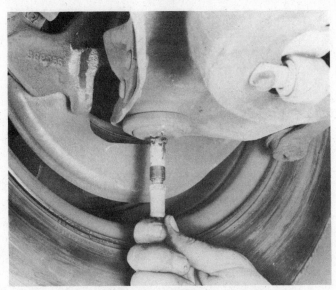

13.6   After wiping the grease fitting clean, push the nozzle firmly into place and pump the grease into the component — usually about two pumps of the gun will be sufficient

store will be able to supply the correct fittings. Straight, as well as angled, fittings are available.

3   For easier access under the vehicle, raise it with a jack and place jackstands under the frame. Make sure it's safely supported by the stands. If the wheels are to be removed at this interval for tire rotation or brake inspection, loosen the lug nuts slightly while the vehicle is still on the ground.

4   Before beginning, force a little grease out of the nozzle to remove any dirt from the end of the gun. Wipe the nozzle clean with a rag.

5   With the grease gun and plenty of clean rags, crawl under the vehicle and begin lubricating the components.

6   Wipe the balljoint grease fitting nipple clean and push the nozzle firmly over it **(see illustration)**. Squeeze the trigger on the grease gun to force grease into the component. The balljoints should be lubricated until the rubber seal is firm to the touch. Do not pump too much grease into the fittings as it could rupture the seal. For all other suspension and steering components, continue pumping grease into the fitting until it oozes out of the joint between the two components. If it escapes around the grease gun nozzle, the nipple is clogged or the nozzle is not completely seated on the fitting. Resecure the gun nozzle to the fitting and try again. If necessary, replace the fitting with a new one.

7   Wipe the excess grease from the components and the grease fitting. Repeat the procedure for the remaining fittings.

8   If equipped with a manual transmission, lubricate the shift linkage with a little multi-purpose grease. Later 4-speed transmissions also have a grease fitting so the grease gun can be used.

9   On manual transmission equipped models, lubricate the clutch linkage pivot points with clean engine oil. Lubricate the pushrod-to-fork contact points with chassis grease.

10   While you are under the vehicle, clean and lubricate the parking brake cable, along with the cable guides and levers. This can be done by smearing some of the chassis grease onto the cable and its related parts with your fingers.

11   The steering gear seldom requires the addition of lubricant, but if there is obvious leakage of grease at the seals, remove the plug or cover and check the lubricant level. If the level is low, add the specified lubricant.

12   Open the hood and smear a little chassis grease on the hood latch mechanism. Have an assistant pull the hood release lever from inside the vehicle as you lubricate the cable at the latch.

13   Lubricate all the hinges (door, hood, etc.) with engine oil to keep them in proper working order.

14   The key lock cylinders can be lubricated with spray graphite or silicone lubricant, which is available at auto parts stores.

15   Lubricate the door weatherstripping with silicone spray. This will reduce chafing and retard wear.

14   Suspension and steering check

1   Indications of a fault in these systems are excessive play in the steering wheel before the front wheels react, excessive sway around corners, body movement over rough roads or binding at some point as the steering wheel is turned.

2   Raise the front of the vehicle periodically and visually check the suspension and steering components for wear. Because of the work to be done, make sure the vehicle cannot fall from the stands.

3   Check the wheel bearings. Do this by spinning the front wheels. Listen for any abnormal noises and watch to make sure the wheel spins true (doesn't wobble). Grab the top and bottom of the tire and pull in-and-out on it. Notice any movement which would indicate a loose wheel bearing assembly. If the bearings are suspect, refer to Section 36 and Chapter 10 for more information.

4   From under the vehicle check for loose bolts, broken or disconnected parts and deteriorated rubber bushings on all suspension and steering components. Look for grease or fluid leaking from the steering assembly. Check the power steering hoses and connections for leaks.

5   Have an assistant turn the steering wheel from side-to-side and check the steering components for free movement, chafing and binding. If the steering doesn't react with the movement of the steering wheel, try to determine where the slack is located.

15   Exhaust system check

1   With the engine cold (at least three hours after the vehicle has been driven), check the complete exhaust system from the manifold to the end of the tailpipe. Be careful around the catalytic converter, which may be hot even after three hours. The inspection should be done with the vehicle on a hoist to permit unrestricted access. If a hoist isn't available, raise the vehicle and support it securely on jackstands.

2   Check the exhaust pipes and connections for signs of leakage and/or corrosion indicating a potential failure. Make sure that all brackets and hangers are in good condition and tight.

3   Inspect the underside of the body for holes, corrosion, open seams, etc. which may allow exhaust gases to enter the passenger compartment. Seal all body openings with silicone or body putty.

4   Rattles and other noises can often be traced to the exhaust system, especially the hangers, mounts and heat shields. Try to move the pipes, mufflers and catalytic converter. If the components can come in contact with the body or suspension parts, secure the exhaust system with new brackets and hangers.

16   Manual transmission lubricant level check

Refer to illustration 16.1

1   The manual transmission has an inspection and fill plug which must be removed to check the oil level **(see illustration)**. If the vehicle is raised to gain access to the plug, be sure to support it safely on jackstands — DO NOT crawl under a vehicle which is supported only by a jack!

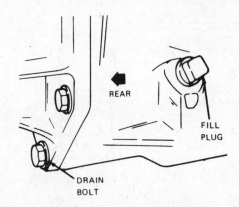

16.1   The manual transmission has two plugs, one for checking and filling and the lower one for draining

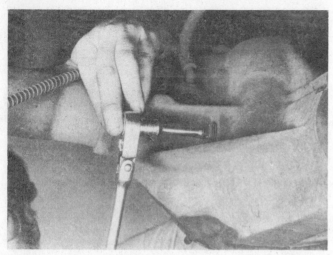

17.2   Use a ratchet or breaker bar and a 3/8-inch drive extension to remove the differential check/fill plug

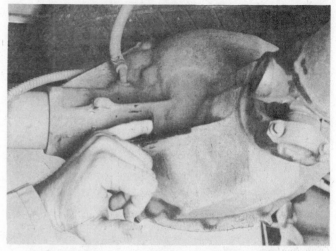

17.3   Use your little finger as a dipstick to make sure the differential oil level is even with the bottom of the opening

2   Remove the plug from the transmission and use your little finger to reach inside the housing to feel the oil level. The level should be at or near the bottom of the plug hole.
3   If it isn't, add the recommended oil through the plug hole with a syringe or squeeze bottle.
4   Install and tighten the plug and check for leaks after the first few miles of driving.

17   Differential oil level check

Refer to illustrations 17.2 and 17.3

1   The differential has a check/fill plug which must be removed to check the oil level. If the vehicle is raised to gain access to the plug, be sure to support it safely on jackstands — DO NOT crawl under the vehicle when it's supported only by the jack.
2   Remove the oil check/fill plug from the side of the differential (**see illustration**).
3   The oil level should be at the bottom of the plug opening (**see illustration**). If not, use a syringe to add the recommended lubricant until it just starts to run out of the opening. On some models a tag is located in the area of the plug which gives information regarding lubricant type, particularly on models equipped with a limited slip differential.
4   Install the plug and tighten it securely.

18   Tire rotation

Refer to illustration 18.2

1   The tires should be rotated at the specified intervals and whenever

uneven wear is noticed.
2   Refer to the accompanying illustration for the preferred tire rotation pattern.
3   Refer to the information in *Jacking and towing* at the front of this manual for the proper procedures to follow when raising the vehicle and changing a tire. If the brakes are to be checked, don't apply the parking brake as stated. Make sure the tires are blocked to prevent the vehicle from rolling as it's raised.
4   Preferably, the entire vehicle should be raised at the same time. This can be done on a hoist or by jacking up each corner and then lowering the vehicle onto jackstands placed under the frame rails. Always use four jackstands and make sure the vehicle is safely supported.
5   After rotation, check and adjust the tire pressures as necessary and be sure to check the lug nut tightness.
6   For additional information on the wheels and tires, refer to Chapter 10.

19   Brake check

Refer to illustrations 19.4, 19.6, 19.11, 19.12 and 19.14
Note: *For detailed photographs of the brake system, refer to Chapter 9.*
Warning: *Brake system dust contains asbestos, which is hazardous to your health. DO NOT blow it out with compressed air and DO NOT inhale it. DO NOT use gasoline or solvents to remove the dust. Use brake system cleaner or denatured alcohol only.*

1   In addition to the specified intervals, the brakes should be inspected every time the wheels are removed or whenever a defect is suspected.
2   To check the brakes, raise the vehicle and place it securely on jackstands. Remove the wheels (see *Jacking and towing* at the front of the manual, if necessary).

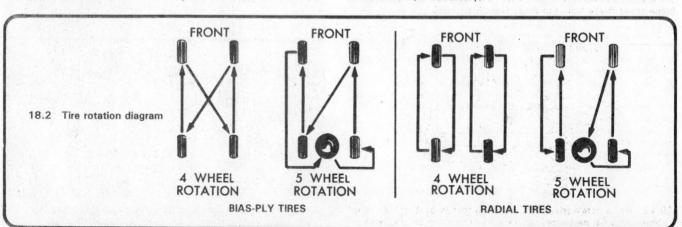

18.2   Tire rotation diagram

FRONT   FRONT   FRONT   FRONT

4 WHEEL ROTATION   5 WHEEL ROTATION   4 WHEEL ROTATION   5 WHEEL ROTATION

BIAS-PLY TIRES   RADIAL TIRES

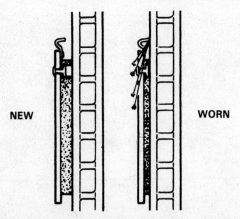

19.4   The front disc brake pad wear sensors will contact the rotors and make a squealing noise when the pad is worn out

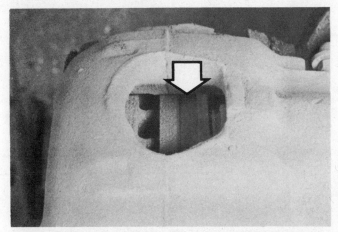

19.6   The front disc brake pads can be checked easily by looking through the inspection window in each caliper

Disc brakes

3   Disc brakes are used on the front wheels. Extensive rotor damage can occur if the pads are not replaced when needed.

4   These vehicles are equipped with a wear sensor attached to the inner pad. This is a small, bent piece of metal which is visible from the inner side of the brake caliper. When the pad wears to the specified limit, the metal sensor rubs against the rotor and makes a squealing sound **(see illustration)**.

5   The disc brake calipers, which contain the pads, are visible with the wheels removed. There is an outer pad and an inner pad in each caliper. All pads should be inspected.

6   Each caliper has a "window" to inspect the pads. Check the thickness of the pad lining by looking into the caliper at each end and down through the inspection window at the top of the housing **(see illustration)**. If the wear sensor is very close to the rotor or the pad material has worn to about 1/8-inch or less, the pads should be replaced.

7   If you're unsure about the exact thickness of the remaining lining material, remove the pads for further inspection or replacement (refer to Chapter 9).

8   Before installing the wheels, check for leakage and/or damage (cracks, splitting, etc.) around the brake hose connections. Replace the hose or fittings as necessary, referring to Chapter 9.

9   Check the condition of the rotor. Look for score marks, deep scratches and burned spots. If these conditions exist, the hub/rotor assembly should be removed for servicing (Section 36).

Drum brakes

10   On rear brakes, remove the drum by pulling it off the axle and brake assembly. If this proves difficult, make sure the parking brake is released, then squirt penetrating oil around the center hub areas. Allow the oil to soak in and try to pull the drum off again.

11   If the drum still cannot be pulled off, the brake shoes will have to be adjusted. This is done by first removing the plug from the backing plate with a hammer and chisel **(see illustration)**.

12   With the plug removed, push the lever off the star wheel and then use a small screwdriver to turn the star wheel, which will move the brake shoes away from the drum **(see illustration)**.

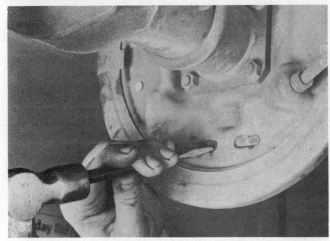

19.11   Use a hammer and chisel to remove the plug from the brake backing plate

13   With the drum removed, do not touch any brake dust (see the Warning at the beginning of this Section).

14   Note the thickness of the lining material on both the front and rear brake shoes. If the material has worn away to within 1/16-inch of the recessed rivets or metal backing, the shoes should be replaced **(see illustration)**. The shoes should also be replaced if they're cracked,

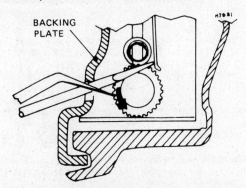

19.12   Use a screwdriver and adjusting tool to back off the rear brake shoes if necessary so the brake drum can be removed

19.14   The brake shoe lining thickness is measured from the outer surface of the lining to the metal shoe

glazed (shiny surface) or contaminated with brake fluid.

15   Make sure that all the brake assembly springs are connected and in good condition.

16   Check the brake components for any signs of fluid leakage. With your finger, carefully pry back the rubber cups on the wheel cylinders located at the top of the brake shoes. Any leakage is an indication that the wheel cylinders should be overhauled immediately (Chapter 9). Also check brake hoses and connections for signs of leakage.

17   Wipe the inside of the drum with a clean rag and brake cleaner or denatured alcohol. Again, be careful not to breath the dangerous asbestos dust.

18   Check the inside of the drum for cracks, score marks, deep scratches and hard spots, which will appear as small discolorations. If these imperfections cannot be removed with fine emery cloth, the drum must be taken to a machine shop equipped to turn the drums.

19   If after the inspection process all parts are in good working condition, reinstall the brake drum (using a metal or rubber plug if the knock-out was removed).

20   Install the wheels and lower the vehicle.

Parking brake

21   The parking brake operates from a foot pedal and locks the rear brake system. The easiest, and perhaps most obvious method of periodically checking the operation of the parking brake assembly is to park the vehicle on a steep hill with the parking brake set and the transmission in Neutral. If the parking brake cannot prevent the vehicle from rolling, it's in need of adjustment (see Chapter 9).

20   Fuel system check

Warning: *There are certain precautions to take when inspecting or servicing the fuel system components. Work in a well ventilated area and don't allow open flames (cigarettes, appliance pilot lights, etc.) in the work area. Mop up spills immediately and don't store fuel soaked rags where they could ignite. On fuel injection equipped models the fuel system is under pressure. No components should be disconnected until the pressure has been relieved (see Chapter 4).*

1   On most models the main fuel tank is located under the left side of the vehicle.

2   The fuel system is most easily checked with the vehicle raised on a hoist so the components underneath the vehicle are readily visible and accessible.

3   If the smell of gasoline is noticed while driving or after the vehicle has been in the sun, the system should be thoroughly inspected immediately.

4   Remove the gas tank cap and check for damage, corrosion and an unbroken sealing imprint on the gasket. Replace the cap with a new one if necessary.

5   With the vehicle raised, check the gas tank and filler neck for punctures, cracks and other damage. The connection between the filler neck and the tank is especially critical. Sometimes a rubber filler neck will leak due to loose clamps or deteriorated rubber, problems a home mechanic can usually rectify. **Warning:** *Do not, under any circumstances, try to repair a fuel tank yourself (except rubber components). A welding torch or any open flame can easily cause the fuel vapors to explode if the proper precautions are not taken!*

6   Carefully check all rubber hoses and metal lines leading away from the fuel tank. Look for loose connections, deteriorated hoses, crimped lines and other damage. Follow the lines to the front of the vehicle, carefully inspecting them all the way. Repair or replace damaged sections as necessary.

7   If a fuel odor is still evident after the inspection, refer to Section 39.

21   Carburetor choke check

Refer to illustration 21.3

1   The choke operates only when the engine is cold, so this check should be performed before the engine has been started for the day.

2   Remove the engine cover and take off the top plate of the air cleaner assembly. It's usually held in place by a wing nut at the center. If any vacuum hoses must be disconnected, make sure you tag the hoses for reinstallation in their original positions. Place the top plate and wing

21.3   The carburetor choke plate is visible after removing the air cleaner top plate

nut aside, out of the way of moving engine components.

3   Look at the center of the air cleaner housing. You will notice a flat plate at the carburetor opening **(see illustration)**.

4   Press the accelerator pedal to the floor. The plate should close completely. Start the engine while you watch the plate at the carburetor. Don't position your face near the carburetor, as the engine could backfire, causing serious burns. When the engine starts, the choke plate should open slightly.

5   Allow the engine to continue running at an idle speed. As the engine warms up to operating temperature, the plate should slowly open, allowing more air to enter through the top of the carburetor.

6   After a few minutes, the choke plate should be fully open to the vertical position. Blip the throttle to make sure the fast idle cam disengages.

7   You'll notice that the engine speed corresponds with the plate opening. With the plate fully closed, the engine should run at a fast idle speed. As the plate opens and the throttle is moved to disengage the fast idle cam, the engine speed will decrease.

8   Refer to Chapter 4 for specific information on adjusting and servicing the choke components.

22   Carburetor/throttle body mounting nut torque check

1   The carburetor or TBI unit is attached to the top of the intake manifold by several bolts or nuts. These fasteners can sometimes work loose from vibration and temperature changes during normal engine operation and cause a vacuum leak.

2   Remove the engine cover (Chapter 11).

3   If you suspect that a vacuum leak exists at the bottom of the carburetor or throttle body, obtain a length of hose. Start the engine and place one end of the hose next to your ear as you probe around the base with the other end. You will hear a hissing sound if a leak exists (be careful of hot or moving engine components).

4   Remove the air cleaner assembly, tagging each hose to be disconnected with a piece of numbered tape to make reassembly easier.

5   Locate the mounting nuts or bolts at the base of the carburetor or throttle body. Decide what special tools or adapters will be necessary, if any, to tighten the fasteners.

6   Tighten the nuts or bolts to the specified torque. Don't overtighten them, as the threads could strip.

7   If, after the nuts or bolts are properly tightened, a vacuum leak still exists, the carburetor or throttle body must be removed and a new gasket installed. See Chapter 4 for more information.

8   After tightening the fasteners, reinstall the air cleaner and return all hoses to their original positions. Install the engine cover.

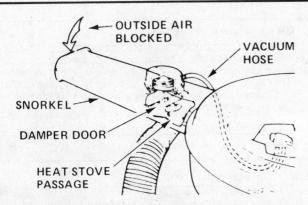

24.5 When the engine is cold, the damper door closes off the snorkel passage, allowing air warmed by the exhaust manifold to enter the carburetor

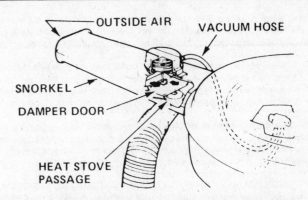

24.6 As the engine warms up, the damper door moves down to close off the heat stove passage and open the snorkel passage so outside air can enter the carburetor

23 Throttle linkage inspection

1   Inspect the throttle linkage for damage and missing parts and for binding and interference when the accelerator pedal is depressed.
2   Lubricate the various linkage pivot points with engine oil.

24 Thermostatic air cleaner check

Refer to illustrations 24.5 and 24.6

1   Some engines are equipped with a thermostatically controlled air cleaner which draws air to the carburetor from different locations, depending on engine temperature.
2   This is a visual check. If access is limited, a small mirror may have to be used.
3   Remove the engine cover and locate the damper door inside the air cleaner assembly. It's inside the long snorkel of the metal air cleaner housing.
4   If there is a flexible air duct attached to the end of the snorkel, leading to an area behind the grille, disconnect it at the snorkel. This will enable you to look through the end of the snorkel and see the damper inside.
5   The check should be done when the engine is cold. Start the engine and look through the snorkel at the damper, which should move to a closed position. With the damper closed, air cannot enter through the end of the snorkel, but instead enters the air cleaner through the flexible duct attached to the exhaust manifold and the heat stove passage **(see illustration)**.
6   As the engine warms up to operating temperature, the damper should open to allow air through the snorkel end **(see illustration)**. Depending on outside temperature, this may take 10-to-15 minutes. To speed up this check you can reconnect the snorkel air duct, drive the vehicle, then check to see if the damper is completely open.
7   If the thermo-controlled air cleaner isn't operating properly see Chapter 6 for more information.

25 Drivebelt check, adjustment and replacement

Refer to illustrations 25.3 and 25.4

Note: *Later models are equipped with one serpentine drivebelt that runs all engine accessories. The belt tension is automatically controlled — no check or adjustment is required.*

1   The drivebelts, or V-belts as they are often called, are located at the front of the engine and play an important role in the overall operation of the engine and accessories. Due to their function and material make-up, the belts are prone to failure after a period of time and should be inspected and adjusted periodically to prevent major engine damage.
2   The number of belts used on a particular vehicle depends on the accessories installed. Drivebelts are used to turn the alternator, power steering pump, water pump and air conditioning compressor. Depending on the pulley arrangement, more than one of these components

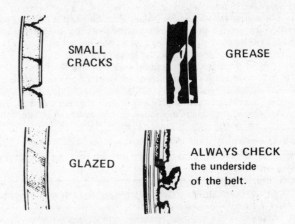

25.3 Here are some of the more common problems associated with drivebelts (check the belts very carefully to prevent an untimely breakdown)

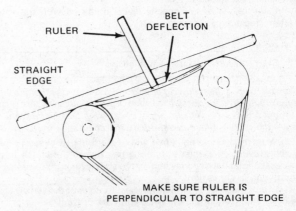

25.4 Drivebelt tension can be checked with a straightedge and ruler

may be driven by a single belt.
3   With the engine off, locate the drivebelts at the front of the engine. Using your fingers (and a flashlight, if necessary), move along the belts checking for cracks and separation of the belt plies. Also check for fraying and glazing, which gives the belt a shiny appearance **(see illustration)**. Both sides of each belt should be inspected, which means you will have to twist the belt to check the underside. Check the pulleys for nicks, cracks, distortion and corrosion.
4   The tension of each belt is checked by pushing on it at a distance halfway between the pulleys. Push firmly with your thumb and see how much the belt moves (deflects) **(see illustration)**. A rule of thumb

1

is that if the distance from pulley center-to-pulley center is between 7 and 11-inches, the belt should deflect 1/4-inch. If the belt travels between pulleys spaced 12-to-16 inches apart, the belt should deflect 1/2-inch.

5   If adjustment is needed, either to make the belt tighter or looser, it's done by moving the belt-driven accessory on the bracket.

6   For each component there will be an adjusting bolt and a pivot bolt. Both bolts must be loosened slightly to enable you to move the component.

7   After the two bolts have been loosened, move the component away from the engine to tighten the belt or toward the engine to loosen the belt. Hold the accessory in position and check the belt tension. If it's correct, tighten the two bolts until just snug, then recheck the tension. If the tension is all right, tighten the bolts.

8   It will often be necessary to use some sort of pry bar to move the accessory while the belt is adjusted. If this must be done to gain the proper leverage, be very careful not to damage the component being moved or the part being pried against.

9   To replace a belt, follow the above procedures for drivebelt adjustment but slip the belt off the pulleys and remove it. Since belts tend to wear out more or less at the same time, it's a good idea to replace all of them at the same time. Mark each belt and the corresponding pulley grooves so the replacement belts can be installed properly.

10   Take the old belts with you when purchasing new ones in order to make a direct comparison for length, width and design.

11   Adjust the belts as described earlier in this Section.

12   When replacing a serpentine drivebelt (used on later models), insert a 1/2-inch drive breaker bar into the tensioner and rotate it counterclockwise to release the belt tension. Make sure the new belt is routed correctly (refer to the label in the engine compartment). Also, the belt must completely engage the grooves in the pulleys.

26   Seatbelt check

1   Check the seatbelts, buckles, latch plates and guide loops for any obvious damage or signs of wear.

2   Make sure the seatbelt reminder light comes on when the key is turned on.

3   The seatbelts are designed to lock up during a sudden stop or impact, yet allow free movement during normal driving. The retractors should hold the belt against your chest while driving and rewind the belt when the buckle is unlatched.

4   If any of the above checks reveal problems with the seatbelt system, replace parts as necessary.

27   Starter/Neutral safety switch check

Warning: *During the following checks there is a chance that the vehicle could lunge forward, possibly causing damage or injuries. Allow plenty of room around the vehicle, apply the parking brake firmly and hold down the regular brake pedal during the checks.*

1   These models are equipped with a starter/Neutral safety switch which prevents the engine from starting unless the clutch pedal is depressed (manual transmission) or the shift lever is in Neutral or Park (automatic transmission).

2   On automatic transmission vehicles, try to start the vehicle in each gear. The engine should crank only in Park or Neutral.

3   If equipped with a manual transmission, place the shift lever in Neutral. The engine should crank only with the clutch pedal depressed.

4   Make sure the steering column lock allows the key to go into the Lock position only when the shift lever is in Park (automatic transmission) or Reverse (manual transmission).

5   The ignition key should come out only in the Lock position.

28   Spare tire and jack check

1   Check the spare tire to make sure it's securely fastened so it cannot come loose when the vehicle is in motion.

2   Make sure the jack and components are secured in place. Lubricate the jack threads with engine oil after each use.

29   Idle speed check and adjustment

Note: *The engine ilde speed on these models is controlled by the ECM and is not adjustable by conventional methods. The manufacturer recommends having the idle speed checked and adjusted at the specified interval by a General Motors dealer service department or properly equipped shop.*

30   Fuel filter replacement

Carburetor equipped vehicles
Refer to illustrations 30.6 and 30.8

1   On these models the fuel filter is located inside the fuel inlet nut at the carburetor. It's made of either pleated paper or porous bronze and cannot be cleaned or reused.

2   The job should be done with the engine cold (after sitting at least three hours) and the engine cover removed (Chapter 11). The necessary tools include open-end wrenches to fit the fuel line nuts. Flare nut wrenches (which wrap around the nut) should be used if available. In addition, you have to obtain the replacement filter (make sure it's for your specific vehicle and engine) and some clean rags.

3   Remove the air cleaner assembly. If vacuum hoses must be disconnected, be sure to note their positions and/or tag them to ensure that they are reinstalled correctly.

4   Follow the fuel line from the fuel pump to the point where it enters the carburetor. In most cases the fuel line will be metal all the way from the fuel pump to the carburetor.

5   Place some rags under the fuel inlet fittings to catch spilled fuel as the fittings are disconnected.

6   With the proper size wrench, hold the fuel inlet nut immediately next to the carburetor body. Now loosen the fitting at the end of the metal fuel line. Make sure the fuel inlet nut next to the carburetor is held securely while the fuel line is disconnected **(see illustration)**.

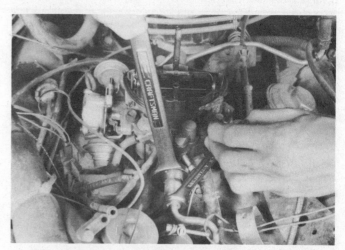

30.6   Two wrenches are required to loosen the carburetor fuel line inlet nut

7   After the fuel line is disconnected, move it aside for better access to the inlet nut. Don't crimp the fuel line.

8   Unscrew the fuel inlet nut, which was previously held steady. As this fitting is drawn away from the carburetor body, be careful not to lose the thin washer-type gasket on the nut or the spring, located behind the fuel filter. Also pay close attention to how the filter is installed **(see illustration)**.

9   Compare the old filter with the new one to make sure they're the same length and design.

10   Reinstall the spring in the carburetor body.

11   Place the filter in position (a gasket is usually supplied with the new filter) and tighten the nut. Make sure it's not cross-threaded. Tighten it securely, but be careful not to overtighten it as the threads can strip easily, causing fuel leaks. Reconnect the fuel line to the fuel inlet nut, again using caution to avoid cross-threading the nut. Use a

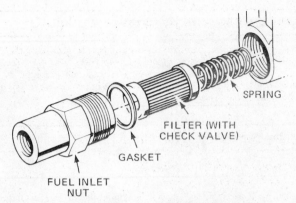

30.8 Carburetor mounted fuel filter component layout

SPRING

FILTER (WITH
CHECK VALVE)

GASKET

FUEL INLET
NUT

back-up wrench on the fuel inlet nut while tightening the fuel line fitting.
12 Start the engine and check carefully for leaks. If the fuel line fitting leaks, disconnect it and check for stripped or damaged threads. If the fuel line fitting has stripped threads, remove the entire line and have a repair shop install a new fitting. If the threads look all right, purchase some thread sealing tape and wrap the threads with it. Inlet nut repair kits are available at most auto parts stores to overcome leaking at the fuel inlet nut.

Fuel injected vehicles

Refer to illustration 30.15
Warning: *Refer to Chapter 4 and relieve the fuel system pressure before proceeding.*

13 Fuel injected engines employ an in-line fuel filter. The filter is located on the left side frame rail, near the engine.
14 With the engine cold, place a container, newspapers or rags under the fuel filter.
15 Use wrenches to disconnect the fuel lines and detach the filter from the frame **(see illustration).**
16 Install the new filter by reversing the removal procedure. Make sure the arrow on the filter points toward the engine, not the fuel tank. Tighten the fittings securely, but don't cross-thread them.

31 Air filter and PCV filter replacement

Refer to illustrations 31.3, 31.5, 31.13 and 31.14
1 At the specified intervals, the air filter and (if equipped) PCV filter should be replaced with new ones. The engine air cleaner also supplies filtered air to the PCV system.

Carbureted and TBI models

2 Remove the engine cover (Chapter 11).
3 The filter is located on top of the carburetor or Throttle Body Injection (TBI) unit and is replaced by unscrewing the wing nut from the top of the filter housing and lifting off the cover **(see illustration).**
4 While the top plate is off, be careful not to drop anything down into the carburetor, TBI or air cleaner assembly.
5 Lift the air filter element out of the housing **(see illustration)** and wipe out the inside of the air cleaner housing with a clean rag.
6 Place the new filter in the air cleaner housing. Make sure it seats properly in the bottom of the housing.
7 The PCV filter is also located inside the air cleaner housing on some models. Remove the top plate and air filter as previously described, then locate the PCV filter on the inside of the housing.
8 Remove the old filter.
9 Install the new PCV filter and the new air filter.
10 Install the top plate and any hoses which were disconnected.
11 Install the engine cover.

Central Port Injection (CPI) models

Note: *The CPI system is used only on some 1992 and later 4.3L V6 models. These models can be identified by the W in the eighth position of the Vehicle Identification Number (VIN).*
12 Loosen the clamp screw on the intake air duct. Disconnect the intake air duct from the air filter cover.

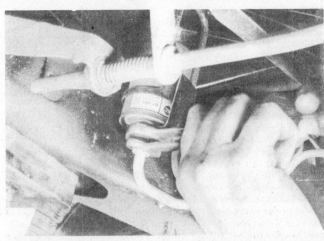

30.15 Use two wrenches to detach the fuel lines from the filter

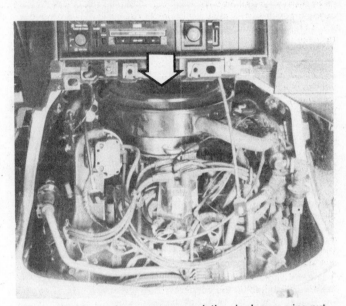

31.3 With the engine cover removed, the air cleaner wing nut (arrow) is visible on top of the air cleaner assembly (carbureted and TBI models)

31.5 Lift the air cleaner element out of the housing; on V6 models it's a tight fit (carbureted and TBI models)

31.13 Detach the cover clips (CPI models)

13   Detach the clips securing the air filter cover and remove the cover **(see illustration)**.
14   Lift the filter out of the housing, noting the direction in which it's installed **(see illustration)**.
15   Installation is the reverse of removal. Note that many replacement filters are marked with an arrow to show the direction of airflow through the filter.

32   Ignition timing check and adjustment

Refer to illustrations 32.4 and 32.5
Note: *If the information in this Section differs from the Vehicle Emission Control Information label in the engine compartment of your vehicle, the label should be considered correct.*
1   The engine must be at normal operating temperature and the air conditioner must be Off. Make sure the idle speed is correct.
2   Apply the parking brake and block the wheels to prevent movement of the vehicle. The transmission must be in Park (automatic) or Neutral (manual).
3   If the SERVICE ENGINE SOON light is on, don't proceed with the ignition timing check (see Chapter 6 for more information).
4   The Electronic Spark Timing (EST) system must be bypassed prior to checking the ignition timing. Remove the engine cover (Chapter 11). Locate the single tan wire with a black stripe that's connected to the distributor and unplug the connector **(see illustration)**. Don't unplug the 4-wire harness connector at the distributor.
5   Locate the timing marks at the front of the engine (they should be visible from above after the hood is opened) **(see illustration)**. The crankshaft pulley or vibration damper has a notch or groove in it and a small metal plate with notches and numbers is attached to the timing cover. Clean the plate with solvent so the numbers are visible.
6   Use chalk or white paint to mark the notch or groove in the pulley/vibration damper.
7   Highlight the notch or point on the timing plate that corresponds to the ignition timing specification on the Emission Control Information label (0° or TDC will most likely be specified).
8   Hook up the timing light by following the manufacturer's instructions (an inductive pick-up timing light is preferred). Generally, the power leads are attached to the battery terminals and the pick-up lead is attached to the number one spark plug wire. On the four-cylinder engine, the number one spark plug is the very front one. On the V6 engine, the number one spark plug is the front one on the driver's side of the engine. **Caution:** *If an inductive pick-up timing light isn't available, don't puncture the spark plug wire to attach the timing light pick-up lead. Instead, use an adapter between the spark plug and plug wire. If the insulation on the plug wire is damaged, the secondary voltage will jump to ground at the damaged point and the engine will misfire.*
9   Make sure the timing light wires are routed away from the drivebelts and fan, then start the engine.
10   Allow the idle speed to stabilize, then point the flashing timing light at the timing marks — be very careful of moving engine components!
11   The mark on the pulley/vibration damper will appear stationary. If it's aligned with the specified point on the timing plate, the ignition timing is correct.
12   If the marks aren't aligned, adjustment is required. Loosen the

31.14 Lift the filter out and note how it's installed (CPI models)

distributor hold-down bolt and turn the distributor very slowly until the marks are aligned. Since access to the bolt is tight, a special distributor wrench may be needed.
13   Tighten the bolt and recheck the timing.
14   Turn off the engine and remove the timing light (and adapter, if used).
15   Reconnect the EST wire harness connector, then clear any ECM trouble codes set during the ignition timing procedure (see Chapter 6).

33   Automatic transmission fluid and filter change

Refer to illustrations 33.7, 33.10 and 33.11
1   At the specified time intervals, the transmission fluid should be drained and replaced. Since the fluid will remain hot long after driving, perform this procedure only after the engine has cooled down completely.
2   Before beginning work, purchase the specified transmission fluid (see *Recommended lubricants and fluids* at the front of this Chapter) and a new filter.
3   Other tools necessary for this job include jackstands to support the vehicle in a raised position, a drain pan capable of holding at least eight pints, newspapers and clean rags.
4   Raise the vehicle and support it securely on jackstands.
5   With a drain pan in place, remove the front and side pan mounting bolts.
6   Loosen the rear pan bolts approximately four turns.
7   Carefully pry the transmission pan loose with a screwdriver, allowing the fluid to drain **(see illustration)**.
8   Remove the remaining bolts, pan and gasket. Carefully clean the gasket surface of the transmission to remove all traces of the old gasket and sealant.
9   Drain the fluid from the transmission pan, clean it with solvent and dry it with compressed air.
10   Remove the filter from the mount inside the transmission **(see illustration)**.

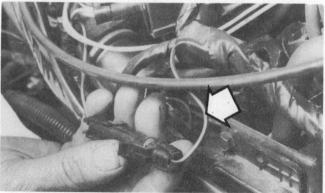

32.4   Unplug the EST wire (arrow) before checking the ignition timing

32.5   The ignition timing marks are located at the front of the engine

33.7   With the rear bolts in place but loose, pull the front of the pan down to let the transmission fluid drain

1

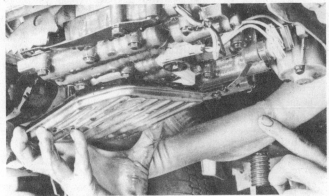

33.10   Rotate the filter out of the retaining clip and then lower it from the transmission

33.11   Reach up into the filter opening with your finger to retrieve the O-ring if it doesn't come out with the filter

11   Install a new filter and O-ring **(see illustration)**.

12   Make sure the gasket surface on the transmission pan is clean, then install a new gasket. Put the pan in place against the transmission and, working around the pan, tighten each bolt a little at a time until the final torque figure is reached.

13   Lower the vehicle and add the specified amount of automatic transmission fluid through the filler tube (Section 6).

14   With the transmission in Park and the parking brake set, run the engine at a fast idle, but don't race it.

15   Move the gear selector through each range and back to Park. Check the fluid level.

16   Check under the vehicle for leaks during the first few trips.

34   Manual transmission lubricant change

1   Raise the vehicle and support it securely on jackstands.

2   Move a drain pan, rags, newspapers and wrenches under the transmission.

3   Remove the transmission drain plug at the bottom of the case (see illustration 16.1) and allow the oil to drain into the pan.

4   After the oil has drained completely, reinstall the plug and tighten it securely.

5   Remove the fill plug from the side of the transmission case. Using a hand pump, syringe or funnel, fill the transmission with the correct amount of the specified lubricant. Reinstall the fill plug and tighten it securely.

6   Lower the vehicle.

7   Drive the vehicle for a short distance then check the drain and fill plugs for leakage.

35   Differential oil change

Refer to illustrations 35.6a, 35.6b, 35.6c and 35.8

1   Some differentials can be drained by removing the drain plug, while on others it's necessary to remove the cover plate on the differential

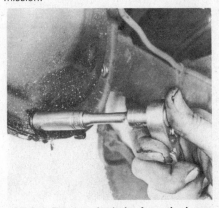

35.6a   Remove the bolts from the lower edge of the cover . . .

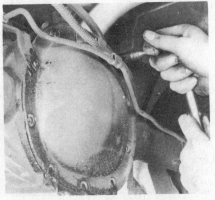

35.6b   . . . then loosen the top bolts and let the oil drain

35.6c   After the oil has drained, remove the cover

housing. As an alternative, a hand suction pump can be used to remove the differential lubricant through the filler hole. If there is no drain plug and a suction pump isn't available, be sure to obtain a new gasket at the same time the gear lubricant is purchased.

2   Raise the vehicle and support it securely on jackstands. Move a drain pan, rags, newspapers and wrenches under the vehicle.

3   Remove the fill plug from the differential.

4   If equipped with a drain plug, remove the plug and allow the differential oil to drain completely. After the oil has drained, install the plug and tighten it securely.

5   If a suction pump is being used, insert the flexible hose. Work the hose down to the bottom of the differential housing and pump the oil out.

6   If the differential is being drained by removing the cover plate, remove the bolts on the lower half of the plate **(see illustration)**. Loosen the bolts on the upper half and use them to keep the cover loosely attached **(see illustration)**. Allow the oil to drain into the pan, then completely remove the cover **(see illustration)**.

7   Using a lint-free rag, clean the inside of the cover and the accessible areas of the differential housing. As this is done, check for chipped gears and metal particles in the lubricant, indicating that the differential should be more thoroughly inspected and/or repaired.

8   Thoroughly clean the gasket mating surfaces of the differential housing and the cover plate. Use a gasket scraper or putty knife to remove all traces of the old gasket **(see illustration)**.

35.8   Carefully scrape the old gasket material off to ensure a leak-free seal with the new gasket

9   Apply a thin layer of RTV sealant to the cover flange and then press a new gasket into position on the cover. Make sure the bolt holes align properly.

10   Place the cover on the differential housing and install the bolts. Tighten the bolts securely.

11   On all models, use a hand pump, syringe or funnel to fill the differential housing with the specified lubricant until it's level with the bottom of the plug hole.

12   Install the filler plug and tighten it securely.

36   Front wheel bearing check, repack and adjustment

Refer to illustrations 36.1, 36.6, 36.7, 36.8, 36.11 and 36.15

1   In most cases the front wheel bearings will not need servicing until the brake pads are changed. However, the bearings should be checked whenever the front of the vehicle is raised for any reason. Several items, including a torque wrench and special grease, are required for this procedure **(see illustration)**.

2   With the vehicle securely supported on jackstands, spin each wheel and check for noise, rolling resistance and free play.

3   Grasp the top of each tire with one hand and the bottom with the other. Move the wheel in-and-out on the spindle. If there's any noticable movement, the bearings should be checked and then repacked with grease or replaced if necessary.

4   Remove the wheel.

5   Fabricate a wood block (1-1/16 inch by 1/2-inch by 2-inches long) which can be slid between the brake pads to keep them separated. Remove the brake caliper (Chapter 9) and hang it out of the way on a piece of wire.

6   Pry the dust cap out of the hub using a screwdriver or hammer and chisel **(see illustration)**.

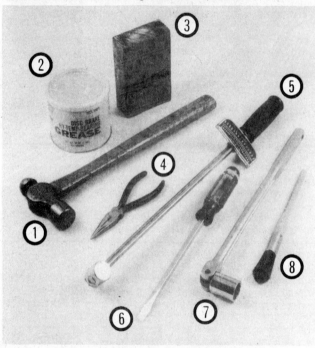

36.1   Tools and materials needed for front wheel bearing maintenance

1   Hammer — A common hammer will do just fine
2   Grease — High-temperature grease which is formulated specially for front wheel bearings should be used
3   Wood block — If you have a scrap piece of 2x4, it can be used to drive the new seal into the hub
4   Needle-nose pliers — Used to straighten and remove the cotter pin in the spindle
5   Torque wrench — This is very important in this procedure; if the bearing is too tight, the wheel won't turn freely — if it is too loose, the wheel will 'wobble' on the spindle. Either way, it could mean extensive damage
6   Screwdriver — Used to remove the seal from the hub (a long screwdriver would be preferred)
7   Socket/breaker bar — Needed to loosen the nut on the spindle if it is extremely tight
8   Brush — Together with some clean solvent, this will be used to remove old grease from the hub and spindle

36.6   Dislodge the dust cap by working around the outer circumference with a hammer and chisel

Common spark plug conditions

NORMAL

Symptoms: Brown to grayish-tan color and slight electrode wear. Correct heat range for engine and operating conditions.

Recommendation: When new spark plugs are installed, replace with plugs of the same heat range.

WORN

Symptoms: Rounded electrodes with a small amount of deposits on the firing end. Normal color. Causes hard starting in damp or cold weather and poor fuel economy.

Recommendation: Plugs have been left in the engine too long. Replace with new plugs of the same heat range. Follow the recommended maintenance schedule.

CARBON DEPOSITS

Symptoms: Dry sooty deposits indicate a rich mixture or weak ignition. Causes misfiring, hard starting and hesitation.

Recommendation: Make sure the plug has the correct heat range. Check for a clogged air filter or problem in the fuel system or engine management system. Also check for ignition system problems.

ASH DEPOSITS

Symptoms: Light brown deposits encrusted on the side or center electrodes or both. Derived from oil and/or fuel additives. Excessive amounts may mask the spark, causing misfiring and hesitation during acceleration.

Recommendation: If excessive deposits accumulate over a short time or low mileage, install new valve guide seals to prevent seepage of oil into the combustion chambers. Also try changing gasoline brands.

OIL DEPOSITS

Symptoms: Oily coating caused by poor oil control. Oil is leaking past worn valve guides or piston rings into the combustion chamber. Causes hard starting, misfiring and hesitation.

Recommendation: Correct the mechanical condition with necessary repairs and install new plugs.

GAP BRIDGING

Symptoms: Combustion deposits lodge between the electrodes. Heavy deposits accumulate and bridge the electrode gap. The plug ceases to fire, resulting in a dead cylinder.

Recommendation: Locate the faulty plug and remove the deposits from between the electrodes.

TOO HOT

Symptoms: Blistered, white insulator, eroded electrode and absence of deposits. Results in shortened plug life.

Recommendation: Check for the correct plug heat range, over-advanced ignition timing, lean fuel mixture, intake manifold vacuum leaks, sticking valves and insufficient engine cooling.

PREIGNITION

Symptoms: Melted electrodes. Insulators are white, but may be dirty due to misfiring or flying debris in the combustion chamber. Can lead to engine damage.

Recommendation: Check for the correct plug heat range, over-advanced ignition timing, lean fuel mixture, insufficient engine cooling and lack of lubrication.

HIGH SPEED GLAZING

Symptoms: Insulator has yellowish, glazed appearance. Indicates that combustion chamber temperatures have risen suddenly during hard acceleration. Normal deposits melt to form a conductive coating. Causes misfiring at high speeds.

Recommendation: Install new plugs. Consider using a colder plug if driving habits warrant.

DETONATION

Symptoms: Insulators may be cracked or chipped. Improper gap setting techniques can also result in a fractured insulator tip. Can lead to piston damage.

Recommendation: Make sure the fuel anti-knock values meet engine requirements. Use care when setting the gaps on new plugs. Avoid lugging the engine.

MECHANICAL DAMAGE

Symptoms: May be caused by a foreign object in the combustion chamber or the piston striking an incorrect reach (too long) plug. Causes a dead cylinder and could result in piston damage.

Recommendation: Repair the mechanical damage. Remove the foreign object from the engine and/or install the correct reach plug.

7   Straighten the bent ends of the cotter pin, then pull the cotter pin out of the locking nut **(see illustration)**. Discard the cotter pin and use a new one during reassembly.
8   Remove the spindle nut and washer from the end of the spindle **(see illustration)**.
9   Pull the hub assembly out slightly, then push it back into its original position. This should force the outer bearing off the spindle enough so it can be removed.
10 Pull the hub off the spindle.

36.7   Remove the cotter pin and discard it — use a new one when the hub is reinstalled

11 Use a screwdriver to pry the seal out of the rear of the hub **(see illustration)**. As this is done, note how the seal is installed.
12 Remove the inner wheel bearing from the hub.
13 Use solvent to remove all traces of the old grease from the bearings, hub and spindle. A small brush may prove helpful; however make sure no bristles from the brush embed themselves inside the bearing rollers. Allow the parts to air dry.
14 Carefully inspect the bearings for cracks, heat discoloration, worn rollers, etc. Check the bearing races inside the hub for wear and damage. If the bearing races are defective, the hubs should be taken to a machine shop with the facilities to remove the old races and press new ones in. Note that the bearings and races come as matched sets and old bearings should never be installed on new races.
15 Use high-temperature front wheel bearing grease to pack the bearings. Work the grease completely into the bearings, forcing it between the rollers, cone and cage from the back side **(see illustration)**.
16 Apply a thin coat of grease to the spindle at the outer bearing seat, inner bearing seat, shoulder and seal seat.
17 Put a small quantity of grease inboard of each bearing race inside the hub. Using your finger, form a dam at these points to provide extra grease availability and to keep thinned grease from flowing out of the bearing.
18 Place the grease-packed inner bearing into the rear of the hub and put a little more grease outboard of the bearing.
19 Place a new seal over the inner bearing and tap the seal evenly into place with a hammer and block of wood until it's flush with the hub.
20 Carefully place the hub assembly onto the spindle and push the grease-packed outer bearing into position.
21 Install the washer and spindle nut. Tighten the nut only slightly (no more than 12 ft-lbs of torque).
22 Spin the hub in a forward direction to seat the bearings and remove any grease or burrs which could cause excessive bearing play later.

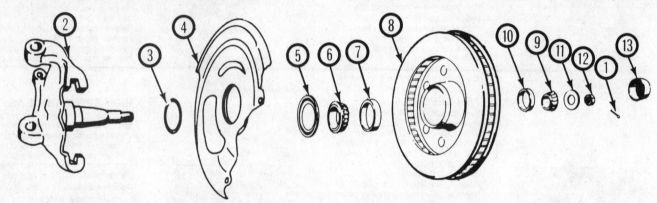

36.8   Front wheel hub and bearing components — exploded view

1 Cotter pin	5 Seal	8 Disc/hub	11 Washer
2 Steering knuckle	6 Inner wheel bearing	9 Outer wheel bearing	12 Spindle nut
3 Gasket	7 Inner wheel bearing race	10 Outer wheel bearing race	13 Dust cap
4 Splash shield			

36.11   Use a screwdriver to pry the grease seal from the rear of the hub

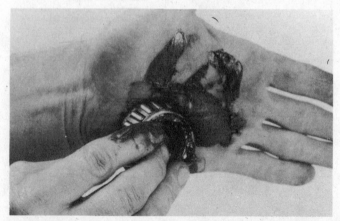

36.15   Work the grease into each bearing until it's full

23 Check to see that the tightness of the spindle nut is still approximately 12 ft-lbs.
24 Loosen the spindle nut until it's just loose, no more.
25 Using your hand (not a wrench of any kind), tighten the nut until it's snug. Install a new cotter pin through the hole in the spindle and spindle nut. If the nut slots don't line up, loosen the nut slightly until they do. From the hand-tight position, the nut should not be loosened more than one-half flat to install the cotter pin.
26 Bend the ends of the cotter pin until they're flat against the nut. Cut off any extra length which could interfere with the dust cap.
27 Install the dust cap, tapping it into place with a hammer.
28 Place the brake caliper near the rotor and carefully remove the wood spacer. Install the caliper (Chapter 9).
29 Install the tire/wheel assembly on the hub and tighten the lug nuts.
30 Grasp the top and bottom of the tire and check the bearings in the manner described earlier in this Section.
31 Lower the vehicle.

37 Cooling system servicing (draining, flushing and refilling)

See illustration 37.4

Warning: *Antifreeze is a corrosive and poisonous solution, so be careful not to spill any of the coolant mixture on the vehicle's paint or your skin. If this happens, rinse immediately with plenty of clean water. Consult local authorities regarding proper disposal procedures for antifreeze before draining the cooling system. In many areas, reclamation centers have been established to collect used oil and coolant mixtures.*

1 Periodically, the cooling system should be drained, flushed and refilled to replenish the antifreeze mixture and prevent formation of rust and corrosion, which can impair the performance of the cooling system and cause engine damage. When the cooling system is serviced, all hoses and the radiator cap should be checked and replaced if necessary.
2 Apply the parking brake and block the wheels. If the vehicle has just been driven, wait several hours to allow the engine to cool down before beginning this procedure.
3 Once the engine is completely cool, remove the radiator cap.
4 Move a large container under the radiator drain to catch the coolant. Attach a 3/8-inch diameter hose to the drain fitting to direct the coolant into the container, then open the drain fitting **(see illustration)** (a pair of pliers may be required to turn it).
5 After the coolant stops flowing out of the radiator, move the container under the engine block drain plug (if so equipped). Remove the plug and allow the coolant in the block to drain.
6 While the coolant is draining, check the condition of the radiator hoses, heater hoses and clamps (refer to Section 9 if necessary).
7 Replace any damaged clamps or hoses.
8 Once the system is completely drained, flush the radiator with fresh water from a garden hose until it runs clear at the drain. The flushing action of the water will remove sediments from the radiator but will not remove rust and scale from the engine and cooling tube surfaces.
9 These deposits can be removed with a chemical cleaner. Follow the procedure outlined in the manufacturer's instructions. If the radiator is severely corroded, damaged or leaking, it should be removed (Chapter 3) and taken to a radiator repair shop.
10 Remove the overflow hose from the coolant recovery reservoir. Drain the reservoir and flush it with clean water, then reconnect the hose.
11 Close and tighten the radiator drain. Install and tighten the block drain plug.
12 Place the heater temperature control in the maximum heat position.
13 Slowly add new coolant (a 50/50 mixture of water and antifreeze) to the radiator until it's full. Add coolant to the reservoir up to the lower mark.
14 Leave the radiator cap off and run the engine in a well-ventilated area until the thermostat opens (coolant will begin flowing through the radiator and the upper radiator hose will become hot).
15 Turn the engine off and let it cool. Add more coolant mixture to bring the level back up to the lip on the radiator filler neck.
16 Squeeze the upper radiator hose to expel air, then add more coolant mixture if necessary. Replace the radiator cap.
17 Start the engine, allow it to reach normal operating temperature and check for leaks.

37.4 The drain fitting (arrow) is located at the lower right corner of the radiator

38.2 The PCV valve fits into the rocker arm cover — place your finger over the opening to feel for suction and shake the valve, listening for a rattling sound

38 Positive Crankcase Ventilation (PCV) valve check and replacement

Refer to illustration 38.2

1 The PCV valve is usually located in the rocker arm cover.
2 With the engine idling at normal operating temperature, pull the valve (with hose attached) from the rubber grommet in the cover **(see illustration)**.
3 Place your finger over the valve opening. If there's no vacuum at the valve, check for a plugged hose, manifold port, or the valve itself. Replace any plugged or deteriorated hoses.
4 Turn off the engine and shake the PCV valve, listening for a rattle. If the valve doesn't rattle, replace it with a new one.
5 To replace the valve, pull it from the end of the hose, noting its installed position and direction.
6 When purchasing a replacement PCV valve, make sure it's for your particular vehicle and engine size. Compare the old valve with the new one to make sure they're the same.
7 Push the valve into the end of the hose until it's seated.
8 Inspect the rubber grommet for damage and replace it with a new one if necessary.
9 Push the PCV valve and hose securely into position.

39.2 The evaporative emissions control system canister is located at the left front corner of the engine compartment (arrow) — inspect the various hoses attached to it and the canister itself for damage

40.2 The EGR diaphragm should move easily with finger pressure

39 Evaporative emissions control system check

Refer to illustration 39.2
1   The function of the evaporative emissions control system is to draw fuel vapors from the gas tank and fuel system, store them in a charcoal canister and route them to the intake manifold during normal engine operation.
2   The most common symptom of a fault in the evaporative emissions system is a strong fuel odor in the engine compartment. If a fuel odor is detected, inspect the charcoal canister, located in the engine compartment **(see illustration)**. Check the canister and all hoses for damage and deterioration.
3   The evaporative emissions control system is explained in more detail in Chapter 6.

40 Exhaust Gas Recirculation (EGR) system check

1   The EGR valve is usually located on the intake manifold, adjacent to the carburetor or TBI unit. Most of the time when a problem develops in this emissions system, it's due to a stuck or corroded EGR valve.

Carbureted and TBI models
Refer to illustration 40.2
2   With the engine cold to prevent burns, push on the EGR valve diaphragm. Using moderate pressure, you should be able to press the diaphragm in-and-out within the housing **(see illustration)**.
3   If the diaphragm doesn't move or moves only with much effort, replace the EGR valve with a new one. If in doubt about the condition of the valve, compare the free movement of your EGR valve with a new valve.
4   Refer to Chapter 6 for more information on the EGR system.

Central Port Injection (CPI) models
5   These models are equipped with a sealed valve which makes it impossible to check the operation of the valve. Make sure the electrical connector is on tight and is free of corrosion.
6   Refer to Chapter 6 for more information on the EGR system.

41 Spark plug replacement

Refer to illustrations 41.2, 41.5a, 41.5b, 41.6 and 41.10
1   Open the hood and remove the engine cover (Chapter 11).
2   In most cases, the tools necessary for spark plug replacement include a spark plug socket which fits onto a ratchet (spark plug sockets are padded inside to prevent damage to the porcelain insulators on the new plugs), various extensions and a gap gauge to check and adjust the gaps on the new plugs **(see illustration)**. A special plug wire removal tool is available for separating the wire boots from the spark plugs,

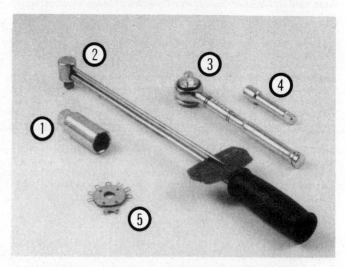

41.2 Tools required for changing spark plugs

*1 **Spark plug socket** — This will have special padding inside to protect the spark plug porcelain insulator*
*2 **Torque wrench** — Although not mandatory, use of this tool is the best way to ensure that the plugs are tightened properly*
*3 **Ratchet** — Standard hand tool to fit the plug socket*
*4 **Extension** — Depending on model and accessories, you may need special extensions and universal joints to reach one or more of the plugs*
*5 **Spark plug gap gauge** — This gauge for checking the gap comes in a variety of styles. Make sure the gap for your engine is included*

but it isn't absolutely necessary. A torque wrench should be used to tighten the new plugs.
3   The best approach when replacing the spark plugs is to purchase the new ones in advance, adjust them to the proper gap and replace them one at a time. When buying the new spark plugs, be sure to obtain the correct plug type for your particular engine. This information can be found on the *Emission Control Information label* located under the hood and in the factory owner's manual. If differences exist between the plug specified on the emissions label and in the owner's manual, assume that the emissions label is correct.
4   Allow the engine to cool completely before attempting to remove

41.5a Spark plug manufacturers recommend using a wire-type gauge when checking the gap — if the wire does not slide between the electrodes with a slight drag, adjustment is required

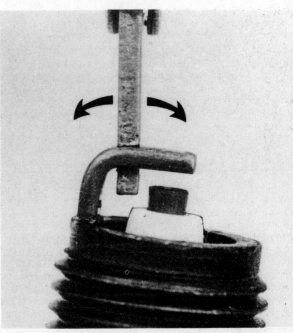

41.5b To change the gap, bend the *side* electrode only, as indicated by the arrows, and be very careful not to crack or chip the porcelain insulator surrounding the center electrode

any of the plugs. While you're waiting for the engine to cool, check the new plugs for defects and adjust the gaps.

5   The gap is checked by inserting the proper thickness gauge between the electrodes at the tip of the plug (**see illustration**). The gap between the electrodes should be the same as the one specified on the *Emissions Control Information label*. The wire should just slide between the electrodes with a slight amount of drag. If the gap is incorrect, use the adjuster on the gauge body to bend the curved side electrode slightly until the proper gap is obtained (**see illustration**). If the side electrode is not exactly over the center electrode, bend it with the adjuster until it is. Check for cracks in the porcelain insulator (if any are found, the plug should not be used).

6   With the engine cool, remove the spark plug wire from one spark plug. Pull only on the boot at the end of the wire — do not pull on the wire. A plug wire removal tool should be used if available (**see illustration**).

7   If compressed air is available, use it to blow any dirt or foreign material away from the spark plug hole. A common bicycle pump will also work. The idea here is to eliminate the possibility of debris falling into the cylinder as the spark plug is removed.

8   Place the spark plug socket over the plug and remove it from the engine by turning it in a counterclockwise direction.

9   Compare the spark plug to those shown in the photos on page 51 to get an indication of the general running condition of the engine.

10   Thread one of the new plugs into the hole until you can no longer turn it with your fingers, then tighten it with a torque wrench (if available) or the ratchet. It might be a good idea to slip a short length of rubber hose over the end of the plug to use as a tool to thread it

into place (**see illustration**). The hose will grip the plug well enough to turn it, but will start to slip if the plug begins to cross-thread in the hole — this will prevent damaged threads and the accompanying repair costs.

11   Before pushing the spark plug wire onto the end of the plug, inspect it following the procedures outlined in Section 42.

12   Attach the plug wire to the new spark plug, again using a twisting motion on the boot until it's seated on the spark plug.

13   Repeat the procedure for the remaining spark plugs, replacing them one at a time to prevent mixing up the spark plug wires.

42 Spark plug wire check and replacement

1   The spark plug wires should be checked at the recommended intervals and whenever new spark plugs are installed in the engine.

2   The wires should be inspected one at a time to prevent mixing up the order, which is essential for proper engine operation.

3   Disconnect the plug wire from one spark plug. To do this, grab the rubber boot, twist slightly and pull the wire free. Do not pull on the wire itself, only on the rubber boot (see illustration 41.6).

4   Check inside the boot for corrosion, which will look like a white crusty powder. Push the wire and boot back onto the end of the spark

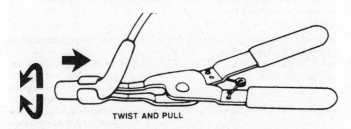

41.6 When removing the spark plug wires, pull only on the boot and use a twisting/pulling motion

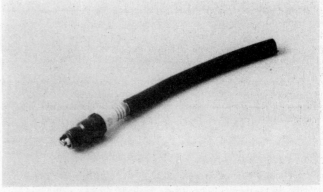

41.10 A length of 3/16-inch ID rubber hose will save time and prevent damaged threads when installing the spark plugs

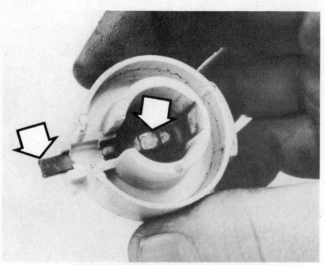

43.4a Check the distributor rotor contacts (arrows) for wear and burn marks (remote coil-type distributor)

43.4b Carbon tracking on the rotor is caused by a leaking arc seal between the distributor cap and the ignition coil (always replace both the seal and rotor when this condition is present) (coil in cap-type distributor)

43.5 This type rotor can be pried off the distributor shaft with a screwdriver — other types have two screws which must be removed (be careful not to drop anything down into the distributor)

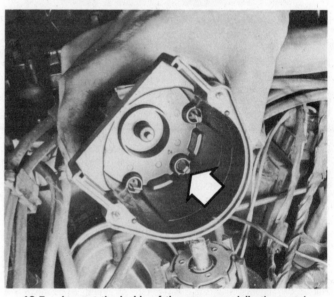

43.7a Inspect the inside of the cap, especially the metal terminals (arrow) for corrosion and wear

plug. It should be a tight fit on the plug. If it isn't, remove the wire and use a pair of pliers to carefully crimp the metal connector inside the boot until it fits securely on the end of the spark plug.

5   Using a clean rag, wipe the entire length of the wire to remove any built-up dirt and grease. Once the wire is clean, check for holes, burned areas, cracks and other damage. Don't bend the wire excessively or the conductor inside might break.

6   Disconnect the wire from the distributor cap. A retaining ring at the top of the distributor may have to be removed to free the wires. Again, pull only on the rubber boot. Check for corrosion and a tight fit in the same manner as the spark plug end. Reattach the wire to the distributor cap.

7   Check the remaining spark plug wires one at a time, making sure they are securely fastened at the distributor and the spark plug when the check is complete.

8   If new spark plug wires are required, purchase a new set for your specific engine model. Wire sets are available pre-cut, with the rubber boots already installed. Remove and replace the wires one at a time to avoid mix-ups in the firing order. The wire routing is extremely im-

portant, so be sure to note exactly how each wire is situated before removing it.

43 Distributor cap and rotor check and replacement

Refer to illustrations 43.4a, 43.4b, 43.5, 43.7a, 43.7b and 43.13
Note: *It's common practice to install a new distributor cap and rotor whenever new spark plug wires are installed. On models that have the ignition coil mounted in the cap, the coil will have to be transferred to the new cap.*

1   Remove the engine cover.

Check

2   To gain access to the distributor cap, especially on a V6 engine, it may be necessary to remove the air cleaner assembly.

3   Loosen the distributor cap mounting screws (note that the screws have a shoulder so they don't come completely out). On some models,

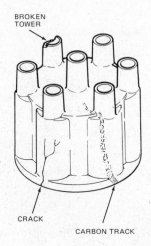

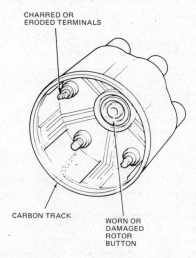

43.7b Shown here are some of the common defects to look for when inspecting the distributor cap (if in doubt about its condition, install a new one)

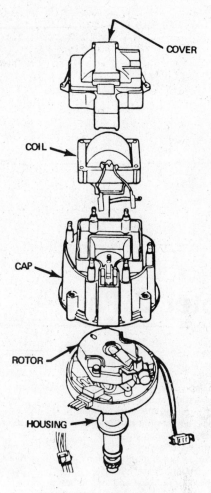

43.13 Coil-in-cap distributor components — exploded view

the cap is held in place with latches that look like screws — to release them, push down with a screwdriver and turn them about 1/2-turn. Pull up on the cap, with the wires attached, to separate it from the distributor, then position it to one side.

4   The rotor is now visible on the end of the distributor shaft. Check it carefully for cracks and carbon tracks. Make sure the center terminal spring tension is adequate and look for corrosion and wear on the rotor tip **(see illustrations)**. If in doubt about its condition, replace it with a new one.

5   If replacement is required, detach the rotor from the shaft and install a new one. On some models, the rotor is press fit on the shaft and can be pried or pulled off **(see illustration)**. On other models, the rotor is attached to the distributor shaft with two screws.

6   The rotor is indexed to the shaft so it can only be installed one way. Press fit rotors have an internal key that must line up with a slot in the end of the shaft (or vice versa). Rotors held in place with screws have one square and one round peg on the underside that must fit into holes with the same shape.

7   Check the distributor cap for carbon tracks, cracks and other damage. Closely examine the terminals on the inside of the cap for excessive corrosion and damage **(see illustrations)**. Slight deposits are normal. Again, if in doubt about the condition of the cap, replace it with a new one. Be sure to apply a small dab of silicone lubricant to each terminal before installing the cap. Also, make sure the carbon brush (center terminal) is correctly installed in the cap — a wide gap between the brush and rotor will result in rotor burn-through and/or damage to the distributor cap.

Replacement

Conventional distributor

8   On models with a separately mounted ignition coil, simply separate the cap from the distributor and transfer the spark plug wires, one at a time, to the new cap. Be very careful not to mix up the wires!

9   Reattach the cap to the distributor, then tighten the screws or reposition the latches to hold it in place.

Coil-in-cap distributor

10   Use your thumbs to push the spark plug wire retainer latches away from the coil cover.

11   Lift the retainer ring away from the distributor cap with the spark plug wires attached to the ring. It may be necessary to work the wires off the distributor cap towers so they remain with the ring.

12   Disconnect the battery/tachometer/coil electrical connector from the distributor cap.

13   Remove the two coil cover screws and lift off the coil cover **(see illustration)**.

14   There are three small spade connectors on wires extending from the coil into the electrical connector hood at the side of the distributor cap. Note which terminals the wires are attached to, then use a small screwdriver to push them free.

15   Remove the four coil mounting screws and lift the coil out of the cap.

16   When installing the coil in the new cap, be sure to install a new rubber arc seal in the cap.

17   Install the coil screws, the wires in the connector hood, and the coil cover.

18   Install the cap on the distributor.

19   Plug in the coil electrical connector to the distributor cap.

20   Install the spark plug wire retaining ring on the distributor cap.

Chapter 2 Part A Four-cylinder engine

Contents

Specifications

General
Cylinder numbers (front-to-rear) 1–2–3–4
Firing order 1–3–4–2

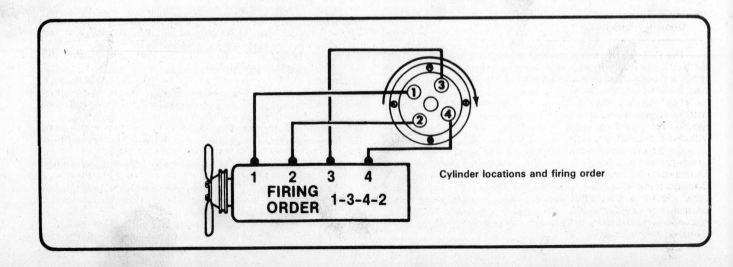

Cylinder locations and firing order

FIRING
ORDER 1-3-4-2

Camshaft

Lobe lift (intake and exhaust)	0.398 in
Bearing journal diameter	1.869 in
Bearing oil clearance.	0.0007 to 0.0027 in
Gear/thrust plate end clearance	0.0015 to 0.0050 in

Torque specifications

Ft-lbs *(unless otherwise noted)*

Cylinder head bolts	
1985	92
1986	90
1987 on **(see illustration 10.25)**	
step 1 — all bolts, in sequence	18
step 2 — all bolts, except 9, in sequence	22
step 2 — bolt 9	30
step 3 — all bolts, except 9, in sequence	Turn an additional 120°
step 3 — bolt 9	Turn an additional 90°
Intake manifold-to-cylinder head bolts	
1985	29
1986 **(see illustration 8.15)**	
Bolts 1, 2 and 6	38
Bolts 3, 4 and 5	25
Bolt 7	37
1987 on	25
Exhaust manifold bolts	
1985	44
1986 on **(see illustration 9.13)**	
Bolts 1, 2 and 7	36
Bolts 3, 4, 5 and 6	32
Flywheel-to-crankshaft bolts	
1985	44
1986	55
1987 on	65
Driveplate-to-crankshaft bolts	
1985	44
1986 on	55
Crankshaft pulley hub-to-crankshaft bolt	160
Lifter guide retainer-to-block stud	90 in-lbs
Oil pan bolts	
1985	75 in-lbs
1986 on	90 in-lbs
Oil pan drain plug	25
Oil pick-up tube bracket nut	37
Oil pump-to-block bolts	22
Pushrod cover nuts	90 in-lbs
Rocker arm bolts	
1985 and 1986	20
1987 on	24
Rocker arm cover bolts	
1985 and 1986	72 in-lbs
1987 on	48 in-lbs
Timing gear cover bolts	90 in-lbs
Camshaft thrust plate bolts	90 in-lbs

2A

1   General information

This Part of Chapter 2 is devoted to in-vehicle repair procedures for the 2.5 liter four-cylinder engine. Information concerning engine removal and installation, as well as engine block and cylinder head overhaul, is in Part C of this Chapter.

The following repair procedures are based on the assumption that the engine is installed in the vehicle. If the engine has been removed from the vehicle and mounted on a stand, many of the steps included in this Part of Chapter 2 will not apply.

The Specifications included in this Part of Chapter 2 apply only to the engine and procedures in this Part. The Specifications necessary for rebuilding the block and cylinder head are found in Part C.

Caution: *If the vehicle is equipped with a Delco Loc II audio system (1992 and later models with a Compact Disc player), be sure the lockout feature is turned off before performing any procedure that requires disconnecting the battery (refer to your owner's manual for further information on this system).*

2   Repair operations possible with the engine in the vehicle

Many major repair operations can be accomplished without removing the engine from the vehicle.

Clean the engine compartment and the exterior of the engine with some type of pressure washer before any work is done. A clean engine will make the job easier and will help keep dirt out of the internal areas of the engine.

Depending on the components involved, remove the engine cover and, if necessary, the hood to improve access to the engine as repairs are performed (refer to Chapter 11 if necessary).

If vacuum, exhaust, oil or coolant leaks develop, indicating a need for gasket or seal replacement, the repairs can generally be made with the engine in the vehicle. The intake and exhaust manifold gaskets, oil pan gasket and cylinder head gasket are all accessible with the engine in place.

Exterior engine components such as the intake and exhaust manifolds, the oil pan (and the oil pump), the water pump, the starter mo-

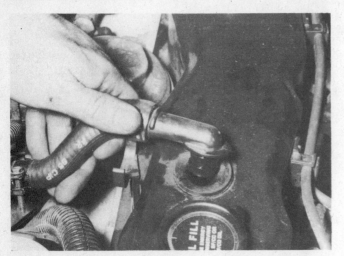

3.3   The PCV valve can be pulled out of the rubber grommet in the rocker arm cover (leave the hose attached to the valve)

tor, the alternator, the distributor and the fuel injection system can be removed for repair with the engine in place.

Since the cylinder head can be removed without pulling the engine, valve component servicing can also be accomplished with the engine in the vehicle.

In extreme cases caused by a lack of necessary equipment, repair or replacement of piston rings, pistons, connecting rods and rod bearings is possible with the engine in the vehicle. However, this practice is not recommended because of the cleaning and preparation work that must be done to the components involved.

3   Rocker arm cover — removal and installation

Refer to illustrations 3.3, 3.8, 3.9, 3.10, 3.11a and 3.11b

1   Disconnect the negative battery cable from the battery, then remove the engine cover and the air cleaner assembly.
2   Unbolt the dipstick and oil filler tubes at the water outlet.
3   Remove the PCV valve from the rocker arm cover **(see illustration)**.
4   Label each spark plug wire before removal to ensure that all wires are reinstalled correctly, then remove the wires from the plugs (refer to Chapter 1). Detach the wires and retaining clips from the rocker arm cover.
5   Remove the EGR valve (Chapter 6).

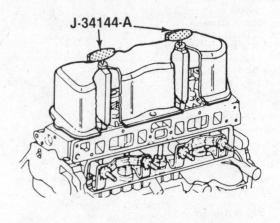

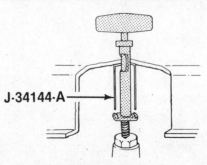

3.8   GM recommends a special tool for rocker arm cover removal — if you're careful not to distort the cover, you can get by without it!

6   Detach the vacuum rail at the intake manifold and water outlet.
7   Remove the rocker arm cover bolts.
8   Starting with 1987 models, a special tool (GM no. J34144-A) is recommended for rocker arm cover removal **(see illustration)**.
9   Remove the rocker arm cover. If it sticks to the head, use a soft-face hammer or a block of wood and a hammer to dislodge it. If the cover still won't come loose, pry on it carefully at several points until the seal is broken, but don't distort the cover flange **(see illustration)**. **Note:** *If you bend the cover, straighten it with a block of wood and a hammer.*
10   Prior to reinstallation, remove all dirt, oil and old gasket material

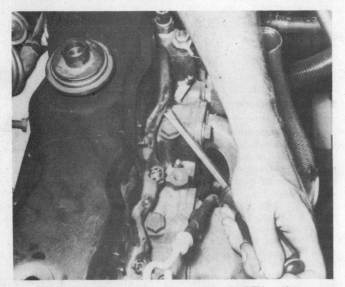

3.9   The rocker arm cover is sealed with RTV — if you have to pry it off the head, try to avoid bending the flange

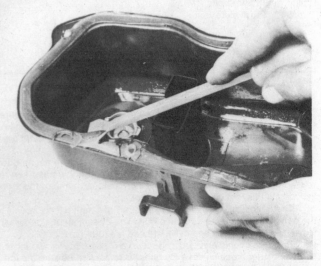

3.10   Remove the old sealant from the rocker arm cover flange and the cylinder head with a gasket scraper, then clean the mating surfaces with lacquer thinner or acetone

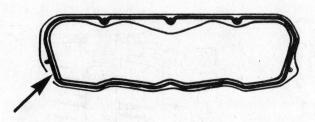

3.11a   Apply a continuous 3/16-in diameter bead of RTV sealant (arrow) to the rocker arm cover flange

from the cover and cylinder head with a scraper **(see illustration)**. Clean the mating surfaces with lacquer thinner or acetone.

11   Apply a continuous 3/16-inch (5 mm) diameter bead of RTV sealant to the flange on the cover. Be sure the sealant is applied to the inside of the bolt holes **(see illustrations)**. **Note:** *Don't get the sealant in the bolt holes in the head or damage to the head may occur.*

12   Place the rocker arm cover on the cylinder head while the sealant is still wet and install the mounting bolts. Tighten the bolts a little at a time until the specified torque is reached.

13   Complete the installation by reversing the removal procedure.

14   Start the engine and check for oil leaks at the rocker arm cover-to-head joint.

---

4   Valve springs, retainers and seals — replacement

Refer to illustrations 4.4, 4.8a, 4.8b, 4.16 and 4.17

Note: *Broken valve springs and defective valve stem seals can be replaced without removing the cylinder head. Two special tools and a compressed air source are normally required to perform this operation, so read through this Section carefully and rent or buy the tools before beginning the job. If compressed air isn't available, a length of nylon rope can be used to keep the valves from falling into the cylinder during this procedure.*

1   Refer to Section 3 and remove the rocker arm cover.

2   Remove the spark plug from the cylinder which has the defective component. If all of the valve stem seals are being replaced, all of the spark plugs should be removed.

3   Turn the crankshaft until the piston in the affected cylinder is at top dead center on the compression stroke (refer to Section 13 for instructions). If you're replacing all of the valve stem seals, begin with cylinder number one and work on the valves for one cylinder at a time. Move from cylinder-to-cylinder following the firing order sequence (1-3-4-2).

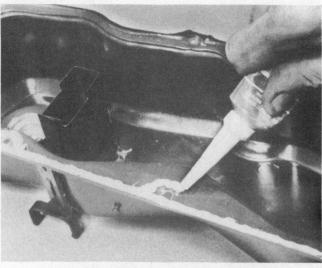

3.11b   Make sure the sealant is applied to the INSIDE of the bolt holes or oil will leak out around the bolt threads

4   Thread an adapter into the spark plug hole and connect an air hose from a compressed air source to it **(see illustration)**. Most auto parts stores can supply the air hose adapter. **Note:** *Many cylinder compression gauges utilize a screw-in fitting that may work with your air hose quick-disconnect fitting.*

5   Remove the bolt, pivot ball and rocker arm for the valve with the defective part and pull out the pushrod. If all of the valve stem seals are being replaced, all of the rocker arms and pushrods should be removed (refer to Section 6).

6   Apply compressed air to the cylinder. The valves should be held in place by the air pressure. If the valve faces or seats are in poor condition, leaks may prevent the air pressure from retaining the valves — refer to the alternative procedure below.

7   If you don't have access to compressed air, an alternative method can be used. Position the piston at a point just before TDC on the compression stroke, then feed a long piece of nylon rope through the spark plug hole until it fills the combustion chamber. Be sure to leave the end of the rope hanging out of the engine so it can be removed easily. Use a large breaker bar and socket to rotate the crankshaft in the normal direction of rotation until slight resistance is felt.

8   Stuff shop rags into the cylinder head holes above and below the valves to prevent parts and tools from falling into the engine, then use a valve spring compressor to compress the spring **(see illustration)**. Remove the keepers with small needle-nose pliers or a magnet **(see**

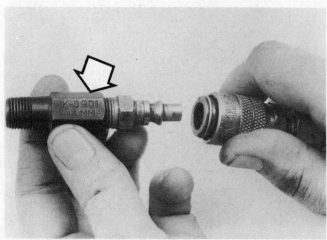

4.4   This is what the air hose adapter that threads into the spark plug hole looks like — they're commonly available from auto parts stores

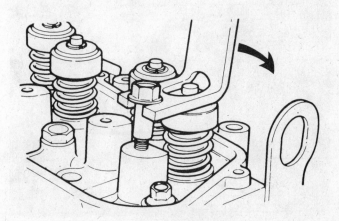

4.8a   A lever-type valve spring compressor is used to compress the spring and remove the keepers to replace valve seals or springs with the head installed

2A

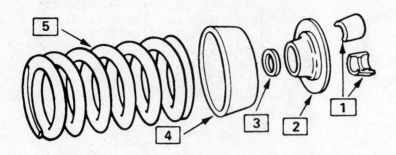 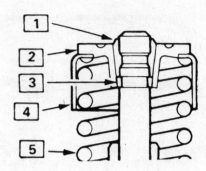

4.8b   Exploded view of a valve and related components (later models are slightly different)

1 *Keepers* 3 *O-ring seal* 5 *Spring*
2 *Retainer* 4 *Shield*

illustration). Note: *A couple of different types of tools are available for compressing the valve springs with the head in place. One type grips the lower spring coils and presses on the retainer as the knob is turned, while the other type, shown here, utilizes the rocker arm bolt for leverage. Both types work very well, although the lever type is usually less expensive.*

9   Remove the valve stem O-ring seal, spring retainer, shield and valve spring, then remove the umbrella type guide seal, if equipped (the O-ring seal will most likely be hardened and will probably break when removed, so plan on installing a new one each time the original is removed). **Note:** *If air pressure fails to hold the valve in the closed position during this operation, the valve face or seat is probably damaged. If so, the cylinder head will have to be removed for additional repair operations.*

10   Wrap a rubber band or tape around the top of the valve stem so the valve will not fall into the combustion chamber, then release the air pressure. **Note:** *If a rope was used instead of air pressure, turn the crankshaft slightly in the direction opposite normal rotation.*

11   Inspect the valve stem for damage. Rotate the valve in the guide and check the end for eccentric movement, which would indicate that the valve is bent.

12   Move the valve up-and-down in the guide and make sure it doesn't bind. If the valve stem binds, either the valve is bent or the guide is damaged. In either case, the head will have to be removed for repair.

13   Reapply air pressure to the cylinder to retain the valve in the closed position, then remove the tape or rubber band from the valve stem. If a rope was used instead of air pressure, rotate the crankshaft in the normal direction of rotation until slight resistance is felt.

14   Lubricate the valve stem with engine oil and install a new umbrella type guide seal, if used.

15   Install the spring and shield in position over the valve.

16   Install the valve spring retainer. Compress the valve spring and carefully install the new O-ring seal in the lower groove of the valve stem. Make sure the seal isn't twisted — it must lie perfectly flat in the groove **(see illustration).**

17   Position the keepers in the upper groove. Apply a small dab of grease to the inside of each keeper to hold it in place if necessary **(see illustration).** Remove the pressure from the spring tool and make sure the keepers are seated. Refer to Chapter 2, Part C, and check the seals with a vacuum pump.

18   Disconnect the air hose and remove the adapter from the spark plug hole. If a rope was used in place of air pressure, pull it out of the cylinder.

19   Refer to Section 6 and install the rocker arm(s) and pushrod(s).

20   Install the spark plug(s) and hook up the wire(s).

21   Refer to Section 3 and install the rocker arm cover.

22   Start and run the engine, then check for oil leaks and unusual sounds coming from the rocker arm cover area.

4.16   Make sure the O-ring seal under the retainer is seated in the groove and not twisted before installing the keepers

4.17   Keepers don't always stay in place, so apply a small dab of grease to each one as shown here before installation — it'll hold them in place on the valve stem as the spring is released

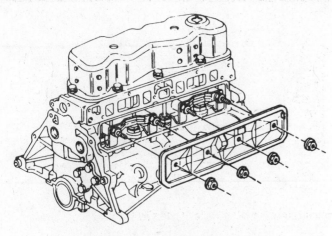

**5.9   The pushrod cover is held in place
with four nuts**

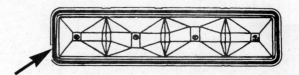

**5.12   The pushrod cover is sealed with RTV — no gasket
is required**

13 Install new rubber pushrod cover seals (see illustration).
14 Install the cover while the sealant is still wet. Make sure the semi-circular cutout in the edge of the pushrod cover is facing down.
15 Tighten the nuts gradually until they're snug, then tighten them to the specified torque.
16 The remaining installation steps are the reverse of removal.
17 Start and run the engine, then check for oil and coolant leaks.

---

5   Pushrod cover — removal and installation

Refer to illustrations 5.9, 5.12 and 5.13

1   Disconnect the negative cable from the battery.
2   Remove the engine cover (Chapter 11).
3   Remove the alternator and brackets (Chapter 5).
4   Remove the intake manifold-to-block brace.
5   Drain the cooling system (Chapter 1).
6   Detach the lower radiator and heater hoses.
7   Remove the oil pressure sending unit.
8   Detach the wiring harness brackets from the cover.
9   Remove the four pushrod cover nuts (see illustration). Flip one nut over so the washer faces out and reinstall it on the long inner stud. Put a second nut on the stud with the washer facing in. Put two 6 mm nuts on the shorter stud. Jam them together with two wrenches. Un-screw the studs by turning the inner nuts until the cover breaks free.
10 Remove the pushrod cover. **Caution:** *Careless prying may damage the sealing surface of the cover. If you bend the cover during removal, place it on a flat surface and straighten it with a soft-face hammer.*
11 Remove all traces of old gasket material with a scraper, then clean the mating surfaces with lacquer thinner or acetone.
12 Apply a continuous 3/16-inch diameter bead of RTV sealant to the mating surface of the pushrod cover (see illustration).

**6   Rocker arms and pushrods — removal,
inspection and installation**

Refer to illustrations 6.3, 6.4a, 6.4b and 6.5
Removal

1   Refer to Section 3 and detach the rocker arm cover from the cylinder head.
2   Beginning at the front of the cylinder head, loosen the rocker arm bolts. **Note:** *If the pushrods are the only items being removed, rotate the rocker arms to one side so the pushrods can be lifted out.*
3   Remove the bolts, the rocker arms and the pivot balls (see illustration) and store them in marked containers (they must be reinstalled in their original locations).

**5.13   Don't forget to install new rubber sealing washers
around the pushrod cover mounting studs or oil will leak
past the studs**

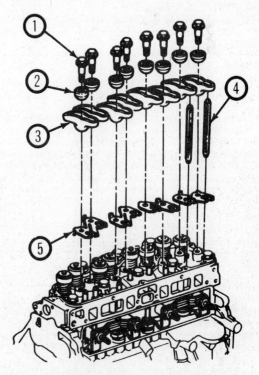

**6.3   Rocker arms, pushrods and related
components — exploded view**

1   Rocker arm bolt   *4   Pushrod*
2   Pivot ball   *5   Pushrod guide*
3   Rocker arm

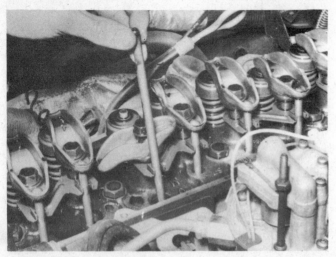

6.4a Loosen the rocker arm bolt, rotate the rocker arm to one side and lift out the pushrod

6.4b If more than one pushrod is being removed, store them in a perforated cardboard box to prevent mixups during installation — note the label indicating the front of the engine

4   Remove the pushrods and store them separately to make sure they don't get mixed up during installation **(see illustrations)**.
5   If the pushrod guides must be removed for any reason, make sure they're marked so they can be reinstalled in their original locations **(see illustration)**.

Inspection

6   Check each rocker arm for wear, cracks and other damage, especially where the pushrods and valve stems contact the rocker arm faces.
7   Make sure the hole at the pushrod end of each rocker arm is open.
8   Check each rocker arm pivot area for wear, cracks and galling. If the rocker arms are worn or damaged, replace them with new ones and use new pivot balls as well.
9   Inspect the pushrods for cracks and excessive wear at the ends. Roll each pushrod across a piece of plate glass to see if it's bent (if it wobbles, it's bent).

Installation

10   Lubricate the lower ends of the pushrods with clean engine oil or moly-base grease and install them in their original locations. Make sure each pushrod seats completely in the lifter socket.
11   Apply moly-base grease to the ends of the valve stems and the upper ends of the pushrods before positioning the rocker arms and installing the bolts.
12   Set the rocker arms in place, then install the pivot balls and bolts. Apply moly-base grease to the pivot balls to prevent damage to the mating surfaces before engine oil pressure builds up. Tighten the bolts to the specified torque.

---

7   Hydraulic lifters — removal, inspection and installation

Removal

Refer to illustrations 7.7a, 7.7b, 7.8 and 7.9

1   A noisy valve lifter can be isolated when the engine is idling. Place a length of hose or tubing near the position of each valve while listening at the other end. Or remove the rocker arm cover and, with the engine idling, place a finger on each of the valve spring retainers, one at a time. If a valve lifter is defective, it'll be evident from the shock felt at the retainer as the valve seats.
2   The most likely cause of a noisy valve lifter is a piece of dirt trapped between the plunger and the lifter body.
3   Remove the rocker arm cover (Section 3).
4   Loosen both rocker arm bolts at the cylinder with the noisy lifter and rotate the rocker arms away from the pushrods.
5   Remove the pushrod guides and pushrods (Section 6).
6   Remove the pushrod cover (Section 5).

6.5 If they're removed, make sure the pushrod guides (arrows) are kept in order also

7   Remove the lifter guide retainer by unscrewing the locknuts on the pushrod cover studs. Remove the lifter guide **(see illustrations)**.
8   There are several ways to extract a lifter from its bore. A special removal tool is available, but isn't always necessary. On newer engines without a lot of varnish buildup, lifters can often be removed with a small magnet or even with your fingers **(see illustration)**. A scribe can also be used to pull the lifter out of the bore. **Caution:** *Don't use pliers of any type to remove a lifter unless you intend to replace it with a new one — they will damage the precision machined and hardened surface of the lifter, rendering it useless.*
9   Store the lifters in a clearly labelled box to insure their reinstallation in the same lifter bores **(see illustration)**.

Inspection

Refer to illustrations 7.11a, 7.11b, 7.11c and 7.13

Conventional lifters

10   Clean the lifters with solvent and dry them thoroughly without mixing them up.
11   Check each lifter wall, pushrod seat and foot for scuffing, score marks and uneven wear. Each lifter foot (the surface that rides on the cam lobe) must be slightly convex, although this can be difficult to determine by eye. If the base of the lifter is concave **(see illustrations)**, the lifters and camshaft must be replaced. If the lifter walls are damaged or worn (which isn't very likely), inspect the lifter bores in the engine block as well. If the pushrod seats **(see illustration)** are worn, check the pushrod ends.

7.7a Pushrod cover stud locknuts (arrows) — manifold removed for clarity

7.7b Remove the lifter guide — if you're removing more than one guide, keep them in order to prevent mixups during installation

2A

7.8 On engines that haven't become sticky with sludge and varnish, the lifters can usually be removed by hand

7.9 If you're removing more than one lifter, keep them in order in a clearly labelled box

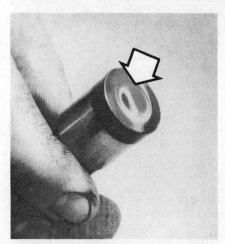

7.11a If the bottom (foot) of any lifter is worn concave, scratched or pitted, replace the entire set with new lifters

7.11b The bottom (foot) of each lifter should be slightly convex — the side of another lifter can be used as a straightedge to check it (if it appears flat, it's worn and should be discarded)

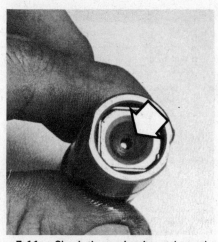

7.11c Check the pushrod seat (arrow) in the top of each lifter for wear

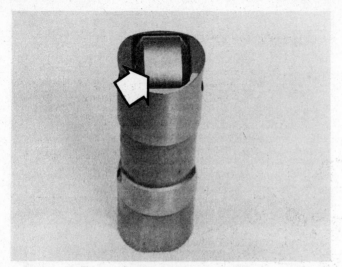

7.13 The roller on roller lifters must turn freely — check for wear and excessive play as well

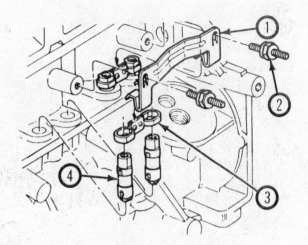

7.18 Hydraulic lifters and related components — exploded view

1 Retainer	3 Lifter guide
2 Stud	4 Lifter

12 If new lifters are being installed, a new camshaft must also be installed. If a new camshaft is installed, then use new lifters as well. Never install used lifters unless the original camshaft is used and the lifters can be installed in their original location!

Roller lifters

13 Check the rollers carefully for wear and damage and make sure they turn freely without excessive play **(see illustration)**. The inspection procedure for conventional lifters also applies to roller lifters.

14 Used roller lifters can be reinstalled with a new camshaft and the original camshaft can be used if new lifters are installed.

Installation

Refer to illustration 7.18

15 The used lifters must be installed in their original bores. Coat them with moly-base grease or engine assembly lube.

16 Lubricate the bearing surfaces of the lifter bores with engine oil.

17 Install the lifter(s) in the lifter bore(s). **Note:** *Make sure that the oil orifice is facing toward the front of the engine.*

18 Install the lifter guide(s) and retainer(s) **(see illustration)**.

19 Install the pushrods, pushrod guides, rocker arms and rocker arm retaining bolts (Section 6). **Caution:** *Make sure that each pair of lifters is on the base circle of the camshaft; that is, with both valves closed, before tightening the rocker arm bolts.*

20 Tighten the rocker arm bolts to the specified torque.

21 Install the pushrod cover (Section 5).

22 Install the rocker arm cover (Section 3).

---

8   Intake manifold — removal and installation

Refer to illustrations 8.10 and 8.15

1   Disconnect the cable from the negative battery terminal, then remove the engine cover (Chapter 11).

2   Remove the air cleaner assembly (Chapter 4).

3   Remove the PCV valve and hose.

4   Drain the cooling system (Chapter 1).

5   Refer to Chapter 4 and detach the fuel lines, vacuum lines and wire leads from the fuel injection assembly. When disconnecting the fuel line be prepared to catch some fuel, then plug the line to prevent contamination.

6   After noting how it's installed, disconnect the fuel injection throttle linkage. Disconnect the cruise control and TVS linkage (if so equipped).

7   Tag and disconnect all remaining vacuum lines and wires hooked to components on the manifold. Remove the coolant hoses from the manifold.

8   Remove the ignition coil. Unbolt the alternator and bracket and set it aside (Chapter 5).

9   Remove the mounting bolts and separate the manifold from the

8.10 Remove the old intake manifold gasket with a scraper — don't leave any material on the mating surfaces

cylinder head. Don't pry between the manifold and head, as damage to the gasket sealing surfaces may result.

10 Remove the old gasket **(see illustration)**.

11 If a new manifold is being installed, transfer all components still attached to the old manifold to the new one.

12 Before installing the manifold, clean the cylinder head and manifold gasket surfaces with lacquer thinner or acetone. All gasket material and sealing compound must be removed prior to installation.

13 Apply a thin coat of RTV sealant to the intake manifold and cylinder head mating surfaces. Make certain that the sealant will not spread into the air or coolant passages when the manifold is installed.

14 Place a new gasket on the manifold, hold the manifold in position against the cylinder head and install the mounting bolts finger tight.

15 Tighten the mounting bolts a little at a time in the correct sequence **(see illustration)** until they're all at the specified torque.

16 Install the remaining components in the reverse order of removal.

17 Fill the radiator with coolant, start the engine and check for leaks.

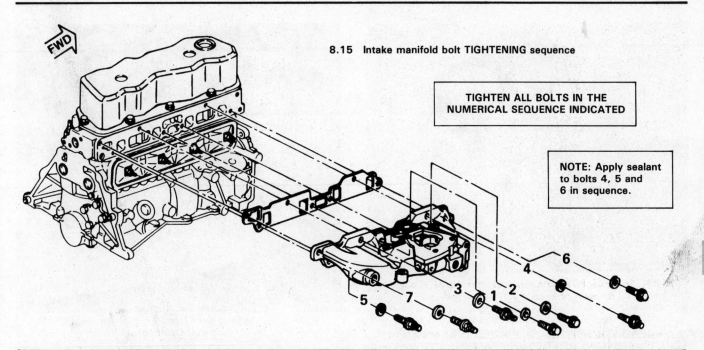

8.15   Intake manifold bolt TIGHTENING sequence

TIGHTEN ALL BOLTS IN THE
NUMERICAL SEQUENCE INDICATED

NOTE: Apply sealant
to bolts 4, 5 and
6 in sequence.

2A

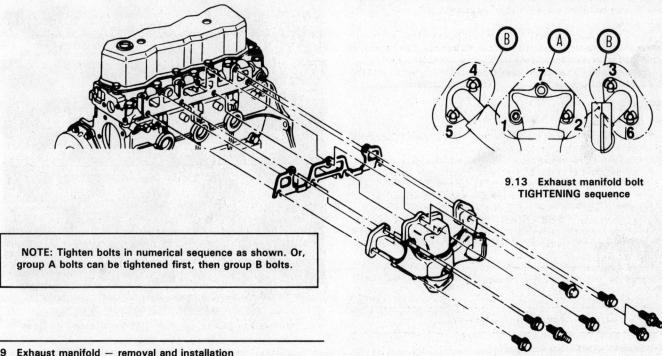

NOTE: Tighten bolts in numerical sequence as shown. Or,
group A bolts can be tightened first, then group B bolts.

9.13   Exhaust manifold bolt TIGHTENING sequence

9   Exhaust manifold — removal and installation

Refer to illustration 9.13

1   Remove the cable from the negative battery terminal.
2   Remove the engine cover (Chapter 11).
3   Remove the heat stove pipe at the exhaust manifold.
4   Raise the vehicle and support it securely on jackstands.
5   Disconnect the oxygen sensor.
6   Label the four spark plug wires, then disconnect them and secure them out of the way.
7   Disconnect the exhaust pipe from the exhaust manifold. You may have to apply penetrating oil to the fastener threads, as they are usually corroded. The exhaust pipe can be hung from the frame with a piece of wire.
8   Remove the rear air conditioning compressor bracket.
9   Remove the exhaust manifold end bolts first, then remove the center bolts and separate the exhaust manifold from the engine.

10   Remove the exhaust manifold gasket.
11   Before installing the manifold, clean the gasket mating surfaces on the cylinder head and manifold. All old gasket material and carbon deposits must be removed. Check the bolt threads for damage.
12   Place a new exhaust manifold gasket in position on the cylinder head, then place the manifold in position and install the mounting bolts finger tight.
13   Tighten the mounting bolts a little at a time in the correct sequence **(see illustration)** until all of the bolts are at the specified torque.
14   Reconnect the exhaust pipe and reinstall the air conditioning compressor bracket.
15   Lower the vehicle.
16   Install the remaining components in the reverse order of removal.
17   Start the engine and check for exhaust leaks between the manifold and cylinder head and between the manifold and exhaust pipe.

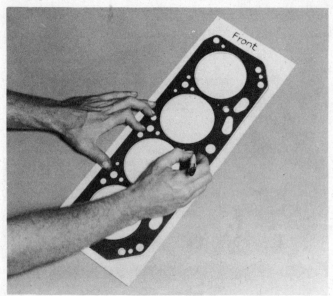

10.15   To avoid mixing up the head bolts, use a new gasket to transfer the bolt hole pattern to a piece of cardboard, then punch holes to accept the bolts . . .

10.16   . . . and push each head bolt through the matching hole in the cardboard

10   Cylinder head — removal and installation

Removal

Refer to illustrations 10.15, 10.16 and 10.17

1   Disconnect the negative cable from the battery and remove the engine cover. .

2   Drain the cooling system (Chapter 1).

3   Remove the air cleaner assembly Chapter 4).

4   Remove the throttle, cruise control and TVS cables (as equipped).

5   Remove the dipstick tube and thermostat housing.

6   Remove the alternator and brackets (Chapter 5).

7   Unbolt the air conditioner compressor and swing it out of the way for clearance. **Caution:** *Don't disconnect any of the air conditioning lines unless the system has been depressurized by a dealer service department or repair shop.*

8   Disconnect all wires and vacuum hoses from the cylinder head and manifold. Be sure to label them to simplify reinstallation. Refer to Chapter 4 and detach the fuel lines from the TBI unit.

9   Remove the upper radiator, water pump bypass and heater hoses.

10   Disconnect the spark plug wires and remove the spark plugs. Be sure to label the plug wires to simplify reinstallation.

11   Remove the rocker arm cover (Section 3).

12   Remove the pushrods (Section 6).

13   Remove the ignition coil (Chapter 5).

14   Raise the vehicle and support it securely on jackstands, then unbolt the exhaust pipe from the manifold.

15   Using a new head gasket, outline the cylinders and bolt pattern on a piece of cardboard **(see illustration)**. Be sure to indicate the front of the engine for reference. Punch holes at the bolt locations.

16   Loosen the cylinder head mounting bolts in 1/4-turn increments until they can be removed by hand. Store the bolts in the cardboard holder as they're removed — this will ensure that they are reinstalled in their original locations **(see illustration)**.

17   Lift the head off the engine. If it's stuck, pry on it only at the overhang on the thermostat end of the head **(see illustration). Caution:** *If you pry on the head anywhere else, damage to the gasket surface may result.*

18   Place the head on a block of wood to prevent damage to the gasket surface. Refer to Part C for cylinder head disassembly and valve service procedures.

10.17   If the head is stuck, pry it up at the overhang just behind and below the thermostat housing

Installation

Refer to illustrations 10.19, 10.23, 10.25 and 10.28

19   If a new cylinder head is being installed, transfer all external parts from the old cylinder head to the new one **(see illustration)**.

20   The mating surfaces of the cylinder head and block must be perfectly clean when the head is installed. It's also a good idea to have the head checked for distortion (warpage) and cracks by an automotive machine shop.

21   Use a gasket scraper to remove all traces of carbon and old gasket material, then clean the mating surfaces with lacquer thinner or acetone. If there's oil on the mating surfaces when the head is installed, the gasket may not seal correctly and leaks may develop. Use a vacuum cleaner to remove any debris that falls into the cylinders.

22   Check the block and head mating surfaces for nicks, deep scratches and other damage. If damage is slight, it can be removed with a file; if it's excessive, machining may be the only alternative.

10.19 Cylinder head and related components — exploded view

1 Outer engine heat stove
2 Bolt
3 Stud
4 Stud
5 Exhaust manifold
6 Inner engine heat stove
7 Exhaust manifold gasket
8 Stud
9 Bolt
10 Thermostat housing cover
11 Gasket
12 Thermostat
13 Thermostat housing
14 Bolt
15 Hose clamp
16 Hose
17 Cylinder head gasket
18 Intake valve
19 Exhaust valve
20 Plug
21 Gasket
22 Coolant temperature sensor
23 NOT USED
24 Cylinder head
25 Cylinder head bolt
26 Spark plug
27 Cylinder head bolt
28 Retainer
29 Valve stem oil seal (O-ring)
30 Valve keepers
31 Rocker arm bolt
32 Rocker arm pivot ball
33 Rocker arm
34 Valve stem oil shield
35 Valve spring
36 Intake valve stem seal
37 Washer
38 Intake manifold bolt
39 Plug
40 NOT USED
41 Plug
42 Intake manifold stud
43 Intake manifold
44 Intake manifold gasket
45 Pushrod guide
46 Cylinder head bolt
47 Pushrod
48 Rocker arm cover

2A

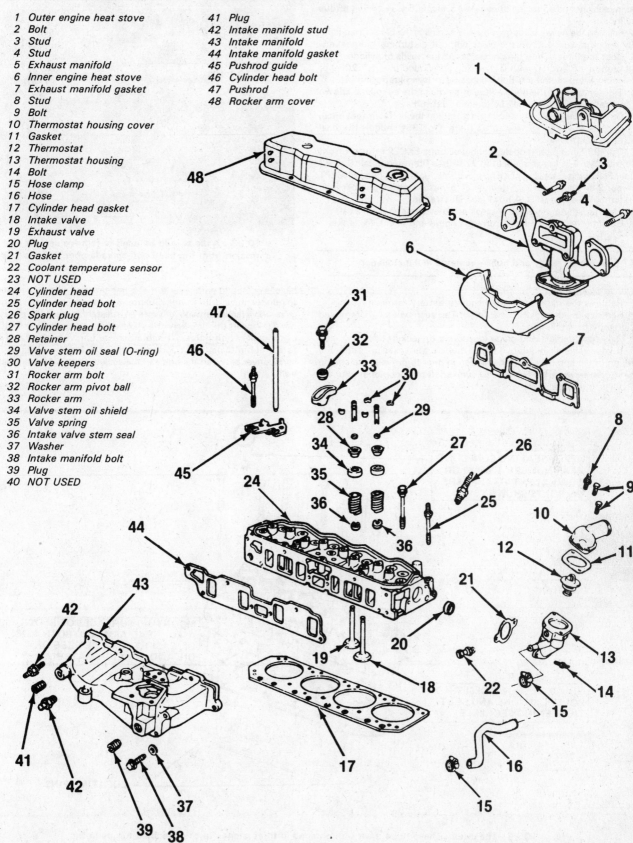

23 Use a tap of the correct size to chase the threads in the head bolt holes. Mount each bolt in a vise and run a die down the threads to remove corrosion and restore the threads **(see illustration)**. Dirt, corrosion, sealant and damaged threads will affect critical head bolt torque readings.
24 Position the new gasket over the dowel pins in the block, then carefully position the head on the block without disturbing the gasket.
25 Coat the threads and the undersides of the heads of cylinder head bolt numbers 9 and 10 with GM sealing compound (no. 1052080 or equivalent) and install the bolts finger tight **(see illustration)**.
26 Tighten each of the bolts a little at a time in the sequence shown in illustration 10.25 until all bolts are at 18 ft-lbs.
27 On 1985 models only, continue tightening the bolts, in sequence, to 40, then to 70 and finally to 92 ft-lbs. On 1986 models the final torque is 90 ft-lbs.
28 On 1987 and later models, tighten all bolts EXCEPT the left front bolt (number 9 in the sequence) to 22 ft-lbs. Tighten number 9 to 30 ft-lbs. Following the sequence one more time, tighten all bolts EXCEPT number 9 an additional 120-degrees (1/3-turn). Tighten number 9 an additional 90-degrees (1/4-turn) **(see illustration)**.
29 The remaining installation steps are the reverse of removal.
30 Change the oil and filter, run the engine and check for leaks.

11   Crankshaft pulley and hub — removal and installation

Refer to illustrations 11.6 and 11.9
1   Remove the cable from the negative battery terminal.
2   Remove the drivebelts (Chapter 1). Tag each belt as it's removed to simplify reinstallation.
3   Raise the vehicle and place it securely on jackstands.
4   If your vehicle is equipped with a manual transmission, apply the parking brake and put the transmission in gear to prevent the engine from turning over, then remove the crankshaft pulley bolts. If your ve-

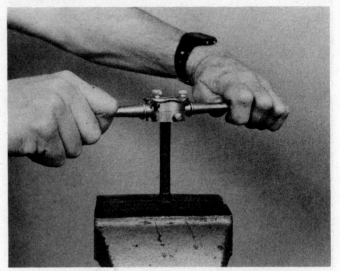

10.23   A die should be used to remove sealant and corrosion from the head bolt threads prior to installation

hicle is equipped with an automatic transmission, it may be necessary to remove the starter motor (Chapter 5) and immobilize the starter ring gear with a large screwdriver while an assistant loosens the pulley bolts.
5   To loosen the crankshaft hub retaining bolt, install a bolt in one of the pulley bolt holes. Attach a breaker bar, extension and socket to the hub retaining bolt and immobilize the hub by wedging a large screwdriver between the bolt and the socket. Remove the hub retaining bolt.

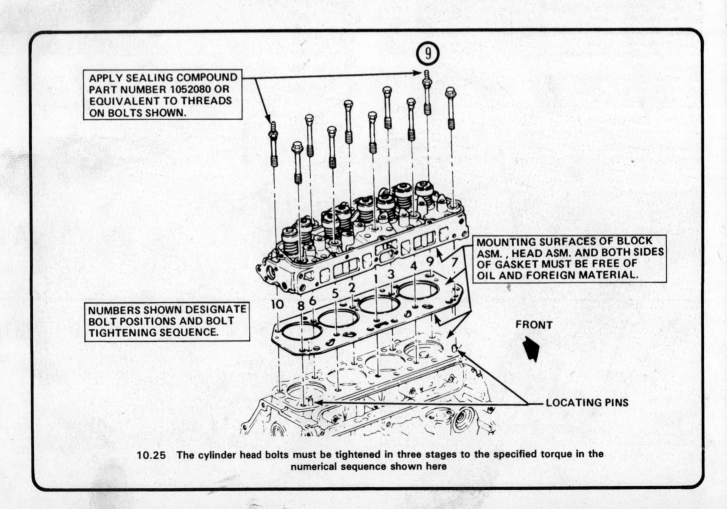

APPLY SEALING COMPOUND PART NUMBER 1052080 OR EQUIVALENT TO THREADS ON BOLTS SHOWN.

MOUNTING SURFACES OF BLOCK ASM., HEAD ASM. AND BOTH SIDES OF GASKET MUST BE FREE OF OIL AND FOREIGN MATERIAL.

NUMBERS SHOWN DESIGNATE BOLT POSITIONS AND BOLT TIGHTENING SEQUENCE.

FRONT

LOCATING PINS

10.25   The cylinder head bolts must be tightened in three stages to the specified torque in the numerical sequence shown here

10.28 The final step in tightening the cylinder head bolts is known as "angle torquing" — all bolts except number 9 should be turned an additional 120-degrees, while bolt 9 should be turned an additional 90-degrees

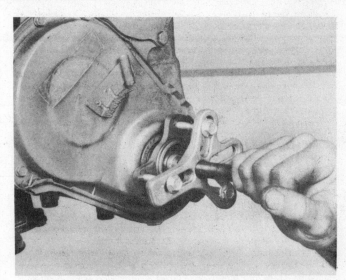

11.6 Use a puller to remove the hub from the crankshaft

2A

6   Remove the crankshaft hub. Use a puller if necessary (see illustration).
7   Refer to Section 12 for the front oil seal replacement procedure.
8   Apply a thin layer of moly-base grease to the seal contact surface of the hub.
9   Slide the pulley hub onto the crankshaft until it bottoms against the crankshaft timing gear. Note that the slot in the hub must be aligned with the Woodruff key in the end of the crankshaft. The hub retaining bolt can also be used to press the hub into position (see illustration).
10 Tighten the hub-to-crankshaft bolt to the specified torque.
11 Install the crankshaft pulley on the hub. Use Locktite on the bolt threads.
12 Install the drivebelts (Chapter 1).

12 Front crankshaft oil seal — replacement

Note: *The front crankshaft oil seal can be replaced with the timing gear cover in place. However, due to the limited amount of room available,* you may conclude that the procedure would be easier if the cover were removed from the engine first. If so, refer to Section 13 for the cover removal and installation procedure.

Timing gear cover in place
Refer to illustration 12.2

1   Disconnect the negative battery cable from the battery, then remove the crankshaft pulley hub (Section 11).
2   Note how the seal is installed — the new one must face the same direction! Carefully pry the oil seal out of the cover with a seal puller or a large screwdriver (see illustration). Be very careful not to distort the cover or scratch the crankshaft!
3   Apply clean engine oil or multi-purpose grease to the outer edge of the new seal, then install it in the cover with the lip (open end) facing IN. Drive the seal into place with a large socket and a hammer (if a large socket isn't available, a piece of pipe will also work). Make sure the seal enters the bore squarely and stop when the front face is flush with the cover.
4   Install the pulley hub (Section 11).

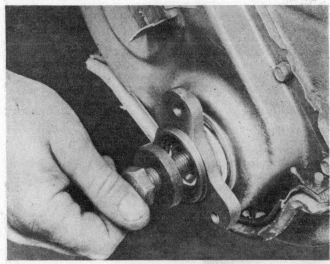

11.9 Use the pulley hub bolt to press the hub onto the crankshaft

12.2 The front crankshaft seal can be removed in the vehicle with a seal removal tool or a large screwdriver (V6 engine shown — four-cylinder similar)

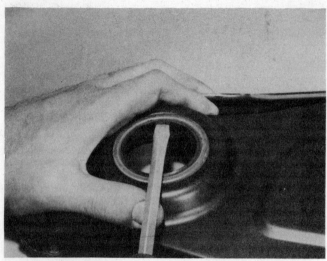

12.6   Once the timing gear cover is removed, place it on a
flat surface and gently pry the old seal out with
a large screwdriver

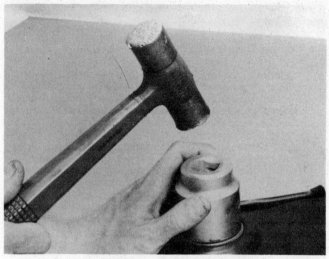

12.8a   Clean the bore, then apply a small amount of oil to
the outer edge of the new seal and drive it squarely into
the opening with a large socket . . .

12.8b   . . . or a block of wood and a hammer — don't
damage the seal in the process!

Timing gear cover removed

Refer to illustrations 12.6, 12.8a and 12.8b

5   Remove the timing gear cover as described in Section 13.
6   Using a large screwdriver, pry the old seal out of the cover **(see
illustration)**. Be careful not to distort the cover or scratch the wall of
the seal bore. If the engine has accumulated a lot of miles, apply
penetrating oil to the seal-to-cover joint and allow it to soak in before
attempting to remove the seal.
7   Clean the bore to remove any old seal material and corrosion. Support the cover on a block of wood and position the new seal in the
bore with the lip (open end) of the seal facing IN. A small amount of
oil applied to the outer edge of the new seal will make installation easier
— don't overdo it!
8   Drive the seal into the bore with a large socket and hammer until
it's completely seated **(see illustration)**. Select a socket that's the same
outside diameter as the seal. A section of pipe or even a block of wood
can be used if a socket isn't available) **(see illustration)**.
9   Reinstall the timing gear cover.

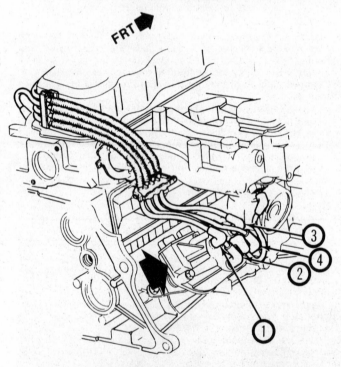

13.4   After you locate the number 1 spark plug wire
terminal on the distributor cap, make a mark (arrow) on the
distributor body directly under the terminal

13 Top Dead Center (TDC) for number 1 piston — locating

Refer to illustrations 13.4 and 13.5

1   Top Dead Center (TDC) is the highest point in the cylinder that
each piston reaches as it travels up-and-down when the crankshaft
turns. Each piston reaches TDC on the compression stroke and again
on the exhaust stroke, but TDC generally refers to piston position on
the compression stroke. The timing marks on the pulley installed on
the front of the crankshaft are referenced to the number one piston
at TDC on the compression stroke.
2   Positioning the piston(s) at TDC is an essential part of many procedures such as rocker arm removal, camshaft and timing gear removal
and distributor removal.

13.5 Turn the crankshaft until the notch in the drivebelt pulley (lower arrow) is directly opposite the zero mark on the timing plate (upper arrow) (note that in this photo, the crankshaft must be turned just a little more to align the marks)

14.9 Timing gear cover bolt locations

2A

3   In order to bring any piston to TDC, the crankshaft must be turned using one of the methods outlined below. When looking at the front of the engine, normal crankshaft rotation is *clockwise.* **Warning:** *Before beginning this procedure, be sure to place the transmission in Neutral and unplug the distributor wire harness connector to disable the ignition system.*

  a) The preferred method is to turn the crankshaft with a large socket and breaker bar attached to the crankshaft pulley hub bolt threaded into the front of the crankshaft.

  b) A remote starter switch, which may save some time, can also be used. Attach the switch leads to the S (switch) and B (battery) terminals on the starter motor. Once the piston is close to TDC, use a socket and breaker bar as described in the previous paragraph.

  c) If an assistant is available to turn the ignition switch to the Start position in short bursts, you can get the piston close to TDC without a remote starter switch. Use a socket and breaker bar as described in Paragraph a) to complete the procedure.

4   Note the position of the terminal for the number one spark plug wire on the distributor cap **(see illustration).** Use a felt-tip pen or chalk to make a mark on the distributor body directly under the terminal. Remove the screws, detach the cap from the distributor and set it aside.

5   Turn the crankshaft (see Paragraph 3 above) until the notch in the crankshaft pulley is aligned with the 0 on the timing plate (located at the front of the engine) **(see illustration).**

6   Look at the distributor rotor — it should be pointing directly at the mark you made on the distributor body. If the rotor is pointing at the terminal for the number four spark plug, the number one piston is at TDC on the exhaust stroke.

7   To get the piston to TDC on the compression stroke, turn the crankshaft one complete turn (360°) clockwise. The rotor should now be pointing at the mark on the distributor. When the rotor is pointing at the number one spark plug wire terminal in the distributor cap and the ignition timing marks are aligned, the number one piston is at TDC on the compression stroke.

8   After the number one piston has been positioned at TDC on the compression stroke, TDC for any of the remaining pistons can be located by turning the crankshaft 180° at a time and following the firing order (1-3-4-2).

---

14 Timing gear cover — removal and installation

Refer to illustrations 14.9, 14.13 and 14.14

1   Detach the cable from the negative terminal of the battery.

2   Remove the power steering reservoir (if equipped). Be prepared

to catch the fluid in a drain pan.

3   Remove the upper fan shroud (Chapter 3).

4   Remove the drivebelts (Chapter 1).

5   Detach the fan and drivebelt pulley.

6   Disconnect and unbolt the alternator and brackets (Chapter 5).

7   Raise the front of the vehicle and support it on jackstands. Apply the parking brake. Drain the coolant (Chapter 1), then detach the lower radiator hose from the water pump.

8   Remove the crankshaft pulley and hub (Section 11).

9   Remove the timing gear cover-to-block bolts **(see illustration).**

10 Remove the cover by carefully prying it off. The cover is sealed with RTV, so it may be stuck to the block. The flange between the cover and oil pan may be bent during removal. Try to minimize damage to the flange or it may be too distorted to be straightened.

11 Use a scraper to remove all old sealant from the cover, oil pan and block, then clean the mating surfaces with lacquer thinner or acetone.

12 Check the cover flanges for distortion, particularly around the bolt holes. If necessary, place the cover on a block of wood and use a hammer to flatten and restore the mating surfaces.

13 Apply a 3/8-inch wide by 3/16-inch thick bead of RTV sealant to the timing gear cover flange that mates with the oil pan. Apply a 1/4-inch wide by 1/8-inch thick bead to the cover-to-block flange **(see illustration).**

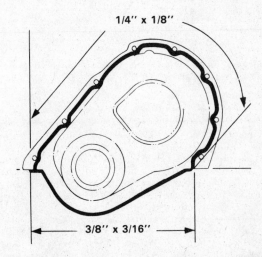

14.13 Apply a 1/4-inch wide by 1/8-inch thick bead of RTV sealant to the timing gear cover flange that contacts the block and a 3/8-inch wide by 3/16-inch thick bead to the cover-to-oil pan flange

14   Apply a dab of sealant to the joints between the oil pan and the engine block **(see illustration)**.
15   Place the cover in position and loosely install a couple of mounting bolts.
16   Install the crankshaft hub to center the cover (Section 11). Be sure to lubricate the seal contact surface of the hub.
17   Install the remaining mounting bolts and tighten them to the specified torque.
18   Install the crankshaft pulley, then hook up the lower radiator hose.
19   Lower the vehicle.
20   Refill the cooling system (Chapter 1).
21   Install the components removed to gain access to the cover.
22   Reattach the cable to the negative terminal of the battery.
23   Start the engine and check for oil leaks at the seal.

15   Camshaft, timing gears and bearings — removal, inspection and installation

Camshaft lobe lift check

Refer to illustration 15.3

1   In order to determine the extent of cam lobe wear, the lobe lift should be checked prior to camshaft removal. Refer to Section 3 and remove the rocker arm cover.
2   Position the number one piston at TDC on the compression stroke (see Section 13).
3   Beginning with the number one cylinder valves, mount a dial indicator on the engine and position the plunger against the top surface of the first rocker arm. The plunger should be directly above and in line with the pushrod **(see illustration)**.
4   Zero the dial indicator, then very slowly turn the crankshaft in the normal direction of rotation (clockwise when looking at the front of the engine) until the indicator needle stops and begins to move in the opposite direction. The point at which it stops indicates maximum cam lobe lift.
5   Record this figure for future reference, then reposition the piston at TDC on the compression stroke.
6   Move the dial indicator to the remaining number one cylinder rocker arm and repeat the check. Be sure to record the results for each valve.
7   Repeat the check for the remaining valves. Since each piston must be at TDC on the compression stroke for this procedure, work from cylinder-to-cylinder following the firing order sequence. Turn the crank-

15.3   When checking the camshaft lobe lift, the dial indicator plunger must be positioned directly above and in line with the pushrod

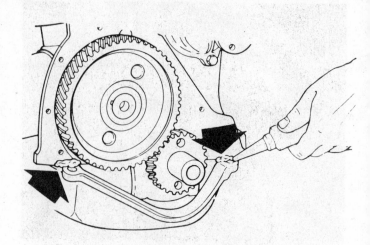

14.14   Put a dab of sealant at the junction between the oil pan and the bottom edge of the block (arrows)

shaft 180-degrees when moving from one cylinder to the next.
8   After the check is complete, compare the results to the Specifications. If camshaft lobe lift is less than specified, cam lobe wear has occurred and a new camshaft should be installed.

Removal

Refer to illustration 15.24

9   Disconnect the negative battery cable from the battery.
10   Remove the engine cover.
11   Detach the power steering reservoir from the fan shroud. Be prepared to catch the fluid in a drain pan.
12   Remove the radiator (Chapter 3).
13   Remove the drivebelts (Chapter 1).
14   Detach the fan and drivebelt pulley (Chapter 3).
15   Remove the air cleaner assembly.
16   Remove the pushrod cover (Section 5).
17   Remove the EGR valve (Chapter 6).
18   Tag and disconnect the vacuum hoses at the intake manifold and thermostat housing.
19   Remove the pushrods and lifters.
20   Refer to Section 14 and detach the timing gear cover.
21   Remove the distributor (Chapter 5) and the oil pump driveshaft (Section 16).
22   Remove the headlight bezels, the grille and the bumper filler panel (Chapter 11).
23   Remove the air conditioning condenser baffles. Unbolt the condenser and support it out of the way — don't disconnect the refrigerant lines!
24   Turn the crankshaft until the holes in the camshaft gear are aligned with the thrust plate bolts, then remove the bolts **(see illustration)**.
25   Carefully pull the camshaft and gear assembly out of the block. **Caution:** *To avoid damage to the camshaft bearings as the lobes pass over them, support the camshaft near the block as it's withdrawn.*
26   The crankshaft gear should slide off the crankshaft without a great deal of resistance.

Inspection

Refer to illustrations 15.28 and 15.32

Camshaft

27   After the camshaft has been removed from the engine, cleaned with solvent and dried, inspect the bearing journals for uneven wear, pitting and evidence of seizure. If the journals are damaged, the bearing inserts in the block are probably damaged as well. Both the camshaft and bearings will have to be replaced.
28   If the journals are in good condition, measure the bearing journals with a micrometer **(see illustration)** to determine their sizes and whether or not they're out-of-round. The inside diameter of each bearing can be measured with a telescoping gauge and micrometer. Subtract each cam journal diameter from the corresponding bearing inside diameter to obtain the bearing oil clearance.

15.24 Turn the camshaft until the holes in the gear are aligned with the thrust plate bolts, then remove them with a ratchet and socket

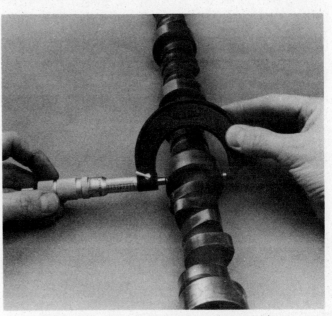

15.28 The camshaft bearing journal diameters are checked to pinpoint excessive wear and out-of-round conditions

2A

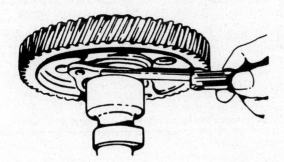

15.32 Use a feeler gauge to check the thrust plate (gear) end clearance

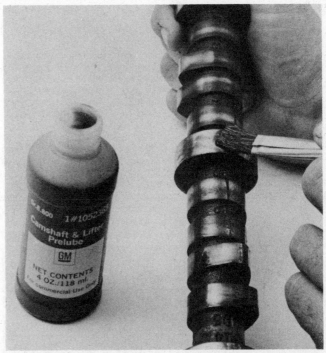

15.34 Be sure to prelube the bearing journals and lobes prior to camshaft installation

29 Compare the clearance for each bearing to the Specifications. If it's excessive for any of the bearings, have new bearings installed by an automotive machine shop.

30 Check the camshaft lobes for heat discoloration, score marks, chipped areas, pitting and uneven wear. If the lobes are in good condition and if the lobe lift measurements are as specified, the camshaft can be reused.

Gears

31 Check the camshaft drive and driven gears for cracks, missing teeth and excessive wear. If the teeth are highly polished, pitted and galled, or if the outer hardened surface of the teeth is flaking off, new parts will be required. If one gear is worn or damaged, replace both gears as a set. Never install one new and one used gear.

32 Check the gear end clearance with a feeler gauge and compare it to the Specifications (**see illustration**). If it's less than the minimum specified, the spacer ring should be replaced. If it's excessive, the thrust plate must be replaced. In either case, the gear will have to be pressed off the camshaft, so take the parts to an automotive machine shop.

Bearing replacement

33 Camshaft bearing replacement requires special tools and expertise that place it outside the scope of the home mechanic. Take the block to an automotive machine shop to ensure that the job is done correctly.

Installation

Refer to illustrations 15.34 and 15.36

34 Lubricate the camshaft bearing journals and cam lobes with moly-base grease, engine assembly lube or GM camshaft and lifter prelube (**see illustration**).

35 Slide the camshaft into the engine. Support the cam near the block and be careful not to scrape or nick the bearings.

15.36   Align the timing marks as shown here when installing the camshaft

16.3   The oil pump driveshaft retainer plate is located on the engine block, just below the pushrod cover and just above the oil filter

36   Install the gear on the end of the crankshaft (if not already done). Don't forget the Woodruff key and don't hammer the gear onto the shaft. Align the timing marks on the gears as the gears mesh (**see illustration**).

37   Line up the access holes in the gear with the thrust plate holes and the bolt holes in the block. Apply Locktite to the threads, then install the thrust plate bolts and tighten them to the specified torque.

38   The remaining installation steps are the reverse of removal.

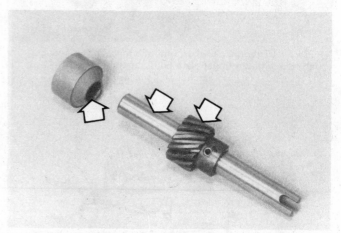

16.6   Inspect the oil pump driveshaft, gear and bushing for wear and damage

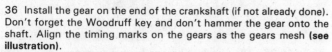

16   Oil pump driveshaft — removal and installation

Refer to illustrations 16.3, 16.6, 16.7 and 16.8

1   Disconnect the cable from the negative terminal of the battery, then remove the engine cover (Chapter 11).

2   Raise the vehicle and support it on jackstands.

3   Remove the oil pump driveshaft retainer plate bolts (**see illustration**).

4   Remove the oil pump driveshaft and bushing with a magnet.

5   Clean the mating surfaces of the block and retainer plate with lacquer thinner or acetone.

6   Check the bushing and driveshaft for wear (**see illustration**). Replace them if they're worn or damaged.

7   Install the bushing and oil pump driveshaft in the block. The shaft driven gear must mesh with the camshaft drive gear and the slot in the lower end of the shaft must mate with the oil pump gear tang (**see illustration**).

8   Apply a 1/16-inch bead of RTV sealant to the retainer plate so it completely seals around the oil pump driveshaft hole in the block (**see illustration**).

9   Install the retainer plate and tighten the mounting bolts securely.

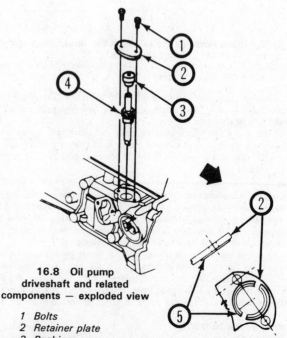

16.8   Oil pump driveshaft and related components — exploded view

1   *Bolts*
2   *Retainer plate*
3   *Bushing*
4   *Driveshaft and gear assembly*
5   *RTV sealant*

16.7   If the slotted oil pump driveshaft is properly mated with the oil pump gear tang, the top of the bushing will be flush with the retainer plate mounting surface

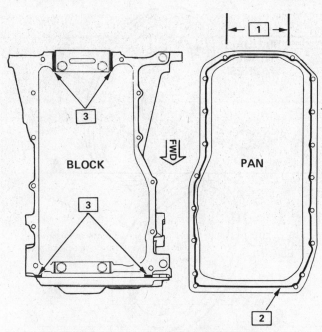

17.8 Oil pan sealant application details

1 3/8-inch wide by 3/16-inch thick

2 3/16-inch wide by 1/8-inch thick

3 1/8-inch bead

17 Oil pan — removal and installation

Refer to illustration 17.8

1   Disconnect the cable from the negative battery terminal.
2   Raise the vehicle and support it securely on jackstands.
3   Drain the engine oil and remove the oil filter (Chapter 1).
4   Disconnect the exhaust pipe at the manifold and hangers and tie the system aside.
5   Remove the starter (Chapter 5) and the bellhousing dust cover.
6   Remove the bolts and detach the oil pan. Don't pry between the block and pan or damage to the sealing surfaces may result and oil leaks could develop. If the pan is stuck, dislodge it with a block of wood and a hammer.
7   Use a scraper to remove all traces of sealant from the pan and block, then clean the mating surfaces with lacquer thinner or acetone.
8   Apply a 3/16-inch wide by 1/8-inch thick bead of RTV sealant to the oil pan flange. Make the bead 3/8-inch wide by 3/16-inch thick between the bolt holes at the rear end of the pan. Apply a 1/8-inch bead of sealant to the block at the rear main bearing cap joints and the timing gear cover joints **(see illustration)**.
9   Install the oil pan and tighten the mounting bolts to the specified torque. Start at the center of the pan and work out toward the ends in a spiral pattern.
10 Install the bellhousing dust cover and the starter, then reconnect the exhaust pipe to the manifold and hanger brackets..
11 Lower the vehicle.
12 Install a new filter and add oil to the engine.
13 Reconnect the negative battery cable.
14 Start the engine and check for leaks.

18 Oil pump — removal and installation

Refer to illustration 18.2

1   Remove the oil pan (Section 15).
2   Remove the two oil pump mounting bolts and the pick-up tube bracket nut from the main bearing cap bolt **(see illustration)**.
3   Detach the oil pump and pick-up assembly from the block.
4   If the pump is defective, replace it with a new one. If the engine

18.2   Remove the oil pump flange mounting bolts and the pick-up tube bracket nut

is being completely overhauled, install a new oil pump — don't reuse the original or attempt to rebuild it.
5   To install the pump, turn the shaft so the gear tang mates with the slot on the lower end of the oil pump driveshaft. The oil pump should slide easily into place over the oil pump driveshaft lower bushing. If it doesn't, pull it off and turn the tang until it's aligned with the pump driveshaft slot.
6   Install the pump mounting bolts and the tube bracket nut. Tighten them to the specified torque.
7   Reinstall the oil pan (Section 17).
8   Add oil, run the engine and check for leaks.

19 Flywheel/driveplate — removal and installation

Refer to illustrations 19.2, 19.3a and 19.3b

1   Refer to Chapter 7 and remove the transmission. If your vehicle has a manual transmission, the pressure plate and clutch will also have to be removed (Chapter 8).
2   Jam a large screwdriver in the starter ring gear or driveplate hole to keep the crankshaft from turning, then remove the mounting bolts **(see illustration)**. Since it's fairly heavy, support the flywheel as the last bolt is removed.

19.2   A large screwdriver wedged in the starter ring gear teeth or one of the holes in the driveplate can be used to keep the flywheel/driveplate from turning as the mounting bolts are removed

2A

19.3a   Don't lose the shim used on automatic transmission equipped vehicles

3   Pull straight back on the flywheel/driveplate to detach it from the crankshaft. Note the shim installed between the driveplate and crankshaft on vehicles equipped with an automatic transmission (**see illustrations**).
4   On manual transmission equipped vehicles, check the pilot bushing and replace it if necessary (Chapter 8).
5   Installation is the reverse of removal. Be sure to align the hole in the flywheel/driveplate with the dowel pin in the crankshaft. Use Locktite on the bolt threads and tighten them to the specified torque in a criss-cross pattern.

20   Rear main oil seal — replacement

Refer to illustrations 20.5, 20.8a and 20.8b

1   The rear main bearing oil seal can be replaced without removing the oil pan or crankshaft.
2   Remove the transmission (Chapter 7).
3   If equipped with a manual transmission, remove the pressure plate and clutch disc (Chapter 8).
4   Remove the flywheel or driveplate (Section 19).
5   Using a seal removal tool or a large screwdriver, carefully pry the seal out of the block (**see illustration**). Don't scratch or nick the crankshaft in the process.

20.5   Carefully pry the oil seal out with a screwdriver — don't nick or scratch the crankshaft or the new seal will be damaged and leaks will develop

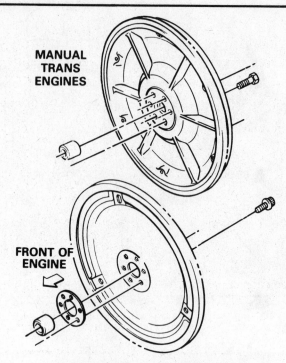

MANUAL TRANS ENGINES

FRONT OF ENGINE

AUTOMATIC TRANS. ENGINES

19.3b   Flywheel/driveplate mounting details

6   Clean the bore in the block and the seal contact surface on the crankshaft. Check the crankshaft surface for scratches and nicks that could damage the new seal lip and cause oil leaks. If the crankshaft is damaged, the only alternative is a new or different crankshaft.
7   Apply a light coat of engine oil or multi-purpose grease to the outer edge of the new seal. Lubricate the seal lip with moly-base grease.
8   Press the new seal into place with GM tool no. J34924 (if available) (**see illustration**). The seal lip must face toward the front of the engine. If the special tool isn't available, carefully work the seal lip over the end of the crankshaft and tap the seal in with a hammer and punch until it's seated in the bore (**see illustration**).
9   Install the flywheel or driveplate.
10   If equipped with a manual transmission, reinstall the clutch disc and pressure plate.
11   Reinstall the transmission as described in Chapter 7.

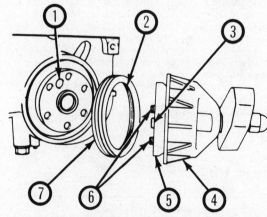

20.8a   Installing the rear main oil seal with GM special tool no. J-34924

1 Alignment hole in crankshaft	*5 Mandrel*
2 Dust lip	*6 Screws*
3 Dowel pin	*7 Oil seal*
4 Collar	

20.8b Tap around the outer edge of the new seal with a hammer and punch to seat it squarely in the bore

21 Engine mounts — replacement

Refer to illustration 21.5

Warning: *Improper lifting methods or devices are hazardous and could result in severe injury or death. DO NOT place any part of your body under the engine/transmission when it's supported only by a jack. Failure of the lifting device could result in serious injury or death.*

1   If the rubber mounts have hardened, cracked or separated from the metal backing plates, they must be replaced. This operation may be carried out with the engine/transmission still in the vehicle.
2   Disconnect the negative cable from the battery.
3   Raise the front of the vehicle and support it securely on jackstands.
4   Support the engine with a jack. Position a block of wood between the jack head and the oil pan.
5   Remove the engine mount-to-chassis bolts **(see illustration)**.
6   Remove the mount-to-engine support bracket bolts. It's not necessary to detach the support bracket from the engine.
7   Raise the engine just enough to clear the bracket, then remove the engine mount.
8   Place the new mount in position.
9   Install the mount-to-engine support bracket bolts and tighten them securely.
10   Tighten the mount-to-chassis bolts securely.
11   Remove the jack.
12   Remove the jackstands and lower the vehicle.

2A

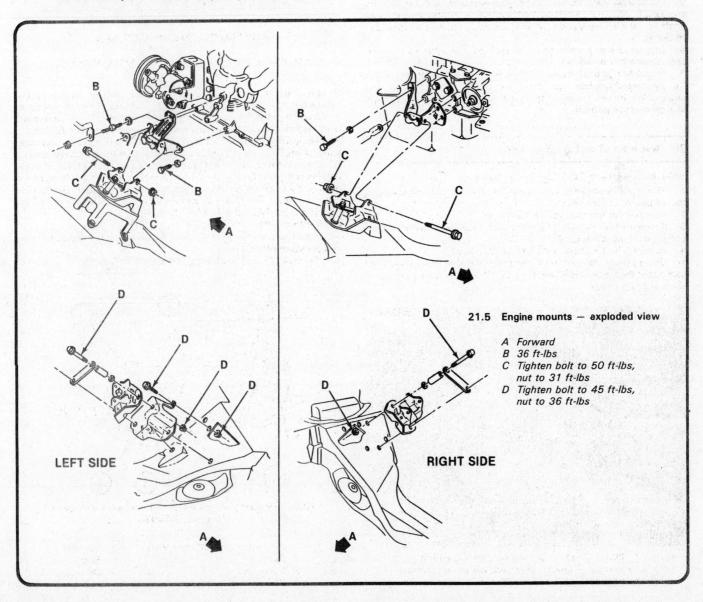

LEFT SIDE

RIGHT SIDE

21.5 Engine mounts — exploded view

A *Forward*
B *36 ft-lbs*
C *Tighten bolt to 50 ft-lbs, nut to 31 ft-lbs*
D *Tighten bolt to 45 ft-lbs, nut to 36 ft-lbs*

Chapter 2 Part B V6 engine

Contents

Specifications

General

Cylinder numbers (front-to-rear)

left (driver's) side	1-3-5
right side..	2-4-6
Firing order	1-6-5-4-3-2

Camshaft

Bearing journal

diameter	1.8682 to 1.8692 in
out-of-round limit	0.001 in

Lobe lift

1990 and earlier

intake	0.357 in
exhaust	0.390 in

1991

LB4 engine

intake...	0.234 in
exhaust	0.257 in

LU2 engine (high output)

intake...	0.269 in
exhaust	0.276 in

1992 on

All except VIN W engine

intake...	0.234 in
exhaust	0.257 in

VIN W engine

intake...	0.288 in
exhaust	0.294 in
End play..	0.004 to 0.012 in

Balancer shaft (VIN W engine)

Rear bearing journal outside diameter	1.4309 to 1.4215 in

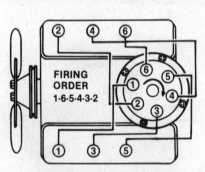

CYLINDER NUMBERS AND DISTRIBUTOR SPARK PLUG WIRE TERMINAL LOCATIONS

Torque specifications

Ft-lbs (unless otherwise noted)

Rocker arm cover bolts

1985	48 in-lbs
1987	100 in-lbs
1986 and 1988 on	90 in-lbs

Intake manifold bolts

1985	30
1986 on	36
Exhaust manifold bolts	20
1985	20

1986 on

center bolts..	26
all others	20
Cylinder head bolts*......................................	65

Timing chain cover bolts

1985	84 in-lbs
1986	92 in-lbs
1987	100 in-lbs
1988 on	120 in-lbs

Camshaft sprocket	
Bolt (all except 1992 and later VIN W engine)............................	18
Bolt and nut (1992 and later VIN W engine)	21
Balancer shaft (1992 and later VIN W engine)	
Retainer bolts	120 in-lbs
Driven gear bolt	15 plus and additional 35-degrees rotation
Drive gear retaining stud	144 in-lbs
Rocker arm nut (1992 and later VIN W engine)	20 ft-lbs
Vibration damper bolt	
1985	60
1986 on	70
Lifter restrictor retainer bolts	145 in-lbs
Oil pan	
1985	
1/4-20 bolts	84 in-lbs
5/16-18 bolts	168 in-lbs
1986 on	
bolts/studs..	100 in-lbs
nuts	200 in-lbs
Oil pump bolt	65
Main bearing cap bolts	
1985	70
1986 and 1987	75
1988 through 1990	80
1991 on	75
Rear main oil seal housing bolts...	135 in-lbs
Flywheel bolts...	65
Driveplate bolts...	55

*Use Permatex number 2 on the bolt threads

1   General information

This Part of Chapter 2 is devoted to in-vehicle repair procedures for the V6 engine. All information concerning engine removal and installation and engine block and cylinder head overhaul can be found in Part C of this Chapter.

The VIN W V6 engine introduced in 1992 is very similar to the other V6 engines in this Chapter, except it is equipped with a balancer shaft and has the Central Port Injection (CPI) fuel injection system. You can identify this engine by its unique intake plenum assembly. If there's any doubt as to whether or not you have this engine, refer to the Vehicle Identification Number (VIN) that is located on the forward edge of the dashboard on the driver's side. The VIN is visible from outside the vehicle, through the windshield. If the eighth position in the alpha-numeric code is a W, you have the VIN W engine.

The following repair procedures are based on the assumption that the engine is installed in the vehicle. If the engine has been removed from the vehicle and mounted on a stand, many of the steps outlined in this Part of Chapter 2 will not apply.

The Specifications included in this Part of Chapter 2 apply only to the procedures contained in this Part. Part C of Chapter 2 contains the Specifications necessary for cylinder head and engine block rebuilding. **Caution:** *If the vehicle is equipped with a Delco Loc II audio system (1992 and later models with a Compact Disc player), be sure the lockout feature is turned off before performing any procedure that requires disconnecting the battery (refer to your owner's manual for further information on this system).*

2   Repair operations possible with the engine in the vehicle

Many major repair operations can be accomplished without removing the engine from the vehicle.

Clean the engine compartment and the exterior of the engine with some type of pressure washer before any work is done. It will make the job easier and help keep dirt out of the internal areas of the engine.

Remove the engine cover and the hood, if necessary, to improve access to the engine as repairs are performed (refer to Chapter 11 if necessary).

If vacuum, exhaust, oil or coolant leaks develop, indicating a need for gasket or seal replacement, the repairs can generally be made with the engine in the vehicle. The intake and exhaust manifold gaskets, timing cover gasket, oil pan gasket, crankshaft oil seals and cylinder head gaskets are all accessible with the engine in place.

Exterior engine components, such as the intake and exhaust manifolds, the oil pan (and the oil pump), the water pump, the starter motor, the alternator, the distributor and the fuel system components can be removed for repair with the engine in place.

Since the cylinder heads can be removed without pulling the engine, valve component servicing can also be accomplished with the engine in the vehicle. Replacement of the timing chain and sprockets is also possible with the engine in the vehicle.

In extreme cases caused by a lack of necessary equipment, repair or replacement of piston rings, pistons, connecting rods and rod bearings is possible with the engine in the vehicle. However, this practice is not recommended because of the cleaning and preparation work that must be done to the components involved.

3   Rocker arm covers — removal and installation

Removal

1   Disconnect the negative cable from the battery.
2   Remove the engine cover (Chapter 11).
3   Remove the air cleaner assembly and heat stove tube (Chapter 4).

Right side

Refer to illustrations 3.4, 3.5, 3.7 and 3.11

4   Working under the hood, unbolt the oil filler tube and the dipstick tube from the alternator bracket (see illustration).

3.4   **Remove the dipstick tube mounting bolt and the oil filler tube bolts (arrows) (some have already been removed in this photo)**

2B

3.5   Unclip the wiring harness to make room for rocker arm cover removal

3.7   The diverter valve (arrow) is mounted near the rear of the right rocker arm cover

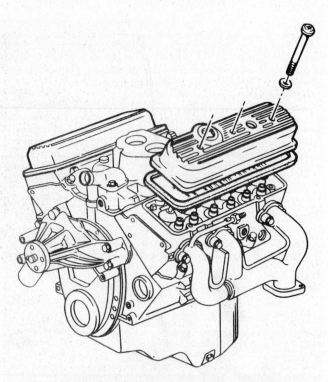

3.11   The rocker arm cover bolts require a special tool for removal (typical)

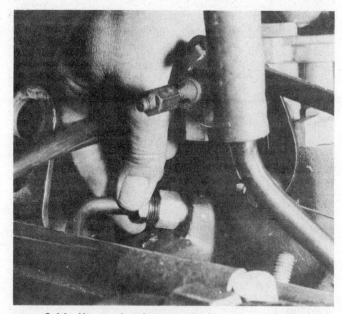

3.14   Unscrewing the power brake booster vacuum line fitting

5   Unclip the wiring harness from the oil filler tube (see illustration), then separate the tube from the rocker arm cover.
6   Disconnect the crankcase ventilation pipe from the rocker arm cover.
7   Working in the passenger compartment, remove the diverter valve, bracket and hoses (see illustration). Refer to Chapter 6 if necessary.
8   Remove the spark plug wire bracket from the right cylinder head.
9   Unbolt the dipstick tube bracket at the cylinder head and move it aside.
10 Finish unclipping the wire harness at the rocker arm cover and move it aside.

11 Use a T-30 TORX bit to remove the rocker arm cover bolts, then detach the cover from the head (see illustration). Note: If the cover is stuck to the head, bump one end with a block of wood and a hammer to jar it loose. If that doesn't work, try to slip a flexible putty knife between the head and cover to break the gasket seal. Don't pry at the cover-to-head joint or damage to the sealing surfaces may occur (leading to oil leaks in the future).

Left side

Refer to illustrations 3.14 and 3.15

12 Unbolt the cruise control servo and bracket (if equipped) and set it aside (see illustration 5.8, if necessary).
13 Remove the A/C compressor rear brace (if so equipped) (see illustration 5.6, if necessary).
14 Detach the power brake booster vacuum line from the intake manifold (see illustration).

3.15   Rear view of left rocker arm cover showing the vacuum brake booster line, the PCV valve, the AIR check valve and tube and the rocker arm cover mounting bolts (arrows)

15 Remove the PCV valve (**see illustration**).
16 Remove the spark plug wire bracket from the cylinder head.
17 Detach the throttle/TV cable bracket from the manifold.
18 Use a T-30 TORX bit to remove the rocker arm cover bolts, then detach the cover from the head. **Note:** *If the cover is stuck to the head, bump one end with a block of wood and a hammer to jar it loose. If that doesn't work, try to slip a flexible putty knife between the head and cover to break the gasket seal. Don't pry at the cover-to-head joint or damage to the sealing surfaces may occur (leading to oil leaks in the future).*

Installation

19 The mating surfaces of each cylinder head and rocker arm cover must be perfectly clean when the covers are installed. Use a gasket scraper to remove all traces of sealant and old gasket material, then clean the mating surfaces with lacquer thinner or acetone. If there's sealant or oil on the mating surfaces when the cover is installed, oil leaks may develop.
20 Clean the mounting bolt threads with a die to remove any corrosion and restore damaged threads. Make sure the threaded holes in the head are clean — run a tap into them to remove corrosion and restore damaged threads.
21 The gaskets should be mated to the covers before the covers are installed. Apply a thin coat of RTV sealant to the cover flange, then position the gasket inside the cover lip and allow the sealant to set up so the gasket adheres to the cover. If the sealant isn't allowed to set, the gasket may fall out of the cover as it's installed on the engine.
22 Carefully position the cover on the head and install the bolts.
23 Tighten the bolts in three or four steps to the specified torque.
24 The remaining installation steps are the reverse of removal.
25 Start the engine and check carefully for oil leaks as the engine warms up.

4   Valve spring, retainer and seals — replacement

Refer to illustrations 4.4, 4.8a, 4.8b, 4.9, 4.16 and 4.17
Note: *Broken valve springs and defective valve stem seals can be replaced without removing the cylinder heads. Two special tools and a compressed air source are normally required to perform this operation, so read through this Section carefully and rent or buy the tools before beginning the job. If compressed air isn't available, a length of nylon rope can be used to keep the valves from falling into the cylinder during this procedure.*

1 Refer to Section 3 and remove the rocker arm cover from the affected cylinder head. If all of the valve stem seals are being replaced, remove both rocker arm covers.
2 Remove the spark plug from the cylinder which has the defective component. If all of the valve stem seals are being replaced, all of the spark plugs should be removed.
3 Turn the crankshaft until the piston in the affected cylinder is at top dead center on the compression stroke (refer to Section 9 for instructions). If you are replacing all of the valve stem seals, begin with cylinder number one and work on the valves for one cylinder at a time. Move from cylinder-to-cylinder following the firing order sequence (1-6-5-4-3-2).
4 Thread an adapter into the spark plug hole (**see illustration**) and connect an air hose from a compressed air source to it. Most auto parts stores can supply the air hose adapter. **Note:** *Many cylinder compression gauges utilize a screw-in fitting that may work with your air hose quick-disconnect fitting.*

4.4   Use compressed air, if available, to hold the valves closed when the springs are removed — the air hose adapter (arrow) threads into the spark plug hole and accepts the hose from the compressor

5 Remove the nut, pivot ball and rocker arm for the valve with the defective part and pull out the pushrod. If all of the valve stem seals are being replaced, all of the rocker arms and pushrods should be removed (refer to Section 7).
6 Apply compressed air to the cylinder. The valves should be held in place by the air pressure. If the valve faces or seats are in poor condition, leaks may prevent air pressure from retaining the valves — refer to the alternative procedure below.
7 If you don't have access to compressed air, an alternative method can be used. Position the piston at a point just before TDC on the compression stroke, then feed a long piece of nylon rope through the spark plug hole until it fills the combustion chamber. Be sure to leave the end of the rope hanging out of the engine so it can be removed easily. Use a large breaker bar and socket to rotate the crankshaft in the normal

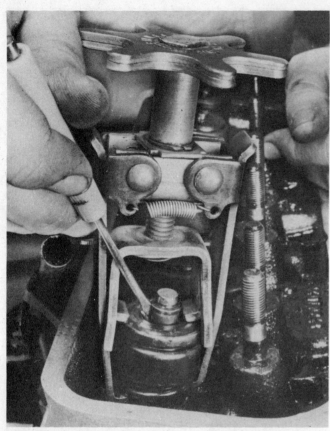

4.8a Once the spring is depressed, the keepers can be
removed with a small magnet or needle-nose pliers
(a magnet is preferred to prevent dropping the keepers)

4.8b The stamped steel lever-type valve spring
compressor is usually less expensive than the type that
grips the spring coils

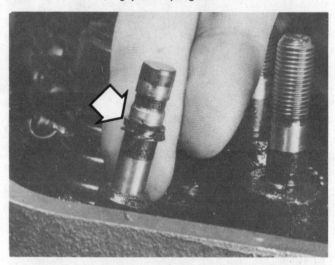

4.9 The O-ring seal (arrow) should be replaced with a
new one each time the keepers and retainer are removed

direction of rotation until **slight** resistance is felt.

8   Stuff shop rags into the cylinder head holes above and below the
valves to prevent parts and tools from falling into the engine, then use
a valve spring compressor to compress the spring/damper assembly.
Remove the keepers with small needle-nose pliers or a magnet (**see
illustration**). **Note:** *A couple of different types of tools are available
for compressing the valve springs with the head in place. One type,
shown here, grips the lower spring coils and presses on the retainer
as the knob is turned, while the other type utilizes the rocker arm stud
and nut for leverage* (**see illustration**). *Both types work very well,
although the lever type is usually less expensive.*

9   Remove the spring retainer or rotator, oil shield and valve spring
assembly, then remove the valve stem O-ring seal and the umbrella-type
guide seal (the O-ring seal will most likely be hardened and will probably
break when removed, so plan on installing a new one each time the
original is removed) (**see illustration**). **Note:** *If air pressure fails to hold
the valve in the closed position during this operation, the valve face
and/or seat is probably damaged. If so, the cylinder head will have to
be removed for additional repair operations.*

10   Wrap a rubber band or tape around the top of the valve stem so
the valve won't fall into the combustion chamber, then release the air
pressure. **Note:** *If a rope was used instead of air pressure, turn the
crankshaft slightly in the direction opposite normal rotation.*

11   Inspect the valve stem for damage. Rotate the valve in the guide
and check the end for eccentric movement, which would indicate that
the valve is bent.

12   Move the valve up-and-down in the guide and make sure it doesn't
bind. If the valve stem binds, either the valve is bent or the guide is
damaged. In either case, the head will have to be removed for repair.

13   Reapply air pressure to the cylinder to retain the valve in the closed
position, then remove the tape or rubber band from the valve stem.
If a rope was used instead of air pressure, rotate the crankshaft in the
normal direction of rotation until **slight** resistance is felt.

14   Lubricate the valve stem with engine oil and install a new umbrella-
type guide seal.

4.16 Make sure the O-ring seal under the retainer is seated
in the groove and not twisted before installing the keepers

4.17 Apply a small dab of grease to each keeper as shown here before installation — it will hold them in place on the valve stem as the spring is released

15 Install the spring/damper assembly and shield in position over the valve.

16 Install the valve spring retainer or rotator. Compress the valve spring assembly and carefully install the new O-ring seal in the lower groove of the valve stem. Make sure the seal isn't twisted — it must lie perfectly flat in the groove (**see illustration**).

17 Position the keepers in the upper groove. Apply a small dab of grease to the inside of each keeper to hold it in place if necessary (**see illustration**). Remove the pressure from the spring tool and make sure the keepers are seated. Refer to Chapter 2, Part C, Section 11 and check the seals with a vacuum pump.

18 Disconnect the air hose and remove the adapter from the spark plug hole. If a rope was used in place of air pressure, pull it out of the cylinder.

19 Refer to Section 7 and install the rocker arm(s) and pushrod(s).

20 Install the spark plug(s) and hook up the wire(s).

21 Refer to Section 3 and install the rocker arm cover(s).

22 Start and run the engine, then check for oil leaks and unusual sounds coming from the rocker arm cover area.

2B

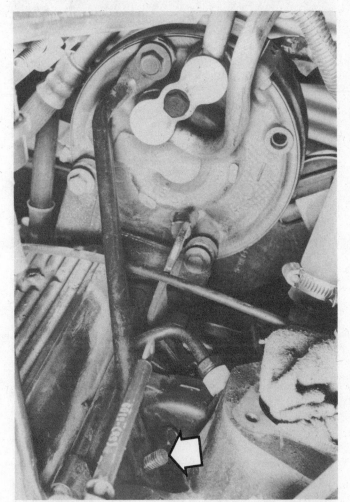

5.6 Rear of A/C compressor showing brace attached to intake manifold stud (arrow) (throttle body removed for clarity)

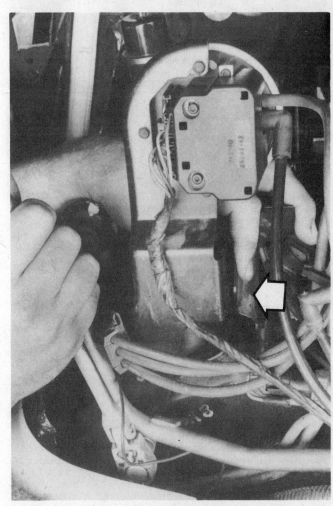

5.8 Arrow points to optional cruise control servo bracket bolt location — socket wrench is on lower bracket mounting bolt

5 Intake manifold – removal and installation

Removal

Refer to illustrations 5.6, 5.8, 5.9, 5.10, 5.11 and 5.17

1 Disconnect the negative cable from the battery and remove the upper fan shroud.

2 Remove the engine cover (Chapter 11).

3 Remove the air filter assembly (carbureted and TBI models) or air intake duct (CPI models) (see Chapter 4).

4 Drain the radiator (Chapter 1).

5 Disconnect the upper radiator and heater hoses at the front of the engine.

6 Remove the rear brace from the A/C compressor (**see illustration**).

7 Remove the spark plug wires, coil and distributor (Chapters 1 and 5).

8 Remove the cruise control servo and brackets, if so equipped (**see illustration**).

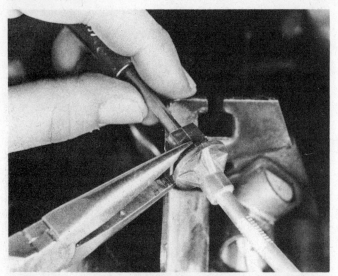

5.9　Pinch the cable tabs together to get them out of the bracket (cable removed for clarity)

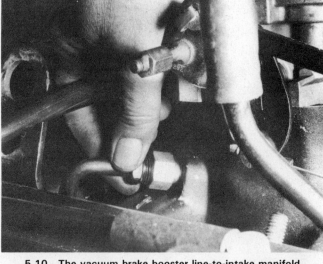

5.10　The vacuum brake booster line-to-intake manifold fitting is to the left of the throttle body

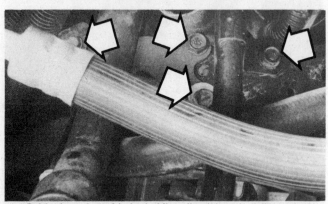

5.11　Location of bolts holding dipstick and oil filler tubes to alternator bracket (arrows)

9   Remove the throttle, cruise control and TV cables from the bracket(s) on the manifold **(see illustration)**.

10   Detach the vacuum brake booster line from the manifold **(see illustration)**.

11   Disconnect the engine oil filler tube at the alternator bracket **(see illustration)**.

12   Disconnect the automatic transmission fluid dipstick tube at the alternator bracket.

13   On models equipped with CPI fuel injection, relieve the fuel system pressure (see Chapter 4), then remove the air intake plenum (see Chapter 4). **Warning:** *On CPI models, never disconnect the fuel lines without first relieving the fuel pressure!*

14   Unbolt the alternator bracket at the manifold and push it aside.

15   Label and disconnect the fuel lines, vacuum hoses/pipes and electrical wires at the manifold and the carburetor, TBI unit or CFI unit (see Chapter 4). **Warning:** *Gasoline is extremely flammable. When disconnecting the fuel lines, observe the fuel warnings in Chapter 4.*

16   On TBI models, unbolt the fuel line from the rear of the cylinder head. It may be necessary to keep the stud from turning with vise-grip pliers.

17   On carbureted and TBI models, remove the coolant tube from the right side of the manifold **(see illustration)**.

18   Loosen the manifold mounting bolts in 1/4-turn increments until they can be removed by hand.

19   The manifold will probably be stuck to the cylinder heads and force may be required to break the gasket seal. A large pry bar can be positioned under the cast-in lug near the left front mounting bolt to pry up the front of the manifold, but make sure all bolts have been removed first! **Caution:** *Don't pry between the block and manifold or the heads and manifold or damage to the gasket sealing surfaces may occur, leading to vacuum leaks.*

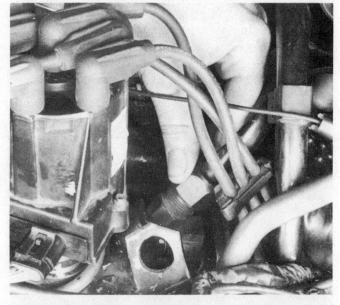

5.17　Disconnect the coolant tube at the manifold and set it aside

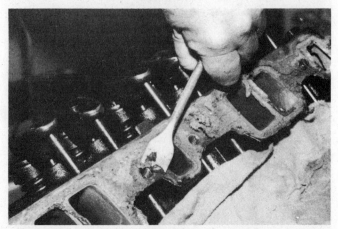

5.20　After covering the lifter valley, use a gasket scraper to remove all traces of sealant and old gasket material from the head and manifold mating surfaces

5.21a   The bolt hole threads must be clean and dry to ensure accurate torque readings when the manifold mounting bolts are installed

5.21b   Clean the bolt holes with compressed air, but be careful – wear safety goggles!

2B

Installation

Refer to illustrations 5.20, 5.21a, 5.21b, 5.22, 5.23, 5.24, 5.25, 5.27a, and 5.27b

Note: *The mating surfaces of the cylinder heads, block and manifold must be perfectly clean when the manifold is installed. Gasket removal solvents in aerosol cans are available at most auto parts stores and may be helpful when removing old gasket material that's stuck to the heads and manifold (since the manifold is made of aluminum, aggressive scraping can cause damage). Be sure to follow the directions printed on the container.*

20   Use a gasket scraper to remove all traces of sealant and old gasket material, then clean the mating surfaces with lacquer thinner or acetone. If there's old sealant or oil on the mating surfaces when the manifold is installed, oil or vacuum leaks may develop. When working on the heads and block, cover the lifter valley with shop rags to keep debris out of the engine **(see illustration)**. Use a vacuum cleaner to remove any gasket material that falls into the intake ports in the heads.

21   Use a tap of the correct size to chase the threads in the bolt holes, then use compressed air (if available) to remove the debris from the holes **(see illustrations)**. **Warning:** *Wear safety glasses or a face shield to protect your eyes when using compressed air!* Remove excessive carbon deposits and corrosion from the exhaust, EGR and coolant passages in the heads and manifold.

22   Apply a 3/16-inch wide bead of RTV sealant to the front and rear manifold mating surfaces of the block **(see illustration)**. Make sure the beads extend up the heads 1/2-inch on each side.

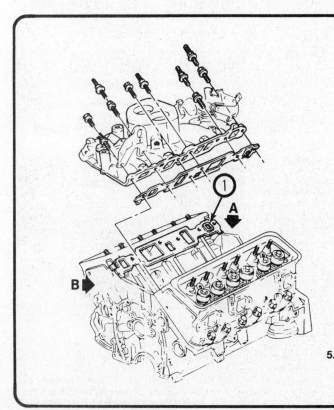

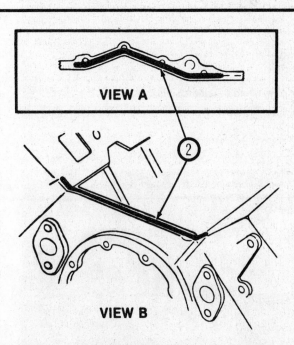

VIEW A

VIEW B

5.22   Intake manifold sealant application details (typical)

1   Port blocking plate
2   RTV sealant

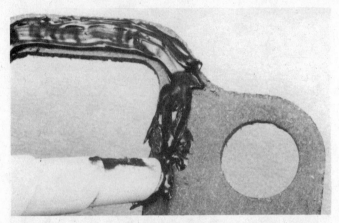

5.23   RTV sealant should be used around the coolant passage holes in the new intake manifold gaskets

23   Apply a thin coat of RTV sealant around the coolant passage holes on the cylinder head side of the new intake manifold gaskets **(see illustration)**.
24   Position the gaskets on the cylinder heads, with the ears at each end overlapping the bead of RTV sealant on the head. The upper side of each gasket will have a THIS SIDE UP label stamped into it to ensure correct installation **(see illustration)**.
25   Make sure all intake port openings, coolant passage holes and bolt holes are aligned correctly. **Note:** *The gaskets used on 1986 and later models have the rear coolant passages blocked off* **(see illustration)**. *Be sure the gaskets are installed with the blocked off passages at the rear of the engine. Some gaskets may have small tabs which must be bent over until they're flush with the rear surface of each head.*
26   Carefully set the manifold in place while the sealant is still wet. **Caution:** *Don't disturb the gaskets and don't move the manifold fore and-aft after it contacts the sealant on the block.*
27   Install the bolts and tighten them to the specified torque following the recommended sequence **(see illustrations)**. On carbureted and TBI models, work up to the final torque in two stages and note that two different tightening sequences must be followed, one in each stage. On CPI models, work up to the final torque in two stages using the same sequence. **Note:** *CPI is used on 1992 and later VIN W engines.*
28   The remaining installation steps are the reverse of removal. Start the engine and check carefully for oil and coolant leaks at the intake manifold joints.

6   Exhaust manifolds – removal and installation

Removal
Refer to illustrations 6.7, 6.10 and 6.12
1   Disconnect the negative battery cable from the battery.

5.25   The rear coolant passages on some models are blocked off – make sure the gasket is installed with the blocked off hole at the rear!

5.24   Be sure to install the gaskets with the marks UP!

2   Remove the engine cover (Chapter 11).
3   Raise the vehicle and support it securely on jackstands.
4   Working under the vehicle, apply penetrating oil to the exhaust pipe-to-manifold studs and nuts (they're usually rusty).
5   Remove the nuts holding the exhaust pipe(s) to the manifold(s). In extreme cases you may have to heat them with a propane or acetylene torch in order to loosen them.

Right side manifold

6   On carbureted and TBI models, remove the air filter assembly and heat stove pipe (see Chapter 4).
7   Release the hose clamp and separate the hose from the AIR system check valve **(see illustration)**.

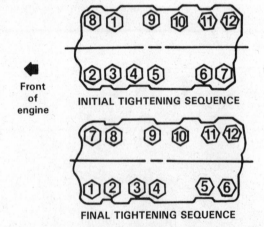

5.27a   Intake manifold bolt tightening sequence – note that the initial sequence differs from the final sequence! (carbureted and TBI models)

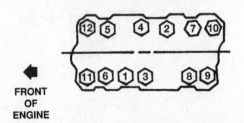

5.27b   Intake manifold bolt tightening sequence (CPI models)

6.7   Right side exhaust manifold mounting details showing the AIR system check valve, spark plug wire bracket and heat stove pipe mount (arrows) (engine removed for clarity)

8   Detach the spark plug wires from the plugs and brackets and position them out of the way (Chapter 1).

Left side manifold

9   Unplug the oxygen sensor wire (Chapter 6).

10 Detach the spark plug wires from the plugs and brackets and position them out of the way **(see illustration)**.

11 Unscrew the fitting at the manifold, release the hose clamp and detach the hose from the AIR system check valve, then remove the bracket bolt and detach the AIR tube and check valve as an assembly.

Both manifolds

12 Bend the lock tabs back **(see illustration)**, then remove the mounting bolts and separate the manifold from the head. The heat shields on the left side manifold will come off after the bolts are removed.

Installation

Refer to illustration 6.14

13 Check the manifold for cracks and make sure the bolt threads are clean and undamaged. The manifold and cylinder head mating surfaces must be clean before the manifolds are reinstalled — use a gasket scraper to remove all carbon deposits.

14 Position the manifold, tab washers and heat shields (if equipped) on the head and install the mounting bolts **(see illustration)**.

6.10   Left side exhaust manifold mounting details showing the spark plug wire brackets, heat shields, AIR system check valve, AIR tube-to-manifold fitting and AIR tube bracket bolt (arrows) (engine removed for clarity)

2B

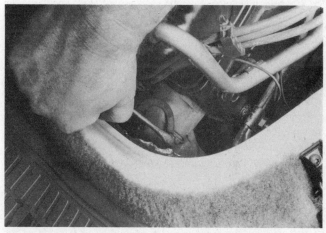

6.12   Flatten the tabs on the lock washers before removing the exhaust manifold mounting bolts

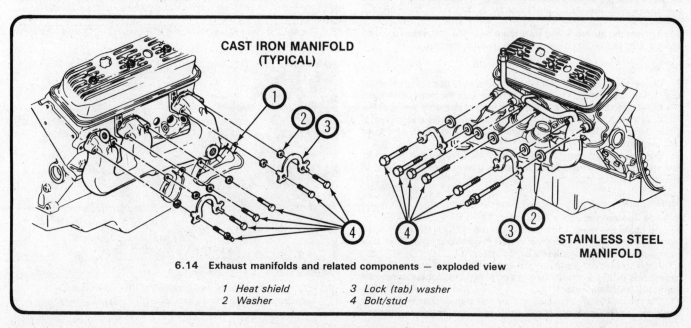

CAST IRON MANIFOLD
(TYPICAL)

STAINLESS STEEL
MANIFOLD

6.14   Exhaust manifolds and related components — exploded view

1 Heat shield	3 Lock (tab) washer
2 Washer	4 Bolt/stud

7.4 A perforated cardboard box can be used to store the pushrods to ensure that they are reinstalled in their original locations — note the label indicating the front of the engine

15 When tightening the mounting bolts, work from the center to the ends and be sure to use a torque wrench. Tighten the bolts in three equal steps until the specified torque is reached.
16 The remaining installation steps are the reverse of removal.
17 Start the engine and check for exhaust leaks.

7 Rocker arms and pushrods — removal, inspection and installation

Removal

Refer to illustration 7.4

1 Refer to Section 3 and detach the rocker arm cover(s) from the cylinder head(s).
2 Beginning at the front of one cylinder head, loosen and remove the rocker arm stud nuts. Store them separately in marked containers to ensure that they will be reinstalled in their original locations. **Note:** *If the pushrods are the only items being removed, loosen each nut just enough to allow the rocker arms to be rotated to the side so the pushrods can be lifted out.*
3 Lift off the rocker arms and pivot balls and store them in the marked containers with the nuts (they must be reinstalled in their original locations).
4 Remove the pushrods and store them separately to make sure they don't get mixed up during installation (**see illustration**).

Inspection

5 Check each rocker arm for wear, cracks and other damage, especially where the pushrods and valve stems contact the rocker arm faces.
6 Make sure the hole at the pushrod end of each rocker arm is open.
7 Check each rocker arm pivot area for wear, cracks and galling. If the rocker arms are worn or damaged, replace them with new ones and use new pivot balls as well.
8 Inspect the pushrods for cracks and excessive wear at the ends. Roll each pushrod across a piece of plate glass to see if it's bent (if it wobbles, it's bent).

Installation

Refer to illustrations 7.10, 7.11 and 7.13

9 Lubricate the lower end of each pushrod with clean engine oil or moly-base grease and install them in their original locations. Make sure each pushrod seats completely in the lifter.
10 Apply moly-base grease to the ends of the valve stems and the upper ends of the pushrods before positioning the rocker arms over the studs (**see illustration**).
11 Set the rocker arms in place, then install the pivot balls and nuts. Apply moly-base grease to the pivot balls to prevent damage to the

7.10 The ends of the pushrods and the valve stems should be lubricated with moly-base grease prior to installation of the rocker arms

mating surfaces before engine oil pressure builds up (**see illustration**). Be sure to install each nut with the **flat** side against the pivot ball.

Valve adjustment (all except VIN W engines)

Note: *On1992 and later VIN W engines, there are no provisions for valve adjustment. The rocker arm studs have a positive stop shoulder for the rocker arm. After valve service, tighten the rocker arm nuts to the torque listed in this Chapter's Specifications. Unless there have been machining operations that significantly altered the valve lash, the adjustment should be correct.*

12 Refer to Section 9 and bring the number one piston to top dead center on the compression stroke.
13 Tighten the rocker arm nuts (number one cylinder only) until all play is removed at the pushrods. This can be determined by rotating each pushrod between your thumb and index finger as the nut is tightened (**see illustration**). At the point where a slight drag is just felt as you spin the pushrod, all lash has been removed.
14 Tighten each nut an additional one full turn (360°) to center the lifters. Valve adjustment for cylinder number one is now complete.
15 Turn the crankshaft 120° in the normal direction of rotation until the next piston in the firing order (number six) is at TDC on the compression stroke. The distributor rotor should be pointing in the direction of terminal number six on the cap (see Section 9 for additional information).
16 Repeat the procedure described in Paragraphs 13 and 14 for the number six cylinder valves.

7.11 Moly-base grease applied to the pivot balls will ensure adequate lubrication until oil pressure builds up when the engine is started

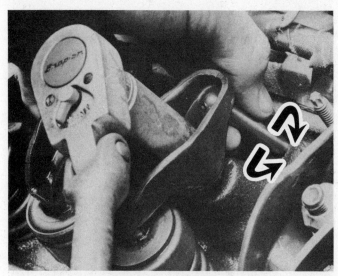

7.13 Rotate each pushrod as the rocker arm nut is tightened to determine the point at which all play is removed, then tighten each nut an additional one full turn

17 Turn the crankshaft another 120° and adjust the number five cylinder valves. Continue turning the crankshaft 120° at a time and adjust both valves for each cylinder before proceeding. Follow the firing order sequence — a cylinder number illustration is also included — in the Specifications.

18 Refer to Section 3 and install the rocker arm covers. Start the engine, listen for unusual valvetrain noises and check for oil leaks at the rocker arm cover joints.

8 Cylinder heads — removal and installation

Note: *The engine must be completely cool when the heads are removed. Failure to allow the engine to cool off could result in head warpage.*

Removal

Refer to illustration 8.13

Both cylinder heads

1 Remove the intake manifold (Section 5).
2 Remove the rocker arm cover (Section 3).
3 Remove the pushrods (Section 7).
4 Raise and support the vehicle on jackstands.

Left (driver's side) cylinder head

5 Remove the A/C and power steering pump drivebelts, if equipped (Chapter 1).
6 Unbolt the power steering pump and lay it aside. Leave the hoses connected (Chapter 10).
7 Remove the A/C compressor, idler pulley and bracket, if equipped (Chapter 3).
8 Remove the exhaust manifold (Section 6).
9 Proceed to Step 13.

Right cylinder head

10 Remove the engine ground wire and electrical harness at the rear of the head.
11 Remove the diverter valve assembly (Chapter 6).
12 Remove the alternator (Chapter 5).

Both cylinder heads

13 Using a new head gasket, outline the cylinders and bolt pattern on a piece of cardboard **(see illustration)**. Be sure to indicate the front of the engine for reference. Punch holes at the bolt locations.
14 Loosen the head bolts in 1/4-turn increments until they can be removed by hand. Work from bolt-to-bolt in a pattern that's the reverse of the tightening sequence shown in illustration 8.24. **Note:** *Don't overlook the row of bolts on the lower edge of each head, near the spark plug holes.* Store the bolts in the cardboard holder as they're removed; this will ensure that the bolts are reinstalled in their original holes.

15 Lift the head(s) off the engine. If resistance is felt, DO NOT pry between the head and block as damage to the mating surfaces will result. To dislodge the head, place a block of wood against the end of it and strike the wood block with a hammer. Store the heads on blocks of wood to prevent damage to the gasket sealing surfaces.
16 Cylinder head disassembly and inspection procedures are covered in detail in Chapter 2, Part C.

Installation

Refer to illustrations 8.20, 8.21a, 8.21b, 8.23 and 8.24

17 The mating surfaces of the cylinder heads and block must be perfectly clean when the heads are installed.
18 Use a gasket scraper to remove all traces of carbon and old gasket material, then clean the mating surfaces with lacquer thinner or acetone. If there's oil on the mating surfaces when the heads are installed, the gaskets may not seal correctly and leaks may develop. When working on the block, cover the lifter valley with shop rags to keep debris out of the engine. Use a vacuum cleaner to remove any debris that falls into the cylinders.
19 Check the block and head mating surfaces for nicks, deep scratches and other damage. If damage is slight, it can be removed with a file — if it's excessive, machining may be the only alternative.
20 Use a tap of the correct size to chase the threads in the head bolt holes. Mount each bolt in a vise and run a die down the threads to remove corrosion and restore the threads **(see illustration)**. Dirt, corrosion, sealant and damaged threads will affect torque readings.

2B

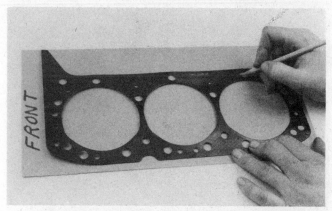

8.13 To avoid mixing up the head bolts, use a new gasket to transfer the bolt hole pattern to a piece of cardboard, then punch holes to accept the bolts

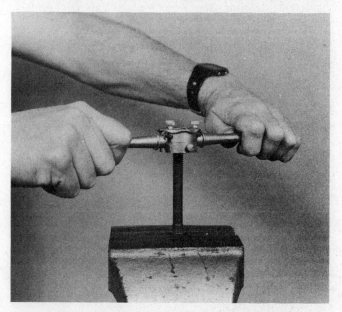

8.20 A die should be used to remove sealant and corrosion from the head bolt threads prior to installation

8.21a Locating dowels (arrows) are used to position the head gaskets on the block

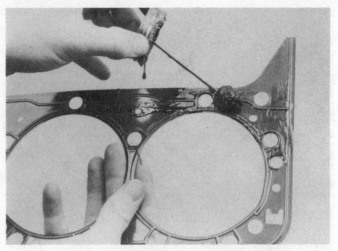

8.21b   Steel gaskets should be coated with a sealant such as K&W Copper Coat before installation

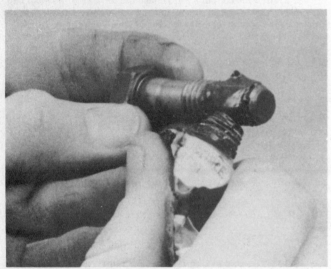

8.23   The head bolts MUST be coated with a non-hardening sealant (such as Permatex no. 2) before they're installed — coolant will leak past the bolts if this isn't done

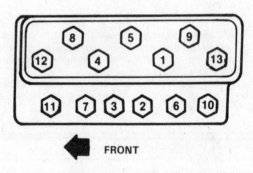

8.24   Cylinder head bolt tightening sequence

21 Position the new gaskets over the dowel pins in the block **(see illustration)**. **Note:** *If a steel gasket is used, apply a thin, even coat of sealant such as K&W Copper Coat to both sides prior to installation* **(see illustration)**. Steel gaskets must be installed with the raised bead UP. The composition gasket must be installed dry — don't use sealant.
22 Carefully position the heads on the block without disturbing the gaskets.
23 Before installing the head bolts, coat the threads with a *non-hardening sealant* such as Permatex no. 2 **(see illustration)**.
24 Install the bolts in their original locations and tighten them finger tight. Follow the recommended sequence and tighten the bolts in several steps to the specified torque **(see illustration)**.
25 The remaining installation steps are the reverse of removal.
26 Change the engine oil and filter (Chapter 1), then start the engine and check carefully for oil and coolant leaks.

9   Top Dead Center (TDC) for number 1 piston — locating

Refer to illustrations 9.4a, 9.4b, 9.6a, 9.6b and 9.7

1   Top Dead Center (TDC) is the highest point in the cylinder that each piston reaches as it travels up-and-down when the crankshaft turns. Each piston reaches TDC on the compression stroke and again

on the exhaust stroke, but TDC generally refers to piston position on the compression stroke. The timing marks on the vibration damper installed on the front of the crankshaft are referenced to the number one piston at TDC on the compression stroke.
2   Positioning the piston(s) at TDC is an essential part of many procedures such as rocker arm removal, valve adjustment, timing chain and sprocket replacement and distributor removal.
3   In order to bring any piston to TDC, the crankshaft must be turned using one of the methods outlined below. When looking at the front of the engine, normal crankshaft rotation is *clockwise*. **Warning:** *Before beginning this procedure, be sure to place the transmission in Neutral and unplug the wire connector at the distributor to disable the ignition system.*

a) The preferred method is to turn the crankshaft with a large socket and breaker bar attached to the vibration damper bolt threaded into the front of the crankshaft.
b) A remote starter switch, which may save some time, can also be used. Attach the switch leads to the S (switch) and B (battery) terminals on the starter motor. Once the piston is close to TDC, use a socket and breaker bar as described in the previous paragraph.
c) If an assistant is available to turn the ignition switch to the Start position in short bursts, you can get the piston close to TDC without a remote starter switch. Use a socket and breaker bar as described in Paragraph a) to complete the procedure.

4   Make a mark on the distributor housing directly below the number one spark plug wire terminal on the distributor cap **(see illustration)**. **Note:** *The terminal numbers are marked on the spark plug wires near the distributor* **(see illustration)**.
5   Remove the distributor cap as described in Chapter 1.

9.4a Make a mark on the distributor housing directly below the number 1 spark plug wire (arrow)

9.4b The spark plug wires are numbered to correspond to their respective cylinders (arrow)

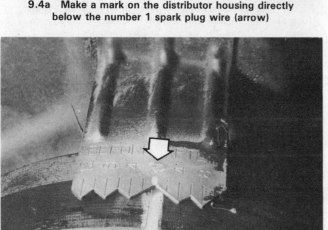

9.6a Turn the crankshaft until the line on the vibration damper is directly opposite the zero mark on the timing plate as shown here

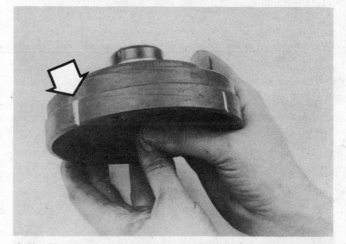

9.6b The vibration damper has two marks — the first one that approaches the timing plate can be disregarded, while the second mark (arrow) is the one that's used to locate TDC

6   Turn the crankshaft (see Paragraph 3 above) until the line on the vibration damper is aligned with the zero mark on the timing plate (**see illustrations**). The timing plate and vibration damper are located low on the front of the engine, near the pulley that turns the drivebelt.

7   The rotor should now be pointing directly at the mark on the distributor housing (**see illustration**). If it isn't, the piston is at TDC on the exhaust stroke.

8   To get the piston to TDC on the compression stroke, turn the crankshaft one complete turn (360°) clockwise. The rotor should now be pointing at the mark. When the rotor is pointing at the number one spark plug wire terminal in the distributor cap (which is indicated by the mark on the housing) and the ignition timing marks are aligned, the number one piston is at TDC on the compression stroke.

9   After the number one piston has been positioned at TDC on the compression stroke, TDC for any of the remaining cylinders can be located by turning the crankshaft 120° at a time and following the firing order (refer to the Specifications).

10 Timing cover, chain and sprockets — removal and installation

Removal
Refer to illustrations 10.2, 10.4, 10.5 and 10.6

1   Refer to Chapter 3 and remove the water pump.
2   Remove the bolts and separate the crankshaft drivebelt pulley from

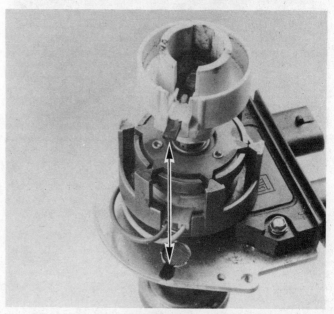

9.7 If the rotor is pointing directly at the mark on the distributor housing, as shown here, the number one piston is at TDC on the compression stroke

10.2   The vibration damper bolt (arrow) is usually very tight,
so use a six-point socket and a breaker bar to loosen it
(the three other bolts hold the pulley to the vibration damper)

10.4   Use the recommended puller to remove the vibration
damper — if a puller that applies force to the outer edge is
used, the damper will be damaged!

the vibration damper (see illustration).

3   Refer to Section 9 and position the *number four* piston at TDC on
the compression stroke. **Caution:** *Once this has been done, DO NOT
turn the crankshaft until the timing chain and sprockets have been
reinstalled!*

4   Remove the bolt from the front of the crankshaft, then use a puller
to detach the vibration damper (see illustration). **Caution:** *Don't use
a puller with jaws that grip the outer edge of the damper. The puller
must be the type shown in the illustration that utilizes bolts to apply
force to the damper hub only.*

5   Remove the bolts and separate the timing chain cover from the
block. It may be stuck – if so, use a putty knife or screwdriver to break

the gasket seal (see illustration). The cover is easily distorted, so be
very careful when prying it off.

6   Remove the three bolts (all except VIN W) or two bolts and one
nut (VIN W) from the end of the camshaft (see illustration), then detach the camshaft sprocket and chain as an assembly. **Note:** *On VIN
W engines, the balancer shaft drive gear will stay attached to the
camshaft and the driven gear will stay attached to the balancer shaft.
The sprocket on the crankshaft can be removed with a two- or three-
jaw puller, but be careful not to damage the threads in the end of the
crankshaft.* **Note:** *If the timing chain cover oil seal has been leaking, refer to Section 14 and install a new one.*

10.5   A putty knife or screwdriver can be used to break
the timing chain cover-to-block seal, but be careful when
prying it off as damage to the cover may result

10.6   Remove the three bolts from the end of the
camshaft (arrows)

Installation

Refer to illustration 10.10

7 Use a gasket scraper to remove all traces of old gasket material and sealant from the cover and engine block. Stuff a shop rag into the opening at the front of the oil pan to keep debris out of the engine. Clean the cover and block sealing surfaces with lacquer thinner or acetone.

8 Check the cover flange for distortion, particularly around the bolt holes. If necessary, place the cover on a block of wood and use a hammer to flatten and restore the gasket surface.

9 If new parts are being installed, be sure to align the keyway in the crankshaft sprocket with the Woodruff key in the end of the crankshaft. Press the sprocket onto the crankshaft with the vibration damper bolt, a large socket and some washers or tap it gently into place until it's completely seated. **Caution:** *If resistance is encountered, DO NOT hammer the sprocket onto the crankshaft. It may eventually move onto the shaft, but it may be cracked in the process and fail later, causing extensive engine damage.*

10 Loop the new chain over the camshaft sprocket, then turn the sprocket until the timing mark is in the 6 o'clock position. Mesh the chain with the crankshaft sprocket and position the camshaft sprocket on the end of the cam. If necessary, turn the camshaft so the dowel pin fits into the sprocket hole with the timing mark in the 6 o'clock position. When correctly installed, the marks on the sprockets will be aligned as shown in illustration 10.10. **Note:** *The number four piston must be at TDC on the compression stroke as the chain and sprockets are installed (see Paragraph 3 above).*

TIMING MARKS

10.10 With the number four piston at TDC on the compression stroke and the timing marks on the cam and crankshaft sprockets in the 6 and 12 o'clock positions, a straight line should pass through the camshaft timing mark, the center of the camshaft, the crankshaft timing mark and the center of the crankshaft as shown here

11 Apply Locktite to the camshaft sprocket bolt (or nut) threads, then install and tighten them to the specified torque. Lubricate the chain with clean engine oil.

12 Check the oil pan-to-block joints to make sure that all excess sealant is removed.

13 Apply RTV sealant to the U-shaped channel on the bottom of the cover.

14 Apply a thin layer of RTV sealant to both sides of the new gasket, then position it on the engine block (the dowel pins and sealant will hold it in place).

15 Since the oil pan seal in the bottom of the cover must be compressed in order to position the cover over the dowel pins and thread the bolts into the block, the cover is nearly impossible to install unless the oil pan is removed first. It can be done, but it's very difficult, time consuming and frustrating.

16 Refer to Section 12 and remove the oil pan, then install the timing chain cover. After the cover bolts have been tightened securely, reinstall the oil pan.

17 Lubricate the oil seal contact surface of the vibration damper hub with moly-base grease or clean engine oil, then install the damper on the end of the crankshaft. The keyway in the damper must be aligned with the Woodruff key in the crankshaft nose. If the damper cannot be seated by hand, slip a large washer over the bolt, install the bolt and tighten it to push the damper into place. Remove the large washer and tighten the bolt to the specified torque.

18 The remaining installation steps are the reverse of removal.

---

11 Camshaft, bearings and lifters — removal, inspection and installation

Camshaft lobe lift check

Refer to illustration 11.3

1 In order to determine the extent of cam lobe wear, the lobe lift should be checked prior to camshaft removal. Refer to Section 3 and remove the rocker arm covers.

2 Position the number one piston at TDC on the compression stroke (see Section 9).

3 Beginning with the number one cylinder valves, mount a dial indicator on the engine and position the plunger against the top surface of the first rocker arm. The plunger should be directly above and in line with the pushrod (**see illustration**).

11.3 When checking the camshaft lobe lift, the dial indicator plunger must be positioned directly above the pushrod

4 Zero the dial indicator, then very slowly turn the crankshaft in the normal direction of rotation until the indicator needle stops and begins to move in the opposite direction. The point at which it stops indicates maximum cam lobe lift.

5 Record this figure for future reference, then reposition the piston at TDC on the compression stroke.

6 Move the dial indicator to the remaining number one cylinder rocker arm and repeat the check. Be sure to record the results for each valve.

7 Repeat the check for the remaining valves. Since each piston must be at TDC on the compression stroke for this procedure, work from cylinder-to-cylinder following the firing order sequence.

8 After the check is complete, compare the results to the Specifications. If camshaft lobe lift is less than specified, cam lobe wear has occurred and a new camshaft should be installed.

2B

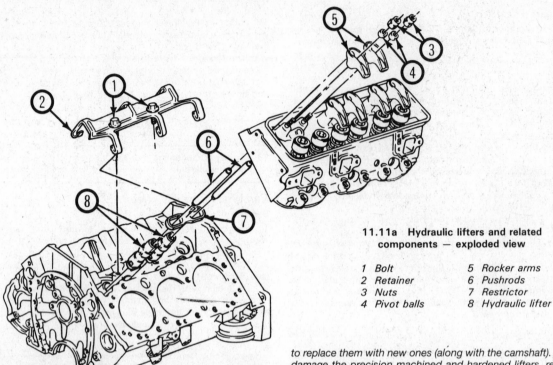

11.11a Hydraulic lifters and related components — exploded view

1 Bolt	5 Rocker arms
2 Retainer	6 Pushrods
3 Nuts	7 Restrictor
4 Pivot balls	8 Hydraulic lifter

Removal

Refer to illustrations 11.11a, 11.11b and 11.13

9   Refer to the appropriate Sections and remove the intake manifold, the rocker arms, the pushrods and the timing chain and camshaft sprocket. The radiator should be removed as well (Chapter 3).

10   There are several ways to extract the lifters from the bores. A special tool designed to grip and remove lifters is manufactured by many tool companies and is widely available, but it may not be required in every case. On newer engines without a lot of varnish buildup, the lifters can often be removed with a small magnet or even with your fingers. A machinist's scribe with a bent end can be used to pull the lifters out by positioning the point under the retainer ring in the top of each lifter. **Caution:** *Don't use pliers to remove the lifters unless you intend*

to replace them with new ones (along with the camshaft). The pliers will damage the precision machined and hardened lifters, rendering them useless.

11   Before removing the lifters, arrange to store them in a clearly labeled box to ensure that they're reinstalled in their original locations. **Note:** *On engines equipped with roller lifters, the retainer and restrictors must be removed before the lifters are withdrawn* **(see illustration).** Remove the lifters and store them where they won't get dirty **(see illustration).** DO NOT attempt to withdraw the camshaft with the lifters in place.

12   On VIN W engines, remove the balancer shaft drive and driven gears (see Section 12).

13   Thread two 6-inch long 5/16-18 bolts into two of the camshaft sprocket bolt holes to use as a handle when removing the camshaft from the block **(see illustration).** Carefully pull the camshaft out. Support the cam near the block so the lobes don't nick or gouge the bearings as it's withdrawn.

11.11b   The lifters on an engine that has accumulated many miles may have to be removed with a special tool — be sure to store the lifters in an organized manner to make sure they are reinstalled in their original locations

11.13   Long bolts can be threaded into the camshaft bolt holes to provide a handle for removal and installation of the camshaft – support the cam near the block as it's withdrawn

11.18 After the camshaft is in place, turn it until the dowel pin (arrow) is in the 3 o'clock position as shown here

Inspection

14   Refer to Part A, Section 15, for the camshaft and bearing inspection procedure. Lifter inspection procedures (for conventional and roller lifters) are covered in Part A, Section 7. The illustrations in Part A also pertain to the V6 engine.

Bearing replacement

15   Camshaft bearing replacement requires special tools and expertise that place it outside the scope of the home mechanic. Take the block to an automotive machine shop to ensure that the job is done correctly.

Installation
Refer to illustration 11.18

16   Lubricate the camshaft bearing journals and cam lobes with moly-base grease or engine assembly lube (see illustration 15.34 in Part A).
17   Slide the camshaft into the engine. Support the cam near the block and be careful not to scrape or nick the bearings.
18   Turn the camshaft until the dowel pin is in the 3 o'clock position **(see illustration)**.
19   On VIN W engines, install the balancer shaft drive and driven gears (see Section 12).
20   Refer to Section 10 and install the timing chain and sprockets.
21   Lubricate the lifters with clean engine oil and install them in the block. If the original lifters are being reinstalled, be sure to return them to their original locations. If a new camshaft was installed, be sure to install new lifters as well (except for engines with roller lifters).
22   The remaining installation steps are the reverse of removal.
23   Before starting and running the engine, change the oil and install a new oil filter (see Chapter 1).

---

12   Balancer shaft – removal and installation (1992 and later VIN W engines)

Removal

1   Remove the air cleaner assembly and air intake duct.
2   Remove the timing cover, chains and sprockets (see Section 10).
3   Remove the hood latch (see Chapter 11).
4   Remove the intake manifold (see Section 5).
5   Remove the radiator grille and headlight bezels (see Chapter 11).
6   Remove the radiator and its support braces, then remove the air conditioning condenser – if equipped – (see Chapter 3).
7   Remove the radiator support crossover.
8   Remove the retaining stud and the balancer shaft drive gear from the camshaft.
9   Remove the retaining bolt and the balancer shaft driven gear.
10   Remove the two bolts securing the balancer shaft retainer and remove the retainer.
11   Unbolt and remove the lifter retainer **(see illustration 11.11a)**.
12   Using a soft-faced mallet, carefully tap the balancer shaft out of the block.

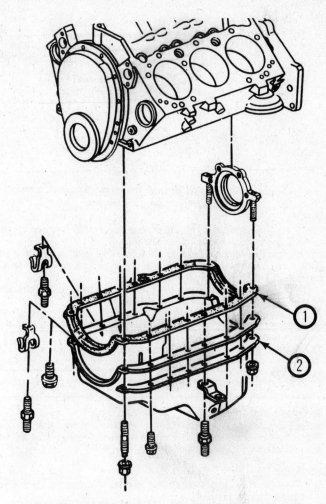

13.5 The gasket (1) is a one-piece molded rubber part and reinforcement strips (2) are used on each side of the oil pan

Inspection

13   After the balancer shaft has been removed from the engine, cleaned with solvent and dried, inspect the rear bearing journal for uneven wear, pitting and evidence of seizure. If the journal is damaged, the rear bearing in the block is probably damaged as well. The bearing will have to be replaced.
14   Check the balancer drive and driven gears for cracks, missing teeth and excessive wear. If the teeth are highly polished, pitted or galled, or if the outer hardened surface of the teeth is flaking off, new parts will be required. If one gear is worn or damaged, replace both gears as a set. Never install one new gear and one used gear.

Bearing replacement

15   Balancer shaft bearing replacement requires special tools and expertise that place it outside the scope of the home mechanic. Take the engine block to a dealer service department or an automotive machine shop to ensure that the job is done correctly.

Installation
Refer to illustration 12.22

16   Lubricate the balancer shaft bearing journals with moly-base grease or engine assembly lube.
17   Slide the balancer shaft into the engine. Support the balancer near the block and be careful not to scrape or nick the bearing. It may be necessary to gently tap on the shaft with a soft-face mallet.
18   Install the balance shaft retainer and two bolts and tighten them to the torque listed in this Chapter's Specifications.
19   Install the lifter retainer and bolts, then tighten the bolts securely.
20   Rotate the balancer shaft by hand to make sure there is sufficient clearance between the balancer shaft and the lifter retainer. Replace the lifter retainer if necessary.

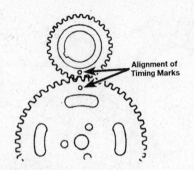

12.22 Make sure the balancer shaft timing marks on both the drive and driven gears are aligned

21   Install the balancer shaft driven gear and tighten the bolt to the torque listed in this Chapter's Specifications.
22   Rotate the camshaft so that, with the drive gear temporarily installed, the timing mark is straight up at the 12 o'clock position **(see illustration)**. Remove the drive gear.
23   Rotate the balancer shaft until the timing mark is facing straight down at the 6 o'clock position **(see illustration 12.22)**.
24   Install the balancer drive gear onto the camshaft and install the retaining stud, then tighten it to the torque listed in this Chapter's Specifications.
25   Install the timing chain, sprockets and cover (see Section 10).

13 Oil pan – removal and installation

Refer to illustration 13.5
Note: *The following procedure is based on the assumption that the engine is in place in the vehicle. If it's been removed, merely unbolt the oil pan and detach it from the block.*

Removal
1   Disconnect the negative battery cable from the battery, then refer to Chapter 1 and drain the oil.
2   Refer to Chapter 5 and remove the starter motor.
3   Remove the cover from the lower part of the bellhousing.
4   Separate the exhaust pipes from the manifolds.
5   Remove the oil pan mounting bolts/nuts. Most models are equipped with a reinforcement strip on each side of the oil pan which may come loose after the bolts/nuts are removed **(see illustration on page 97)**.
6   Carefully separate the pan from the block. Don't pry between the block and pan or damage to the sealing surfaces may result and oil leaks could develop. You may have to turn the crankshaft slightly to maneuver the front of the pan past the crank counterweights.

Installation
7   Clean the gasket sealing surfaces with lacquer thinner or acetone. Make sure the bolt holes in the block are clean.

15.2   The front crankshaft oil seal can be removed in the vehicle with a seal removal tool (shown here) or a large screwdriver

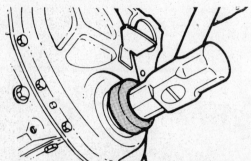

15.4   Installing the front crankshaft oil seal using GM tool no. J-23042A

8   Check the oil pan flange for distortion, particularly around the bolt holes. If necessary, place the pan on a block of wood and use a hammer to flatten and restore the gasket surface.
9   The rubber gasket should be checked carefully and replaced with a new one if damage is noted. Apply a small amount of RTV sealant to the corners of the semi-circular cutouts at both ends of the pan, then attach the rubber gasket to the pan.
10   Carefully position the pan against the block and install the bolts/nuts finger tight (don't forget the reinforcement strips, if used). Tighten the bolts/nuts in three steps to the specified torque. Start at the center of the pan and work out toward the ends in a spiral pattern.
11   The remaining steps are the reverse of removal. **Caution:** *Don't forget to refill the engine with oil before starting it (see Chapter 1).*
12   Start the engine and check carefully for oil leaks at the oil pan.

14 Oil pump – removal and installation

1   Remove the oil pan as described in Section 13.
2   While supporting the oil pump, remove the pump-to-rear main bearing cap bolt. On some models, the oil pan baffle must be removed first, since it's also held in place by the pump mounting bolt.
3   Lower the pump and remove it along with the pump driveshaft.
4   If a new oil pump is installed, make sure the pump driveshaft is mated with the shaft inside the pump.
5   Position the pump on the engine and make sure the slot in the upper end of the driveshaft is aligned with the tang on the lower end of the distributor shaft. The distributor drives the oil pump, so it is absolutely essential that the components mate properly.
6   Install the mounting bolt and tighten it to the specified torque.
7   Install the oil pan.

15 Crankshaft oil seals – replacement

Front seal – timing cover in place
Refer to illustrations 15.2 and 15.4
1   Remove the vibration damper as described in Section 10.
2   Carefully pry the seal out of the cover with a seal removal tool or a large screwdriver **(see illustration)**. Be careful not to distort the cover

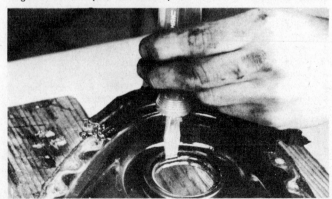

15.6   While supporting the cover near the seal bore, drive the old seal out from the inside with a hammer and punch or screwdriver

15.8 Clean the bore, then apply a small amount of oil to the outer edge of the seal and drive it squarely into the opening with a large socket and hammer – DO NOT damage the seal in the process!

or scratch the wall of the seal bore. If the engine has accumulated a lot of miles, apply penetrating oil to the seal-to-cover joint and allow it to soak in before attempting to pull the seal out.

3   Clean the bore to remove any old seal material and corrosion. Position the new seal in the bore with the open end of the seal facing IN. A small amount of oil applied to the outer edge of the new seal will make installation easier – don't overdo it!

4   Drive the seal into the bore with GM tool no. J-23042A or a large socket and hammer until it's completely seated **(see illustration)**. Select a socket that's the same outside diameter as the seal (a section of pipe can be used if a socket isn't available).

5   Reinstall the vibration damper.

Front seal – timing cover removed

Refer to illustrations 15.6 and 15.8

6   Use a punch or screwdriver and hammer to drive the seal out of the cover from the back side. Support the cover as close to the seal bore as possible **(see illustration)**. Be careful not to distort the cover or scratch the wall of the seal bore. If the engine has accumulated a lot of miles, apply penetrating oil to the seal-to-cover joint on each side and allow it to soak in before attempting to drive the seal out.

7   Clean the bore to remove any old seal material and corrosion. Support the cover on blocks of wood and position the new seal in the bore with the open end of the seal facing IN. A small amount of oil applied to the outer edge of the new seal will make installation easier – don't overdo it!

8   Drive the seal into the bore with a large socket and hammer until it's completely seated **(see illustration)**. Select a socket that's the same outside diameter as the seal (a section of pipe can be used if a socket isn't available).

Rear seal

1985 models

Refer to illustrations 15.12, 15.14, 15.15a, 15.15b, 15.16, 15.17 and 15.19

15.15a   Using the tool like a "shoehorn", attach the seal section to the bearing cap . . .

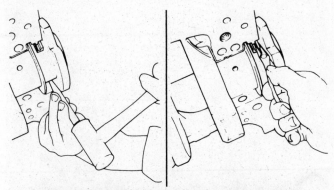

15.12   Tap the seal end with a brass punch or wood dowel and hammer (left), until it can be gripped with a pair of pliers and pulled out (right)

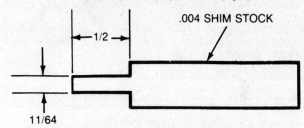

15.14   If the new seal did not include an installation tool, make one from a piece of brass shim stock 0.004-inch thick

9   The rear main seal on these models can be replaced with the engine in the vehicle. Refer to the appropriate Sections and remove the oil pan and oil pump.

10   Remove the bolts and detach the rear main bearing cap from the engine.

11   The seal section in the bearing cap can be pried out with a screwdriver.

12   To remove the seal section in the block, tap on one end with a hammer and brass punch or wood dowel until the other end protrudes far enough to grip it with a pair of pliers and pull it out **(see illustration)**. Be very careful not to nick or scratch the crankshaft journal or seal surface as this is done.

13   Inspect the bearing cap and engine block mating surfaces, as well as the cap seal grooves, for nicks, burrs and scratches. Remove any defects with a fine file or deburring tool.

14   A small seal installation tool is usually included when a new seal is purchased. If you didn't receive one, they can also be purchased separately at most auto parts stores or you can make one from an old feeler gauge or a piece of brass shim stock **(see illustration)**.

15   Using the tool, install one seal section in the cap with the lip facing the front of the engine (if the seal has two lips, the one with the helix must face the front) **(see illustrations)**. The ends should be flush

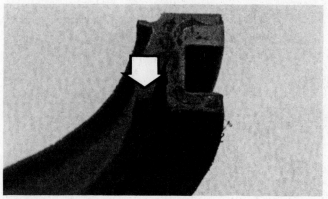

15.15b   . . . with the oil seal lip pointing toward the front of the engine

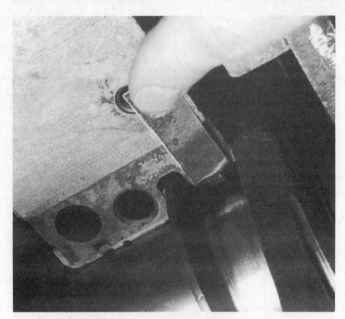

15.16   Position the tool to protect the back side of the seal as it passes over the sharp edge of the ridge – note that the seal straddles the ridge

15.17   Make sure the seal lip faces the front of the engine and hold the tool in place to protect the seal as it's installed

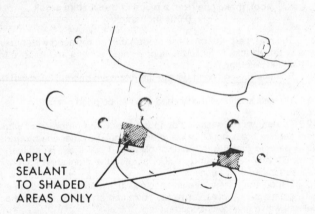

APPLY
SEALANT
TO SHADED
AREAS ONLY

15.19   Before installing the rear main bearing cap, apply the specified sealant to the shaded areas of the block (or the equivalent areas on the cap)

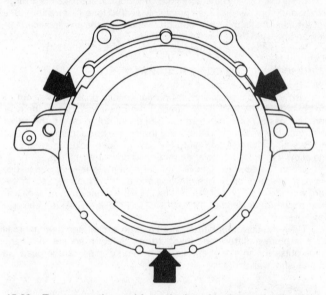

15.23   To remove the seal from the housing, insert the tip of the screwdriver into each notch (arrows) and lever the seal out

with the mating surface of the cap. Make sure it's completely seated.

16   Position the narrow end of the tool so that it will protect the back side of the seal as it passes over the sharp edge of the ridge in the block **(see illustration)**.

17   Lubricate the seal lips and the groove in the back side with moly-base grease or clean engine oil – don't get any lubricant on the seal ends. Insert the seal into the block, over the tool **(see illustration)**. **Caution:** *Make sure that the lip points toward the front of the engine when the seal is installed.*

18   Push the seal into place, using the tool like a -shoehorn". Turning the crankshaft may help to draw the seal into place. When both ends of the seal are flush with the block surface, remove the tool.

19   Apply a thin, even coat of anaerobic-type gasket sealant to the areas of the cap or block indicated in the accompanying illustration. Do not get any sealant on the bearing face, crankshaft journal, seal ends or seal lips. Also, lubricate the cap seal lips with moly-base grease or clean engine oil.

20   Carefully position the bearing cap on the block, install the bolts and tighten them to 10-to-12 ft-lbs only. Tap the crankshaft forward and backward with a lead or brass hammer to line up the main bearing and crankshaft thrust surfaces, then tighten the rear bearing cap bolts to the specified torque.

21   Install the oil pump and oil pan.

1986 and later models

Refer to illustrations 15.23, 15.25 and 15.26

Note: *Some 1987 models may begin to leak oil at the rear main oil seal due to a manufacturing defect. If you suspect that your vehicle falls into this category, take it to a dealer service department. Tell them to consult Chevrolet Dealer Service Bulletin no. 88-10, Section 6A, dated April, 1987.*

22   Later models are equipped with a one-piece seal that requires an entirely different installation procedure. The transmission (Chapter 7) must be removed to gain access to the seal housing.

23   The old seal can be removed from the housing by inserting a large screwdriver into the notches provided and prying it out **(see illustration)**. Be sure to note how far it's recessed into the housing bore before removing it; the new seal will have to be recessed an equal amount. Be very careful not to scratch or otherwise damage the bore in the housing or oil leaks could develop.

24   Check the seal contact surface very carefully for scratches and nicks that could damage the new seal lip and cause oil leaks. If the

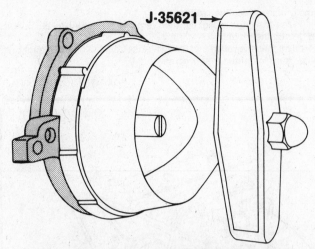

J-35621

15.25 GM tool no. J-35621 is recommended for seal installation with the housing attached to the engine

crankshaft is damaged, the only alternative is a new or different crankshaft.

25 Make sure the housing is clean, then apply a thin coat of engine oil to the outer edge of the new seal. Apply moly-based grease to the seal lips. The seal must be pressed squarely into the housing bore, so hammering it into place is not recommended. If your don't have access to GM tool no. J-35621 **(see illustration)**, remove the oil pan (Section 12) and unbolt the seal housing from the block. Sandwich the housing and seal between two smooth pieces of wood and press the seal into place with the jaws of a large vise. The pieces of wood must be thick enough to distribute the force evenly around the entire circumference of the seal. Work slowly and make sure the seal enters the bore squarely.

26 The seal lips must be lubricated with clean engine oil or moly-based grease before the seal/housing is slipped over the crankshaft and bolted to the block. Use a new gasket – no sealant is required – and make sure the dowel pins are in place before installing the housing **(see illustration)**.

27 Tighten the nuts/screws a little at a time until they're all snug.

16 Flywheel/driveplate – removal and installation

1 Refer to Chapter 7 and remove the transmission. If your vehicle has a manual transmission, the pressure plate and clutch will also have to be removed (Chapter 8).

2 Jam a large screwdriver in the starter ring gear to keep the crankshaft from turning, then remove the mounting bolts. Since it's fairly heavy, support the flywheel as the last bolt is removed.

3 Pull straight back on the flywheel/driveplate to detach it from the crankshaft.

4 Installation is the reverse of removal. The driveplate must be mounted with the torque converter pads facing the transmission. Be sure to align the hole in the flywheel/driveplate with the dowel pin in the crankshaft. Use Locktite on the bolt threads and tighten them to the specified torque in a criss-cross pattern.

17 Engine mounts – check and replacement

Refer to illustration 17.7

1 Engine mounts seldom require attention, but broken or deteriorated mounts should be replaced immediately or the added strain placed on the driveline components may cause damage.

Check

2 During the check, the engine must be raised slightly to remove the weight from the mounts. Refer to Chapter 11 and remove the engine cover before raising the engine.

3 Raise the vehicle and support it securely on jackstands, then position the jack under the engine oil pan. Place a large block of wood between the jack head and the oil pan, then carefully raise the engine just enough to take the weight off the mounts.

4 Check the mounts to see if the rubber is cracked, hardened or separated from the metal plates. Sometimes the rubber will split right down the center. Rubber preservative or WD-40 should be applied to the mounts to slow deterioration.

5 Check for relative movement between the mount plates and the engine or frame (use a large screwdriver or pry bar to attempt to move the mounts). If movement is noted, lower the engine and tighten the mount fasteners.

2B

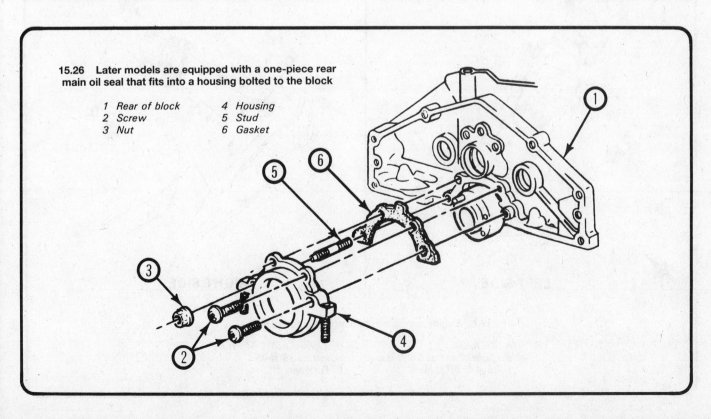

15.26 Later models are equipped with a one-piece rear main oil seal that fits into a housing bolted to the block

1 Rear of block   4 Housing
2 Screw   5 Stud
3 Nut   6 Gasket

Replacement

6   Disconnect the negative battery cable from the battery, then raise the vehicle and support it securely on jackstands.

7   Remove the nut and withdraw the mount through bolt from the frame bracket **(see illustration)**.

8   Raise the engine slightly, then remove the mount-to-block bolts and detach the mount.

9 Installation is the reverse of removal. Use Locktite on the mount bolts and be sure to tighten them securely.

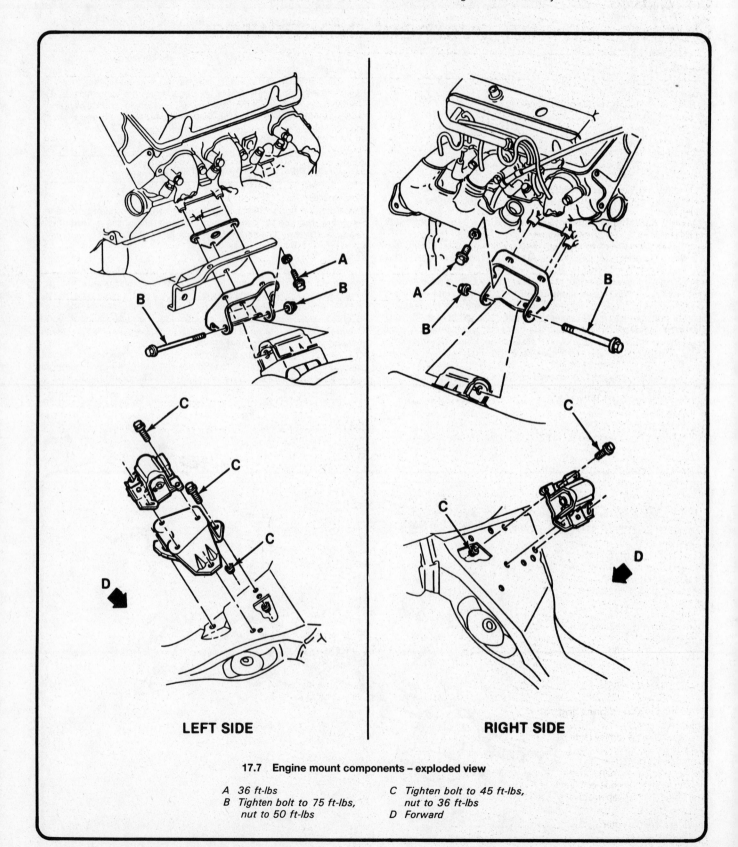

LEFT SIDE   **RIGHT SIDE**

17.7   Engine mount components – exploded view

A 36 ft-lbs
B Tighten bolt to 75 ft-lbs,
   nut to 50 ft-lbs

C Tighten bolt to 45 ft-lbs,
   nut to 36 ft-lbs
D Forward

Chapter 2   Part C
General engine overhaul procedures

Contents

2C

Specifications

Four-cylinder engine

General
Bore and stroke	4.00 x 3.00 in
Oil pressure	36 to 41 psi at 2000 rpm
Compression pressure	140 psi at 160 rpm

Cylinder head and valve train
Head warpage limit	0.006 in
Valve face angle	45-degrees
Valve seat angle	
1985 and 1986	45-degrees
1987 on	46-degrees
Minimum valve margin width	1/32 in
Valve stem-to-guide clearance	
intake	0.001 to 0.0027 in
exhaust	0.001 to 0.0027 in
Valve seat width	
intake	0.035 to 0.075 in
exhaust	
1985 and 1986	0.058 to 0.097 in
1987 on	0.085 to 0.105 in
Valve spring free length	1.78 in
Valve spring installed height	
1985 and 1986	1.690 in
1987 on	1.440 in
Valve spring pressure and length (intake and exhaust)	
valve closed	
1985 and 1986	78 to 86 lbs at 1.66 in
1987 on	71 to 78 lbs at 1.44 in
valve open	
1985 and 1986	170 to 180 lbs at 1.26 in
1987 on	158 to 170 lbs at 1.040 in

Crankshaft and connecting rods
Crankshaft end play	0.0035 to 0.0085 in
Connecting rod end play (side clearance)	0.006 to 0.022 in
Main bearing journal diameter	2.3 in
Main bearing oil clearance	0.0005 to 0.0022 in
Connecting rod journal diameter	2.0 in
Connecting rod bearing oil clearance	0.0005 to 0.0026 in
Crankshaft journal taper/out-of-round limit	0.005 in

Engine block
Cylinder bore diameter	4.0 in
Out-of-round limit	0.001 in
Taper limit	0.005 in

Pistons and rings

Piston-to-bore clearance
    1985
        top of bore .... 0.0025 to 0.0033 in
        bottom of bore .... 0.0017 to 0.0041 in
    1986 on .... 0.0014 to 0.0022 in
Ring side clearance
    top compression ring
        1985 .... 0.0015 to 0.003 in
        1986 on .... 0.002 to 0.003 in
    second compression ring
        1985 .... 0.0015 to 0.003 in
        1986 on .... 0.001 to 0.003 in
    oil ring... 0.015 to 0.055 in
Compression ring end gap .... 0.010 to 0.020 in
Oil ring end gap
    1985 .... 0.015 to 0.055 in
    1986 on .... 0.020 to 0.060 in

Torque specifications*

Ft-lbs

Main bearing cap bolts.. 70
Connecting rod cap nuts 32
Oil pump-to-block bolts 22
Oil pick-up tube bracket nut 37

*Note: *Refer to Part A for additional torque specifications.*

V6 engine

General

Bore and stroke .... 4.000 x 3.480 in
Oil pressure (minimum)
    All except VIN W .... 10 psi at 500 rpm; 30 to 55 psi at 2000 rpm
    VIN W .... 20 to 50 psi at 1200 rpm; 42 to 60 psi at 2400 to 5000 rpm
Compression pressure .... Lowest-reading cylinder must be at least 70% of highest-reading cylinder (100 psi minimum)

Engine block

Cylinder bore diameter
    Through 1991 .... 3.9995 to 4.0025 in
    1992 and later .... 4.0004 to 4.0017 in
Taper limit .... 0.001 in
Out-of-round limit .... 0.002 in

Pistons and rings

Piston-to-cylinder bore clearance
    standard .... 0.0007 to 0.0017 in
    service limit .... 0.0027 in
Piston ring-to-groove side clearance
    all except VIN W
        standard
            compression rings .... 0.0012 to 0.0032 in
            oil control ring... 0.002 to 0.007 in
        service limit
            compression rings .... 0.0033 in
            oil control ring... 0.008 in
    VIN W
        standard
            compression rings .... 0.0014 to 0.0032 in
            oil control ring... 0.002 to 0.007 in
        service limit
            compression rings .... 0.0042 in
            oil control ring... 0.008 in
Piston ring end gap
    standard
        all except VIN W
            top compression ring .... 0.010 to 0.020 in
            second compression ring .... 0.010 to 0.025 in
            oil control ring... 0.015 to 0.055 in
        VIN W
            top compression ring .... 0.010 to 0.020 in
            second compression ring .... 0.018 to 0.026 in
            oil control ring... 0.015 to 0.055 in
    service limit
        top compression ring... 0.030 in
        second compression ring .... 0.035 in
        oil control ring .... 0.065 in
Piston pin
    diameter .... 0.9270 to 0.9273 in
    pin-to-piston clearance limit .... 0.001 in
    pin-to-rod interference fit... 0.0008 to 0.0016 in

Crankshaft

Main journal	
diameter	
all except VIN W	
no. 1 journal	2.4484 to 2.4493 in
no. 2 and 3 journals	2.4481 to 2.4490 in
no. 4 journal	2.4479 to 2.4488 in
VIN W	
no. 1 journal	2.4488 to 2.4495 in
no. 2 and 3 journals	2.4485 to 2.4494 in
no. 4 journal	2.4480 to 2.4489 in
taper limit	0.001 in
out-of-round limit	0.001 in
Main bearing oil clearance	
standard	
no. 1 journal	0.0008 to 0.0020 in
no. 2 and 3 journals	0.0011 to 0.0023 in
no. 4 journal	0.0017 to 0.0032 in
service limit	
no. 1 journal	0.001 to 0.0015 in
no. 2 and 3 journals	0.001 to 0.0025 in
no. 4 journal	0.0025 to 0.0035 in
Connecting rod journal	
diameter	2.2487 to 2.2497 in
taper limit	0.001 in
out-of-round limit	0.001 in
Connecting rod bearing oil clearance	
standard	0.0013 to 0.0035 in
service limit	0.0035 in
Connecting rod end play (side clearance)	0.006 to 0.014 in
Crankshaft end play	0.002 to 0.006 in

Cylinder head and valve train

Head warpage limit	0.003 in per 6 in span/0.006 in overall
Valve seat angle	46°
Valve seat width	
intake	1/32 to 1/16 (0.0313 to 0.0625) in
exhaust	1/16 to 3/32 (0.0625 to 0.0938) in
Valve seat runout limit	0.002 in
Valve face angle	45~
Minimum valve margin width	1/32 in
Valve stem-to-guide clearance	
standard	
all except VIN W	0.0010 to 0.0027 in
VIN W	0.0011 to 0.0027 in
service limit	
all except VIN W	
intake	0.0037 in
exhaust	0.0047 in
VIN W (intake and exhaust)	0.0029 in
Valve spring free length	2.030 in
Valve spring damper (inner spring) free length	1.860 in
Valve spring installed height	
intake	1-23/32 (1.7188) in
exhaust	1-19/32 (1.5938) in
Valve spring pressure and length (intake and exhaust)	
closed	76 to 84 lbs. at 1.70 in
open	194 to 206 lbs. at 1.25 in

Torque specifications *

	Ft-lbs
Rocker arm studs	
All except VIN W	50
VIN W	35
Main bearing cap bolts	
1985	70
1986 and 1987	75
1988 through 1990	80
1991 on	75
Connecting rod cap nuts	
1990 and earlier	45
1991	20 plus an additional 60-degrees rotation
1992 on	20 plus an additional 70-degrees rotation
Oil pump bolts	65

* Note: *Refer to Part B for additional torque specifications*

2C

2.4   The oil pressure can be checked by attaching the gauge to the fitting block near the distributor (V6 engine shown)

3.3   If your engine has a coil-in-cap distributor, disconnect the wire from the BAT terminal on the distributor cap when checking the compression

3.4   A compression gauge with a threaded fitting for the plug hole is preferred over the type that requires hand pressure to maintain the seal

1   General information

Included in this portion of Chapter 2 are the general overhaul procedures for the cylinder head(s) and internal engine components.

The information ranges from advice concerning preparation for an overhaul and the purchase of replacement parts to detailed, step-by-step procedures covering removal and installation of internal engine components and the inspection of parts.

The following Sections have been written based on the assumption that the engine has been removed from the vehicle. For information concerning in-vehicle engine repair, as well as removal and installation of the external components necessary for the overhaul, see Part A or B of this Chapter and Section 7 of this Part.

The Specifications included here in Part C are only those necessary for the inspection and overhaul procedures which follow. Refer to Parts A and B for additional Specifications.

2   Engine overhaul — general information

Refer to illustration 2.4

It's not always easy to determine when, or if, an engine should be completely overhauled, as a number of factors must be considered.

High mileage is not necessarily an indication that an overhaul is needed, while low mileage doesn't preclude the need for an overhaul. Frequency of servicing is probably the most important consideration. An engine that's had regular and frequent oil and filter changes, as well as other required maintenance, will most likely give many thousands of miles of reliable service. Conversely, a neglected engine may require an overhaul very early in its life.

Excessive oil consumption is an indication that piston rings, valve seals and/or valve guides are in need of attention. Make sure that oil leaks aren't responsible before deciding that the rings and/or guides are bad. Have a cylinder compression or leakdown test performed by an experienced tune-up mechanic to determine the extent of the work required.

If the engine is making obvious knocking or rumbling noises, the connecting rod and/or main bearings may be at fault. Check the oil pressure with a gauge installed in place of the oil pressure sending unit (**see illustration**) and compare it to the Specifications. If it's extremely low, the bearings and/or oil pump are probably worn out.

Loss of power, rough running, excessive valve train noise and high fuel consumption rates may also point to the need for an overhaul, especially if they're all present at the same time. If a complete tune-up doesn't remedy the situation, major mechanical work is the only solution.

An engine overhaul involves restoring the internal parts to the specifications of a new engine. During an overhaul, the piston rings are replaced and the cylinder walls are reconditioned (rebored and/or honed). If a rebore is done, new pistons are required. The main bearings, connecting rod bearings and camshaft bearings are generally replaced with new ones and, if necessary, the crankshaft may be reground to restore the journals. Generally, the valves are serviced as well, since

they're usually in less-than-perfect condition at this point. While the engine is being overhauled, other components, such as the distributor, starter and alternator, can be rebuilt as well. The end result should be a like new engine that will give many trouble free miles. **Note:** *Critical cooling system components such as the hoses, drivebelts, thermostat and water pump MUST be replaced with new parts when an engine is overhauled. The radiator should be checked carefully to ensure that it isn't clogged or leaking; if in doubt, replace it with a new one. Also, we don't recommend overhauling the oil pump — always install a new one when an engine is rebuilt.*

Before beginning the engine overhaul, read through the entire procedure to familiarize yourself with the scope and requirements of the job. Overhauling an engine isn't difficult, but it is time consuming. Plan on the vehicle being tied up for a minimum of two weeks, especially if parts must be taken to an automotive machine shop for repair or reconditioning. Check on availability of parts and make sure that any necessary special tools and equipment are obtained in advance. Most work can be done with typical hand tools, although a number of precision measuring tools are required for inspecting parts to determine if they must be replaced. Often an automotive machine shop will handle the inspection of parts and offer advice concerning reconditioning and replacement. **Note:** *Always wait until the engine has been completely disassembled and all components, especially the engine block, have been inspected before deciding what service and repair operations must be performed by an automotive machine shop.* Since the block's condition will be the major factor to consider when determining whether to overhaul the original engine or buy a rebuilt one, never purchase parts or have machine work done on other components until the block has been thoroughly inspected. As a general rule, time is the primary cost of an overhaul, so it doesn't pay to install worn or substandard parts.

As a final note, to ensure maximum life and minimum trouble from a rebuilt engine, everything must be assembled with care in a spotlessly clean environment.

3   Cylinder compression check

Refer to illustrations 3.3 and 3.4

1   A compression check will tell you what mechanical condition the upper end (pistons, rings, valves, head gaskets) of your engine is in. Specifically, it can tell you if the compression is down due to leakage caused by worn piston rings, defective valves and seats or a blown head gasket. **Note:** *The engine must be at normal operating temperature and the battery must be fully charged for this check. Also, if the engine is equipped with a carburetor, the choke valve must be all the way open to get an accurate compression reading (if the engine's warm, the choke should be open).*

2   Begin by cleaning the area around the spark plugs before you remove them (compressed air should be used, if available, otherwise a small brush or even a bicycle tire pump will work). The idea is to prevent dirt from getting into the cylinders as the compression check is being done. Remove all of the spark plugs from the engine (Chapter 1).

3   Block the throttle wide open. If the ignition coil is an integral part

of the distributor cap, disconnect the wire from the BAT terminal on the cap (**see illustration**). If the ignition coil is mounted separately, unplug the coil-to-distributor wire harness at the distributor.

4   With the compression gauge in the number one spark plug hole (**see illustration**), depress the accelerator pedal all the way to the floor to open the throttle valve. Crank the engine over at least four compression strokes and watch the gauge. The compression should build up quickly in a healthy engine. Low compression on the first stroke, followed by gradually increasing pressure on successive strokes, indicates worn piston rings. A low compression reading on the first stroke, which doesn't build up during successive strokes, indicates leaking valves or a blown head gasket (a cracked head could also be the cause). Record the highest gauge reading obtained.

5   Repeat the procedure for the remaining cylinders and compare the results to the Specifications.

6   Add some engine oil (about three squirts from a plunger-type oil can) to each cylinder, through the spark plug hole, and repeat the test.

7   If the compression increases after the oil is added, the piston rings are definitely worn. If the compression doesn't increase significantly, the leakage is occurring at the valves or head gasket. Leakage past the valves may be caused by burned valve seats and/or faces or warped, cracked or bent valves.

8   If two adjacent cylinders have equally low compression, there's a strong possibility that the head gasket between them is blown. The appearance of coolant in the combustion chambers or the crankcase would verify this condition.

9   If the compression is unusually high, the combustion chambers are probably coated with carbon deposits. If that's the case, the cylinder head(s) should be removed and decarbonized.

10   If compression is way down or varies greatly between cylinders, it would be a good idea to have a leak-down test performed by an automotive repair shop. This test will pinpoint exactly where the leakage is occurring and how severe it is.

4   Engine removal — methods and precautions

If you've decided that an engine must be removed for overhaul or major repair work, several preliminary steps should be taken.

Locating a suitable place to work is extremely important. Adequate work space, along with storage space for the vehicle, will be needed. If a shop or garage isn't available, at the very least a flat, level, clean work surface made of concrete or asphalt is required.

Cleaning the engine compartment and engine before beginning the removal procedure will help keep tools clean and organized.

An engine hoist or A-frame will also be necessary. Make sure the equipment is rated in excess of the combined weight of the engine and accessories. Safety is of primary importance, considering the potential hazards involved in lifting the engine out of the vehicle.

If the engine is being removed by a novice, a helper should be available. Advice and aid from someone more experienced would also be helpful. There are many instances when one person cannot simultaneously perform all of the operations required when lifting the engine out of the vehicle.

Plan the operation ahead of time. Arrange for or obtain all of the tools and equipment you'll need prior to beginning the job. Some of the equipment necessary to perform engine removal and installation safely and with relative ease are (in addition to an engine hoist) a heavy duty floor jack, complete sets of wrenches and sockets as described in the front of this manual, wooden blocks and plenty of rags and cleaning solvent for mopping up spilled oil, coolant and gasoline. If the hoist must be rented, make sure that you arrange for it in advance and perform beforehand all of the operations possible without it. This will save you money and time.

Plan for the vehicle to be out of use for quite a while. A machine shop will be required to perform some of the work which the do-it-yourselfer can't accomplish without special equipment. These shops often have a busy schedule, so it would be a good idea to consult them before removing the engine in order to accurately estimate the amount of time required to rebuild or repair components that may need work.

Always be extremely careful when removing and installing the engine. Serious injury can result from careless actions. Plan ahead, take your time and a job of this nature, although major, can be accomplished successfully.

5   Engine – removal and installation

Refer to illustrations 5.3 and 5.30

Warning 1: *The engine is very heavy. Use proper lifting equipment. Never place any part of your body under the engine or transmission when it's supported only by a hoist – it could shift or fall, causing serious injury or even death! Also, the air conditioning system is under high pressure and opening the system will cause a sudden discharge of refrigerant. If the refrigerant gets in your eyes it could cause blindness, so have the system discharged by a service station before disconnecting any hoses or lines.*

Warning 2: *Later models may be equipped with airbags. Impact sensors for the airbag system are located in the area of the radiator support/grille. The airbag(s) could accidently deploy if these sensors are disturbed, so be extremely careful when working in this area. Air bag system components are also located in the steering wheel, steering column and base of the steering column, so be extremely careful in these areas and don't disturb any airbag system components or wiring. You could easily be injured if an airbag accidently deploys, and the airbag might not deploy correctly in a collision if any components or wiring in the system have been disturbed.*

Caution: *If the vehicle is equipped with a Delco Loc II audio system (1992 and later models with a Compact Disc player), be sure the lockout feature is turned off before performing any procedure that requires disconnecting the battery (refer to your owner's manual for further information on this system).*

1   Detach the negative battery cable from the battery.

2   Remove the engine cover (Chapter 11).

3   Remove the headlight bezels, grille, lower grille panel, radiator support brace, core support braces, horns, lower tie bar and hood latch mechanism (**see illustration**). For further information refer to Chapter 11.

4   Drain the coolant and engine oil and discard the oil filter (Chapter 1).

5   Remove the radiator, air deflector panels and fan shroud (Chapter 3).

6   Remove the accelerator pedal kick panel.

7   Remove the air cleaner assembly (Chapter 4).

8   Refer to Chapter 4 and disconnect the fuel lines from the engine. Be sure to relieve the system pressure on fuel injected models before releasing the fittings.

9   On automatic transmission equipped models, disconnect the oil cooler lines from the right (passenger) side of the radiator (Chapter 3).

10   Label and disconnect the vacuum lines and wire harnesses connected to the engine.

11   Disconnect the throttle, TV and cruise control cables as applicable.

12   Disconnect the radiator and heater hoses from the engine.

13   Remove the power steering pump, if equipped (Chapter 10).

14   Remove the A/C compressor with the bracket and the condensor (Chapter 3).

15   On V6 models, remove the distributor cap (Chapter 1).

16   Refer to Chapter 6 and remove the diverter valve and AIR check valves (V6 engine only).

17   Remove the transmission dipstick tube (automatic only).

18   Remove the oil filler neck and thermostat outlet (four-cylinder engine only).

19   Raise the vehicle and support it securely on jackstands.

5.3   Tie the horizontal wiring harness (arrow) up out of the way after removing the front body and trim components

2C

5.30 The automatic transmission torque converter is supported following engine removal by a pipe laid across the frame rails — stick bolts through the holes in each side of the bellhousing (arrows)

20   Disconnect the exhaust pipe(s) from the manifold(s).
21   Remove the bellhousing cover.
22   Remove the starter (Chapter 5).
23   Disconnect the strut rods at the bellhousing cover, if equipped.
24   On automatic transmission equipped models, unbolt the torque converter (Chapter 7).
25   Remove the engine mount through bolts and nuts.
26   Support the front of the transmission with a jack. Unbolt the transmission from the engine. On automatic transmission equipped models, separate the torque converter from the transmission by gently prying against the driveplate.
27   Attach a hoist to the engine and lift the engine slightly while pulling it forward. The engine should separate from the transmission (leaving the torque converter with the transmission on automatic transmission equipped models).
28   Lift the engine out of the vehicle. If anything hangs up, stop and correct it now. Don't use brute force alone or you'll damage something. The engine hoist boom should be approximately parallel to the floor when lifting the engine.
29   Carefully place the engine on an engine stand or a sturdy workbench.
30   Support the transmission with a pipe laid across the frame rails **(see illustration)**.
31   Installation is the reverse of removal. Be sure to tighten all fasteners and double-check to make sure all wires and hoses are connected.
32   Refill the cooling system, add oil and transmission fluid as needed.
33   Start the engine, check for leaks and test all systems for proper operation.
34   Have the A/C system (if equipped) evacuated, recharged and leak tested by a service station.

6   Engine rebuilding alternatives

The do-it-yourselfer is faced with a number of options when performing an engine overhaul. The decision to replace the engine block, piston/connecting rod assemblies and crankshaft depends on a number of factors, with the number one consideration being the condition of the block. Other considerations are cost, access to machine shop facilities, parts availability, time required to complete the project and the extent of prior mechanical experience on the part of the do-it-yourselfer.
Some of the rebuilding alternatives include:
Individual parts — If the inspection procedures reveal that the engine block and most engine components are in reusable condition, purchasing individual parts may be the most economical alternative. The block, crankshaft and piston/connecting rod assemblies should all be inspected carefully. Even if the block shows little wear, the cylinder bores should be surface honed.
Crankshaft kit — This rebuild package consists of a reground crankshaft and a matched set of pistons and connecting rods. The

pistons will already be installed on the connecting rods. Piston rings and the necessary bearings will be included in the kit. These kits are commonly available for standard cylinder bores, as well as for engine blocks which have been bored to a regular oversize.
Short block — A short block consists of an engine block with a crankshaft and piston/connecting rod assemblies already installed. All new bearings are incorporated and all clearances will be correct. The existing camshaft, valve train components, cylinder head(s) and external parts can be bolted to the short block with little or no machine shop work necessary.
Long block — A long block consists of a short block plus an oil pump, oil pan, cylinder head(s), rocker arm cover(s), camshaft and valve train components, timing sprockets and chain or gears and timing cover. All components are installed with new bearings, seals and gaskets incorporated throughout. The installation of manifolds and external parts is all that's necessary.
Give careful thought to which alternative is best for you and discuss the situation with local automotive machine shops, auto parts dealers and experienced rebuilders before ordering or purchasing replacement parts.

7   Engine overhaul — disassembly sequence

1   It's much easier to disassemble and work on the engine if it's mounted on a portable engine stand. A stand can often be rented quite cheaply from an equipment rental yard. Before the engine is mounted on a stand, the flywheel/driveplate should be removed from the engine.
2   If a stand isn't available, it's possible to disassemble the engine with it blocked up on a sturdy workbench or on the floor. Be extra careful not to tip or drop the engine when working without a stand.
3   If you're going to obtain a rebuilt engine, all external components must come off first, to be transferred to the replacement engine, just as they will if you're doing a complete engine overhaul yourself. These include:
   Alternator and brackets
   Emissions control components
   Distributor, spark plug wires and spark plugs
   Thermostat and housing cover
   Water pump
   EFI components or carburetor
   Intake/exhaust manifolds
   Oil filter
   Engine mounts
   Clutch and flywheel/driveplate
Note: *When removing the external components from the engine, pay close attention to details that may be helpful or important during installation. Note the installed position of gaskets, seals, spacers, pins, brackets, washers, bolts and other small items.*
4   If you're obtaining a short block, which consists of the engine block, crankshaft, pistons and connecting rods all assembled, then the cylinder head(s), oil pan and oil pump will have to be removed as well. See *Engine rebuilding alternatives* for additional information regarding the different possibilities to be considered.
5   If you're planning a complete overhaul, the engine must be disassembled and the internal components removed in the following order:
   Rocker arm cover(s)
   Intake and exhaust manifolds
   Rocker arms and pushrods
   Valve lifters
   Cylinder head(s)
   Timing cover
   Timing chain and sprockets (V6 engine only)
   Camshaft
   Oil pan
   Oil pump
   Piston/connecting rod assemblies
   Crankshaft and main bearings
6   Before beginning the disassembly and overhaul procedures, make sure the following items are available:
   Common hand tools
   Small cardboard boxes or plastic bags for storing parts
   Gasket scraper
   Ridge reamer

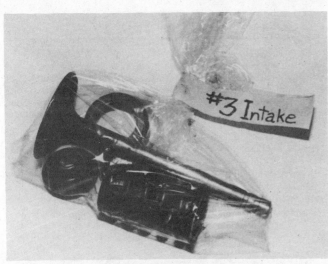

8.2 A small plastic bag, with an appropriate label, can be used to store the valve train components so they can be kept together and reinstalled in the correct guide

Vibration damper puller
Micrometers
Telescoping gauges
Dial indicator set
Valve spring compressor
Cylinder surfacing hone
Piston ring groove cleaning tool
Electric drill motor
Tap and die set
Wire brushes
Oil gallery brushes
Cleaning solvent

8 Cylinder head — disassembly

Refer to illustrations 8.2, 8.3a and 8.3b

Note: *New and rebuilt cylinder heads are commonly available for most engines at dealerships and auto parts stores. Due to the fact that some specialized tools are necessary for the disassembly and inspection procedures, and replacement parts may not be readily available, it may be more practical and economical for the home mechanic to purchase replacement head(s) rather than taking the time to disassemble, inspect and recondition the original(s).*

1   Cylinder head disassembly involves removal of the intake and exhaust valves and related components. If they're still in place, remove the rocker arm nuts, pivot balls and rocker arms from the cylinder head studs. Label the parts or store them separately so they can be reinstalled in their original locations.
2   Before the valves are removed, arrange to label and store them, along with their related components, so they can be kept separate and reinstalled in the same valve guides they are removed from (**see illustration**).
3   Compress the springs on the first valve with a spring compressor and remove the keepers (**see illustration**). Carefully release the valve spring compressor and remove the retainer (V6 exhaust valves have rotators), the shield, the springs and the spring seat. Next, remove the O-ring seal from the upper end of the valve stem (just under the keeper groove) and the umbrella-type seal from the guide (not used on V6 exhaust valves), then pull the valve out of the head. If the valve binds in the guide (won't pull through), push it back into the head and deburr the area around the keeper groove with a fine file or whetstone (**see illustration**).
4   Repeat the procedure for the remaining valves. Remember to keep all the parts for each valve together so they can be reinstalled in the same locations.
5   Once the valves and related components have been removed and stored in an organized manner, the head should be thoroughly cleaned and inspected. If a complete engine overhaul is being done, finish the

8.3a Use a valve spring compressor to compress the spring, then remove the keepers from the valve stem

8.3b If the valve won't pull through the guide, deburr the edge of the stem end and the area around the top of the keeper groove with a file

engine disassembly procedures before beginning the cylinder head cleaning and inspection process.

9 Cylinder head — cleaning and inspection

Refer to illustrations 9.12, 9.14, 9.15a, 9.15b, 9.16, 9.17, 9.18 and 9.19

1   Thorough cleaning of the cylinder head(s) and related valve train components, followed by a detailed inspection, will enable you to decide how much valve service work must be done during the engine overhaul.

Cleaning

2   Scrape all traces of old gasket material and sealing compound off the head gasket, intake manifold and exhaust manifold sealing surfaces. Be very careful not to gouge the cylinder head. Special gasket removal solvents that soften gaskets and make removal much easier are available at auto parts stores.
3   Remove all built up scale from the coolant passages.
4   Run a stiff wire brush through the various holes to remove deposits that may have formed in them.
5   Run an appropriate size tap into each of the threaded holes to remove corrosion and thread sealant that may be present. If compressed air is available, use it to clear the holes of debris produced by this operation.
6   Clean the rocker arm pivot stud threads with a wire brush.
7   Clean the cylinder head with solvent and dry it thoroughly. Compressed air will speed the drying process and ensure that all holes and recessed areas are clean. **Note:** *Decarbonizing chemicals are available and may prove very useful when cleaning cylinder heads and valve train components. They are very caustic and should be used with caution. Be sure to follow the instructions on the container.*
8   Clean the rocker arms, pivot balls, nuts and pushrods with solvent and dry them thoroughly (don't mix them up during the cleaning pro-

2C

9.12 Check the cylinder head gasket surface for warpage by trying to slip a feeler gauge under the straightedge (see the Specifications for the maximum warpage allowed and use a feeler gauge of that thickness)

9.14 A dial indicator can be used to determine the valve stem-to-guide clearance (move the valve stem as indicated by the arrows)

cess). Compressed air will speed the drying process and can be used to clean out the oil passages.
9   Clean all the valve springs, shields, keepers and retainers (or rotators) with solvent and dry them thoroughly. Do the components from one valve at a time to avoid mixing up the parts.
10   Scrape off any heavy deposits that may have formed on the valves, then use a motorized wire brush to remove deposits from the valve heads and stems. Again, make sure the valves don't get mixed up.

Inspection

Cylinder head
11   Inspect the head very carefully for cracks, evidence of coolant leakage and other damage. If cracks are found, a new cylinder head should be obtained. **Note:** *GM has determined that some 1986 Astro vans equipped with a four-cylinder engine may have been produced with blocked cylinder head coolant passages, which results in audible spark knock and/or engine overheating. As long as the head is off the engine, it may be a good idea to take it to a dealer service department for inspection. Tell them to refer to Chevrolet Dealer Product Campaign Bulletin number 86C14(a)6A, dated December, 1986.*
12   Using a straightedge and feeler gauge, check the head gasket mating surface for warpage **(see illustration)**. If the warpage exceeds the specified limit, it can be resurfaced at an automotive machine shop. **Note:** *If the V6 engine heads are resurfaced, the intake manifold flanges will also require machining.*
13   Examine the valve seats in each of the combustion chambers. If they're pitted, cracked or burned, the head will require valve service that is beyond the scope of the home mechanic.
14   Check the valve stem-to-guide clearance by measuring the lateral movement of the valve stem with a dial indicator attached securely to the head **(see illustration)**. The valve must be in the guide and approximately 1/16-inch off the seat. The total valve stem movement indicated by the gauge needle must be divided by two to obtain the actual clearance. After this is done, if there's still some doubt regarding the condition of the valve guides they should be checked by an automotive machine shop (the cost should be minimal). **Note:** *Some 1987 vehicles with a four-cylinder engine may experience premature exhaust valve guide wear. The condition could be caused by puddled chrome on the valve stems, which results in a rough surface and accelerates wear. The engine may exhibit valve train noise, misfiring or a rough idle. A Chevrolet Dealer Service Bulletin, number 87-1556A, dated June, 1987, has been issued, so ask your dealer service department for assistance. Engines with a build sequence number higher than 3200559 should be immune to the problem.*

Valves
15   Carefully inspect each valve face for uneven wear, deformation, cracks, pits and burned areas **(see illustrations)**. Check the valve stem for scuffing and galling and the neck for cracks. Rotate the valve and check for any obvious indication that it's bent. Look for pits and excessive wear on the end of the stem. The presence of any of these conditions indicates the need for valve service by an automotive

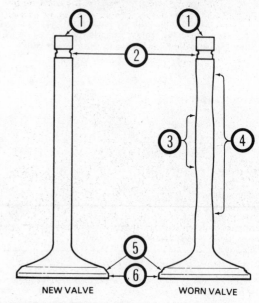

9.15a Check for valve wear at the points shown here

1 Valve tip
2 Keeper groove
3 Stem (least worn area)
4 Stem (most worn area)
5 Valve face
6 Margin

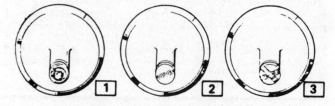

9.15b Valve stem tip wear patterns

1 Proper tip pattern (rotator functioning properly)
2 No rotation pattern (replace rotator and check rotation)
3 Partial rotation pattern (replace rotator and check rotation)

machine shop.
16   Measure the margin width on each valve **(see illustration)**. Any valve with a margin narrower than 1/32-inch will have to be replaced with a new one.

Valve components
17   Check each valve spring for wear (on the ends) and pits. Measure the free length and compare it to the Specifications **(see illustration)**.

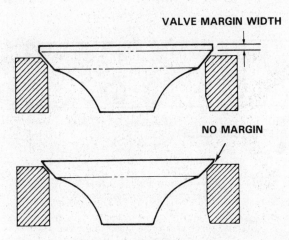

VALVE MARGIN WIDTH

NO MARGIN

9.16 The margin width on each valve must be as specified (if no margin exists, the valve cannnot be reused)

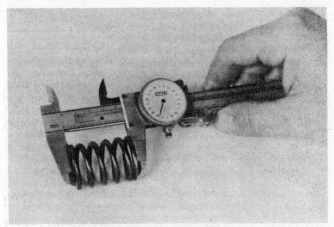

9.17 Measure the free length of each valve spring with a dial or vernier caliper

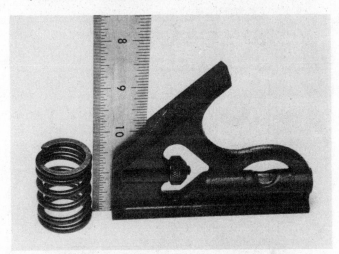

9.18 Check each valve spring for squareness

9.19 The exhaust valve rotators can be checked by turning the inner and outer sections in opposite directions — feel for smooth movement and excessive play

Any springs that are shorter than specified have sagged and should not be reused. The tension of all springs should be checked with a special fixture before deciding that they're suitable for use in a rebuilt engine (take the springs to an automotive machine shop for this check).
18 Stand each spring on a flat surface and check it for squareness (**see illustration**). If any of the springs are distorted or sagged, replace all of them with new parts.
19 Check the spring retainers (or rotators) and keepers for obvious wear and cracks. Any questionable parts should be replaced with new ones, as extensive damage will occur if they fail during engine operation. Make sure the rotators operate smoothly with no binding or excessive play (**see illustration**).

Rocker arm components
20 Check the rocker arm faces (the areas that contact the pushrod ends and valve stems) for pits, wear, galling, score marks and rough spots. Check the rocker arm pivot contact areas and pivot balls as well. Look for cracks in each rocker arm and nut.
21 Inspect the pushrod ends for scuffing and excessive wear. Roll each pushrod on a flat surface, like a piece of plate glass, to determine if it's bent.
22 Check the rocker arm studs in the cylinder heads for damaged threads and secure installation.
23 Any damaged or excessively worn parts must be replaced with new ones.
24 If the inspection process indicates that the valve components are in generally poor condition and worn beyond the limits specified, which is usually the case in an engine that's being overhauled, reassemble the valves in the cylinder head and refer to Section 10 for valve servicing recommendations.

25 If the inspection turns up no excessively worn parts, and if the valve faces and seats are in good condition, the valve train components can be reinstalled in the cylinder head without major servicing. Refer to the appropriate Section for the cylinder head reassembly procedure.

10 Valves — servicing

1 Because of the complex nature of the job and the special tools and equipment needed, servicing of the valves, the valve seats and the valve guides, commonly known as a valve job, is best left to a professional.
2 The home mechanic can remove and disassemble each head, do the initial cleaning and inspection, then reassemble and deliver it to a dealer service department or an automotive machine shop for the actual valve servicing.
3 The dealer service department, or automotive machine shop, will remove the valves and springs, recondition or replace the valves and valve seats, recondition the valve guides, check and replace the valve springs, spring retainers or rotators and keepers (as necessary), replace the valve seals with new ones, reassemble the valve components and make sure the installed spring height is correct. The cylinder head gasket surface will also be resurfaced if it's warped.
4 After the valve job has been performed by a professional, the head will be in like new condition. When the head is returned, be sure to clean it again before installation on the engine to remove any metal particles and abrasive grit that may still be present from the valve service or head resurfacing operations. Use compressed air, if available, to blow out all the oil holes and passages.

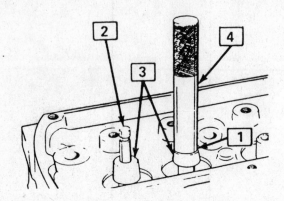

11.3   Make sure the new valve stem seals are seated against the tops of the valve guides

1 *Valve seal seated in tool*
2 *Deburr the end of the valve stem before installing the seal*
3 *Seal*
4 *Valve seal installation tool*

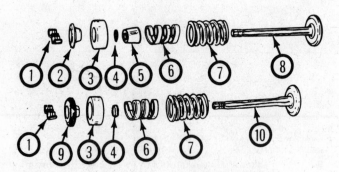

11.5b   V6 engine valves and related components — exploded view

1 *Keeper*   6 *Damper*
2 *Retainer*   7 *Spring*
3 *Oil shield*   8 *Intake valve*
4 *O-ring oil seal* 9 *Rotator*
5 *Umbrella seal* 10 *Exhaust valve*

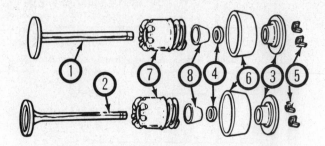

11.5a   Four-cylinder engine valves and related components — exploded view

1 *Intake valve*   5 *Keepers*
2 *Exhaust valve*   6 *Oil shield*
3 *Retainer*   7 *Valve spring (with damper)*
4 *O-ring oil seal* 8 *Umbrella seal*

11.6   Make sure the O-ring seal under the retainer is seated in the groove and not twisted before installing the keepers

11   Cylinder head — reassembly

Refer to illustrations 11.3, 11.5a, 11.5b, 11.6, 11.8 and 11.9

1   Regardless of whether or not a head was sent to an automotive repair shop for valve servicing, make sure it's clean before beginning reassembly.
2   If a head was sent out for valve servicing, the valves and related components will already be in place. Begin the reassembly procedure with Step 8.
3   Install new seals on each of the intake valve guides. Using a hammer and a deep socket or seal installation tool, gently tap each seal into place until it's completely seated on the guide (see illustration). Don't twist or cock the seals during installation or they won't seal properly on the valve stems. The umbrella-type seals (if used) are installed over the valves after the valves are in place.
4   Beginning at one end of the head, lubricate and install the first valve. Apply moly-base grease or clean engine oil to the valve stem.
5   Drop the spring seat or shim(s) over the valve guide and set the valve springs, shield and retainer (or rotator) in place (see illustrations).
6   Compress the springs with a valve spring compressor and carefully install the O-ring oil seal in the lower groove of the valve stem. Make

sure the seal isn't twisted — it must lie perfectly flat in the groove (see illustration). Position the keepers in the upper groove, then slowly release the compressor and make sure the keepers seat properly. Apply a small dab of grease to each keeper to hold it in place if necessary.
7   Repeat the procedure for the remaining valves. Be sure to return the components to their original locations — don't mix them up!
8   Once all the valves are in place in both heads, the valve stem O-ring seals must be checked to make sure they don't leak. This procedure requires a vacuum pump and special adapter (GM tool no. J-23994), so it may be a good idea to have it done by a dealer service department, repair shop or automotive machine shop. The adapter is positioned on each valve retainer or rotator and vacuum is applied with the hand pump (see illustration). If the vacuum can't be maintained, the seal is leaking and must be checked/replaced before the head is installed on the engine.
9   Check the installed valve spring height with a ruler graduated in 1/32-inch increments or a dial caliper. If the head was sent out for service work, the installed height should be correct (but don't automatically assume that it is). The measurement is taken from the top of each spring seat or shim(s) to the top of the oil shield (or the bottom of the retainer/rotator, the two points are the same) (see illustration). If the height is greater than specified, shims can be added under the springs to correct it. **Caution:** *Don't, under any circumstances, shim the springs to the point where the installed height is less than specified.*

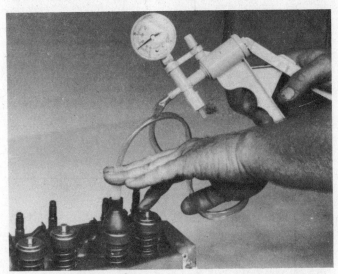

11.8   A special adapter and vacuum pump are required to check the O-ring valve stem seals for leaks

11.9   Be sure to check the valve spring installed height (the distance from the top of the seat/shims to the top of the shield)

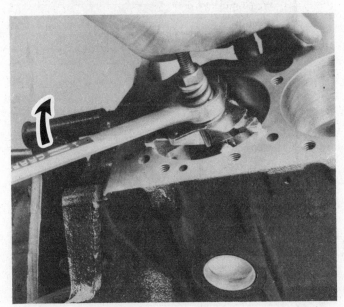

12.1   A ridge reamer is required to remove the ridge from the top of the cylinder — do this before removing the pistons!

12.3   Check the connecting rod side clearance with a feeler gauge as shown

2C

10   Apply moly-base grease to the rocker arm faces and the pivot balls, then install the rocker arms and pivots on the cylinder head studs. Thread the nuts on three or four turns only (when the heads are installed on a V6 engine, the nuts will be tightened following a specific procedure).

12   Piston/connecting rod assembly — removal

Refer to illustrations 12.1, 12.3 and 12.5

Note: *Prior to removing the piston/connecting rod assemblies, remove the cylinder head(s), the oil pan and the oil pump by referring to the appropriate Sections in Chapter 2, Part A or B.*

1   Completely remove the ridge at the top of each cylinder with a ridge reaming tool (**see illustration**). Follow the manufacturer's instructions provided with the tool. Failure to remove the ridge before attempting to remove the piston/connecting rod assemblies may result in piston breakage.

2   After the cylinder ridges have been removed, turn the engine upside-down so the crankshaft is facing up.

3   Before the connecting rods are removed, check the end play with feeler gauges. Slide them between the first connecting rod and the crankshaft throw until the play is removed (**see illustration**). The end play is equal to the thickness of the feeler gauge(s). If the end play exceeds the service limit, new connecting rods will be required. If new rods (or a new crankshaft) are installed, the end play may fall under the specified minimum (if it does, the rods will have to be machined to restore it — consult an automotive machine shop for advice if necessary). Repeat the procedure for the remaining connecting rods.

4   Check the connecting rods and caps for identification marks. If they aren't plainly marked, use a small center punch to make the appropriate number of indentations on each rod and cap (1 — 4 or 6, depending on the engine type and cylinder they're associated with).

5   Loosen each of the connecting rod cap nuts 1/2-turn at a time until they can be removed by hand. Remove the number one connecting rod cap and bearing insert. Don't drop the bearing insert out of the cap. Slip a short length of plastic or rubber hose over each connecting rod cap bolt to protect the crankshaft journal and cylinder wall as the

12.5   To prevent damage to the crankshaft journals and
cylinder walls, slip sections of hose over the rod bolts
before removing the pistons

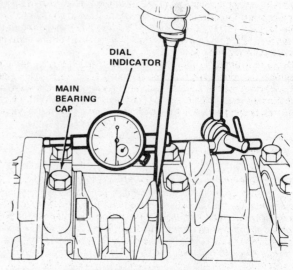

13.1   Checking crankshaft end play with a dial indicator

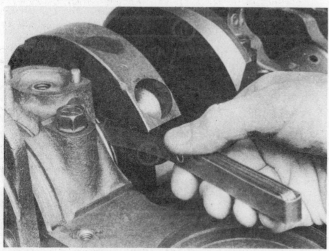

13.3   Checking crankshaft end play with a feeler gauge

13.4a   Use a center punch or number stamping dies to
mark the main bearing caps to ensure that they're
reinstalled in their original locations on the block
(make the punch marks near one of the bolt heads)

13.4b   Mark the caps in order from the front of the engine
to the rear (one mark for the front cap, two for the second
one and so on) — the rear cap doesn't have to be marked
since it can't be installed in any other location

13.4c   The arrow on the main bearing cap indicates the
front of the engine

piston is removed (**see illustration**). Push the connecting rod/piston assembly out through the top of the engine. Use a wooden hammer handle to push on the upper bearing insert in the connecting rod. If resistance is felt, double-check to make sure that all of the ridge was removed from the cylinder.

6   Repeat the procedure for the remaining cylinders. After removal, reassemble the connecting rod caps and bearing inserts in their respective connecting rods and install the cap nuts finger tight. Leaving the old bearing inserts in place until reassembly will help prevent the connecting rod bearing surfaces from being accidentally nicked or gouged.

13   Crankshaft — removal

Refer to illustrations 13.1, 13.3, 13.4a, 13.4b and 13.4c

Note: *The crankshaft can be removed only after the engine has been removed from the vehicle. It's assumed that the flywheel or driveplate, vibration damper/crankshaft pulley hub, timing chain (V6 engine only), oil pan, oil pump and piston/connecting rod assemblies have already been removed. If your engine is equipped with a one-piece rear main oil seal (later model V6 engines only), the seal housing must be unbolted and separated from the block before proceeding with crankshaft removal.*

1   Before the crankshaft is removed, check the end play. Mount a dial indicator with the stem in line with the crankshaft and just touching one of the crank throws (**see illustration**).

2   Push the crankshaft all the way to the rear and zero the dial indicator. Next, pry the crankshaft to the front as far as possible and check the reading on the dial indicator. The distance that it moves is the end play. If it's greater than specified, check the crankshaft thrust surfaces for wear. If no wear is evident, new main bearings should correct the end play.

3   If a dial indicator isn't available, feeler gauges can be used. Gently pry or push the crankshaft all the way to the front of the engine. Slip feeler gauges between the crankshaft and the front face of the thrust main bearing to determine the clearance (**see illustration**).

4   Check the main bearing caps to see if they're marked to indicate their locations. They should be numbered consecutively from the front of the engine to the rear. If they aren't, mark them with number stamping dies or a center punch (**see illustrations**). Main bearing caps generally have a cast-in arrow, which points to the front of the engine (**see illustration**). Loosen each of the main bearing cap bolts 1/4-turn at a time each, until they can be removed by hand.

5   Gently tap the caps with a soft-face hammer, then separate them from the engine block. If necessary, use the bolts as levers to remove the caps. Try not to drop the bearing inserts if they come out with the caps.

6   Carefully lift the crankshaft out of the engine. It's a good idea to have an assistant available, since the crankshaft is quite heavy. With

the bearing inserts in place in the engine block and main bearing caps, return the caps to their respective locations on the engine block and tighten the bolts finger tight.

14   Engine block — cleaning

Refer to illustrations 14.8 and 14.10

Note: *The core plugs (also known as freeze or soft plugs) may be difficult or impossible to retrieve if they're driven into the block coolant passages.*

1   Drill a small hole in the center of each core plug and pull them out with an auto body type dent puller.

2   Using a gasket scraper, remove all traces of gasket material from the engine block. Be very careful not to nick or gouge the gasket sealing surfaces.

3   Remove the main bearing caps and separate the bearing inserts from the caps and the engine block. Tag the bearings, indicating which cylinder they were removed from and whether they were in the cap or the block, then set them aside.

4   Using a 1/4-inch drive breaker bar or ratchet, remove all of the threaded oil gallery plugs from the rear of the block. The plugs are usually very tight — they may have to be drilled out and the holes re-tapped. Discard the plugs and use new ones when the engine is reassembled..

5   If the engine is extremely dirty it should be taken to an automotive machine shop to be steam cleaned or hot tanked.

6   After the block is returned, clean all oil holes and oil galleries one more time. Brushes specifically designed for this purpose are available at most auto parts stores. Flush the passages with warm water until the water runs clear, dry the block thoroughly and wipe all machined surfaces with a light, rust preventative oil. If you have access to compressed air, use it to speed the drying process and to blow out all the oil holes and galleries.

7   If the block isn't extremely dirty or sludged up, you can do an adequate cleaning job with hot soapy water and a stiff brush. Take plenty of time and do a thorough job. Regardless of the cleaning method used, be sure to clean all oil holes and galleries very thoroughly, dry the block completely and coat all machined surfaces with light oil.

8   The threaded holes in the block must be clean to ensure accurate torque readings during reassembly. Run the proper size tap into each of the holes to remove any rust, corrosion, thread sealant or sludge and to restore any damaged threads (**see illustration**). If possible, use compressed air to clear the holes of debris produced by this operation. Now is a good time to clean the threads on the head bolts and the main bearing cap bolts as well.

9   Reinstall the main bearing caps and tighten the bolts finger tight.

10   After coating the sealing surfaces of the new core plugs with RTV sealant, install them in the engine block (**see illustration**). Make sure

14.8 All bolt holes in the block — particularly the main bearing cap and head bolt holes — should be cleaned and restored with a tap (be sure to remove debris from the holes after this is done)

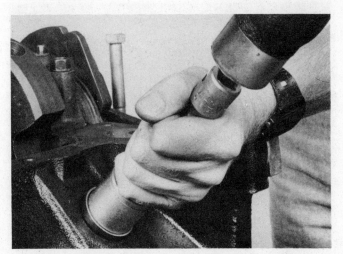

14.10 A large socket on an extension can be used to drive the new soft plugs into the bores

they're driven in straight and seated properly or leakage could result. Special tools are available for this purpose, but equally good results can be obtained using a large socket, with an outside diameter that will just slip into the core plug, a 1/2-inch drive extension and a hammer.

11 Apply non-hardening sealant (such as Permatex number 2 or Teflon tape) to the new oil gallery plugs and thread them into the holes at the rear of the block. Make sure they're tightened securely.

12 If the engine isn't going to be reassembled right away, cover it with a large plastic trash bag to keep it clean.

15 Engine block — inspection

Refer to illustrations 15.4a, 15.4b and 15.4c

1 Before the block is inspected, it should be cleaned as described in Section 14. Double-check to make sure the ridge at the top of each cylinder has been completely removed.

2 Visually check the block for cracks, rust and corrosion. Look for stripped threads in the threaded holes. It's also a good idea to have the block checked for hidden cracks by an automotive machine shop that has the special equipment to do this type of work. If defects are found, have the block repaired, if possible, or replaced.

3 Check the cylinder bores for scuffing and scoring.

4 Measure the diameter of each cylinder at the top (just under the ridge area), center and bottom of the cylinder bore, parallel to the crankshaft axis (**see illustrations**). Next, measure each cylinder's diameter at the same three locations *across* the crankshaft axis. Compare the results to the Specifications. If the cylinder walls are badly scuffed or scored, or if they're out-of-round or tapered beyond the limits

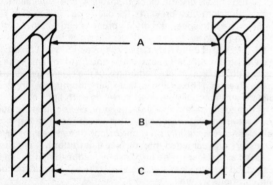

15.4a Measure the diameter of each cylinder just under the wear ridge (A), at the center (B) and at the bottom (C)

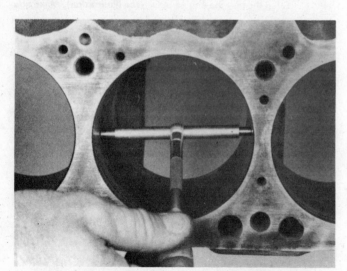

15.4b The ability to ''feel'' when the telescoping gauge is at the correct point will be developed over time, so work slowly and repeat the check until you're satisfied that the bore measurement is accurate

given in the Specifications, have the engine block rebored and honed at an automotive machine shop. If a rebore is done, oversize pistons and rings will be required.

5 If the cylinders are in reasonably good condition and not worn to the outside of the limits, and if the piston-to-cylinder clearances can be maintained properly, then they don't have to be rebored. Honing is all that's necessary (Section 16).

16 Cylinder honing

Refer to illustrations 16.3a and 16.3b

1 Prior to engine reassembly, the cylinder bores must be honed so the new piston rings will seat correctly and provide the best possible combustion chamber seal. **Note:** *If you don't have the tools or don't want to tackle the honing operation, most automotive machine shops will do it for a reasonable fee.*

2 Before honing the cylinders, install the main bearing caps and tighten the bolts to the specified torque.

3 Two types of cylinder hones are commonly available — the flex hone or ''bottle brush'' type and the more traditional surfacing hone with spring-loaded stones. Both will do the job, but for the less experienced mechanic the ''bottle brush'' hone will probably be easier to use. You'll also need plenty of light oil or honing oil, some rags and an electric drill motor. Proceed as follows:

a) Mount the hone in the drill motor, compress the stones and slip it into the first cylinder **(see illustration)**. Be sure to wear safety goggles or a face shield!

b) Lubricate the cylinder with plenty of oil, turn on the drill and move the hone up-and-down in the cylinder at a pace that will produce a fine crosshatch pattern on the cylinder walls. Ideally, the crosshatch lines should intersect at approximately a 60° angle **(see illustration)**. Be sure to use plenty of lubricant and don't take off any more material than is absolutely necessary to produce the desired finish. **Note:** *Piston ring manufacturers may specify a smaller crosshatch angle than the traditional 60° — read and follow any instructions included with the new rings.*

c) Don't withdraw the hone from the cylinder while it's running. Instead, shut off the drill and continue moving the hone up-and-down in the cylinder until it comes to a complete stop, then compress the stones and withdraw the hone. If you're using a ''bottle brush'' type hone, stop the drill motor, then turn the chuck in the normal direction of rotation while withdrawing the hone from the cylinder.

d) Wipe the oil out of the cylinder and repeat the procedure for the remaining cylinders.

4 After the honing job is complete, chamfer the top edges of the cylinder bores with a small file so the rings won't catch when the

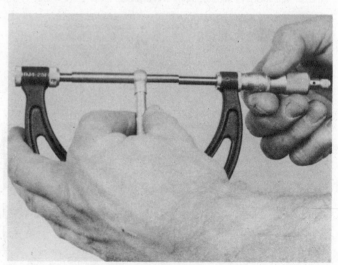

15.4c The gauge is then measured with a micrometer to determine the bore size

16.3a A "bottle brush" hone will produce better results if you've never done cylinder honing before

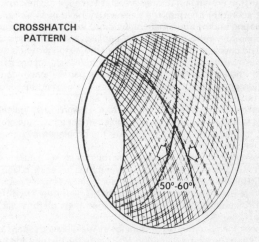

16.3b The cylinder hone should leave a smooth, crosshatch pattern with the lines intersecting at approximately a 60-degree angle

2C

pistons are installed. **Be very careful not to nick the cylinder walls with the end of the file.**

5   The entire engine block must be washed again very thoroughly with warm, soapy water to remove all traces of the abrasive grit produced during the honing operation. **Note:** *The bores can be considered clean when a white cloth — dampened with clean engine oil — used to wipe them out doesn't pick up any more honing residue, which will show up as gray areas on the cloth.* Be sure to run a brush through all oil holes and galleries and flush them with running water.

6   After rinsing, dry the block and apply a coat of light rust preventive oil to all machined surfaces. Wrap the block in a plastic trash bag to keep it clean and set it aside until reassembly.

17 Piston/connecting rod assembly — inspection

Refer to illustrations 17.4a, 17.4b, 17.10 and 17.11

1   Before the inspection process can be carried out, the piston/connecting rod assemblies must be cleaned and the original piston rings removed from the pistons. **Note:** *Always use new piston rings when the engine is reassembled.*

2   Using a piston ring installation tool, carefully remove the rings from the pistons. Be careful not to nick or gouge the pistons in the process.

3   Scrape all traces of carbon from the top of the piston. A handheld wire brush or a piece of fine emery cloth can be used once the majority of the deposits have been scraped away. Do not, under any circumstances, use a wire brush mounted in a drill motor to remove deposits from the pistons. The piston material is soft and will be eroded away by the wire brush.

4   Use a piston ring groove cleaning tool to remove carbon deposits from the ring grooves. If a tool isn't available, a piece broken off the old ring will do the job. Be very careful to remove only the carbon deposits — don't remove any metal and do not nick or scratch the sides of the ring grooves (**see illustrations**).

5   Once the deposits have been removed, clean the piston/rod assemblies with solvent and dry them with compressed air (if available). Make sure the oil return holes in the back sides of the ring grooves are clear.

6   If the pistons and cylinder walls aren't damaged or worn excessively, and if the engine block is not rebored, new pistons won't be necessary. Normal piston wear appears as even vertical wear on the piston thrust surfaces and slight looseness of the top ring in its groove. New piston rings, on the other hand, should always be used when an engine is rebuilt.

7   Carefully inspect each piston for cracks around the skirt, at the pin bosses and at the ring lands.

8   Look for scoring and scuffing on the thrust faces of the skirt, holes

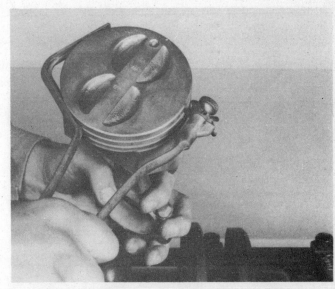

17.4a The piston ring grooves can be cleaned with a special tool, as shown here, . . .

17.4b . . . or a section of a broken ring

in the piston crown and burned areas at the edge of the crown. If the skirt is scored or scuffed, the engine may have been suffering from overheating and/or abnormal combustion, which caused excessively high operating temperatures. The cooling and lubrication systems should be checked thoroughly. A hole in the piston crown is an indication that abnormal combustion (preignition) was occurring. Burned areas at the edge of the piston crown are usually evidence of spark knock (detonation). If any of the above problems exist, the causes must be corrected or the damage will occur again.

9   Corrosion of the piston, in the form of small pits, indicates that coolant is leaking into the combustion chamber and/or the crankcase. Again, the cause must be corrected or the problem may persist in the rebuilt engine.

10 Measure the piston ring side clearance by laying a new piston ring in each ring groove and slipping a feeler gauge in beside it (**see illustration**). Check the clearance at three or four locations around each groove. Be sure to use the correct ring for each groove; they are different. If the side clearance is greater than specified, new pistons will have to be used.

11 Check the piston-to-bore clearance by measuring the bore (see Section 15) and the piston diameter. Make sure the pistons and bores are correctly matched. Measure the piston across the skirt, at a 90° angle to and in line with the piston pin (**see illustration**). Subtract the piston diameter from the bore diameter to obtain the clearance. If it's greater than specified, the block will have to be rebored and new pistons and

rings installed.

12 Check the piston-to-rod clearance by twisting the piston and rod in opposite directions. Any noticeable play indicates excessive wear, which must be corrected. The piston/connecting rod assemblies should be taken to an automotive machine shop to have the pistons and rods rebored and new pins installed.

13 If the pistons must be removed from the connecting rods for any reason, they should be taken to an automotive machine shop. While they are there have the connecting rods checked for bend and twist, since automotive machine shops have special equipment for this purpose. **Note:** *Unless new pistons and/or connecting rods must be installed, do not disassemble the pistons and connecting rods.*

14 Check the connecting rods for cracks and other damage. Temporarily remove the rod caps, lift out the old bearing inserts, wipe the rod and cap bearing surfaces clean and inspect them for nicks, gouges and scratches. After checking the rods, replace the old bearings, slip the caps into place and tighten the nuts finger tight.

18   Crankshaft — inspection

Refer to illustration 18.2

1   Clean the crankshaft with solvent and dry it with compressed air (if available). Be sure to clean the oil holes with a stiff brush and flush them with solvent. Check the main and connecting rod bearing journals for uneven wear, scoring, pits and cracks. Check the rest of the crankshaft for cracks and other damage.

2   Using a micrometer, measure the diameter of the main and connecting rod journals and compare the results to the Specifications (**see illustration**). By measuring the diameter at a number of points around each journal's circumference, you'll be able to determine whether or not the journal is out-of-round. Take the measurement at each end of the journal, near the crank throws, to determine if the journal is tapered.

18.2   Measure the diameter of each crankshaft journal at several points to detect taper and out-of-round conditions

3   If the crankshaft journals are damaged, tapered, out-of-round or worn beyond the limits given in the Specifications, have the crankshaft reground by an automotive machine shop. Be sure to use the correct size bearing inserts if the crankshaft is reconditioned.

4   Refer to Section 19 and examine the main and rod bearing inserts.

19   Main and connecting rod bearings — inspection

1   Even though the main and connecting rod bearings should be replaced with new ones during the engine overhaul, the old bearings should be retained for close examination, as they may reveal valuable information about the condition of the engine.

2   Bearing failure occurs because of lack of lubrication, the presence of dirt or other foreign particles, overloading the engine and corrosion. Regardless of the cause of bearing failure, it must be corrected before the engine is reassembled to prevent it from happening again.

3   When examining the bearings, remove them from the engine block,

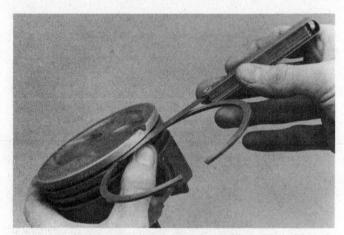

17.10   Check the ring side clearance with a feeler gauge at several points around the groove

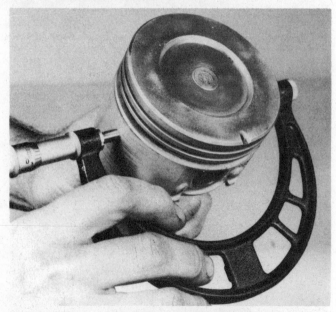

17.11   Measure the piston diameter at a 90° angle to the piston pin and in line with it

the main bearing caps, the connecting rods and the rod caps and lay them out on a clean surface in the same general position as their location in the engine. This will enable you to match any bearing problems with the corresponding crankshaft journal.

4   Dirt and other foreign particles get into the engine in a variety of ways. It may be left in the engine during assembly, or it may pass through filters or the PCV system. It may get into the oil, and from there into the bearings. Metal chips from machining operations and normal engine wear are often present. Abrasives are sometimes left in engine components after reconditioning, especially when parts are not thoroughly cleaned using the proper cleaning methods. Whatever the source, these foreign objects often end up embedded in the soft bearing material and are easily recognized. Large particles will not embed in the bearing and will score or gouge the bearing and journal. The best prevention for this cause of bearing failure is to clean all parts thoroughly and keep everything spotlessly clean during engine assembly. Frequent and regular engine oil and filter changes are also recommended.

5   Lack of lubrication (or lubrication breakdown) has a number of interrelated causes. Excessive heat (which thins the oil), overloading (which squeezes the oil from the bearing face) and oil leakage or throw off (from excessive bearing clearances, worn oil pump or high engine speeds) all contribute to lubrication breakdown. Blocked oil passages, which usually are the result of misaligned oil holes in a bearing shell, will also oil starve a bearing and destroy it. When lack of lubrication is the cause of bearing failure, the bearing material is wiped or extruded from the steel backing of the bearing. Temperatures may increase to the point where the steel backing turns blue from overheating.

6   Driving habits can have a definite effect on bearing life. Full throttle, low speed operation (lugging the engine) puts very high loads on bearings, which tends to squeeze out the oil film. These loads cause the bearings to flex, which produces fine cracks in the bearing face (fatigue failure). Eventually the bearing material will loosen in pieces and tear away from the steel backing. Short trip driving leads to corrosion of bearings because insufficient engine heat is produced to drive off the condensed water and corrosive gases. These products collect in the engine oil, forming acid and sludge. As the oil is carried to the engine bearings, the acid attacks and corrodes the bearing material.

7   Incorrect bearing installation during engine assembly will lead to bearing failure as well. Tight fitting bearings leave insufficient bearing oil clearance and will result in oil starvation. Dirt or foreign particles trapped behind a bearing insert result in high spots on the bearing which lead to failure.

20   Engine overhaul — reassembly sequence

1   Before beginning engine reassembly, make sure you have all the necessary new parts, gaskets and seals as well as the following items on hand:

Common hand tools
A 1/2-inch drive torque wrench
Piston ring installation tool
Piston ring compressor
Short lengths of rubber or plastic hose
   to fit over connecting rod bolts
Plastigage
Feeler gauges
A fine-tooth file
New engine oil
Engine assembly lube or moly-base grease
RTV-type gasket sealant
Anaerobic-type gasket sealant
Thread locking compound

2   In order to save time and avoid problems, engine reassembly must be done in the following general order:

New camshaft bearings (must be done by automotive machine shop)
Piston rings
Crankshaft and main bearings
Piston/connecting rod assemblies
Oil pump
Camshaft and lifters
Oil pan
Timing chain and sprockets (V6 engine only)
Cylinder head(s), pushrods and rocker arms

Timing cover
Intake and exhaust manifolds
Rocker arm cover(s)
Flywheel/driveplate

21   Piston rings — installation

Refer to illustrations 21.3, 21.4, 21.5, 21.9a, 21.9b and 21.12

1   Before installing the new piston rings, the ring end gaps must be checked. It's assumed that the piston ring side clearance has been checked and verified correct (Section 17).

2   Lay out the piston/connecting rod assemblies and the new ring sets so the ring sets will be matched with the same piston and cylinder during the end gap measurement and engine assembly.

3   Insert the top (number one) ring into the first cylinder and square it up with the cylinder walls by pushing it in with the top of the piston (**see illustration**). The ring should be near the bottom of the cylinder, at the lower limit of ring travel.

4   To measure the end gap, slip feeler gauges between the ends of the ring until a gauge equal to the gap width is found (**see illustration**). The feeler gauge should slide between the ring ends with a slight amount of drag. Compare the measurement to the Specifications. If the gap is larger or smaller than specified, double-check to make sure you have the correct rings before proceeding.

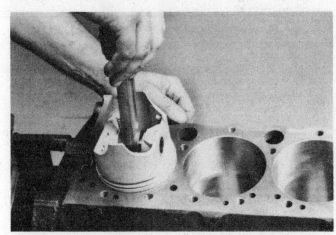

21.3   When checking piston ring end gap, the ring must be square in the cylinder bore (this is done by pushing the ring down with the top of a piston as shown)

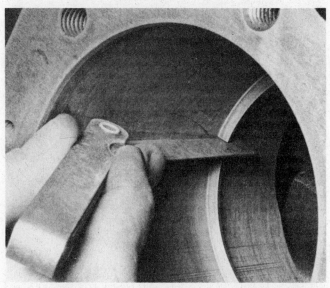

21.4   With the ring square in the cylinder, measure the end gap with a feeler gauge

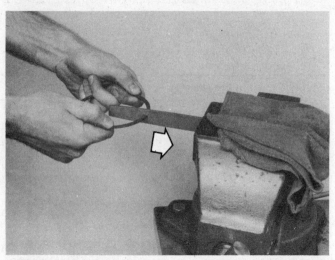

21.5   If the end gap is too small, clamp a file in a vise and file the ring ends (from the outside in only) to enlarge the gap slightly

21.9b   DO NOT use a piston ring installation tool when installing the oil ring side rails

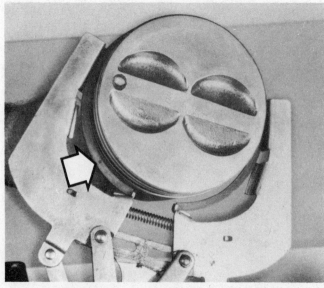

21.12   Installing the compression rings with a ring expander — the mark (arrow) must face up

21.9a   Installing the spacer/expander in the oil control ring groove

5   If the gap is too small, it must be enlarged or the ring ends may come in contact with each other during engine operation, which can cause serious damage to the engine. The end gap can be increased by filing the ring ends very carefully with a fine file. Mount the file in a vise equipped with soft jaws, slip the ring over the file with the ends contacting the file face and slowly move the ring to remove material from the ends. When performing this operation, file only from the outside in (**see illustration**).

6   Excess end gap isn't critical unless it's greater than 0.040-inch. Again, double-check to make sure you have the correct rings for your engine.

7   Repeat the procedure for each ring that will be installed in the first cylinder and for each ring in the remaining cylinders. Remember to keep rings, pistons and cylinders matched up.

8   Once the ring end gaps have been checked/corrected, the rings can be installed on the pistons.

9   The oil control ring (lowest one on the piston) is installed first. It's composed of three separate components. Slip the spacer/expander into the groove (**see illustration**). If an anti-rotation tang is used, make sure it's inserted into the drilled hole in the ring groove. Next, install the lower side rail. Don't use a piston ring installation tool on the oil ring side rails, as they may be damaged. Instead, place one end of the side rail into the groove between the spacer/expander and the ring land, hold it firmly in place and slide a finger around the piston while pushing the rail into the groove (**see illustration**). Next, install the upper side rail in the same manner.

10   After the three oil ring components have been installed, check to make sure that both the upper and lower side rails can be turned smoothly in the ring groove.

11   The number two (middle) ring is installed next. It's stamped with a mark which must face up, toward the top of the piston. **Note:** *Always follow the instructions printed on the ring package or box — different manufacturers may require different approaches. Do not mix up the top and middle rings, as they have different cross sections.*

12   Use a piston ring installation tool and make sure the identification mark is facing the top of the piston, then slip the ring into the middle groove on the piston (**see illustration**). Don't expand the ring any more than is necessary to slide it over the piston.

13   Install the number one (top) ring in the same manner. Make sure the mark is facing up. Be careful not to confuse the number one and number two rings.

14   Repeat the procedure for the remaining pistons and rings.

22   Crankshaft — installation and main bearing oil clearance check

Refer to illustrations 22.10 and 22.14

1   Crankshaft installation is the first step in engine reassembly. It's assumed at this point that the engine block and crankshaft have been

cleaned, inspected and repaired or reconditioned. **Note:** *If your engine has a two-piece rear main oil seal (1985 V6 models), refer to Section 23 and install the oil seal sections in the cap and block before proceeding with crankshaft installation.*

2   Position the engine with the bottom facing up.

3   Remove the main bearing cap bolts and lift out the caps. Lay them out in the proper order to ensure correct installation.

4   If they're still in place, remove the old bearing inserts from the block and the main bearing caps. Wipe the main bearing surfaces of the block and caps with a clean, lint free cloth. They must be kept spotlessly clean.

5   Clean the back sides of the new main bearing inserts and lay one bearing half in each main bearing saddle in the block. Lay the other bearing half from each bearing set in the corresponding main bearing cap. Make sure the tab on the bearing insert fits into the recess in the block or cap. Also, the oil holes in the block must line up with the oil holes in the bearing insert. Do not hammer the bearing into place and do not nick or gouge the bearing faces. No lubrication should be used at this time.

6   The flanged thrust bearing must be installed in the rear cap and saddle.

7   Clean the faces of the bearings in the block and the crankshaft main bearing journals with a clean, lint free cloth. Check or clean the oil holes in the crankshaft, as any dirt here can go only one way — straight through the new bearings.

8   Once you're certain the crankshaft is clean, carefully lay it in position in the main bearings.

9   Before the crankshaft can be permanently installed, the main bearing oil clearance must be checked.

10   Trim several pieces of the appropriate size of Plastigage (they must be slightly shorter than the width of the main bearings) and place one piece on each crankshaft main bearing journal, parallel with the journal axis (**see illustration**).

11   Clean the faces of the bearings in the caps and install the caps in their respective positions (don't mix them up) with the arrows pointing toward the front of the engine. Don't disturb the Plastigage.

12   Starting with the center main and working out toward the ends, tighten the main bearing cap bolts, in three steps, to the specified torque. Don't rotate the crankshaft at any time during this operation.

13   Remove the bolts and carefully lift off the main bearing caps. Keep them in order. Don't disturb the Plastigage or rotate the crankshaft. If any of the main bearing caps are difficult to remove, tap them gently from side-to-side with a soft-face hammer to loosen them.

14   Compare the width of the crushed Plastigage on each journal to the scale printed on the Plastigage container to obtain the main bearing oil clearance (**see illustration**). Check the Specifications to make sure it's correct.

15   If the clearance is not as specified, the bearing inserts may be the wrong size (which means different ones will be required). Before deciding that different inserts are needed, make sure that no dirt or oil was between the bearing inserts and the caps or block when the clearance was measured. If the Plastigage was wider at one end than the other, the journal may be tapered (refer to Section 18).

16   Carefully scrape all traces of the Plastigage material off the main bearing journals and/or the bearing faces. Don't nick or scratch the bearing faces.

17   Carefully lift the crankshaft out of the engine. Clean the bearing faces in the block, then apply a thin, uniform layer of clean moly-base grease or engine assembly lube to each of the bearing surfaces. Be sure to coat the thrust faces as well as the journal face of the rear bearing.

18   If not already done, refer to Section 23 and install the rear main oil seal sections in the block and bearing cap (1985 V6 engine only). Lubricate the seal faces with moly-base grease, engine assembly lube or clean engine oil.

19   Make sure the crankshaft journals are clean, then lay the crankshaft back in place in the block. Clean the faces of the bearings in the caps, then apply lubricant to them. Install the caps in their respective positions with the arrows pointing toward the front of the engine. Note that the rear cap must have a special sealant applied (see Chapter 2B). Install the bolts.

20   Tighten all except the rear cap bolts (the one with the thrust bearing) to the specified torque (work from the center out and approach the final torque in three steps). Tighten the rear cap bolts to 10-to-12 ft-lbs. Tap the ends of the crankshaft forward and backward with a lead or brass hammer to line up the main bearing and crankshaft thrust

22.10   Lay the Plastigage strips (arrow) on the main bearing journals, parallel to the crankshaft centerline

22.14   Compare the width of the crushed Plastigage to the scale on the container to determine the main bearing oil clearance (always take the measurement at the widest point of the Plastigage); be sure to use the correct scale — standard and metric scales are included

surfaces. Retighten all main bearing cap bolts to the specified torque, starting with the center main and working out toward the ends.

21   On manual transmission equipped models, install a new pilot bearing in the end of the crankshaft (see Chapter 8).

22   Rotate the crankshaft a number of times by hand to check for any obvious binding.

23   The final step is to check the crankshaft end play with a feeler gauge or a dial indicator as described in Section 13. The end play should be correct if the crankshaft thrust faces aren't worn or damaged and new bearings have been installed.

24   If you have a V6 engine with a one-piece rear main oil seal, refer to Section 23 and install the new seal, then bolt the housing to the block.

---

23   Rear main oil seal installation

Four-cylinder engine

1   Clean the bore in the block and seal contact surface on the crankshaft. Check the crankshaft surface for scratches and nicks that could

damage the new seal lip and cause oil leaks. If the crankshaft is damaged, the only alternative is a new or different crankshaft.
2   Apply a light coat of engine oil or multi-purpose grease to the outer
edge of the new seal. Lubricate the seal lip with moly-base grease.
3   Press the new seal into place with GM tool no. J34924 (if available)
(see illustration 20.8a in Chapter 2, Part A). The seal lip must face
toward the front of the engine. If the special tool isn't available, carefully
work the seal lip over the end of the crankshaft and tap the seal in
with a hammer and punch until it's seated in the bore (see illustration
20.8b in Part A).

V6 engine

1985

4   Inspect the rear main bearing cap and engine block mating surfaces,
as well as the seal grooves, for nicks, burrs and scratches. Remove
any defects with a fine file or deburring tool.
5   Install one seal section in the block with the lip facing the front
of the engine (if the seal has two lips, the one with the helix must face
the front) (see illustration 14.15b in Chapter 2, Part B). Leave one end
protruding from the block approximately 1/4 to 3/8-inch and make sure
it's completely seated.
6   Repeat the procedure to install the remaining seal half in the rear
main bearing cap. In this case, leave the opposite end of the seal protruding from the cap the same distance the block seal is protruding
from the block.
7   During final installation of the crankshaft (after the main bearing
oil clearances have been checked with Plastigage) as described in Section 22, apply a thin, even coat of anaerobic-type gasket sealant to
the areas of the cap or block indicated in illustration 14.19 (Part B of
Chapter 2). Don't get any sealant on the bearing face, crankshaft journal, seal ends or seal lips. Also, lubricate the seal lips with moly-base
grease or clean engine oil.

1986 on

8   Later models are equipped with a one-piece seal that requires an
entirely different installation procedure. The crankshaft must be installed first and the main bearing caps bolted in place, then the new
seal should be installed in the housing and the housing bolted to the
block (see illustration 14.26 in Chapter 2, Part B).
9   Before installing the crankshaft, check the seal contact surface
very carefully for scratches and nicks that could damage the new seal
lip and cause oil leaks. If the crankshaft is damaged, the only alternative is a new or different crankshaft.
10   The old seal can be removed from the housing by inserting a large
screwdriver into the notches provided and prying it out (see illustration
14.23 in Part B). Be sure to note how far it's recessed into the housing
bore before removing it; the new seal will have to be recessed an equal
amount. Be very careful not to scratch or otherwise damage the bore
in the housing or oil leaks could develop.
11   Make sure the housing is clean, then apply a thin coat of engine
oil to the outer edge of the new seal. The seal must be pressed squarely
into the housing bore, so hammering it into place is not recommended.
If you don't have access to a press, sandwich the housing and seal
between two smooth pieces of wood and press the seal into place with
the jaws of a large vise. The pieces of wood must be thick enough
to distribute the force evenly around the entire circumference of the
seal. Work slowly and make sure the seal enters the bore squarely.
12   The seal lips must be lubricated with clean engine oil or moly-based
grease before the seal/housing is slipped over the crankshaft and bolted
to the block. Use a new gasket — no sealant is required — and make
sure the dowel pins are in place before installing the housing.
13   Tighten the nuts/screws a little at a time until they're all snug.

**24   Piston/connecting rod assembly — installation and
        rod bearing oil clearance check**

Refer to illustrations 24.5, 24.8, 24.9, 24.11 and 24.13

1   Before installing the piston/connecting rod assemblies, the cylinder
walls must be perfectly clean, the top edge of each cylinder must be
chamfered, and the crankshaft must be in place.
2   Remove the connecting rod cap from the end of the number one
connecting rod. Remove the old bearing inserts and wipe the bearing
surfaces of the connecting rod and cap with a clean, lint free cloth.
They must be kept spotlessly clean.

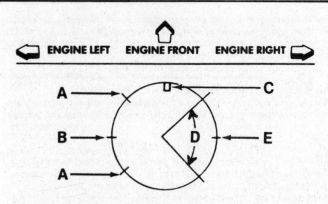

24.5   Position the piston ring gaps as shown here before
installing the piston/connecting rod assemblies in the engine

A   Oil ring rail gaps   D   Oil ring spacer gap
B   2nd compression ring gap   (tang in hole or slot with arc)
C   Notch in piston   E   Top compression ring gap

3   Clean the back side of the new upper bearing half, then lay it in
place in the connecting rod. Make sure the tab on the bearing fits into
the recess in the rod. Don't hammer the bearing insert into place and
be very careful not to nick or gouge the bearing face. Don't lubricate
the bearing at this time.
4   Clean the back side of the other bearing insert and install it in the
rod cap. Again, make sure the tab on the bearing fits into the recess
in the cap, and don't apply any lubricant. It's critically important that
the mating surfaces of the bearing and connecting rod are perfectly
clean and oil free when they're assembled.
5   Position the piston ring gaps at 120° intervals around the piston
(see illustration), then slip a section of plastic or rubber hose over each
connecting rod cap bolt.
6   Lubricate the piston and rings with clean engine oil and attach a
piston ring compressor to the piston. Leave the skirt protruding about
1/4-inch to guide the piston into the cylinder. The rings must be compressed until they're flush with the piston.
7   Rotate the crankshaft until the number one connecting rod journal
is at BDC (bottom dead center) and apply a coat of engine oil to the
cylinder walls.
8   With the notch on top of the piston **(see illustration)** facing the
front of the engine, gently insert the piston/connecting rod assembly
into the number one cylinder bore and rest the bottom edge of the ring
compressor on the engine block. Tap the top edge of the ring compressor to make sure it's contacting the block around its entire circumference.

24.8   The notch in each piston must face the FRONT of
the engine as the pistons are installed

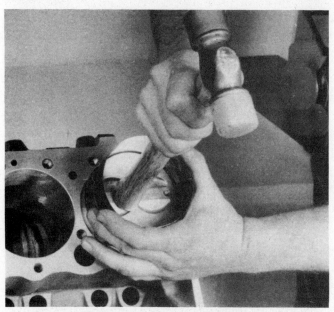

24.9 The piston can be driven (gently) into the cylinder bore with the end of a wooden hammer handle

24.11 Lay the Plastigage strips on each rod bearing journal, parallel to the crankshaft centerline

9   Carefully tap on the top of the piston with the end of a wooden hammer handle (**see illustration**) while guiding the end of the connecting rod into place on the crankshaft journal. The piston rings may try to pop out of the ring compressor just before entering the cylinder bore, so keep some downward pressure on the ring compressor. Work slowly, and if any resistance is felt as the piston enters the cylinder, stop immediately. Find out what's hanging up and fix it before proceeding. Do not, for any reason, force the piston into the cylinder, as you might break a ring and/or the piston.

10   Once the piston/connecting rod assembly is installed, the connecting rod bearing oil clearance must be checked before the rod cap is permanently bolted in place.

11   Cut a piece of the appropriate size Plastigage slightly shorter than the width of the connecting rod bearing and lay it in place on the number one connecting rod journal, parallel with the journal axis (**see illustration**).

12   Clean the connecting rod cap bearing face, remove the protective hoses from the connecting rod bolts and install the rod cap. Make sure the mating mark on the cap is on the same side as the mark on the connecting rod. Install the nuts and tighten them to the specified torque, working up to it in three steps. **Note:** *Use a thin-wall socket to avoid erroneous torque readings that can result if the socket is wedged between the rod cap and nut.* Do not rotate the crankshaft at any time during this operation.

13   Remove the rod cap, being very careful not to disturb the Plastigage. Compare the width of the crushed Plastigage to the scale printed on the Plastigage container to obtain the oil clearance (**see illustration**). Compare it to the Specifications to make sure the clearance is correct. If the clearance is not as specified, the bearing inserts may be the wrong size (which means different ones will be required). Before deciding that different inserts are needed, make sure that no dirt or oil was between the bearing inserts and the connecting rod or cap when the clearance was measured. Also, recheck the journal diameter. If the Plastigage was wider at one end than the other, the journal may be tapered (refer to Section 18).

14   Carefully scrape all traces of the Plastigage material off the rod journal and/or bearing face. Be very careful not to scratch the bearing — use your fingernail or a piece of hardwood. Make sure the bearing faces are perfectly clean, then apply a uniform layer of clean moly-base grease or engine assembly lube to both of them. You'll have to push the piston into the cylinder to expose the face of the bearing insert in the connecting rod — be sure to slip the protective hoses over the rod bolts first.

15   Slide the connecting rod back into place on the journal, remove the protective hoses from the rod cap bolts, install the rod cap and tighten the nuts to the specified torque. Again, work up to the torque in three steps.

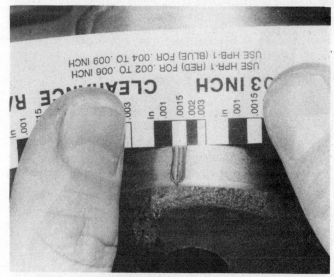

24.13 Measuring the width of the crushed Plastigage to determine the rod bearing oil clearance (be sure to use the correct scale — standard and metric scales are included)

16   Repeat the entire procedure for the remaining piston/connecting rod assemblies. Keep the back sides of the bearing inserts and the inside of the connecting rod and cap perfectly clean when assembling them. Make sure you have the correct piston for the cylinder and that the notch on the piston faces to the front of the engine when the piston is installed. Remember, use plenty of oil to lubricate the piston before installing the ring compressor. Also, when installing the rod caps for the final time, be sure to lubricate the bearing faces adequately.

17   After all the piston/connecting rod assemblies have been properly installed, rotate the crankshaft a number of times by hand to check for any obvious binding.

18   As a final step, the connecting rod end play must be checked. Refer to Section 12 for this procedure. Compare the measured end play to the Specifications to make sure it's correct. If it was correct before disassembly and the original crankshaft and rods were reinstalled, it should still be right. If new rods or a new crankshaft were installed, the end play may be too small. If so, the rods will have to be removed and taken to an automotive machine shop for resizing.

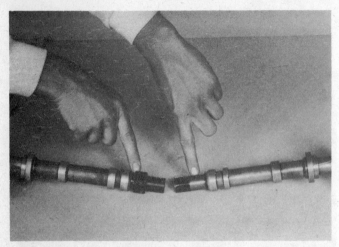

25.3 The pre-oil distributor (right) has the gear and advance weights (if equipped) removed

25   Pre-oiling engine after overhaul

Refer to illustrations 25.3, 25.5 and 25.6
Note: *This procedure applies to the V6 engine only.*

1   After an overhaul it's a good idea to pre-oil the engine before it is installed in the vehicle and started for the first time. Pre-oiling will reveal any problems with the lubrication system at a time when corrections can be made easily and will prevent major engine damage. It will also allow the internal engine parts to be lubricated thoroughly in the normal fashion without the heavy loads associated with combustion placed on them.
2   The engine should be completely assembled with the exception of the distributor and rocker arm covers. The oil filter and oil pressure sending unit must be in place and the specified amount of oil must be in the crankcasè (see Chapter 1).
3   A modified small block Chevrolet V8 distributor will be needed for this procedure — a junkyard should be able to supply one for a reasonable price. In order to function as a pre-oil tool, the distributor must have the gear on the lower end of the shaft and, if equipped, the advance weights on the upper end of the shaft removed **(see illustration)**.
4   Install the pre-oil distributor in place of the original distributor and make sure the lower end of the shaft mates with the upper end of the oil pump driveshaft. Turn the distributor shaft until they're aligned and the distributor body seats on the block. Install the distributor hold-down clamp and bolt.
5   Mount the upper end of the shaft in the chuck of an electric drill and use the drill to turn the pre-oil distributor shaft, which will drive the oil pump and circulate the oil throughout the engine **(see illustration)**. **Note:** *The drill must turn in a clockwise direction.*
6   It may take two or three minutes, but oil should soon start to flow out of all of the rocker arm holes, indicating that the oil pump is working properly **(see illustration)**. Let the oil circulate for several seconds, then shut off the drill motor.
7   Remove the pre-oil distributor, then install the rocker arm covers.

26   Initial start-up and break-in after overhaul

1   Once the engine has been installed in the vehicle, double-check the engine oil and coolant levels.
2   With the spark plugs out of the engine and the ignition system disabled (see Section 3), crank the engine until oil pressure registers on the gauge.
3   Install the spark plugs, hook up the plug wires and restore the ignition system functions (Section 3).
4   Start the engine. It may take a few moments for the gasoline to reach the carburetor or injectors, but the engine should start without a great deal of effort.

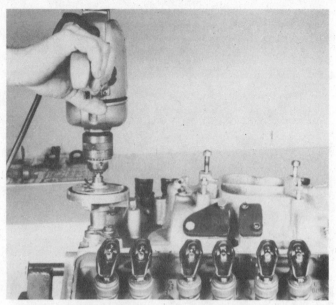

25.5 A drill motor connected to the modified distributor shaft drives the oil pump — make sure it turns clockwise as viewed from above

25.6 Oil, assembly lube or grease will begin to flow from all of the rocker arm holes if the oil pump and lubrication system are functioning properly

5   After the engine starts, it should be allowed to warm up to normal operating temperature. While the engine is warming up, make a thorough check for oil and coolant leaks.
6   Shut the engine off and recheck the engine oil and coolant levels.
7   Drive the vehicle to an area with minimum traffic, accelerate at full throttle from 30 to 50 mph, then allow the vehicle to slow to 30 mph with the throttle closed. Repeat the procedure 10 or 12 times. This will load the piston rings and cause them to seat properly against the cylinder walls. Check again for oil and coolant leaks.
8   Drive the vehicle gently for the first 500 miles (no sustained high speeds) and keep a constant check on the oil level. It is not unusual for an engine to use oil during the break-in period.
9   At approximately 500 to 600 miles, change the oil and filter.
10 For the next few hundred miles, drive the vehicle normally. Do not pamper it or abuse it.
11 After 2000 miles, change the oil and filter again and consider the engine fully broken in.

Chapter 3
Cooling, heating and air conditioning systems

Contents

Specifications

General

Coolant capacity	See Chapter 1
Radiator cap pressure rating	15 psi
Thermostat rating	195° F

Torque specifications

	Ft-lbs
Air conditioner compressor mounting bolts	
four-cylinder engine	
front bolts	37
rear bolts	20
V6 engine	
top bolt	25
bottom bolt	37
Compressor line manifold bolt	18
Fan assembly-to-water pump hub	
four-cylinder engine without fan clutch	20
four-cylinder engine with fan clutch	18
V6 engine	22
Fan-to-fan clutch	
four-cylinder engine	7
V6 engine	18
Thermostat housing cover bolts	
All except VIN W	22
VIN W	15
Water pump-to-block bolts	
four-cylinder engine	17
V6 engine	22

1 General information

Engine cooling system

The Astro/Safari employs a pressurized engine cooling system with thermostatically controlled coolant circulation. An impeller type water pump mounted on the front of the block pumps coolant through the engine. The coolant flows around each cylinder and toward the rear of the engine. Cast-in coolant passages direct coolant around the in-

take and exhaust ports, near the spark plug areas and in close proximity to the exhaust valve guide inserts.

A wax pellet type thermostat is located at the front of the engine. During warm up, the closed thermostat prevents coolant from circulating through the radiator. When the engine reaches normal operating temperature, the thermostat opens and allows hot coolant to travel through the radiator, where it is cooled before returning to the engine.

The aluminum radiator is a crossflow type, with tanks on either side of the core.

The cooling system is sealed by a pressure type radiator cap. This raises the boiling point of the coolant and the higher boiling point of the coolant increases the cooling efficiency of the radiator.

If the system pressure exceeds the cap pressure relief value, the excess pressure in the system forces the spring-loaded valve inside the cap off its seat and allows the coolant to escape through the overflow tube into a coolant reservoir. When the system cools the excess coolant is automatically drawn from the reservoir back into the radiator.

The coolant reservoir does double duty as both the point at which fresh coolant is added to the cooling system to maintain the proper fluid level and as a holding tank for overheated coolant. This type of cooling system is known as a *closed* design because coolant that escapes past the pressure cap is saved and reused.

Heating system

The heating system consists of a blower fan and heater core located under the dashboard, the inlet and outlet hoses connecting the heater core to the engine cooling system and the heater/air conditioning control head on the dashboard. Hot engine coolant is circulated through the heater core at all times. When the heater mode is activated, a flap door opens to expose the heater box to the passenger compartment. A fan switch on the control head activates the blower motor, which forces air through the core, heating the air.

Air conditioning system

The air conditioning system consists of a condenser mounted in front of the radiator, an evaporator mounted under the dash, a compressor mounted on the engine, a filter-drier (accumulator) which contains a high pressure relief valve and the plumbing connecting all of the above.

A blower fan forces the warmer air of the passenger compartment through the evaporator core (sort of a radiator-in-reverse), transferring the heat from the air to the refrigerant. The liquid refrigerant boils off into low pressure vapor, taking the heat with it when it leaves the evaporator.

Caution: *If the vehicle is equipped with a Delco Loc II audio system (1992 and later models with a Compact Disc player), be sure the lock-out feature is turned off before performing any procedure that requires disconnecting the battery (refer to your owner's manual for further information on this system).*

2   Antifreeze — general information

Warning: *Don't allow antifreeze to come in contact with your skin or painted surfaces of the vehicle. Flush contacted areas immediately with plenty of water. Don't store new coolant or leave old coolant lying around where it's easily accessible to children and pets — they are attracted by its sweet taste. Ingestion of even a small amount can be fatal. Wipe up garage floor and drip pan coolant spills immediately. Keep antifreeze containers covered and repair leaks in your cooling system immediately. Antifreeze is flammable — be sure to read the precautions on the container.*

The cooling system should be filled with a water/ethylene glycol based antifreeze solution which will prevent freezing down to at least −20°F. It also provides protection against corrosion and increases the coolant boiling point.

The cooling system should be drained, flushed and refilled at least every other year (see Chapter 1). The use of antifreeze solutions for periods of longer than two years is likely to cause damage and encourage the formation of rust and scale in the system.

Before adding antifreeze to the system, check all hose connections. Antifreeze can leak through very minute openings.

The exact mixture of antifreeze to water which you should use depends on the relative weather conditions. The mixture should contain at least 50 percent antifreeze, but should never contain more than 70 percent antifreeze. Refer to the antifreeze ratio table on the coolant container.

3   Thermostat — check and replacement

Refer to illustrations 3.9a and 3.9b

Note: *Don't drive the vehicle without a thermostat! The computer will stay in open loop and emissions and fuel economy will suffer.*

Check

1   Before condemning the thermostat, check the coolant level, drivebelt tension and temperature gauge (or light) operation.
2   If the engine takes a long time to warm up, the thermostat is probably stuck open. Replace the thermostat.

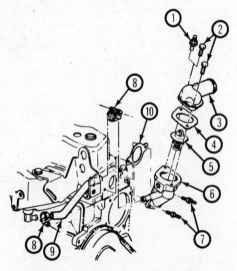

3.9a Four-cylinder engine thermostat and related components — exploded view

1 Stud	4 Gasket	7 Bolt
2 Bolt	5 Thermostat	8 Hose clamp
3 Thermostat	6 Thermostat	9 Hose
housing cover	housing	10 Gasket

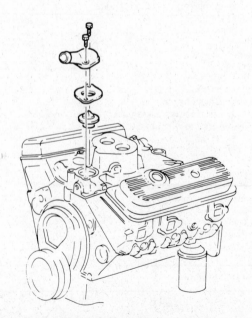

3.9b V6 engine thermostat and related components — exploded view

3   If the engine runs too hot, check the temperature of the upper radiator hose. If the hose isn't hot, the thermostat is probably stuck shut. Replace the thermostat.

4   If the upper radiator hose is hot, it means the coolant is circulating and the thermostat is open. Refer to the troublshooting section for the cause of overheating.

5   If an engine has been overheated, you may find damage such as leaking head gaskets, scuffed pistons and warped or cracked heads.

Replacement

Warning: *The engine must be completely cool before beginning this procedure!*

6   Disconnect the negative battery cable from the battery.

7   Drain about two quarts of coolant from the cooling system (Chapter 1).

8   Loosen the hose clamp and detach the upper radiator hose from the thermostat housing cover fitting.

9   Remove the bolts, then detach the thermostat housing cover and gasket **(see illustrations).** Note: *If the cover is difficult to remove, tap it gently with a soft-face hammer or a block of wood. Don't try to pry the cover loose or damage to the gasket sealing surfaces may result and leaks could develop.*.

10 Note how it's installed (which end is facing up), then lift out the thermostat.

11 Remove all traces of old gasket material and sealant from the housing and cover with a gasket scraper, then clean the gasket mating surfaces with lacquer thinner or acetone.

12   Apply a thin layer of RTV sealant to the gasket mating surfaces of the housing and cover, then install the new thermostat in the housing. Make sure the correct end faces up - the spring is normally directed down, into the housing/intake manifold.

13 Position a new gasket on the housing and make sure the bolt holes line up.

14 Carefully position the cover on the housing and install the bolts. Tighten them a little at a time to the specified torque — don't over-tighten them or the cover may be distorted!

15 Reattach the radiator hose to the cover fitting and tighten the hose clamp. Now may be a good time to check and replace all of the cooling system hoses and clamps (see Chapter 1).

16 Refer to Chapter 1 and refill the system, then run the engine and check carefully for leaks.

4   Engine cooling fan and clutch — check and replacement

Refer to illustrations 4.10a and 4.10b

Check

1   All V6 and some four-cylinder engines are equipped with thermo-statically controlled fan clutches.

2   Begin the clutch check with a lukewarm engine (start it when cold and let it run for two minutes only).

3   Remove the key from the ignition switch for safety purposes.

4   Turn the fan blades and note the resistance. There should be moderate resistance, depending on temperature.

5   Drive the vehicle until the engine is warmed up. Shut it off and remove the key.

6   Turn the fan blades and again note the resistance. There should be a noticeable increase in resistance.

7   If the fan clutch fails this check or is locked up solid, replacement is indicated. If excessive fluid is leaking from the hub or lateral play over 1/4-inch is noted, replace the fan clutch.

8   If any fan blades are bent, don't straighten them! The metal will be weakened and blades could fly off during engine operation. Replace the fan with a new one.

4.10a   The fan is attached to the clutch assembly or water pump hub with four nuts or bolts (arrow)

3

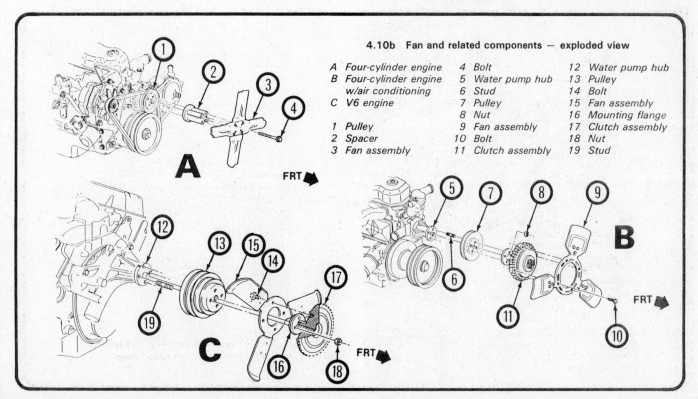

4.10b   Fan and related components — exploded view

A	Four-cylinder engine	4	Bolt	12	Water pump hub
B	Four-cylinder engine w/air conditioning	5	Water pump hub	13	Pulley
		6	Stud	14	Bolt
C	V6 engine	7	Pulley	15	Fan assembly
		8	Nut	16	Mounting flange
1	Pulley	9	Fan assembly	17	Clutch assembly
2	Spacer	10	Bolt	18	Nut
3	Fan assembly	11	Clutch assembly	19	Stud

Replacement

9   Remove the upper fan shroud.
10 Remove the fasteners holding the fan assembly to the water pump hub **(see illustrations)**.
11 Detach the fan and clutch assembly.
12 Unbolt the fan from the clutch (if equipped).
13 Installation is the reverse of removal.
14 Tighten all fasteners to the specified torque.

5   Radiator - removal and installation

Refer to illustrations 5.4a, 5.4b, 5.4c, 5.4d, 5.6 and 5.7
Warning 1: *The engine must be completely cool before beginning this procedure!*

Warning 2: *Later models may be equipped with airbags. Impact sensors for the airbag system are located in the area of the radiator support/grille. The airbag(s) could accidently deploy if these sensors are disturbed, so be extremely careful when working in this area. Air bag system components are also located in the steering wheel, steering column and base of the steering column, so be extremely careful in these areas and don't disturb any airbag system components or wiring. You could easily be injured if an airbag accidently deploys, and the airbag might not deploy correctly in a collision if any components or wiring in the system have been disturbed.*

1   Disconnect the negative battery cable from the battery, then refer to Chapter 9 and remove the brake master cylinder.
2   Drain the coolant from the radiator (Chapter 1).
3   Remove the coolant overflow hose from the fitting on the filler neck.

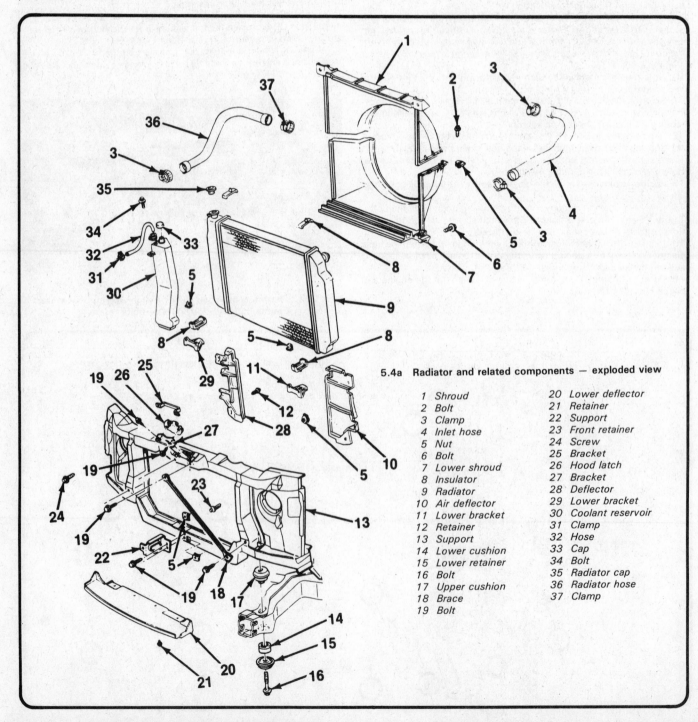

5.4a   Radiator and related components — exploded view

1 Shroud	20 Lower deflector
2 Bolt	21 Retainer
3 Clamp	22 Support
4 Inlet hose	23 Front retainer
5 Nut	24 Screw
6 Bolt	25 Bracket
7 Lower shroud	26 Hood latch
8 Insulator	27 Bracket
9 Radiator	28 Deflector
10 Air deflector	29 Lower bracket
11 Lower bracket	30 Coolant reservoir
12 Retainer	31 Clamp
13 Support	32 Hose
14 Lower cushion	33 Cap
15 Lower retainer	34 Bolt
16 Bolt	35 Radiator cap
17 Upper cushion	36 Radiator hose
18 Brace	37 Clamp
19 Bolt	

4   Remove the upper fan shroud. There are two bolts at the top hidden by the wiring harness and two bolts on each side at the bottom **(see illustrations)**.

5   Loosen the hose clamps and detach the radiator hoses from the radiator. If they're hard to remove, grasp each hose, at the fitting, with a large pair of water pump pliers and twist it to break the seal, then pull it off.

6   On vehicles with an automatic transmission, disconnect the transmission cooler lines from the right (passenger) side of the radiator **(see illustration)**. It may be easier if you remove the two bolts holding the lower fan shroud and pull it out of the way. Be careful not to twist the lines or damage the fittings – it's a good idea to use a flare nut wrench rather than an open end wrench. Plug the lines to prevent leakage and keep dirt out of the transmission.

7   Disconnect the engine oil cooler lines from the left (driver's) side of the radiator **(see illustration)**. Not all vehicles are equipped with an engine oil cooler.

8   Lift the radiator out, tilting it so the filler neck end is up.

9   Pull out the snap-fasteners to remove the air deflector panels for access to the engine.

10   Carefully check the radiator for signs of leakage, deterioration of the tubes and fins and rust and corrosion (particularly on the inside). Inspect the cooling fins for distortion and damage. In most cases, a radiator repair shop should handle any needed repairs. Radiator flushing is covered in Chapter 1.

11   Installation is the reverse of removal.

12   Add coolant, test run the engine and check for leaks.

13   Recheck the automatic transmission fluid and oil levels.

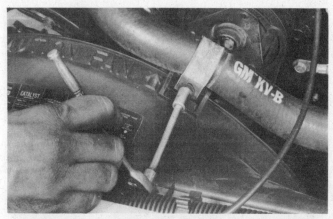

5.4b   Unbolt the radiator hose bracket prior to removing the upper fan shroud

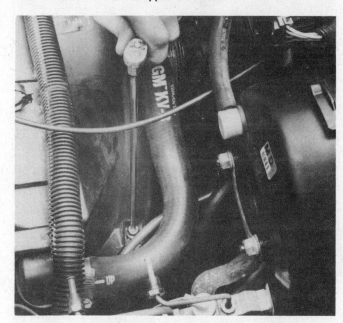

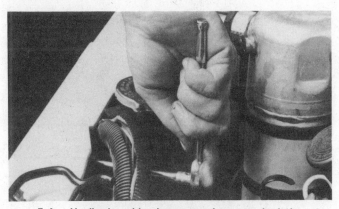

5.4c   Unclip the wiring harness and remove the bolts above each end of the radiator, . . .

5.4d   . . . then use a long extension to reach the two lower mounting bolts on each side of the shroud

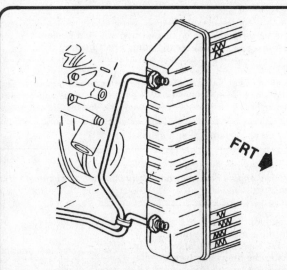

5.6   The automatic transmission cooler lines are attached to the right (passenger) side of the radiator

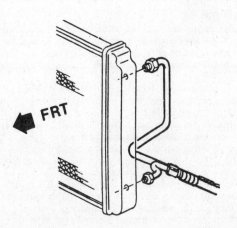

5.7   The optional engine oil cooler lines are attached to the left (driver's) side of the radiator

3

6.1   Coolant reservoir mounting details — note that the windshield washer reservoir must be raised first

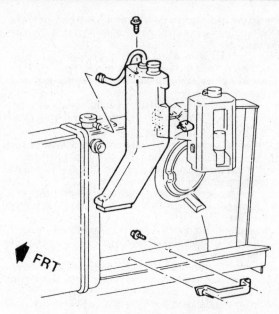

6.2   Make sure the lower end of the reservoir fits into the U-shaped bracket before installing the mounting bolt

6   Coolant reservoir — removal and installation

Refer to illustrations 6.1 and 6.2

Warning: *The engine must be completely cool before beginning this procedure!*

1   Detach the overflow hose from the reservoir **(see illustration)**.

2   Remove the mounting bolt and lift up on the reservoir to separate it from the lug on the windshield washer fluid reservoir **(see illustration)**. The reservoir can't be lifted all the way out yet because the air conditioning system line is in the way.

3   Remove the windshield washer reservoir mounting bolts, then lift the reservoir up to allow clearance for removal of the coolant reservoir. Don't detach any wires or hoses from the windshield washer reservoir.

4   Installation is the reverse of removal. Be sure the lower end of the coolant reservoir slips into the U-shaped bracket **(see illustration 6.2)**.

7   Water pump — check

Refer to illustration 7.3

1   Water pump failure can cause overheating of and serious damage to the engine. There are three ways to check the operation of the water pump while it's installed on the engine. If any one of the three following quick checks indicates water pump failure, it should be replaced immediately.

2   Start the engine and warm it up to normal operating temperature. Squeeze the upper radiator hose. If the water pump is working properly, a pressure surge should be felt as the hose is released.

3   A seal protects the water pump impeller shaft bearing from contamination by engine coolant. If the seal fails, weep holes in the top and bottom of the water pump snout **(see illustration)** will leak coolant under the vehicle. If the weep hole is leaking, shaft bearing failure will follow. Replace the water pump immediately.

4   Besides contamination by coolant after a seal failure, the water pump impeller shaft bearing can also be prematurely worn out by an improperly tensioned drivebelt. When the bearing wears out, it emits a high pitched squealing sound. If noise is coming from the water pump during engine operation, the shaft bearing has failed. Replace the water pump immediately.

5   To identify excessive bearing wear before the bearing actually fails, grasp the water pump pulley and try to force it up-and-down or from

7.3   The water pump weep hole (arrow) will drip coolant when the mechanical seal for the pump shaft bearing fails

side-to-side. If the pulley can be moved either horizontally or vertically, the bearing is nearing the end of its service life. Replace the water pump.

8   Water pump — removal and installation

Refer to illustrations 8.8, 8.9a and 8.9b

Warning: *The engine must be completely cool before beginning this procedure.*

Removal

1   Disconnect the negative battery cable from the battery.

2   Drain the coolant (Chapter 1).

3   Remove the upper fan shroud (Section 5).

4   Remove the drivebelts (see Chapter 1).

5   Remove the fan (and fan clutch — if equipped) as outlined in Section 4.

6   Pull the water pump pulley off the hub.

7   Loosen the hose clamps and detach the lower radiator hose and

8.8   Several brackets must be removed before the water pump can be detached (V6 engine shown)

8.9a   V6 engine water pump mounting bolt locations (arrows)

3

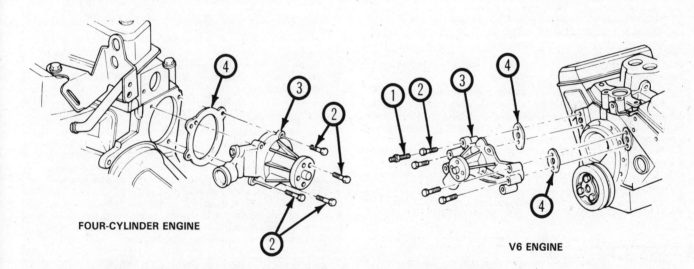

FOUR-CYLINDER ENGINE

V6 ENGINE

8.9b   Water pump and related components — exploded view (be sure to use a new gasket when installing the pump)

1. *Stud*
2. *Bolt*
3. *Water pump*
4. *Gasket*

heater hose from the water pump fittings. If they're hard to remove, grasp each hose, at the fitting, with a large pair of water pump pliers and twist it to break the seal, then pull it off.

8   Remove the alternator, air pump, power steering pump and A/C compressor brackets, as needed **(see illustration)**.

9   Remove the bolts and detach the pump from the engine **(see illustrations)**.

Installation

10   Using a gasket scraper, remove all traces of old gasket material and sealant from the engine block. Clean the mounting surface(s) with lacquer thinner or acetone.

11   When installing the new pump, use a new gasket (the V6 engine requires two gaskets). Coat both sides of the gasket(s) with a thin layer of RTV sealant.

12   Apply a thin coat of sealant (GM no. 1052080 or equivalent) to the mounting bolts.

13   Install the bolts and tighten them to the specified torque in a criss-cross pattern. Don't overtighten them or the pump may be distorted.

14   Reinstall all parts removed for access to the pump.

15   Refill the cooling system, run the engine and check for leaks.

9   Coolant temperature sending unit — check and replacement

Refer to illustration 9.1

Temperature warning light system check

1   If the light doesn't come on when the ignition switch is turned on, check the bulb. If the light stays on even with the engine cold, unplug

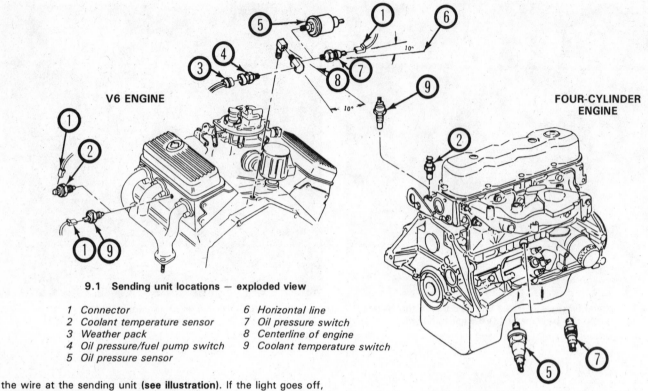

9.1 Sending unit locations — exploded view

1 Connector
2 Coolant temperature sensor
3 Weather pack
4 Oil pressure/fuel pump switch
5 Oil pressure sensor
6 Horizontal line
7 Oil pressure switch
8 Centerline of engine
9 Coolant temperature switch

the wire at the sending unit (**see illustration**). If the light goes off, replace the sending unit. If the light stays on, the wire is grounded somewhere in the harness.

Temperature gauge system check

2   If the gauge is inoperative, check the fuse (Chapter 12).
3   If the fuse is OK, unplug the wire connected to the sending unit and ground it with a jumper wire. Turn on the ignition switch. The gauge should now register at maximum. If it does, replace the sending unit. If it's still inoperative, the gauge or wiring may be faulty.

Sending unit replacement

4   Allow the engine to cool completely.
5   Remove the engine cover (Chapter 11).
6   Unplug the wire connected to the sending unit.
7   Unscrew the sending unit and quickly install the new unit to prevent loss of coolant.
8   Connect the wire and install the engine cover.

10   Heater and air conditioner blower motor — removal and installation

Refer to illustrations 10.3 and 10.4

1   Disconnect the negative battery cable from the battery.
2   Remove the windshield washer reservoir (see Section 6, since the coolant reservoir is attached to it, and note that the windshield washer reservoir has a hose and wire harness that must be detached).
3   Unplug the wires from the blower motor (**see illustration**).
4   Remove the mounting screws and pull out the fan assembly. Due to limited room, it's necessary to remove the fan retaining nut (**see illustration**), pull the fan off and place it back in the blower housing. Now the fan motor can be lifted out of the engine compartment.
5   Installation is the reverse of removal.

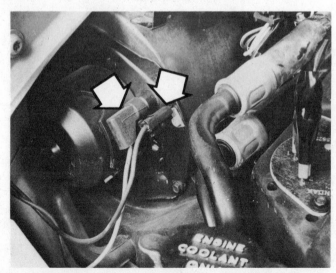

10.3   Air conditioner/heater blower motor wire harness connectors (arrows)

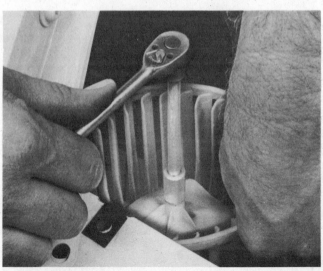

10.4   Due to limited space, the fan must be removed from the motor before the motor can be lifted out

11   Heater core — removal and installation

Refer to illustrations 11.5, 11.6 and 11.11

Warning: *The engine must be completely cool before beginning this procedure!*

Main heater

1   Disconnect the negative battery cable from the battery.
2   Drain the coolant (Chapter 1).
3   Remove the coolant reservoir (Section 6).
4   Remove the windshield washer fluid reservoir mounting bolts and move it aside.
5   Loosen the clamps and detach the heater hoses from the core tubes. Plug the core tubes **(see illustration)**.
6   Working in the passenger compartment, under the dash, remove the heater core cover screws **(see illustration)**.

11.5   The heater hoses are attached to the core tubes with hose clamps — remove the top hose first, followed by the bottom one

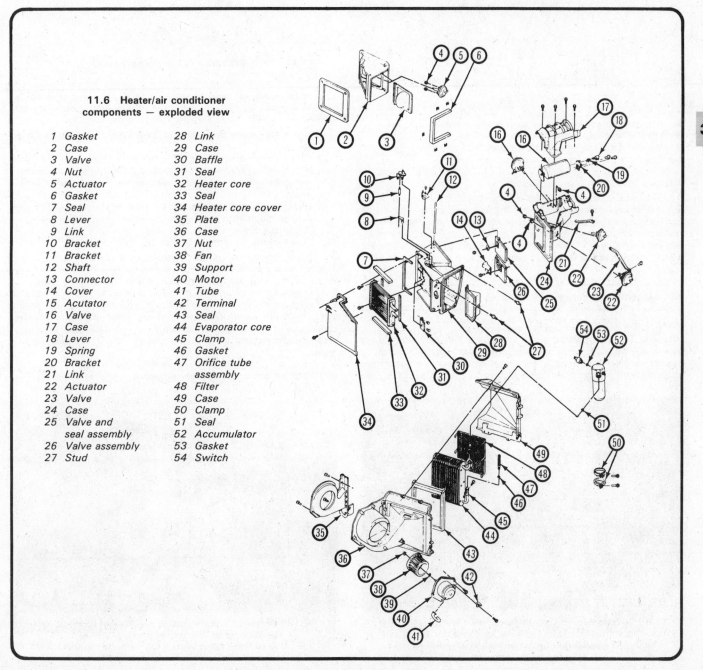

11.6   Heater/air conditioner components — exploded view

1	Gasket	28	Link
2	Case	29	Case
3	Valve	30	Baffle
4	Nut	31	Seal
5	Actuator	32	Heater core
6	Gasket	33	Seal
7	Seal	34	Heater core cover
8	Lever	35	Plate
9	Link	36	Case
10	Bracket	37	Nut
11	Bracket	38	Fan
12	Shaft	39	Support
13	Connector	40	Motor
14	Cover	41	Tube
15	Acutator	42	Terminal
16	Valve	43	Seal
17	Case	44	Evaporator core
18	Lever	45	Clamp
19	Spring	46	Gasket
20	Bracket	47	Orifice tube assembly
21	Link	48	Filter
22	Actuator	49	Case
23	Valve	50	Clamp
24	Case	51	Seal
25	Valve and seal assembly	52	Accumulator
26	Valve assembly	53	Gasket
27	Stud	54	Switch

3

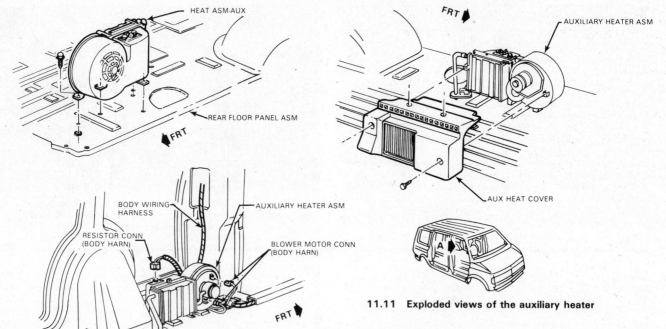

7   Remove the core mounting screws at the rear of the core.
8   Lift the core out of the housing.
9   Installation is the reverse of removal.
10   Refill the cooling system and check for leaks.

Auxiliary heater

11   The optional auxiliary heater is floor mounted just ahead of the left rear wheel housing **(see illustration)**. The 3-speed fan and engine compartment mounted water valve are controlled from a dash mounted switch.
12   Follow Steps 1, 2, 5 and 6 above to remove the heater core.
13   Installation is the reverse of removal.

---

12   Air conditioning system — check and maintenance

Refer to illustrations 12.9 and 12.12
Warning: *The air conditioning system is under high pressure. Do not loosen any hose fittings or remove any components until after the system has been discharged by a dealer service department, automotive air conditioning shop or service station.*

11.11   Exploded views of the auxiliary heater

1   The following maintenance steps should be performed on a regular basis to ensure that the air conditioner continues to operate at peak efficiency.
   a) Check the tension of the drivebelt and adjust it if necessary (Chapter 1).
   b) Check the condition of the hoses. Look for cracks, hardening and deterioration. **Warning:** *Don't replace A/C hoses until the system has been discharged by a dealer service department or repair shop.*
   c) Check the fins of the condenser for leaves, bugs and any other foreign material. A soft brush and compressed air can be used to remove them.
   d) Maintain the correct refrigerant charge.

2   The system should be run for about 10 minutes at least once a month. This is particularly important during the winter months because long term non-use can cause hardening and failure of the seals.
3   Because of the complexity of the air conditioning system and the special equipment necessary to service it, troubleshooting and repairs should be done by a professional mechanic. The most common cause of poor cooling is low refrigerant charge. If a noticeable drop in system cooling ability occurs, the following procedure will help pinpoint the cause.
4   Warm the engine to normal operating temperature.
5   The hood and doors should be open.

12.9   To determine if the refrigerant level is adequate, feel the evaporator inlet pipe with one hand and the surface of the accumulator (arrows) with the other and note the temperature of each

12.12   A typical aftermarket air conditioner recharge kit hooked up to the Schrader valve (arrow)

13.3 Use a back-up wrench when loosening/tightening the A/C line fittings (accumulator shown)

13.4 The accumulator is held in place with two brackets — loosen the bolts to withdraw it

6 Operate the A/C mode control.
7 Move the temperature selector lever to the coolest position.
8 Turn the fan control to the High position.
9 With the compressor engaged, feel the evaporator inlet pipe between the orifice and the evaporator. Put your other hand on the surface of the accumulator can (see illustration).
10 If both surfaces feel about the same temperature and if both feel a little cooler than the surrounding air, the refrigerant level is probably okay. The problem is elsewhere.
11 If the inlet pipe has frost accumulation or feels cooler than the accumulator surface, the refrigerant charge is low. Add refrigerant as follows.
12 Buy an automotive air conditioner recharge kit and hook it up to the evaporator inlet pipe fitting in accordance with the kit manufacturer's instructions (see illustration). Add refrigerant until both the accumulator surface and the evaporator inlet pipe feel about the same temperature. Allow stabilization time between each addition.
13 Add one additional can of refrigerant.

13 Air conditioner accumulator — removal and installation

Refer to illustrations 13.3 and 13.4
Warning: The air conditioning system is under high pressure. Do not loosen any hose fittings or remove any components until after the system has been discharged by a dealer service department, automotive air conditioning shop or service station. After the system has been discharged, residual pressure may still remain — be sure to wear eye protection when loosening line fittings!
1 Have the system discharged.

2 Disconnect the negative battery cable from the battery.
3 Disconnect the accumulator inlet and outlet lines (see illustration). Immediately cap the open lines.
4 Loosen the bolts and lift the accumulator out of the bracket (see illustration). Pour the oil out of the accumulator into a measuring cup, noting the amount.
5 Pour an equal amount of fresh 525 viscosity refrigerant oil into the new accumulator, plus an additional two ounces.
6 Use new O-rings lubricated with refrigerant oil during installation.
7 Installation is the reverse of removal.
8 Have the system evacuated and recharged by an air conditioning shop or service station.

14 Air conditioner compressor — removal and installation

Refer to illustrations 14.5, 14.6, 14.7a, 14.7b, 14.7c and 14.7d
Warning: The air conditioning system is under high pressure. Do not loosen any hose fittings or remove any components until after the system has been discharged by a dealer service department, automotive air conditioning shop or service station. After the system has been discharged, residual pressure may still remain — be sure to wear eye protection when loosening line fittings!
1 Have the system discharged.
2 Disconnect the negative battery cable from the battery.
3 Remove the engine cover (Chapter 11).
4 Remove the drivebelt (Chapter 1).
5 Detach the wire harness from the compressor (see illustration).
6 Unbolt the refrigerant hose manifold from the compressor and cap all the fittings (see illustration).

14.5 Detach the wire harness and ground wire (arrows) before removing the compressor drivebelt and mounting bolts (arrows)

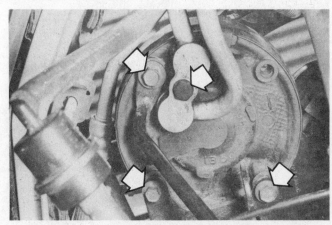

14.6 Rear view of the compressor (V6 engine) showing the manifold bolt, brace bolt and mounting bolts (arrows)

7　Unbolt the compressor and remove it from the vehicle (**see illustrations**).

8　Installation is the reverse of removal. Refer to Chapter 1 and adjust the drivebelt.

9　Have the system evacuated and recharged by an air conditioning shop or service station.

15　Air conditioner condenser - removal and installation

Refer to illustrations 15.4, 15.5a and 15.5b

Warning 1: *The air conditioning system is under high pressure. Do not loosen any hose fittings or remove any components until after the sys-* tem has been discharged by a dealer service department, automotive air conditioning shop or service station. After the system has been discharged, residual pressure may still remain - be sure to wear eye protection when loosening line fittings!

Warning 2: *Later models may be equipped with airbags. Impact sensors for the airbag system are located in the area of the radiator support/grille. The airbag(s) could accidently deploy if these sensors are disturbed, so be extremely careful when working in this area. Air bag system components are also located in the steering wheel, steering column and base of the steering column, so be extremely careful in these areas and don't disturb any airbag system components or wiring. You could easily be injured if an airbag accidently deploys, and the airbag might not deploy correctly in a collision if any components or wiring in the system have been disturbed.*

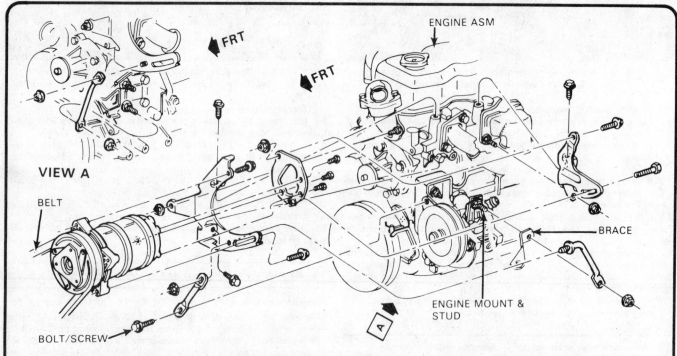

14.7a　Air conditioner compressor and related components — exploded view (1985 and 1986 four-cylinder engine)

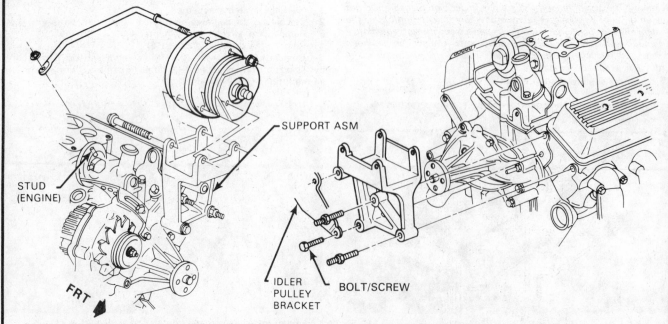

14.7b　Air conditioner compressor and related components — exploded view (1985 and 1986 V6 engine)

1   Have the system discharged.
2   Disconnect the negative battery cable from the battery.
3   Remove the grille as described in Chapter 11.
4   Remove the radiator tie bar support and horns **(see illustration)**.
5   Disconnect the refrigerant lines from the condenser (one fitting is located just in front of and slightly below the brake master cylinder and the other is located in front of the accumulator on the passenger side of the vehicle) **(see illustrations)**. Use a back-up wrench to prevent twisting the tubing.

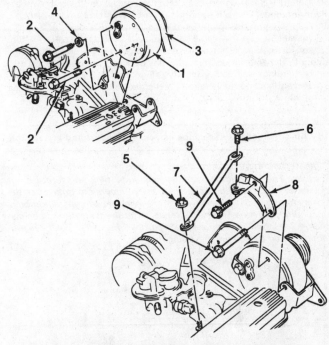

14.7d   Air conditioner compressor and related components - exploded view (typical 1987 and later V6 engine)

1 *Compressor*	4 *Washer*	7 *Brace*
2 *Bolts*	5 *Nut*	8 *Bracket*
3 *Drivebelt*	6 *Bolts*	9 *Bolts*

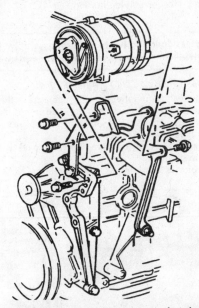

14.7c   Air conditioner compressor mounting details (1987-on four-cylinder engine)

15.4   Remove the radiator support bolts (arrows) to gain access to the condensor

15.5a   Disconnect the refrigerant lines (this is the left one) before lifting out the condensor

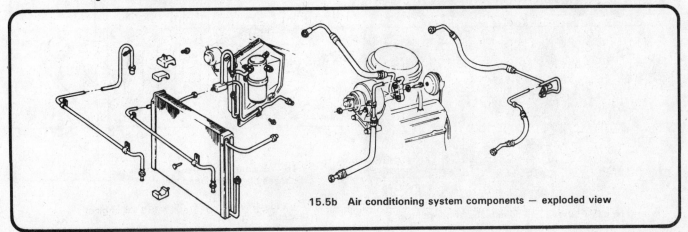

15.5b   Air conditioning system components — exploded view

6   Carefully lift the condensor out of the vehicle. Don't lose the rubber mounting pads. Store it upright so the oil won't run out.
7   Cap all open fittings to keep dirt and moisture out.
8   Installation is the reverse of removal. If you're replacing the condensor, drain the oil out of it into a measuring cup and record the amount. The amount drained, plus one ounce, must be replaced during recharging. Use 525 viscosity refrigerant oil.
9   Have the system evacuated, recharged and leak tested by an air conditioning shop or service station.

16   Air conditioner orifice tube screen — removal and installation

Refer to illustration 16.2

Warning: *The air conditioning system is under high pressure. Do not loosen any hose fittings or remove any components until after the system has been discharged by a dealer service department, automotive air conditioning shop or service station. After the system has been discharged, residual pressure may still remain — be sure to wear eye protection when loosening line fittings!*

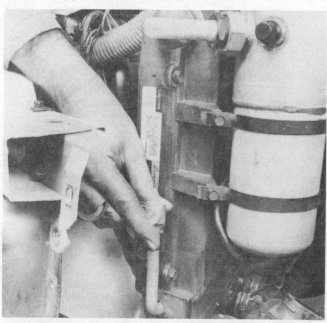

16.2   The orifice tube screen is located inside this tube (which is taped over to seal out dirt) (the radiator has been removed for clarity)

17.4a   The cable (arrow) can be detached after removing the press on retainer from the arm

Note: *The orifice tube screen is a filtering device that may clog and cause insufficient cooling. It can be removed and cleaned or replaced if necessary.*

1   Have the system discharged.
2   Disconnect the refrigerant line at the evaporator inlet and remove the orifice tube screen from the inlet tube **(see illustration)**.
3   Installation is the reverse of removal. Be sure to install the end marked ''shorter screen end'' first.
4   Have the system evacuated, recharged and leak tested by an air conditioning shop or service station.

17   Air conditioner and heater control assembly — removal and installation

Refer to illustrations 17.3, 17.4a and 17.4b

1   Disconnect the negative battery cable from the battery.
2   Remove the trim ring around the instrument cluster.
3   Remove the screws and pull the control assembly out of the dashboard **(see illustration)**.
4   Disconnect the control cable, vacuum hoses and wire harnesses **(see illustrations)**.
5   Installation is the reverse of removal.

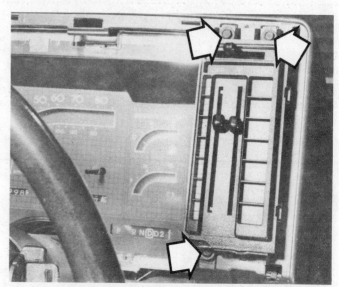

17.3   Air conditioner/heater control mounting screws (arrows)

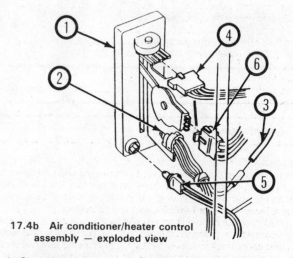

17.4b   Air conditioner/heater control assembly — exploded view

1 Control assembly	4 Blower switch connector
2 Vacuum harness	5 Light
3 Vacuum hose	6 Mode selector wiring harness

Chapter 4 Fuel and exhaust systems

Contents

Specifications

General

Fuel injection system pressure	
TBI..	9 to 13 psi
CPI..	55 to 61 psi
Fuel pump flow rate (TBI only).........................	1/2-pint or more in 15 seconds
Non-adjustable TPS output check	
Model 300 and 700................................	less than 1.25 volt
Model 220..	less than 1.00 volt
IAC valve pintle dimension	
Model 300 and 220................................	less than 1-1/8 in
Model 700..	less than 1-1/10 in
Minimum idle speed adjustment (fuel injected models)	
Model 700..	650 rpm ±25 rpm
Model 220	
manual transmission	600 to 650 rpm
automatic transmission	500 to 550 rpm

Torque specifications

	Ft-lbs (unless otherwise specified)
CPI air intake plenum fasteners......................	88 in-lbs
Carburetor mounting bolts	
long bolts..	7
short bolts	11
Model 300 TBI assembly	
TBI mounting bolts...............................	10 to 15
TBI mounting stud................................	3 to 6
TBI mounting nut.................................	10 to 15
Model 700 TBI mounting studs	12
Model 220 TBI assembly	
IAC valve	13
fuel inlet nut...................................	30
fuel outlet nut..................................	21
mounting bolts	12

1 General information

Fuel system

The fuel system on carbureted vehicles consists of a fuel tank, mechanical fuel pump, fuel feed, return and vapor lines between the tank and the carburetor, an in-line fuel filter, air cleaner assembly and either a Model E4ME or E4MED Quadrajet carburetor.

Fuel systems on fuel injected vehicles include a fuel tank, electrically operated fuel pump inside the tank, fuel pump relay, fuel feed, return and vapor lines between the tank and the engine, an in-line fuel filter, air cleaner assembly and either a Central Port Injection (CPI) system)(some 1992 and later models) or a Model 300 or 700 (single injector) or 220 (twin injector) Throttle Body Injection (TBI) system. The Model 300 TBI system is used on all earlier 4-cylinder engines and the Model 700 system is used on later 4-cylinder engines. The Model 220 is used on V6 engines.

Exhaust system

The exhaust system, which is similar for both 4-cylinder and V6 powered vehicles, includes an exhaust manifold fitted with an oxygen sensor, the exhaust pipe itself, a catalytic converter and a muffler. The exhaust system is supported by several rubber mountings, which permit some movement of the exhaust system but do not permit transfer of noise and vibration into the passenger compartment.

The catalytic converter is an emission control device added to the exhaust system to reduce hydrocarbon and carbon monoxide pollutants from the exhaust gas stream.

Caution: *If the vehicle is equipped with a Delco Loc II audio system*

2.12 On CPI models, disconnect the electrical connector from the fuel pump relay (arrow)

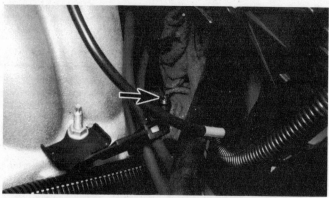

2.13 On CPI models, use a screwdriver to bleed the remaining fuel out of the fuel line fitting - be sure to absorb the fuel with a shop towel

(1992 and later models with a Compact Disc player), be sure the lockout feature is turned off before performing any procedure that requires disconnecting the battery (refer to your owner's manual for further information on this system).

2   Fuel pressure relief procedure

1   Before servicing any component on a fuel injected vehicle it is necessary to relieve the fuel pressure to minimize the risk of fire or personal injury.

Model 300 TBI (earlier 4-cylinder engine)

2   Remove the fuse marked Fuel Pump from the fuse block in the passenger compartment.
3   Crank the engine over. It will start and run until the fuel supply remaining in the fuel lines is depleted.
4   After the engine stops, engage the starter again for another three seconds to assure that any remaining pressure is dissipated.
5   Turn the ignition to Off.
6   Replace the fuel pump fuse.

Model 700 TBI (later 4-cylinder engines)

7   Place the transmission in Park (automatic) or Neutral (manual), set the parking brake and block the drive wheels.
8   Detach the three terminal electrical connector at the fuel tank.
9   Start the engine and allow it to run until it stops for lack of fuel.
10   Engage the starter for three seconds to dissipate fuel pressure in lines.

Model 220 TBI (All except 1992 and later VIN W V6 engines)

11   The Model 220 TBI contains a constant bleed feature in the pressure regulator that relieves pressure. No special procedure is required to relieve the fuel pressure.

Central Port Injection (CPI) – 1992 and later VIN W V6 engines
Refer to illustrations 2.12 and 2.13
Warning: *Gasoline is extremely flammable, so take extra precautions when you work on any part of the fuel system. Don't smoke or allow open flames or bare light bulbs near the work area, and don't work in a garage where a natural gas-type appliance (such as a water heater or clothes dryer) with a pilot light is present. If you spill any fuel on your skin, rinse it off immediately with soap and water. When you perform any kind of work on the fuel system, wear safety glasses and have a Class B type fire extinguisher on hand.*
12   CPI systems are equipped with a special fitting built into the fuel line at the rear of the air intake plenum. Connect a special fuel pressure gauge (J-34730-1) to the threaded fitting adapter (J-34730-250). This tool is available at a dealer parts department. The gauge assembly is equipped with a bleed-off valve. If the tool is not available, disconnect the fuel pump relay and crank the engine over **(see illustration)**.

13   Place a shop towel around the fitting and bleed the remaining fuel out of the fuel line by placing the tip of a screwdriver on the valve **(see illustration)**. Be careful not to let the fuel spray into the engine compartment.

3   Fuel system – check

Fuel pump flow check (TBI models only)
1   If your vehicle is equipped with a 4-cylinder engine, relieve the system fuel pressure (see Section 2).
2   Detach the fuel feed line from the TBI unit and connect a hose to it, then put the end of the hose in a graduated container.
3   Apply battery voltage to fuel pump test terminal G of the ALDL. If necessary, refer to Chapter 6 for the location of the ALDL.
4   The fuel pump should supply the minimum specified amount of fuel in the specified time period.
5   If the flow is below the minimum required, inspect the fuel lines and fittings (see Section 4) for a restriction. If there is no restriction, check the fuel pump pressure.

Fuel pump pressure check (TBI models only)
6   Turn the engine off.
7   If your vehicle is equipped with a 4-cylinder engine, relieve the fuel system pressure (see Section 2).
8   Remove the air cleaner (see Section 8) and plug the THERMAC vacuum port on the TBI unit.
9   Install a Kent-Moore J-29548-A, or equivalent, fuel pressure gauge.
10   Start the engine and note the fuel pressure. Compare your reading to the specified fuel pressure.
11   If the pressure is not within the specified range, see *Fuel system diagnosis.*
12   If the pressure is within the specified range, relieve the system fuel pressure (see Section 2), remove the fuel pressure gauge, attach the fuel line to the TBI and install the air cleaner. Don't forget to remove the plug from the THERMAC vacuum port.

Fuel system diagnosis
Four-cylinder engine
Refer to illustrations 3.13a, 3.13b and 3.13c
13   Diagnostic charts 3.13a, 3.13b and 3.13c **(see illustrations)** diagram the testing procedures for the throttle body injection system used on 4-cylinder engines.
V6 engines
Refer to illustrations 3.14a and 3.14b
14   Diagnostic charts 3.14a and 3.14b (see illustrations) diagram the testing procedures for the throttle body injection system used on most V6 engines.
15   Fuel system diagnosis on the Central Port Injection (CPI) system used on VIN W V6 engines requires special tools and expertise that place it outside the scope of the home mechanic. Take the vehicle to a dealer service department or other qualified shop.

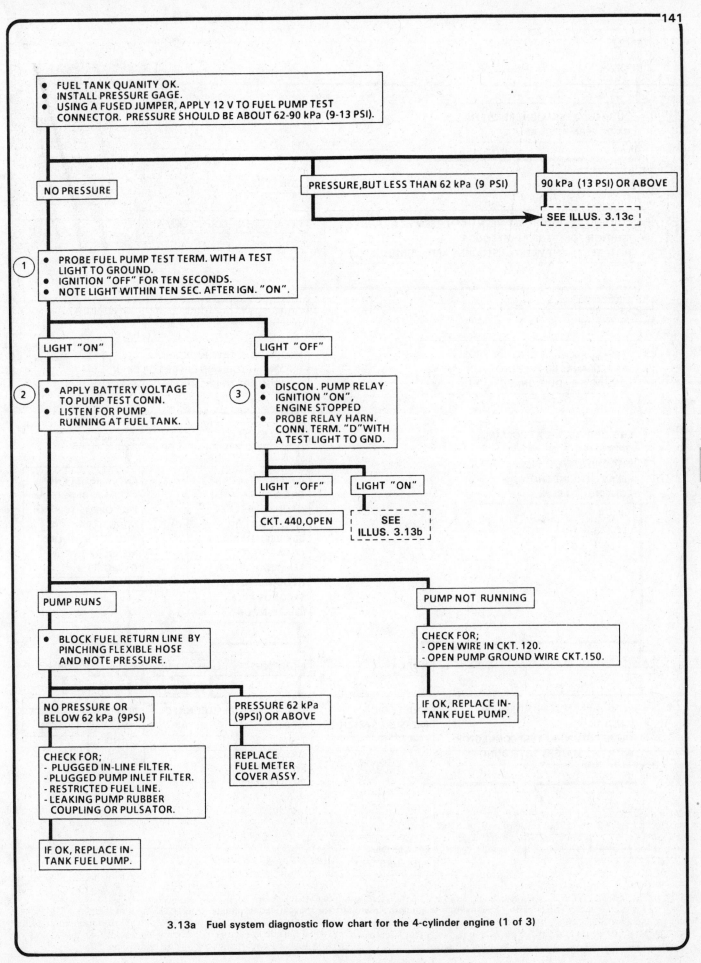

3.13a   Fuel system diagnostic flow chart for the 4-cylinder engine (1 of 3)

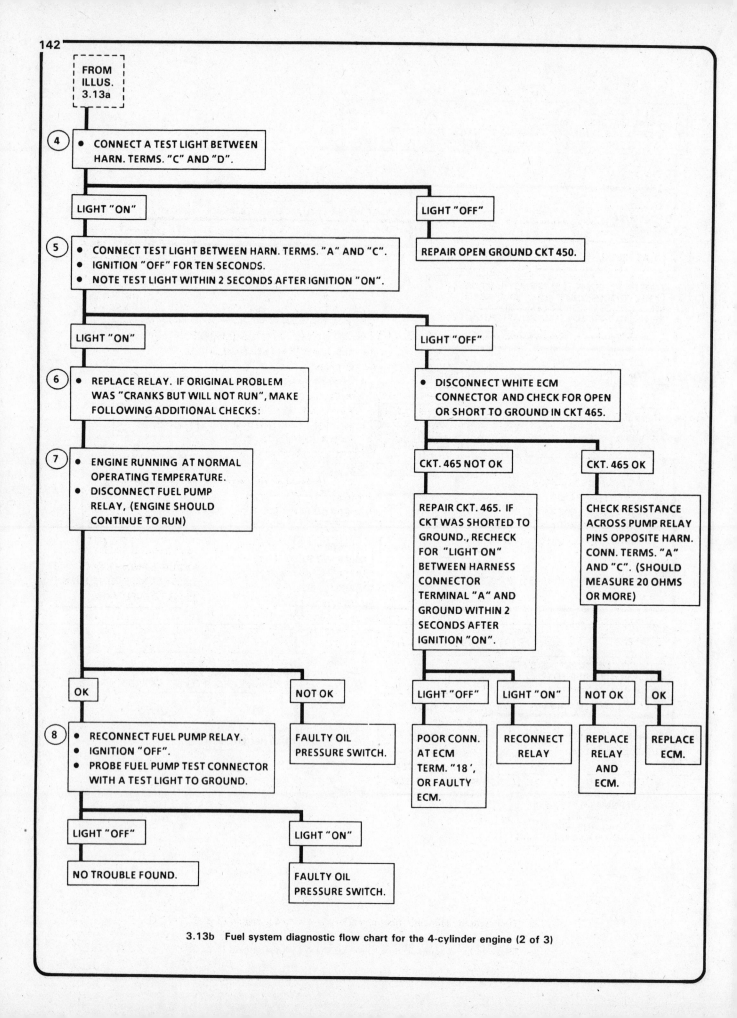

3.13b Fuel system diagnostic flow chart for the 4-cylinder engine (2 of 3)

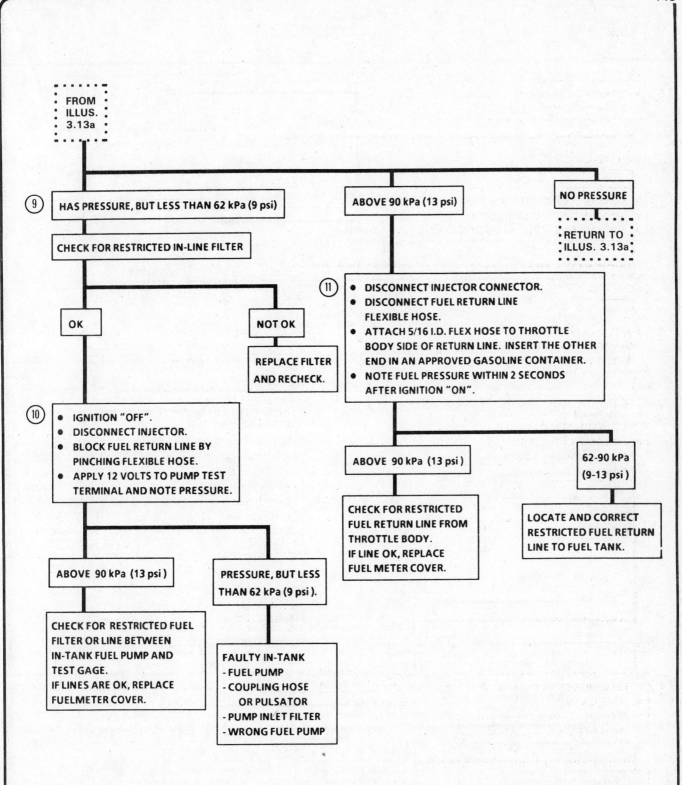

3.13c Fuel system diagnostic flow chart for the 4-cylinder engine (3 of 3)

4

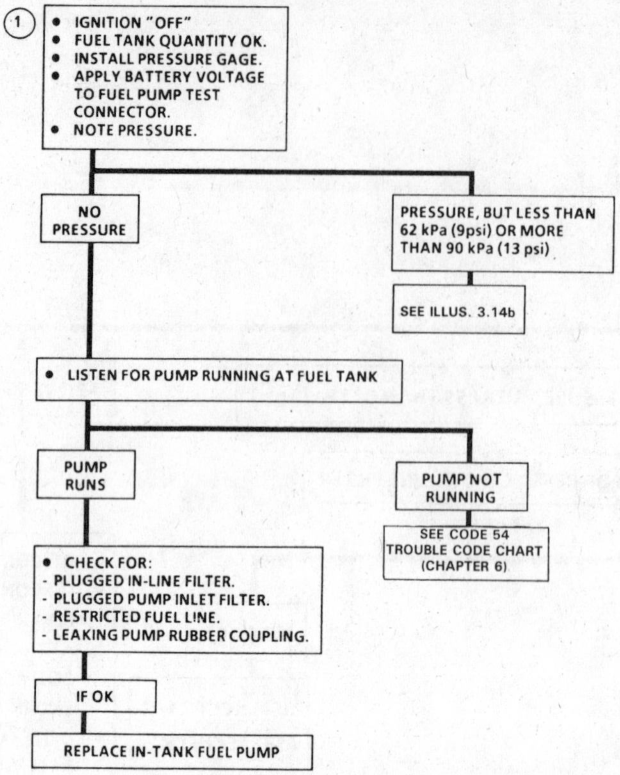

① • IGNITION "OFF"
   • FUEL TANK QUANTITY OK.
   • INSTALL PRESSURE GAGE.
   • APPLY BATTERY VOLTAGE
     TO FUEL PUMP TEST
     CONNECTOR.
   • NOTE PRESSURE.

NO PRESSURE

PRESSURE, BUT LESS THAN 62 kPa (9psi) OR MORE THAN 90 kPa (13 psi)

SEE ILLUS. 3.14b

• LISTEN FOR PUMP RUNNING AT FUEL TANK

PUMP RUNS

PUMP NOT RUNNING

SEE CODE 54 TROUBLE CODE CHART (CHAPTER 6)

• CHECK FOR:
  - PLUGGED IN-LINE FILTER.
  - PLUGGED PUMP INLET FILTER.
  - RESTRICTED FUEL LINE.
  - LEAKING PUMP RUBBER COUPLING.

IF OK

REPLACE IN-TANK FUEL PUMP

3.14a   Fuel system diagnostic flow chart for the V6 engine with
TBI fuel injection

FROM ILLUS. 3.14a

FUEL PRESSURE IS BELOW 62 kPa (9psi) OR ABOVE 89 kPa (13 psi).

① HAS PRESSURE, BUT LESS THAN 62 kPa (9 PSI)

ABOVE 89 kPa (13 PSI)

CHECK FOR RESTRICTED IN-LINE FILTER

③ • DISCONNECT INJECTOR CONNECTOR.
   • DISCONNECT FUEL RETURN LINE
     FLEXIBLE HOSE.
   • ATTACH 5/16 I.D. FLEX HOSE TO THROTTLE
     BODY SIDE OF RETURN LINE. INSERT THE OTHER
     END IN AN APPROVED GASOLENE CONTAINER.
   • NOTE FUEL PRESSURE WITHIN 2 SECONDS
     AFTER IGNITION "ON".

OK

NOT OK

② • IGNITION "OFF".
   • DISCONNECT INJECTOR.
   • BLOCK FUEL REUURN LINE BY
     PINCHING FLEXIBLE HOSE.
   • APPLY 12 VOLTS TO FUEL PUMP TEST
     CONNECTOR AND NOTE PRESSURE.

REPLACE FILTER AND RECHECK.

ABOVE 89 KPa (13 PSI)

62-89 kPa (9-13 PSI)

ABOVE 89 kPa (13 PSI)

PRESSURE, BUT LESS THAN 62 kPa (9 PSI)

CHECK FOR RESTRICTED FUEL RETURN LINE FROM THROTTLE BODY.

LOCATE AND CORRECT RESTRICTED FUEL RETURN LINE TO FUEL TANK.

CHECK FOR RESTRICTED FUEL FILTER OR LINE BETWEEN IN-TANK FUEL PUMP AND TEST GAGE.

FAULTY IN-TANK
- FUEL PUMP
- COUPLING HOSE
- PUMP INLET FILTER
- WRONG FUEL PUMP

IF LINE OK, REPLACE FUEL METER COVER.

IF LINES ARE OK, REPLACE FUEL METER COVER.

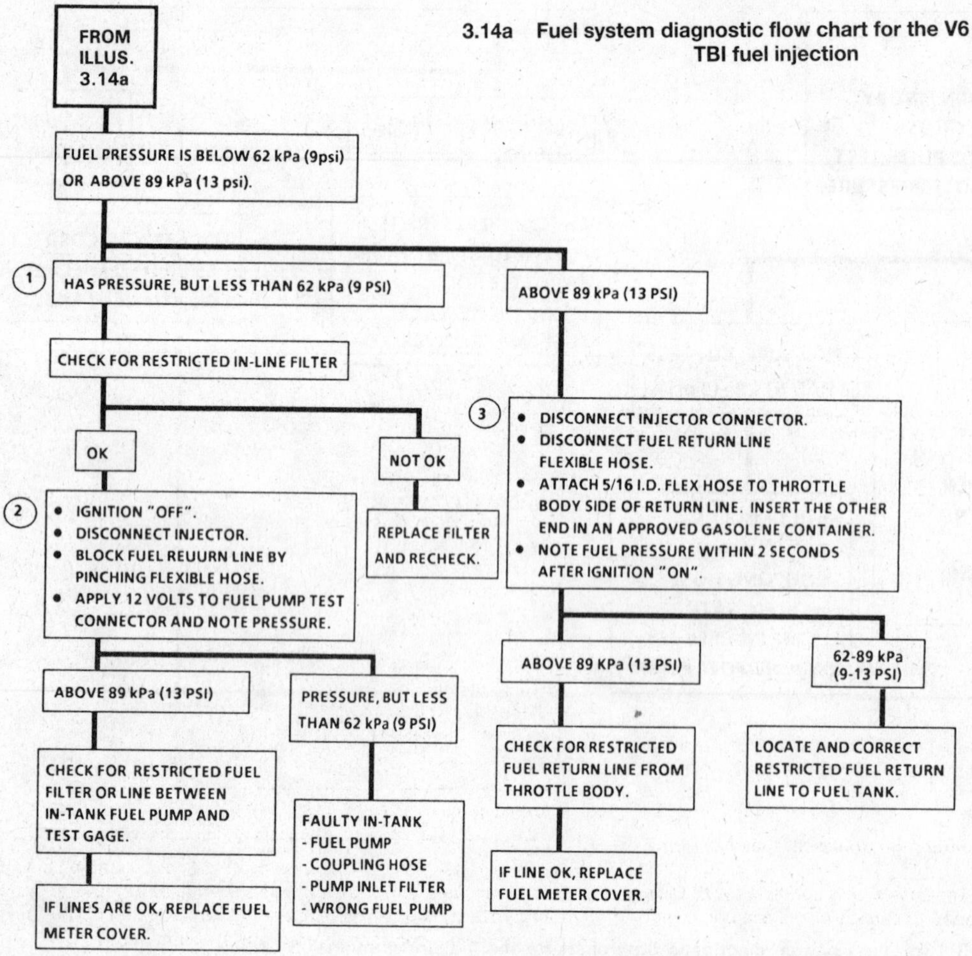

3.14b   Fuel system diagnostic flow chart for the V6 engine with
TBI fuel injection (continued)

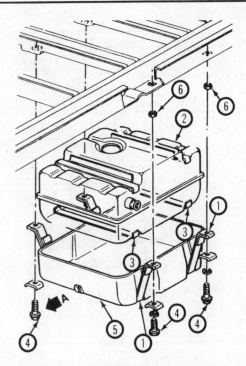

5.5a   Fuel tank assembly component details

A	Front	2	Tank	5	Lower shield
1	Strap	3	Insulator	6	Nuts
		4	Bolts		

4   Fuel lines and fittings — repair and replacement

Metal fuel and vapor lines

Caution: *Fuel and vapor lines are specially manufactured. It is important to use replacement lines meeting GM specifications. Lines not meeting GM specifications can cause premature failure or failure to meet emission standards.*

1   When replacing fuel feed and return lines, always use welded steel tubing meeting GM Specification 124M or its equivalent. The replacement line must have the same type fittings as the original lines to ensure the integrity of the connection.
2   Never replace fuel lines with copper or aluminum tubing.
3   Check and replace any damaged O-rings or washers.
4   Fuel lines should be inspected occasionally for leaks, dents or kinks.
5   Follow the same routing as the original line.
6   Lines must be properly secured to the frame to prevent chafing. A minimum clearance of 1/4-inch must be maintained to prevent contact and chafing.

Fuel and vapor hoses

Caution: *Fuel and vapor hoses are specially manufactured. It is important to use replacement hoses meeting GM Specification 6163-M. These hoses are identified by the word ''Fluorelastomer'' marked on them. Hoses not so marked could cause premature failure or failure to meet emission standards.*

7   Do not use rubber hose within 4-inches of any part of the exhaust system or within 10-inches of the catalytic converter.

TBI fuel lines

8   Because TBI fuel lines are under high pressure, these systems require special consideration.
9   Many of the feed and return lines use screw couplings with O-rings. Any time these fittings are loosened to service or replace components, make sure that:
   a)   A backup wrench is used to loosen and tighten the fitting.
   b)   Check all O-rings for cuts or any damage and replace any that appear worn or damaged.
   c)   If the lines are replaced, always use the original equipment parts, or parts that meet GM specifications.

5.5b   Unclip the lower shield from the fuel tank and pull it down far enough to detach the fuel feed, return, vapor canister and filler neck breather hoses

5.6   Loosen the hose clamp (arrow) and detach the filler neck hose from the fuel tank

5   Fuel tank — removal and installation

Refer to illustrations 5.5a, 5.5b and 5.6
1   Relieve the system fuel pressure (see Section 2).
2   Detach the cable from the negative terminal of the battery.
3   Raise the vehicle and support it securely on jackstands.
4   Support the fuel tank with a transmission jack, a floor jack or a pair of jackstands.
5   Unclip the lower shield from the right side of the tank and pull it down far enough to remove the the fuel feed, return and vapor hoses **(see illustrations)**.
6   Loosen the filler neck hose clamp **(see illustration)** and detach the filler neck hose from the pipe on the tank.
7   Remove the fuel tank support strap bolts and remove the support straps.
8   Carefully lower the tank enough to disconnect the fuel pump lead, sending unit lead and ground wire.
9   Remove the fuel tank from the vehicle.
10   Installation is the reverse of removal.

6   Fuel tank — cleaning and repair

1   Any repairs to the fuel tank or filler neck should be carried out by a professional who has experience in this critical and potentially dangerous work. Even after cleaning and flushing of the fuel tank, explosive fumes can remain and ignite during repair.
2   If the fuel tank is removed from the vehicle, it should not be placed in an area where sparks or open flames could ignite the fumes coming out of the tank. Be especially careful inside garages where a natural gas-type appliance is located, because the pilot light could cause an explosion.

4

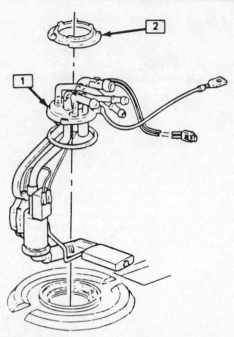

7.15   To remove the fuel pump and sender (1), turn the lock ring (2) counterclockwise, then lift the pump/sender assembly out

---

7 Fuel pump — removal and installation

Warning: *Gasoline is extremely flammable, so extra precautions must be taken when working on any part of the fuel system. Do not smoke or allow open flames or bare light bulbs near the work area. Also, do not work in a garage if a natural gas type appliance with a pilot light is present.*

Mechanical pump (carburetor equipped models)

1   The fuel pump is a sealed unit and cannot be rebuilt. It's mounted on the right (passenger) side of the engine at the very front.
2   To remove the pump, first isolate the battery by disconnecting the negative battery cable.
3   Detach the fuel inlet hose, the outlet line and the vapor return hose (if equipped). Hold the fitting on the pump with a back-up wrench as the outlet line is disconnected. Also, if possible, use a flare-nut wrench on the fuel line fitting.
4   Remove the two mounting bolts and detach the fuel pump. As the pump is removed, the pushrod may fall out — be sure to retrieve it.
5   Remove the gasket and mounting plate.
6   Remove all traces of old gasket and sealant with a scraper, then clean the block mounting surface with lacquer thinner or acetone.
7   Apply a dab of heavy grease to the pushrod to hold it in place as the pump is installed.
8   Position the new gasket, the mounting plate and the pump on the block, then install the bolts and tighten them 1/4-turn at a time until they're secure.
9   Reattach the inlet hose, the outlet line and the vapor return hose to the pump. Be sure to tighten the fitting on the outlet line and the clamps on the hoses securely.
10 Start the engine and check for fuel leaks at the hose and line connections.

Electric pump (fuel injected models)
Refer to illustrations 7.15 and 7.18

11 Relieve the fuel pressure (Section 2).
12 Remove the cable from the negative battery terminal.
13 Remove the fuel tank (Section 5).
14 The fuel pump/sending unit assembly is located inside the fuel tank. It is held in place by a cam lock ring mechanism consisting of an inner ring with three locking cams and an outer ring with three tangs. The outer ring is welded to the tank and can't be turned.
15 To unlock the fuel pump/sending unit assembly, turn the inner ring counterclockwise until the locking cams are free of the tangs **(see il-**

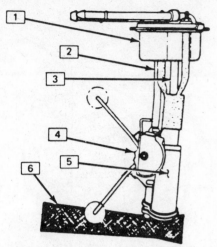

7.18   **Typical fuel pumper/sender unit**

1 Vapor separator	4 Fuel level sender
2 Fuel return tube	5 Electric fuel pump
3 Fuel feed tube	6 Filter strainer

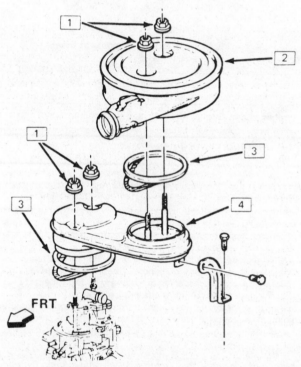

8.3a   **Exploded view of a typical air cleaner assembly for the 4-cylinder engine**

| 1 Nuts | 3 Gaskets |
| 2 Air cleaner housing assembly | 4 Adapter |

lustration). Warning: *If the rings are locked together too tightly to release them by hand, gently knock them loose with a rubber or brass hammer. Do not use a steel hammer to knock the lock rings loose. A spark could cause an explosion!*
16 Extract the fuel pump/sending unit assembly from the fuel tank.
Caution: *The fuel level float and sending unit are delicate. Do not bump them into the lock ring during removal or the accuracy of the sending unit may be affected.*
17 Inspect the condition of the rubber gasket around the mouth of the lock ring mechanism. If it is dried, cracked or deteriorated, replace it.
18 Inspect the strainer on the lower end of the fuel pump **(see illustration)**. If it is dirty, remove it, clean it with a suitable solvent and blow it out with compressed air. If it is too dirty to be cleaned, replace it.

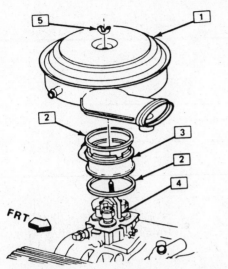

8.3b Exploded view of a typical air cleaner housing assembly for the V6 engine

1 Air cleaner housing assembly	3 Adapter
	4 Stud
2 Seal	5 Nut

19 If it is necessary to separate the fuel pump and sending unit, remove the pump from the sending unit by pulling the fuel pump assembly into the rubber connector and sliding the pump away from the bottom support. Care should be taken to prevent damage to the rubber insulator and fuel strainer during removal. After the pump assembly is clear of the bottom support, pull the pump assembly out of the rubber connector.
20 Insert the fuel pump/sending unit assembly into the fuel tank.
21 Turn the inner lock ring clockwise until the locking cams are fully engaged by the retaining tangs. **Note:** *If you have installed a new O-ring type rubber gasket, it may be necessary to push down on the inner lock ring until the locking cams slide under the retaining tangs.*
22 Install the fuel tank (Section 5).

8 Air cleaner housing assembly — removal and installation

Refer to illustrations 8.3a and 8.3b

1 Detach the cable from the negative terminal of the battery.
2 Detach the fresh air intake duct from the mouth of the air cleaner housing assembly.
3 Remove the air cleaner cover nuts or wing nut **(see illustrations)**.
4 Remove the air cleaner assembly and the gasket between the air cleaner housing and the adapter.
5 Discard the old gasket. Be sure to remove the paper from the new gasket before installing it.
6 If you are replacing the air cleaner housing assembly, installation is the reverse of removal.
7 If you are planning to remove the TBI unit, the intake manifold, a cylinder head, etc. remove the adapter nuts, the adapter assembly and the gasket between the adapter and the TBI assembly.
8 Discard the old gasket. Be sure to remove the paper from the new gasket before installing it.
9 Installation is the reverse of removal.

9 Carburetor — removal and installation

Warning: *Gasoline is extremely flammable, so extra precautions must be taken when working on any part of the fuel system. Do not smoke or allow open flames or bare light bulbs in or near the work area. Also, don't work in a garage if a natural gas appliance such as a water heater or clothes dryer is present.*

1 Remove the battery (see Chapter 5).
2 Remove the air cleaner assembly (see Section 8).
3 Detach the accelerator linkage.
4 Detach the transmission detent cable (see Chapter 7 Part B).
5 Detach the cruise control cable, if equipped.

6 Clearly label, then detach, all vacuum lines.
7 Disconnect the fuel line at the carburetor inlet.
8 Clearly label, then unplug all electrical connectors.
9 Remove the four carburetor mounting bolts.
10 Remove the carburetor from the intake manifold.
11 Installation is the reverse of removal. Be sure to replace the carburetor base gasket and tighten the carburetor mounting bolts to the specified torque.

10 Carburetor — overhaul and adjustments

Warning: *Gasoline is extremely flammable, so extra precautions must be taken when working on any part of the fuel system. Do not smoke or allow open flames or bare light bulbs in or near the work area. Also, don't work in a garage if a natural gas appliance such as a water heater or clothes dryer is present.*

Overhaul

1 If you are going to overhaul the carburetor yourself, first obtain a good quality carburetor rebuild kit (which will include all necessary gaskets, internal parts, instructions and a parts list). You will also need some solvent and a means of blowing out the internal passages of the carburetor with air.
2 Because carburetor designs are constantly modified by the manufacturer in order to meet emissions regulations, it isn't feasible for us to do a step-by-step overhaul of each type. You'll receive a detailed set of instructions with any quality carburetor overhaul kit. They will apply in a more specific manner to the carburetor on your vehicle.
3 An alternative is to obtain a new or rebuilt carburetor. They are readily available from dealers and auto parts stores. Make sure the exchange carburetor is identical to the original. A tag is usually attached to the top of the carburetor. It will aid in determining the exact type of carburetor you have. When obtaining a rebuilt carburetor or a rebuild kit, take time to make sure that the kit or carburetor matches your application exactly. Seemingly insignificant differences can make a large difference in the performance of your engine.
4 If you choose to overhaul your own carburetor, allow enough time to disassemble the carburetor carefully, soak the necessary parts in the cleaning solvent (usually for at least one-half day or according to the instructions listed on the carburetor cleaner) and reassemble it, which will usually take much longer than disassembly. When disassembling the carburetor, match each part with the illustration in the carburetor kit and lay the parts out in order on a clean work surface.

Adjustments

5 Because there are a number of different configurations for Federal and California carburetors and because a considerable number of special

11.2a Typical Model 300 TBI unit on earlier vehicles with a 4-cylinder engine

A Fuel injector	D Throttle Position Sensor (TPS)
B Fuel pressure regulator	E Fuel meter cover
C Idle Air Control (IAC) valve	

4

11.2b Typical Model 220 TBI unit on V6 powered vehicles

A Fuel injectors
B Fuel pressure regulator
   (under fuel meter cover)
C Idle Air Control (IAC) valve
D Throttle Position Sensor (TPS)

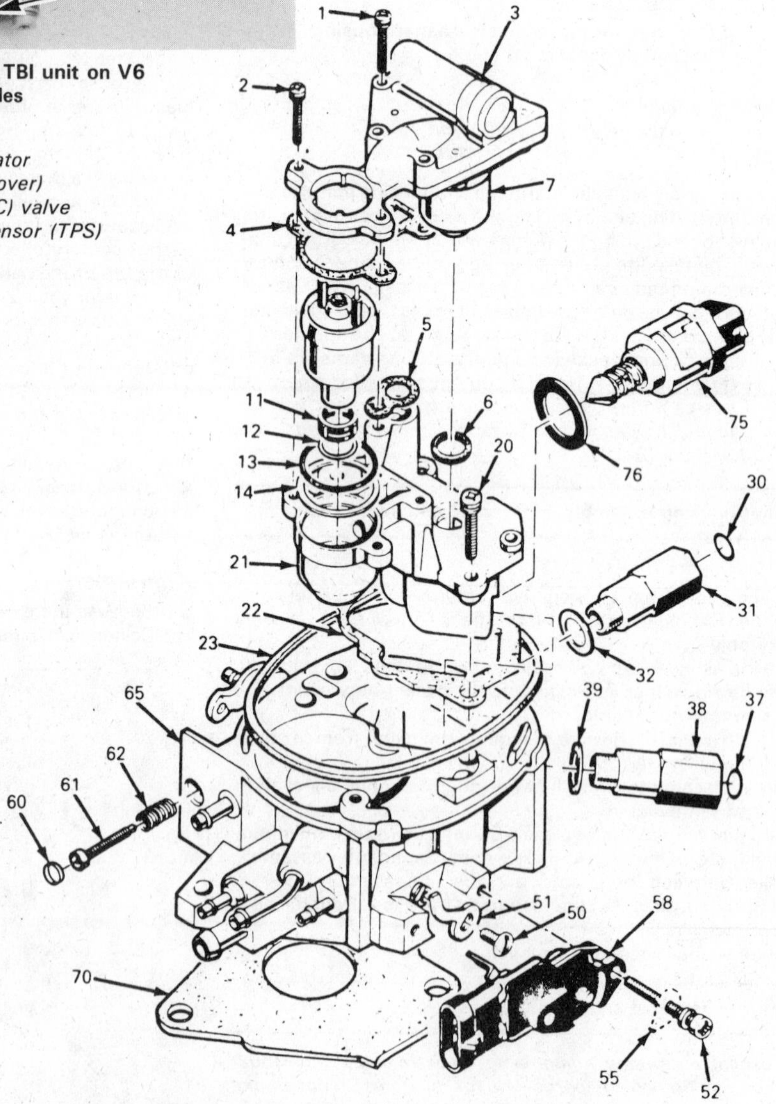

12.5 Exploded view of the Model 300 TBI assembly (earlier 4-cylinder engines)

1   Long screw and washer
2   Short screw and washer
3   Fuel meter cover
4   Fuel meter cover gasket
5   Fuel meter outlet gasket
6   Pressure regulator dust seal
7   Pressure regulator
11 Fuel injector nozzle filter
12 Lower O-ring
13 Upper O-ring
14 Fuel injector back-up washer
20 Attaching screw and washer
21 Fuel meter body
22 Fuel meter body gasket
23 Air filter gasket
30 Fuel return line O-ring
31 Fuel return nut
32 Fuel return nut gasket
37 Fuel inlet line O-ring
38 Fuel inlet nut
39 Fuel inlet nut gasket
50 TPS lever attaching screw
51 TPS lever
52 Attaching screw and washer
55 TPS attaching screw retainer

58 Throttle position sensor
60 Idle stop screw plug
61 Throttle stop screw
62 Throttle stop screw spring

65 Throttle body assembly
70 Flange mounting gasket
75 Idle air control valve
76 IAC to throttle body gasket

12.7   The fuel pressure regulator is installed in the fuel meter cover and pre-adjusted by the factory — do not remove the four retaining screws (arrows) or you may damage the regulator

tools and tuning equipment is necessary to adjust these carburetors, it is impossible to include a detailed step-by-step procedure outlining every adjustment. Aside from idle speed adjustment and other adjustments shown in the carburetor overhaul kit, do not attempt to adjust the carburetor on your vehicle. If adjustments are needed other than those listed above, take the vehicle to a professional mechanic. The procedure for adjusting the idle speed on your vehicle is located on the VECI label.

11   Fuel injection system — general information

Refer to illustrations 11.2a and 11.2b

Electronic fuel injection provides optimum air/fuel mixture ratios at all stages of combustion and offers better throttle response characteristics than carburetion. It also enables the engine to run at the leanest possible air/fuel mixture ratio, greatly reducing exhaust gas emissions.

All non-carbureted vehicles employ a type of fuel injection known as Throttle Body Injection (TBI) **(see illustrations)**. Three types of TBI units are employed on the vehicles covered by this manual. The Model 300 is used on earlier vehicles powered by the 4-cylinder engine; the Model 700 is used on later vehicles with the 4-cylinder engine.

Both the 300 and the 700 are single injector designs. All fuel injected V6 engines utilize the Model 220 twin-injector model.

Although they differ somewhat in design, there is very little difference in function between these three TBI units.

All three TBI systems are controlled by an Electronic Control Module (ECM), which monitors engine performance and adjusts the air/fuel mixture accordingly during all engine operating conditions.

An electric fuel pump located in the fuel tank with the fuel gauge sending unit pumps fuel to the TBI unit through the fuel feed line and an in-line fuel filter. A pressure regulator in the TBI keeps fuel available to the injector(s) at a constant pressure between 9 and 13 psi. Fuel in excess of injector needs is returned to the fuel tank by a separate line.

12   Model 300 Throttle Body Injection (TBI) — removal, overhaul and installation

Refer to illustrations 12.5, 12.7, 12.8a, 12.8b, 12.10, 12.11, 12.17, 12.18, 12.19, 12.25, 12.26 and 12.35

Note: *Because of its relative simplicity, a throttle body assembly need be neither removed from the intake manifold nor completely disassembled during component replacement. However, for the sake of clarity, the following procedures are shown with the TBI assembly removed from the vehicle.*

1   Relieve the fuel pressure (Section 2).
2   Detach the cable from the negative terminal of the battery.
3   Remove the air cleaner housing assembly, adapter and gaskets.

12.8a   The best way to remove the fuel injector is to pry on it with a screwdriver, using a second screwdriver as a fulcrum

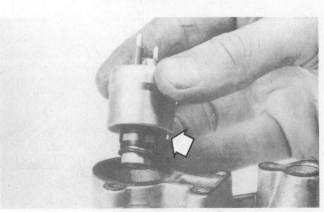

12.8b   Note the position of the terminals on top and the dowel pin on bottom of the injector in relation to the fuel meter cover when you lift the injector out of the cover

Fuel meter cover and fuel injector
Disassembly

4   Remove the injector electrical connector (on top of the TBI) by squeezing the two tabs together and pulling straight up.
5   Unscrew the five fuel meter cover retaining screws and lockwashers securing the fuel meter cover to the fuel meter body. Note the location of the two short screws **(see illustration)**.
6   Remove the fuel meter cover. **Caution:** *Do not immerse the fuel meter cover in solvent. It might damage the pressure regulator diaphragm and gasket.*
7   The fuel meter cover contains the fuel pressure regulator, which is pre-set and plugged at the factory. If a malfunction occurs, it cannot be serviced, and must be replaced as a complete assembly. **Warning:** *Do not remove the screws securing the pressure regulator to the fuel meter cover* **(see illustration)**. *It has a large spring inside under heavy compression.*
8   With the old fuel meter cover gasket in place to prevent damage to the casting, carefully pry the injector from the fuel meter body with a screwdriver until it can be lifted free **(see illustrations)**. **Caution:** *Use care in removing the injector to prevent damage to the electrical connector terminals, the injector fuel filter, the O-ring and the nozzle.*
9   The fuel meter body should be removed from the throttle body if it needs to be cleaned. To remove it, remove the fuel feed and return line fittings and the Torx screws that attach the fuel meter body to the throttle body.

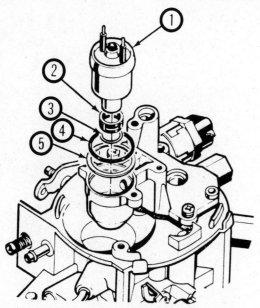

12.10   Remove the large O-ring and steel back up washer from the injector cavity of the fuel meter body

1 Fuel injector   4 Large O-ring
2 Filter   5 Steel back-up washer
3 Small O-ring

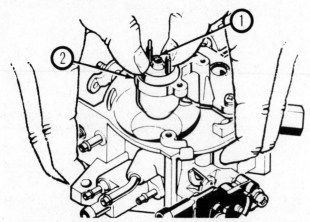

12.17   Push straight down with both thumbs to install the injector in the fuel meter body cavity

1 Fuel injector   2 Fuel meter body

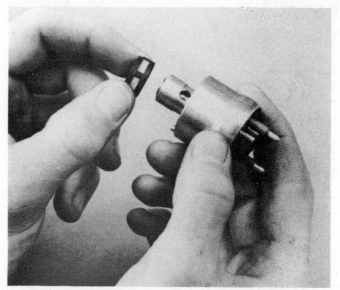

12.11   Gently rotate the fuel injector filter back and forth and carefully pull it off the nozzle

12.18   Position the fuel outlet passage gasket (A) and the fuel meter cover gasket (B) properly

10 Remove the old gasket from the fuel meter cover and discard it. Remove the large O-ring and steel back-up washer from the upper counterbore of the fuel meter body injector cavity (see illustration). Clean the fuel meter body thoroughly in solvent and blow dry.

11 Remove the small O-ring from the nozzle end of the injector. Carefully rotate the injector fuel filter back and forth and remove the filter from the base of the injector (see illustration). Gently clean the filter in solvent and allow it to drip dry. It is too small and delicate to dry with compressed air. **Caution:** *The fuel injector itself is an electrical component. Do not immerse it in any type of cleaning solvent.*

12 The fuel injector is not serviceable. If it is malfunctioning, replace it as an assembly.

Reassembly

13 Install the clean fuel injector nozzle filter on the end of the fuel injector with the larger end of the filter facing the injector so that the filter covers the raised rib at the base of the injector. Use a twisting motion to position the filter against the base of the injector.

14 Lubricate a new small O-ring with automatic transmission fluid. Push the O-ring onto the nozzle end of the injector until it presses against the injector fuel filter.

15 Insert the steel backup washer in the top counterbore of the fuel meter body injector cavity.

16 Lubricate a new large O-ring with automatic transmission fluid and install it directly over the backup washer. Be sure that the O-ring is seated properly in the cavity and is flush with the top of the fuel meter body casting surface. **Caution:** *The back-up washer and large O-ring must be installed before the injector or improper seating of the large O-ring could cause fuel to leak.*

17 Install the injector in the cavity in the fuel meter body, aligning the raised lug on the injector base with the cast-in notch in the fuel meter body cavity. Push straight down on the injector with both thumbs (see illustration) until it is fully seated in the cavity. **Note:** *The electrical terminals of the injector should be approximately parallel to the throttle shaft.*

18 Install a new fuel outlet passage gasket on the fuel meter cover and a new fuel meter cover gasket on the fuel meter body (see illustration).

12.19   Install a new dust seal into the recess of the fuel meter body

12.25   Remove the IAC valve with a large wrench, but be careful — it's a delicate device

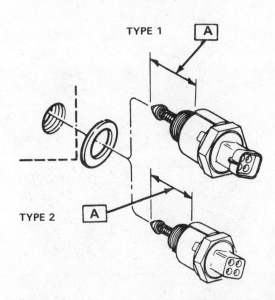

12.26   Distance A should be less than 1-1/8 inch for either type of Idle Air Control valve — if it isn't, determine what kind of IAC valve you have and adjust it accordingly
Type 1 — with electrical terminal collar
Type 2 — without electrical terminal collar

19 Install a new dust seal into the recess on the fuel meter body **(see illustration)**.
20 Install the fuel meter cover onto the fuel meter body, making sure that the pressure regulator dust seal and cover gaskets are in place.
21 Apply a thread locking compound to the threads of the fuel meter cover attaching screws. Install the screws (the two short screws go next to the injector) and tighten them securely. **Note:** *Service repair kits include a small vial of thread compound with directions for use. If this material is not available, use Loctite 262, GM part number 1052624, or equivalent. Do not use a higher strength locking compound than recommended, as this may prevent subsequent removal of the attaching screws or cause breakage of the screwhead if removal becomes necessary.*
22 Plug in the electrical connector to the injector.
23 Install the air cleaner.

Idle Air Control (IAC) valve
Removal
24 Unplug the electrical connector at the IAC valve.
25 Remove the IAC valve with a wrench on the hex surface only **(see illustration).**
Adjustment
26 Before installing a new IAC valve, measure the distance the valve is extended **(see illustration)**. The measurement should be made from the motor housing to the end of the cone. The distance should be no greater than 1-1/8 inch. If the cone is extended too far, damage may occur to the valve when it is installed.
27 Identify the replacement IAC valve as either a Type I (with a collar at the electric terminal end) or a Type II (without a collar) **(see illustration 10.26)**. If the measured dimension "A" is greater than 1-1/8 inch, the distance must be reduced as follows:
   Type I — Exert firm pressure on the valve to retract it (a slight side-to-side movement may be helpful).
   Type II — Compress the retaining spring of the valve while turning the valve in a clockwise direction. Return the spring to its original position with the straight portion of the spring aligned with the flat surface of the valve.
Installation
28 Install the new IAC valve to the throttle body. Use the new gasket supplied with the assembly.
29 Plug in the electrical connector.
30 Install the air cleaner.
31 Start the engine and allow it to reach normal operating temperature. The Electronic Control Module (ECM) will reset the idle speed when the vehicle is driven above 35 mph.

Throttle Position Sensor (TPS)
32 The Throttle Position Sensor (TPS) is connected to the throttle shaft on the TBI unit. As the throttle valve angle is changed (as the accelerator pedal is moved), the output of the TPS also changes. At a closed throttle position, the output of the TPS is below 1.25 volts. As the throttle valve opens, the output increases so that, at wide-open throttle, the output voltage is approximately 5 volts.
33 A broken or loose TPS can cause intermittent bursts of fuel from the injector and an unstable idle, because the ECM thinks the throttle is moving. A problem in any of the TPS circuits will set either a Code 21 or 22 (see "Trouble Codes," Chapter 6).
34 The TPS is not adjustable. The ECM uses the reading at idle for the zero reading. If the TPS malfunctions, it is replaced as a unit.

35 Unscrew the two Torx screws **(see illustration)** and remove the TPS.
36 Install the new TPS. **Note:** *Make sure that the tang on the lever is properly engaged with the stop on the TBI* **(see illustration)**.
37 Install the air cleaner assembly.
38 Attach the cable to the negative terminal of the battery.
39 With the ignition switch on and the engine off, check for fuel leaks.

13 Model 700 Throttle Body Injection (TBI) — removal, overhaul and installation

Refer to illustrations 13.5, 13.6, 13.32, 13.33, 13.51 and 13.62

Note: *Because of its relative simplicity, the throttle body does not need to be removed from the intake manifold or disassembled for component replacement. However, for the sake of clarity, the following procedures are shown with the TBI assembly removed from the vehicle.*

1 Relieve the fuel pressure (Section 2).
2 Detach the cable from the negative terminal of the battery.
3 Remove the air cleaner housing assembly, adapter and gaskets.

Fuel injector

4 Unplug the electrical connector from the fuel injector.
5 Remove the injector retainer screw and retainer **(see illustration)**.

12.35 The Throttle Position Sensor (TPS) is mounted to the side of the TBI with two Torx screws

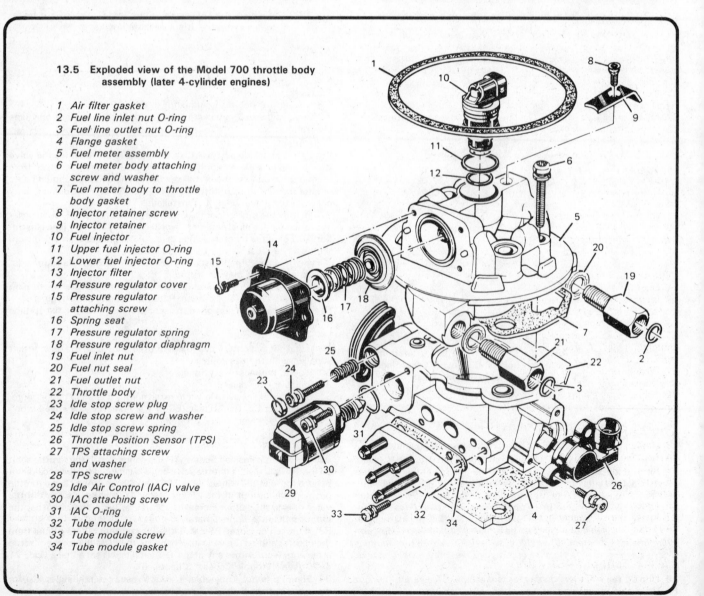

13.5 Exploded view of the Model 700 throttle body assembly (later 4-cylinder engines)

1 *Air filter gasket*
2 *Fuel line inlet nut O-ring*
3 *Fuel line outlet nut O-ring*
4 *Flange gasket*
5 *Fuel meter assembly*
6 *Fuel meter body attaching screw and washer*
7 *Fuel meter body to throttle body gasket*
8 *Injector retainer screw*
9 *Injector retainer*
10 *Fuel injector*
11 *Upper fuel injector O-ring*
12 *Lower fuel injector O-ring*
13 *Injector filter*
14 *Pressure regulator cover*
15 *Pressure regulator attaching screw*
16 *Spring seat*
17 *Pressure regulator spring*
18 *Pressure regulator diaphragm*
19 *Fuel inlet nut*
20 *Fuel nut seal*
21 *Fuel outlet nut*
22 *Throttle body*
23 *Idle stop screw plug*
24 *Idle stop screw and washer*
25 *Idle stop screw spring*
26 *Throttle Position Sensor (TPS)*
27 *TPS attaching screw and washer*
28 *TPS screw*
29 *Idle Air Control (IAC) valve*
30 *IAC attaching screw*
31 *IAC O-ring*
32 *Tube module*
33 *Tube module screw*
34 *Tube module gasket*

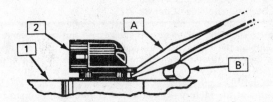

13.6   To remove the fuel injector unit (2) from the fuel meter body (1), insert a screwdriver (A) under the fuel injector flange as shown, place a fulcrum (B) behind the tip and pry the injector loose

6   To remove the fuel injector assembly, place a screwdriver blade under the ridge opposite the connector (**see illustration**) and carefully pry it out.

7   Remove the upper and lower O-rings from the injector and from the fuel injector cavity and discard them.

8   Inspect the fuel injector filter for evidence of dirt and contamination. If present, look for the presence of dirt in the fuel lines and the fuel tank.

9   Lubricate new upper and lower O-rings with transmission fluid and install them on the injector. Make sure that the upper O-ring is in the groove and the lower one is flush up against the filter.

10   To install the injector assembly, push it straight into the fuel injector cavity. Be sure that the electrical connector end on the injector is facing in the general direction of the cut-out in the fuel meter body for the wire grommet. **Note:** *If you are installing a new injector, be sure to replace the old unit with an identical part. Injectors from other models will fit in the Model 700 TBI assembly but are calibrated for different flow rates.*

11   Using thread locking compound on the retainer attaching screw, install the injector retainer and tighten the retaining screw.

12   Install the air cleaner housing assembly, adapter and gaskets.

13   With the engine off and the ignition on, check for fuel leaks.

Fuel pressure regulator

14   Remove the four pressure regulator attaching screws while keeping the pressure regulator compressed. **Caution:** *The pressure regulator contains a large spring under heavy compression. Use care when removing the screws to prevent personal injury.*

15   Remove the pressure regulator cover assembly.

16   Remove the pressure regulator spring, seat, and the pressure regulator diaphragm.

17   Using a magnifying glass, if necessary, inspect the pressure regulator seat in the fuel meter body cavity for pitting, nicks or irregularities. If any damage is present, the entire fuel body casting must be replaced.

18   Install the new pressure regulator diaphragm assembly. Make sure it is seated in the groove in the fuel meter body.

19   Install the regulator spring seat and spring into the cover assembly.

20   Install the cover assembly over the diaphragm while aligning the mounting holes. **Caution:** *Use care while installing the pressure regulator to prevent misalignment and possible leaks.*

21   While maintaining pressure on the regulator spring, install the four screw assemblies that have been coated with thread locking compound.

22   Reconnect the negative battery cable. With the engine off and the ignition on, check for fuel leaks.

Throttle Position Sensor (TPS)

23   Unplug the electrical connector from the throttle position sensor.

24   Remove the two TPS attaching screws and remove the TPS from the throttle body.

25   With the throttle valve closed, install the TPS on the throttle shaft. Rotate it counterclockwise to align the mounting holes.

26   Install the two TPS attaching screws.

27   Install the air cleaner housing assembly, adapter and gaskets.

28   Attach the cable to the negative terminal of the battery. **Note:** *See non-adjustable TPS output check at end of this section.*

Idle Air Control (IAC) valve

29   Unplug the electrical connector from the IAC valve and remove the IAC valve mounting screws and the IAC valve.

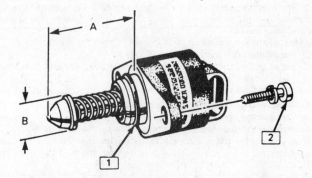

13.32   Typical flange-type IAC valve for the Model 700 TBI unit

1 O-ring	A Distance of pintle extension
2 Screw and washer	B Diameter of pintle

30   Remove the O-ring from the IAC valve and discard it.

31   Clean the IAC valve seating surfaces on the throttle body to assure proper sealing of the new O-ring and proper contact of the IAC valve flange.

32   Before installing a new IAC valve, measure the distance between the tip of the valve pintle and the flange mounting surface when the pintle is fully extended (**see illustration**). If dimension "A" is greater than given in the Specifications, it must be reduced to prevent damage to the valve.

33   To retract the IAC valve, grasp the IAC valve as shown and exert firm pressure with your thumb, using a slight side-to-side movement on the valve pintle (**see illustration**).

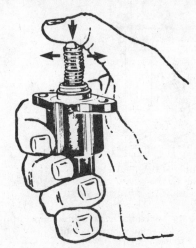

13.33   To adjust the IAC valve pintle, grasp it as shown and, using a side-to-side motion with your thumb, press it firmly down into the valve

34   Lubricate a new O-ring with transmission fluid and install it on the IAC valve.

35   Install the IAC valve to the throttle body. Coat the IAC valve attaching screws with thread locking compound. Install and tighten them securely. Plug in the IAC valve electrical connector.

36   Install the air cleaner housing assembly, adapter and gaskets.

37   Attach the cable to the negative terminal of the battery.

38   Start the engine, allow it to reach operating temperature, then take the vehicle for a drive. When the engine reaches normal operating temperature the ECM will set the proper idle speed.

Tube module assembly

39   Remove the tube module assembly attaching screws and remove the tube module.

40　Remove the tube module gasket and discard it. Clean any old gasket material from the surface of the throttle body to insure proper sealing of the new gasket.
41　Install the new tube module gasket.
42　Install the tube module.
43　Install the air cleaner housing assembly, adapter and gaskets.

Fuel meter assembly

44　Remove the throttle body injection unit.
45　Remove the two fuel meter body attaching screws and washers and remove the fuel meter assembly from the throttle body.
46　If you are installing a new fuel meter, remove the fuel pressure regulator and the fuel outlet nut and transfer them to the new fuel meter.
47　Remove the fuel meter body-to-throttle body gasket and discard it.
48　Install a new fuel meter-to-throttle body gasket. Match the cutout portions of the gasket with the openings in the throttle body.
49　Install the fuel meter onto the throttle body and tighten the attaching screws.

Throttle body assembly

50　Unplug the electrical connectors from the fuel injector, IAC and TPS.
51　Remove the throttle body mounting studs (**see illustration**).

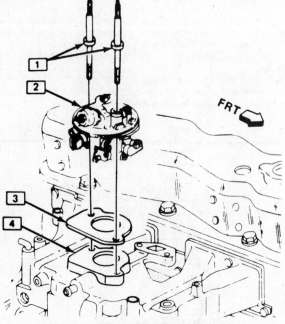

**13.51　Exploded view of the Model 700
mounting installation**

1	*Mounting studs*	*3*	*Gasket*
2	*TBI unit*	*4*	*Intake manifold*

52　Remove and discard the throttle body-to-intake manifold gasket. Place the TBI assembly on a clean work surface.
53　Remove the fuel injector, fuel meter assembly, TPS, IAC valve and the tube module.
54　Install the new tube module assembly, IAC valve and TPS on the new throttle body assembly.
55　Install a new fuel meter body-to-throttle body gasket.
56　Install the fuel meter assembly and fuel injector.
57　Install a new throttle body-to-intake manifold gasket and install the throttle body assembly on the intake manifold. Tighten the mounting studs to the specified torque.

Minimum idle speed adjustment

Note: *This adjustment should be performed only when the throttle body assembly has been replaced. The engine should be at normal operating temperature before making the adjustment.*
58　Plug any vacuum line ports as required (see the VECI label).

59　With the IAC valve connected, ground the diagnostic terminal of the ALDL connector (see Chapter 6).
60　Turn the ignition on but do not start the engine. Wait at least 30 seconds to allow the IAC valve pintle to extend and seat in the throttle body. Unplug the IAC valve electrical connector.
61　Remove the ground jumper from the diagnostic terminal and start the engine.
62　The throttle stop screw used for regulating minimum idle speed is adjusted at the factory. The screw is covered with a plug to discourage unauthorized adjustments. To remove the plug, pierce it with an awl (**see illustration**), then apply leverage.

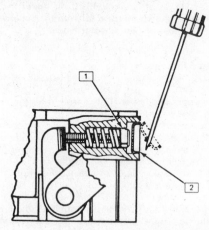

**13.62　To gain access to the factory sealed idle stop
screw (1), remove the plug (2) by piercing it with an awl,
then levering it loose**

63　With the transmission in Neutral (manual) or Park (automatic), adjust the idle stop screw to obtain the specified rpm.
64　Turn the ignition off and reconnect the IAC valve electrical connector, unplug any plugged vacuum line ports and install the air cleaner housing assembly, adapter and gaskets.

Non-adjustable TPS output check

Note: *This check should be performed only when the throttle body or the throttle position sensor has been replaced or after the minimum idle speed has been adjusted.*

65　Connect a digital voltmeter from center terminal ''B'' to outside terminal ''A'' of the TPS connector.
66　With the ignition on and the engine stopped, the TPS voltage should be as listed in the Specifications. If the voltage is greater than specified, replace the TPS.

14　Model 220 Throttle Body Injection (TBI) — removal, overhaul and installation

---

Refer to illustrations 14.5, 14.6, 14.7, 14.14, 14.16, 14.21, 14.22, 14.23, 14.24, 14.25, 14.37, 14.40, 14.41a, 14.41b, 14.41c, 14.50, 14.52, 14.65 and 14.66

Note: *Because of its relative simplicity, the throttle body assembly does not need to be removed from the intake manifold or disassembled for component replacement. However, for the sake of clarity, the following procedures are shown with the TBI assembly removed from the vehicle.*

1　Relieve system fuel pressure (see Section 2).
2　Detach the cable from the negative terminal of the battery.
3　Remove the air cleaner housing assembly, adapter and gaskets.

Fuel meter cover/fuel pressure regulator assembly

Note: *The fuel pressure regulator is housed in the fuel meter cover. Whether you are replacing the meter cover or the regulator itself, the entire assembly must be replaced. The regulator must not be removed from the cover.*

4　Unplug the electrical connectors to the fuel injectors.
5　Remove the long and short fuel meter cover screws (**see illustration**) and remove the fuel meter cover.

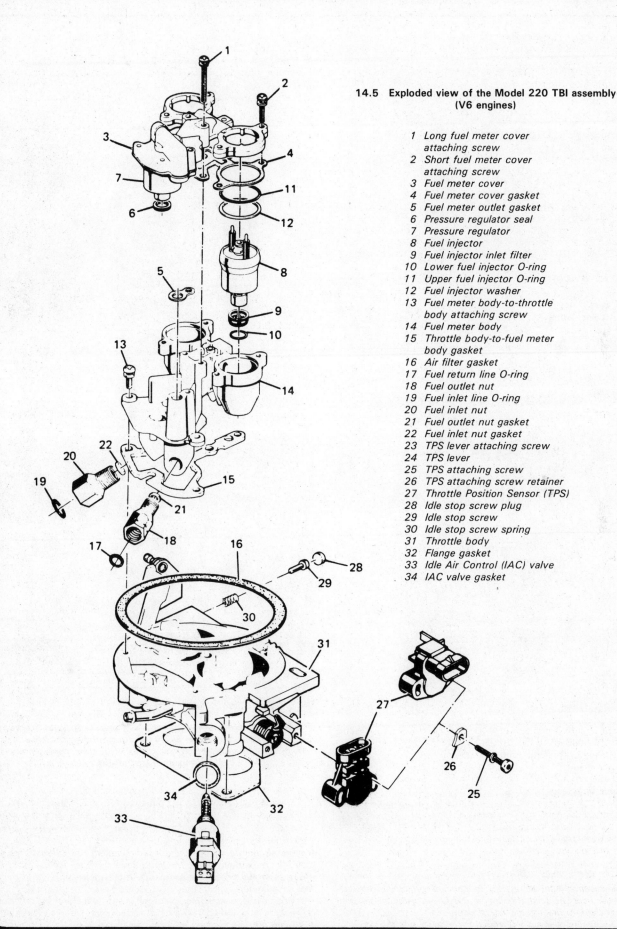

14.5 Exploded view of the Model 220 TBI assembly (V6 engines)

1 Long fuel meter cover attaching screw
2 Short fuel meter cover attaching screw
3 Fuel meter cover
4 Fuel meter cover gasket
5 Fuel meter outlet gasket
6 Pressure regulator seal
7 Pressure regulator
8 Fuel injector
9 Fuel injector inlet filter
10 Lower fuel injector O-ring
11 Upper fuel injector O-ring
12 Fuel injector washer
13 Fuel meter body-to-throttle body attaching screw
14 Fuel meter body
15 Throttle body-to-fuel meter body gasket
16 Air filter gasket
17 Fuel return line O-ring
18 Fuel outlet nut
19 Fuel inlet line O-ring
20 Fuel inlet nut
21 Fuel outlet nut gasket
22 Fuel inlet nut gasket
23 TPS lever attaching screw
24 TPS lever
25 TPS attaching screw
26 TPS attaching screw retainer
27 Throttle Position Sensor (TPS)
28 Idle stop screw plug
29 Idle stop screw
30 Idle stop screw spring
31 Throttle body
32 Flange gasket
33 Idle Air Control (IAC) valve
34 IAC valve gasket

4

14.6   Carefully peel away the old fuel meter outlet passage gasket and fuel meter cover gasket with a razor blade

14.7   Never remove the four pressure regulator screws (arrows) from the fuel meter cover

14.14   To remove either injector electrical connector, depress the two tabs on the front and rear of each connector and lift straight up

14.16   To remove an injector, slip the tip of a flat-bladed screwdriver under the lip of the lug on top of the injector and, using another screwdriver as a fulcrum, carefully pry the injector up and out

6   Remove the fuel meter outlet passage gasket, cover gasket and pressure regulator seal. Carefully remove any old gasket material that is stuck with a razor blade **(see illustration)**. **Caution:** *Do not attempt to re-use either of these gaskets.*

7   Inspect the cover for dirt, foreign material and casting warpage. If it is dirty, clean it with a clean shop rag soaked in solvent. Do not immerse the fuel meter cover in cleaning solvent — it could damage the pressure regulator diaphragm and gasket. **Warning:** *Do not remove the four screws (see illustration) securing the pressure regulator to the fuel meter cover. The regulator contains a large spring under compression which, if accidentally released, could cause injury. Disassembly might also result in a fuel leak between the diaphragm and the regulator*

housing. The new fuel meter cover assembly will include a new pressure regulator.

8   Install the new pressure regulator seal, fuel meter outlet passage gasket and cover gasket.

9   Install the fuel meter cover assembly using Loctite 262 or equivalent on the screws. **Note:** *The short screws go next to the injectors.*

10   Attach the electrical connectors to both injectors.

11   Attach the cable to the negative terminal of the battery.

12   With the engine off and the ignition on, check for leaks around the gasket and fuel line couplings.

13   Install the air cleaner, adapter and gaskets.

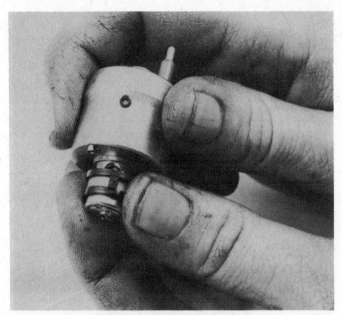

14.21 Slide the new filter onto the nozzle of the fuel injector

14.22 Lubricate the lower O-ring with transmission fluid then place it on the shoulder in the bottom of the injector cavity

14.23 Place the steel back-up washer on the shoulder near the top of the injector cavity

14.24 Lubricate the upper O-ring with transmission fluid then install it on top of the steel washer

Fuel injector assembly

14 To unplug the electrical connectors from the fuel injectors, squeeze the plastic tabs and pull straight up **(see illustration)**. **Note:** *Do not remove the fuel meter cover assembly gasket — leave it in place to protect the casting from damage during injector removal.*

15 Remove the fuel meter cover/pressure regulator assembly.

16 Use a screwdriver and fulcrum **(see illustration)** to pry out the injector.

17 Remove the upper (larger) and lower (smaller) O-rings and filter from the injector.

18 Remove the steel backup washer from the top of the injector cavity.

19 Inspect the fuel injection filter for evidence of dirt and contamination. If present, check for the presence of dirt in the fuel lines and fuel tank.

20 Be sure to replace the fuel injector with an identical part. Injectors from other models can fit in the Model 220 TBI assembly but are calibrated for different flow rates.

21 Slide the new filter into place on the nozzle of the injector **(see illustration)**.

22 Lubricate the new lower (smaller) O-ring with automatic transmission fluid and place it on the small shoulder at the bottom of the fuel injector cavity in the fuel meter body **(see illustration)**.

23 Install the steel back-up washer in the injector cavity **(see illustration)**.

24 Lubricate the new upper (larger) O-ring with automatic transmission fluid and install it on top of the steel back-up washer **(see illustration)**. **Note:** *The backup washer and the large O-ring must be installed before the injector. If they aren't, improper seating of the large O-ring could cause fuel leakage.*

25 To install the injector, align the raised lug on the injector base with the notch in the fuel meter body cavity **(see illustration)**. Push down on the injector until it is fully seated in the fuel meter body. **Note:** *The electrical terminals should be parallel with the throttle shaft.*

26 Install the fuel meter cover assembly and gasket.

27 Attach the cable to the negative terminal of the battery.

28 With the engine off and the ignition on, check for fuel leaks.

29 Attach the electrical connectors to the fuel injector(s).

30 Install the air cleaner housing assembly, adapter and gaskets.

Throttle Position Sensor (TPS)

31 Remove the two TPS attaching screws and retainers and remove the TPS from the throttle body.

32 If you intend to re-use the same TPS, do not attempt to clean it by soaking it in any liquid cleaner or solvent. The TPS is a delicate electrical component and can be damaged by solvents.

33 Install the TPS on the throttle body while lining up the TPS lever with the TPS drive lever.
34 Install the two TPS attaching screws and retainers.
35 Install the air cleaner housing assembly, adapter and gaskets.
36 Attach the cable to the negative terminal of the battery. **Note:** *See non-adjustable TPS output check at end of this section.*

Idle Air Control (IAC) valve

37 Unplug the electrical connector from the IAC valve and remove the IAC valve **(see illustration)**.
38 Remove and discard the old IAC valve gasket. Clean any old gasket material from the surface of the throttle body assembly to insure proper sealing of the new gasket.
39 All pintles in IAC valves on Model 220 TBI units have the same dual taper. However, the pintles on some units have a 12mm diameter and the pintles on others have a 10mm diameter. A replacement IAC

valve must have the appropriate pintle taper and diameter for proper seating of the valve in the throttle body.
40 Measure the distance between the tip of the pintle and the housing mounting surface with the pintle fully extended **(see illustration)**. If dimension ''A'' is greater than the specified dimension, it must be reduced to prevent damage to the valve.
41 If the pintle must be adjusted, determine whether your valve is a Type I (collar around the electrical terminal) or a Type II (no collar around the electrical terminal).
a) To adjust the pintle of an IAC valve with a collar, grasp the valve and exert firm pressure on the pintle with the thumb. Use a slight side-to-side movement on the pintle as you press it in with your thumb **(see illustration)**.
b) To adjust the pintle of an IAC valve without a collar, compress the retaining spring while turning the pintle clockwise **(see illustration)**. Return the spring end to its original position with the straight

14.25 Make sure that the lug is aligned with the groove in the bottom of the fuel injector cavity

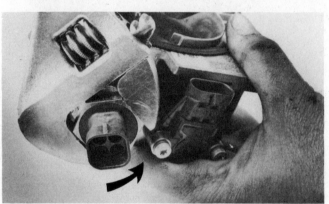

14.37 The IAC valve can be removed with an adjustable wrench (shown) or a 1-1/4 inch wrench

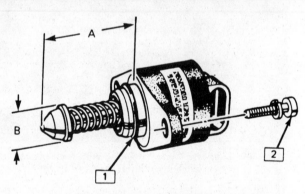

14.40 Typical flange type IAC valve for the Model 220 TBI

1 O-ring   A Distance of pintle extension
2 Screw and washer   B Diameter of pintle

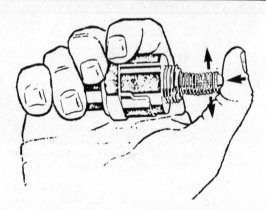

14.41a To adjust an IAC valve with a collar, retract the valve pintle by exerting firm pressure while using a slight side-to-side movement on the pintle

14.41b To adjust an IAC valve without a collar, compress the valve retaining spring while turning the valve clockwise . . .

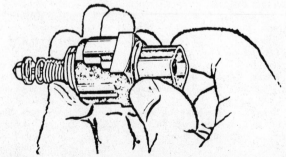

14.41c . . . then return the spring to its original position with the straight portion aligned in the slot under the flat surface of the valve

portion aligned in the slot under the flat surface of the valve **(see illustration)**.

42 Install the IAC valve and tighten it to the specified torque. Attach the electrical connector.

43 Install the air cleaner housing assembly, adapter and gaskets.

44 Attach the cable to the negative terminal of the battery.

45 Start the engine and allow it to reach operating temperature, then turn it off. No adjustment of the IAC valve is required after installation. The IAC valve is reset by the ECM when the engine is turned off.

Fuel meter body assembly

46 Unplug the electrical connectors from the fuel injectors.

47 Remove the fuel meter cover/pressure regulator assembly, fuel meter cover gasket, fuel meter outlet gasket and pressure regulator seal.

48 Remove the fuel injectors.

49 Unscrew the fuel inlet and return line threaded fittings, detach the lines and remove the O-rings.

50 Remove the fuel inlet and outlet nuts and gaskets from the fuel meter body assembly **(see illustration)**. Note the locations of the nuts to ensure proper reassembly. The inlet nut has a larger passage than the outlet nut.

51 Remove the gasket from the inner end of each fuel nut.

52 Remove the fuel meter body-to-throttle body attaching screws and remove the fuel meter body from the throttle body **(see illustration)**.

53 Install the new throttle body-to-fuel meter body gasket. Match the cut-out portions in the gasket with the openings in the throttle body.

54 Install the fuel meter body on the throttle body. Coat the fuel meter body-to-throttle body attaching screws with thread locking compound before installing them.

55 Install the fuel inlet and outlet nuts, with new gaskets, in the fuel meter body and tighten the nuts to the specified torque. Install the fuel inlet and return line threaded fittings with new O-rings. Use a back-up wrench to prevent the nuts from turning.

56 Install the fuel injectors.

57 Install the fuel meter cover/pressure regulator assembly.

59 Attach the cable to the negative terminal of the battery.

58 Attach the electrical connectors to the fuel injectors.

60 With the engine off and the ignition on, check for leaks around the fuel meter body, the gasket and around the fuel line nuts and threaded fittings.

61 Install the air cleaner housing assembly, adapters and gaskets.

Throttle body assembly

62 Unplug all electrical connectors — the IAC valve, TPS and fuel injectors. Detach the grommet with the wires from the throttle body.

63 Detach the throttle linkage, return spring(s), transmission control cable (automatics) and, if equipped, cruise control.

64 Clearly label, then detach, all vacuum hoses.

65 Using a backup wrench, detach the inlet and outlet fuel line nuts **(see illustration)**. Remove the fuel line O-rings from the nuts and discard them.

66 Remove the TBI mounting bolts **(see illustration)** and lift the TBI unit from the intake manifold. Remove and discard the TBI manifold gasket.

67 Place the TBI unit on a holding fixture (Kent-Moore J-9789-118 or BT-3553 or equivalent). **Note:** *If you don't have a holding fixture,*

and decide to place the TBI directly on a work bench surface, be extremely careful when servicing it. The throttle valve can be easily damaged.

68 Remove the fuel meter body-to-throttle body attaching screws and separate the fuel meter body from the throttle body.

69 Remove the throttle body-to-fuel meter body gasket and discard it.

70 Remove the TPS.

71 Invert the throttle body on a flat surface for greater stability and remove the IAC valve.

72 Clean the throttle body assembly in a cold immersion cleaner. Clean the metal parts thoroughly and blow dry with compressed air. Be sure that all fuel and air passages are free of dirt or burrs. **Caution:** *Do not place the TPS, IAC valve, pressure regulator diaphragm, fuel injectors or other components containing rubber in the solvent or cleaning bath. If the throttle body requires cleaning, soaking time in the cleaner should be kept to a minimum. Some models have throttle shaft dust seals that could lose their effectiveness by extended soaking.*

73 Inspect the mating surfaces for damage that could affect gasket sealing. Inspect the throttle lever and valve for dirt, binds, nicks and other damage.

74 Invert the throttle body on a flat surface for stability and install the IAC valve and the TPS.

75 Install a new throttle body-to-fuel meter body gasket and place the fuel meter body assembly on the throttle body assembly. Coat the fuel meter body-to-throttle body attaching screws with thread locking compound and tighten them securely.

76 Install the TBI unit and tighten the mounting bolts to the specified torque. Use a new TBI-to-manifold gasket.

77 Install new O-rings on the fuel line nuts. Install the fuel line and outlet nuts by hand to prevent stripping the threads. Using a backup wrench, tighten the nuts to the specified torque once they have been correctly threaded into the TBI unit.

78 Attach the vacuum hoses, throttle linkage, return spring(s), transmission control cable (automatics) and, if equipped, cruise control cable. Attach the grommet, with wire harness, to the throttle body.

79 Plug in all electrical connectors, making sure that the connectors are fully seated and latched.

80 Check to see if the accelerator pedal is free by depressing the pedal to the floor and releasing it with the engine off.

81 Connect the negative battery cable, and, with the engine off and the ignition on, check for leaks around the fuel line nuts.

82 Adjust the minimum idle speed and check the TPS output (see Steps 84 through 93).

83 Install the air cleaner housing assembly, adapter and gaskets.

Minimum idle speed adjustment

Note: *This adjustment should be performed only when the throttle body has been replaced. The engine should be at normal operating temperature before making the adjustment.*

84 Remove the air cleaner housing assembly, adapter and gaskets.

85 Plug any vacuum ports as required by the VECI label.

86 With the IAC valve connected, ground the diagnostic terminal of the ALDL connector (see Chapter 6). Turn on the ignition but do not start the engine. Wait at least 30 seconds to allow the IAC valve pintle to extend and seat in the throttle body. Disconnect the IAC valve electrical connector. Remove the ground from the diagnostic terminal and

14.50 Remove the fuel inlet and outlet nuts from the fuel meter body

14.52 Once the fuel inlet and outlet nuts are off, pull the fuel meter body straight up to separate it from the throttle body

14.65 When disconnecting the fuel feed and return lines from the fuel inlet and outlet nuts, be sure to use a backup wrench to prevent damage to the lines

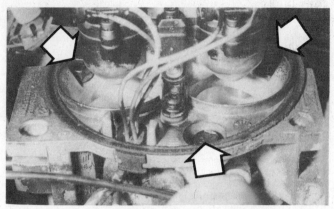

14.66 To remove the Model 220 throttle body from the intake manifold, remove the three bolts (arrows)

start the engine.
87 Remove the plug by first piercing it with an awl **(see illustration in Section 13)**, then applying leverage.
88 Adjust the idle stop screw to obtain the specified rpm in neutral (manual) or in Drive (automatic).
89 Turn the ignition off and reconnect the IAC valve electrical connector.
90 Unplug any plugged vacuum line ports.
91 Install the air cleaner housing assembly, adapter and new gaskets (see Section 8).

Non-adjustable TPS output check

Note: *This check should be performed only when the throttle body or the TPS has been replaced or after the minimum idle speed has been adjusted.*

92 Connect a digital voltmeter from the TPS connector center terminal ''B'' to outside terminal ''A'' (you'll have to fabricate jumpers for terminal access).
93 With the ignition on and the engine off, TPS voltage should be less than the specified voltage. If it's more than the specified voltage, check the minimum idle speed before replacing the TPS.

15   Central Port Injection (CPI) - general information and CPI unit removal and installation

General information

Refer to illustration 15.6
1 Central Port Injection (CPI) is used on 1992 and later V6 engines with VIN code W. The CPI unit's function is to control fuel delivery to the engine. The CPI system is controlled by the Electronic Control Module (ECM) located in the passenger compartment. The ECM is the control center of the Computer Command Control system (CCCS).
2 The ECM monitors voltage from several sensors to determine how much fuel the engine needs. When the key is turned ''ON'', the ECM turns on the fuel pump relay for two seconds and the fuel pump builds up pressure to the CPI unit. The ECM monitors the Coolant Temperature Sensor (CTS), the Intake Air Temperature Sensor (IATS), Throttle Position Sensor (TPS) and Manifold Absolute Pressure (MAP) sensor and then determines the proper air/fuel ratio for starting.
3 The fuel control system has an electric fuel pump, located in the fuel tank on the fuel gauge sending unit. The pump provides pressure above the regulated pressure needed by the CPI injector.
4 The intake manifold is designed with an upper and lower manifold assembly. The upper manifold is a variable-tuned split-plenum design that also includes an intake manifold tuning valve, MAP sensor and a throttle valve attached to the plenum.
5 The throttle valve is used to control air flow into the engine and consequently engine output. During engine idle, the throttle valve is almost completely closed and air flow control is handled by the Idle Air Control (IAC) valve.
6 Most of the CPI components are housed directly under the air intake plenum **(see illustration)**. In order to service the CPI unit, it will be necessary to remove the air intake plenum from the intake mani-

fold. The pressure regulator assembly consists of ta fuel meter body, gasket seal, fuel pressure regulator, fuel injector and six poppet nozzles with fuel tubes. The CPI unit is not repairable and must be replaced as an assembly if found to be defective. Be sure to contact a dealer service department for any service contracts or warranties that might cover the repair of the fuel system before attempting it on your own.
7 The CPI system has a low-gain fuel pressure regulator to maintain pressure at the fuel injector through a range of fuel recirculation rates from the in-tank fuel pump. With the ignition ''ON'' and the engine NOT running, the fuel pressure should be 55 to 61 psi. Fuel enters the fuel meter body through the fuel inlet line and flows directly into the injector cavity. When the ECM de-energizes the injector solenoid, fuel is recirculated through the pressure regulator. Fuel pressure applied to the regulator diaphragm acts against the spring force and opens the valve from its seat. This allows fuel to return to the fuel tank by way of the fuel meter body outlet and the return line. While the ECM energizes the injector solenoid, the armature lifts off the six fuel tube seats and delivers fuel through the fuel meter body out to the six poppet nozzles.
8 When the ECM energizes the injector solenoid, pressurized fuel flows through the fuel tubes to each poppet nozzle. There are six poppet nozzles (one for each cylinder). An increase in fuel pressure will cause the poppet nozzle ball to lift from its seat against spring force and spray fuel at approximately 52 psi. De-energizing the injector solenoid closes the armature and reduces the fuel pressure on the poppet nozzle ball.

CPI unit removal and installation

Refer to illustrations 15.10, 15.11, 15.12, 15.22, 15.24, 15.25
Note: *Do not attempt to disassemble the CPI unit. It is a non-serviceable part.*
Removal
9 Relieve the fuel pressure (see Section 2). Remove the Torx screws and lift off the plastic cover from the air intake plenum.
10 Disconnect the electrical connectors on the TPS, IAC motor, MAP sensor and intake manifold tuning valve assembly **(see illustration)**.
11 Disconnect the TV linkage, cruise control cable (if so equipped) and accelerator cable **(see illustration)** from the throttle valve assembly.
12 Remove the bolts that retain the bracket to the air intake plenum **(see illustration)**.
13 Remove the intake air ducts from the plenum and the fan shroud.
14 Remove the ignition coil (see Chapter 5).
15 Disconnect the PCV hose from the plenum and the valve cover.
16 Disconnect the vacuum lines from the front and rear of the air intake plenum.
17 Remove the ignition wire and harness bracket from the plenum. Be sure to mark the position of each stud and nut.
18 Remove the bolts and nuts from the air intake plenum. Start on the front bolt and work your way counter-clockwise (standing directly in front of the engine compartment) around the circumference of the plenum.
19 Lift the air intake plenum from the intake manifold. Remove the

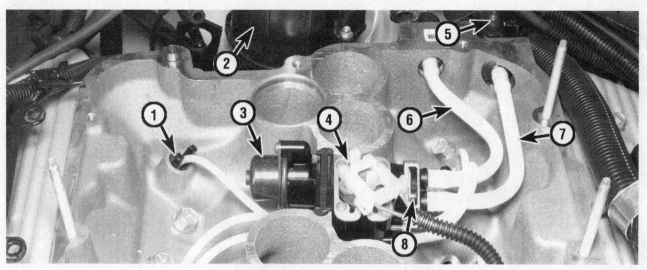

15.6 Central Port Injection (CPI) system details

1 Poppet nozzle	3 Fuel pressure regulator	5 Fuel line access fitting	7 Inlet fuel line
2 Distributor	4 Central Port Injection unit	6 Fuel return line	8 Fuel inlet and return line clip

15.10 Disconnect the MAP sensor electrical connector

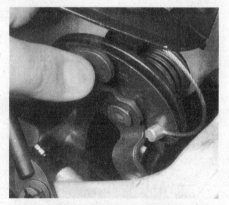

15.11 While pulling the throttle back, lift the accelerator cable from the notch on the throttle valve

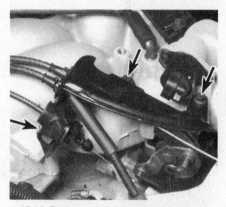

15.12 Remove the three bolts (arrows) from the plenum and lift the bracket assembly off the plenum

15.22 Squeeze the tab (arrow) to disconnect the injector electrical connector

15.24 Carefully remove the inlet and return lines from the injector assembly

15.25 Squeeze the two tabs and lift to remove the poppet nozzle from the intake manifold

gasket from the intake manifold.

20   Inspect the gasket surface on the plenum and the intake manifold for any chips, burrs or cracks. If the plenum is damaged, replace it with a new unit.

21   Clean the gasket surface on the plenum and the intake manifold with a soft cloth and solvent.

22   Detach the electrical connector from the CPI assembly **(see illustration)**.

23   Disconnect the fuel fitting clip and discard it.

24   Disconnect the fuel inlet and outlet lines from the CPI assembly **(see illustration)**. Remove the O-ring seals and discard them. Use new seals for assembly.

25   Squeeze the poppet nozzle locking tabs **(see illustration)** while lifting the nozzle out of the intake manifold.

26   After disconnecting the six poppet nozzles, lift the CPI assembly out of the intake manifold as a single unit.

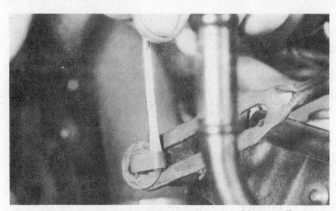

**16.8   To remove the clip, pop it loose with a small
screwdriver and slide the cable end off the linkage stud**

Installation

27   Align the CPI assembly grommet with the casting grommet slots
and push down until it is seated at the bottom of the guide hole.

28   Push the poppet nozzles into the casing sockets. **Caution:** *Be
sure the poppet nozzles are seated and secured in the casting sockets
before installing the plenum. Check by pulling each poppet nozzle
firmly until it is in its correct place. This will prevent fuel leaks and consequently any fire danger.*

29   Connect the fuel inlet and outlet lines to the CPI assembly. Be
sure to install new O-rings. Coat the new O-rings with clean engine oil.

30   Install the new fuel fitting clip.

31   Be sure the fuel pump relay is connected and pressurize the fuel
pump by turning the ignition "ON". Do not start the engine. Check all
the fittings for fuel leaks before installing the air intake plenum.

32   Install the air intake plenum. Be sure to use a new gasket. Tighten
the plenum fasteners to the torque listed in this Chapter's Specifications. **Note:** *Be sure the plenum does not pinch any fuel lines or nozzles.*

---

16   Throttle cable – removal and installation

Refer to illustrations 16.8 and 16.11

1   The accelerator control system is the cable type. There are no
linkage adjustments. Because there are no adjustments, only the specific replacement part will work.

2   When work has been performed on the accelerator controls, always check to ensure that all components are installed the same way
they were removed and that all linkage and cables are neither rubbing
nor binding.

Accelerator cable

3   When performing service on the accelerator cable, observe the
following:

a) The retainer must be installed with the tangs secured over the
head of the stud.

b) The conduit fitting at both ends of the cable must have its locking
tangs expanded and locked in the attaching holes.

c) The braided portion of the accelerator cable must not come in
contact with the front of the dash sealer during assembly, repair
or replacement.

d) Flexible components (hoses, wires, conduits, etc.) must not be
routed within two inches of the moving parts of the accelerator
linkage outboard of the support bracket unless the routing is pos-
itively controlled.

Accelerator pedal

4   When performing service on the accelerator pedal, observe the
following:

a) The mounting surface between the support and the dash panel
must be free of insulation. The carpet and padding in the pedal
and tunnel area must be positioned to lay flat and be free of wrin-
kles and bunches.

b) Slip the accelerator control cable through the slot in the rod and
then install the retainer in the rod, being sure that it is seated.

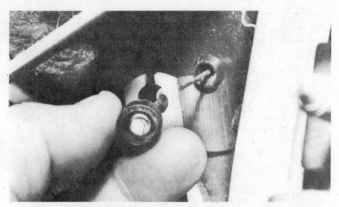

**16.11   To detach the throttle cable from the accelerator
pedal, pull the small plastic bush loose from the upper end
of pedal lever then lift the cable up and out of the groove
in the lever**

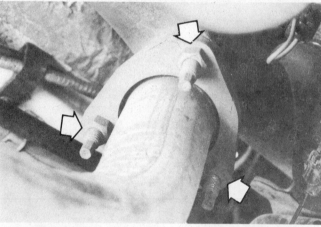

**17.3   To detach the forward end of the exhaust pipe from the
exhaust manifold, remove the three nuts (V6 engine shown)**

Care must be utilized in pressing the retainer into the hole in the
rod to assure that the cable is not kinked or damaged in any way.

c) After all components of the accelerator linkage are secured, the
linkage must operate freely without binding between closed throttle and wide open throttle.

Replacement (typical)

5   Detach the cable from the negative terminal of the battery.

6   On carbureted and TBI models, remove the air filter housing and
adapter.

7   Locate the forward end of the throttle cable at the carburetor, TBI
or CPI linkage.

8   On carbureted and TBI models, pop the retaining clip on the end
of the throttle linkage stud loose with a small screwdriver **(see illustration)**.

9   On CPI models, disconnect the retainer from the throttle lever
stud, then disconnect the throttle cable from the notch on the throttle
valve **(see illustration 15.11)**.

10   The cable is held in the cable bracket with a small plastic ferrule.
Pinch the two locking tabs of the ferrule together and pull the cable
through the hole in the bracket.

11   Inside the vehicle locate the upper end of the accelerator pedal
lever. Pull the small plastic bush out of the top of the lever, push the
lever forward and lift the cable free of the slot in the top of the lever
(see illustration).

12   Locate the spot immediately above and forward of the upper end
of the accelerator pedal lever where the cable comes through the firewall. Note that the cable comes through a large rubber washer (for insulation against water). Pull this washer loose. The cable is retained at
its hole in the firewall with a ferrule similar to the one used with the cable bracket at the carburetor/TBI unit. Pinch the locking tabs together
and pull the cable through the firewall.

13   Installation is the reverse of removal.

17 Exhaust system – removal and installation

Refer to illustrations 17.3 and 17.4

1   Detach the cable from the negative terminal of the battery.
2   Raise the vehicle and place it securely on jackstands.
3   Detach the exhaust manifold-to-exhaust pipe nuts **(see illustration)**.
4   Remove the exhaust pipe hanger located in front of the muffler **(see illustration)** and the hanger behind the muffler.
5   Unbolt and remove the rear exhaust hanger.
6   Remove the exhaust system.
7   Installation is the reverse of removal.

18 Catalytic converter – bottom cover replacement

Refer to illustrations 18.1, 18.3, 18.4 and 18.5

1   If the bottom cover of the catalytic converter is torn or punctured, it can be replaced with a repair kit. Remove the bottom cover by cutting close to the bottom outside edges **(see illustration)**. The depth of the cut must be very shallow to prevent damage to the inner shell of the converter. **Note:** *On the dual bed converter, follow the contour of the air inlet tube carefully so that it is not punctured.*
2   Remove the insulation. Inspect the inner shell of the converter for damage. Do not remove the filler plug. If there is damage to the inner shell, the converter assembly must be replaced.
3   Place new insulation in the replacement cover. Apply a bead of sealing compound all the way around the cover after the insulation is in position **(see illustration)**. Apply extra sealer at the front and rear opening for the pipes. On the dual bed converter, also apply extra sealer around the air inlet tube.
4   Install the replacement cover on the converter and install the cover retaining channels on both sides of the converter **(see illustration)**.
5   On the single bed converter, attach two clamps over the retaining channels at each end of the converter **(see illustration)**. On the dual bed converter, attach two clamps over the retaining channels at each end of the converter plus one clamp without a retaining channel between the air inlet tube and exhaust inlet pipe.

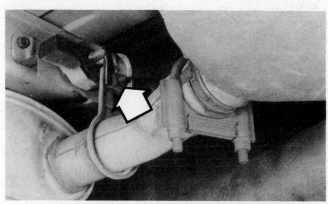

17.4   To detach the forward exhaust hanger from its insulator, remove the hanger mounting bolt (arrow)

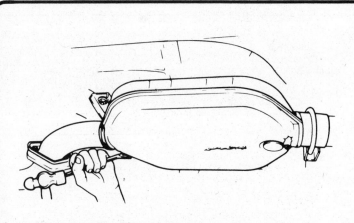

18.1   To remove the catalytic converter cover, you'll have to cut it off with a chisel

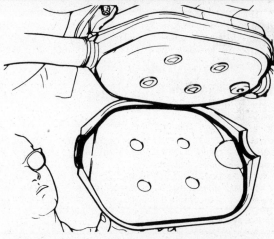

18.3   Be sure to apply a bead of sealant on the new cover in the area indicated by the darkened line

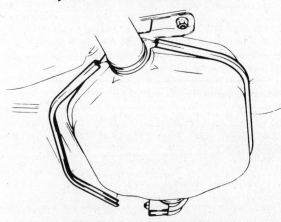

18.4   Install the retaining channels along the edges of the new cover

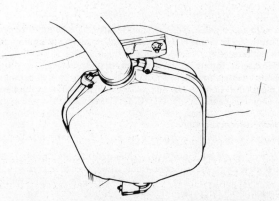

18.5   Install clamps over the retaining channels at both ends of the converter

Chapter 5   Engine electrical systems

Specifications

General

Cylinder numbers	See Chapter 2
Firing order	See Chapter 2
Distributor rotation	clockwise

Torque specifications

Ft-lbs

Alternator mounting bolts
four-cylinder engine
upper bolt	20
lower bolt	37

V6 engine
upper bolt	18
lower bolt	35

---

1   Ignition system — general information

The engines in all vehicles covered in this manual are equipped with High Energy Ignition (HEI) systems consisting of an ignition switch, battery, coil, primary (low tension) and secondary (high tension) wiring circuits, a distributor and spark plugs.

High Energy Ignition (HEI) distributor

HEI equipped vehicles use a special HEI distributor with Electronic Spark Timing (EST). Some HEI distributors combine all the ignition components into one unit with the ignition coil in the distributor cap. On other HEI distributors, the coil is mounted separately.

All spark timing changes in the HEI/EST distributor are carried out by the Electronic Control Module (ECM), which monitors data from various engine sensors, computes the desired spark timing and signals the distributor to change the timing accordingly. No vacuum or mechanical advance is used.

Electronic Spark Control (ESC)

Some engines are equipped with an Electronic Spark Control (ESC), which uses a knock sensor in connection with the ECM to control spark timing to allow the engine to have maximum spark advance without spark knock. This improves driveability and fuel economy.

Secondary (spark plug) wiring

The secondary (spark plug) wire used with the HEI system is a car-
bon impregnated cord conductor encased in an 8 mm diameter rubber jacket with an outer silicone jacket. This type of wire will withstand very high temperatures and provides an excellent insulator for the HEI's high voltage. **Warning:** *Because of the very high voltage generated by the HEI system, extreme care should be taken whenever an operation involving ignition components is performed. This not only includes the distributor, coil, control module and spark plug wires, but related items that are connected to the systems as well, such as the plug connections, tachometer and testing equipment.*

---

2   Battery - removal and installation

Warning: *Hydrogen gas is produced by the battery, so keep open flames and lighted cigarettes away from it at all times. Always wear eye protection when working around a battery. Rinse off spilled electrolyte immediately with large amounts of water.*
Caution: *If the vehicle is equipped with a Delco Loc II audio system (1992 and later models with a Compact Disc player), be sure the lockout feature is turned off before performing any procedure that requires disconnecting the battery (refer to your owner's manual for further information on this system).*
1   Detach the cable from the negative terminal of the battery.
2   Detach the cable from the positive terminal of the battery.
3   Remove the battery hold-down retainer.

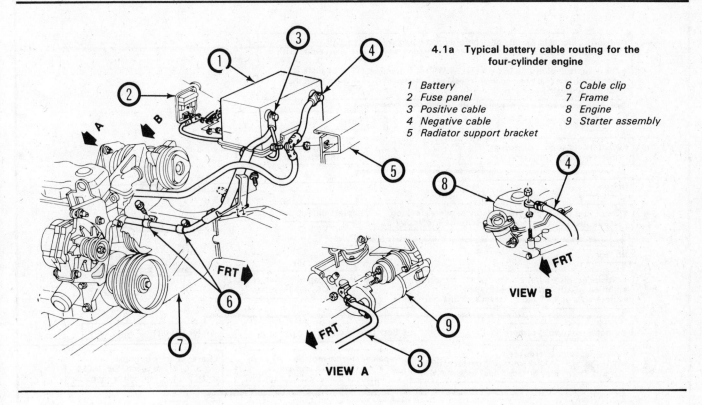

4.1a Typical battery cable routing for the four-cylinder engine

1	Battery	6	Cable clip
2	Fuse panel	7	Frame
3	Positive cable	8	Engine
4	Negative cable	9	Starter assembly
5	Radiator support bracket		

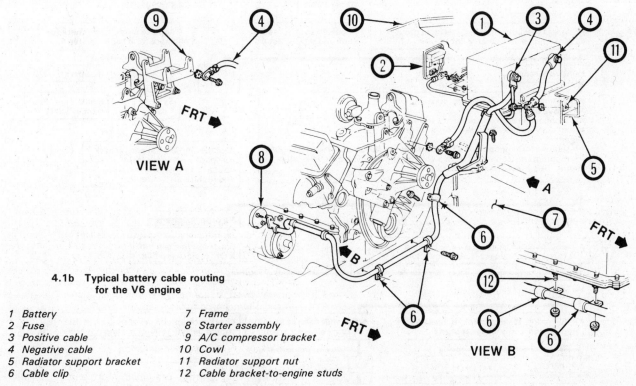

4.1b Typical battery cable routing for the V6 engine

1	Battery	7	Frame
2	Fuse	8	Starter assembly
3	Positive cable	9	A/C compressor bracket
4	Negative cable	10	Cowl
5	Radiator support bracket	11	Radiator support nut
6	Cable clip	12	Cable bracket-to-engine studs

5

4 Remove the battery.
5 Installation is the reverse of removal.

3 Battery — emergency jump starting

Refer to the *Booster battery (jump) starting* procedure at the front of this manual.

4 Battery cables — check and replacement

Refer to illustrations 4.1a and 4.1b
1 Periodically inspect the entire length of each battery cable for damage, cracked or burned insulation and corrosion **(see illustrations)**. Poor battery cable connections can cause starting problems and decreased engine performance.

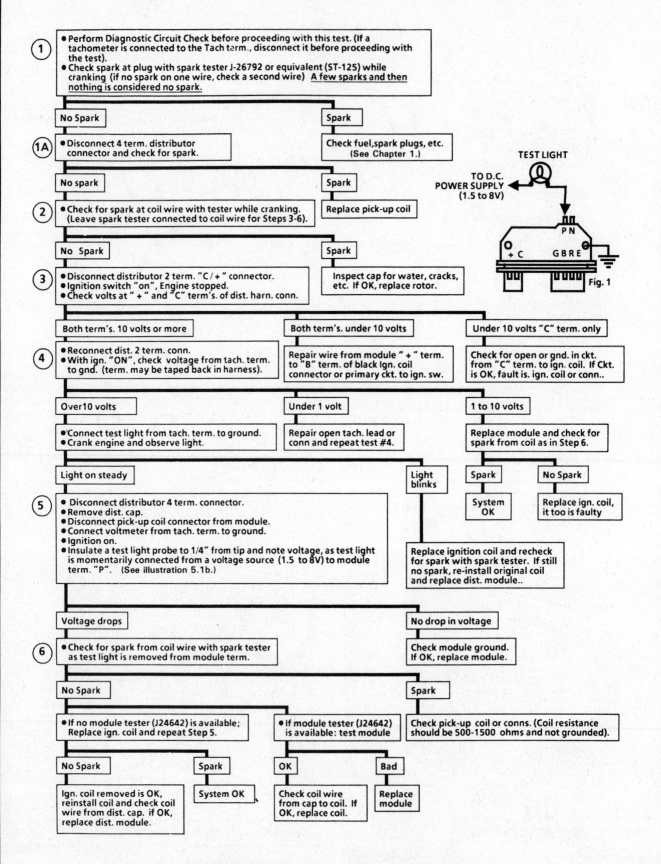

① • Perform Diagnostic Circuit Check before proceeding with this test. (If a tachometer is connected to the Tach term., disconnect it before proceeding with the test).
 • Check spark at plug with spark tester J-26792 or equivalent (ST-125) while cranking (if no spark on one wire, check a second wire) A few sparks and then nothing is considered no spark.

No Spark | Spark

①A • Disconnect 4 term. distributor connector and check for spark.

Check fuel, spark plugs, etc. (See Chapter 1.)

TEST LIGHT

TO D.C. POWER SUPPLY (1.5 to 8V)

No spark | Spark

② • Check for spark at coil wire with tester while cranking. (Leave spark tester connected to coil wire for Steps 3-6).

Replace pick-up coil

P N
+ C   G B R E

Fig. 1

No Spark | Spark

③ • Disconnect distributor 2 term. "C / +" connector.
 • Ignition switch "on", Engine stopped.
 • Check volts at " + " and "C" term's. of dist. harn. conn.

Inspect cap for water, cracks, etc. If OK, replace rotor.

Both term's. 10 volts or more | Both term's. under 10 volts | Under 10 volts "C" term. only

④ • Reconnect dist. 2 term. conn.
 • With ign. "ON", check voltage from tach. term. to gnd. (term. may be taped back in harness).

Repair wire from module " + " term. to "B" term. of black Ign. coil connector or primary ckt. to ign. sw.

Check for open or gnd. in ckt. from "C" term. to ign. coil. If Ckt. is OK, fault is. ign. coil or conn..

Over 10 volts | Under 1 volt | 1 to 10 volts

 • Connect test light from tach. term. to ground.
 • Crank engine and observe light.

Repair open tach. lead or conn and repeat test #4.

Replace module and check for spark from coil as in Step 6.

Light on steady | Light blinks | Spark | No Spark

⑤ • Disconnect distributor 4 term. connector.
 • Remove dist. cap.
 • Disconnect pick-up coil connector from module.
 • Connect voltmeter from tach. term. to ground.
 • Ignition on.
 • Insulate a test light probe to 1/4" from tip and note voltage, as test light is momentarily connected from a voltage source (1.5 to 8V) to module term. "P". (See illustration 5.1b.)

System OK | Replace ign. coil, it too is faulty

Replace ignition coil and recheck for spark with spark tester. If still no spark, re-install original coil and replace dist. module..

Voltage drops | No drop in voltage

⑥ • Check for spark from coil wire with spark tester as test light is removed from module term.

Check module ground. If OK, replace module.

No Spark | Spark

 • If no module tester (J24642) is available; Replace ign. coil and repeat Step 5.

 • If module tester (J24642) is available: test module

Check pick-up coil or conns. (Coil resistance should be 500-1500 ohms and not grounded).

No Spark | Spark | OK | Bad

Ign. coil removed is OK, reinstall coil and check coil wire from dist. cap. if OK, replace dist. module.

System OK

Check coil wire from cap to coil. If OK, replace coil.

Replace module

5.1a Diagnostic flow chart for checking the ignition system

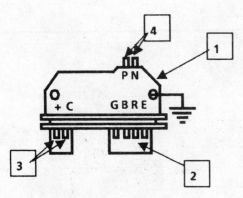

5.1b   HEI distributor module

1 *Module*	3 *Ignition coil terminals*
2 *EST terminals*	4 *Pick-up coil terminals*

2   Check the cable-to-terminal connections at the ends of the cables for cracks, loose wire strands and corrosion. The presence of white, fluffy deposits under the insulation at the cable terminal connection is a sign the cable is corroded and should be replaced. Check the terminals for distortion, missing mounting bolts or nuts and corrosion.

3   If only the positive cable is to be replaced, be sure to disconnect the negative cable from the battery first.

4   Disconnect and remove the cable. Make sure the replacement cable is the same length and diameter.

5   Clean the threads of the starter or ground connection with a wire brush to remove rust and corrosion. Apply a light coat of petroleum jelly to the threads to ease installation and prevent future corrosion.

6   Attach the cable to the starter or ground connection and tighten the mounting nut securely.

7   Before connecting the new cable to the battery, make sure it reaches the terminals without having to be stretched.

8   Connect the positive cable first, followed by the negative cable. Tighten the nuts and apply a thin coat of petroleum jelly to the terminal and cable connection.

5   Ignition system — check

Refer to illustrations 5.1a and 5.1b

Warning: *Because of the very high voltage generated by the ignition system, extreme care should be taken whenever an operation is performed involving ignition components. This not only includes the distributor, coil, control module and spark plug wires, but related items that are connected to the system as well, such as the plug connections, tachometer and any test equipment.*

Diagnostic chart 5.1a **(see illustration)** diagrams the testing procedures for the HEI ignition system. Also shown is the terminal identification for testing the ignition module **(see illustration)**.

6   Distributor — removal and installation

Four-cylinder engine
Refer to illustrations 6.4 and 6.5
Removal

1   Disconnect the cable from the negative battery terminal.

2   Remove the coil wire from the distributor cap.

3   Remove the distributor cap.

4   Note the position of the rotor and the distributor-to-block alignment. Make an alignment mark on the distributor to indicate the position of the rotor **(see illustration)**.

5   Remove the distributor hold-down clamp bolt and clamp **(see illustration)**. Remove the distributor from the engine. **Caution:** *Do not turn the crankshaft while the distributor is removed from the engine. If the crankshaft is turned, the position of the rotor will be altered and the engine will have to be retimed.*

Installation (crankshaft not turned after distributor removal)

6   Insert the distributor into the engine in exactly the same relation to the block in which it was removed. To mesh the gears, it may be necessary to turn the rotor slightly. At this point the distributor may not seat down against the block completely. This is due to the lower end of the distributor shaft not mating properly with the oil pump shaft. If this is the case, check again to make sure the distributor is aligned

5

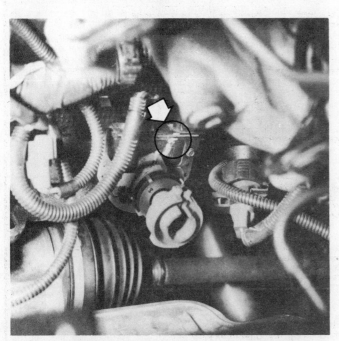

6.4   Mark the position of the rotor with respect to the distributor before removing the rotor

6.5   The distributor hold-down clamp and bolt must be removed before the distributor can be removed from the engine

with the block in the same position it was in before removal and that the rotor is correctly aligned with the distributor body. The gear on the distributor shaft is engaged with the gear on the camshaft, and this relationship cannot change as long as the distributor is not lifted from the engine. Use a socket and breaker bar on the crankshaft bolt to turn the engine over in the normal direction of rotation. The rotor will turn, but the oil pump shaft will not because the two shafts are not engaged. When the proper alignment is reached the distributor will drop down over the oil pump shaft, and the distributor body will seat properly against the block.

7   Install the hold-down clamp and tighten the bolt securely.
8   Install the distributor cap and coil wire.
9   Connect the cable to the negative terminal of the battery.

Installation (crankshaft turned after distributor removal)
10 Remove the number one spark plug.
11 Place your finger over the spark plug hole while turning the crankshaft in the normal direction of rotation with a wrench on the pulley bolt at the front of the engine.
12 When you feel compression, continue turning the crankshaft slowly until the timing mark on the crankshaft pulley is aligned with the ''0'' on the engine timing indicator.
13 Position the rotor to point to between the number one and number three distributor terminals.
14 Insert the distributor into the engine in exactly the same relation to the block in which it was removed. To mesh the gears, it may be necessary to turn the rotor slightly. If the distributor does not seat fully against the block it is because the oil pump shaft has not seated in the distributor shaft. Make sure the distributor drive gear is fully engaged with the camshaft gear, then use a socket on the crankshaft bolt to turn the engine over in the normal direction of rotation until the two shafts engage and the distributor seats against the block.
15 Install the hold-down clamp and tighten the bolt securely.
16 Install the distributor cap and coil wire.
17 Connect the cable to the negative terminal of the battery.

V6 engine
Refer to illustrations 6.22 and 6.23
Removal
18 Detach the cable from the negative terminal of the battery.
19 Remove the air cleaner housing assembly, adapter and gaskets (see Chapter 4).
20 Unplug the wiring harness connectors from the side of the distributor base.
21 Remove the distributor cap (see Chapter 1) and move it out of the way.
22 Scribe a mark on the distributor housing base to show the direction the rotor is pointing **(see illustration)**.

6.22   Make a mark on the distributor housing base (arrow) to show the direction the rotor is pointing before removing the distributor

6.23   Mark the position of the distributor in relation to the engine (arrow) before loosening the distributor hold-down clamp

23 Mark the position of the distributor housing in relation to the engine **(see illustration)**.
24 Remove the distributor hold-down bolt and clamp.
25 Remove the distributor. **Caution:** *Avoid turning the crankshaft while the distributor is removed. Turning the crankshaft while the distributor is removed will change the timing position of the rotor and require re-timing the engine.*

Installation (crankshaft not turned after distributor removal)
26 Position the rotor in the exact location it was in when the distributor was removed.
27 Lower the distributor into the engine. To mesh the gears at the bottom of the distributor it may be necessary to turn the rotor slightly. It is possible that the distributor may not seat down fully against the block because the lower part of the distributor shaft has not properly engaged the oil pump shaft. Make sure the distributor and rotor are properly aligned with the marks made earlier, then use a large socket and breaker bar on the crankshaft bolt to turn the engine in the normal direction of rotation until the two shafts engage and the distributor drops down against the block.
28 With the base of the distributor seated against the engine block turn the distributor housing to align the marks made on the distributor base and the engine block.
29 Place the hold-down clamp in position and loosely install the hold-down bolt.
30 Reconnect the ignition wiring harness.
31 Install the distributor cap.
32 Reconnect the coil connector.
33 With the distributor in its original position, tighten the hold-down bolt.
34 Check the ignition timing (Chapter 1).

Installation (crankshaft turned after distributor removal)
35 Remove the number one spark plug.
36 Place your finger over the spark plug hole while turning the crankshaft with a wrench on the pulley bolt at the front of the engine.
37 When you feel compression, continue turning the crankshaft slowly until the timing mark on the vibration damper is aligned with the ''0'' on the engine timing indicator.
38 Position the rotor between the number one and six spark plug terminals on the cap.
39 Lower the distributor into the engine. To mesh the gears at the bottom of the distributor, it may be necessary to turn the rotor slightly. If the distributor does not drop down flush against the block it is because the distributor shaft has not mated to the oil pump shaft. Place

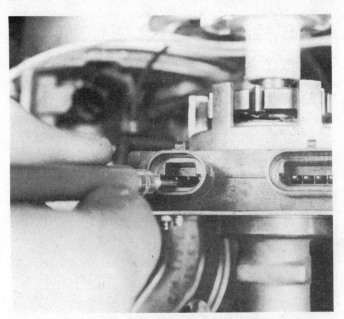

7.4 To check the module for voltage, touch the voltmeter probe to the module positive terminal

a large socket and breaker bar on the crankshaft bolt and turn the engine over in the normal direction of rotation until the two shafts engage properly, allowing the distributor to seat flush against the block.

40 With the base of the distributor properly seated against the engine block, turn the distributor housing to align the marks made on the distributor base and the engine block.

41 Place the hold-down clamp in position and loosely install the hold-down bolt.

42 Reconnect the ignition wiring harness.

43 Install the distributor cap. If the secondary wiring harness was removed from the cap, reinstall it.

44 Reconnect the coil connector.

45 With the distributor in its original position, tighten the hold-down bolt and check the ignition timing.

7 Ignition module — check and replacement

Refer to illustrations 7.4, 7.11, 7.15 and 7.16

Note: *It is not necessary to remove the distributor to check or replace the module.*

Check

1 Disconnect the tachometer lead (if so equipped) at the distributor.

2 Check for a spark at the coil and spark plug wires (Section 5).

3 If there is no spark, remove the distributor cap. Remove the ignition module from the distributor but leave the connector plugged in.

4 With the ignition switch turned On, check for voltage at the module positive terminal **(see illustration)**.

5 If the reading is less than ten volts, there is a fault in the wire between the module positive (+) terminal and the ignition coil positive connector or the ignition coil and primary circuit-to-ignition switch.

6 If the reading is ten volts or more, check the ''C'' terminal on the module **(see illustration 5.1b)**.

7 If the reading is less than one volt, there is an open or grounded lead in the distributor-to-coil ''C'' terminal connection or ignition coil or an open primary circuit in the coil itself.

8 If the reading is one to ten volts, replace the module with a new one and check for a spark (Section 5). If there is a spark the module was faulty and the system is now operating properly. If there is no spark, there is a fault in the ignition coil.

9 If the reading in Step 4 is 10 volts or more, unplug the pick-up coil connector from the module. Check the ''C'' terminal voltage with the ignition switch On and watch the voltage reading as a test light is momentarily (five seconds or less) connected between the battery positive (+) terminal and the module ''P'' terminal **(see illustration 5.1b)**.

10 If there is no drop in voltage, check the module ground and, if it is good, replace the module with a new one.

11 If the voltage drops, check for spark at the coil wire as the test light is removed from the module terminal. If there is no spark, the module is faulty and should be replaced with a new one. If there is a spark, the pick-up coil or connections are faulty or not grounded **(see illustration)**.

Replacement

12 Detach the cable from the negative terminal of the battery.

13 Remove the distributor cap and rotor (see Chapter 1).

14 Remove both module attaching screws and lift the module up and away from the distributor.

15 Disconnect both electrical leads from the module **(see illustration)**. Note that the leads cannot be interchanged.

5

7.11 As the test light is removed, check for a spark at the coil wire (arrow)

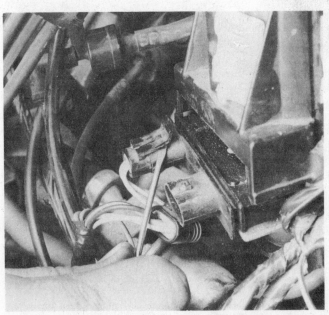

7.15 Unplug both electrical connectors from the module

16 Do not wipe the grease from the module or the distributor base if the same module is to be reinstalled. If a new module is to be installed, a package of silicone grease will be included with it. Wipe the distributor base and the new module clean, then apply the silicone grease on the face of the module and on the distributor base where the module seats **(see illustration)**. This grease is necessary for heat dissipation.

17 Install the module and attach both electrical leads.

18 Install the distributor rotor and cap (see Chapter 1).

19 Attach the cable to the negative terminal of the battery.

---

8   Ignition pick-up coil - check and replacement

Refer to illustrations 8.4, 8.5a, 8.5b, 8.5c, 8.9, 8.10a, 8.10b, 8.10c, 8.11a, 8.11b and 8.12

1 Detach the cable from the negative terminal of the battery.

2 Remove the distributor cap and rotor (see Chapter 1).

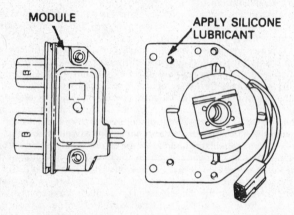

7.16   Silicone lubricant applied to the distributor base in the area under the ignition module dissipates heat — this is a distributor with a separately mounted coil

3 Remove the distributor from the engine (see Section 6).

4 Detach the pick-up coil leads from the module **(see illustration)**.

Check

5 Connect one lead of an ohmmeter to the terminal of the pick-up coil lead and the other to ground as shown **(see illustrations)**. Flex the leads by hand to check for intermittent opens. The ohmmeter should indicate infinite resistance at all times. If it doesn't, the pick-up coil is defective and must be replaced.

6 Connect the ohmmeter leads to both terminals of the pick-up coil lead. Flex the leads by hand to check for intermittent opens. The ohm-

8.4   Before removing the pick-up coil, unplug the lead from the ignition module

TESTING PICKUP COIL

8.5a   Testing the pick-up coil on a typical four-cylinder distributor

TESTING PICKUP COIL

8.5b   Testing the pick-up coil on a typical V6 distributor (1990 and earlier)

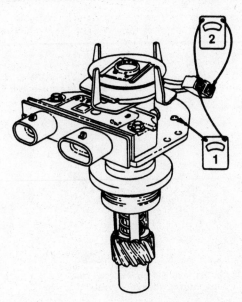

8.5c Testing the pick-up coil on a typical V6 distributor (1991 and later)

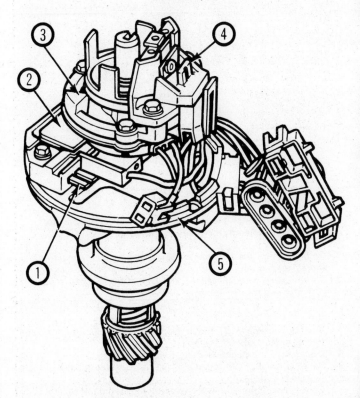

8.9 A typical HEI/EST distributor equipped with a Hall Effect switch

1 "P" terminal
2 Module
3 Pick-up coil assembly

4 Hall Effect switch
5 Pick-up coil leads

meter should read one steady value between 500 and 1500 ohms as the leads are flexed by hand. If it doesn't, the pick-up coil is defective and must be replaced.

Replacement

7   Remove the spring from the distributor shaft.
8   Mark the distributor tang drive and shaft so that they can be re-assembled in the same position.

9   If the distributor is equipped with a Hall Effect switch **(see illustration)**, remove it.
10   Carefully mount the distributor in a soft-jawed vise and, using a hammer and punch, remove the roll pin from the distributor shaft and gear **(see illustrations)**. Remove the distributor shaft **(see illustration)**.

8.10a To remove the pick-up coil, mount the distributor shaft in a soft-jawed vise and, using a drift punch and hammer, knock out the roll pin

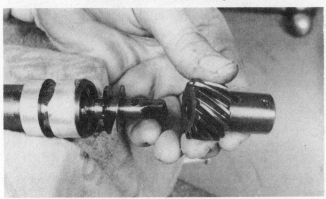

8.10b Remove the driven gear and spacer washers from the end of the shaft, making sure to note the order in which you remove any spacers

8.10c Remove the shaft from the distributor

5

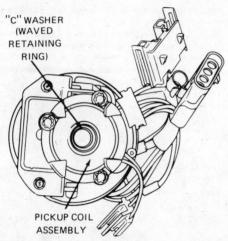

8.11a To remove the pick-up coil from a 4-cylinder engine distributor, remove the thin "C" washer (waved retaining ring)

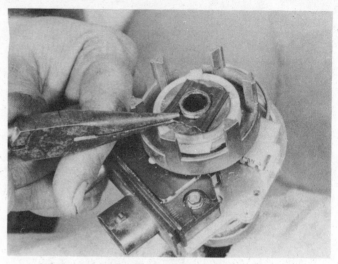

8.11b To remove the pick-up coil from a V6 engine distributor, remove the retaining clip

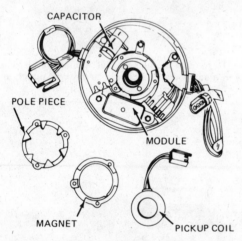

8.12 Lift out the pick-up coil parts — pick-up coil, magnet and pole piece — one by one (don't forget the order in which you remove the parts and their relationship to each other)

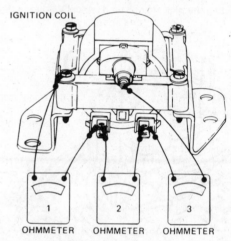

9.12 To check the ignition coil, use an ohmmeter to perform the following three checks

1 *On high scale, the ohmmeter should read infinity*
2 *On low scale, should read very low or zero*
3 *On high scale, should not read infinite. If the coil fails any of these tests, replace it*

11 To remove the pick-up coil, remove the thin "C" washer or the retaining clip **(see illustrations)**.
12 Lift the pick-up coil assembly straight up and remove it from the distributor. Note the order in which you remove the pieces **(see illustration)**.
13 Reassembly is the reverse of disassembly.
14 Installation is the reverse of removal.

---

9 Ignition coil — removal, check and installation

Refer to illustration 9.12

1 Disconnect the cable from the negative terminal of the battery.

Removal

2 On models with a separately mounted coil, unplug the coil high tension wire and both electrical leads from the coil.
3 Remove both mounting nuts and remove the coil from the engine.
4 On models with the coil in the distributor cap, remove the coil cover screws and lift off the cover. **Note:** *If you are just checking the coil, it is not necessary to remove the coil from the cap. Refer to the checking procedure below.*
5 Push the coil electrical leads through the top of the hood with a small screwdriver.
6 Remove the coil mounting screws and lift the coil, with the leads, from the cap.

Check

7 It is not necessary to remove the coil from the distributor cap on coil-in-cap models to test the coil.
8 Disconnect the negative cable from the battery.
9 Remove the distributor cap and turn it over so the coil electrical connectors are visible.
10 Connect an ohmmeter to the two outercoil terminals. It should indicate zero resistance. If it doesn't, replace the coil.
11 Connect the ohmmeter between one of the outer terminals and the central coil-to-rotor contact with the ohmmeter on the high scale. Repeat the test using the other terminal. If both terminals show infinite resistance, replace the coil.
12 On models with a separately mounted coil, check the coil for opens and grounds by performing the following three tests with an ohmmeter **(see illustration)**.
13 Using the ohmmeter's high scale, hook up the ohmmeter leads as illustrated (see test #1 in illustration 9.12). The ohmmeter should indicate a very high, or infinite, resistance value. If it doesn't, replace the coil.
14 Using the low scale, hook up the leads as illustrated (see test #2 in illustration 9.12). The ohmmeter should indicate a very low, or zero, resistance value. If it doesn't, replace the coil.
15 Using the high scale, hook up the leads as illustrated (see test #3

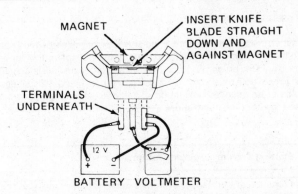

MAGNET

INSERT KNIFE BLADE STRAIGHT DOWN AND AGAINST MAGNET

TERMINALS UNDERNEATH

12 V

BATTERY   VOLTMETER

10.2 To test the Hall Effect switch, connect a 12-volt power supply and voltmeter as shown (check the polarity markings carefully before making any connections)

in illustration 9.12). The ohmmeter should not indicate an infinite resistance. If it does, replace the coil.

Installation

16 Installation of the coil is the reverse of the removal procedure.

10 Hall effect switch — check and replacement

Refer to illustration 10.2

1   Some HEI distributors are equipped with a Hall effect switch which is located above the pickup coil assembly. The Hall effect switch is used in place of the *R* terminal of the HEI distributor to send engine RPM information to the ECM.

2   Test the switch by connecting a 12-volt power supply and voltmeter as shown **(see illustration)**. Check the polarity markings carefully before making any connections.

3   When the knife blade is *not* inserted as shown, the voltmeter should read less than 0.5 volts. If the reading is more, the Hall effect switch is faulty and must be replaced by a new one.

4   With the knife blade inserted, the voltmeter should read within 0.5 volts of battery voltage. Replace the switch with a new one if the reading is more.

5   Remove the Hall effect switch by unplugging the connector and removing the retaining screws.

6   Installation is the reverse of removal.

11 Charging system — general information and precautions

The charging system consists of a belt-driven alternator with an integral voltage regulator and the battery. These components work together to supply electrical power for the ignition system, the lights and all accessories.

There are two types of alternators used. Earlier vehicles use the SI type and later models are equipped with the CS type. There are two types of CS alternators in use, the CS-130 and the CS-144. All types use a conventional pulley and fan.

To determine which type of alternator is installed on your vehicle, look at the fasteners employed to attach the two halves of the alternator housing. All CS models use rivets instead of screws. CS alternators are rebuildable once the rivets are drilled out. However, we don't recommend this practice. For all intents and purposes, CS types should be considered non-serviceable and, if defective, should be exchanged as cores for new or rebuilt units.

The purpose of the voltage regulator is to limit the alternator's voltage to a preset value. This prevents power surges, circuit overloads, etc., during peak voltage output. On all models with which this manual is concerned, the voltage regulator is contained within the alternator housing.

The charging system does not ordinarily require periodic maintenance. The drivebelts, electrical wiring and connections should, however, be inspected at the intervals suggested in Chapter 1.

Take extreme care when making circuit connections to a vehicle equipped with an alternator and note the following. When making connections to the alternator from a battery, always match correct polarity. Before using arc welding equipment to repair any part of the vehicle, disconnect the wires from the alternator and the battery terminal. Never start the engine with a battery charger connected. Always disconnect both battery leads before using a battery charger.

The charging indicator lamp on the dash lights when the ignition switch is turned on and goes out when the engine starts. If the lamp stays on or comes on once the engine is running, a charging system problem has occurred. See Section 12 for the proper diagnosis procedure for each type of alternator.

12 Charging system — check

Refer to illustration 12.5

1   If a malfunction occurs in the charging circuit, do not immediately assume that the alternator is causing the problem. First check the following items:

   a) The battery cables where they connect to the battery. Make sure the connections are clean and tight.
   b) The battery electrolyte specific gravity. If it is low, charge the battery.
   c) Check the external alternator wiring and connections. They must be in good condition.
   d) Check the drivebelt condition and tension (Chapter 1).
   e) Make sure the alternator mounting bolts are tight.
   f) Run the engine and check the alternator for abnormal noise (may be caused by a loose drive pulley, loose mounting bolts, worn or dirty bearings, defective diode or defective stator).

2   Using a voltmeter, check the battery voltage with the engine off. It should be approximately 12 volts.

3   Start the engine and check the battery voltage again. It should now be approximately 14 to 15 volts.

4   Locate the test hole in the back of the alternator. **Note:** *If there is no test hole, your vehicle is equipped with a newer CS type alternator. Further testing of this type of alternator must be done by a dealer or automotive electrical shop.*

5   Ground the tab that is located inside the hole by inserting a screwdriver blade into the hole and touching the tab and the case at the same time **(see illustration). Caution:** *Do not run the engine with the tab grounded any longer than necessary to obtain a voltmeter reading. If the alternator is charging, it is running unregulated during the test. This condition may overload the electrical system and cause damage to the components.*

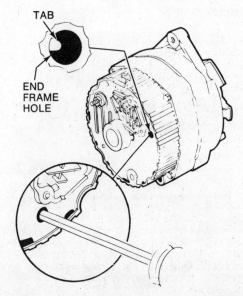

TAB

END FRAME HOLE

12.5 To full field an SI-type alternator, ground the tab located inside the hole by inserting a screwdriver blade into the hole and touching the tab and case at the same time

5

6   The reading on the voltmeter should be 15 volts or higher with the tab grounded in the test hole.

7   If the voltmeter indicates low battery voltage, the alternator is faulty and should be replaced with a new one (Section 15).

8   If the voltage reading is 15 volts or higher and a no charge condition is present, the regulator or field circuit is the problem. Remove the alternator (Section 13) and have it checked further by an auto electric shop.

13   Alternator — removal and installation

1   Detach the cable from the negative terminal of the battery.
2   Remove the upper radiator shroud (see Chapter 3).
3   Remove the two-terminal plug and the battery lead on the back of the alternator.
4   Loosen the alternator adjuster bolt.
5   Remove the alternator drive belt from the alternator pulley.
6   Remove the alternator pivot bolt and adjuster bolt.
7   Remove the alternator.
8   Installation is the reverse of removal. For information regarding alternator belt adjustment, see Chapter 1.

14   Alternator brushes — replacement

Refer to illustrations 14.2, 14.3a, 14.3b, 14.4, 14.5, 14.6, 14.7 and 14.10

Note: *The following procedure applies only to SI type alternators. CS types have riveted housings and cannot be disassembled.*

1   Remove the alternator from the vehicle (Section 15).
2   Scribe or paint marks on the front and rear end frame housings of the alternator to facilitate reassembly **(see illustration)**.
3   Remove the four through-bolts holding the front and rear end frames together, then separate the drive end frame from the rectifier end frame **(see illustrations)**.
4   Remove the bolts holding the stator to the rear end frame and separate the stator from the end frame **(see illustration)**.
5   Remove the nuts attaching the diode trio to the rectifier bridge and remove the trio **(see illustration)**.
6   Remove the screws attaching the resistor (not used on all models) and brush holder to the end frame and remove the brush holder **(see illustration)**.
7   Remove the brushes from the brush holder by slipping the brush retainer off the brush holder **(see illustration)**.
8   Remove the springs from the brush holder.

9   Installation is the reverse of the removal procedure, noting the following:
10   When installing the brushes in the brush holder, install the brush closest to the end frame first. Slip the paper clip through the rear of the end frame to hold the brush, then insert the second brush and push the paper clip in to hold both brushes while reassembly is completed. The paper clip should not be removed until the front and rear end frames have been bolted together **(see illustration)**.

15   Starting system — general information

The function of the starting system is to crank the engine. The starting system is composed of a starting motor, solenoid and battery. The battery supplies the electrical energy to the solenoid, which then completes the circuit to the starting motor, which does the actual work of cranking the engine.

The solenoid and starting motor are mounted together at the lower front side of the engine. No periodic lubrication or maintenance is required.

The electrical circuitry of the vehicle is arranged so that the starter motor can only be operated when the clutch pedal is depressed (manual transmission) or the transmission selector lever is in Park or Neutral (automatic transmission).

Never operate the starter motor for more than 30 seconds at a time without pausing to allow it to cool for at least two minutes. Excessive cranking can cause overheating, which can seriously damage the starter.

16   Starter motor — testing in vehicle

Refer to illustration 16.6

1   If the starter motor does not turn at all when the switch is operated, make sure that the shift lever is in Neutral or Park (automatic transmission) or that the clutch pedal is depressed (manual transmission).
2   Make sure that the battery is charged and that all cables, both at the battery and starter solenoid terminals, are secure.
3   If the starter motor spins but the engine is not cranking, the over-running clutch in the starter motor is slipping and the motor must be removed from the engine for replacement.
4   If, when the switch is actuated, the starter motor does not operate at all but the solenoid clicks, then the problem lies with either the battery, the main solenoid contacts or the starter motor itself. **Note:** *Before diagnosing starter problems, make sure that the battery is fully charged.*

14.2   Mark the drive end frame and rectifier end frame assemblies with a scribe or paint before separating the two halves

14.3a   Carefully separate the drive end frame and the rectifier end frame assemblies

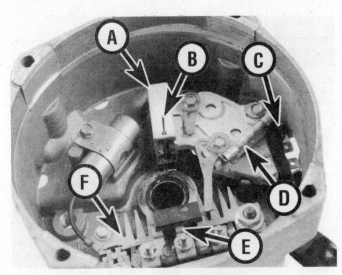

14.3b Inside the typical SI–type alternator

A Brush holder
B Paper clip retaining brushes
C Regulator
D Resistor (not all models)
E Diode trio
F Rectifier bridge

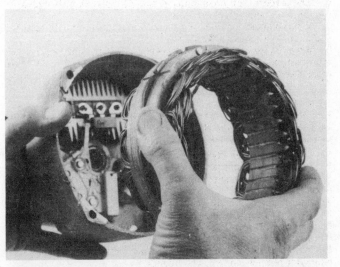

14.4 After removing the bolts holding the stator assembly to the end frame, remove the stator

14.5 Remove the nuts attaching the diode trio to the rectifier bridge and remove the trio

14.6 After removing the screws that attach the brush holder and the resistor (if equipped) to the end frame, remove the brush holder

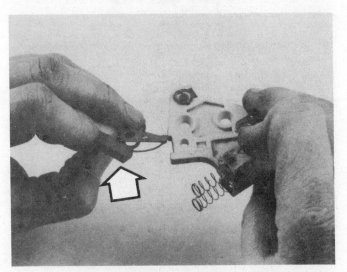

14.7 Slip the brush retainer off the brush holder and remove the brushes

14.10 To hold the brushes in place during reassembly, insert a paper clip like this through the hole in the end frame nearest the rotor shaft

5

5   If the solenoid plunger cannot be heard when the switch is actuated, the solenoid itself is defective or the solenoid circuit is open.

6   To check the solenoid, connect a jumper lead between the battery (+) and the "S" terminal on the solenoid (see illustration). If the starter motor now operates, the solenoid is OK and the problem is in the ignition switch, neutral start switch or in the wiring.

7   If the starter motor still does not operate, remove the starter/solenoid assembly for disassembly, testing and repair.

8   If the starter motor cranks the engine at an abnormally slow speed, first make sure that the battery is charged and that all terminal connections are tight. If the engine is partially seized, or has the wrong viscosity oil in it, it will crank slowly.

9   Run the engine until normal operating temperature is reached, then disconnect the coil wire from the distributor cap and ground it on the engine.

10 Connect a voltmeter positive lead to the starter motor terminal of the solenoid and then connect the negative lead to ground.

11 Crank the engine and take the voltmeter readings as soon as a steady figure is indicated. Do not allow the starter motor to turn for more than 30 seconds at a time. A reading of 9 volts or more, with the starter motor turning at normal cranking speed, is normal. If the reading is 9 volts or more but the cranking speed is slow, the motor is faulty. If the reading is less than 9 volts and the cranking speed is slow, the solenoid contacts are probably burned.

17   Starter motor — removal and installation

Refer to illustration 17.4

1   Detach the cable from the negative terminal of the battery.
2   Remove the starter braces or shields, if equipped.
3   Raise the vehicle and place it securely on jackstands.
4   Detach the wires from the starter solenoid.
5   Remove the two bolts, nuts, washers and shims holding the starter to the engine (see illustration).
6   Remove the starter from the engine.
7   Installation is the reverse of removal.

18   Starter solenoid — removal and installation

Refer to illustration 18.5

1   Disconnect the cable from the negative terminal of the battery.
2   Remove the starter motor (Section 17).

16.6   Typical starter solenoid "S" terminal location (arrow)

Removal

3   Disconnect the strap from the solenoid to the starter motor terminal.
4   Remove the two screws which secure the solenoid to the starter motor.
5   Twist the solenoid in a clockwise direction to disengage the flange from the starter body (see illustration).

Installation

6   To install, first make sure the return spring is in position on the plunger, then insert the solenoid body into the starter housing and turn the solenoid counterclockwise to engage the flange.
7   Install the two solenoid screws and connect the motor strap.

17.4   To remove the starter from the engine, detach the electrical wires from the solenoid terminals, then remove both mounting bolts (arrows)

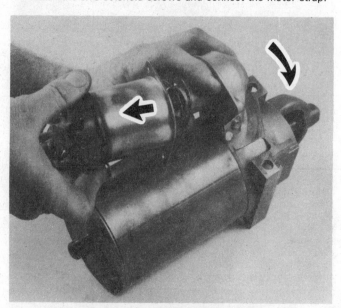

18.5   To remove the starter solenoid from the starter motor, remove the solenoid-to-starter frame mounting screws, then turn the solenoid in a clockwise direction and pull

Chapter 6 Emissions control systems

Contents

1 General information

Refer to illustration 1.6

To prevent pollution of the atmosphere from incompletely burned and evaporating gases, and to maintain good driveability and fuel economy, a number of emission control devices are incorporated. They include the:

Electronic Spark Timing (EST)
Electronic Spark Control (ESC) system
Exhaust Gas Recirculation (EGR) system
Evaporative Emission Control System (EECS)
Positive Crankcase Ventilation (PCV) system
Transmission Converter Clutch (TCC)
Catalytic converter
Air Injection Reaction (AIR) (carbureted V6)
Air management system (V6 with fuel injection)
Thermostatic air cleaner
Air conditioning control

All of these systems are linked, directly or indirectly, to the Computer Command Control (CCC or C3) system.

The Sections in this Chapter include general descriptions, checking procedures within the scope of the home mechanic and component replacement procedures (when possible) for each of the systems listed above.

Before assuming that an emissions control system is malfunctioning, check the fuel and ignition systems carefully. The diagnosis of some emission control devices requires specialized tools, equipment and training. If checking and servicing become too difficult or if a procedure is beyond the scope of your skills, consult your dealer service department.

This doesn't mean, however, that emission control systems are particularly difficult to maintain and repair. You can quickly and easily perform many checks and do most (if not all) of the regular maintenance at home with common tune-up and hand tools. **Note:** *The most frequent cause of emissions problems is simply a loose or broken vacuum hose or wiring connection, so always check the hose and wiring connections first.*

Pay close attention to any special precautions outlined in this Chapter. It should be noted that the illustrations of the various systems may not exactly match the system installed on your vehicle because of changes made by the manufacturer during production or from year-to-year.

A Vehicle Emissions Control Information label is located in the engine compartment **(see illustration)**. This label contains important emissions specifications and ignition timing procedures, as well as a vacuum hose schematic and emissions components identification guide. When servicing the engine or emissions systems, the VECI label in your particular vehicle should always be checked for up-to-date information. **Caution:** *If the vehicle is equipped with a Delco Loc II audio system (1992 and later models with a Compact Disc player), be sure the lockout feature is turned off before performing any procedure that requires disconnecting the battery (refer to your owner's manual for further information on this system).*

2 Computer Command Control (CCC) system and trouble codes

Refer to illustrations 2.1a, 2.1b, 2.1c, 2.1d, 2.1e, 2.5a and 2.5b

The Computer Command Control (CCC) system consists of an Electronic Control Module (ECM) and information sensors which monitor

1.6 The Vehicle Emission Control Information (VECI) label is located on the fan shroud and contains information on idle speed adjustment, ignition timing, location of emission devices on your vehicle, vacuum line routing, etc.

6

various functions of the engine and send data back to the ECM **(see illustrations)**.

There are two types of ECMs used. Vehicles equipped with a 4-cylinder engine have an ECM with a MEM-CAL (Memory and Calibration) unit. Vehicles equipped with a V6 engine have an ECM with a PROM and a CALPAK.

The ECM controls the following systems:

Fuel control
Electronic spark timing
Electronic spark control (V6 only)
Air management (V6 only)
Exhaust gas recirculation
Transmission converter clutch

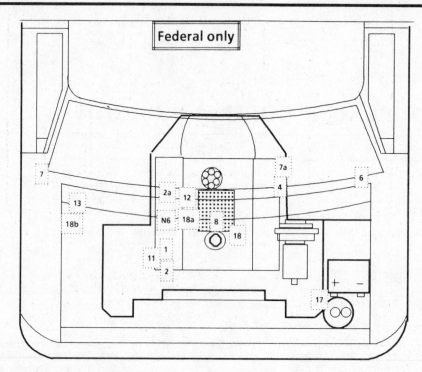

2.1a   Emission control component location on carbureted Federal V6 engine

EMISSIONS DEVICES

1   Crankcase vent valve (PCV)
2   Air injection pump
2a Air injection divert valve
3   Deceleration valve
4   EFE valve
6   Fuse panel
7   Electronic Spark Control module
7a ESC knock sensor
8   Accelerator pump solenoid
12 EGR solenoid
13 Distributor thermal vacuum switch
17 Fuel vapor canister
18 Throttle kicker
18a Throttle kicker solenoid
18b Throttle kicker relay

◎ Exhaust Gas Recirculation valve

2.1b   Emission control component location on carbureted California V6 engine

COMPUTER HARNESS

C1 Electronic Control Module (ECM)
C2 ALCL diagnostic connector
C3 "CHECK ENGINE" light
C5 ECM harness ground
C6 Fuse panel
C7 "C.E." lamp driver
C10 Diagnostic dwell connector

ECM CONTROLLED

1   Mixture control solenoid
5   Trans. Conv. Clutch connector
6   Electronic Spark Timing
7   Electronic Spark Control module
9   Air injection divert solenoid
10 Throttle kicker relay
12 Exhaust Gas Recirculation solenoid
17a Fuel vapor canister
17 Fuel vapor canister solenoid
18 Throttle kicker
18a Throttle kicker solenoid

◎ Exhaust Gas Recirculation valve

EMISSION SYSTEMS
(NOT ECM CONTROLLED)

N1 Crankcase vent valve (PCV)
N2 EFE valve
N3 Deceleration valve
N8 Air injection pump

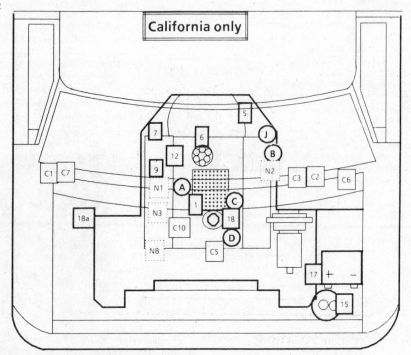

○ INFORMATION SENSORS

A Manifold differential pressure
B Exhaust oxygen
C Throttle position
D Coolant temperature
J ESC knock

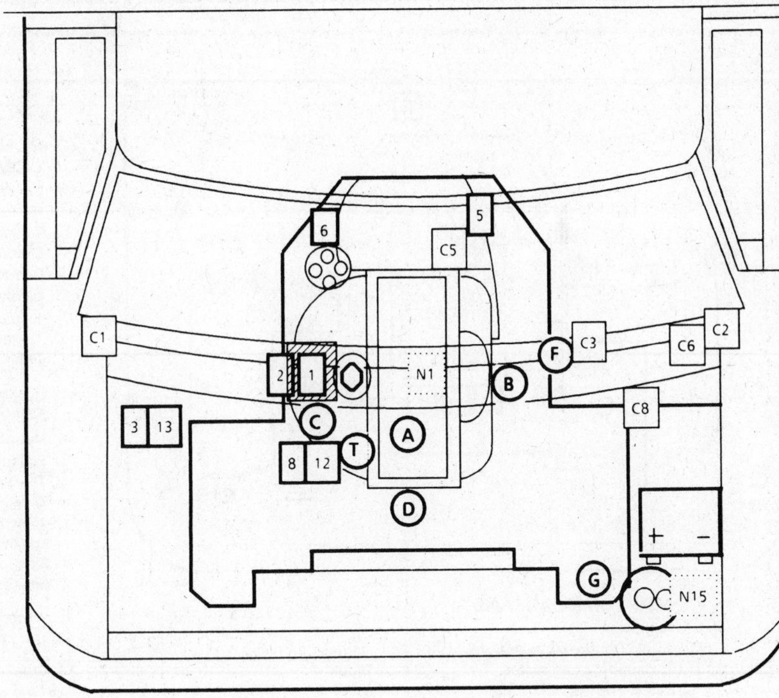

2.1c Emission control component location on fuel injected four-cylinder engine

☐ COMPUTER COMMAND CONTROL

C1 Electronic Control Module (E.C.M.)
C2 ALDL diagnostic connector
C3 "SERVICE ENGINE SOON" light
C5 ECM harness ground
C6 Fuse panel
C8 Fuel pump test connector

☐ ECM CONTROLLED COMPONENTS

1   Fuel injector
2   Idle air control
3   Fuel pump relay
5   Transmission Converter Clutch Connector
6   Electronic Spark Timing Distributor (E.S.T.)
8   Oil pressure switch
12 Exhaust Gas Recirculation Vacuum Solenoid
13 A/C relay

◯ ECM INFORMATION SENSORS

A Manifold pressure (M.A.P.)
B Exhaust oxygen
C Throttle position (T.P.S.)
D Coolant temperature
F Vehicle speed (V.S.S.)
G Power Steering Pressure
T Manifold Air Temperature (M.A.T.)

⬚ EMISSION COMPONENTS (NOT ECM CONTROLLED)

N1   Crankcase vent (PCV) valve
N15 Fuel vapor canister

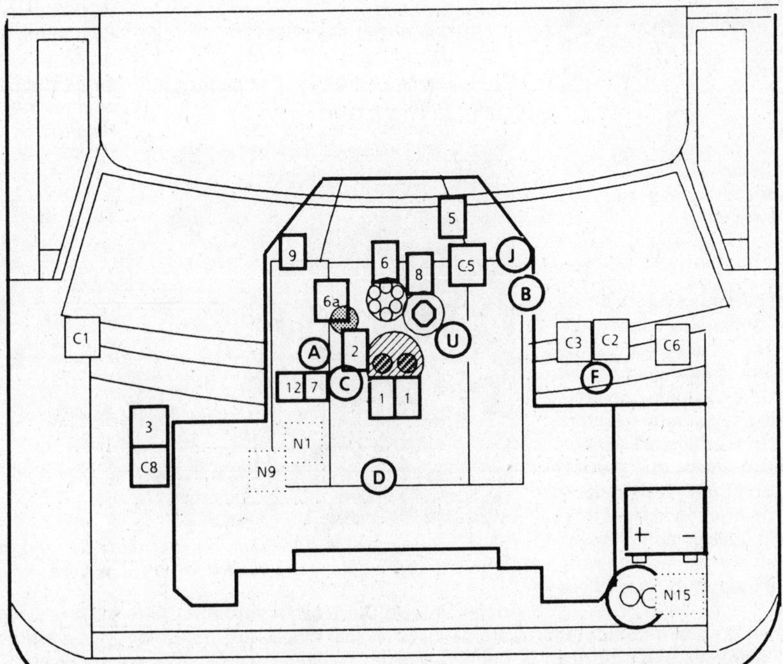

2.1d Emission control component locations on TBI fuel injected V6 engines

☐ COMPUTER COMMAND CONTROL

C1 Electronic Control Module (E.C.M.)
C2 ALDL diagnostic connector
C3 "SERVICE ENGINE SOON" light
C5 ECM harness ground
C6 Fuse panel
C8 Fuel pump test connector

☐ ECM CONTROLLED COMPONENTS

1   Fuel injector
2   Idle air control
3   Fuel pump relay
5   Transmission Converter Clutch Connector
6   Electronic Spark Timing Distributor (E.S.T.)
6a   Remote ignition coil
7   Electronic Spark Control module (E.S.C.)
8   Oil pressure switch
9   Electric Air Control solenoid (E.A.C.)
12   Exhaust Gas Recirculation Vacuum Solenoid

◯ ECM INFORMATION SENSORS

A Manifold Absolute Pressure (M.A.P.)
B Exhaust oxygen
C Throttle position (T.P.S.)
D Coolant temperature
F Vehicle speed (V.S.S.)
J Electronic Spark Control Knock (E.S.C.)

⬚ EMISSION COMPONENTS (NOT ECM CONTROLLED)

N1   Crankcase vent valve (PCV)
N9   Air Pump
N15 Fuel Vapor Canister

6

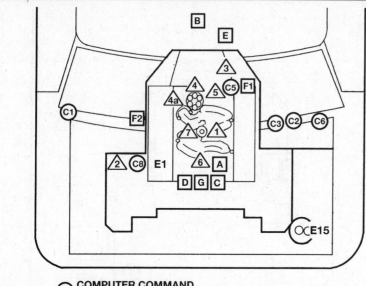

2.1e Emission control component locations on CPI fuel-injected V6 engines (VIN W)

△ **ECM CONTROLLED COMPONENTS**
1 Intake manifold tuning valve
2 Fuel pump relay
3 Transmission connector
4 Electronic Spark Timing (EST) distributor
4a Remote ignition coil
5 Oil pressure switch
6 Linear Exhast Gas Recirculation (EGR)
7 Central Port Injection CPI injector assembly (internal)

☐ **ECM INFORMATION SENSORS**
A Manifold Absolute Pressure (MAP)
B Exhaust oxygen (O₂) sensor
C Throttle Position Sensor (TPS)
D Coolant Temperature Sensor (CTS)
E Vehicle Speed Sensor (VSS)
F1 Electronic Spark Control (ESC) knock (1 of 2)
F2 Electronic Spark Control (ESC) knock (2 of 2)
G Intake Air Temperature (IAT)

EMISSION COMPONENTS (NOT ECM CONTROLLED)
E1 Crankcase Vent Valve (PVC)
E15 Fuel vapor canister

○ **COMPUTER COMMAND CONTROL**
C1 Electronic Control Module (ECM)
C2 ALDL diagnostic connector
C3 "SERVICE ENGINE SOON" light
C5 ECM harness ground
C6 Fuse block
C8 Fuel pump test connector

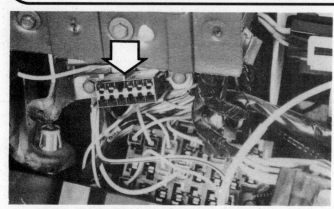

2.5a The Assembly Line Data Link (arrow) is located under the dash near the fuse panel

Manual transmission shift light
Air conditioning clutch control

The CCC system is analogous to the central nervous system in the human body. The sensors (nerve endings) constantly relay information to the ECM (brain), which processes the data and, if necessary, sends out a command to change the operating parameters of the engine (body).

Here's a specific example of how one portion of this system operates: An oxygen sensor, located in the exhaust manifold, constantly monitors the oxygen content of the exhaust gas. If the percentage of oxygen in the exhaust gas is incorrect, an electrical signal is sent to the ECM. The ECM takes this information, processes it and then sends a command to the fuel injection system, telling it to change the air/fuel mixture. This happens in a fraction of a second and it goes on continuously when the engine is running. The end result is an air/fuel mixture ratio which is constantly maintained at a predetermined ratio, regardless of driving conditions.

One might think that a system which uses an on-board computer and electrical sensors would be difficult to diagnose. This is not necessarily the case. The CCC system has a built-in diagnostic feature which indicates a problem by flashing a *Service Engine Soon* light on the instrument panel. When this light comes on during normal vehicle operation, a fault in one of the information sensor circuits or the ECM itself has been detected. More importantly, the source of the malfunction is stored in the ECM's memory.

To retrieve this information from the ECM memory, you must use a short jumper wire to ground a diagnostic terminal. This terminal is part of a wiring connector known as the Assembly Line Communica-

2.5b The Assembly Line Data Link (ALDL) terminal identification

A Ground
B Diagnostic terminal
C AIR (if used)
D Check Engine light (if used)
E Serial data (special tool required — do not use)
F TCC (if used)
G Fuel pump (if used)
H Brake sense speed input
M Serial data (four-cylinder engine only, special tool required — do not use)

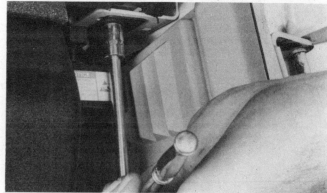

3.4 Remove this door lock control relay (if equipped) bracket bolt and drop the relay down where it will be out of the way

tions Link (ALCL) **(see illustrations)**. The ALCL is located underneath the dashboard, just below the instrument panel and to the left of the center console. To use the ALCL, remove the plastic cover by sliding it toward you. With the connector exposed to view, push one end of the jumper wire into the diagnostic terminal and the other end into the ground terminal.

When the diagnostic terminal is grounded with the ignition on and the engine stopped, the system will enter the *Diagnostic Mode*. In this mode the ECM will display a "Code 12" by flashing the *Service Engine Soon* light, indicating that the system is operating. A code 12 is simply one flash, followed by a brief pause, then two flashes in quick succession. This code will be flashed three times. If no other codes are

Trouble codes	Circuit or system	Probable cause
Code 12 (1 flash, pause, 2 flashes)	No distributor reference pulses to ECM	This code will flash whenever the diagnostic terminal is grounded with the ignition turned On and the engine not running. If additional trouble codes are stored in the ECM they will appear after this code has flashed three times. If this code appears while the engine is running, no reference pulses from the distributor are reaching the ECM.
Code 13 (1 flash, pause, 3 flashes)	Oxygen sensor circuit	Check for a sticking or misadjusted throttle position sensor. Check the wiring and connectors from the oxygen sensor. Replace the oxygen sensor.
Code 14 (1 flash, pause, 4 flashes)	Coolant sensor/high temp	If the engine is experiencing overheating problems the problem must be rectified before continuing. Check all wiring and connectors associated with the coolant temperature sensor. Replace the coolant temperature sensor.*
Code 15 (1 flash, pause, 5 flashes)	Coolant sensor/low temp	See above, then check the wiring connections at the ECM.
Code 21 (2 flashes, pause, 1 flash)	Throttle position sensor/voltage high	Check for a sticking or misadjusted TPS plunger. Check all wiring and connections between the TPS and the ECM. Adjust or replace the TPS (see Chapter 4).*
Code 22 (2 flashes, pause, 2 flashes)	Throttle position sensor/voltage low	Check the TPS adjustment (Chapter 4). Check the ECM connector. Replace the TPS (Chapter 4).*
Code 23 (carbureted) (2 flashes, pause, 3 flashes)	Mixture control solenoid	The mixture control solenoid is open or grounded.
Code 23 (fuel injected) (2 flashes, pause, 3 flashes)	MAT low temp indication	Sets if the manifold air temperature sensor, connections or wires are open for 3 seconds.
Code 24 (2 flashes, pause, 4 flashes)	Vehicle speed sensor	A fault in this circuit should be indicated only when the vehicle is in motion. Disregard Code 24 if it is set when the drive wheels are not turning. Check the connections at the ECM. Check the TPS setting.
Code 25 (2 flashes, pause, 5 flashes)	Manifold/high air temperature	High temperature indication. Sets if the sensor or signal line becomes grounded for 3 seconds.
Code 32 (carbureted) (3 flashes, pause, 2 flashes)	BARO circuit low	Barometric pressure sensor circuit low.
Code 32 (fuel injected) (3 flashes, pause, 2 flashes)	EGR	Vacuum switch shorted to ground on start-up, switch not closed after the ECM has commanded the EGR for a specified period of time or the EGR solenoid circuit is open for specified period of time. Replace the EGR valve.*
Code 33 (3 flashes, pause, 3 flashes)	MAP sensor	Check the vacuum hoses from the MAP sensor. Check the electrical connections at the ECM. Replace the MAP sensor.*
Code 34 (3 flashes, pause, 4 flashes)	Vacuum sensor or MAP sensor	Code 34 will set when the signal voltage from the MAP sensor is too low. Instead the ECM will substitute a fixed MAP value and use the TPS to control fuel delivery. Replace the MAP sensor.*
Code 35 (carbureted) (3 flashes, pause, 5 flashes)	ISC valve	Idle Speed Control error. Replace the ISC.*
Code 35 (fuel injected) (3 flashes, pause, 5 flashes)	IAC valve	Idle Air Control error. Code will set when closed throttle speed is 50 rpm above or below the correct idle speed for 30 seconds. Replace the IAC.*
Code 41 (4 flashes, pause, 1 flash)	EST circuit	No distributor reference pulses to the ECM at specified engine vacuum.
Code 42 (4 flashes, pause, 2 flashes)	Electronic Spark Timing	Electronic Spark Timing bypass circuit or EST circuit is grounded or open. A malfunctioning HEI module can cause this code.
Code 43 (4 flashes, pause, 3 flashes)	Electronic spark control unit	The ESC retard signal has been on for too long or the system has failed a functional check.
Code 44 (4 flashes, pause, 4 flashes)	Lean exhaust	Check the ECM wiring connections, particularly terminals 15 and 8. Check for vacuum leakage at the TBI base gasket, vacuum hoses or the intake manifold gasket. Replace the oxygen sensor.*
Code 45 (4 flashes, pause, 5 flashes)	Rich exhaust	Check the evaporative charcoal canister and its components for the presence of fuel. Replace the oxygen sensor.*
Code 51 (5 flashes, pause, 1 flash)	PROM or MEM-CAL	Make sure that the PROM or MEM-CAL is properly installed in the ECM. Replace the PROM or MEM-CAL.*
Code 52 (5 flashes, pause, 2 flashes)	CALPAK	Check the CALPAK to insure proper installation. Replace the CALPAK.*
Code 53 (5 flashes, pause, 3 flashes)	EGR valve	Exhaust Gas Recirculation valve vacuum sensor has received improper EGR vacuum.
Code 54 (5 flashes, pause, 4 flashes)	Fuel pump	Low fuel pump voltage. Sets when the fuel pump voltage is less than 2 volts when reference pulses are being received.
Code 55 (5 flashes, pause, 5 flashes)	ECM	Be sure that the ECM ground connections are tight. If they are, replace the ECM.*

6

* Component replacement may not cure the problem in all cases. For this reason, you may want to seek professional advice before purchasing replacement parts.

stored, Code 12 will continue to flash until the diagnostic terminal ground is removed.

After flashing Code 12 three times, the ECM will display any stored trouble codes. Each code will be flashed three times, then Code 12 will be flashed again, indicating that the display of any stored trouble codes has been completed.

When the ECM sets a trouble code, the *Service Engine Soon* light will come on and a trouble code will be stored in memory. If the problem is intermittent, the light will go out after 10 seconds, when the fault goes away. However, the trouble code will stay in the ECM memory until the battery voltage to the ECM is interrupted. Removing battery voltage for 10 seconds will clear all stored trouble codes. Trouble codes should always be cleared after repairs have been completed. **Caution:** *To prevent damage to the ECM, the ignition switch must be Off when disconnecting power to the ECM.*

Following is a list of the typical trouble codes which may be encountered while diagnosing the Computer Command Control System.

Also included are simplified troubleshooting procedures. If the problem persists after these checks have been made, more detailed service procedures will have to be done by a dealer service department.

3   Electronic Control Module (ECM)/Programmable Read Only Memory (PROM)/CALPAK/MEM-CAL

Refer to illustrations 3.4, 3.5, 3.6a, 3.6b, 3.7, 3.8a, 3.8b, 3.13, 3.14, 3.17, 3.29 and 3.32

1   The Electronic Control Module (ECM) is located inside the body in front of the right front door.
2   Disconnect the negative battery cable from the battery.
3   Remove the screws from the trim panel under the right end of the dash.
4   Remove the mounting bolt from the door lock relay bracket **(see illustration)**.

3.5   Remove the right hush panel by pulling it out from the bulkhead (it has two pop fasteners) and straight back

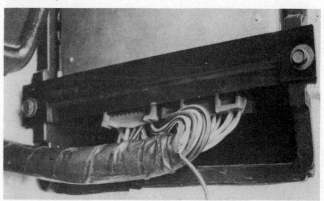

3.6a   Remove the two retainer bracket bolts and the retainer bar

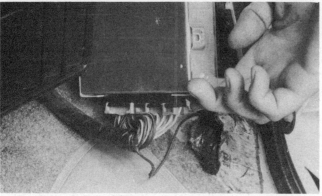

3.6b   Pull the ECM out of the housing assembly

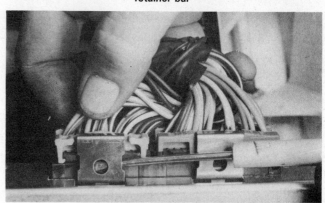

3.7   Use a small screwdriver to pry back the clips and unplug the ECM electrical connectors

3.8a   If you are replacing the ECM compare the service numbers on the label on the old unit to the numbers on the new one

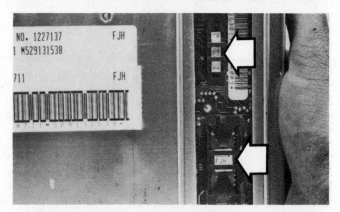

3.8b   The CALPAK (top) and PROM (bottom) inside an ECM for a V6 (ECMs for the 4-cylinder are similar but have a MEM-CAL instead of a PROM and CALPAK

5   Remove the right hush panel retaining screw and detach the panel **(see illustration)**.
6   Remove the retaining bolts **(see illustration)** and carefully slide the ECM out far enough to unplug the electrical connector **(see illustration)**.
7   Unplug both electrical connectors **(see illustration)** from the ECM.
 Caution: *The ignition switch must be turned off when pulling out or plugging in the connectors to prevent damage to the ECM.*

PROM

8   To allow one model of ECM to be used for many different vehicles **(see illustration)**, a device called a PROM (Programmable Read Only Memory) is used. To access the PROM remove the cover. The PROM **(see illustration)** is located inside the ECM and contains information on the vehicle's weight, engine, transmission, axle ratio, etc. One ECM part number can be used by many GM vehicles but the PROM is very specific and must be used only in the vehicle for which it was designed. For this reason, it is essential to check the latest parts book and Service Bulletin information for the correct part number when replacing a PROM. An ECM purchased at the dealer is purchased without a PROM. The PROM from the old ECM must be carefully removed and installed in the new ECM.

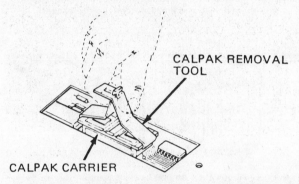

3.13 Using a PROM removal tool, grasp the PROM carrier at the narrow ends and gently rock the removal tool until the PROM is unplugged from the socket

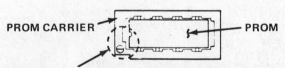

3.14 Note how the notch in the PROM is matched up with the smaller notch in the carrier

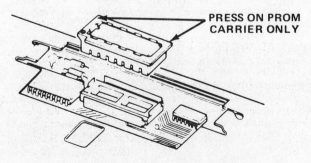

3.17 Press only on the ends of the PROM carrier — pressure on the area in between could result in bent or broken pins or damage to the PROM

CALPAK (V6)

9   A device known as a CALPAK **(see illustration 3.8b)** is used to allow fuel delivery if other parts of the ECM are damaged. The CALPAK has an access door in the ECM and replacement is the same as that described for the PROM.

MEM-CAL (four-cylinder)

10 The MEM-CAL contains the functions of the PROM, CALPAK and ESC module used on other GM applications. Like the PROM, it contains the calibrations needed for a specific vehicle as well as the back-up fuel control circuitry required if the rest of the ECM becomes damaged or faulty.

ECM/PROM/CALPAK replacement

11 Turn the ECM so that the bottom cover is facing up and place it on a clean work surface.
12 Remove the PROM/CALPAK access cover.
13 Using a PROM removal tool (available at your dealer), grasp the PROM carrier at the narrow ends **(see illustration)**. Gently rock the carrier from end to end while applying firm upward force. The PROM carrier and PROM should lift off the PROM socket easily. **Caution:** *The PROM carrier should only be removed with the special rocker-type PROM removal tool. Removal without this tool or with any other type of tool may damage the PROM or the PROM socket.*
14 Note the reference end of the PROM carrier **(see illustration)** before setting it aside.
15 If you are replacing the ECM, remove the new ECM from its container and check the service number to make sure that it is the same as the number on the old ECM.
16 If you are replacing the PROM, remove the new PROM from its container and check the service number to make sure that it is the same as the number of the old PROM.
17 Position the PROM/PROM carrier assembly squarely over the PROM socket with the small notched end of the carrier aligned with the small notch in the socket at the pin 1 end. Press on the PROM carrier until it seats firmly in the socket **(see illustration)**.
18 If the PROM is new, make sure that the notch in the PROM is matched to the small notch in the carrier. **Caution:** *If the PROM is installed backwards and the ignition switch is turned on, the PROM will be destroyed.*
19 Using the tool, install the new PROM carrier in the PROM socket of the ECM. The small notch of the carrier should be aligned with the small notch in the socket. Press on the PROM carrier until it is firmly seated in the socket. **Caution:** *Do not press on the PROM — press only on the carrier.*
20 Attach the access cover to the ECM and tighten the two screws.
21 Install the ECM in the support bracket, plug in the electrical connectors to the ECM and install the hush panel.
22 Start the engine.
23 Enter the diagnostic mode by grounding the diagnostic lead of the ALCL (see Section 2). If no trouble codes occur, the PROM is correctly installed.
24 If Trouble Code 51 occurs, or if the *Service Engine Soon* light comes on and remains constantly lit, the PROM is not fully seated, is installed backwards, has bent pins or is defective.
25 If the PROM is not fully seated, pressing firmly on both ends of the carrier should correct the problem.
26 If the pins have been bent, remove the PROM, straighten the pins and reinstall the PROM. If the bent pins break or crack when you attempt to straighten them, discard the PROM and replace it with a new one.
27 If careful inspection indicates that the PROM is fully seated, has not been installed backwards and has no bent pins, but the *Service Engine Soon* light remains lit, the PROM is probably faulty and must be replaced.

MEM-CAL replacement

Note: *With respect to removal of the ECM from the vehicle, MEM-CAL replacement is similar to the procedure described for the PROM or CALPAK. However, the actual removal and installation steps for the MEM-CAL and the functional check to ensure that the MEM-CAL is installed properly differ in detail from the Steps for the PROM and CALPAK.*

6

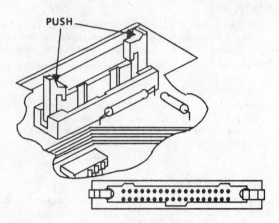

3.29 Push the retaining clips (arrows) back away from the MEM-CAL and simultaneously grasp it at both ends and lift it out of the socket

28 Remove the MEM-CAL access cover.
29 Using two fingers, push both retaining clips back away from the MEM-CAL **(see illustration)**. At the same time, grasp the MEM-CAL at both ends and lift it up out of its socket. Do not remove the MEM-CAL cover itself. **Caution:** *Use of unapproved removal or installation methods may damage the MEM-CAL or socket.*
30 Verify that the numbers on the old ECM and new ECM match up (or that the numbers of the old and new MEM-CALs match up, depending on what component(s) you're replacing) as described in the procedure for removing and installing the PROM and CALPAK.
31 To install the MEM-CAL in the MEM-CAL socket, press only on the ends of the MEM-CAL.
32 The small notches in the MEM-CAL must be aligned with the small notches in the MEM-CAL socket. Press on the ends of the MEM-CAL until the retaining clips snap into the ends of the MEM-CAL. Do not press on the middle of the MEM-CAL — press only on the ends **(see illustration)**.
33 The remainder of the installation is similar to that for the PROM/ CALPAK.
34 Once the new MEM-CAL is installed in the old ECM (or the old MEM-CAL is installed in the new ECM), check your installation to verify that it has been installed properly by doing the following test:
   a) Turn the ignition switch on.
   b) Enter the diagnostics mode at the ALCL (see Section 2).
   c) Allow Code 12 to flash four times to verify that no other codes are present. This indicates that the MEM-CAL is installed properly and the ECM is functioning properly.
35 If trouble codes 41, 42, 43, 51 or 55 occur, or if the *Service Engine Soon* light is on constantly but is flashing no codes, the MEM-CAL is either not fully seated or is defective. If it's not fully seated, press firmly on the ends of the MEM-CAL. If it is necessary to remove the MEM-CAL, follow the above Steps again.

---

4   Information sensors

Refer to illustrations 4.1, 4.3, 4.5a, 4.5b, 4.5c, 4.7, 4.8, 4.12, 4.23a, 4.23b, 4.24, 4.36a, 4.36b, 4.41a and 4.41b
Note: *See component location illustrations in Section 2 for the location of the following information sensors.*

Engine coolant temperature sensor

1   The coolant sensor **(see illustration)** is a thermistor (a resistor which varies the value of its voltage output in accordance with temperature changes). A failure in the coolant sensor circuit should set either a Code 14 or a Code 15. These codes indicate a failure in the coolant temperature circuit, so the appropriate solution to the problem will be either repair of a wire or replacement of the sensor.
2   To remove the sensor, release the locking tab, unplug the electrical connector, then carefully unscrew the sensor. **Caution:** *Handle the coolant sensor with care. Damage to this sensor will affect the operation of the entire fuel injection system.*

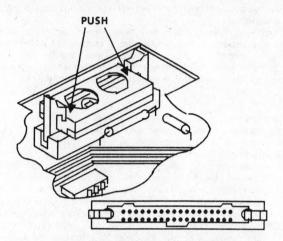

3.32 To install the MEM-CAL, press only the ends (arrows) — make sure that the notches in the MEM-CAL are aligned with the small notches in the socket

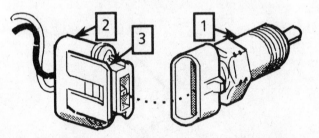

4.1 To remove the engine coolant temperature ECM sensor (1) pry open the locking tab (3) with a small screwdriver and unplug the harness connector (2), then carefully unscrew the sensor with a deep socket or wrench

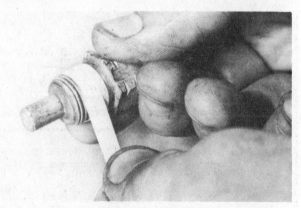

4.3 To prevent leakage, wrap the threads of the coolant temperature sensor with Teflon tape before installing it

3   Before installing the new sensor, wrap the threads with Teflon sealing tape to prevent leakage and thread corrosion **(see illustration)**.
4   Installation is the reverse of removal.

Manifold Absolute Pressure (MAP) sensor

5   The Manifold Absolute Pressure (MAP) sensor **(see illustrations)** monitors the intake manifold pressure changes resulting from changes in engine load and speed and converts the information into a voltage output. The ECM uses the MAP sensor to control fuel delivery and ignition timing.
6   A failure in the MAP sensor circuit should set a Code 33 or a Code 34.
7   Diagnostic chart 4.7 **(see illustration)** diagrams the testing procedures for the MAP sensor.

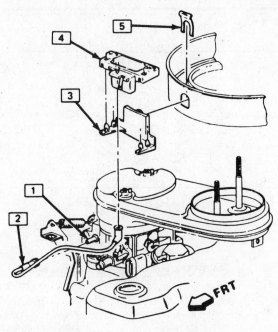

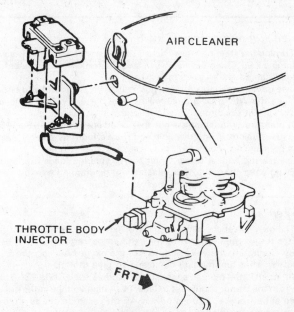

4.5b Exploded view of the MAP sensor assembly for the V6 engine with TBI fuel injection

4.5a Exploded view of the Manifold Absolute Pressure (MAP) sensor assembly on a 4-cylinder engine

1 Port "J"
2 Harness assembly
3 Mounting bracket
4 MAP sensor
5 Retainer clip

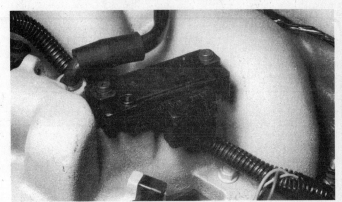

4.5c Location of the MAP sensor assembly on the V6 with CPI fuel injection

6

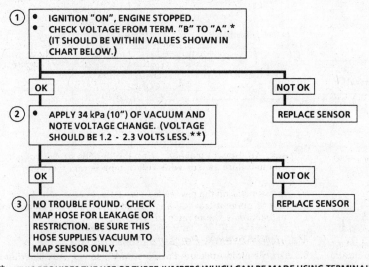

① • IGNITION "ON", ENGINE STOPPED.
• CHECK VOLTAGE FROM TERM. "B" TO "A".*
(IT SHOULD BE WITHIN VALUES SHOWN IN CHART BELOW.)

OK

NOT OK → REPLACE SENSOR

② • APPLY 34 kPa (10") OF VACUUM AND NOTE VOLTAGE CHANGE. (VOLTAGE SHOULD BE 1.2 - 2.3 VOLTS LESS.**)

OK

NOT OK → REPLACE SENSOR

③ NO TROUBLE FOUND. CHECK MAP HOSE FOR LEAKAGE OR RESTRICTION. BE SURE THIS HOSE SUPPLIES VACUUM TO MAP SENSOR ONLY.

* THIS REQUIRES THE USE OF THREE JUMPERS WHICH CAN BE MADE USING TERMINALS 12014836 AND 12014837.
** IF VOLTAGE DOES NOT IMMEDIATELY FOLLOW VACUUM CHANGE, SENSOR IS FAULTY.

CLEAR CODES AND CONFIRM "CLOSED LOOP" OPERATION AND NO "SERVICE ENGINE SOON" LIGHT.

4.7 Diagnostic flow chart for checking MAP output

ALTITUDE		VOLTAGE RANGE
Meters	Feet	
Below 305	Below 1,000	3.8---5.5V
305--- 610	1,000--2,000	3.6---5.3V
610--- 914	2,000--3,000	3.5---5.1V
914--1219	3,000--4,000	3.3---5.0V
1219--1524	4,000--5,000	3.2---4.8V
1524--1829	5,000--6,000	3.0---4.6V
1829--2133	6,000--7,000	2.9---4.5V
2133--2438	7,000--8,000	2.8---4.3V
2438--2743	8,000--9,000	2.6---4.2V
2743--3048	9,000--10,000	2.5---4.0V

LOW ALTITUDE = HIGH PRESSURE = HIGH VOLTAGE

Power steering pressure switch

8   Turning the steering wheel increases power steering fluid pressure and engine load. The pressure switch **(see illustration)** will close before the load can cause an idle problem.

9   The power steering switch is normally open to ground and circuit 495 (see the Wiring Diagrams) will be near battery voltage. Closing the switch causes circuit 495 to read less than 1 volt.

10   A pressure switch that will not open or an open circuit 495 or 450, will cause timing to retard at idle and may affect idle quality.

11   A pressure switch that will not close or an open circuit 450 or 495 may cause the engine to die when power steering loads are high.

12   Diagnostic chart 4.12 **(see illustration)** diagrams the testing procedure for the power steering pressure switch.

Oxygen sensor

13   The oxygen sensor is mounted in the exhaust system where it can monitor the oxygen content of the exhaust gas stream.

14   By monitoring the voltage output of the oxygen sensor, the ECM will know what fuel mixture command to give the injector.

15   An open in the oxygen sensor circuit should set a Code 13. A low voltage in the circuit should set a Code 44. A high voltage in the circuit should set a Code 45. Codes 44 and 45 may also be set as a result of fuel system problems.

16   See Section 5 for the oxygen sensor replacement procedure.

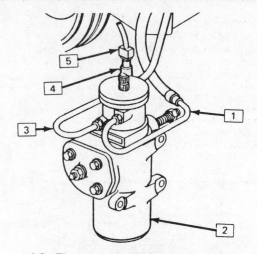

4.8   The power steering pressure switch (4-cylinder engine)

1 Outlet pipe	4 Power steering
2 Power steering gear	pressure switch
3 Inlet pipe	5 Electrical connector

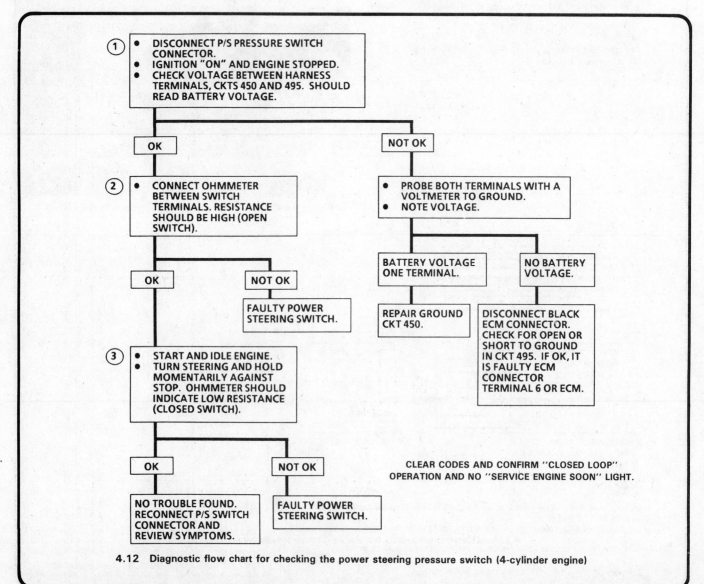

4.12   Diagnostic flow chart for checking the power steering pressure switch (4-cylinder engine)

Throttle Position Sensor (TPS)

17 The Throttle Position Sensor (TPS) is located on the end of the throttle shaft on the TBI unit.

18 By monitoring the output voltage from the TPS, the ECM can determine fuel delivery based on throttle valve angle (driver demand). A broken or loose TPS can cause intermittent bursts of fuel from the injector and an unstable idle because the ECM thinks the throttle is moving.

19 A problem in any of the TPS circuits will set a Code 21 or 22.

20 Once a trouble code is set, the ECM will use an artificial default value for TPS and some vehicle performance will return.

21 Should the TPS require replacement, the complete procedure is contained in Chapter 4.

Park/Neutral switch (automatic transmission equipped vehicles only)

22 The Park/Neutral (P/N) switch, located on the steering column indicates to the ECM when the transmission is in Park or Neutral. This information is used for Transmission Converter Clutch (TCC), Exhaust Gas Recirculation (EGR) and Idle Air Control (IAC) valve operation. Caution: *The vehicle should not be driven with the Park/Neutral switch disconnected because idle quality will be adversely affected and a false Code 24 (failure in the Vehicle Speed Sensor circuit) may be set.*

23 The switch is closed to ground in Park or Neutral and open in Drive ranges (see illustrations).

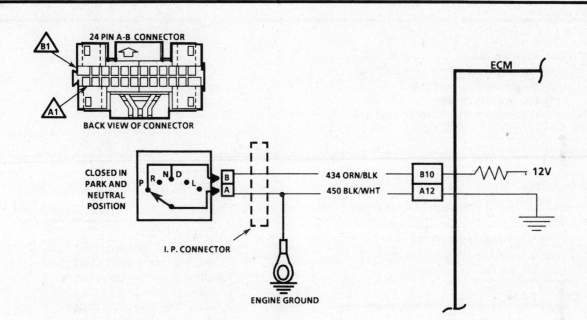

4.23a Electrical schematic for the Park/Neutral switch on 4-cylinder engines

6

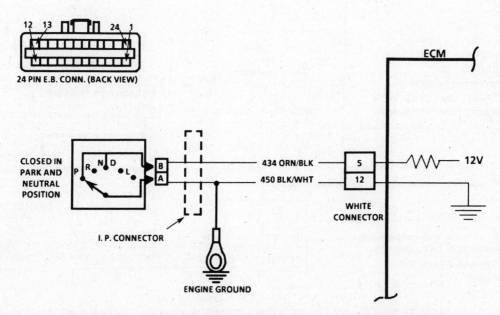

4.23b Electrical schematic for the Park/Neutral switch on V6 engines

24 Diagnostic chart 4.24 (see illustration) diagrams the test procedures for the Park/Neutral switch.

Adjustment

25 To adjust the Park/Neutral switch, move the switch housing all the way toward the low gear position.

26 Move the gear selector to the Park position. The main housing and the housing back should ratchet, providing proper switch adjustment.

Replacement

27 To replace the switch, place the gear selector in Neutral.

28 Unplug the electrical connectors.

29 Spread the tangs on the housing and pull the switch out.

30 To install a new switch, align the actuator on the switch with the hole in the shift tube.

31 Position the rearward portion of the switch (the connector side) to fit into the cutout in the lower jacket.

32 Push down on the front of the switch to engage the two tangs.

33 Move the gear selector to Park and the switch is adjusted.

34 Plug in the electrical connectors.

Air conditioning control

A/C clutch control (4-cylinder engine)

35 During A/C operation, the ECM controls the application of the A/C compressor clutch.

36 Diagnostic charts 4.36a and 4.36b (see illustrations) diagram the testing procedures for the A/C clutch control.

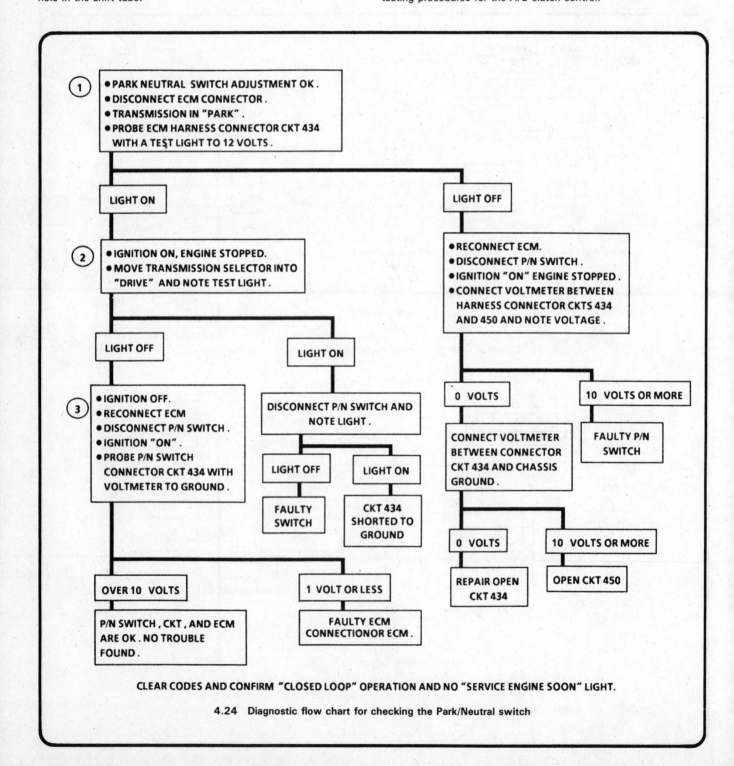

4.24   Diagnostic flow chart for checking the Park/Neutral switch

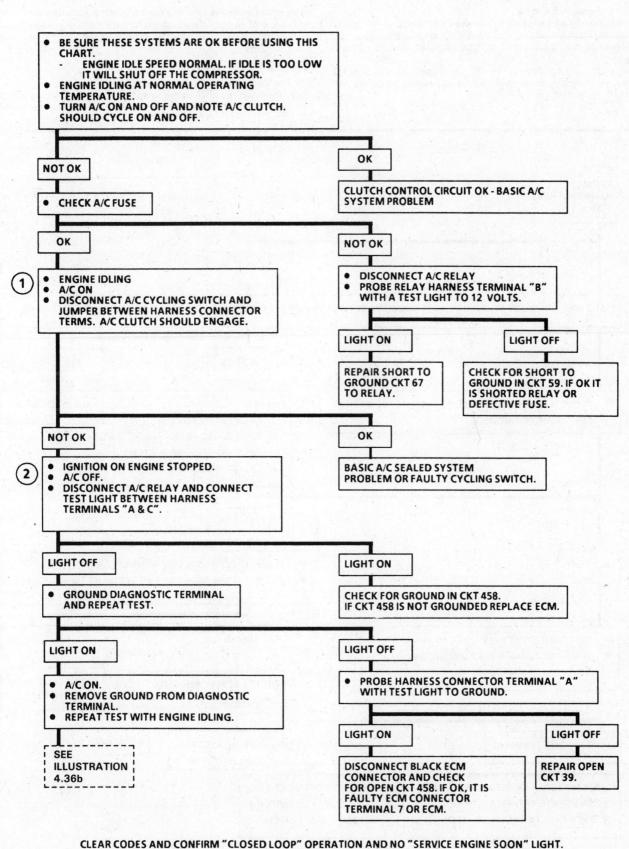

- BE SURE THESE SYSTEMS ARE OK BEFORE USING THIS CHART.
  - ENGINE IDLE SPEED NORMAL. IF IDLE IS TOO LOW IT WILL SHUT OFF THE COMPRESSOR.
- ENGINE IDLING AT NORMAL OPERATING TEMPERATURE.
- TURN A/C ON AND OFF AND NOTE A/C CLUTCH. SHOULD CYCLE ON AND OFF.

NOT OK

- CHECK A/C FUSE

OK

(1)
- ENGINE IDLING
- A/C ON
- DISCONNECT A/C CYCLING SWITCH AND JUMPER BETWEEN HARNESS CONNECTOR TERMS. A/C CLUTCH SHOULD ENGAGE.

OK

CLUTCH CONTROL CIRCUIT OK - BASIC A/C SYSTEM PROBLEM

NOT OK

- DISCONNECT A/C RELAY
- PROBE RELAY HARNESS TERMINAL "B" WITH A TEST LIGHT TO 12 VOLTS.

LIGHT ON

REPAIR SHORT TO GROUND CKT 67 TO RELAY.

LIGHT OFF

CHECK FOR SHORT TO GROUND IN CKT 59. IF OK IT IS SHORTED RELAY OR DEFECTIVE FUSE.

NOT OK

(2)
- IGNITION ON ENGINE STOPPED.
- A/C OFF.
- DISCONNECT A/C RELAY AND CONNECT TEST LIGHT BETWEEN HARNESS TERMINALS "A & C".

OK

BASIC A/C SEALED SYSTEM PROBLEM OR FAULTY CYCLING SWITCH.

LIGHT OFF

- GROUND DIAGNOSTIC TERMINAL AND REPEAT TEST.

LIGHT ON

CHECK FOR GROUND IN CKT 458. IF CKT 458 IS NOT GROUNDED REPLACE ECM.

LIGHT ON

- A/C ON.
- REMOVE GROUND FROM DIAGNOSTIC TERMINAL.
- REPEAT TEST WITH ENGINE IDLING.

LIGHT OFF

- PROBE HARNESS CONNECTOR TERMINAL "A" WITH TEST LIGHT TO GROUND.

LIGHT ON

DISCONNECT BLACK ECM CONNECTOR AND CHECK FOR OPEN CKT 458. IF OK, IT IS FAULTY ECM CONNECTOR TERMINAL 7 OR ECM.

LIGHT OFF

REPAIR OPEN CKT 39.

SEE ILLUSTRATION 4.36b

CLEAR CODES AND CONFIRM "CLOSED LOOP" OPERATION AND NO "SERVICE ENGINE SOON" LIGHT.

4.36a   Diagnostic flow chart for checking the A/C clutch control (4-cylinder engine)

6

A/C ''On'' signal (V6 engine)

37 Turning on the air conditioning supplies battery voltage to the A/C compressor clutch and to terminal B8 of ECM connector through circuit 59 (see the Wiring Diagrams) to increase idle air rate and maintain idle speed.

38 The ECM does not control the A/C compressor clutch, so if the A/C does not function, the problem is probably related to the air conditioning system and not the ECM.

39 If the A/C is operating properly and idle is too low when the A/C compressor turns on or is too high when the A/C compressor turns off, check for an open circuit 59 (see the Wiring Diagrams) to the ECM. If the circuit is okay, either ECM connector terminal B8 or the ECM itself is faulty.

Vehicle Speed Sensor (VSS)

40 The Vehicle Speed Sensor (VSS) is located next to the speedometer cable fitting on the back of the instrument cluster. It sends a pulsing voltage signal to the ECM, which the ECM converts to miles per hour.

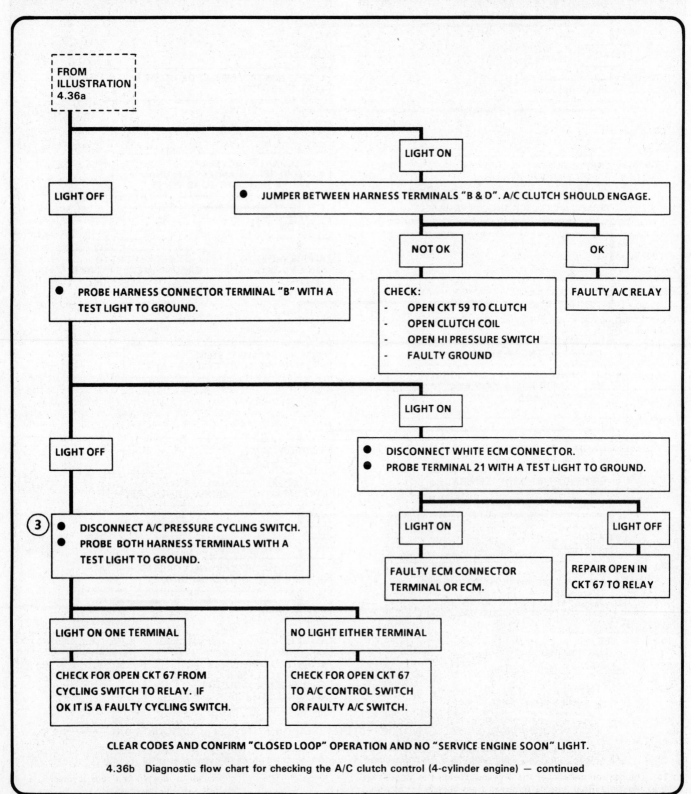

4.36b Diagnostic flow chart for checking the A/C clutch control (4-cylinder engine) — continued

4.41a To replace the Vehicle Speed Sensor remove the sensor mounting screw . . .

4.41b . . . then trace the sensor pigtail lead to the electrical connector and unplug it from the wire harness

The VSS is part of the Transmission Converter Clutch (TCC) system.
41 To replace the VSS, remove the instrument cluster (see Chapter 12). Detach the sensor retaining screw **(see illustration)** and unplug the sensor **(see illustration)**. Trace the pigtail of the VSS to its connector with the main wiring harness and unplug it.
42 Installation is the reverse of removal.

Distributor reference signal

43 The distributor sends a signal to the ECM to tell it both engine rpm and crankshaft position. See Electronic Spark Timing (Section 6), for further information.

5   Oxygen sensor

Refer to illustrations 5.1a and 5.1b

General description

1   The oxygen sensor, which is located in the exhaust manifold **(see illustrations)**, monitors the oxygen content of the exhaust gas stream.

The oxygen content in the exhaust reacts with the oxygen sensor to produce a voltage output which varies from 0.1 volt (high oxygen, lean mixture) to 0.9 volts (low oxygen, rich mixture). The ECM constantly monitors this variable voltage output to determine the ratio of oxygen to fuel in the mixture. The ECM alters the air/fuel mixture ratio by controlling the pulse width (open time) of the fuel injectors. A mixture ratio of 14.7 parts air to 1 part fuel is the ideal mixture ratio for minimizing exhaust emissions, thus allowing the catalytic converter to operate at maximum efficiency. It is this ratio of 14.7 to 1 which the ECM and the oxygen sensor attempt to maintain at all times.
2   The oxygen sensor produces no voltage when it is below its normal operating temperature of about 600°F (360°C). During this initial period before warm-up, the ECM operates in open loop mode.
3   If the engine reaches normal operating temperature and/or has been running for two or more minutes, and if the oxygen sensor is producing a steady signal voltage between 0.35 and 0.55-volts, even though the TPS indicates that the engine is not at idle, the ECM will set a Code 13.
4   A delay of two minutes or more between engine start-up and normal operation of the sensor, followed by a low voltage signal or a short in the sensor circuit, will cause the ECM to set a Code 44. If a high voltage signal occurs, the ECM will set a Code 45.

6

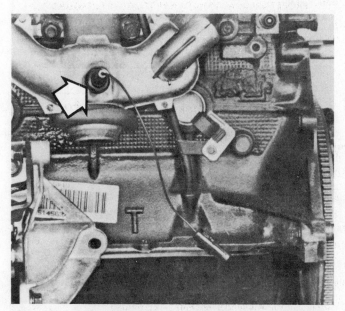

5.1a The oxygen sensor for the 4-cylinder engine is located in the exhaust manifold (engine removed from vehicle for clarity)

5.1b The oxygen sensor on the V6 engine is located in the left exhaust manifold

5   When any of the above codes occur, the ECM operates in the open loop mode — that is it controls fuel delivery in accordance with a programmed default value instead of feedback information from the oxygen sensor.

6   The proper operation of the oxygen sensor depends on four conditions:

   a) **Electrical** — The low voltages generated by the sensor depend upon good, clean connections which should be checked whenever a malfunction of the sensor is suspected or indicated.

   b) **Outside air supply** — The sensor is designed to allow air circulation to the internal portion of the sensor. Whenever the sensor is removed and installed or replaced, make sure the air passages are not restricted.

   c) **Proper operating temperature** — The ECM will not react to the sensor signal until the sensor reaches approximately 600 °F (315 °C). This factor must be taken into consideration when evaluating the performance of the sensor.

   d) **Unleaded fuel** — The use of unleaded fuel is essential for proper operation of the sensor. Make sure the fuel you are using is of this type.

7   In addition to observing the above conditions, special care must be taken whenever the sensor is serviced.

   a) The oxygen sensor has a permanently attached pigtail and connector which should not be removed from the sensor. Damage or removal of the pigtail or connector can adversely affect operation of the sensor.

   b) Grease, dirt and other contaminants should be kept away from the electrical connector and the louvered end of the sensor.

   c) Do not use cleaning solvents of any kind on the oxygen sensor.

   d) Do not drop or roughly handle the sensor.

   e) The silicone boot must be installed in the correct position to prevent the boot from being melted and to allow the sensor to operate properly.

Replacement

Note: *Because it is installed in the exhaust manifold or pipe, which contracts when cool, the oxygen sensor may be very difficult to loosen when the engine is cold. Rather than risk damage to the sensor (assuming you are planning to reuse it in another manifold or pipe), start and run the engine for a minute or two, then shut it off. Be careful not to burn yourself during the following procedure.*

8   Disconnect the cable from the negative terminal of the battery.

9   Raise the vehicle and place it securely on jackstands.

10   Carefully unsnap the electrical connector from the sensor.

11   Carefully unscrew the sensor from the exhaust manifold. **Caution:** *Excessive force may damage the threads.*

12   Anti-seize compound must be used on the threads of the sensor to facilitate future removal. The threads of new sensors will already be coated with this compound, but if an old sensor is removed and reinstalled, recoat the threads.

13   Install the sensor and tighten it securely.

14   Reconnect the electrical connector of the pigtail lead to the main engine wiring harness.

15   Lower the vehicle and reconnect the cable to the negative terminal of the battery.

6 Electronic Spark Timing (EST)

General description

Note: *Always consult the VECI label for the exact timing procedure for your vehicle.*

1   To provide improved engine performance, fuel economy and control of exhaust emissions, the Electronic Control Module (ECM) controls distributor spark advance (ignition timing) with the Electronic Spark Timing (EST) system.

2   The EST system consists of the distributor HEI module, an ECM and the connecting wires. The four terminals for the EST are lettered on the module. The distributor four-terminal connector is lettered left-to-right, A-B-C-D. These circuits perform the following functions:

   a) **Terminal A** — Reference Ground Low. This wire is grounded in the distributor and insures that the ground circuit has no voltage drop which could affect performance. It is open, it may cause poor performance.

   b) **Terminal B** — Bypass. At about 400 rpm the ECM applies 5-volts to this circuit to switch spark timing control from the HEI module to the ECM. An open or grounded bypass circuit will set a Code 42 and the engine will run at base timing, plus a small amount of advance built into the HEI module.

   c) **Terminal C** — Distributor Reference High. This provides the ECM with rpm and crankshaft position information.

   d) **Terminal D** — EST. This circuit triggers the HEI module. The ECM doesn't know what the actual timing is, but it does know when it gets the reference signal. It advances or retards the spark from that point. If the base timing is set incorrectly, the entire spark curve will be incorrect.

3   The ECM receives a reference pulse from the distributor, which indicates both engine rpm and crankshaft position. The ECM then determines the proper spark advance for the engine operating conditions and sends an EST pulse to the distributor.

Checking

4   The ECM will set spark timing at a specified value when the diagnostic "Test" terminal in the ALCL connector is grounded. To check for EST operation, the timing should be checked at 2000 rpm with the terminal ungrounded. Then ground the test terminal. If the timing changes at 2000 rpm, the EST is operating. A fault in the EST system will usually set Trouble Code 42.

Setting base timing

5   To set the initial base timing, locate, then disconnect the timing connector (the location and wire color of the timing connector is on the VECI label).

6   Set the timing as specified on the VECI label. This will cause a Code 42 to be stored in the ECM memory. Be sure to clear the memory after setting the timing (see Section 2).

7   For further information regarding the testing and component replacement procedures for either the HEI/EST distributor or the distributorless (DIS or C3I) ignition systems, refer to Chapter 5.

7 Electronic Spark Control (ESC) system (V6 engine)

Refer to illustrations 7.3, 7.6 and 7.13

General description

1   Irregular octane levels in modern gasoline can cause detonation in an engine. Detonation is sometimes referred to as "spark knock."

2   The Electronic Spark Control (ESC) system is designed to retard spark timing up to 20 ° to reduce spark knock in the engine. This allows the engine to use maximum spark advance to improve driveability and fuel economy.

3   The ESC knock sensor **(see illustration)** sends a voltage signal of 8 to 10-volts to the ECM when no spark knock is occurring and the ECM provides normal advance. When the knock sensor detects ab-

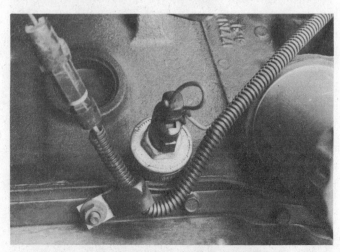

7.3   The Electronic Spark Control (ESC) knock sensor on the V6 engine is located on the right side of the block, forward of the oil cooler

normal vibration (spark knock), the ESC module turns off the circuit to the ECM and the voltage at ECM terminal B7 drops to zero volts. The ECM then retards the EST distributor until spark knock is eliminated.
4 Failure of the ESC knock sensor signal or loss of ground at the ESC module will cause the signal to the ECM to remain high. This condition will result in the ECM controlling the EST as if no spark knock is occurring. Therefore, no retard will occur and spark knock may become severe under heavy engine load conditions. At this point, the ECM will

set a Code 43.
5 Loss of the ESC signal to the ECM will cause the ECM to constantly retard EST. This will result in sluggish performance and cause the ECM to set a Code 43.

Checking
6 Diagnostic chart 7.6 (see illustration) diagrams the testing procedures for the ESC system.

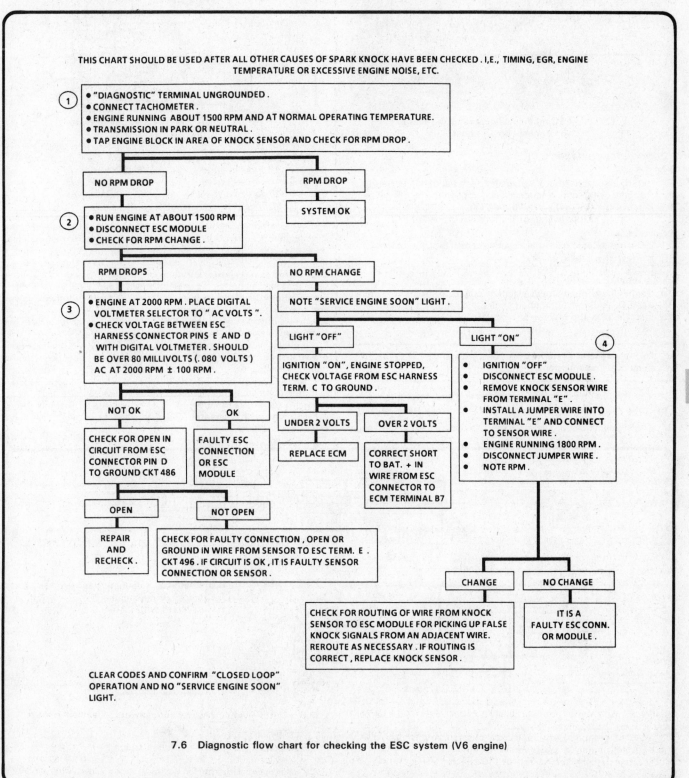

7.6 Diagnostic flow chart for checking the ESC system (V6 engine)

7.13 The ESC module is located at the rear of the engine compartment

Component replacement

ESC sensor
7   Detach the cable from the negative terminal of the battery.
8   Disconnect the wiring harness connector from the ESC sensor.
9   Remove the ESC sensor from the block.
10 Installation is the reverse of the removal procedure.

ESC module
11 Detach the cable from the negative terminal of the battery.
12 Remove the engine cover.
13 Locate the module (**see illustration**) at the rear of the engine compartment.
14 Detach the wiring harness electrical connector from the module.
15 Remove the module mounting bolts and remove the module.
16 Installation is the reverse of removal.

8   Air management system (V6 — California and all manual transmissions)

Refer to illustrations 8.2, 8.6, 8.7, 8.27, 8.43, 8.45 and 8.51

General description
1   The air management system is used to reduce carbon monoxide

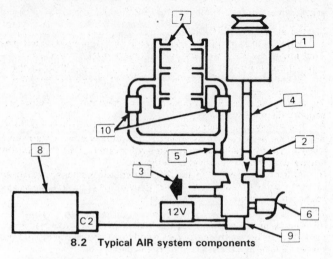

8.2 Typical AIR system components

1 Air pump	7 Air injection pipes
2 EAC valve	(air to exhaust ports)
3 Air to air cleaner	8 ECM
4 Air to EAC valve	9 EAC solenoid
5 Air to exhaust ports	10 Check valves
6 Manifold vacuum signal	

and hydrocarbon emissions. The system used on these vehicles, the Air Injection Reaction (AIR) system, adds air to the exhaust manifold to continue combustion after the exhaust gases leave the combustion chamber.
2   The AIR system (**see illustration**) consists of an air pump, a diverter valve (Federal/carbureted) or an Electric Air Control (EAC) valve (California/carbureted and all fuel injected vehicles), a pair of check valves and the plumbing between these components.
3   A belt-driven air pump supplies air through a centrifugal filter fan to the EAC valve.
4   A check valve on either side of the engine prevents the back flow of exhaust into the air pump if there is an exhaust backfire or pump drivebelt failure.
5   To help prevent backfiring during high vacuum conditions, Federal/carbureted engines utilize a deceleration (gulp) valve to allow air to flow into the intake manifold. This air enters the air/fuel mixture to lean the rich condition created by high vacuum when the throttle valve closes on deceleration.

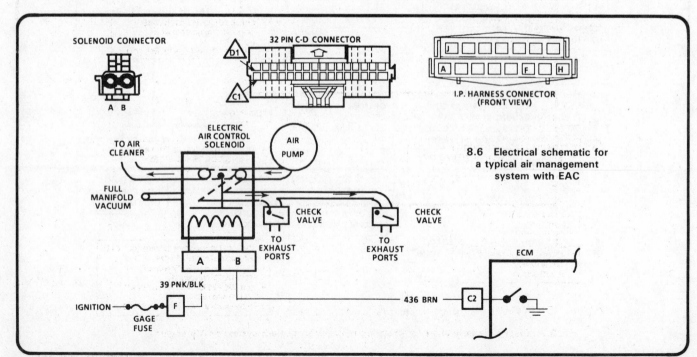

8.6 Electrical schematic for a typical air management system with EAC

Checking

Electric air control (EAC) valve

6   During cold starting, the ECM completes the ground circuit **(see illustration)**, the EAC solenoid is energized and air is directed to the exhaust ports. As the coolant temperature increases the ECM opens the ground circuit, the EAC solenoid is de-energized and air goes to the air cleaner.

7   Diagnostic chart 8.7 **(see illustration)** diagrams the testing procedures for the EAC valve.

8   The AIR system is not completely noiseless. Under normal conditions, noise rises in pitch as engine speed increases. To determine if the excessive noise is the fault of the AIR system pump, operate the engine with the pump drivebelt removed.

9   If the noise is caused by the AIR system pump, check for a seized air pump, proper mounting and bolt torque of the pump and the proper routing and connections of the hoses.

Air pump

10   The air pump is a permanently-lubricated positive displacement vane type design which requires no periodic maintenance. If it is making noise, replace it. Do not attempt to lubricate it.

11   To check air flow from the hoses, accelerate the engine to about 1500 rpm and note the air flow from the hoses. If air flow increases as the engine is accelerated, the pump is operating satisfactorily. If air flow does not increase or is not present, proceed as follows:

12   Check the drivebelt for proper tension (see Chapter 1).

13   Inspect the pressure relief valve for air leaks. If the valve is leaking, you can hear it leak when the pump is running.

Check valve

14   Inspect the check valve(s) whenever the corresponding hose is disconnected or whenever check valve failure is suspected. A pump that has become inoperative and shows indications of having exhaust gases in the pump indicates check valve failure.

15   Blow through the check valve (toward the cylinder head), then attempt to suck back through the check valve. Flow should only be in one direction (toward the exhaust manifold). Replace the valve if it does not operate properly.

Deceleration valve

16   Remove the air cleaner housing assembly and adapter (see Chapter 4), plug the air cleaner vacuum source and connect a tachometer.

17   With the engine running at the specified idle speed, remove the

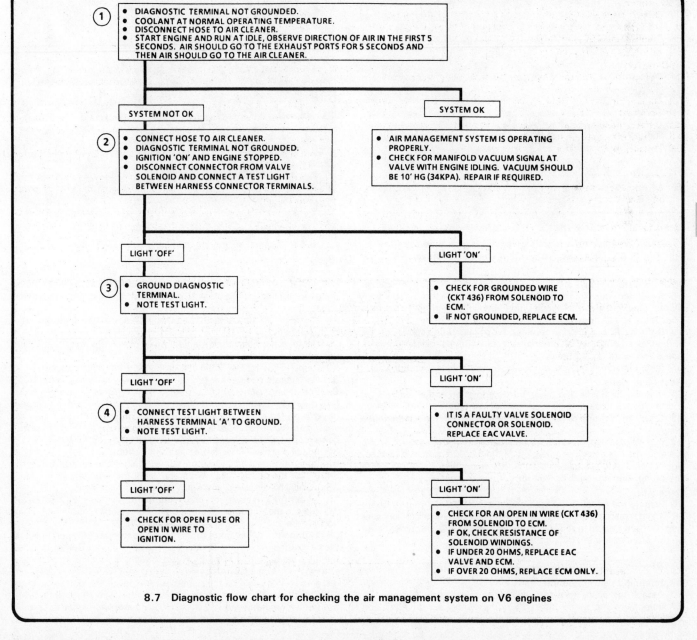

8.7   Diagnostic flow chart for checking the air management system on V6 engines

8.27   To remove the drivebelt loosen the adjusting bolt and mounting brace bolts (arrows)

8.43   A typical EAC valve

8.45   To detach the manifold vacuum signal tube from the EAC valve, pry it off with a small screwdriver

8.51   Typical air management system check valve — V6 engine shown

small deceleration valve signal hose from the manifold vacuum source.

18 Reconnect the signal hose and listen for air flow through the ventilation pipe and into the deceleration valve. There should also be a noticeable speed drop when the signal hose is reconnected.

19 If the air flow does not continue for at least one second, or the engine speed does not drop noticeably, check the deceleration valve hoses for restrictions or leaks.

20 If no restrictions or leaks are found, replace the deceleration valve.

Hoses and pipes

21 Inspect the hoses and pipes for deterioration and holes.

22 Inspect all hose and pipe clamps for tightness.

23 Check the routing of all hoses and pipes. Interference can cause wear.

24 If a leak is suspected on the pressure side of the system, or if a hose or pipe has been disconnected on the pressure side, the connections should be checked for leaks with a soapy water solution. With the pump running, bubbles will form if a leak exists.

Drivebelt

25 Inspect the drivebelt for wear, cracks or deterioration (see Chapter 1) and replace as necessary. When installing a new belt, make sure that it is fully seated in the V-belt grooves of the A/C compressor, air pump, alternator and crankshaft pulleys.

Component replacement

Air pump and centrifugal filter fan

26 Detach the cable from the negative terminal of the battery.

27 Immobilize the pump pulley by compressing the drivebelt and loosen the pump pulley bolts. Loosen the drivebelt tension adjusting

bolt and, if necessary, the mounting brace bolts **(see illustration)**. Pivot the air pump toward the block to remove belt tension and remove the drivebelt.

28 Clearly label, then detach, the pump hoses, vacuum lines and electrical connectors.

29 Remove the belt tension adjusting bolt and the mounting brace bolt and remove the air pump.

30 Remove the pulley bolts, the pulley and the pulley spacer.

31 Use needle nose pliers to pull the filter fan from the pump hub. **Caution:** *Do not allow any filter fragments to enter the air pump intake hole during removal. Do not remove the filter fan by inserting a screwdriver between the pump and the filter fan. You will damage the pump sealing lip. Do not attempt to clean the centrifugal filter fan with either compressed air or solvents. If it is dirty, it must be replaced.*

32 Install the new filter fan on the pump hub.

33 Install the spacer and pump pulley against the centrifugal fan.

34 Install the pump pulley bolts and snug them finger tight.

35 Install the air pump and snug the bolts finger tight.

36 Install the drivebelt and adjust the belt tension (see Chapter 1).

37 Tighten the air pump mounting brace bolt and belt tension adjusting bolt securely.

38 Tighten the pulley bolts to the specified torque. This compresses the centrifugal filter fan onto the pump hole. Do not attempt to drive the filter fan on with a hammer. **Note:** *A slight amount of interference with the housing bore is normal.*

39 Attach the cable to the negative terminal of the battery.

40 Check the air management system for proper operation. **Note:** *After a new filter fan has been installed, it may squeal upon initial operation until the sealing lip has worn in.*

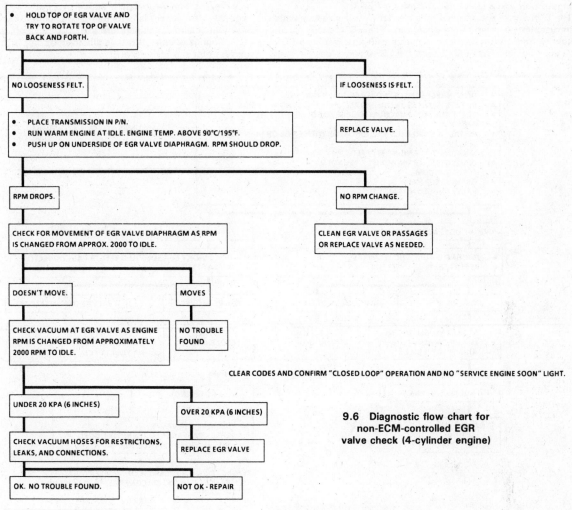

- HOLD TOP OF EGR VALVE AND TRY TO ROTATE TOP OF VALVE BACK AND FORTH.

NO LOOSENESS FELT. → IF LOOSENESS IS FELT. → REPLACE VALVE.

- PLACE TRANSMISSION IN P/N.
- RUN WARM ENGINE AT IDLE. ENGINE TEMP. ABOVE 90°C/195°F.
- PUSH UP ON UNDERSIDE OF EGR VALVE DIAPHRAGM. RPM SHOULD DROP.

RPM DROPS. / NO RPM CHANGE. → CLEAN EGR VALVE OR PASSAGES OR REPLACE VALVE AS NEEDED.

CHECK FOR MOVEMENT OF EGR VALVE DIAPHRAGM AS RPM IS CHANGED FROM APPROX. 2000 TO IDLE.

DOESN'T MOVE. / MOVES → NO TROUBLE FOUND.

CHECK VACUUM AT EGR VALVE AS ENGINE RPM IS CHANGED FROM APPROXIMATELY 2000 RPM TO IDLE.

CLEAR CODES AND CONFIRM "CLOSED LOOP" OPERATION AND NO "SERVICE ENGINE SOON" LIGHT.

UNDER 20 KPA (6 INCHES) / OVER 20 KPA (6 INCHES) → REPLACE EGR VALVE

CHECK VACUUM HOSES FOR RESTRICTIONS, LEAKS, AND CONNECTIONS.

OK. NO TROUBLE FOUND. / NOT OK - REPAIR

9.6 Diagnostic flow chart for non-ECM-controlled EGR valve check (4-cylinder engine)

EAC valve
41 Detach the cable from the negative terminal of the battery.
42 Remove the engine cover (see Chapter 11).
43 Locate the EAC valve (see illustration) on the right side of the engine bay.
44 Detach the electrical connector from the terminal on the lower front of the valve.
45 Detach the manifold vacuum signal hose (see illustration).
46 Detach the air inlet and outlet hoses from the valve.
47 Remove the EAC valve.
48 Installation is the reverse of removal.

Check valve
49 Detach the cable from the negative terminal of the battery.
50 Remove the engine cover (see Chapter 11).
51 Locate the check valve you wish to replace (see illustration).
52 Release the clamp and detach the hose from the valve.
53 Using a backup wrench, unscrew the valve from the threaded fitting on the air injection pipe.
54 Installation is the reverse of removal.

Air injection pipe assembly
55 Detach the cable from the negative terminal of the battery.
56 Remove the engine cover (see Chapter 11).
57 Locate the pipe assembly you wish to replace.
58 Unscrew the check valve.
59 Unscrew the pipe assembly threaded fitting from the manifold.
60 Remove the pipe assembly mounting bracket bolts.
61 Remove the pipe assembly.
62 Installation is the reverse of removal.

Deceleration valve
63 Detach the cable from the negative terminal of the battery.
64 Remove the engine cover (see Chapter 11).
65 Detach the vacuum hoses from the valve.
66 Remove the screws securing the valve to the engine bracket.
67 Remove the deceleration valve.
68 Installation is the reverse of removal.

9 Exhaust Gas Recirculation (EGR) system

Refer to illustrations 9.6, 9.8, 9.12, 9.13, 9.30 and 9.39

General description

1 The EGR system is used to lower NOx (oxides of nitrogen) emission levels caused by high combustion temperatures. It does this by decreasing combustion temperatures.
2 The EGR system consists of a negative backpressure EGR valve, a ported manifold vacuum source tube and, on the V6, a solenoid which controls this vacuum source.

Checking

3 Too much EGR flow tends to weaken combustion, causing the engine to run rough or stop. When EGR flow is excessive, the engine can stop after a cold start or at idle after deceleration, the vehicle can surge at cruising speeds or the idle may be rough. If the EGR valve remains constantly open, the engine may not idle at all.
4 Too little or no EGR flow allows combustion temperatures to get too high during acceleration and load conditions. This can cause spark knock (detonation), engine overheating or emission test failure.
5 A procedure for performing a check of the EGR is contained in Chapter 1. The following additional checks can help pinpoint the source of an EGR problem.
4-cylinder engine EGR valve check (non-ECM-controlled EGR)
6 See the accompanying diagnostic flow chart for checking the non-ECM controlled EGR valve on the four-cylinder engine (see illustration).

6

V6 engine EGR valve check (ECM-controlled EGR)

7   The EGR valve is controlled by a normally open solenoid which allows vacuum to pass when energized. The ECM energizes the solenoid to turn on the EGR and monitors EGR flow with the EGR temperature switch. The ECM controls the EGR when three conditions are present: engine coolant is above 113°F, the TPS is at part throttle and the MAP sensor is in its mid-range. Code 32 will detect a faulty vacuum solenoid, temperature switch or vacuum supply.

8   Diagnostic chart 9.8 (see illustration) diagrams the testing procedures for the EGR valve.

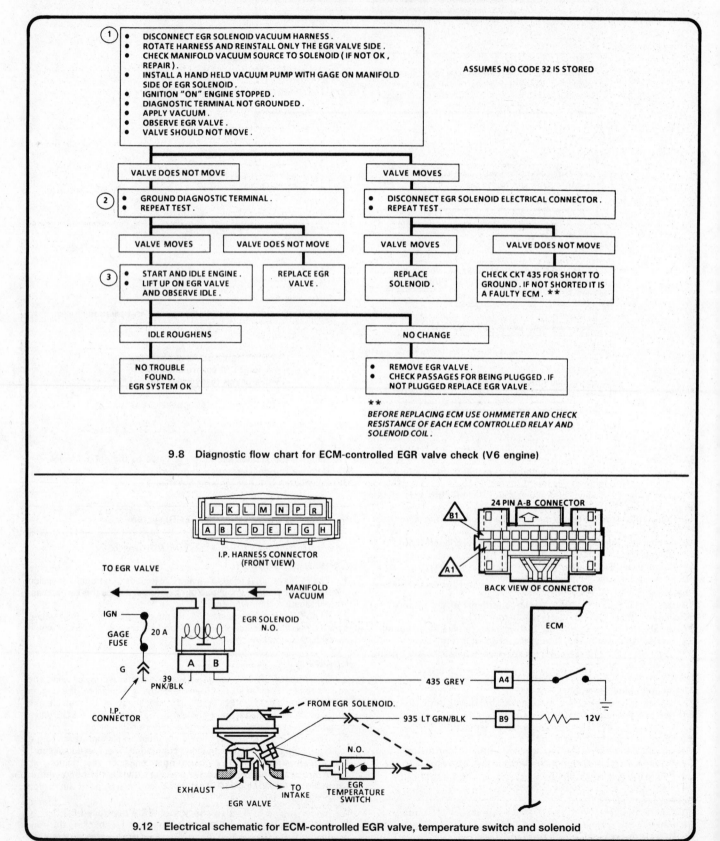

9.8 Diagnostic flow chart for ECM-controlled EGR valve check (V6 engine)

9.12 Electrical schematic for ECM-controlled EGR valve, temperature switch and solenoid

1992 and later CPI equipped V6 engine with linear EGR valve

9   The EGR valve is a normally closed electric solenoid and is controlled by the Electronic Control Module (ECM). The ECM monitors various engine parameters; throttle position sensor, manifold absolute pressure, coolant temperature sensor and pintle position sensor. Output messages from these sensors are sent to the EGR system to indicate the correct amount of exhaust gas recirculation that is necessary to lower combustion temperatures.

10   The ECM energizes the EGR valve and the valve's pintle is raised to allow a controlled amount of exhaust gases to flow from the exhaust manifold into the intake manifold. The linear valve EGR valve is unique since the ECM continuously monitors the pintle height and corrects it to maintain an accurate flow of exhaust gases.

EGR system failure (carbureted and TBI models)

11   If a Code 32 is displayed by the Service Engine Soon light, the EGR temperature switch was closed during start-up or the switch was not detected closed under when the coolant temperature exceeded 194°F and the EGR duty cycle commanded by the ECM was greater than 50% (both conditions must be met for about 4 minutes).

12   The EGR vacuum control solenoid uses an ECM controlled pulse width modulated EGR solenoid. The valve is normally open and the vacuum source is a ported signal. The ECM will turn the EGR on and off (the "duty cycle") by grounding circuit 435 (see illustration). The duty cycle should be zero percent (no EGR) when in Park or Neutral, when the TPS input is below the specified value or when Wide Open Throttle (WOT) is indicated.

13   Diagnostic chart 9.11 (see illustration) diagrams the testing procedures for an EGR system failure.

EGR system failure (1992 and later CPI-equipped V6 engine)

14   Testing of this EGR system requires special tools and expertise that place it outside the scope of the home mechanic. Take the vehicle to a dealer service department or other qualified shop.

Component replacement

EGR valve (carbureted and TBI models)

15   When buying a new EGR valve, make sure that you have the right EGR valve.

16   Detach the cable from the negative terminal of the battery.

17   Remove the engine cover (see Chapter 11).

18   Remove the air cleaner housing assembly and adapter (see Chapter 4).

19   Detach the vacuum line from the EGR valve vacuum tube.

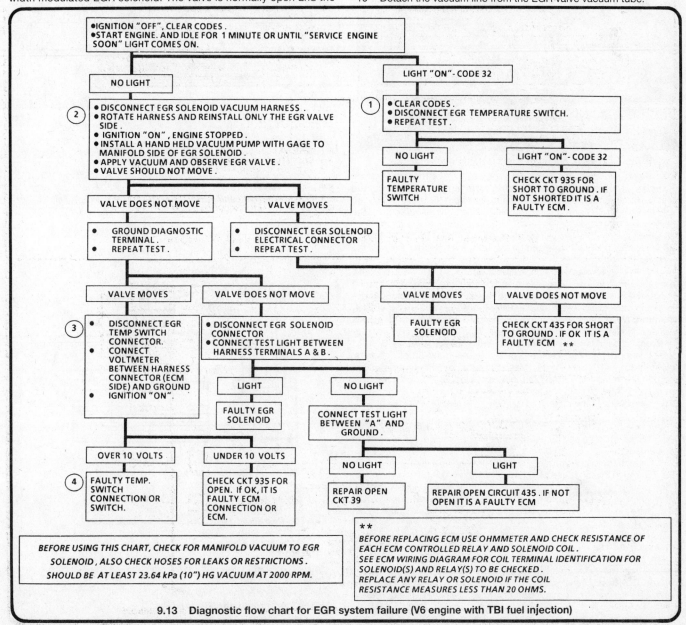

9.13   Diagnostic flow chart for EGR system failure (V6 engine with TBI fuel injection)

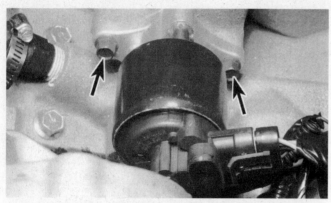

**9.30 Disconnect the electrical connector from the EGR valve,
then remove the mounting bolts (arrows)**

9.39   EGR valve solenoid electrical connector (arrow)

20   If you are replacing the EGR valve itself, trace the temperature switch pigtail lead to the main engine wire harness and unplug the electrical connector, then remove the switch from the valve. If you are replacing the EGR valve gasket, unplug the lead but do not remove the switch from the valve.

21   Remove the EGR valve mounting bolts.

22   Remove the EGR valve and gasket from the manifold. Discard the gasket.

23   With a wire wheel, buff the exhaust deposits from the EGR valve mounting surface on the manifold and, if you plan to reuse the same valve, the mounting surface of the valve itself. Look for exhaust deposits in the valve outlet. Remove deposit build-up with a screwdriver. **Caution:** *Never wash the valve in solvents or degreaser - both agents will permanently damage the diaphragm. Sand blasting is also not recommended because it will affect the operation of the valve.*

24   If the EGR passage evinces an excessive build-up of deposits, clean it out with a wire wheel. Make sure that all loose particles are completely removed to prevent them from clogging the EGR valve or from being ingested into the engine.

25   Installation is the reverse of removal.

EGR valve (1992 and later CPI-equipped V6 engine)

26   When buying a new EGR valve, make sure you get the correct replacement part.

27   Detach the cable from the negative battery terminal.

28   Remove the air intake plenum (see Chapter 4).

29   Disconnect the electrical connector from the EGR valve.

30   Remove the EGR valve mounting bolts **(see illustration)**.

31   Remove the EGR valve and gasket from the intake manifold. Discard the gasket.

32   With a wire wheel, buff the exhaust deposits from the EGR valve mounting surface on the intake manifold and, if you plan to reuse the same valve, the mounting surface of the valve itself. Look for exhaust deposits in the valve outlet. Remove deposit build-up with a screwdriver. **Caution:** *Never wash the valve in solvent or degreaser and sandblasting is not recommended because it will affect the operation of the valve.*

33   If the valve was cleaned, make sure all loose particles are com-

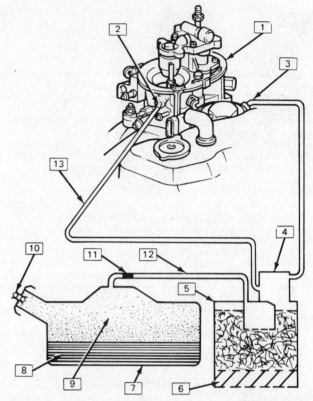

10.2a   Typical evaporative system for the 4-cylinder engine

1 TBI unit	6 Purge air	10 Pressure/vacuum
2 Canister purge port	7 Fuel tank	relief gas cap
3 Vacuum signal	8 Fuel	11 Vent restricter
4 Purge valve	9 Vapor	12 Fuel tank vent
5 Vapor storage canister		13 Purge line

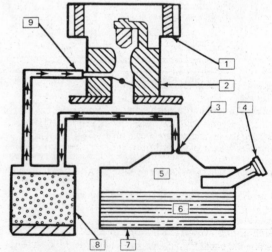

10.2b   Typical evaporative system for the V6 engine

1 Air cleaner	5 Vapor
2 TBI unit	6 Fuel
3 Restricter	7 Fuel tank
4 Pressure/vacuum	8 Charcoal canister
relief gas cap	9 Purge

pletely removed to prevent them from clogging the EGR valve or from being ingested into the engine.

34   Installation is the reverse of removal.

Hoses (carbureted and TBI models)

35   When replacing hoses, use hose identified with the word "Fluore-

10.15   To remove the charcoal canister, label and detach the vacuum lines, then remove the canister clamp bolt (arrow) and lift the canister out (grille, radiator and condenser removed for clarity)

10.16   To replace the canister filter, peel it out and install a new one

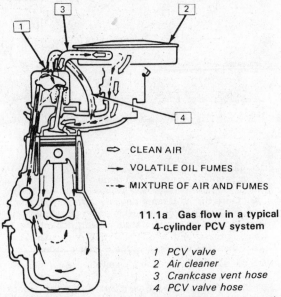

⇨ CLEAN AIR

→ VOLATILE OIL FUMES

--→ MIXTURE OF AIR AND FUMES

11.1a   Gas flow in a typical 4-cylinder PCV system

1   *PCV valve*
2   *Air cleaner*
3   *Crankcase vent hose*
4   *PCV valve hose*

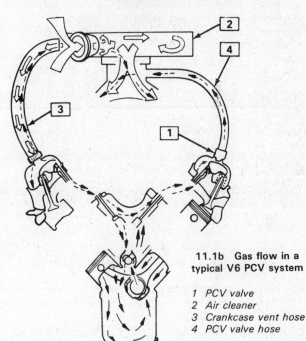

11.1b   Gas flow in a typical V6 PCV system

1   *PCV valve*
2   *Air cleaner*
3   *Crankcase vent hose*
4   *PCV valve hose*

6

lastomer." Use the VECI label (on the fan shroud) as a hose routing guide. For further information regarding hose inspection and service, see Chapter 1.

EGR vacuum solenoid (carbureted and TBI models)

36   Detach the cable from the negative terminal of the battery.
37   Remove the engine cover (see Chapter 11).
38   Remove the air cleaner housing assembly and adapter (see Chapter 4).
39   Unplug the electrical connector from the solenoid **(see illustration)**.
40   Clearly label, then detach, both vacuum hoses.
41   Remove the solenoid mounting screw and remove the solenoid.
42   Installation is the reverse of removal.

EGR temperature switch (carbureted and TBI models)

43   Detach the cable from the negative terminal of the battery.
44   Remove the engine cover (see Chapter 11).
45   Trace the pigtail lead to the main engine wire harness and unplug the electrical connector.
46   Remove the switch.
47   Installation is the reverse of removal. Be sure to use anti-seize compound on the switch threads.

---

10   Evaporative Emission Control System (EECS)

Refer to illustrations 10.2a, 10.2b, 10.15 and 10.16

General description

1   This system is designed to trap and store fuel vapors that evaporate

from the fuel tank, throttle body and intake manifold.
2   The Evaporative Emission Control System (EECS) consists of a charcoal-filled canister and the lines connecting the canister to the fuel tank, ported vacuum and intake manifold vacuum **(see illustrations)**.
3   Fuel vapors are transferred from the fuel tank, throttle body and intake manifold to a canister where they are stored when the engine is not operating. When the engine is running, the fuel vapors are purged from the canister by intake air flow and consumed in the normal combustion process.

Checking

4   Poor idle, stalling and poor driveability can be caused by an inoperative purge valve, a damaged canister, split or cracked hoses or hoses connected to the wrong tubes.
5   Evidence of fuel loss or fuel odor can be caused by liquid fuel leaking from fuel lines or the TBI, a cracked or damaged canister, an inoperative bowl vent valve, an inoperative purge valve, disconnected, misrouted, kinked, deteriorated or damaged vapor or control hoses or an improperly seated air cleaner or air cleaner gasket.
6   Inspect each hose attached to the canister for kinks, leaks and breaks along its entire length. Repair or replace as necessary.
7   Inspect the canister. If it is cracked or damaged, replace it.
8   Look for fuel leaking from the bottom of the canister. If fuel is leaking, replace the canister and check the hoses and hose routing.
9   Check the filter at the bottom of the canister. If it's dirty, plugged or damaged, replace the filter. **Note:** *Some later models don't have replaceable filters.*

10 Apply a short length of hose to the lower tube of the purge valve assembly and attempt to blow through it. Little or no air should pass into the canister (a small amount of air will pass because the canister has a constant purge hole).

11 With a hand vacuum pump, apply vacuum through the control vacuum signal tube to the purge valve diaphragm.

12 If the diaphragm does not hold vacuum for at least 20 seconds, the diaphragm is leaking and the canister must be replaced.

13 If the diaphragm holds vacuum, again try to blow through the hose while vacuum is still being applied. An increased flow of air should be noted. If it isn't, replace the canister.

Component replacement

14 Clearly label, then detach, all vacuum lines from the canister.

15 Loosen the canister mounting clamp bolt (see illustration) and pull the canister out.

16 Check the filter and replace it if it is dirty (see illustration).

17 Installation is the reverse of removal.

---

11 Positive Crankcase Ventilation (PCV) system

Refer to illustrations 11.1a and 11.1b

1 The Positive Crankcase Ventilation (PCV) system reduces hydrocarbon emissions by scavenging crankcase vapors. It does this by circulating fresh air from the air cleaner through the crankcase, where it mixes with blow-by gases and is then rerouted through a PCV valve to the intake manifold **(see illustrations)**.

2 The main components of the PCV system are the PCV valve, a fresh air filtered inlet and the vacuum hoses connecting these two components with the engine and the EECS system.

3 To maintain idle quality, the PCV valve restricts the flow when the intake manifold vacuum is high. If abnormal operating conditions arise, the system is designed to allow excessive amounts of blow-by gases to flow back through the crankcase vent tube into the air cleaner to be consumed by normal combustion.

4 Checking and replacement of the PCV valve and filter is covered in Chapter 1.

---

12 Thermostatic air cleaner (THERMAC)(carbureted and TBI models)

Refer to illustrations 12.2, 12.18, 12.27 and 12.28

General description

1 A heated air intake system is used to provide good driveability under varying climatic conditions. By having a uniform inlet air temperature, the fuel system can be calibrated to reduce exhaust emissions and to eliminate throttle valve icing.

2 The THERMAC air cleaner **(see illustration)** is operated by heated air and manifold vacuum. Air can enter the air cleaner from outside the engine compartment or from a heat stove built around the exhaust manifold. A temperature sensor located inside the air cleaner housing determines the operational mode of the THERMAC.

Checking

3 If the engine hesitates during warm-up:
 a) The heat stove tube could be disconnected.
 b) The vacuum diaphragm motor could be inoperative, leaving the snorkel (mouth) of the air cleaner housing open to outside air.
 c) There may be no manifold vacuum.
 d) The damper door does not move.
 e) The air cleaner housing assembly-to-TBI adapter seal may be missing.
 f) The air cleaner housing assembly cover seal may be missing.
 g) The air cleaner housing assembly cover may be loose.
 h) The air cleaner housing assembly may be loose.

4 Lack of power and/or sluggish or spongy throttle response can be caused by:
 a) A stuck damper door that does not open to outside air.
 b) A temperature sensor that does not bleed off vacuum.

5 Inspect the system to be sure that all hoses and the heat stove tube are connected. Check for kinked, plugged or deteriorated hoses.

6 Check for the presence and condition of air cleaner to carburetor gasket seal.

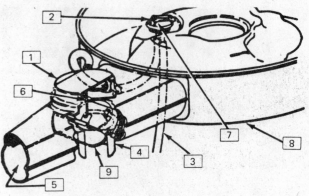

12.2 Typical THERMAC air cleaner

1 Vacuum diaphragm motor
2 Temperature sensor
3 Vacuum hose (to manifold vacuum)
4 Heat stove duct
5 Snorkel
6 Linkage
7 Air bleed valve
8 Air cleaner assembly
9 Damper door

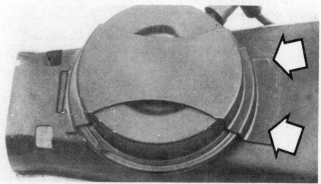

12.18 Once the air cleaner housing assembly is removed from the TBI unit, turn it upside down and detach the vacuum line from the temperature sensor, drill out the spot welds (arrows) with a 1/16-inch drill, then enlarge as necessary to remove the retaining strap

7 With the air cleaner assembly installed, the damper door should be open to outside air.

8 Start the engine. Watch the damper door in the air cleaner snorkel. When the engine is first started, the damper door should move and close off outside air. As the air cleaner warms up, the damper door should open slowly to the outside air.

9 If the air cleaner fails to operate as described above, the door may not be moving at the right temperature. If the driveability problem is during warm-up, make the temperature sensor check below.

10 With the engine off, disconnect the vacuum hose at the vacuum diaphragm motor.

11 Apply at least 7 inches of vacuum to the vacuum diaphragm motor. The damper door should completely block off outside air when vacuum is applied. If it doesn't, check to see if the linkage is hooked up correctly.

12 With vacuum still applied, trap vacuum in the vacuum diaphragm motor by bending the hose. The damper door should remain closed. If it doesn't, replace the vacuum diaphragm motor assembly. Failure of the vacuum diaphragm motor is more likely to be caused from binding linkage or a corroded snorkel than from a failed diaphragm. Check this first before replacing the diaphragm.

13 If the vacuum motor checks out okay, check the vacuum hoses and connections. If they're okay, replace the temperature sensor.

14 Start the test with the air cleaner temperature below 86°F. If the engine has been run recently, remove the air cleaner cover and place the thermometer as close as possible to the sensor. Let the air cleaner cool until the thermometer reads below 86°F for about 5 to 10 minutes. Reinstall the air cleaner.

15 Start and idle the engine. The damper door should move to close off outside air immediately if the engine is cool enough. When the damper door starts to open the snorkel passage (in a few minutes), remove the air cleaner and read the thermometer. It must read about 131°F.

**12.27   Pry off the sensor retaining clips with
a small screwdriver**

16 If the damper door is not open to outside air at the indicated
temperature, the temperature sensor is malfunctioning and must be
replaced.

Component replacement

Vacuum diaphragm motor

17 Remove the air cleaner (see Chapter 4).
18 Detach the vacuum tube from the motor **(see illustration)**.
19 Drill out the two spot welds with a 1/16-inch drill, then enlarge
as required to remove the retaining strap. Do not damage the snorkel
tube.
20 Bend the strap up and out of the way.
21 Lift up the motor, cocking it to one side to unhook the motor linkage
at the control damper assembly.
22 To install a new motor, drill a 7/64-inch hole in the snorkel tube
at the center of the vacuum motor retaining strap.
23 Install the vacuum motor linkage into the control damper assembly.
24 Use the motor retaining strap and sheet metal screw provided in
the motor service package to secure the motor to the snorkel tube.
Make sure that the screw does not interfere with the operation of the
damper assembly. Shorten the screw if necessary.
25 Install the air cleaner housing assembly (see Chapter 4). Be sure
to attach the vacuum hose to the motor.

Sensor

26 Remove the air cleaner housing assembly (see Chapter 4).
27 Note the position **(see illustration)** of the sensor in the air cleaner
housing to facilitate reinstallation.
28 Pry up the tabs on the sensor retaining clip **(see illustration)**.
Remove the clip and sensor from the air cleaner.
29 Installation is the reverse of removal. Be sure to attach the two
vacuum lines to the sensor pipes.

13 Transmission Converter Clutch (TCC)

General description

1   The Transmission Converter Clutch (TCC) uses a solenoid-operated
valve in the automatic transmission to mechanically couple the engine
flywheel to the output shaft of the transmission through the torque
converter. This reduces the slippage losses in the converter, reducing
emissions because engine rpm at any given speed is reduced. It also
increases fuel economy.
2   For the converter clutch to operate properly, two conditions must
be met:
   a) The engine must be warmed up before the clutch can apply. The
       engine coolant temperature sensor (see Section 4) tells the ECM
       when the engine is at operating temperature.
   b) The vehicle must be traveling at the necessary minimum speed
       to raise the pressure to the level necessary to apply the valve.
       If the hydraulic pressure is correct, the ECM signals the solenoid
       to apply the converter clutch.
3   After the converter clutch applies, the ECM uses the information
from the TPS to release the clutch when the car is accelerating or de-
celerating at a certain rate.
4   Another switch used in the TCC circuit is a brake switch which
opens the power supply to the TCC solenoid when the brake is applied.
5   The transmission on the V6 engine uses a 4th gear switch to send

**12.28   Note the position of the sensor in the air
cleaner housing**

a signal to the ECM telling it what gear the transmission is in. The ECM
uses this information to vary the conditions under which the clutch
applies or releases. However, the transmission does not have to be
in high gear in order for the ECM to turn on the clutch. Transmissions
using gear select switches can be identified by three wires coming out
of the TCC connector.
6   The transmission also uses a 4-3 pulse switch to open the TCC
solenoid circuit momentarily during a downshift.
7   A third gear switch is placed in series on the battery side of the
TCC solenoid to prevent TCC application until the transmission is in
third gear.

Checking

8   If the converter clutch is applied at all times, the engine will stall
immediately, just like a manual transmission with the clutch applied.
9   If the converter clutch does not apply, fuel economy may be lower
than expected. If the Vehicle Speed Sensor (VSS) (see Section 4) fails,
the TCC will not apply.
10   A TCC-equipped transmission has different operating characteristics than an automatic transmission without TCC. If you detect a
''chuggle'' or ''surge'' condition, perform the following check.
11   Install a tachometer.
12   Drive the vehicle until normal operating temperature is reached,
then maintain a 50 to 55 mph speed.
13   Lightly touch the the brake pedal and check it for a slight bumpy
sensation, indicating that the the TCC is releasing. A slight increase
in rpm should also be noted.
14   Release the brake and check for reapplication of the converter
clutch and a slight decrease in engine rpm.
15   If the TCC fails to perform satisfactorily during this test, take your
vehicle to a dealer to have the TCC serviced.

14 Catalytic converter

General description

1   The catalytic converter is an emission control device added to the
exhaust system to reduce pollutants from the exhaust gas stream. A
single-bed converter design is used in combination with a three-way
(reduction) catalyst. The catalytic coating on the three-way catalyst
contains platinum and rhodium, which lowers the levels of oxides of
nitrogen (NOx) as well as hydrocarbons (HC) and carbon monoxide
(CO).

Checking

2   The test equipment for a catalytic converter is expensive and highly
sophisticated. If you suspect that the converter on your vehicle is malfunctioning, take it to a dealer or authorized emissions inspection facility
for diagnosis and repair.
3   Whenever the vehicle is raised for servicing of underbody components, check the converter for leaks, corrosion and other damage.
If damage is discovered, the converter should be replaced.
4   Because the converter part of the exhaust system, converter
replacement requires removal of the exhaust pipe assembly (see
Chapter 4). Take the vehicle, or the exhaust pipe system, to a dealer
or a muffler shop.

6

Chapter 7 Part A Manual transmission

Contents

Specifications

Torque specifications

	Ft-lbs
Drain and fill plugs	17
Transmission-to-bellhousing bolts	50
Extension housing-to-case bolts	
4-speed	45
5-speed	25
Control assembly mounting bolts (5-speed)	23
Shifter-to-shift bracket bolts (4-speed)	33
Cover-to-case bolts (4-speed)	15

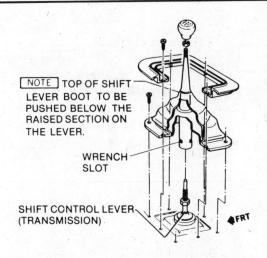

NOTE TOP OF SHIFT LEVER BOOT TO BE PUSHED BELOW THE RAISED SECTION ON THE LEVER.

WRENCH SLOT

SHIFT CONTROL LEVER (TRANSMISSION)

FRT

2.2   Shift lever and boot installation details (5-speed)

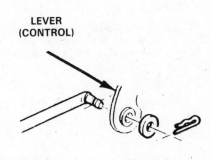

LEVER (CONTROL)

3.5   Pull the retaining clips from the linkage rods, remove the washers and separate the rods from the shifter control levers

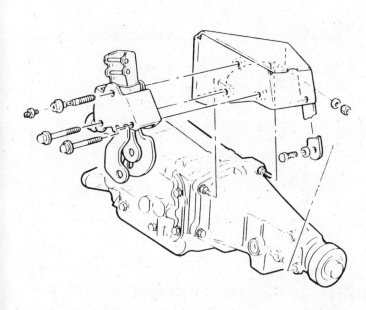

3.6   Shift control and bracket mounting details (4-speed)

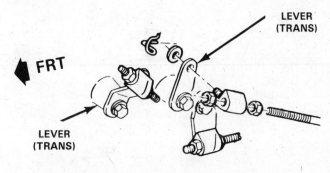

LEVER (TRANS)

FRT

LEVER (TRANS)

3.7   Mark the position of the linkage rods, remove the clips and washers from the adjuster studs then separate the rods and adjusters from the transmission levers

Installation

3   Turn the nut on the transmission shift control lever to the bottom of its thread travel.
4   Install the upper shift lever and thread it down the shaft until it seats against the nut. Turn the lever counterclockwise to align the shift pattern on the knob, then, while holding the upper shift lever with a wrench, tighten the lower lever nut securely against the shift lever.
5   Install the shift lever boot and retainer.

3   Shift linkage and control (4-speed) — removal, installation and adjustment

Refer to illustrations 3.5, 3.6, 3.7, 3.9 and 3.10

Removal

1   Disconnect the cable from the negative terminal of the battery.
2   Unscrew the shift knob from the shift lever.
3   Remove the shift boot attaching bolts and carefully pull the boot off the shift lever.
4   Raise the vehicle and support it securely on jackstands.
5   Remove the clips and washers from the shift linkage rods and disconnect the rods from the shifter control levers (**see illustration**). It is a good idea to mark the rods with tape to ensure correct installation.
6   Remove the shift control mounting bolts (**see illustration**) and guide the assembly downward until the shift lever is clear of the floorpan.
7   To remove the shift linkage rods from the transmission, remove the clips and washers that retain the rods to the transmission levers (**see illustration**). It is not necessary to remove the nuts from the threaded portion of the rods. Again, be sure to mark the rods as to their relative positions so they can be reinstalled properly.

1   General information

The vehicles covered in this manual equipped with manual transmissions are available with either a 76mm 4-speed or a 77mm 5-speed (the figure represents the distance between the mainshaft and the countershaft centerlines). The 4-speed transmission utilizes an adjustable external gearshift linkage, while the 5-speed shift control is in a housing bolted to the rear of the transmission.

2   Shift lever (5-speed) — removal and installation

Refer to illustration 2.2

Removal

1   Remove the screws from the shift lever boot retainer and slide the boot and retainer up the lever as far as possible.
2   Using a wrench on the slots provided at the bottom of the upper shift lever, loosen the lever locknut and unscrew the upper lever from the transmission shift control lever (**see illustration**).

7A

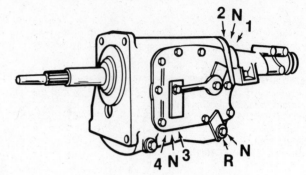

3.9 When reinstalling and/or adjusting the shift linkage and control, place the transmission shift levers in Neutral

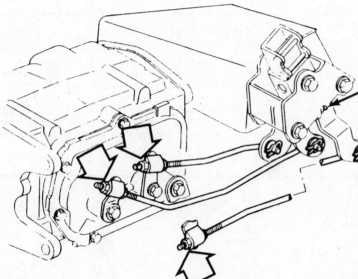

GAGE PIN HOLE

3.10 Insert a 1/4-inch drill bit into the gage pin hole, making sure it passes through all three levers — to lengthen or shorten the linkage rods, turn the adjusting nuts (arrows) accordingly

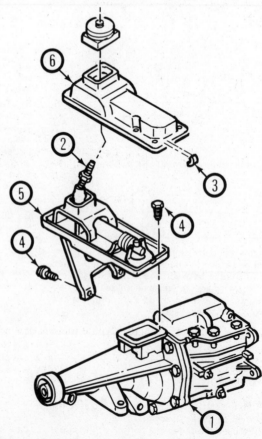

4.2 Shift control assembly mounting details (5-speed transmission)

1 *Transmission*
2 *Control lever*
3 *Clip*
4 *Bolt*
5 *Shift control assembly*
6 *Dust cover*

Installation and adjustment

8   To install the shift linkage rods and/or the shift control, reverse the removal procedure then adjust the linkage as described in the next two Steps.
9   Place the shift control and the transmission levers in the Neutral positions **(see illustration)**. If the linkage rods are too short or too long, loosen the adjuster nuts on the shift rods and back them off so the levers will remain in the Neutral position.
10 Insert a 1/4-inch drill bit into the gauge pin hole. It should pass through the hole freely. If it does not, lengthen or shorten the shift rods accordingly **(see illustration)**.
11 Tighten the shift rod adjuster nuts.

4   Shift control assembly (5-speed) — removal and installation

Refer to illustration 4.2

Removal

1   Remove the transmission as outlined in Section 5.
2   Carefully pry off the clips that retain the dust cover to the control assembly **(see illustration)**.
3   Remove the shift control-to-transmission housing bolts and lift the control from the transmission.
4   Clean all traces of old RTV sealer from the dust cover and control.

Installation

5   Mount the shift control assembly to the transmission and tighten the bolts securely.
6   Apply a bead of RTV sealer to the groove in the dust cover, position the cover on the control assembly and install the retaining clips.
7   Install the transmission.

5   Transmission — removal and installation

Refer to illustrations 5.10 and 5.11

Removal

1   Disconnect the cable from the negative terminal of the battery.
2   Drain the transmission lubricant (Chapter 1).
3   Remove the shift lever (5-speed models). Refer to Section 2.
4   Raise the vehicle and support it securely on jackstands.
5   Disconnect the shift linkage rods from the transmission levers and the shift control assembly (4-speed models). Refer to Section 3.
6   Remove the shift control assembly (4-speed models).
7   Remove the driveshaft (refer to Chapter 8).
8   Disconnect the speedometer cable from the transmission.
9   Remove the exhaust system (refer to Chapter 4).
10 Remove the transmission-to-engine support braces **(see illustration)**. Note the position of any washers and spacers.

7A

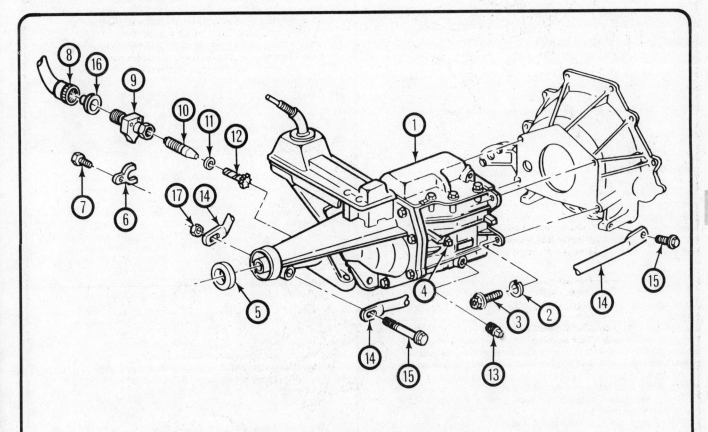

5.10   Typical transmission mounting details

1 Transmission	7 Screw	12 Gear
2 Spring washer	8 Speedometer cable	13 Drain plug
3 Bolt	9 Adapter	14 Support brace
4 Filler plug	10 Sleeve	15 Bolt
5 Output shaft seal	11 Seal	16 Seal
6 Retainer		17 Nut

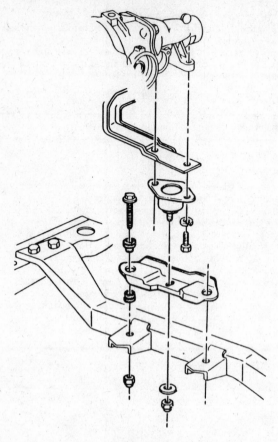

5.11 Remove the transmission mount from the rear crossmember

11 Support the transmission with a floor jack, unbolt the transmission mount from the crossmember **(see illustration)** then remove the cross-member from the vehicle.

12 Slowly lower the floor jack slightly (maintain contact with the transmission) then remove the transmission-to-bellhousing bolts. Do not let the transmission hang unsupported, as damage to the input shaft may result.

13 Pull the transmission straight back and out of the clutch hub splines and lower it to the ground.

Installation

14 Fill the transmission with the recommended lubricant (Chapter 1).

15 Apply a light coat of high temperature grease to the input shaft splines.

16 Set the transmission on the floor jack and raise it into position with the input shaft in alignment with the clutch disc splined hub. Slide the transmission forward until it is seated against the bellhousing. If it doesn't slide in easily, don't apply excessive force. Try engaging the transmission in gear and turning the output shaft to line up the input shaft splines with those in the clutch disc hub.

17 Install the transmission-to-bellhousing bolts and tighten them to the specified torque.

18 Raise the transmission on the jack and install the rear mount and the crossmember.

19 The remainder of installation is the reverse of the removal procedure.

6 Transmission overhaul — general information

Refer to illustrations 6.4a and 6.4b

Overhauling a manual transmission is a difficult job for a do-it-yourselfer. It involves the disassembly and reassembly of many small parts. Numerous clearances must be precisely measured and, if necessary,

6.4a Exploded view of the 77 mm 5-speed transmission

1 Transmission cover
2 Seal
3 Shift shaft
4 3rd and 4th shift fork
5 Shift fork plate
6 Control selector arm
7 Gear selector interlock plate
8 1st and 2nd shift fork
9 Shift fork insert
10 Roll pin
11 Synchromesh spring
12 Reverse sliding gear
13 Output shaft
14 Anti-rattle spring/ball
15 1st gear
16 Thrust washer
17 Rear bearing
18 5th gear
19 Snap ring
20 Speedometer drive gear
21 Speedometer drive gear clip
22 Main shaft roller bearing
23 Main drive gear thrust needle bearing
24 Main drive gear bearing race
25 3rd and 4th synchromesh ring
26 3rd and 4th synchromesh spring
27 3rd and 4th synchromesh hub
28 3rd and 4th synchromesh key
29 3rd and 4th synchromesh sleeve
30 3rd gear
31 Snap ring
32 2nd speed gear thrust washer
33 2nd gear
34 1st and 2nd synchromesh key
35 1st speed gear thrust washer retaining pin
36 Counter gear front bearing
37 Counter gear front thrust washer
38 Counter gear
39 Counter gear bearing front bearing spacer
40 Counter gear rear bearing
41 Counter gear bearing rear spacer
42 Snap ring
43 5th speed drive gear
44 5th speed synchromesh ring
45 5th speed synchromesh key
46 5th speed synchromesh hub
47 5th speed synchromesh spring
48 5th speed synchromesh sleeve
49 5th speed synchromesh key retainer
50 5th speed synchromesh thrust bearing front race
51 5th speed synchromesh needle thrust bearing
52 5th speed synchromesh thrust bearing rear race
53 Snap ring
54 Oiling funnel
55 Nut
56 Magnet
57 Transmission case
58 Fill and drain plug
59 Reverse lock spring
60 Reverse shift fork
61 Fork roller
62 Reverse fork pin
63 Shift rail pin
64 Rail pin roller
65 5th and reverse shift rail
66 Shift fork insert
67 Roll pin
68 5th shift fork
69 5th and reverse relay lever
70 Reverse relay lever retaining ring
71 Reverse idler gear shaft
72 Reverse idler gear
73 5th speed shift lever pivot pin
74 Ventilator
75 Steel ball
76 Detent spring
77 Control lever boot retainer
78 Control lever boot
79 Control lever boot lower retainer
80 Transmission lever and housing control
81 Shift lever damper sleeve
82 Offset shift lever
83 Detent and guide plate
84 Output seal
85 Extension housing bushing
86 Extension housing
87 Main drive gear
88 Front bearing
89 Bearing shim
90 Drive gear bearing retainer
91 Drive gear bearing oil seal

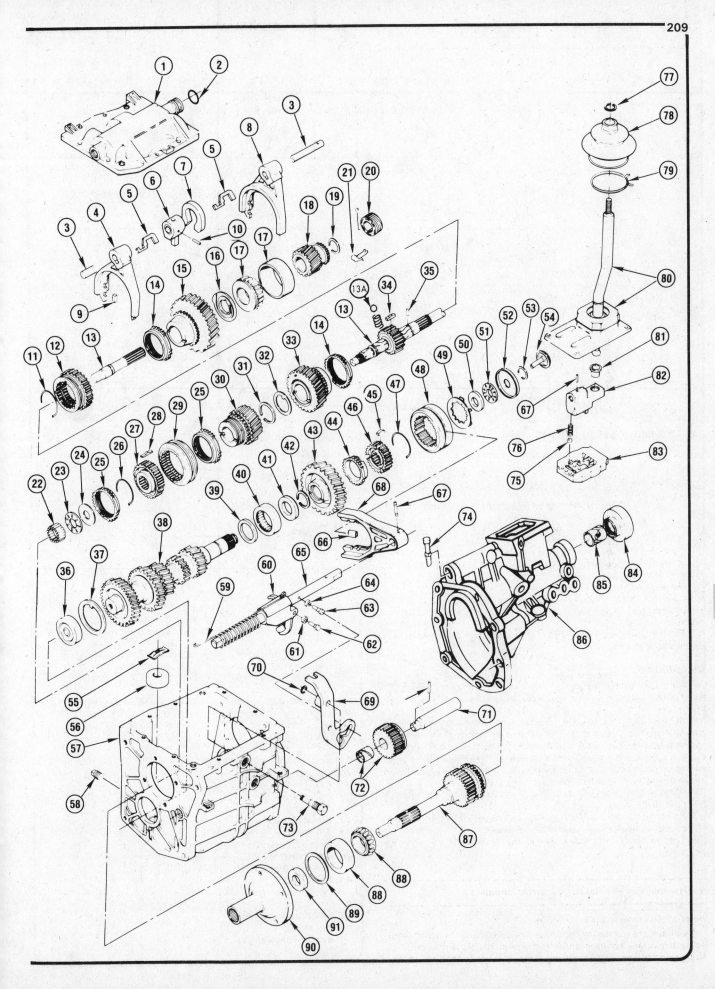

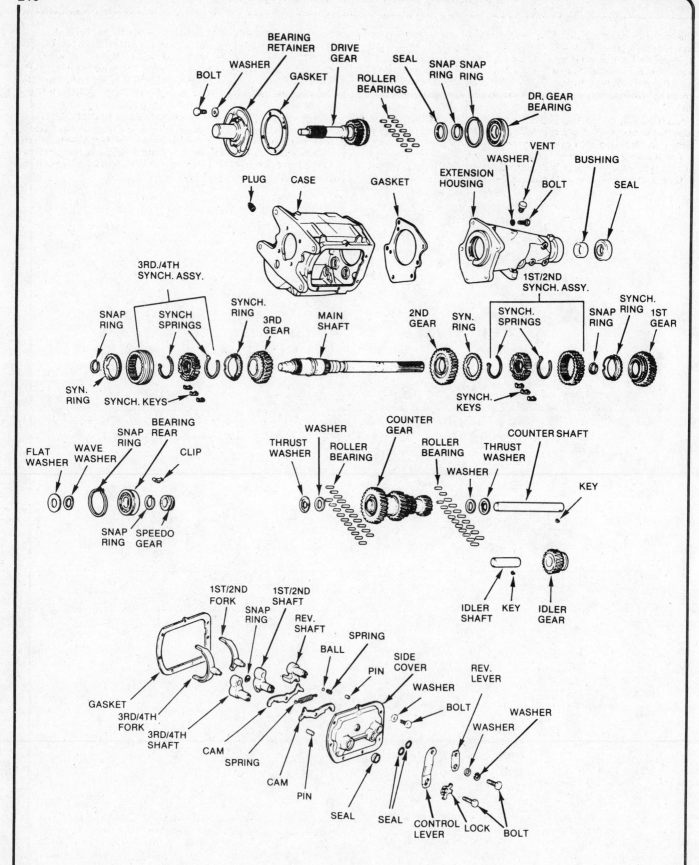

6.4b Exploded view of the 76 mm 4-speed transmission

changed with select fit spacers and snap-rings. As a result, if transmission problems arise, it can be removed and installed by a competent do-it-yourselfer, but overhaul should be left to a transmission repair shop. Rebuilt transmissions may be available — check with your dealer parts department and auto parts stores. At any rate, the time and money involved in an overhaul is almost sure to exceed the cost of a rebuilt unit.

Nevertheless, it's not impossible for an inexperienced mechanic to rebuild a transmission if the special tools are available and the job is done in a deliberate step-by-step manner so nothing is overlooked.

The tools necessary for an overhaul include internal and external snap-ring pliers, a bearing puller, a slide hammer, a set of pin punches, a dial indicator and possibly a hydraulic press. In addition, a large, sturdy workbench and a vise or transmission stand will be required.

During disassembly of the transmission, make careful notes of how each piece comes off, where it fits in relation to other pieces and what holds it in place. Exploded views are included (**see illustrations**) to show where the parts go — but actually noting how they are installed when you remove the parts will make it much easier to get the transmission back together.

Before taking the transmission apart for repair, it will help if you have some idea what area of the transmission is malfunctioning. Certain problems can be closely tied to specific areas in the transmission, which can make component examination and replacement easier. Refer to the *Troubleshooting* section at the front of this manual for information regarding possible sources of trouble.

7A

Chapter 7 Part B   Automatic transmission

Contents

Specifications

Torque specifications

	Ft-lbs
Torque converter-to-driveplate bolts	
1985	39
1986 on	46
Transmission-to-engine bolts	
four-cylinder engine	55
V6 engine	35
Transmission oil pan-to-case bolts	8
Converter shield bolts	10

1   General information

Refer to illustration 1.1

The automatic transmission installed in this vehicle is a 4-speed overdrive unit with a clutch-type torque converter **(see illustration)**. The clutch is designed to engage at speeds above 25 mph and provides a direct connection between the engine and the drive wheels for better efficiency and fuel economy. When the shift lever is in the "Overdrive D" position, the overdrive gear range is automatically selected when the vehicle reaches a steady speed above 40 mph.

Due to the complexity of the clutches and the hydraulic control system, and because of the special tools and expertise required to perform an automatic transmission overhaul, it should not be undertaken by the home mechanic. Therefore, the procedures in this Chapter are limited to general diagnosis, routine maintenance, adjustment and transmission removal and installation.

If the transmission requires major repair work, it should be left to a dealer service department or a transmission repair shop. You can, however, remove and install the transmission yourself and save the expense, even if the repair work is done by a transmission specialist.

Adjustments that the home mechanic can perform include those involving the throttle valve (TV) cable and the shift linkage. **Caution 1:** *Never tow a disabled vehicle with an automatic transmission at speeds greater than 30 mph or distances over 50 miles.*
Caution 2: *If the vehicle is equipped with a Delco Loc II audio system (1992 and later models with a Compact Disc player), be sure the lockout feature is turned off before performing any procedure that requires*
disconnecting the battery (refer to your owner's manual for further information on this system).

2   Diagnosis - general

1   Automatic transmission malfunctions may be caused by a number of conditions, such as poor engine performance, improper adjustments, hydraulic malfunctions and mechanical problems.
2   The first check should be of the transmission fluid level and condition. Refer to Chapter 1 for more information. Unless the fluid and filter have been recently changed, drain the fluid and replace the filter (also in Chapter 1).
3   Road test the vehicle and drive in all the gear ranges, noting discrepancies in operation. Check as follows:
Overdrive range: While stopped, position the lever in the overdrive range and accelerate. Check for a 1-2 shift, 2-3 shift and 3-4 shift. Also, the converter clutch should apply in 2nd or 3rd gear, depending on calibration. Check for part-throttle downshift by depressing the accelerator 3/4 of the way - the transmission should downshift. Check for a full detent downshift by depressing the throttle all the way - the transmission should immediately downshift.
Drive range: At road speed in Fourth gear (Overdrive range), manually shift the transmission to Drive range. The transmission should shift to Third gear immediately. It should not shift back to Overdrive. Also check for part throttle and full throttle downshifts in this range.
Drive 2 range: While in the Third gear range, shift to Second gear,

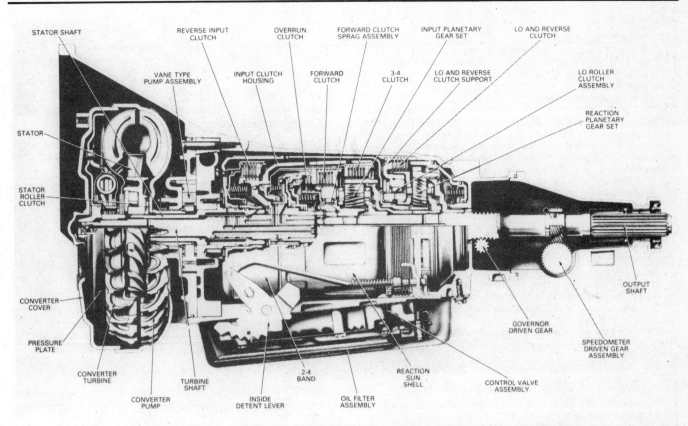

1.1 The Turbo Hydramatic (700-R4, 4L60, 4L60-E) automatic transmission used in the Astro/Safari

The transmission should downshift immediately. While in the Second gear range, check for downshift at part and full throttle.

Low range: Position the lever in Low (1) position and check the operation.

Overrun braking: This can be checked by manually shifting to a lower range. Engine rpm should increase and a braking effect should be noticed.

Reverse: Position the shifter in Reverse and check operation.

4 Verify that the engine is not at fault. If the engine has not received a tune-up recently, refer to Chapter 1 and make sure all engine components are functioning properly.

5 Check the adjustment of the throttle valve (TV) cable (Section 3).

6 Check the condition of all electrical wires and connectors at the transmission, or leading to it.

7 Check for proper adjustment of the shift linkage (Section 5).

8 If at this point a problem remains, there is one final check before the transmission is removed for overhaul. The vehicle should be taken to a specialist who will connect a special oil pressure gauge and check the line pressure in the transmission under different driving conditions.

---

3 Throttle valve (TV) cable — description, inspection and adjustment

---

Description

1 The throttle valve cable used on these transmissions should not be thought of as merely a "downshift" cable, as in earlier transmissions. The TV cable controls line pressure, shift points, shift feel, part throttle downshifts and detent downshifts.

2 If the TV cable is broken, sticky, misadjusted or is the incorrect part, the vehicle will experience a number of problems.

Inspection

Refer to illustration 3.4

3 Remove the engine cover (Chapter 11). Inspection should be made with the engine running at idle speed with the selector lever in Neutral.

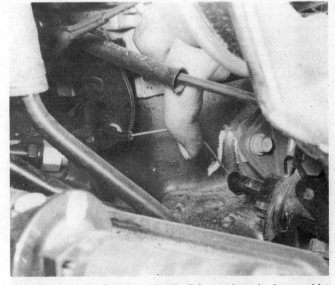

3.4 To check for free operation, pull forward on the inner cable, feeling for smooth operation through the full range of travel — the cable should retract evenly and rapidly when released

Set the parking brake firmly and block the wheels to prevent any vehicle movement. As an added precaution, have an assistant in the driver's seat applying the brake pedal.

4 Grab the inner cable a few inches behind where it attaches to the throttle linkage and pull the cable forward. It should easily slide through the cable housing with no binding or jerky operation **(see illustration)**.

5 Release the cable and it should return to its original location with the cable stop against the cable terminal.

6 If the TV cable does not operate as above, the cause is a defective or misadjusted cable or damaged components at either end of the cable.

7B

Adjustment
Refer to illustration 3.8

7   The engine should not be running during this adjustment.
8   Depress the re-adjust tab and move the slider back through the fitting away from the throttle linkage until the slider stops against the fitting **(see illustration)**.
9   Release the re-adjust tab.
10   Turn the throttle lever to the ''wide open throttle'' position, which will automatically adjust the cable. Release the throttle lever. **Caution:** *Don't use excessive force at the throttle lever to adjust the TV cable. If great effort is required to adjust the cable, disconnect the cable at the transmission end and check for free operation. If it's still difficult, replace the cable. If it's now free, suspect a bent TV link in the transmission or a problem with the throttle lever.*
11   After adjustment check for proper operation as described in Steps 3 through 6 above.

4   Throttle valve (TV) cable — replacement

1   Disconnect the cable from the negative terminal of the battery.
2   Lift off the engine cover and remove the air cleaner housing to gain access to the TV cable end (refer to Chapter 4 if necessary).
3   Disconnect the cable terminal from the throttle lever by pushing forward and then off.
4   Push in on the re-adjust tab and move the slider back through the fitting in the direction away from the throttle lever (towards the rear of the vehicle).
5   Compress the locking tabs and disconnect the cable assembly from the bracket.
6   Raise the vehicle and place it securely on jackstands.
7   Release the cable from the mounting clips, noting how it's routed.
8   Remove the screw and washer securing the cable to the transmission. Pull the cable up and disconnect it from the link at the end of the cable.
9   Place a new seal in the transmission case hole.
10   Connect the transmission end of the cable to the link and secure it to the transmission case with the screw. Tighten the screw securely.
11   Route the new cable up and secure it to the mounting clips.
12   Pass the cable through the bracket and secure it at the bracket with the locking tabs.
13   Connect the cable terminal to the throttle lever and adjust the cable as described in the previous Section.
14   Connect the negative battery cable and check for proper operation.

3.8   Depress the throttle valve (TV) cable re-adjust tab (A) and pull the slider back (arrow) until it rests on its stop — release the tab and open the throttle completely

5   Shift linkage — removal, installation and adjustment

Removal
Refer to illustrations 5.2, 5.3 and 5.4

1   Apply the parking brake, raise the vehicle and support it securely on jackstands.
2   Pull the retaining clip from the shift linkage rod at the lower end of the steering column and separate the rod from the column lever **(see illustration)**.
3   Loosen the nut or the swivel on the linkage rod and separate the rod from the equalizer lever **(see illustration)**.

5.2   To disconnect the shift linkage rod from the shift lever on the steering column (arrow), pull out the retaining clip, remove the washer and pry the rod from the lever

5.3   Loosen the nut securing the shift rod swivel to the equalizer lever then slide the rod out of the swivel

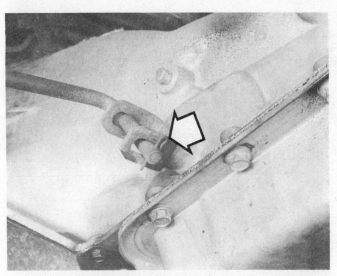

5.4 To remove the equalizer lever from the transmission shift lever, pull out the retaining clip (arrow) and push the equalizer lever up and out

6.3 Use a seal removal tool or a long screwdriver to carefully pry the seal out of the end of the transmission

4   Remove the retaining clip from the equalizer lever and push the equalizer lever out of the shift lever on the transmission **(see illustration)**.

Installation

5   Before reassembling, clean the rubber or nylon parts with soapy water. Check them for cracks and wear, replacing them with new ones if necessary. The metal parts can be washed in solvent.

6   To install the shift linkage, reverse the removal procedure, then adjust it as described in the following Steps.

Adjustment

Refer to illustration 5.9

7   Loosen the nut securing the shift rod swivel to the equalizer lever.

8   Place the column selector lever in the Neutral position gate (don't use the indicator to find the position).

9   Put the transmission shift lever in the Neutral position by turning the bottom of the lever to the forward (Park) position, then back to the second detent (two clicks) **(see illustration)**.

10   Hold the rod tightly in the swivel and tighten the swivel nut securely.

11   Shift the selector lever into the Park position and check the adjustment with the engine running and your foot on the brake. The column

selector lever must go into all of the positions easily.

12   Make sure the engine starts in the Park and Neutral positions only. If the engine cranks over in any other positions, adjust the Neutral safety switch as outlined in Section 9.

13   Align the indicator needle if necessary.

---

6   Transmission output shaft seal — replacement

Refer to illustrations 6.3 and 6.5

1   Raise the vehicle and support it securely on jackstands.

2   Remove the driveshaft (see Chapter 8).

3   Using a seal removal tool or a long screwdriver, pry the old seal from the end of the transmission **(see illustration)**.

4   Compare the new seal with the old to make sure they are the same.

5   Drive the new seal into position using a large socket or a piece of pipe which is the same diameter as the seal **(see illustration)**.

6   Once in position, coat the lips of the new seal with automatic transmission fluid.

7   Reinstall the various components in the reverse order of removal, referring to the necessary Chapters as needed.

7B

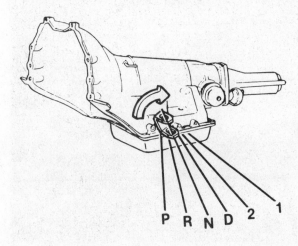

5.9 Shift positions on the transmission shift lever

P R N D 2 1

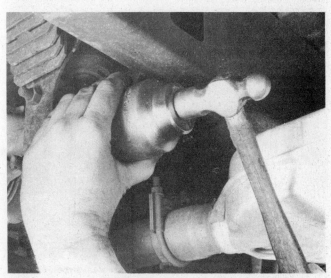

6.5 A large socket works well for installing the seal — the socket should contact the outer edge of the seal

7.11   Remove the angled bracket bolts on both sides of the vehicle (arrows) and the crossmember mounting bolts

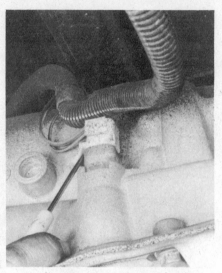

7.15   Unplug the torque converter clutch electrical connector at the left side of the transmission — there's a wire harness retaining bolt just above the connector which also must be removed

7.17   The transmission damper is retained by two bolts and nuts

7   Transmission — removal and installation

Refer to illustrations 7.11, 7.15, 7.17, 7.19a, 7.19b and 7.20

Removal

1   Disconnect the cable from the negative battery terminal.
2   Remove the engine cover and the air cleaner housing.
3   Disconnect the TV cable terminal at the throttle lever.
4   Remove the transmission fluid dipstick.
5   Raise the vehicle and support it securely on jackstands.
6   Drain the transmission fluid (Chapter 1).
7   Disconnect the TV cable at the transmission.
8   Remove the shift linkage rod and the equalizer lever (refer to Section 5). Remove the driveshaft as outlined in Chapter 8.
9   Remove the exhaust system hanger bolt from the bracket just ahead of the muffler.
10 Position a transmission jack under the transmission and secure the transmission to the jack. Raise the transmission slightly.
11 Unbolt the transmission mount from the transmission (see Section 8), remove the two angular brackets behind the crossmember and the crossmember mounting bolts, then remove the crossmember from the vehicle **(see illustration)**.
12 Slowly lower the transmission far enough to gain access to the other components. Be careful not to stretch any wires or cables.
13 Pull the dipstick tube up and out of the transmission case and position it out of the way. Plug the opening to prevent foreign material from entering the transmission.
14 On models so equipped, disconnect the speedometer cable and secure it out of the way. On models equipped with a speed sensor, disconnect the electrical connector from the sensor and secure the electrical wire out of the way.
15 Disconnect the torque converter clutch wire harness at the transmission **(see illustration)** and remove the bracket bolt directly above it.
16 Disconnect and plug the oil cooler lines, located on the right side of the transmission case. Use a flare nut wrench on the tube nut and a back-up wrench on the fitting to avoid damaging the nut or line. Plug the fittings in the transmission case as well as the cooler lines.
17 Remove the damper and support, if used **(see illustration)**.
18 Remove the transmission-to-engine support braces, noting how all of the spacers and washers are installed.
19 Remove the converter housing cover and carefully scribe or paint a mark on the driveplate and torque converter so they can be returned to their original positions **(see illustrations)**.

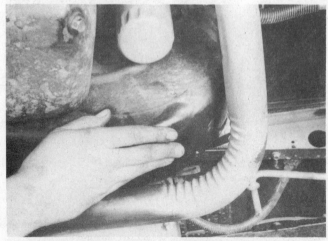

7.19a   Remove the four converter housing cover bolts and carefully work the cover toward the left side of the vehicle — it's a tight fit, but it will come out!

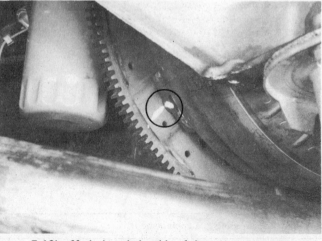

7.19b   Mark the relationship of the torque converter to the driveplate

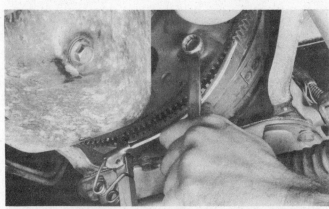

7.20 Remove the converter-to-driveplate retaining bolts (here, a flywheel wrench is being used to prevent the driveplate from turning, but a wrench on the crankshaft vibration damper bolt will also work)

20 Remove the torque converter-to-driveplate bolts (**see illustration**), turning the engine over by hand with a wrench on the crankshaft vibration damper as necessary.

21 Support the engine with a floor jack and a block of wood or an engine hoist so movement will be kept to a minimum.

22 Remove the transmission-to-engine bolts.

23 Make a final check that all wires, cables, etc. are disconnected from the transmission, then separate the transmission from the engine. As this is done, the torque converter must be held back against the transmission. A special holding fixture is available or you can use a piece of bar stock across the front of the transmission for this purpose.

Installation

24 If the torque converter was removed for any reason, position it on the input shaft and gently push it in while rotating it. The converter is seated after two clunks are felt (the converter mating with the splined shafts).

25 Raise the transmission into position and push it forward onto the locating pins. Before installing the driveplate-to-converter bolts, make sure the weld nuts on the converter are flush with the driveplate and the converter rotates freely (this is another way to confirm that the converter is completely seated). Align the marks you made during removal and install the driveplate-to-converter bolts, tightening them finger tight. Once all bolts are installed, tighten them to the specified torque.

26 Install a new oil filler tube O-ring in the case bore.

27 Install the various components in the reverse order of removal, referring to the proper Chapters where necessary for additional information.

28 After all components are installed, adjust the shift linkage and the TV cable referring to Sections 5 and 3 of this Chapter.

29 If the transmission has been drained and a new torque converter installed or the fluid has been drained from the existing one, a slightly different fluid filling procedure is required.

   a) Add approximately 5-1/2 quarts of transmission fluid through the filler tube.

   b) Start the engine and, with the shifter in Park, depress the accelerator enough to get the engine operating at a fast idle speed — do not race the engine.

   c) With your foot firmly on the brake pedal, move the shifter through each range.

   d) After 1 to 3 minutes of running at idle, check the fluid level with the shifter in Park (engine still running).

   e) Add enough fluid to bring the level to a point between the two marks on the dipstick. Add fluid only a little at a time, waiting 1 to 3 minutes, to prevent overfilling the transmission.

---

8 Transmission mount — replacement

Refer to illustrations 8.3, 8.4, 8.5 and 8.6

1 Raise the vehicle and support it securely on jackstands.

8.3 The transmission mount-to-support bracket nut (center) should be removed before the support bracket bolts are removed

8.4 Mount-to-transmission bolt locations (arrows)

7B

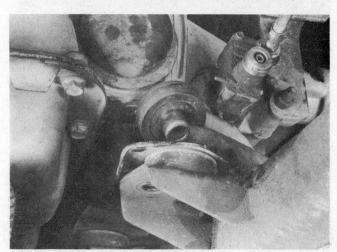

8.5 Remove the two support bracket insulators

2 Support the transmission with a floor jack and a block of wood.

3 Remove the mount-to-support bracket nut and the two support bracket-to-crossmember nuts and bolts (**see illustration**).

4 Remove the two mount-to-transmission bolts (**see illustration**).

5 Remove the two upper support bracket insulators from the support bracket (**see illustration**).

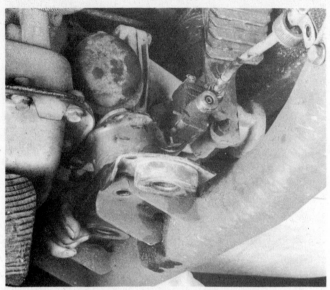

8.6   Jack up the transmission and slide the bracket and mount out far enough to allow mount removal

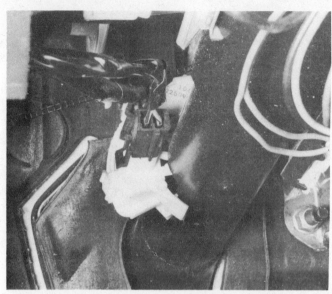

9.2   The Neutral safety switch is located on the lower steering column mast

6   Slide the support bracket and mount out from between the transmission and the crossmember **(see illustration)**.
7   Pull the mount from the support bracket. Installation is the reverse of the removal procedure.

9   Neutral safety switch - replacement

Refer to illustration 9.2

1   When the switch is operating properly, the engine should crank over with the gear selector lever in Park or Neutral only. Also, the backup lights should come on when the lever is in Reverse.
2   The switch is mounted on the lower part of the steering column **(see illustration)**. To replace the switch, unplug the electrical connectors, pry the locking tabs in and separate the switch from the column.
3   Move the shift lever to the Neutral position.
4   Insert the tang on the switch into the shift tube slot in the steering column then press down on the switch to engage the locking tabs.
5   Check to be sure the engine only cranks over in Park or Neutral.

10   Speedometer driven gear - removal and installation

Refer to illustrations 10.2 and 10.4

1   Raise the vehicle and support it securely on jackstands.
2   Unscrew the speedometer cable from the sleeve and remove the cable housing retaining bolt from the crossmember **(see illustration)**.
3   Remove the sleeve retainer screw and retainer. Pull the sleeve and seal from the bore.
4   Slide the driven gear out of the sleeve **(see illustration)**. Inspect the gear for missing or damaged teeth, replacing it if necessary.
5   Installation is the reverse of the removal procedure. Be sure to install a new seal and check the transmission fluid level.

11   Vehicle speed sensor - removal and installation

1   Raise the vehicle and support it securely on jackstands.
2   Disconnect the electrical connector from the sensor.
3   Remove the sensor retaining bolt.
4   Withdraw the sensor from the transmission housing bore.
5   Installation is the reverse of the removal procedure. Be sure to install a new O-ring seal and check the transmission fluid level.

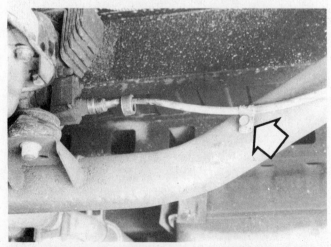

10.2   Unscrew the speedometer cable from the sleeve and remove the cable housing retaining bolt (arrow), then pull the cable out

10.4   Slide the driven gear out of the sleeve and inspect it for damage

Chapter 8 Clutch and drivetrain

Contents

Specifications

Clutch

Fluid type	See Chapter 1
Clutch disc runout limit	0.020 in
Slave cylinder pushrod travel	1.03 in

Torque specifications	**Ft-lbs**
Pressure plate-to-flywheel bolts	
four-cylinder engine	18
V6 engine	30
Belhousing-to-engine bolts	
four-cylinder engine	46
V6 engine (carburetor equipped)	46
V6 engine (TBI equipped)	55
Clutch master cylinder nuts	13
Clutch slave cylinder nuts	13

Driveshaft

Torque specifications	**Ft-lbs**
Universal joint strap bolts	
1985	12 to 17
1986 on	27

Rear axle

Torque specifications	**Ft-lbs**
Differential cover bolts	20
Pinion shaft lock bolt	25
Inner U-bolt nuts	41
Outer U-bolt nuts	48

8

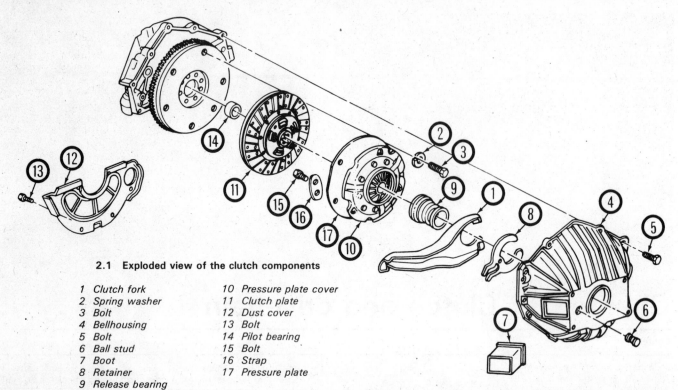

2.1 Exploded view of the clutch components

1 Clutch fork	10 Pressure plate cover
2 Spring washer	11 Clutch plate
3 Bolt	12 Dust cover
4 Bellhousing	13 Bolt
5 Bolt	14 Pilot bearing
6 Ball stud	15 Bolt
7 Boot	16 Strap
8 Retainer	17 Pressure plate
9 Release bearing	

1   General information

The information in this Chapter deals with the components from the rear of the engine to the rear wheels, except for the transmission, which is dealt with in the previous Chapter. For the purposes of this Chapter, these components are grouped into three categories; clutch, driveshaft and rear axle. Separate Sections within this Chapter offer general descriptions and checking procedures for each of these three groups.

Since nearly all the procedures covered in this Chapter involve working under the vehicle, make sure it's securely supported on sturdy jackstands or on a hoist where the vehicle can be easily raised and lowered. **Caution:** *If the vehicle is equipped with a Delco Loc II audio system (1992 and later models with a Compact Disc player), be sure the lockout feature is turned off before performing any procedure that requires disconnecting the battery (refer to your owner's manual for further information on this system).*

2   Clutch — description and check

Refer to illustration 2.1

1 All models equipped with a manual transmission feature a single dry plate, diaphragm spring-type clutch (**see illustration**). The actuation is through a hydraulic system.

2 When the clutch pedal is depressed, hydraulic fluid (under pressure from the clutch master cylinder) flows into the slave cylinder. Because the slave cylinder is connected to the clutch fork, the fork moves the release bearing into contact with the pressure plate release fingers, disengaging the clutch plate.

3 The hydraulic system locates the clutch pedal and provides clutch adjustment automatically, so no adjustment of the linkage or pedal is required.

4 Terminology can be a problem regarding the clutch components because common names have in some cases changed from that used by the manufacturer. For example, the driven plate is also called the clutch plate or disc, the clutch release bearing is sometimes called a throwout bearing, the slave cylinder is sometimes called the operating cylinder.

5 Other than to replace components with obvious damage, some preliminary checks should be performed to diagnose a clutch system failure.

  a) The first check should be of the fluid level in the clutch master cylinder. If the fluid level is low, add fluid as necessary and re-test. If the master cylinder runs dry, or if any of the hydraulic components are serviced, bleed the hydraulic system as described in Section 8.

  b) To check "clutch spin down time", run the engine at normal idle speed with the transmission in Neutral (clutch pedal up — engaged). Disengage the clutch (pedal down), wait nine seconds and shift the transmission into Reverse. No grinding noise should be heard. A grinding noise would indicate component failure in the pressure plate assembly or the clutch disc.

  c) To check for complete clutch release, run the engine (with the brake on to prevent movement) and hold the clutch pedal approximately 1/2-inch from the floor mat. Shift the transmission between 1st gear and Reverse several times. If the shift is not smooth, component failure is indicated. Measure the slave cylinder pushrod travel. With the clutch pedal completely depressed the slave cylinder pushrod should extend 1.03-inches (26.16 mm). If the pushrod will not extend this far check the fluid level in the clutch master cylinder.

  d) Visually inspect the clutch pedal bushing at the top of the clutch pedal to make sure there is no sticking or excessive wear.

  e) Under the vehicle, check that the clutch fork is solidly mounted on the ball stud.

3   Clutch components — removal, inspection and installation

Warning: *Dust produced by clutch wear and deposited on clutch components contains asbestos, which is hazardous to your health. DO NOT blow it out with compressed air and DO NOT inhale it. DO NOT use gasoline or petroleum-based solvents to remove the dust. Brake system cleaner should be used to flush the dust into a drain pan. After the clutch components are wiped clean with a rag, dispose of the contaminated rags and cleaner in a covered container.*

Removal
Refer to illustration 3.7

1 Access to the clutch components is normally accomplished by removing the transmission, leaving the engine in the vehicle. If, of

3.7 After removal of the transmission, this will be the view of the clutch components

1 Pressure plate   2 Flywheel

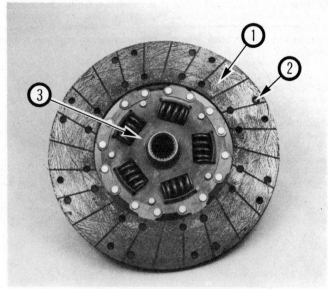

3.12 The clutch plate

1 *Lining — this will wear down in use*
2 *Rivets — these secure the lining and will damage the flywheel or pressure plate if allowed to contact the surfaces*
3 *Markings — ''Flywheel side'' or something similar*

3.14 The machined face of the pressure plate must be inspected for score marks and other damage — if damage is slight, a machine shop can make the surface smooth again

course, the engine is being removed for major overhaul, then the opportunity should always be taken to check the clutch for wear and replace worn components as necessary. The following procedures assume that the engine will stay in place.

2   Referring to Chapter 7 Part A, remove the transmission from the vehicle. Support the engine while the transmission is out. Preferably, an engine hoist should be used to support it from above. However, if a jack is used underneath the engine, make sure a piece of wood is used between the jack and oil pan to spread the load. **Caution:** *The pickup for the oil pump is very close to the bottom of the oil pan. If the pan is bent or distorted in any way, engine oil starvation could occur.*

3   Remove the slave cylinder (see Section 6).

4   Remove the bellhousing-to-engine bolts and then detach the housing. It may have to be gently pried off the alignment dowels with a screwdriver or pry bar.

5   The clutch fork and release bearing can remain attached to the housing for the time being.

6   To support the clutch plate during removal, install a clutch alignment tool through the clutch plate hub.

7   Carefully inspect the flywheel and pressure plate for indexing marks. The marks are usually an X, an O or a white letter. If they cannot be found, scribe marks yourself so the pressure plate and the flywheel will be in the same alignment during installation (**see illustration**).

8   Turning each bolt only 1/2-turn at a time, slowly loosen the pressure plate-to-flywheel bolts. Work in a diagonal pattern and loosen each bolt a little at a time until all spring pressure is relieved. Then hold the pressure plate securely and completely remove the bolts, followed by the pressure plate and clutch plate.

Inspection

Refer to illustrations 3.12 and 3.14

9   Ordinarily, when a problem occurs in the clutch, it can be attributed to wear of the clutch driven plate assembly (clutch plate). However, all components should be inspected at this time.

10 Inspect the flywheel for cracks, heat checking, grooves or other signs of obvious defects. If the imperfections are slight, a machine shop can machine the surface flat and smooth, which is highly recommended regardless of the surface appearance. Refer to Chapter 2 for the flywheel removal and installation procedure.

11 Inspect the pilot bearing (Section 5).

12 Inspect the lining on the clutch plate. There should be at least 1/16-inch of lining above the rivet heads. Check for loose rivets, distortion, cracks, broken springs and other obvious damage (**see illustration**). As mentioned above, ordinarily the clutch plate is replaced as a matter of course, so if in doubt about the condition, replace it with a new one.

13 Ordinarily, the release bearing is also replaced along with the clutch plate (see Section 4).

14 Check the machined surfaces of the pressure plate (**see illustration**). If the surface is grooved or otherwise damaged, take it to a machine shop for possible machining or replacement. Also check for obvious damage, distortion, cracking, etc. Light glazing can be removed with medium grit emery cloth. If a new pressure plate is indicated, new or factory-rebuilt units are available.

Installation

Refer to illustration 3.16

15 Before installation, carefully wipe the flywheel and pressure plate machined surfaces clean. It's important that no oil or grease is on these surfaces or the lining of the clutch plate. Handle these parts only with clean hands.

8

16 Position the clutch plate and pressure plate with the clutch held in place with an alignment tool **(see illustration)**. Make sure it's installed properly (most replacement clutch plates will be marked "flywheel side" or something similar — if not marked, install the clutch with the damper springs toward the transmission).
17 Tighten the pressure plate-to-flywheel bolts only finger tight, working around the pressure plate.
18 Center the clutch plate by inserting the alignment tool through the splined hub and into the pilot bearing in the crankshaft. Tighten the pressure plate-to-flywheel bolts a little at a time, working in a criss-cross pattern to prevent distorting the cover. After all of the bolts are snug, tighten them to the specified torque. Remove the alignment tool.
19 Using high temperature grease, lubricate the inner groove of the release bearing (refer to Section 4). Also place grease on the fork fingers.
20 Install the clutch release bearing as described in Section 4.
21 Install the bellhousing and tighten the bolts to the proper torque specification.
22 Install the transmission, slave cylinder and all components removed previously, tightening all fasteners to the proper torque specifications.

3.16 A clutch alignment tool can be purchased at most auto parts stores and eliminates all guesswork when centering the clutch plate in the pressure plate

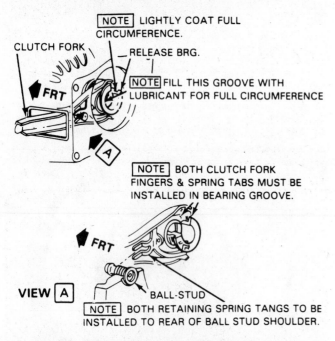

4.6 Release bearing and fork installation and lubrication details

4.7 When installing the release bearing, make sure the fingers and the tabs fit into the bearing recess

4 Clutch release bearing — removal and installation

Refer to illustrations 4.6 and 4.7

Removal

1 Disconnect the negative cable from the battery.
2 Remove the transmission (Chapter 7).
3 Remove the bellhousing (Section 3).
4 Remove the clutch release fork from the ball stud.
5 Hold the center of the bearing and spin the outer portion. If the bearing doesn't turn smoothly or if it's noisy, replace it with a new one. Wipe the bearing with a clean rag and inspect it for damage, wear and cracks. Don't immerse the bearing in solvent — it's sealed for life and to do so would ruin it.

Installation

6 Lubricate the clutch fork ends where they contact the bearing lightly with white lithium base grease. Pack the inner diameter of the bearing with the same grease **(see illustration)**.
7 Install the release bearing on the clutch fork so that both of the fork tabs fit into the bearing recess **(see illustration)**.
8 Lubricate the clutch release fork ball socket with high temperature grease and push the fork onto the ball stud until it's firmly seated.
9 Install the bellhousing and tighten the bolts to the specified torque.
10 The remainder of the installation is the reverse of the removal procedure, tightening all bolts to the specified torque.

5 Pilot bearing — removal, inspection and installation

Refer to illustration 5.9

1 The clutch pilot bearing is an oil impregnated type bearing which is pressed into the rear of the crankshaft. Its primary purpose is to support the front of the transmission input shaft. The pilot bearing should be inspected whenever the clutch components are removed from the engine. Due to its inaccessibility, if you are in doubt as to its condition, replace it with a new one. **Note:** *If the engine has been removed from the vehicle, disregard the following steps which do not apply.*
2 Remove the transmission (refer to Chapter 7 Part A)
3 Remove the clutch components (Section 3).
4 Using a clean rag, wipe the bearing clean and inspect for any excessive wear, scoring or obvious damage. A flashlight will be helpful to direct light into the recess.
5 Removal can be accomplished with a special puller but an alternative method also works very well.
6 Find a solid steel bar which is slightly smaller in diameter than the bearing (19/32-inch should be very close). Alternatives to a solid bar would be a wood dowel or a socket with a bolt fixed in place to make it solid.
7 Check the bar for fit — it should just slip into the bearing with very little clearance.

8   Pack the bearing and the area behind it (in the crankshaft recess) with heavy grease. Pack it tightly to eliminate as much air as possible.

9   Insert the bar into the bearing bore and lightly hammer on the bar, which will force the grease to the backside of the bearing and push it out (**see illustration**). Remove the bearing and clean all grease from the crankshaft recess.

10 To install the new bearing, lubricate the outside surface with oil then drive it into the recess with a soft-face hammer.

11 Install the clutch components, transmission and all other components removed to gain access to the pilot bearing.

6   Clutch slave cylinder — removal, overhaul and installation

Note: *Before beginning this procedure, contact local parts stores and dealer service departments concerning the purchase of a rebuild kit or a new slave cylinder. Availability and cost of the necessary parts may dictate whether the cylinder is rebuilt or replaced with a new one. If it's decided to rebuild the cylinder, inspect the bore as described in Step 9 before purchasing parts.*

Removal

Refer to illustration 6.3

1   Disconnect the negative cable from the battery. Place the cable out of the way so it cannot accidently come into contact with the terminal, which would again allow current to flow.

2   Raise the vehicle and support it securely on jackstands.

3   Disconnect the hydraulic line at the slave cylinder (**see illustration**). Have a small can and rags handy, as some fluid will be spilled as the line is removed.

4   With your fingers, work the rubber dust boot out of the clutch housing, then remove the two mounting nuts.

5   Remove the slave cylinder.

5.9   Pack the recess behind the pilot bearing with heavy grease and force it out hydraulically with a steel rod slightly smaller than the bore in the bearing — when the hammer strikes the rod, the bearing will pop out of the crankshaft

Overhaul

Refer to illustration 6.7

6   Slide the shield off the slave cylinder and remove the pushrod and the rubber dust cover.

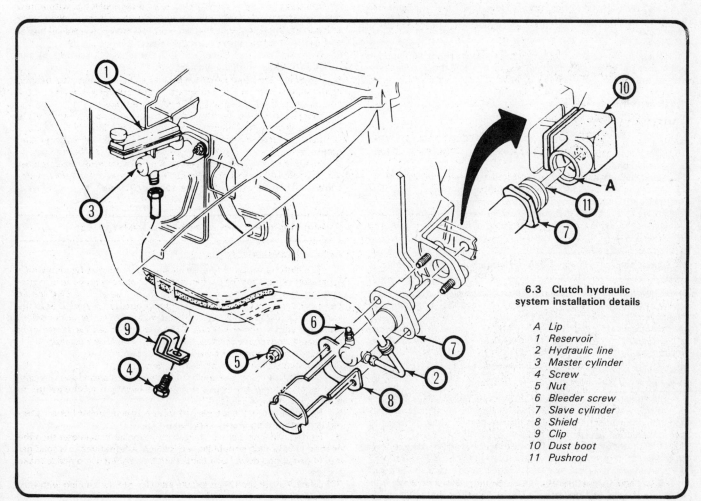

6.3   Clutch hydraulic system installation details

A   Lip
1   Reservoir
2   Hydraulic line
3   Master cylinder
4   Screw
5   Nut
6   Bleeder screw
7   Slave cylinder
8   Shield
9   Clip
10 Dust boot
11 Pushrod

8

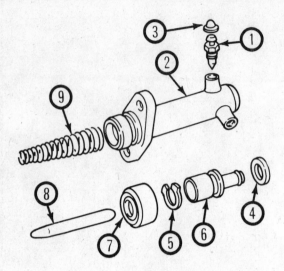

6.7 Exploded view of the clutch slave cylinder

1 Bleeder valve	6 Plunger
2 Slave cylinder body	7 Dust cover
3 Cap	8 Pushrod
4 Seal	9 Spring
5 Retaining clip	

7   Remove the retaining clip (**see illustration**) with a small screwdriver.

8   Tap the cylinder on a block of wood to eject the plunger and seal. Also remove the spring from inside the cylinder.

9   Carefully inspect the bore of the cylinder. Check for deep scratches, score marks and ridges. The bore must be smooth to the touch. If any imperfections are found, the slave cylinder must be replaced with a new one.

10 Using the new parts in the rebuild kit, assemble the components using plenty of fresh brake fluid for lubrication. Note the installed direction of the spring and the seal.

Installation

11 Previous to installation, the system must be bled of all air.

12 Connect the hydraulic line to the slave cylinder. Tighten the connection.

13 Fill the clutch master cylinder with brake fluid (conforming to DOT 3 specifications).

14 Bleed the system as described in Section 8.

15 Install the slave cylinder on the clutch housing, working the rubber dust boot into place and tightening the nuts to the specified torque. Make sure the pushrod is seated in the release fork pocket.

16 Lower the vehicle and connect the negative battery cable.

---

7   Clutch master cylinder — removal, overhaul and installation

---

Note: *Before beginning this procedure, contact local parts stores and dealer service departments concerning the purchase of a rebuild kit or a new master cylinder. Availability and cost of the necessary parts may dictate whether the cylinder is rebuilt or replaced with a new one. If it's decided to rebuild the cylinder, inspect the bore as described in Step 12 before purchasing parts.*

Removal

Refer to illustration 7.4

1   Disconnect the negative cable from the battery. Place the cable out of the way so it cannot accidentally come in contact with the negative terminal of the battery, as this would once again allow power into the electrical system of the vehicle.

2   Under the dashboard, disconnect the pushrod from the top of the clutch pedal. It's held in place with a spring clip.

3   Disconnect the hydraulic line at the clutch master cylinder. If available, use a flare nut wrench on the fitting, which will prevent the fitting from being rounded off. Have rags handy as some fluid will be

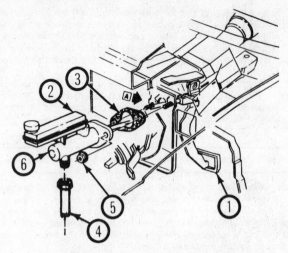

7.4 Master cylinder mounting details

1 Clutch pedal	4 Hydraulic line
2 Reservoir	5 Nut
3 Gasket	6 Master cylinder

lost as the line is removed. **Caution:** *Don't allow brake fluid to come into contact with paint as it will damage the finish.*

4   Remove the two bolts which secure the master cylinder to the engine firewall (**see illustration**). Remove the master cylinder, again being careful not to spill any of the fluid.

Overhaul

Refer to illustration 7.6

5   Remove the reservoir cap and drain all fluid from the master cylinder. Pry the reservoir from the master cylinder body.

6   Pull back the dust cover on the pushrod (**see illustration**) and remove the snap-ring (**see illustration**).

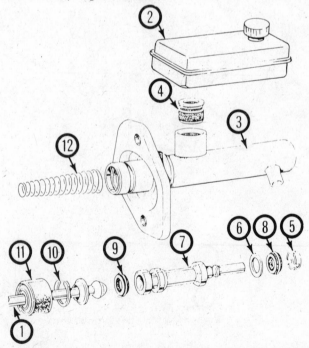

7.6 Clutch master cylinder components — exploded view

1 Pushrod	5 Spring support	9 Seal
2 Reservoir	6 Shim	10 Snap-ring
3 Master cylinder body	7 Plunger	11 Dust cover
4 Seal	8 Seal	12 Spring

7   Remove the retaining washer and the pushrod from the cylinder.
8   Tap the master cylinder on a block of wood to eject the plunger assembly from inside the bore.
9   Separate the spring from the plunger.
10   Remove the spring support, seal and shim from the pushrod.
11   Carefully remove the seal from the plunger.
12   Inspect the bore of the master cylinder for deep scratches, score marks and ridges. The surface must be smooth to the touch. If the bore isn't perfectly smooth, the master cylinder must be replaced with a new or factory rebuilt unit.
13   If the cylinder will be rebuilt, use the new parts contained in the rebuild kit and follow any specific instructions which may have accompanied the rebuild kit.
14   Attach the plunger seal to the plunger.
15   Assemble the shim, spring support and spring on the other end of the plunger.
16   Lubricate the bore of the cylinder and the seals with plenty of fresh brake fluid (DOT 3).
17   Carefully guide the plunger assembly into the bore, being careful not to damage the seals. Make sure the spring end is installed first, with the pushrod end of the plunger closest to the opening.
18   Position the pushrod and retaining washer in the bore, compress the spring and install a new snap-ring.
19   Apply a liberal amount of Girling Rubber Grease or equivalent to the inside of the dust cover and attach it to the master cylinder.

Installation

20   Install the master cylinder on the firewall, installing the two mounting nuts finger tight.
21   Connect the hydraulic line to the master cylinder, moving the cylinder slightly as necessary to thread the fitting properly into the bore. Don't cross-thread the fitting as it's installed.
22   Tighten the two mounting nuts to the specified torque.
23   Inside the vehicle, connect the pushrod to the clutch pedal.
24   Fill the clutch master cylinder reservoir with brake fluid conforming to DOT 3 specifications and bleed the clutch system as outlined in Section 8.

8   Clutch hydraulic system — bleeding

Refer to illustration 8.5

1   The hydraulic system should be bled to remove all air whenever any part of the system has been removed or if the fluid level has fallen so low that air has been drawn into the master cylinder. The procedure is very similar to bleeding a brake system.

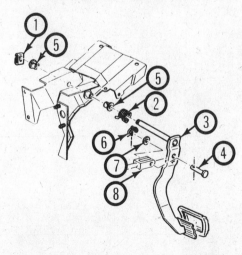

9.4   Exploded view of the clutch pedal components — make sure all bushings and retainers are in good condition before reassembly

1 Pedal pivot pin	3 Clutch pedal	6 Spring clip
retainer clip	4 Pin	7 Washer
2 Spring	5 Bushing	8 Pushrod

2   Fill the master cylinder with new brake fluid conforming to DOT 3 specifications. **Caution:** *Don't re-use any of the fluid coming from the system during the bleeding operation. Also, don't use fluid which has been inside an open container for an extended period of time.*
3   Raise the vehicle and place it securely on jackstands to gain access to the slave cylinder, which is located on the left side of the clutch housing.
4   With your fingers, pry the rubber dust cover out of the clutch cover and then remove the two slave cylinder mounting bolts.
5   Remove the dust cap which fits over the bleeder valve and push a length of plastic hose over the valve. Place the other end of the hose in a clear container with about two inches of brake fluid. The hose end must be in the fluid at the bottom of the container. Hold the slave cylinder up at a 45° angle with the bleeder valve at its highest point (**see illustration**).

8.5   When bleeding the hydraulic clutch system, hold the slave cylinder as shown in order to get the bleed screw at the highest position

6   Have an assistant depress the clutch pedal and hold it. Open the bleeder valve on the slave cylinder, allowing fluid to flow through the hose. Close the bleeder valve when the flow of bubbles or old fluid ceases. Once closed, have your assistant release the pedal.
7   Continue this process until all air is evacuated from the system, indicated by a full, solid stream of fluid being ejected from the bleeder valve each time and no air bubbles in the hose or container. Keep a close watch on the fluid level inside the master cylinder; if the level drops too low, air will be sucked back into the system and the process will have to be started all over again.
8   Install the slave cylinder and lower the vehicle. Check carefully for proper operation before placing the vehicle in normal service.

9   Clutch pedal — removal and installation

Refer to illustration 9.4

1   Disconnect the negative cable from the battery. Place the cable out of the way so it cannot accidentally come in contact with the negative terminal of the battery, as this would once again allow power into the electrical system of the vehicle.
2   Disconnect and remove the starter safety switch (see Section 10).
3   Disconnect the pushrod which goes into the master cylinder. It's held by a pin and spring clip.
4   Remove the pedal pivot pin retainer clip and slide the pedal to the left to remove it. Insert a long screwdriver or rod through the opposite side of the bracket to hold the brake pedal in place while the clutch pedal is removed (**see illustration**).
5   Wipe clean all parts; however, don't use cleaning solvent on the bushings. Replace all worn parts with new ones.

8

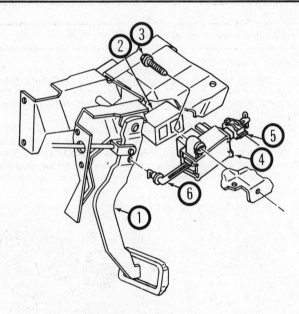

10.2 Starter safety switch installation details

1 *Clutch pedal*   4 *Starter safety switch*
2 *Connector*   5 *Slider*
3 *Screw*   6 *Shaft*

6   Installation is the reverse of removal. Check that the starter safety switch allows the vehicle to be started only with the clutch pedal fully depressed.

10 Starter safety switch — removal, installation and adjustment

Refer to illustration 10.2

1   Disconnect the cable from the negative terminal of the battery.
2   Unplug the electrical connector from the switch **(see illustration)**.
3   Remove the mounting screw and rotate the switch down, dislodging the shaft from the clutch pedal.
4   To install the switch, reverse the removal procedure.
5   To adjust the switch, move the slider to the rear of the switch shaft. Depress the clutch pedal to the floor and hold it there, then move the slider down the shaft to contact the switch. **Note:** *All carpets and floor mats must be in place to achieve an accurate adjustment.*

11 Driveshaft and universal joints — description and check

1   The driveshaft is a tube running between the transmission and the rear end. Universal joints are located at either end of the driveshaft and permit power to be transmitted to the rear wheels at varying angles.
2   The driveshaft features a splined yoke at the front, which slips into the extension housing of the transmission. This arrangement allows the driveshaft to slide back-and-forth within the transmission as the vehicle is in operation.
3   An oil seal is used to prevent leakage of fluid at this point and to keep dirt and contaminants from entering the transmission. If leakage is evident at the front of the driveshaft, replace the oil seal referring to the procedures in Chapter 7.
4   The driveshaft assembly requires very little service. The universal joints are lubricated for life and must be replaced if problems develop. The driveshaft must be removed from the vehicle for this procedure.
5   Since the driveshaft is a balanced unit, it's important that no undercoating, mud, etc. be allowed to stay on it. When the vehicle is raised for service it's a good idea to clean the driveshaft and inspect it for any obvious damage. Also check that the small weights used to originally balance the driveshaft are in place and securely attached. Whenever the driveshaft is removed it's important that it be reinstalled in the same relative position to preserve this balance.

6   Problems with the driveshaft are usually indicated by a noise or vibration while driving the vehicle. A road test should verify if the problem is the driveshaft or another vehicle component:
   a) On an open road, free of traffic, drive the vehicle and note the engine speed (rpm) at which the problem is most evident.
   b) With this noted, drive the vehicle again, this time manually keeping the transmission in 1st, then 2nd, then 3rd gear ranges and running the engine up to the engine speed noted.
   c) If the noise or vibration occurs at the same engine speed regardless of which gear the transmission is in, the driveshaft is not at fault because the speed of the driveshaft varies in each gear.
   d) If the noise or vibration decreased or was eliminated, visually inspect the driveshaft for damage, material on the shaft which would effect balance, missing weights and damaged universal joints. Another possibility for this condition would be tires which are out-of-balance.
7   To check for worn universal joints:
   a) On an open road, free of traffic, drive the vehicle slowly until the transmission is in High gear. Let off on the accelerator, allowing the vehicle to coast, then accelerate. A clunking or knocking noise will indicate worn universal joints.
   b) Drive the vehicle at a speed of about 10 to 15 mph and then place the transmission in Neutral, allowing the vehicle to coast. Listen for abnormal driveline noises.
   c) Raise the vehicle and support it securely on jackstands. With the transmission in Neutral, manually turn the driveshaft, watching the universal joints for excessive play.

12 Driveshaft — removal and installation

Refer to illustration 12.3

Removal

1   Disconnect the negative cable from the battery. Place the cable out of the way so it cannot accidentally come in contact with the negative terminal of the battery, as this would once again allow power into the electrical system of the vehicle.
2   Raise the vehicle on a hoist or support it securely on jackstands. Place the transmission in Neutral with the parking brake off.
3   Using a sharp scribe or a hammer and punch, place marks on the driveshaft and the differential flange in line with each other **(see illustration)**. This is to make sure the driveshaft is reinstalled in the same position to preserve the balance.

12.3   Before removing the driveshaft, mark the relationship of the driveshaft yoke to the differential flange — to prevent the driveshaft from turning when loosening the strap bolts, insert a screwdriver through the yoke

4   Remove the rear universal joint strap bolts and the straps. Turn the driveshaft (or tires) as necessary to bring the bolts into the most accessible position.

5   Tape the bearing caps to the spider to prevent the caps from coming off during removal.

6   Lower the rear of the driveshaft and then slide the front out of the transmission.

7   To prevent loss of fluid and protect against contamination while the driveshaft is out, wrap a plastic bag over the transmission housing and hold it in place with a rubber band.

Installation

8   Remove the plastic bag on the transmission and wipe the area clean. Inspect the oil seal carefully. Procedures for replacement of this seal can be found in Chapter 7.

9   Slide the front of the driveshaft into the transmission.

10   Raise the rear of the driveshaft into position, checking to be sure that the marks are in perfect alignment. If not, turn the rear wheels to match the pinion flange and the driveshaft.

11   Remove the tape securing the bearing caps and install the straps and bolts. Tighten the bolts to the specified torque.

13.4   To press the universal joint out of the driveshaft, set it up in a vise with the small socket (on the right) pushing the joint and bearing cap into the large socket

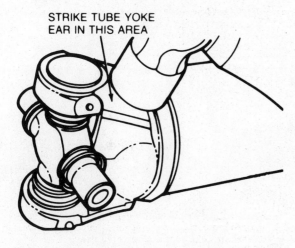

13.9   To relieve stress produced by pressing the bearing caps into the yokes, strike the yoke in the area shown

13   Universal joints — replacement

Refer to illustrations 13.2, 13.4 and 13.9

Note: *A press or large vise will be required for this procedure. It may be advisable to take the driveshaft to a local dealer or machine shop where the universal joints can be replaced for you, normally at a reasonable charge.*

1   Remove the driveshaft as discussed in the previous Section.

2   Using a small pair of pliers, remove the snap-rings from the spider **(see illustration)**. Original front universal joints utilize injected plastic retainers instead of snap-rings. During reassembly, use the snap-rings supplied with the new universal joint.

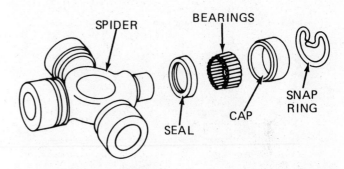

13.2   Exploded view of the universal joint components

3   Supporting the driveshaft, place it in position on either an arbor press or on a workbench equipped with a vise.

4   Place a piece of pipe or a large socket with the same inside diameter over one of the bearing caps. Position a socket which is of slightly smaller diameter than the cap on the opposite bearing cap **(see illustration)** and use the vise or press to force the cap out (inside the pipe or large socket), stopping just before it comes completely out of the yoke. Use the vise or large pliers to work the cap the rest of the way out.

5   Transfer the sockets to the other side and press the opposite bearing cap out in the same manner.

6   Pack the new universal joint bearings with grease. Ordinarily, specific instructions for lubrication will be included with the universal joint servicing kit and should be followed carefully.

7   Position the spider in the yoke and partially install one bearing cap in the yoke.

8   Start the spider into the bearing cap and then partially install the other cap. Align the spider and press the bearing caps into position, being careful not to damage the dust seals.

9   Install the snap-rings. If difficulty is encountered in seating the snap-rings, strike the driveshaft yoke sharply with a hammer. This will spring the yoke ears slightly and allow the snap-rings to seat in the groove **(see illustration)**.

10   Follow the same procedures to replace the rear universal joint, noting that only one-half of the spider needs to be pressed out, since the other two ends are held to the pinion flange with straps and bolts.

11   Install the driveshaft and all components previously removed.

14   Rear axle — description and check

Refer to illustration 14.3

Description

1   The rear axle assembly is a hypoid, semi-floating type (the centerline of the pinion gear is below the centerline of the ring gear). The differential carrier is a casting with a pressed steel cover and the axle tubes are made of steel, pressed and welded into the carrier.

2   An optional locking rear axle is also available. This differential allows for normal differential operation until one wheel loses traction. The unit utilizes multi-disc clutch packs and a speed sensitive engagement mechanism which locks both axleshafts together, applying equal rotational power to both wheels.

8

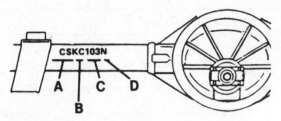

A. Axle Code
B. 7½″ (190 mm) Chevrolet St. Catherines
C. Day Built
D. Shift (D = Day, N = Night)

14.3   Location of the rear axle identification number

15.3a   Remove the pinion shaft lock bolt, . . .

15.3b   . . . then carefully remove the pinion shaft from the differential carrier (don't turn the wheels or the carrier after the shaft has been removed, or the spider gears may fall out)

3   In order to undertake certain operations, particularly replacement of the axleshafts, it's important to know the axle identification number. It's located on the front face of the right side axle tube **(see illustration)**.

Check

4   Many times a fault is suspected in the rear axle area when, in fact, the problem lies elsewhere. For this reason, a thorough check should be performed before assuming a rear axle problem.
5   The following noises are those commonly associated with rear axle diagnosis procedures:
   a) Road noise is often mistaken for mechanical faults. Driving the vehicle on different surfaces will show whether the road surface is the cause of the noise. Road noise will remain the same if the vehicle is under power or coasting.
   b) Tire noise is sometimes mistaken for mechanical problems. Tires which are worn or low on pressure are particularly susceptible to emitting vibrations and noises. Tire noise will remain about the same during varying driving situations, where rear axle noise will change during coasting, acceleration, etc.
   c) Engine and transmission noise can be deceiving because it will travel along the driveline. To isolate engine and transmission noises, make a note of the engine speed at which the noise is most pronounced. Stop the vehicle and place the transmission in Neutral and run the engine to the same speed. If the noise is the same, the rear axle is not at fault.
6   Overhaul and general repair of the rear axle is beyond the scope of the home mechanic due to the many special tools and critical measurements required. Thus, the procedures listed here will involve axleshaft removal and installation, axleshaft oil seal replacement, axleshaft bearing replacement and removal of the entire unit for repair or replacement.

15   Axleshaft — removal and installation

Refer to illustrations 15.3a, 15.3b, 15.4 and 15.5

1   Raise the rear of the vehicle, support it securely and remove the wheel and brake drum (refer to Chapter 9).
2   Remove the pressed steel cover from the differential carrier and allow the oil to drain into a container.
3   Remove the lock bolt from the differential pinion shaft. Remove the pinion shaft **(see illustrations)**.
4   Push the outer (flanged) end of the axleshaft in and remove the C-lock from the inner end of the shaft **(see illustration)**.

15.4   Push the axle flange in, then remove the C-lock from the inner end of the axleshaft

5   Withdraw the axleshaft, taking care not to damage the oil seal in the end of the axle housing as the splined end of the axleshaft passes through it **(see illustration)**.
6   Installation is the reverse of removal. Tighten the lock bolt to the specified torque.
7   Always use a new cover gasket and tighten the cover bolts to the specified torque.
8   Refill the axle with the correct quantity and grade of lubricant (Chapter 1).

16   Axleshaft oil seal — replacement

Refer to illustrations 16.2 and 16.3

1   Remove the axleshaft as described in the preceding Section.
2   Pry the old oil seal out of the end of the axle housing, using a large screwdriver or the inner end of the axleshaft itself as a lever **(see illustration)**.
3   Using a large socket as a seal driver, tap the seal into position so that the lips are facing in and the metal face is visible from the end of the axle housing **(see illustration)**. When correctly installed, the face of the oil seal should be flush with the end of the axle housing. Lubricate the lips of the seal with gear oil.
4   Installation of the axleshaft is described in the preceding Section.

15.5   Carefully pull the axleshaft from the housing to avoid damaging the seal

16.2   The axleshaft oil seal can sometimes be pried out with the end of the axle

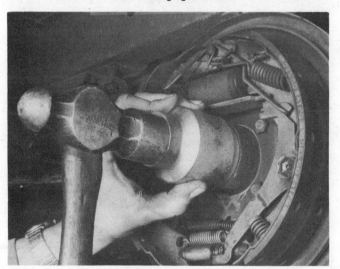

16.3   A large socket can be used to install the new seal squarely

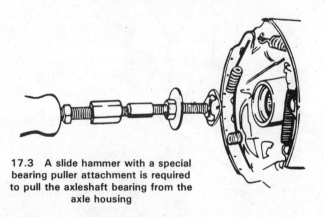

17.3   A slide hammer with a special bearing puller attachment is required to pull the axleshaft bearing from the axle housing

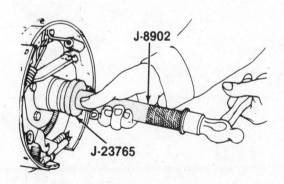

17.4   A special bearing driver is needed to install the axleshaft bearing without damaging it

17   Axleshaft bearing — replacement

Refer to illustrations 17.3 and 17.4

1   Remove the axleshaft (refer to Section 15) and the oil seal (refer to Section 16).
2   A bearing puller will be required or a tool which will engage behind the bearing will have to be fabricated.
3   Attach a slide hammer and pull the bearing from the axle housing **(see illustration)**.
4   Clean out the bearing recess and drive in the new bearing using GM tool no. J8902 and J23765 or equivalent **(see illustration)**. **Caution:** *Failure to use this tool could result in bearing damage.* Lubricate the

8

new bearing with gear lubricant. Make sure that the bearing is tapped into the full depth of its recess and that the numbers on the bearing are visible from the outer end of the housing.

5   Discard the old oil seal and install a new one, then install the axle-shaft.

18   Rear axle assembly — removal and installation

Refer to illustrations 18.6 and 18.10

Removal

1   Loosen the rear wheel lug nuts, raise the rear of the vehicle and support it securely on jackstands positioned under the frame. Remove the wheels.
2   Remove the brake drums (refer to Chapter 9 if any difficulty is encountered).
3   Disconnect the vent hose from the top of the axle housing.
4   Remove the lower shock absorber nuts and bolts and separate the shock absorbers from their mounts.
5   Mark the driveshaft yoke and pinion flange relationship and remove the four universal joint strap bolts (refer to Section 12). Slide the driveshaft as far forward as possible and suspend it with a piece of wire.
6   Disconnect the brake lines at the junction block bolted to the differential cover and unbolt the brake hose from the support bracket **(see illustration)**. Plug the holes in the fitting to prevent excessive fluid loss or hydraulic system contamination.
7   Disconnect the parking brake cables at the equalizer (Chapter 9).
8   Remove the rear stabilizer bar, if so equipped (refer to Chapter 10).
9   Support the rear axle assembly with a jack positioned under the differential housing.
10   Remove the anchor plate nuts and U-bolt nuts and remove the anchor plates from the top of the leaf springs **(see illustration)**. Use caution while doing this, as the axle will be balancing on the floor jack after the anchor plates have been removed.
11   Carefully lower the rear axle assembly to the floor.

Installation

12   Raise the rear axle assembly into place.
13   Install the U-bolts and anchor plates and tighten the nuts to the specified torque. **Note:** *If the vehicle is equipped with a stabilizer bar, it should be installed before tightening any of the bolts.*

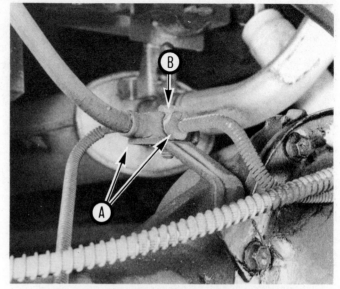

18.6   Loosen the two tube nuts (A) and separate the hydraulic lines from the junction block, then remove the bolt (B) securing the hose to the support bracket

14   Connect the brake hose junction block to the support bracket, install the two hydraulic lines in the junction block and tighten the tube nuts securely.
15   Connect the driveshaft to the pinion flange, lining up the marks made during removal. Tighten the strap bolts to the specified torque.
16   Connect the parking brake cables at the equalizer.
17   Install the shock absorbers and tighten the nuts securely.
18   Install the vent hose on the differential housing.
19   Install the brake drums and rear wheels. Tighten the lug nuts to the specified torque.
20   Check the rear axle lubricant level (Chapter 1).
21   Bleed the brakes as outlined in Chapter 9.
22   Adjust the parking brake if necessary, following the procedure outlined in Chapter 9.

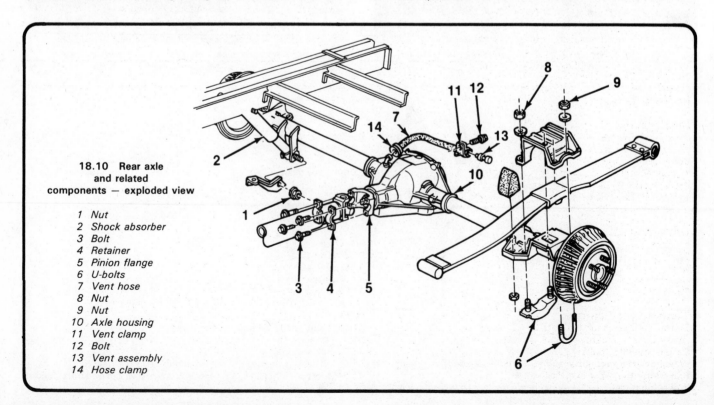

18.10   Rear axle and related components — exploded view

1   Nut
2   Shock absorber
3   Bolt
4   Retainer
5   Pinion flange
6   U-bolts
7   Vent hose
8   Nut
9   Nut
10 Axle housing
11 Vent clamp
12 Bolt
13 Vent assembly
14 Hose clamp

Chapter 9   Brakes

Contents

Specifications

Brake fluid type .... See Chapter 1

Disc brakes

Minimum brake pad thickness .... See Chapter 1
Rotor thickness after resurfacing...................... 0.980 in minimum
Rotor discard thickness .... 0.965 in
Lateral runout....................................... 0.004 in maximum
Rotor thickness variation (parallelism) .... 0.0005 in
Caliper-to-knuckle clearance (clearance on each
   end added together for total) .... 0.010 to 0.024 in

Drum brakes

Minimum brake lining thickness .... See Chapter 1
Drum diameter after resurfacing .... 9.56 in maximum
Drum discard thickness .... 9.59 in
Out-of-round .... 0.006 in maximum
Taper .... 0.003 in maximum

Torque specifications   **Ft-lbs**

Master cylinder mounting nuts 21
Power booster mounting nuts 21
Caliper mounting bolts 37
Wheel cylinder mounting bolts 13
Brake hose-to-caliper inlet fitting bolt 32
Wheel lug nuts .... 90 to 100

9

1   General information

The vehicles covered by this manual are equipped with hydraulically operated front and rear brake systems. The front brakes are disc type and the rear brakes are drum type. Both the front and rear brakes are self adjusting. The front disc brakes automatically compensate for pad wear, while the rear drum brakes incorporate an adjustment mechanism which is activated as the brakes are applied when the vehicle is driven in reverse.

Hydraulic system

The hydraulic system consists of separate front and rear circuits. The master cylinder has separate reservoirs for the two circuits and in the event of a leak or failure in one hydraulic circuit, the other circuit will remain operative. A visual warning of circuit failure or air in the system is given by a warning light activated by displacement of the piston in the pressure differential switch portion of the combination valve from its normal ''in balance'' position.

Combination valve

A combination valve, located in the engine compartment below the master cylinder, consists of three sections providing the following functions: The metering section limits pressure to the front brakes until a predetermined front input pressure is reached and until the rear brakes are activated. There is no restriction at inlet pressures below 3 psi, allowing pressure equalization during non-braking periods. The proportioning section proportions outlet pressure to the rear brakes after a predetermined rear input pressure has been reached, preventing early rear wheel lock-up under heavy brake loads. The valve is also designed to assure full pressure to one brake system should the other system fail. The pressure differential warning switch incorporated into the combination valve is designed to continuously compare the front and rear brake pressure from the master cylinder and energize the dash warning light in the event of either a front or rear brake system failure. The design of the switch and valve are such that the switch will stay in the ''warning'' position once a failure has occurred. The only way to turn the light off is to repair the cause of the failure and apply a brake pedal force of 450 psi.

Power brake booster

The power brake booster, utilizing engine manifold vacuum and atmospheric pressure to provide assistance to the hydraulically operated brakes, is mounted on the firewall in the engine compartment.

Parking brake

The parking brake operates the rear brakes only, through cable actuation. It's activated by a pedal mounted on the left side kick panel.

Service

After completing any operation involving disassembly of any part of the brake system, always test drive the vehicle to check for proper braking performance before resuming normal driving. When testing the brakes, perform the tests on a clean, dry flat surface. Conditions other than these can lead to inaccurate test results.

Test the brakes at various speeds with both light and heavy pedal pressure. The vehicle should stop evenly without pulling to one side or the other. Avoid locking the brakes because this slides the tires and diminishes braking efficiency and control of the vehicle.

Tires, vehicle load and front-end alignment are factors which also affect braking performance.

2   Disc brake pads — replacement

Refer to illustrations 2.5 and 2.6a through 2.6g

Warning: *Disc brake pads must be replaced on both front wheels at the same time — never replace the pads on only one wheel. Also, the dust created by the brake system contains asbestos, which is harmful to your health. Never blow it out with compressed air and don't inhale any of it. An approved filtering mask should be worn when working on the brakes. Do not, under any circumstances, use petroleum-based solvents to clean brake parts. Use brake cleaner or denatured alcohol only!*

Note: *When servicing the disc brakes, use only high quality, nationally recognized brand name pads.*

1   Remove the covers from the brake fluid reservoir.
2   Loosen the wheel lug nuts, raise the front of the vehicle and support it securely on jackstands.
3   Remove the front wheels. Work on one brake assembly at a time, using the assembled brake for reference if necessary.
4   Inspect the rotor carefully as outlined in Section 4. If machining is necessary, follow the information in that Section to remove the rotor, at which time the pads can be removed from the calipers as well.
5   Push the piston back into its bore. If necessary, a C-clamp can be used, but a flat bar will usually do the job **(see illustration)**. As the piston is depressed to the bottom of the caliper bore, the fluid in the master cylinder will rise. Make sure that it doesn't overflow. If necessary, siphon off some of the fluid.
6   Follow the accompanying photos, beginning with illustration 2.6a, for the actual pad replacement procedure. Be sure to stay in order and read the caption under each illustration.
7   When reinstalling the caliper, be sure to tighten the mounting bolts to the specified torque. After the job has been completed, firmly depress the brake pedal a few times to bring the pads into contact with the rotor.

2.5   Using a large C-clamp, push the piston back into the caliper bore — note that one end of the clamp is on the flat area near the brake hose fitting and the other end (screw end) is pressing against the outer brake pad

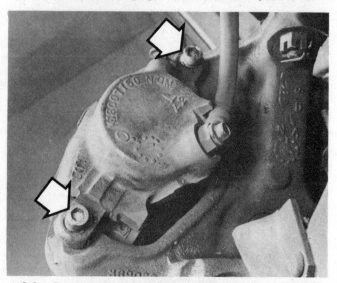

2.6a   Remove the two caliper-to-steering knuckle mounting bolts (arrows) (this will require the use of an Allen head socket wrench)

2.6b   Slide the caliper up and off the rotor

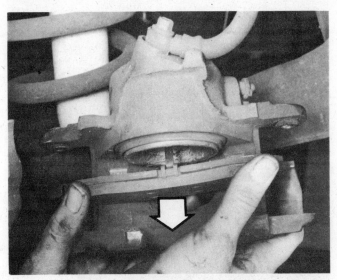

2.6c   Pull the inner pad straight out, disengaging the retainer spring from the caliper piston

2.6d   Transfer the retainer spring from the old inner pad to the new one — hook the end of the spring in the hole at the top of the pad, then insert the two prongs of the spring into the slot on the pad backing plate

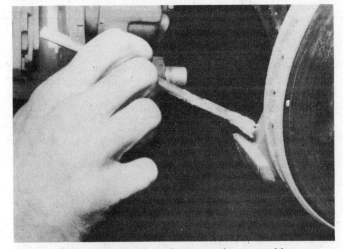

2.6e   Lubricate the caliper mounting ears with multi-purpose grease

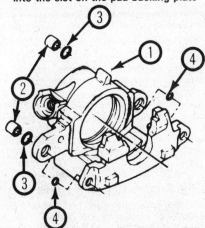

2.6f   Push the mounting bolt sleeves out of the bores, remove the old bushings and install the new ones supplied with the brake pads

1	Caliper	3	Bushings
2	Sleeves	4	Bushings

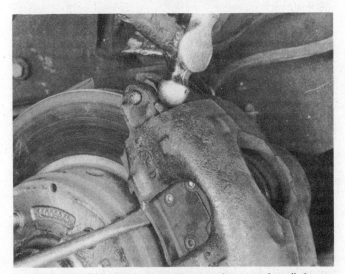

2.6g   Slide the caliper assembly over the rotor, install the mounting bolts, then insert a screwdriver between the rotor and outer brake pad, pry up and strike the pad ears with a hammer to eliminate all play between the pad and caliper

9

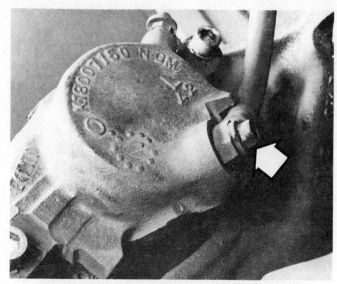

3.4   It's easier to remove the brake hose inlet fitting bolt
(arrow) before removing the caliper mounting bolts

3.8   With the caliper padded to catch the piston, use
compressed air to force the piston out of the bore — make sure
your hands or fingers are not between the piston and caliper!

3.9   When prying the dust boot out of the caliper, be very
careful not to scratch the bore surface

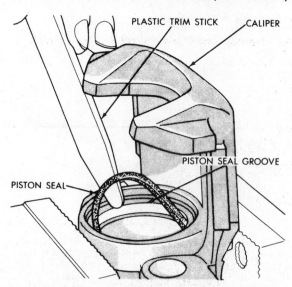

3.10   Remove the piston seal with a wooden or plastic
tool to avoid scratching the bore and seal groove

3   Disc brake caliper — removal, overhaul and installation

Warning: *Dust created by the brake system contains asbestos, which is harmful to your health. Never blow it out with compressed air and don't inhale any of it. An approved filtering mask should be worn when working on the brakes. Do not, under any circumstances, use petroleum-based solvents to clean brake parts. Use brake cleaner or denatured alcohol only!*

Note: *If an overhaul is indicated (usually because of fluid leakage) explore all options before beginning the job. New and factory rebuilt calipers are available on an exchange basis, which makes this job quite easy. If it's decided to rebuild the calipers, make sure that a rebuild kit is available before proceeding. Always rebuild the calipers in pairs — never rebuild just one of them.*

Removal

Refer to illustration 3.4

1   Remove the cover from the brake fluid reservoir, siphon off two-thirds of the fluid into a container and discard it.
2   Loosen the wheel lug nuts, raise the front of the vehicle and support

it securely on jackstands. Remove the front wheels.
3   Bottom the piston in the caliper bore **(see illustration 2.5)**.
4   Remove the brake hose inlet fitting bolt and detach the hose **(see illustration)**. Have a rag handy to catch spilled fluid and wrap a plastic bag tightly around the end of the hose to prevent fluid loss and contamination.
5   Remove the two mounting bolts and detach the caliper from the vehicle (refer to Section 2 if necessary).

Overhaul

Refer to illustrations 3.8, 3.9, 3.10, 3.11, 3.15, 3.16, 3.17 and 3.18

6   Refer to Section 2 and remove the brake pads from the caliper.
7   Clean the exterior of the caliper with brake cleaner or denatured alcohol. **Never use gasoline, kerosene or petroleum-based cleaning solvents.** Place the caliper on a clean workbench.
8   Position a wooden block or several shop rags in the caliper as a cushion, then use compressed air to remove the piston from the caliper **(see illustration)**. Use only enough air pressure to ease the piston out of the bore. If the piston is blown out, even with the cushion in place, it may be damaged. **Warning:** *Never place your fingers in front of the*

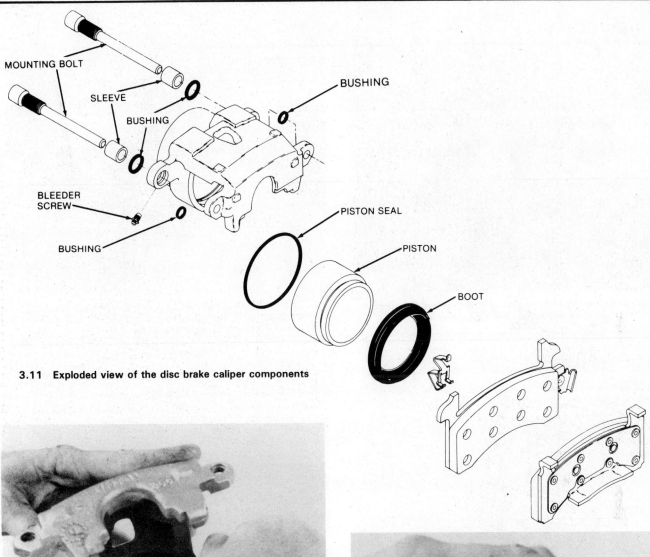

3.11   Exploded view of the disc brake caliper components

3.15   Position the seal in the caliper bore groove, making sure it isn't twisted

3.16   Install the new dust boot in the piston groove (note that the folds are at the open end of the piston)

piston in an attempt to catch or protect it when applying compressed air, as serious injury could occur.

9   Carefully pry the dust boot out of the caliper bore **(see illustration)**.
10 Using a wood or plastic tool, remove the piston seal from the groove in the caliper bore **(see illustration)**. Metal tools may cause bore damage.
11 Remove the caliper bleeder screw, then remove and discard the sleeves and bushings from the caliper ears. Discard all rubber parts **(see illustration)**.
12 Clean the remaining parts with brake system cleaner or denatured alcohol then blow them dry with compressed air.
13 Carefully examine the piston for nicks and burrs and loss of plating. If surface defects are present, the parts must be replaced.
14 Check the caliper bore in a similar way. Light polishing with crocus cloth is permissible to remove light corrosion and stains. Discard the mounting bolts if they're corroded or damaged.
15 When assembling, lubricate the piston bores and seal with clean brake fluid. Position the seal in the caliper bore groove **(see illustration)**.
16 Lubricate the piston with clean brake fluid, then install a new boot in the piston groove with the fold toward the open end of the piston **(see illustration)**.

9

3.17   Install the piston squarely in the caliper bore then bottom it by pushing down evenly

3.18   Seat the boot in the counterbore (a seal driver is being used in this photo, but a drift punch will work if care is exercised)

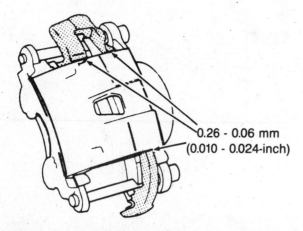

0.26 - 0.06 mm
(0.010 - 0.024-inch)

3.23   Measure the gap between the top and bottom of the caliper and the steering knuckle, then add the measurements together — the total should be within the specified limit

17 Insert the piston squarely in the caliper bore, then apply force to bottom the piston in the bore (see illustration).
18 Position the dust boot in the caliper counterbore, then use a drift to drive it into position (see illustration). Make sure the boot is recessed evenly below the caliper face.
19 Install the bleeder screw.
20 Install new bushings in the mounting bolt holes and fill the area between the bushings with the silicone grease supplied in the rebuild kit. Push the sleeves into the mounting bolt holes.

Installation

Refer to illustration 3.23

21 Inspect the mounting bolts for excessive corrosion.
22 Place the caliper in position over the rotor and mounting bracket, install the bolts and tighten them to the specified torque.
23 Check to make sure the total clearance between the caliper and the bracket stops is between 0.010 and 0.024 inch (see illustration).
24 Install the brake hose and inlet fitting bolt, using new copper washers, then tighten the bolt to the specified torque. Be sure to bleed the brakes (Section 10). .
25 Install the wheels and lower the vehicle.
26 After the job has been completed, firmly depress the brake pedal a few times to bring the pads into contact with the rotor.

---

4   Brake rotor (disc) — inspection, removal and installation

Inspection

Refer to illustrations 4.3, 4.4a, 4.4b and 4.5

1.   Loosen the wheel lug nuts, raise the vehicle and support it securely on jackstands. Remove the wheel.
2   Remove the brake caliper as outlined in Section 3. It's not necessary to disconnect the brake hose. After removing the caliper bolts, suspend the caliper out of the way with a piece of wire. Don't let the caliper hang by the hose and don't stretch or twist the hose.
3   Visually check the rotor surface for score marks and other damage. Light scratches and shallow grooves are normal after use and may not always be detrimental to brake operation, but deep score marks — over 0.015-inch (0.38 mm) — require rotor removal and refinishing by an automotive machine shop. Be sure to check both sides of the rotor (see illustration). If pulsating has been noticed during application of the brakes, suspect rotor runout.

4.3   Check the rotor for deep grooves and score marks (be sure to inspect both sides of the rotor)

4.4a Check rotor runout with a dial indicator — if the reading exceeds the maximum allowable runout, the rotor will have to be resurfaced or replaced

4.4b Using a swirling motion, remove the glaze from the rotor with medium-grit emery cloth

4   To check rotor runout, place a dial indicator at a point about 1/2-inch from the outer edge of the rotor **(see illustration)**. Set the indicator to zero and turn the rotor. The indicator reading should not exceed the specified allowable runout limit. If it does, the rotor should be refinished by an automotive machine shop. **Note:** *Professionals recommend resurfacing of brake rotors regardless of the dial indicator reading, (to produce a smooth, flat surface, that will eliminate brake pedal pulsations and other undesirable symptoms related to questionable rotors). At the very least, if you elect not to have the rotors resurfaced, deglaze the brake pad surface with medium-grit emery cloth (use a swirling motion to ensure a non-directional finish)* **(see illustration)**.
5   The rotor must not be machined to a thickness less than the specified minimum refinish thickness. The minimum wear (or discard) thickness is cast into the inside of the rotor. It should not be confused with the minimum refinish thickness. The rotor thickness can be checked with a micrometer **(see illustration)**.

Removal

6   Refer to Chapter 1, Section 36, for the rotor removal procedure (it's part of the hub and comes off when the hub is removed).

Installation

7   Install the rotor and hub assembly and adjust the wheel bearing (Chapter 1).
8   Install the caliper and brake pad assembly over the rotor and position it on the steering knuckle (refer to Section 3 for the caliper installation procedure, if necessary). Tighten the caliper bolts to the specified torque.
9   Install the wheel, then lower the vehicle to the ground. Depress the brake pedal a few times to bring the brake pads into contact with the rotor. Bleeding of the system will not be necessary unless the brake hose was disconnected from the caliper. Check the operation of the brakes carefully before placing the vehicle into normal service.

---

5   Rear brake shoes — inspection and replacement

Refer to illustrations 5.4a through 5.4v

Warning: *Drum brake shoes must be replaced on both wheels at the same time — never replace the shoes on only one wheel. Also, the dust created by the brake system contains asbestos, which is harmful to your health. Never blow it out with compressed air and don't inhale any of it. An approved filtering mask should be worn when working on the brakes. Do not, under any circumstances, use petroleum-based*

4.5   A micrometer is used to measure rotor thickness — this can be done on the vehicle (as shown) or on the bench (the minimum thickness is cast into the inside of the rotor)

9

solvents to clean brake parts. Use brake cleaner or denatured alcohol only!
Caution: *Whenever the brake shoes are replaced, the retractor and holddown springs should also be replaced. Due to the continuous heating/cooling cycle that the springs are subjected to, they lose their tension over a period of time and may allow the shoes to drag on the drum and wear at a much faster rate than normal. When replacing the rear brake shoes, use only high quality nationally recognized brand-name parts.*

1   Loosen the wheel lug nuts, raise the rear of the vehicle and support it securely on jackstands. Block the front wheels to keep the vehicle from rolling.
2   Release the parking brake.
3   Remove the wheel. **Note:** *All four rear brake shoes must be replaced at the same time, but to avoid mixing up parts, work on only one brake assembly at a time.*

4   Follow the accompanying photos (illustrations 5.4a through 5.4v) for the inspection and replacement of the brake shoes. Be sure to stay in order and read the caption under each illustration. **Note:** *If the brake drum cannot be easily pulled off the axle and shoe assembly, make sure that the parking brake is completely released, then squirt some penetrating oil around the center hub area. Allow the oil to soak in and try to pull the drum off. If the drum still cannot be pulled off, the brake shoes will have to be retracted. This is accomplished by first removing the plug from the backing plate with a hammer and chisel. With the plug removed, pull the lever off the adjusting screw wheel with one small screwdriver while turning the adjusting wheel with another small screwdriver, moving the shoes away from the drum. The drum should now come off.*

5   Before reinstalling the drum it should be checked for cracks, score marks, deep scratches and hard spots, which will appear as small discolored areas. If the hard spots cannot be removed with fine emery cloth or if any of the other conditions listed above exist, the drum must be taken to an automotive machine shop to have it turned. **Note:** *Professionals recommend resurfacing the drums whenever a brake job is done. Resurfacing will eliminate the possibility of out-of-round drums.*

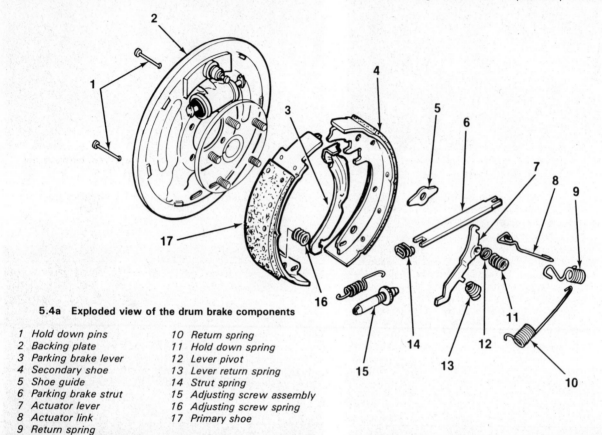

5.4a   Exploded view of the drum brake components

1	Hold down pins	10	Return spring
2	Backing plate	11	Hold down spring
3	Parking brake lever	12	Lever pivot
4	Secondary shoe	13	Lever return spring
5	Shoe guide	14	Strut spring
6	Parking brake strut	15	Adjusting screw assembly
7	Actuator lever	16	Adjusting screw spring
8	Actuator link	17	Primary shoe
9	Return spring		

5.4b   Remove the shoe return springs — the spring tool shown here is available at most auto parts stores and makes this job much easier and safer

5.4c   Pull the bottom of the actuator lever toward the secondary brake shoe, compressing the lever return spring — the actuator link can now be removed

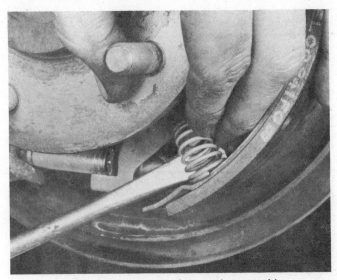

5.4d Pry the actuator lever spring out with a large screwdriver

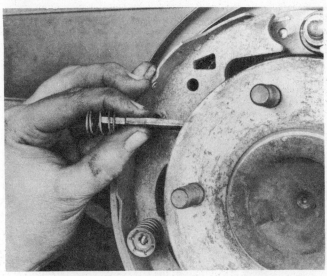

5.4e Slide the parking brake strut out from between the axle flange and primary shoe

5.4f Remove the hold down springs and pins — the hold down spring tool shown here is available at most auto parts stores

5.4g Remove the actuator lever and pivot — be careful not to let the pivot fall out of the lever

5.4h Spread the top of the shoes apart and slide the assembly around the axle

5.4i Unhook the parking brake lever from the secondary shoe

9

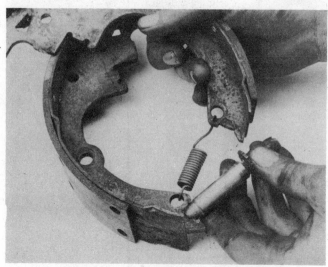

5.4j   Spread the bottom of the shoes apart and remove
the adjusting screw assembly

5.4k   Clean the adjusting screw with solvent, dry it off
and lubricate the threads and end with multi-purpose
grease, then reinstall the adjusting screw assembly
between the new brake shoes

5.4l   Lubricate the shoe contact points on the backing
plate with high-temperature brake grease

5.4m   Insert the parking brake lever into the opening in the
secondary brake shoe

5.4n   Spread the shoes apart and slide them into position
on the backing plate

5.4o   Install the hold down pin and spring through the
backing plate and primary shoe

5.4p Insert the lever pivot into the actuator lever, place the lever over the secondary shoe hold down pin and install the hold down spring

5.4q Guide the parking brake strut behind the axle flange and engage the rear end of it in the slot on the parking brake lever — spread the shoes enough to allow the other end to seat against the primary shoe

5.4r Place the shoe guide over the anchor pin

5.4s Hook the lower end of the actuator link to the actuator lever, then loop the top end over the anchor pin

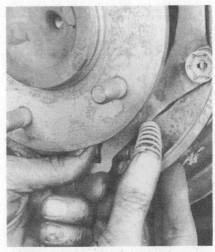

5.4t Install the lever return spring over the tab on the actuator lever, then push the spring up onto the brake shoe

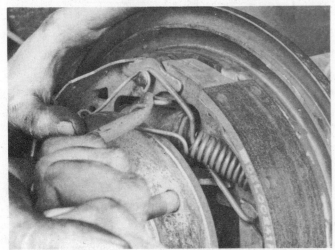

5.4u Install the primary and secondary shoe return springs

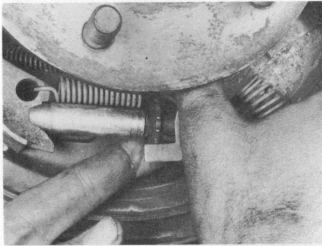

5.4v Pull out on the actuator lever to disengage it from the adjusting screw wheel, turn the wheel to adjust the shoes in or out as necessary — the brake drum should slide over the shoes and turn with a very slight amount of drag

9

If the drums are worn so much that thay can't be resurfaced without exceeding the maximum allowable diameter (stamped into the drum), then new ones will be required. At the very least, if your elect not to have the drums resurfaced, remove the glazing from the surface with medium-grit emery cloth using a swirling motion.

6   Install the brake drum on the axle flange.
7   Mount the wheel, install the lug nuts, then lower the vehicle.
8   Make a number of forward and reverse stops to adjust the brakes until satisfactory pedal action is obtained.

6   Wheel cylinder — removal, overhaul and installation

Note: *If an overhaul is indicated (usually because of fluid leakage or sticky operation) explore all options before beginning the job. New wheel cylinders are available, which makes this job quite easy. If it's decided to rebuild the wheel cylinder, make sure that a rebuild kit is available before proceeding. Never overhaul only one wheel cylinder — always rebuild both of them at the same time.*

Removal

Refer to illustration 6.4

1   Raise the rear of the vehicle and support it securely on jackstands. Block the front wheels to keep the vehicle from rolling.
2   Remove the brake shoe assembly (Section 5).
3   Remove all dirt and foreign material from around the wheel cylinder.
4   Disconnect the brake line **(see illustration)**. Don't pull the brake line away from the wheel cylinder.
5   Remove the wheel cylinder mounting bolts.
6   Detach the wheel cylinder from the brake backing plate and place it on a clean workbench. Immediately plug the brake line to prevent fluid loss and contamination.

Overhaul

Refer to illustration 6.7

7   Remove the bleeder valve, seals, pistons, boots and spring assembly from the wheel cylinder body **(see illustration)**.
8   Clean the wheel cylinder with brake fluid, denatured alcohol or brake system cleaner. **Warning:** *Do not, under any circumstances, use petroleum based solvents to clean brake parts!*
9   Use compressed air to remove excess fluid from the wheel cylinder and to blow out the passages.
10 Check the cylinder bore for corrosion and score marks. Crocus cloth can be used to remove light corrosion and stains, but the cylinder must

be replaced with a new one if the defects cannot be removed easily, or if the bore is scored.
11 Lubricate the new seals with brake fluid.
12 Assemble the brake cylinder components. Make sure the seal lips face in.

Installation

13 Place the wheel cylinder in position and install the bolts.
14 Connect the brake line and install the brake shoe assembly.
15 Bleed the brakes.

7   Master cylinder — removal, overhaul and installation

Note: *Before deciding to overhaul the master cylinder, investigate the availability and cost of a new or factory rebuilt unit and also the availability of a rebuild kit.*

Removal

Refer to illustrations 7.2, 7.4, 7.7, 7.8 and 7.9

1   Place rags under the brake line fittings and prepare caps or plastic bags to cover the ends of the lines once they are disconnected. **Caution:** *Brake fluid will damage paint. Cover all body parts and be careful not to spill fluid during this procedure.*
2   Loosen the tube nuts at the ends of the brake lines where they enter the master cylinder. To prevent rounding off the flats on these nuts, a flare-nut wrench, which wraps around the nut, should be used **(see illustration)**.
3   Pull the brake lines away from the master cylinder slightly and plug the ends to prevent contamination.
4   Remove the two master cylinder mounting nuts disconnect the pushrod from the brake pedal (non-power brakes), move the bracket retaining the combination valve forward slightly, taking care not to bend the hydraulic lines running to the combination valve, and remove the master cylinder from the vehicle **(see illustration)**.
5   Remove the reservoir covers and reservoir diaphragms, then discard any fluid remaining in the reservoir.

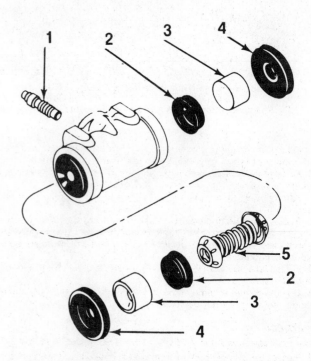

6.7   Exploded view of the wheel cylinder components

1 Bleeder valve	*4 Boot*
2 Seal	*5 Spring assembly*
3 Piston	

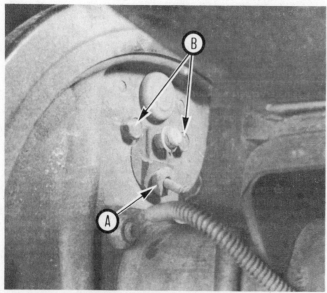

6.4   Completely loosen the brake line fitting (A) then remove the two wheel cylinder mounting bolts (B)

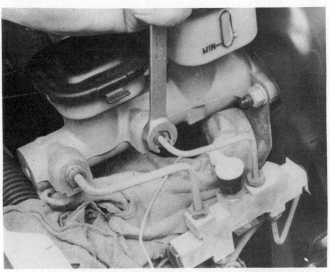

7.2 Disconnect the brake lines from the master cylinder — a flare-nut wrench should be used

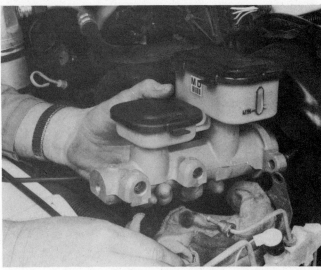

7.4 Pull the combination valve forward, being careful not to bend or kink the lines, then slide the master cylinder off the mounting studs

7.7 Push the primary piston in and remove the lock ring

7.8 Pull the primary piston and spring assembly out of the bore

6   Mount the master cylinder in a vise. Be sure to line the vise jaws with blocks of wood to prevent damage to the cylinder body.

7   Remove the primary piston lock ring by depressing the piston and prying the ring out with a screwdriver (see illustration).

8   Remove the primary piston assembly from the cylinder bore (see illustration).

9   Remove the secondary piston assembly from the cylinder bore. It may be necessary to remove the master cylinder from the vise and invert it, carefully tapping it against a block of wood to expel the piston (see illustration).

10   Pry the reservoir from the cylinder body with a screwdriver. Remove the grommets.

11   Do not attempt to remove the quick take-up valve from the master cylinder body — it's not serviceable.

Overhaul

Refer to illustrations 7.14, 7.15a, 7.15b, 7.15c, 7.15d, 7.16 and 7.17

12   Inspect the cylinder bore for corrosion and damage. If any corrosion or damage is found, replace the master cylinder body with a new one, as abrasives cannot be used on the bore.

13   Lubricate the new reservoir grommets with silicone lubricant and press them into the master cylinder body. Make sure they're properly seated.

9

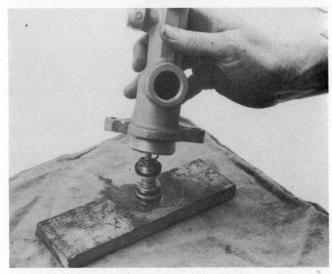

7.9 To remove the secondary piston, tap the cylinder against a block of wood

7.14   Lay the reservoir face down on the bench, with the secondary reservoir propped up on a block of wood — push the master cylinder straight down over the reservoir tubes using a rocking motion

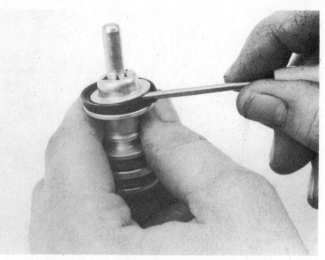

7.15a   Pry the secondary piston spring retainer off with a small screwdriver, then remove the seal

7.15b   Remove the secondary seals from the piston (some only have one seal)

7.15c   Install the secondary seals with the lips facing away from each other (on the single seal design, the seal lip should face away from the center of the piston)

7.15d   Install a new primary seal on the secondary piston with the seal lip facing in the direction shown

7.16   Install a new spring retainer over the end of the secondary piston and push it into place with a socket

14   Lay the reservoir on a hard surface and press the master cylinder body onto the reservoir, using a rocking motion (see illustration).

15   Remove the old seals from the secondary piston assembly and install the new secondary seals with the lips facing **away** from each other (see illustrations). The lip on the primary seal must face in (see illustration).

16   Attach the spring retainer to the secondary piston assembly (see illustration).

17   Lubricate the cylinder bore with clean brake fluid and install the spring and secondary piston assembly (see illustration).

18   Install the primary piston assembly in the cylinder bore, depress it and install the lock ring.

19   Inspect the reservoir cover and diaphragm for cracks and deformation. Replace any damaged parts with new ones and attach the diaphragm to the cover.

20   **Note:** *Whenever the master cylinder is removed, the complete hydraulic system must be bled. The time required to bleed the system can be reduced if the master cylinder is filled with fluid and bench bled (refer to Steps 21 through 25) before the master cylinder is installed on the vehicle.*

21   Insert threaded plugs of the correct size into the cylinder outlet

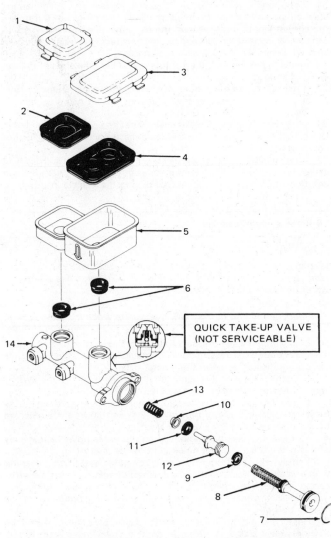

QUICK TAKE-UP VALVE
(NOT SERVICEABLE)

7.17 Exploded view of the master cylinder assembly

1 *Reservoir cover*	8 *Primary piston assembly*
2 *Reservoir diaphragm*	9 *Secondary seal*
3 *Reservoir cover*	10 *Spring retainer*
4 *Reservoir diaphragm*	11 *Primary seal*
5 *Reservoir*	12 *Secondary piston*
6 *Reservoir grommet*	13 *Spring*
7 *Lock ring*	14 *Cylinder body*

holes and fill the reservoirs with brake fluid. The master cylinder should be supported in such a manner that brake fluid will not spill during the bench bleeding procedure.

22 Loosen one plug at a time and push the piston assembly into the bore to force air from the master cylinder. To prevent air from being drawn back into the cylinder, the appropriate plug must be replaced before allowing the piston to return to its original position.

23 Stroke the piston three or four times for each outlet to ensure that all air has been expelled.

24 Since high pressure is not involved in the bench bleeding procedure, an alternative to the removal and replacement of the plugs with each stroke of the piston assembly is available. Before pushing in on the piston assembly, remove one of the plugs completely. Before releasing the piston, however, instead of replacing the plug, simply put your finger tightly over the hole to keep air from being drawn back into the master cylinder. Wait several seconds for the brake fluid to be drawn from the reservoir to the piston bore, then repeat the procedure. When you push down on the piston it will force your finger off the hole, allowing the air inside to be expelled. When only brake fluid is being ejected

from the hole, replace the plug and go on to the other port.

25 Refill the master cylinder reservoirs and install the diaphragm and cover assembly. **Note:** *The reservoirs should only be filled to the top of the reservoir divider to prevent overflowing when the cover is installed.*

Installation

26 Carefully install the master cylinder by reversing the removal steps, then bleed the brakes (refer to Section 10).

8   Combination valve — check and replacement

Check

1   Disconnect the wire from the pressure differential switch. **Note:** *When unplugging the connector, squeeze the side lock releases, moving the inside tabs away from the switch, then pull up.* Pliers may be used as an aid if necessary.

2   Using a jumper wire, connect the switch wire to a good ground, such as the engine block.

3   Turn the ignition key to the On position. The warning light in the instrument panel should light.

4   If the warning light does not light, either the bulb is burned out or the electrical circuit is defective. Replace the bulb (refer to Chapter 10) or repair the electrical circuit as necessary.

5   When the warning light functions correctly, turn the ignition switch off, disconnect the jumper wire and reconnect the wire to the switch terminal.

6   Make sure the master cylinder reservoirs are full, then attach a bleeder hose to one of the rear wheel bleeder valves and immerse the other end of the hose in a container partially filled with clean brake fluid.

7   Turn the ignition switch on.

8   Open the bleeder valve while a helper applies moderate pressure to the brake pedal. The brake warning light on the instrument panel should light.

9   Close the bleeder valve before the helper releases the brake pedal.

10 Reapply the brake pedal with moderate to heavy pressure. The brake warning light should go out.

11 Attach the bleeder hose to one of the front brake bleeder valves and repeat Steps 8 through 10. The warning light should react in the same manner as in Steps 8 and 10.

12 Turn the ignition switch off.

13 If the warning light did not come on in Steps 8 and 11, but does light when a jumper is connected to ground, the warning light switch portion of the combination valve is defective and the combination valve must be replaced with a new one since the components of the combination valve are not individually serviceable.

Replacement

14 Place a container under the combination valve and protect all painted surfaces with newspapers or rags.

15 Disconnect the hydraulic lines at the combination valve, then plug the lines to prevent further loss of fluid and to protect the lines from contamination.

16 Disconnect the electrical connector from the pressure differential switch.

17 Remove the bolt holding the valve to the mounting bracket and remove the valve from the vehicle.

18 Installation is the reverse of the removal procedure.

19 Bleed the entire brake system.

9   Brake hoses and lines — inspection and replacement

Inspection

1   About every six months, with the vehicle raised and supported securely on jackstands, the rubber hoses which connect the steel brake lines with the front and rear brake assemblies should be inspected for cracks, chafing of the outer cover, leaks, blisters and other damage. These are important and vulnerable parts of the brake system and inspection should be complete. A light and mirror will be helpful for a thorough check. If a hose exhibits any of the above conditions, replace it with a new one.

9

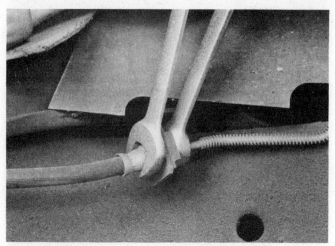

9.2   Place a wrench on the hose fitting to prevent it from turning and disconnect the line with a flare-nut wrench

Replacement

Front brake hose

Refer to illustration 9.2

2   Using a back-up wrench, disconnect the brake line from the hose fitting, being careful not to bend the frame bracket or brake line **(see illustration)**.
3   Use a pair of pliers to remove the U-clip from the female fitting at the bracket, then detach the hose from the bracket.
4   At the caliper end of the hose, remove the bolt from the fitting block, then remove the hose and the copper washers on either side of the fitting block.
5   When installing the hose, always use new copper washers on either side of the fitting block and lubricate all bolt threads with clean brake fluid before installation.
6   With the fitting flange engaged with the caliper locating ledge, attach the hose to the caliper.
7   Without twisting the hose, install the female fitting in the hose bracket. It will fit the bracket in only one position.
8   Install the U-clip retaining the female fitting to the frame bracket.
9   Using a back-up wrench, attach the brake line to the hose fitting.
10   When the brake hose installation is complete, there should be no kinks in the hose. Make sure the hose doesn't contact any part of the suspension. Check this by turning the wheels to the extreme left and right positions. If the hose makes contact, remove the hose and correct the installation as necessary.

Rear brake hose

11   Using a back-up wrench, disconnect the hose at the frame bracket, being careful not to bend the bracket or steel lines.
12   Remove the U-clip with a pair of pliers and separate the female fitting from the bracket.
13   Disconnect the two hydraulic lines at the junction block, then unbolt and remove the hose.
14   Without twisting the hose, install the female end of the hose in the frame bracket. It will fit the bracket in only one position. Bolt the junction block to the support bracket and connect the lines, tightening them securely.
15   Install the U-clips retaining the female end to the bracket.
16   Using a back-up wrench, attach the steel line fittings to the female fittings. Again, be careful not to bend the bracket or steel line.
17   Make sure the hose installation did not loosen the frame bracket. Tighten the bracket if necessary.
18   Fill the master cylinder reservoir and bleed the system (refer to Section 10).

Metal brake lines

19   When replacing brake lines be sure to use the correct parts. Don't use copper tubing for any brake system components. Purchase steel brake lines from a dealer or auto parts store.
20   Prefabricated brake line, with the tube ends already flared and fittings installed, is available at auto parts stores and dealers. These lines are also bent to the proper shapes.

21   If prefabricated lines are not available, obtain the recommended steel tubing and fittings to match the line to be replaced. Determine the correct length by measuring the old brake line (a piece of string can usually be used for this) and cut the new tubing to length, allowing about 1/2-inch extra for flaring the ends.
22   Install the fitting over the cut tubing and flare the ends of the line with a flaring tool.
23   If necessary, carefully bend the line to the proper shape. A tube bender is recommended for this. **Warning:** *Do not crimp or damage the line.*
24   When installing the new line make sure it's securely supported in the brackets and has plenty of clearance between moving or hot components.
25   After installation, check the master cylinder fluid level and add fluid as necessary. Bleed the brake system as outlined in the next Section and test the brakes carefully before driving the vehicle in traffic.

10 Brake system bleeding

Refer to illustration 10.8

Warning: *Wear eye protection when bleeding the brake system. If the fluid comes in contact with your eyes, immediately rinse them with water and seek medical attention.*

Note: *Bleeding the hydraulic system is necessary to remove any air that manages to find its way into the system when it's been opened during removal and installation of a hose, line, caliper or master cylinder.*

1   It will probably be necessary to bleed the system at all four brakes if air has entered the system due to low fluid level, or if the brake lines have been disconnected at the master cylinder.
2   If a brake line was disconnected only at a wheel, then only that caliper or wheel cylinder must be bled.
3   If a brake line is disconnected at a fitting located between the master cylinder and any of the brakes, that part of the system served by the disconnected line must be bled.
4   Remove any residual vacuum from the brake power booster by applying the brake several times with the engine off.
5   Remove the master cylinder reservoir cover and fill the reservoir with brake fluid. Reinstall the cover. **Note:** *Check the fluid level often during the bleeding operation and add fluid as necessary to prevent the fluid level from falling low enough to allow air bubbles into the master cylinder.*
6   Have an assistant on hand, as well as a supply of new brake fluid, an empty clear plastic container, a length of 3/16-inch plastic, rubber or vinyl tubing to fit over the bleeder valve and a wrench to open and close the bleeder valve.
7   Beginning at the right rear wheel, loosen the bleeder valve slightly, then tighten it to a point where it is snug but can still be loosened quickly and easily.
8   Place one end of the tubing over the bleeder valve and submerge the other end in brake fluid in the container **(see illustration)**.

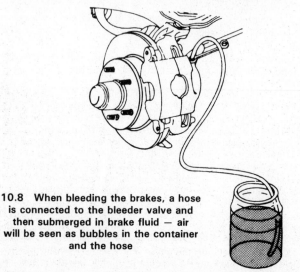

10.8   When bleeding the brakes, a hose is connected to the bleeder valve and then submerged in brake fluid — air will be seen as bubbles in the container and the hose

9 Have the assistant pump the brakes slowly a few times to get pressure in the system, then hold the pedal firmly depressed.

10 While the pedal is held depressed, open the bleeder valve just enough to allow a flow of fluid to leave the valve. Watch for air bubbles to exit the submerged end of the tube. When the fluid flow slows after a couple of seconds, close the valve and have your assistant release the pedal.

11 Repeat Steps 9 and 10 until no more air is seen leaving the tube, then tighten the bleeder valve and proceed to the left rear wheel, the right front wheel and the left front wheel, in that order, and perform the same procedure. Be sure to check the fluid in the master cylinder reservoir frequently.

12 Never use old brake fluid. It contains moisture which will deteriorate the brake system components.

13 Refill the master cylinder with fluid at the end of the operation.

14 Check the operation of the brakes. The pedal should feel solid when depressed, with no sponginess. If necessary, repeat the entire process.

Warning: *Do not operate the vehicle if you are in doubt about the effectiveness of the brake system.*

11 Parking brake — adjustment

Refer to illustration 11.4

1 Apply the parking brake lever exactly two ratchet clicks.

2 Raise the vehicle and support it securely on jackstands.

3 Before adjusting, make sure the equalizer nut groove is lubricated liberally with multi-purpose grease.

4 Tighten the adjusting nut (**see illustration**) until the left rear wheel can just be turned backwards with two hands, but locks when forward motion is attempted.

5 Release the parking brake lever and make sure the rear wheels turn freely in both directions with no drag.

6 Lower the vehicle.

12 Parking brake cables — replacement

Rear cables

Refer to illustrations 12.4 and 12.5

1 Loosen the wheel lug nuts, raise the rear of the vehicle and support it securely on jackstands. Remove the wheel(s).

2 Loosen the equalizer nut to slacken the cables, then disconnect

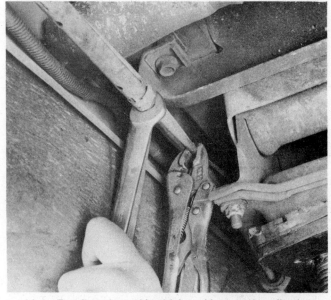

11.4 To adjust the parking brake cable, turn the adjusting nut on the equalizer while preventing the cable from turning with a pair of locking pliers clamped to the end of the adjuster rod

the cable to be replaced from the equalizer.

3 Remove the brake drum from the axle flange. Refer to Section 5 if any difficulty is encountered.

4 Remove the brake shoe assembly far enough to disconnect the cable end from the parking brake lever (**see illustration**).

5 Depress the tangs on the cable housing retainer and push the housing and cable through the backing plate (**see illustration**).

6 To install the cable, reverse the removal procedure and adjust the cable as described in the preceding Section.

Front cable

Refer to illustration 12.9

7 Raise the vehicle and support it securely on jackstands.

8 Loosen the equalizer assembly to provide slack in the cable.

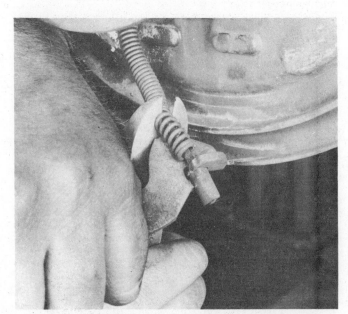

12.4 To disconnect the cable end from the parking brake lever, pull back on the return spring and maneuver the cable out of the slot in the lever

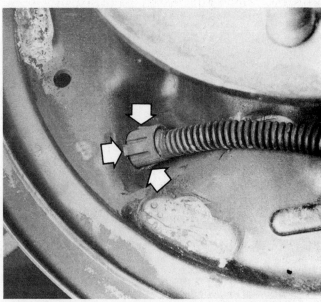

12.5 Depress the retention tangs (arrows) to free the cable and housing from the backing plate

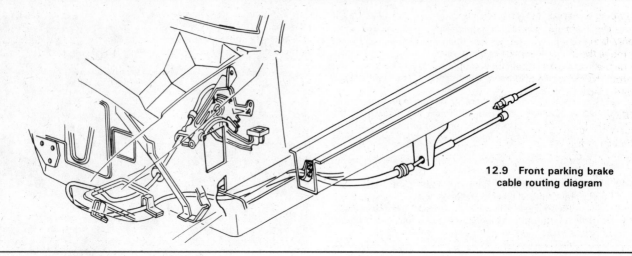

12.9   Front parking brake
cable routing diagram

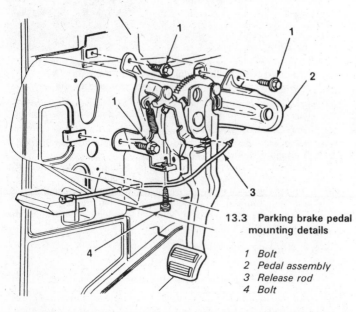

13.3   Parking brake pedal
mounting details

1 Bolt
2 Pedal assembly
3 Release rod
4 Bolt

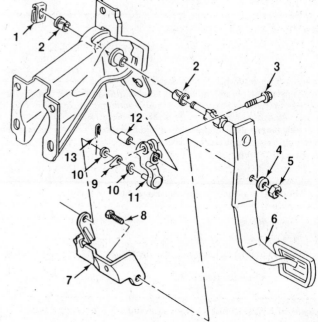

14.2   Brake pedal mounting details

1 Retaining clip	8 Bolt
2 Bushing	9 Pushrod
3 Pinch bolt	10 Washer
4 Washer	11 Actuator lever
5 Nut	12 Spacer
6 Brake pedal	13 Retaining clip
7 Actuator	

9   Disconnect the front cable from the cable joiner near the equalizer **(see illustration)**.
10 Disconnect the cable from the pedal assembly.
11 Free the cable from the routing clips and push the cable and
grommet through the firewall.
12 To install the cable, reverse the removal procedure and adjust
the cable as described in the preceding Section.

13   Parking brake pedal – removal and installation

Refer to illustration 13.3

1   Disconnect the cable from the negative terminal of the battery.
2   Refer to Chapter 11 and remove the instrument panel and dash
assembly.
3   Disconnect the release rod from the pedal assembly **(see illustration)**.
4   Unplug the electrical connector from the parking brake switch.
5   Remove the three pedal mechanism mounting bolts.
6   Disconnect the parking brake cable then depress the tangs on
the cable housing, pushing the housing through the pedal bracket.
7   Remove the pedal assembly.
8   To install the pedal assembly, reverse the removal procedure
and adjust the parking brake cable as outlined in Section 11.

14   Brake pedal – removal and installation

Refer to illustration 14.2
Note: *On vehicles equipped with a manual transmission, the clutch
pedal must be removed first. Refer to Chapter 8 for the clutch pedal
removal and installation procedure.*

Removal

1   Disconnect the cable from the negative battery terminal.
2   Remove the actuator-to-brake pedal nut and bolt **(see illustration)**.

3   Remove the master cylinder pushrod
retaining clip from the actuator lever and slide the pushrod and
washers off the pin.
4   Remove the actuator lever pinch bolt.
5   Slide the brake pedal retaining clip off the pivot pin and pull the
pedal from the mounting bracket. Note how the bushings, actuator
lever and spacers are situated.

Installation

6   Insert the pedal pivot bushings into the mounting bracket, position the actuator lever and spacer between the two bushings and
slide the brake pedal pivot pin through them. Install the retaining
clip.
7   Install the actuator lever pinch bolt and tighten it securely.
8   Attach the master cylinder pushrod to the actuator lever (with a
washer on each side of it) and install the clip. Insert the actuator-to-
brake pedal bolt and tighten the nut securely.

---

15   Power brake booster – inspection, removal and installation

1   The power brake booster unit requires no special maintenance
apart from periodic inspection of the vacuum hose and the case.
2   Dismantling of the power unit requires special tools and is not
ordinarily done by the home mechanic. If a problem develops, install
a new or factory rebuilt unit.
3   Remove the nuts attaching the master cylinder to the booster
and carefully pull the master cylinder forward until it clears the
mounting studs. Don't bend or kink the brake lines.
4   Disconnect the vacuum hose where it attaches to the power
brake booster.
5   From the passenger compartment, disconnect the power brake
pushrod from the top of the brake pedal.
6   Also from this location, remove the nuts attaching the booster to
the firewall.
7   Carefully lift the booster unit away from the firewall and out of
the engine compartment.
8   Place the booster in position and tighten the nuts. Connect the
brake pedal.
9   Install the master cylinder and vacuum hose.
10   Carefully test the operation of the brakes before placing the vehicle in normal service.

---

16   Brake light switch - removal, installation and adjustment

Refer to illustration 16.3

Removal

Caution: *If the vehicle is equipped with a Delco Loc II audio system
(1992 and later models with a Compact Disc player), be sure the lockout feature is turned off before performing any procedure that requires
disconnecting the battery (refer to your owner's manual for further information on this system).*
1   The brake light switch is located on a bracket at the top of the
brake pedal. The switch activates the brake lights at the rear of the vehicle whenever the pedal is depressed.
2   Disconnect the negative battery cable and secure it out of the
way so it cannot come into contact with the battery terminal.
3   Locate the switch at the top of the brake pedal **(see illustration)**.
If equipped with cruise control, there will be another switch very similar
in appearance. The brake light switch is the one on the left of the
bracket.
4   Disconnect the wire harnesses at the brake light switch.
5   Depress the brake pedal and pull the switch out of the clip. The
switch appears to be threaded, but it's designed to be pushed into
and out of the clip and not turned.

Installation and adjustment

6   With the brake pedal depressed, push the new switch into the
clip. Note that audible clicks will be heard as this is done.

7   Pull the brake pedal all the way to the rear against the pedal stop
until the clicking sounds can no longer be heard. This action will automatically move the switch the proper amount and no further adjustment will be required. **Note:** *Do not apply excessive force during
this adjustment procedure, as power booster damage may result.*
8   Connect the wires at the switch and the battery. Have an assistant check that the rear brake lights are functioning properly.

---

17   Anti-lock brake system – general information

Refer to illustrations 17.4a and 17.4b

Description

The Anti-lock brake system is designed to maintain vehicle ma-
neuverability, directional stability and optimum deceleration under
severe braking conditions on most road surfaces. It does so by monitoring the rotational speed of the wheels and controlling the brake
line pressure during braking. This prevents the wheels from locking
up prematurely.
Two types of systems are used: Rear Wheel Anti-Lock (RWAL) and
Four Wheel Anti-Lock (4WAL). RWAL only controls lockup on the rear
wheels, whereas 4WAL prevents lockup on all four wheels.

Components

Actuator assembly

The actuator assembly includes the master cylinder and a control
valve which consists of a dump valve and an isolation valve. The
valve operates by changing the brake fluid pressure in response to
signals from the control unit.

Control unit

The control unit for the anti-lock brakes is called the Electro-Hy-
draulic Control Unit (EHCU) on 4WAL systems and Control module
on RWAL systems. The unit is mounted in the engine compartment
below the master cylinder and is the "brain" for the system **(see illustrations)**. The function of the control unit is to accept and process information received from the speed sensor(s) and brake light switch
to control the hydraulic line pressure, avoiding wheel lockup. The
control unit also constantly monitors the system, even under normal
driving conditions, to find faults within the system.
If a problem develops within the system, the BRAKE (RWAL system) or ANTI-LOCK (4WAL system) warning light will glow on the
dashboard. A diagnostic code will also be stored, which, when re-
trieved by a service technician, will indicate the problem area or component.

Speed sensor

On 4WAL systems, each wheel has a speed sensor. On RWAL systems, a rear wheel speed sensor is located in the transmission extension housing on 2WD models and in the transfer case on All-Wheel
Drive models. The speed sensor(s) sends a signal to the control unit
indicating wheel rotational speed.

**16.3   Unplug the brake light switch electrical connectors
(arrows) and pull the switch out of the mounting bracket**

9

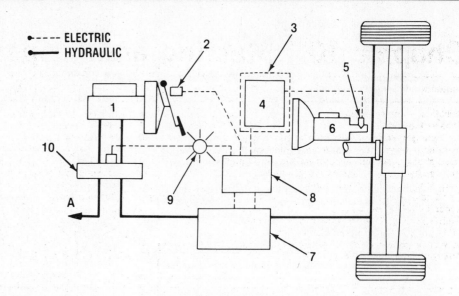

● - - - - ELECTRIC
●———— HYDRAULIC

**17.4a Rear wheel anti-lock
brake system diagram**

  A   To front brakes
  1   Master cylinder
  2   Brake light switch
  3   Instrument cluster
  4   Digital ratio adapter (part of
      instrument cluster)
  5   Speed sensor
  6   Transmission
  7   Isolation/dump valve
  8   RWAL control unit
  9   Brake warning light
 10   Combination valve

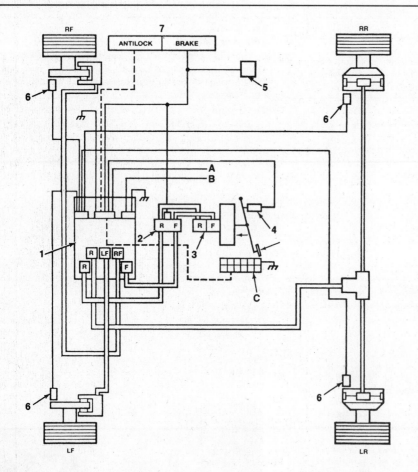

**17.4b – Four wheel anti-lock
brake system diagram**

  A   To ignition switch (B+)
  B   To battery (B+)
  C   Assembly line diagnostic
      link (ALDL)
  1   4WAL EHCU valve
  2   Combination valve
  3   Master cylinder
  4   Brake pedal switch
  5   Parking brake switch
  6   Wheel speed sensors
  7   Warning lights

Brake light switch

The brake light switch signals the control unit when the driver steps on the brake pedal. Without this signal the anti-lock system won't activate.

Diagnosis and repair

If the BRAKE or ANTI-LOCK warning light on the dashboard comes on and stays on, make sure the parking brake is released and there's no problem with the brake hydraulic system. If neither of these is the cause, the anti-lock system is probably malfunctioning. Although special test procedures are necessary to properly diagnose

the system, the home mechanic can perform a few preliminary checks before taking the vehicle to a dealer service department.

  a) Make sure the brakes, calipers and wheel cylinders are in good condition.
  b) Check the electrical connectors at the control unit.
  c) Check the fuses.
  d) Follow the wiring harness to the speed sensor(s) and brake light switch and make sure all connections are secure and the wiring isn't damaged.

If the above preliminary checks don't rectify the problem, the vehicle should be diagnosed by a dealer service department.

Chapter 10   Steering and suspension systems

Contents

Specifications

Front suspension

Torque specifications	Ft-lbs
Upper control arm-to-frame nuts	
1985 through 1987	66
1988 on	75
Lower control arm pivot bolt nuts	96
Replacement balljoint-to-upper control arm bolts	
1985 through 1988	8
1989	17
1990	22
1991 and 1992	17
1993	22
Lower balljoint-to-steering knuckle nut	
1985 through 1987	81
1988 on	90
Upper balljoint-to-steering knuckle nut	
1985 through 1987	52
1988 on	65

Rear suspension

Torque specifications	Ft-lbs
Spring retainer-to-hanger assembly nuts	18 to 28
Hanger assembly-to-frame nuts	81
Shackle nuts (all through 1988)	81
Shackle-to-spring nuts	
1989 through 1992	103
1993	81
Shackle-to-frame nuts (1989 on)	81
U-bolt-to-anchor plate nuts	
1989 through 1992	48
1993	52
Lower plate-to-anchor plate nuts	114

Steering

Torque specifications	Ft-lbs
Steering wheel-to-steering shaft nut	30
Intermediate shaft pinch bolts	30
Steering gear-to-frame bolts	
1985	70
1986 on	55
Tie-rod end-to-steering knuckle nut	30 to 35
Tie-rod adjuster tube clamp nuts	13
Tie-rod-to-relay rod	
1985 through 1987	66
1988 on	35
Idler arm-to-relay rod	
1985 through 1987	66
1988 on	35

1   General Information

Warning 1: *Whenever any of the suspension or steering fasteners are loosened or removed they must be inspected and if necessary, replaced with new ones of the same part number or of original equipment quality and design. Torque specifications must be followed for proper reassembly and component retention. Never attempt to heat; straighten or weld any suspension or steering component. Instead, replace any bent or damaged part with a new one.*

Warning 2: *Later models may be equipped with airbags. Impact sensors for the airbag system are located in the area of the radiator support/grille. The airbag(s) could accidently deploy if these sensors are disturbed, so be extremely careful when working in this area. Air bag system components are also located in the steering wheel, steering column and base of the steering column, so be extremely careful in these areas and don't disturb any airbag system components or wiring. You could easily be injured if an airbag accidently deploys, and the airbag might not deploy correctly in a collision if any components or wiring in the system have been disturbed.*

Caution: *If the vehicle is equipped with a Delco Loc II audio system (1992 and later models with a Compact Disc player), be sure the lockout feature is turned off before performing any procedure that requires disconnecting the battery (refer to your owner's manual for further information on this system).*

The front suspension is independent, allowing each wheel to compensate for road surface changes without appreciably affecting the other **(see illustration)**. Each wheel is connected to the frame by a steering knuckle, balljoints and upper and lower control arms. Each side uses a coil spring mounted between the lower control arm and the frame. Shock absorbers are positioned in the center of the coil spring, with the upper end fastened to the chassis and the lower end bolted to the lower control arm. Body side roll is controlled by a stabilizer bar.

The rear suspension is comprised of the axle, two composite single leaf springs, shock absorbers and an optional stabilizer bar **(see illustration)**. The front of each leaf spring is anchored to the chassis by a hanger assembly, while the rear is attached to a moveable shackle.

The steering system consists of the steering wheel, steering column, an articulated intermediate shaft, the steering gear (either power or manual), power steering pump and the steering linkage.

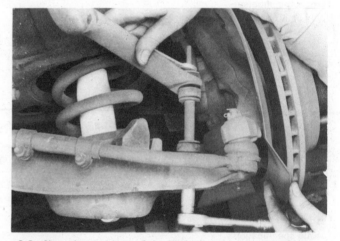

2.2   Note the positions of the bushings, spacers and washers before removing the stabilizer bar-to-control arm nut/bolt

2   Front stabilizer bar — removal and installation

Refer to illustrations 2.2 and 2.3

Removal

1   Raise the vehicle and support it securely on jackstands. Apply the parking brake.

2   Remove the stabilizer bar-to-lower control arm nuts and bolts, noting how the spacers, washers and bushings are positioned **(see illustration)**.

3   Remove the stabilizer bar bracket bolts and detach the bar from the vehicle **(see illustration)**.

4   Pull the brackets off the stabilizer bar and inspect the bushings for cracks, hardening and other signs of deterioration. If the bushings are damaged, replace them.

Installation

5   Position the stabilizer bar bushings on the bar with the slits facing the front of the vehicle. **Note:** *the offset in the bar must face down.*

2.3   Remove the stabilizer bar bracket bolts — the nuts are welded to the frame, so there's no need to put a wrench on them to prevent them from turning

1.1 Front suspension components

1 Stabilizer bar
2 Relay rod
3 Connecting rod
4 Pitman arm

5 Steering gear
6 Idler arm
7 Upper control arm

8 Upper suspension balljoint
9 Shock absorber
10 Steering knuckle

11 Coil spring
12 Lower suspension balljoint
13 Lower control arm
14 Tie-rod

10

1.2 Rear suspension components

1 Composite leaf spring   3 Rear axle tube   5 U-bolt
2 Shock absorber   4 Lower plate   6 Anchor plate

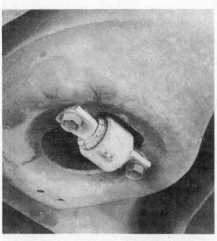

3.3 The bottom of the shock absorber is bolted to the lower control arm

4.4 A special tool (GM tool J-23742) is required to push the balljoints out of the steering knuckle (an alternative tool can be fabricated from a large bolt, nut, washer and socket)

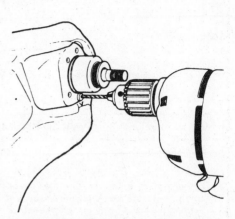

4.5 Drill into the balljoint rivets with a 1/8-inch drill bit, then use a 1/2-inch drill bit to cut the rivet heads off — be careful not to enlarge the holes in the control arm

6   Push the brackets over the bushings and raise the bar up to the frame. Install the bracket bolts but don't tighten them completely at this time.
7   Install the stabilizer bar-to-lower control arm bolts, washers, spacers and rubber bushings and tighten the nuts securely.
8   Tighten the bracket bolts.

3   Front shock absorbers — removal and installation

Refer to illustration 3.3

Removal

1   Loosen the wheel lug nuts, raise the vehicle and support it securely on jackstands. Apply the parking brake. Remove the wheel.
2   Remove the upper shock absorber stem nut. Use an open end wrench to keep the stem from turning. If the nut won't loosen because of rust, squirt some penetrating oil on the stem threads and allow it to soak in for awhile. It may be necessary to keep the stem from turning with a pair of locking pliers, since the flats provided for a wrench are quite small.
3   Remove the two lower shock mount bolts **(see illustration)** and pull the shock absorber out through the bottom of the lower control arm. Remove the washers and the rubber grommets from the top of the shock absorber.

Installation

4   Extend the new shock absorber as far as possible. Position a new washer and rubber grommet on the stem and guide the shock up through the coil spring and into the upper mount.
5   Install the upper rubber grommet and washer and wiggle the stem back-and-forth to ensure that the grommets are centered in the mount. Tighten the stem nut securely.
6   Install the lower mounting bolts and tighten them securely.

4   Balljoints — replacement

Refer to illustrations 4.4, 4.5 and 4.8

Upper balljoint

1   Loosen the wheel lug nuts, raise the vehicle and support it securely on jackstands. Apply the parking brake. Remove the wheel.
2   Place a jack or a jackstand under the lower control arm. **Note:** *The jack or jackstand must remain under the control arm during removal and installation of the balljoint to hold the spring and control arm in position.*
3   Remove the cotter pin from the balljoint stud and back off the nut two turns.

4   Separate the balljoint from the steering knuckle (use GM tool no. J-23742 or equivalent to press the balljoint out of the steering knuckle) **(see illustration)**. An equivalent tool can be fabricated from a large bolt, nut, washer and socket. Countersink the center of the bolt head with a large drill bit to prevent it from slipping off the balljoint stud. Install the tool as shown in the illustration, hold the bolt head with a wrench and tighten the nut against the washer until the balljoint pops out. Notice that the balljoint nut hasn't been completely removed.
5   Using a 1/8-inch drill bit, drill a 1/4-inch deep hole in the center of each rivet head **(see illustration)**.
6   Using a 1/2-inch diameter drill bit, drill off the rivet heads.
7   Use a punch to knock the rivet shanks out, then remove the balljoint from the control arm.
8   Position the new balljoint on the control arm and install the bolts and nuts supplied in the kit **(see illustration)**. Be sure to tighten the nuts to the torque specified on the balljoint kit instruction sheet.
9   Insert the balljoint stud into the steering knuckle and install the nut, tightening it to the specified torque.
10   Install a new cotter pin, tightening the nut slightly if necessary to align a slot in the nut with the hole in the balljoint stud.
11   Install the balljoint grease fitting and fill the joint with grease.

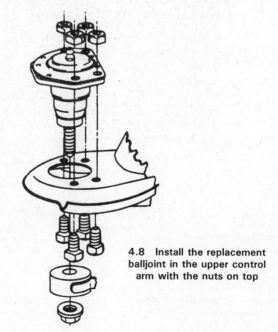

4.8 Install the replacement balljoint in the upper control arm with the nuts on top

10

12　Install the wheel, tightening the lug nuts to the specified torque.
13　Drive the vehicle to an alignment shop to have the front end alignment checked and, if necessary, adjusted.

Lower balljoint

14　The lower balljoint is a press fit in the lower control arm and requires special tools to remove and replace it. Refer to Section 6, remove the lower control arm and take it to an automotive machine shop to have the old balljoint pressed out and the new balljoint pressed in.

5　Upper control arm — removal and installation

Refer to illustration 5.4

Removal

1　Loosen the wheel lug nuts, raise the front of the vehicle and support it securely on jackstands. Apply the parking brake. Remove the wheel.
2　Support the lower control arm with a jack or jackstand. The support point must be as close to the balljoint as possible to give maximum leverage on the lower control arm.
3　Disconnect the upper balljoint from the steering knuckle (refer to Section 4). **Note:** *DO NOT use a ''pickle fork'' type balljoint separator — it may damage the balljoint seals.*
4　Remove the control arm-to-frame nuts and bolts, recording the position of any alignment shims. They must be reinstalled in the same location to maintain wheel alignment **(see illustration)**.

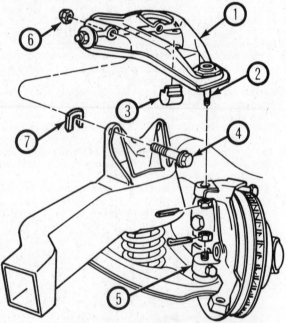

5.4　Upper control arm mounting details (note the positions of the alignment shims and return them to their original positions)

1　Upper control arm	5　Steering knuckle
2　Upper balljoint	6　Nut
3　Bumper	7　Alignment shim
4　Bolt	

5　Detach the control arm from the vehicle. **Note:** *The control arm bushings are pressed into place and require special tools for removal and installation. If the bushings must be replaced, take the control arm to a dealer service department or an automotive machine shop to have the old bushings pressed out and the new ones pressed in.*

Installation

6　Position the control arm on the frame and install the bolts and nuts. Install any alignment shims that were removed. Tighten the nuts to the specified torque.
7　Insert the balljoint stud into the steering knuckle and tighten the

nut to the specified torque. Install a new cotter pin, tightening the nut slightly, if necessary, to align a slot in the nut with the hole in the balljoint stud.
8　Install the wheel and lug nuts and lower the vehicle. Tighten the lug nuts to the specified torque.
9　Drive the vehicle to an alignment shop to have the front end alignment checked and, if necessary, adjusted.

6　Lower control arm — removal and installation

Refer to illustration 6.6

Removal

1　Loosen the wheel lug nuts, raise the vehicle and support it securely on jackstands. Apply the parking brake. Remove the wheel.
2　Unbolt the shock absorber from the lower control arm and push it up into the coil spring.
3　Disconnect the stabilizer bar from the lower control arm (Section 2).
4　Remove the coil spring as described in Section 8.
5　Remove the cotter pin and back off the lower control arm balljoint stud nut two turns. Using GM tool no. J-23742, break the balljoint loose from the steering knuckle and remove the nut.
6　Remove the control arm from the vehicle **(see illustration)**. **Note:** *The control arm bushings are pressed into place and require special tools for removal and installation. If the bushings must be replaced, take the control arm to a dealer service department or an automotive machine shop to have the old bushings pressed out and the new ones pressed in.*

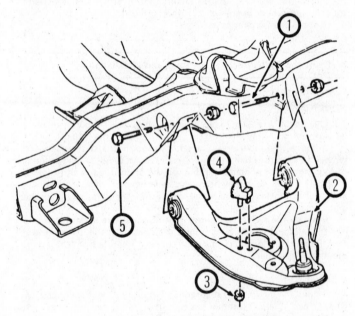

6.6　Lower control arm mounting details

1　Pivot bolt	4　Bumper
2　Lower control arm	5　Pivot bolt
3　Nut	

Installation

7　Insert the balljoint stud into the steering knuckle, tighten the nut to the specified torque and install a new cotter pin. If necessary, tighten the nut slightly to align a slot in the nut with the hole in the balljoint stud.
8　Install the coil spring (Section 8) and the lower control arm pivot bolts and nuts, but don't completely tighten them at this time.
9　Connect the stabilizer bar to the lower control arm.
10　Install the wheel and lug nuts, lower the vehicle and tighten the lug nuts to the specified torque.
11　With the vehicle at normal ride height, tighten the lower control arm pivot bolt nuts to the specified torque.
12　Drive the vehicle to an alignment shop to have the front end alignment checked and, if necessary, adjusted.

7 Steering knuckle — removal and installation

Removal

1 Loosen the wheel lug nuts, raise the vehicle and support it securely on jackstands placed under the frame. Apply the parking brake. Remove the wheel.

2 Remove the brake caliper and place it on top of the upper control arm (see Chapter 9 if necessary).

3 Remove the brake rotor and hub assembly (see Chapter 1).

4 Remove the splash shield from the steering knuckle.

5 Separate the tie-rod end from the steering arm (see Section 17).

6 If the steering knuckle must be replaced, remove the dust seal from the spindle by prying it off with a screwdriver. If it's damaged, replace it with a new one.

7 Position a floor jack under the lower control arm and raise it slightly to take the spring pressure off the suspension stop. The jack must remain in this position throughout the entire procedure.

8 Remove the cotter pins from the upper and lower balljoint studs and back off the nuts two turns each.

9 Break the balljoints loose from the steering knuckle with GM tool no. J-23742 or an equivalent balljoint separator. **Note:** *A pickle fork type balljoint separator may damage the balljoint seals.*

10 Remove the nuts from the balljoint studs, separate the control arms from the steering knuckle and remove the knuckle from the vehicle.

Installation

11 Place the knuckle between the upper and lower control arms and insert the balljoint studs into the knuckle, beginning with the lower balljoint. Install the nuts and tighten them to the specified torque. Install new cotter pins, tightening the nuts slightly to align the slots in the nuts with the holes in the balljoint studs, if necessary.

12 Install the splash shield.

13 Connect the tie-rod end to the steering arm and tighten the nut to the specified torque. Be sure to use a new cotter pin.

14 Install the brake rotor and adjust the wheel bearings following the procedure outlined in Chapter 1.

15 Install the brake caliper.

16 Install the wheel and lug nuts. Lower the vehicle to the ground and tighten the nuts to the specified torque.

8 Coil spring — removal and installation

Refer to illustration 8.4

Removal

1 Loosen the wheel lug nuts, raise the vehicle and support it securely on jackstands placed under the frame. Apply the parking brake. Remove the wheel.

2 Remove the lower shock absorber mounting bolts and push the shock absorber up into the control arm as far as possible.

3 Disconnect the stabilizer bar from the lower control arm (Section 2).

4 Position a jack equipped with GM tool no. J-23028 under the lower control arm bushings **(see illustration)**. **Warning:** *Failure to use this tool could result in severe injury.*

5 Loop a length of safety chain up through the control arm and coil spring and bolt the ends of the chain together. Make sure there's

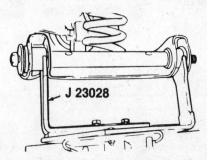

8.4 This fixture, GM tool no. J-23028, attaches to a floor jack and cradles the lower control arm under the bushings — it *must be used* to safely remove the coil spring!

enough slack in the chain so it won't inhibit spring extension when the control arm is lowered.

6 Raise the jack slightly to relieve spring pressure from the control arm pivot bolts and remove the bolts and nuts.

7 Slowly lower the jack until the coil spring is fully extended.

8 Unbolt the safety chain and maneuver the coil spring out. Do not apply downward pressure on the lower control arm as it may damage the balljoint. If the upper coil spring insulator is not on the top of the spring, reach up in the spring pocket and retrieve it.

Installation

9 Place the insulator on top of the coil spring (the top of the spring is flat on the end, with a gripper notch near the end of the spring coil).

10 Install the top of the spring into the spring pocket and the bottom in the lower control arm. The end of the lower spring coil must cover all or part of one drain hole, while the other drain hole must remain unobstructed.

11 Place the jack with GM tool no. J-23028 attached to it under the lower control arm bushings and slowly raise the control arm into place. When the bolt holes are aligned, install the bolts with the bolt heads towards the front of the vehicle. Do not completely tighten the nuts at this time.

12 Pull the shock absorber down through the control arm and install the mounting bolts, tightening them securely.

13 Attach the stabilizer bar to the lower control arm (Section 2).

14 Install the wheel and lug nuts. Lower the vehicle and tighten the lug nuts to the specified torque.

15 Reach under the vehicle and tighten the lower control arm pivot bolt nuts to the specified torque.

16 Drive the vehicle to an alignment shop to have the front end alignment checked and, if necessary, adjusted.

9 Rear stabilizer bar — removal and installation

Refer to illustration 9.2

1 Raise the rear of the vehicle and support it securely on jackstands. Block the front wheels to keep the vehicle from rolling.

2 Remove the upper link-to-frame bracket bolts **(see illustration)**.

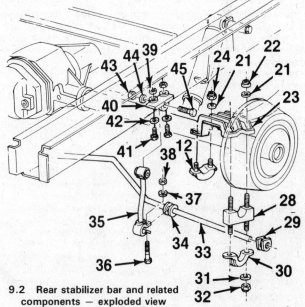

9.2 Rear stabilizer bar and related components — exploded view

12 Lower plate	31 Washer	39 Rivnuts
21 Washer	32 Nut	40 Link bracket
22 Nut	33 Stabilizer bar	41 Bolt
23 Anchor plate	34 Link insulator	42 Washer
24 Nut	35 Link assembly	43 Nut
28 Anchor block	36 Bolt	44 Washer
29 Insulator	37 Washer	45 Bolt
30 Clamp	38 Nut	

10

10.2a   The left side lower shock absorber mount (if the vehicle is equipped with gas-filled shock absorbers it may be necessary to raise the shock with a jack to insert the bolt through the mounting hole)

3   Remove the nuts and clamps from the anchor block studs and detach the stabilizer bar from the vehicle.
4   Inspect all of the rubber bushings and grommets for cracks, hardening and general deterioration, replacing any faulty components as necessary.
5   Installation is the reverse of the removal procedure.

10   Rear shock absorbers — removal and installation

Refer to illustrations 10.2a and 10.2b

1   Raise the rear of the vehicle and support it securely on jackstands. Block the front wheels to keep the vehicle from rolling.
2   Remove the shock absorber lower mounting nut and bolt. On the right side shock absorber, remove the parking brake cable bracket **(see illustrations).**
3   Remove the shock absorber upper mounting nut and slide the shock absorber off the bolt that protrudes through the frame.
4   Installation is the reverse of the removal procedure.

11.2   The bumper bracket must be removed to allow the lower shackle bolt to be pulled out

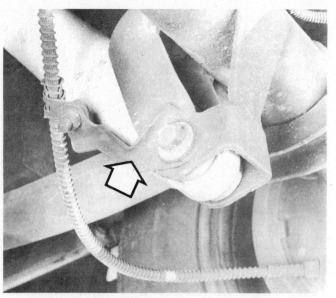

10.2b   The right side lower shock absorber mounting bolt also holds the right parking brake cable bracket

11   Leaf spring — removal and installation

Caution: *The leaf springs are constructed of a fiberglass composite material. Be extremely careful not to scratch or gouge the spring when working near it, as spring failure may occur during vehicle operation.*

Removal

Refer to illustrations 11.2, 11.5, 11.6, 11.8a and 11.8b

1   Raise the rear of the vehicle and support it securely on jackstands placed underneath the frame. Block the front wheels to keep the vehicle from rolling.
2   Remove the bumper bracket **(see illustration)**
3   Remove the shock absorber lower mounting bolt (Section 10).
4   Support the rear axle assembly with a floor jack positioned under the axle tube on the side being worked on.
5   Remove the U-bolt nuts and the lower plate nuts **(see illustration)**.
6   Remove the anchor plate **(see illustration)**, then lower the jack just enough to relieve spring pressure on the axle. Make sure the axle doesn't stretch the brake hose.

11.5   Remove the U-bolt nuts and the lower plate nuts (arrows), . . .

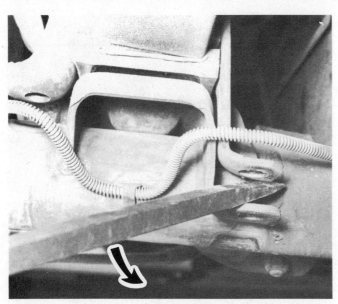

11.6 . . . then pry the anchor plate off the spring and axle

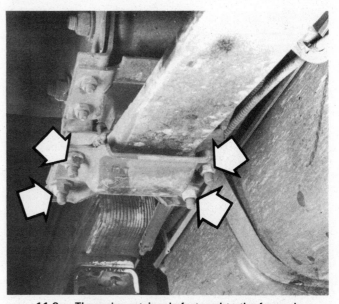

11.8a The spring retainer is fastened to the forward spring hanger with four nuts (arrows)

7   Loosen, but don't remove the shackle nuts.
8   Remove the four spring retainer nuts, then pry the retainer off **(see illustrations)**.
9   Allow the spring to hang down and remove the lower spring-to-shackle nut, washers and bolt. Detach the spring from the vehicle.

Installation

Refer to illustrations 11.12 and 11.14

10 Insert the rear of the spring into the shackle and install the bolt, washers and nut. Don't tighten the nut at this time.
11 Place the other end of the spring into the spring hanger and install the retainer, washers and nuts. Tighten the nuts to the specified torque.
12 Raise the axle to the spring, ensuring that the locating lug on the spring engages with the pocket on the axle **(see illustration)**.
13 Install the anchor plate over the top of the spring. Position the U-bolt and lower plate and install the nuts and bolts, tightening them to the specified torque.
14 Raise the rear axle until the top of the axle is 5.9-inches (150 mm) from the bottom of the frame **(see illustration)**, then tighten the shackle nuts to the specified torque. This adjusts the rear suspension trim height.
15 Install the shock absorber.

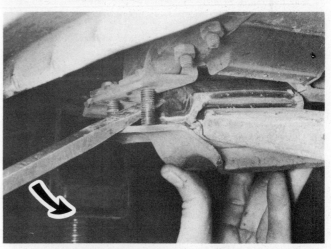

11.8b Carefully pry the spring retainer off (pry between the retainer and hanger, not against the spring)

11.12 When raising the axle into position, the lug on the spring must engage with the pocket in the axle

11.14 Before tightening the shackle nuts, raise the axle until the distance between the axle and the frame is 5.9-inches

10

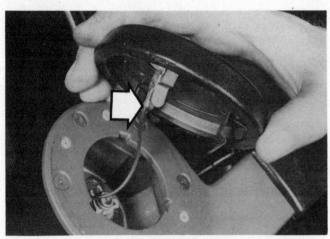

12.2   The horn pad is removed by gripping it firmly and pulling it from the steering wheel — detach the horn wire (arrow)

12.3   A pair of snap-ring pliers can be used to remove the safety clip from the shaft

12.4   Check to be sure that there are alignment marks on the steering shaft and steering wheel (arrow) — if there aren't any or if they don't match up, scribe or paint a line from the shaft to the steering wheel

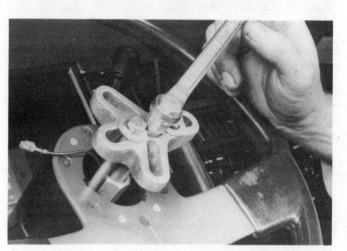

12.5   Remove the wheel from the shaft with a puller — DO NOT hammer on the shaft!

12   Steering wheel – removal and installation

Refer to illustrations 12.2, 12.3, 12.4 and 12.5

Warning: *If the vehicle is equipped with an airbag (supplemental restraint system), do not attempt to remove the steering wheel, since personal injury or damage to the airbag components could result. Take the vehicle to a dealer service department that's equipped to service this system.*

1   Disconnect the cable from the negative terminal of the battery.
2   Pull the horn pad from the steering wheel and disconnect the wire to the horn switch **(see illustration)**.
3   Remove the safety clip from the steering shaft **(see illustration)**.
4   Remove the steering wheel retaining nut then mark the relationship of the steering shaft to the hub (if marks don't already exist or don't line up) to simplify installation and ensure steering wheel alignment **(see illustration)**.
5   Use a puller to disconnect the steering wheel from the shaft **(see illustration)**.
6   To install the wheel, align the mark on the steering wheel hub with the mark on the shaft and slip the wheel onto the shaft. Install the hub nut and tighten it to the specified torque. Install the safety clip.

7   Connect the horn wire and install the horn pad.
8   Connect the negative battery cable.

13   Intermediate shaft – removal and installation

Refer to illustration 13.2

Warning: *On models equipped with airbags, make sure that the steering shaft is not turned while the intermediate shaft is removed or you could damage the airbag system. One way to prevent the shaft from turning is to run the seat belt through the steering wheel and clip the seat belt into place.*

1   Turn the front wheels to the straight ahead position.
2   Using white paint, place alignment marks on the upper universal joint, the steering shaft, the lower universal joint and the steering gear input shaft **(see illustration)**.
3   Remove the upper and lower universal joint pinch bolts.
4   Remove the steering gear-to-frame mounting bolts (Section 14) and lower the steering gear enough to allow intermediate shaft removal.
5   Pry the intermediate shaft off the steering shaft with a large screwdriver, then pull the shaft from the steering gearbox in the same manner.
6   Installation is the reverse of the removal procedure. Be sure to align the marks and tighten the pinch bolts to the specified torque.

13.2   Mark the relationship of the intermediate shaft to the steering shaft and also to the steering gear input shaft

14.2   The power steering pressure and return line fittings (arrows) can be reached from under the vehicle

14.4   Place alignment marks on the Pitman arm and the shaft, then remove the nut and washer

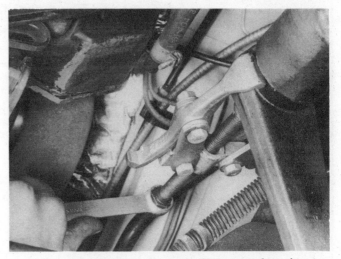

14.5   Use a puller to remove the Pitman arm from the Pitman shaft

14   Steering gear – removal and installation

Refer to illustrations 14.2, 14.4 and 14.5

Warning: *On models equipped with airbags, make sure that the steering shaft is not turned while the steering gear is removed or you could damage the airbag system. One way to prevent the shaft from turning is to run the seat belt through the steering wheel and clip the seat belt into place.*

Removal

1   Raise the front of the vehicle and support it securely on jackstands. Apply the parking brake.

2   Place a drain pan under the steering gear (power steering only). Remove the power steering pressure and return lines and cap the ends to prevent excessive fluid loss and contamination **(see illustration)**.

3   Mark the relationship of the lower intermediate shaft universal joint to the steering gear input shaft. Remove the lower intermediate shaft pinch bolt.

4   Mark the relationship of the Pitman arm to the Pitman shaft so it can be installed in the same position **(see illustration)**. Remove the nut and washer.

5   Remove the Pitman arm from the shaft with a two-jaw puller **(see illustration)**.

6   Support the steering gear and remove the steering gear-to-frame mounting bolts. Lower the unit, separate the intermediate shaft from the steering gear input shaft and remove the steering gear from the vehicle.

Installation

7   Raise the steering gear into position and connect the intermediate shaft, aligning the marks.

8   Install the mounting bolts and washers and tighten them to the specified torque.

9   Slide the Pitman arm onto the Pitman shaft, ensuring that the marks are aligned. Install the washer and nut and tighten the nut to the specified torque.

10   Install the lower intermediate shaft pinch bolt and tighten it to the specified torque.

11   Connect the power steering pressure and return hoses to the steering gear and fill the power steering pump reservoir with the recommended fluid (Chapter 1).

12   Lower the vehicle and bleed the steering system as outlined in Section 16.

10

5   Power steering pump- removal and installation

Refer to illustrations 15.3, 15.4a and 15.4b

Removal

1   Disconnect the cable from the negative terminal of the battery.
2   Place a drain pan under the power steering pump. Remove the drivebelt.
3   On 1990 and earlier V6 engines only, remove the pump rear brace **(see illustration)**.
4   Remove the pump mounting bolts **(see illustrations)** and move the pump out to gain access to the power steering hose connections. Dis-

connect the hoses from the pump and plug the ends to prevent contaminants from entering.
5   Remove the pump from the vehicle, taking care not to spill fluid on the painted surfaces.

Installation

6   Connect the hoses to the pump. Tighten the fittings securely.
7   Position the pump in the mounting bracket and install the bolts. Tighten the bolts securely.
8   On V6 engines only, install the rear brace and tighten the nut and bolts.
9   Fill the power steering reservoir with the recommended fluid and bleed the system following the procedure described in the next Section.

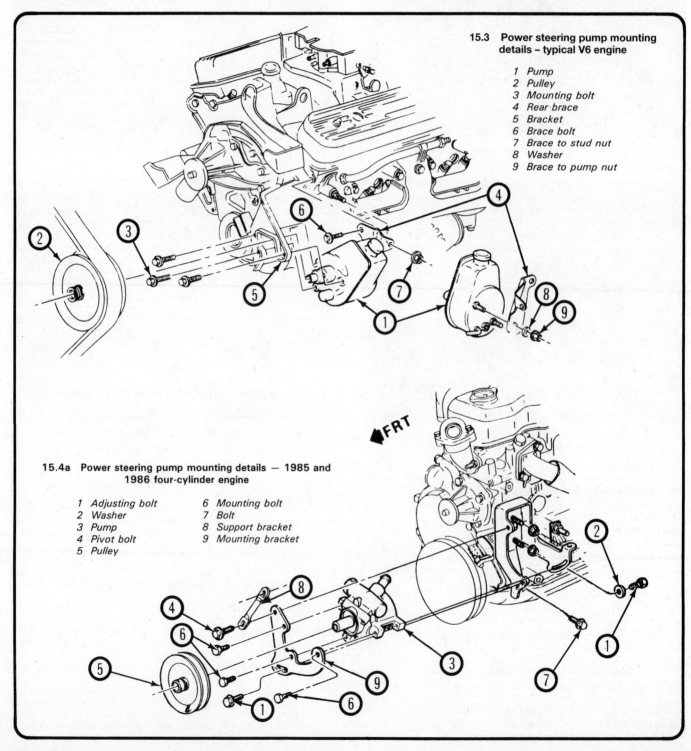

15.3   Power steering pump mounting details – typical V6 engine

1 Pump
2 Pulley
3 Mounting bolt
4 Rear brace
5 Bracket
6 Brace bolt
7 Brace to stud nut
8 Washer
9 Brace to pump nut

15.4a   Power steering pump mounting details — 1985 and 1986 four-cylinder engine

1 Adjusting bolt
2 Washer
3 Pump
4 Pivot bolt
5 Pulley
6 Mounting bolt
7 Bolt
8 Support bracket
9 Mounting bracket

**15.4b   Power steering pump mounting details — 1987 on
four-cylinder engine**

1 *Pump*   3 *Mounting bolt*
2 *Pulley*   4 *Mounting bracket*

16   Power steering system — bleeding

1   Following any operation in which the power steering fluid lines have
been disconnected, the power steering system must be bled to remove
all air and obtain proper steering performance.
2   With the front wheels in the straight ahead position, check the
power steering fluid level and, if low, add fluid until it reaches the Cold
mark on the dipstick.

3   Start the engine and allow it to run at fast idle. Recheck the fluid
level and add more if necessary to reach the Cold mark on the dipstick.
4   Bleed the system by turning the wheels from side-to-side, without
hitting the stops. This will work the air out of the system. Keep the
reservoir full of fluid as this is done.
5   When the air is worked out of the system, return the wheels to
the straight ahead position and leave the vehicle running for several
more minutes before shutting it off.
6   Road test the vehicle to be sure the steering system is functioning
normally and noise free.
7   Recheck the fluid level to be sure it is up to the Hot mark on the
dipstick while the engine is at normal operating temperature. Add fluid
if necessary (see Chapter 1).

17   Steering linkage — inspection, removal and installation

Warning: *Whenever any of the suspension or steering fasteners are
loosened or removed they must be inspected and if necessary, replaced
with new ones of the same part number or of original equipment quality
and design. Torque specifications must be followed for proper
reassembly and component retention. Never attempt to heat, straighten
or weld any suspension or steering component. Instead, replace any
bent or damaged part with a new one.*
Caution: *DO NOT use a ''pickle fork'' type balljoint separator — it may
damage the balljoint seals.*

Inspection
Refer to illustrations 17.1 and 17.5

1   The steering linkage connects the steering gear to the front wheels
and keeps the wheels in proper relation to each other **(see illustration)**.
The linkage consists of the Pitman arm, fastened to the steering gear
shaft, which moves the relay rod back-and-forth through the connecting
rod. The relay rod is supported on each end by frame-mounted idler
arms. The back-and-forth motion of the relay rod is transmitted to the
steering knuckles through a pair of tie-rod assemblies. Each tie-rod is
made up of an inner and outer tie-rod end, a threaded adjuster tube
and two clamps.

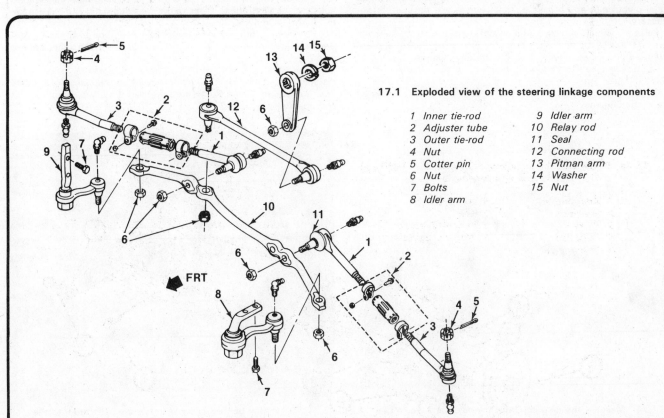

17.1   Exploded view of the steering linkage components

1 *Inner tie-rod*   9 *Idler arm*
2 *Adjuster tube*   10 *Relay rod*
3 *Outer tie-rod*   11 *Seal*
4 *Nut*   12 *Connecting rod*
5 *Cotter pin*   13 *Pitman arm*
6 *Nut*   14 *Washer*
7 *Bolts*   15 *Nut*
8 *Idler arm*

10

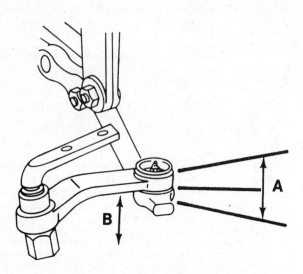

17.5   To check for play in the idler arms, apply approximately 25 lbs. of force up and down (B) on the idler arm — if the total idler arm movement (A) is greater than 1/4-inch, replace the idler arm

17.9   Using a puller, separate the tie-rod end from the steering knuckle; notice that the nut hasn't been completely removed — this will prevent violent separation of the parts!

2   Set the wheels in the straight ahead position and lock the steering wheel.

3   Raise one side of the vehicle until the tire is approximately 1-inch off the ground.

4   Mount a dial indicator with the needle resting on the outside edge of the wheel. Grasp the front and rear of the tire and using light pressure, wiggle the wheel back-and-forth and note the dial indicator reading. The gauge reading should be less than 0.108-inch. If the play in the steering system is more than specified, inspect each steering linkage pivot point and ball stud for looseness and replace parts if necessary.

5   Raise the vehicle and support it on jackstands. Push up, then pull down on the relay rod end of the idler arm, exerting a force of approximately 25 pounds each way. Measure the total distance the end of the arm travels **(see illustration)**. If the play is greater than 1/4-inch, replace the idler arm.

6   Check for torn ball stud boots, frozen joints and bent or damaged linkage components.

Removal and installation
Refer to illustrations 17.9, 17.11, 17.13, 17.15a and 17.15b
Tie-rod

7   Loosen the wheel lug nuts, raise the vehicle and support it securely on jackstands. Apply the parking brake. Remove the wheel.

8   Remove the cotter pin and loosen, but do not remove, the castellated nut from the ball stud.

9   Using a two jaw puller, separate the tie-rod end from the steering knuckle **(see illustration)**. Remove the castellated nut and pull the tie-rod end from the knuckle.

10   Remove the nut securing the inner tie-rod end to the relay rod. Separate the inner tie-rod end from the relay rod in the same manner as in Step 9.

11   If the inner or outer tie-rod end must be replaced, measure the distance from the end of the adjuster tube to the center of the ball stud and record it **(see illustration)**. Loosen the adjuster tube clamp and unscrew the tie-rod end.

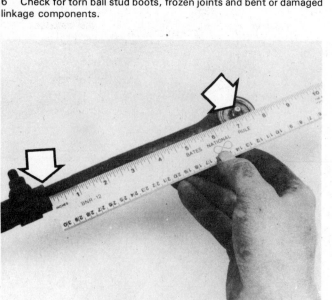

17.11   Measure the distance from the adjuster tube to the ball stud centerline so the new tie-rod end can be set to this dimension

17.13   It may be necessary to force the ball stud into the hole to keep it from spinning when tightening the nut

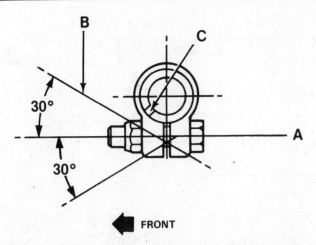

17.15a   Tie-rod adjuster tube and clamp position details

A   *Horizontal*
B   *The clamp bolts must be within 30° of horizontal*
C   *The adjuster tube slot MUST NOT line up with the gap in the clamps*

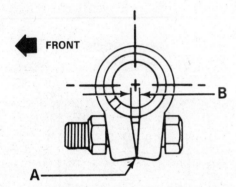

17.15b   The clamp ends (A) may touch when tightened, but there must be a gap between the inner portions of the clamp next to the adjuster tube (B)

12 Lubricate the threaded portion of the tie-rod end with chassis grease. Screw the new tie-rod end into the adjuster tube and adjust the distance from the tube to the ball stud to the previously measured dimension. The number of threads showing on the inner and outer tie-rod ends should be equal within three threads. Don't tighten the clamp yet.
13 To install the tie-rod, insert the inner tie-rod end ball stud into the relay rod until it's seated. Install the nut and tighten it to the specified torque. If the ball stud spins when attempting to tighten the nut, force it into the tapered hole with a large pair of pliers (**see illustration**).
14 Connect the outer tie-rod end to the steering knuckle and install the castellated nut. Tighten the nut to the specified torque and install a new cotter pin. If necessary, tighten the nut slightly to align a slot in the nut with the hole in the ball stud.
15 Tighten the clamp nuts. The center of the bolt should be nearly horizontal and the adjuster tube slot must not line up with the gap in the clamps (**see illustrations**).
16 Install the wheel and lug nuts, lower the vehicle and tighten the lug nuts to the specified torque. Drive the vehicle to an alignment shop to have the front end alignment checked and, if necessary, adjusted.

Idler arm
17 Raise the vehicle and support it securely on jackstands. Apply the parking brake.
18 Loosen but do not remove the idler arm-to-relay rod nut.
19 Separate the idler arm from the relay rod with a two jaw puller (**see illustration 17.9**). Remove the nut.
20 Remove the idler arm-to-frame bolts.
21 To install the idler arm, position it on the frame and install the bolts, tightening them to the specified torque.
22 Insert the idler arm ball stud into the relay rod and install the nut.

Tighten the nut to the specified torque. If the ball stud spins when attempting to tighten the nut, force it into the tapered hole with a large pair of pliers.

Relay rod
23 Raise the vehicle and support it securely on jackstands. Apply the parking brake.
24 Separate the two inner tie-rod ends from the relay rod.
25 Separate the connecting rod from the relay rod.
26 Separate both idler arms from the relay rod.
27 Installation is the reverse of the removal procedure. If the ball studs spin when attempting to tighten the nuts, force them into the tapered holes with a large pair of pliers. Be sure to tighten all of the nuts to the specified torque.

Connecting rod
28 Raise the front of the vehicle and support it securely on jackstands. Apply the parking brake.
29 Loosen, but do not remove, the nut securing the connecting rod ball stud to the relay rod. Separate the joint with a two jaw puller then remove the nut.
30 Separate the connecting rod from the Pitman arm.
31 Installation is the reverse of the removal procedure. If the ball studs spin when attempting to tighten the nuts, force them into the tapered holes with a large pair of pliers. Be sure to tighten all of the nuts to the specified torque.

Pitman arm
32 Refer to Section 14 of this Chapter for the Pitman arm removal procedure.

---

18   Wheels and tires — general information

Refer to illustration 18.1

All vehicles covered by this manual are equipped with metric-sized fiberglass or steel belted radial tires (**see illustration**). Use of other size or type of tires may affect the ride and handling of the vehicle. Don't mix different types of tires, such as radials and bias belted, on the same vehicle as handling may be seriously affected. It's recommended that tires be replaced in pairs on the same axle, but if only one tire is being replaced, be sure it's the same size, structure and tread design as the other.

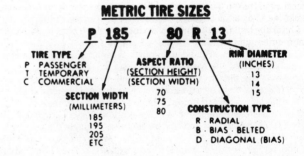

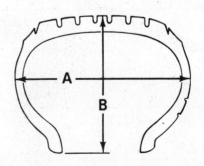

18.1   Metric tire size code

A *Section width*
B *Section height*

10

Because tire pressure has a substantial effect on handling and wear, the pressure on all tires should be checked at least once a month or before any extended trips (see Chapter 1).

Wheels must be replaced if they are bent, dented, leak air, have elongated bolt holes, are heavily rusted, out of vertical symmetry or if the lug nuts won't stay tight. Wheel repairs that use welding or peening are not recommended.

Tire and wheel balance is important in the overall handling, braking and performance of the vehicle. Unbalanced wheels can adversely affect handling and ride characteristics as well as tire life. Whenever a tire is installed on a wheel, the tire and wheel should be balanced by a shop with the proper equipment.

All vehicles covered by this manual are equipped with a compact spare tire, which is designed to save space as well as being easier to handle due to its lighter weight. The spare tire pressure should be checked at least once a month, and maintained at 60 psi. The compact spare tire and wheel are designed for use with each other only, and neither the tire nor the wheel should be coupled with other types or size of wheels and tires. Because the compact spare is designed as a temporary replacement for an out-of-service standard wheel and tire, the compact spare should be used on the vehicle only until the standard wheel and tire are repaired or replaced. Continuous use of the compact spare at speeds of over 50 mph is not recommended. In addition, the expected tread life of the compact spare is only 3000 miles.

19   Front end alignment — general information

Refer to illustration 19.1

A front end alignment refers to the adjustments made to the front wheels so they are in proper angular relationship to the suspension and the ground. Front wheels that are out of proper alignment not only affect steering control, but also increase tire wear. The front end adjustments normally required are camber, caster and toe-in **(see illustration)**.

Getting the proper front wheel alignment is a very exacting process, one in which complicated and expensive machines are necessary to perform the job properly. Because of this, you should have a technician with the proper equipment perform these tasks. We will, however, use this space to give you a basic idea of what is involved with front end alignment so you can better understand the process and deal intelligently with the shop that does the work.

Toe-in is the turning in of the front wheels. The purpose of a toe specification is to ensure parallel rolling of the front wheels. In a vehicle with zero toe-in, the distance between the front edges of the wheels will be the same as the distance between the rear edges of the wheels. The actual amount of toe-in is normally only a fraction of an inch. Toe-in adjustment is controlled by the tie-rod end position on the inner tie-rod. Incorrect toe-in will cause the tires to wear improperly by making them scrub against the road surface.

Camber is the tilting of the front wheels from the vertical when viewed from the front of the vehicle. When the wheels tilt out at the top, the camber is said to be positive (+). When the wheels tilt in at the top the camber is negative (−). The amount of tilt is measured in degrees from the vertical and this measurement is called the camber angle. This angle affects the amount of tire tread which contacts the road and compensates for changes in the suspension geometry when the vehicle is cornering or travelling over an undulating surface.

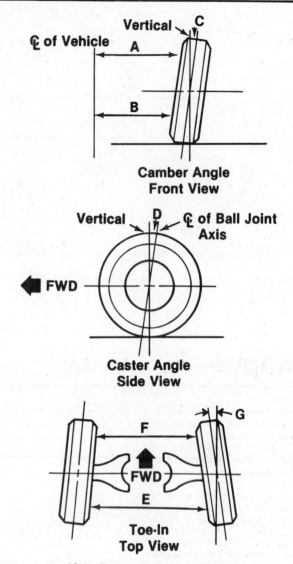

19.1   Front end alignment details

A minus B = C (degrees camber)
D = caster (measured in degrees)
E minus F = toe-in (measured in inches)
G = toe-in (expressed in degrees)

Caster is the tilting of the front steering axis from the vertical. A tilt toward the rear is positive caster and a tilt toward the front is negative caster.

Caster is adjusted by moving shims from one end of the upper control arm mount to the other.

Chapter 11 Body

Contents

Specifications

Torque specifications

	Ft-lbs
Front bumper bolts	26
Rear bumper bolts	26
Lock striker-to-body pillar bolt	49
Front seat nuts	26

1 General information

The vehicles covered in this manual have a separate frame and body.

As with other parts of the vehicle, proper maintenance of body components plays an important part in preserving the vehicle's market value. It's far less costly to handle small problems before they grow into larger ones. Information in this Chapter will tell you all you need to know to keep seals sealing, body panels aligned and general appearance up to par.

Major body components which are particularly vulnerable in accidents are removable. These include the hood, fenders, grille and doors. It's often cheaper and less time consuming to replace an entire panel than it is to attempt a restoration of the old one. However, this must be decided on a case-by-case basis. **Caution:** *If the vehicle is equipped with a Delco Loc II audio system (1992 and later models with a Compact Disc player), be sure the lockout feature is turned off before performing any procedure that requires disconnecting the battery (refer to your owner's manual for further information on this system).*

2 Body and frame - maintenance

1   The condition of your vehicle's body is very important, because it's on this that the second hand value will mainly depend. It's much

more difficult to repair a neglected or damaged body than it is to repair mechanical components. The hidden areas of the body, such as the fender wells, the frame, and the engine compartment, are equally important, although they obviously don't require as frequent attention as the rest of the body.

2   Once a year, or every 12,000 miles, it's a good idea to have the underside of the body and the frame steam cleaned. All traces of dirt and oil will be removed and the underside can then be inspected carefully for rust, damaged brake lines, frayed electrical wiring, damaged cables and other problems. The front suspension components should be greased after this job is done.

3   At the same time, clean the engine and the engine compartment with either a steam cleaner or a water soluble degreaser.

4   The fender wells should be given particular attention, as undercoating can peel away and stones and dirt thrown up by the tires can cause the paint to chip and flake, allowing rust to set in. If rust is found, clean down to the bare metal and apply an anti-rust paint.

5   The body should be washed as needed. Wet the vehicle thoroughly to soften the dirt, then wash it down with a soft sponge and plenty of clean soapy water. If the surplus dirt is not washed off very carefully, it will in time wear down the paint.

6   Spots of tar or asphalt coating thrown up from the road should be removed with a cloth soaked in solvent.

7   Once every six months, give the body and chrome trim a thorough waxing. If a chrome cleaner is used to remove rust from any of the vehicle's plated parts, remember that the cleaner also removes part of the chrome, so use it sparingly.

3 Upholstery and carpets — maintenance

1   Every three months remove the carpets or mats and clean the interior of the vehicle (more frequently if necessary). Vacuum the upholstery and carpets to remove loose dirt and dust.

2   If the upholstery is soiled, apply upholstery cleaner with a damp sponge and wipe it off with a clean, dry cloth.

4 Body repair – minor damage

See photo sequence

Repair of minor scratches

1   If the scratch is superficial and does not penetrate to the metal of the body, repair is very simple. Lightly rub the scratched area with a fine rubbing compound to remove loose paint and built up wax. Rinse the area with clean water.

2   Apply touch-up paint to the scratch, using a small brush. Continue to apply thin layers of paint until the surface of the paint in the scratch is level with the surrounding paint. Allow the new paint at least two weeks to harden, then blend it into the surrounding paint by rubbing with a very fine rubbing compound. Finally, apply a coat of wax to the scratch area.

3   If the scratch has penetrated the paint and exposed the metal of the body, causing the metal to rust, a different repair technique is required. Remove all loose rust from the bottom of the scratch with a pocket knife, then apply rust inhibiting paint to prevent the formation of rust in the future. Using a rubber or nylon applicator, coat the scratched area with glaze-type filler. If required, the filler can be mixed with thinner to provide a very thin paste, which is ideal for filling narrow scratches. Before the glaze filler in the scratch hardens, wrap a piece of smooth cotton cloth around the tip of a finger. Dip the cloth in thinner and then quickly wipe it along the surface of the scratch. This will ensure that the surface of the filler is slightly hollow. The scratch can now be painted over as described earlier in this section.

Repair of dents

4   When repairing dents, the first job is to pull the dent out until the affected area is as close as possible to its original shape. There is no point in trying to restore the original shape completely as the metal in the damaged area will have stretched on impact and cannot be restored to its original contours. It is better to bring the level of the dent up to a point which is about 1/8-inch below the level of the surrounding metal. In cases where the dent is very shallow, it is not worth trying to pull it out at all.

5   If the back side of the dent is accessible, it can be hammered out gently from behind using a soft-face hammer. While doing this, hold a block of wood firmly against the opposite side of the metal to absorb the hammer blows and prevent the metal from being stretched.

6   If the dent is in a section of the body which has double layers, or some other factor makes it inaccessible from behind, a different technique is required. Drill several small holes through the metal inside the damaged area, particularly in the deeper sections. Screw long, self tapping screws into the holes just enough for them to get a good grip in the metal. Now the dent can be pulled out by pulling on the protruding heads of the screws with locking pliers.

7   The next stage of repair is the removal of paint from the damaged area and from an inch or so of the surrounding metal. This is easily done with a wire brush or sanding disk in a drill motor, although it can be done just as effectively by hand with sandpaper. To complete the preparation for filling, score the surface of the bare metal with a screwdriver or the tang of a file or drill small holes in the affected area. This will provide a good grip for the filler material. To complete the repair, see the Section on filling and painting.

Repair of rust holes or gashes

8   Remove all paint from the affected area and from an inch or so of the surrounding metal using a sanding disk or wire brush mounted in a drill motor. If these are not available, a few sheets of sandpaper will do the job just as effectively.

9   With the paint removed, you will be able to determine the severity of the corrosion and decide whether to replace the whole panel, if possible, or repair the affected area. New body panels are not as expensive as most people think and it is often quicker to install a new panel than to repair large areas of rust.

10   Remove all trim pieces from the affected area except those which will act as a guide to the original shape of the damaged body, such as headlight shells, etc. Using metal snips or a hacksaw blade, remove all loose metal and any other metal that is badly affected by rust. Hammer the edges of the hole inward to create a slight depression for the filler material.

11   Wire brush the affected area to remove the powdery rust from the surface of the metal. If the back of the rusted area is accessible, treat it with rust-inhibiting paint.

12   Before filling is done, block the hole in some way. This can be done with sheet metal riveted or screwed into place, or by stuffing the hole with wire mesh.

13   Once the hole is blocked off, the affected area can be filled and painted. See the following sub-section on filling and painting.

Filling and painting

14   Many types of body fillers are available, but generally speaking, body repair kits which contain filler paste and a tube of resin hardener are best for this type of repair work. A wide, flexible plastic or nylon applicator will be necessary for imparting a smooth and contoured finish to the surface of the filler material. Mix up a small amount of filler on a clean piece of wood or cardboard (use the hardener sparingly). Follow the manufacturer's instructions on the package, otherwise the filler will set incorrectly.

15   Using the applicator, apply the filler paste to the prepared area. Draw the applicator across the surface of the filler to achieve the desired contour and to level the filler surface. As soon as a contour that approximates the original one is achieved, stop working the paste. If you continue, the paste will begin to stick to the applicator. Continue to add thin layers of paste at 20-minute intervals until the level of the filler is just above the surrounding metal.

16   Once the filler has hardened, the excess can be removed with a body file. From then on, progressively finer grades of sandpaper should be used, starting with a 180-grit paper and finishing with 600-grit wet-or-dry paper. Always wrap the sandpaper around a flat rubber or wooden block, otherwise the surface of the filler will not be completely flat. During the sanding of the filler surface, the wet-or-dry paper should be periodically rinsed in water. This will ensure that a very smooth finish is produced in the final stage.

17   At this point, the repair area should be surrounded by a ring of bare metal, which in turn should be encircled by the finely feathered edge of good paint. Rinse the repair area with clean water until all of the dust produced by the sanding operation is gone.

18   Spray the entire area with a light coat of primer. This will reveal any imperfections in the surface of the filler. Repair the imperfections

with fresh filler paste or glaze filler and once more smooth the surface with sandpaper. Repeat this spray-and-repair procedure until you are satisfied that the surface of the filler and the feathered edge of the paint are perfect. Rinse the area with clean water and allow it to dry completely.

19 The repair area is now ready for painting. Spray painting must be carried out in a warm, dry, windless and dust free atmosphere. These conditions can be created if you have access to a large indoor work area, but if you are forced to work in the open, you will have to pick the day very carefully. If you are working indoors, dousing the floor in the work area with water will help settle the dust which would otherwise be in the air. If the repair area is confined to one body panel, mask off the surrounding panels. This will help minimize the effects of a slight mismatch in paint color. Trim pieces such as chrome strips, door handles, etc., will also need to be masked off or removed. Use masking tape and several thicknesses of newspaper for the masking operations.

20 Before spraying, shake the paint can thoroughly, then spray a test area until the spray painting technique is mastered. Cover the repair area with a thick coat of primer. The thickness should be built up using several thin layers of primer rather than one thick one. Using 600-grit wet-or-dry sandpaper, rub down the surface of the primer until it is very smooth. While doing this, the work area should be thoroughly rinsed with water and the wet-or-dry sandpaper periodically rinsed as well. Allow the primer to dry before spraying additional coats.

21 Spray on the top coat, again building up the thickness by using several thin layers of paint. Begin spraying in the center of the repair area and then, using a circular motion, work out until the whole repair area and about two inches of the surrounding original paint is covered. Remove all masking material 10 to 15 minutes after spraying on the final coat of paint. Allow the new paint at least two weeks to harden, then use a very fine rubbing compound to blend the edges of the new paint into the existing paint. Finally, apply a coat of wax.

5 Body and frame repair — major damage

1 Major damage must be repaired by an auto body/frame repair shop with the necessary welding and hydraulic straightening equipment.

2 If the damage has been serious, it's vital that the frame be checked for proper alignment or the vehicle's handling characteristics may be adversely affected. Other problems, such as excessive tire wear and wear in the driveline and steering may occur.

3 Due to the fact that all of the major body components (hood, fenders, etc.) are separate and replaceable units, any seriously damaged components should be replaced rather than repaired. Sometimes these components can be found in a wrecking yard that specializes in used vehicle components, often at considerable savings over the cost of new parts.

6 Hinges and locks — maintenance

Every 3000 miles or three months, the door and hood hinges should be lubricated with a few drops of oil. Lubricate the locks with graphite spray. The door striker plates should also be given a thin coat of white lithium-base grease to reduce wear and ensure free movement.

7 Windshield and fixed glass — removal and installation

1 Replacement of the windshield and fixed glass requires the use of special fast-setting adhesive/caulk materials. These operations should be left to a dealer service department or a shop specializing in glass work.

2 Windshield mounted rear view mirror support removal is also best left to experts, as the bond to the glass also requires special tools and adhesives.

8 Hood — removal and installation

1 Remove the windshield wiper arms (Chapter 12).
2 Remove the antenna (Chapter 12).
3 Remove the cowl ventilator grille (Section 10).
4 Remove the two mounting bolts and lift the hood off.
5 To install the hood, lower it into place and install the mounting bolts. Tighten the bolts securely.
6 The remainder of installation is the reverse of removal.

9 Hood release latch and cable — removal and installation

Refer to illustrations 9.1, 9.4 and 9.9

1 Working in the engine compartment, pry the cable housing out of the clip on the latch and disconnect the cable end **(see illustration)**.
2 Pry the cable grommet out of the firewall and the cut grommet to release it.
3 Fasten a piece of string or very fine wire to the end of the cable long enough to pull the new cable through.
4 Working in the passenger compartment, release the cable handle by compressing the tabs on the back, then pull the cable through **(see illustration)**.

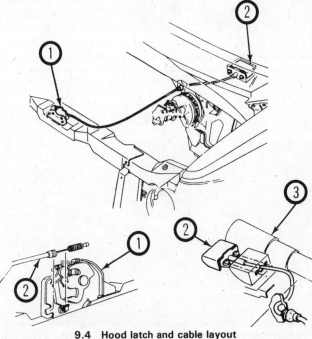

9.4 Hood latch and cable layout

1 Hood latch	*3 Steering column*
2 Cable assembly	

9.1 Use a screwdriver to pry the cable out of the clip

These photos illustrate a method of repairing simple dents. They are intended to supplement *Body repair - minor damage* in this Chapter and should not be used as the sole instructions for body repair on these vehicles.

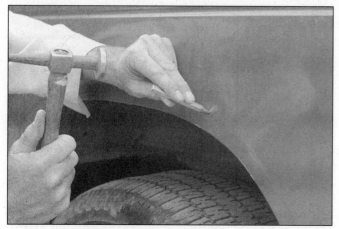

1   If you can't access the backside of the body panel to hammer out the dent, pull it out with a slide-hammer-type dent puller. In the deepest portion of the dent or along the crease line, drill or punch hole(s) at least one inch apart . . .

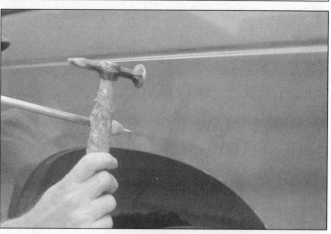

2   . . . then screw the slide-hammer into the hole and operate it. Tap with a hammer near the edge of the dent to help 'pop' the metal back to its original shape. When you're finished, the dent area should be close to its original contour and about 1/8-inch below the surface of the surrounding metal

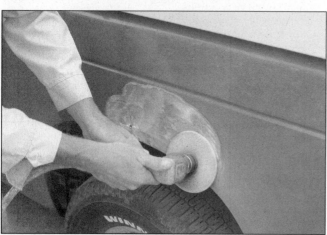

3   Using coarse-grit sandpaper, remove the paint down to the bare metal. Hand sanding works fine, but the disc sander shown here makes the job faster. Use finer (about 320-grit) sandpaper to feather-edge the paint at least one inch around the dent area

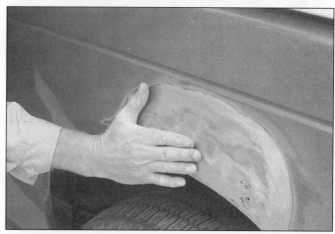

4   When the paint is removed, touch will probably be more helpful than sight for telling if the metal is straight. Hammer down the high spots or raise the low spots as necessary. Clean the repair area with wax/silicone remover

5   Following label instructions, mix up a batch of plastic filler and hardener. The ratio of filler to hardener is critical, and, if you mix it incorrectly, it will either not cure properly or cure too quickly (you won't have time to file and sand it into shape)

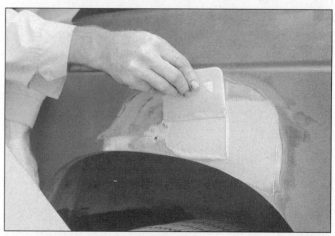

6   Working quickly so the filler doesn't harden, use a plastic applicator to press the body filler firmly into the metal, assuring it bonds completely. Work the filler until it matches the original contour and is slightly above the surrounding metal

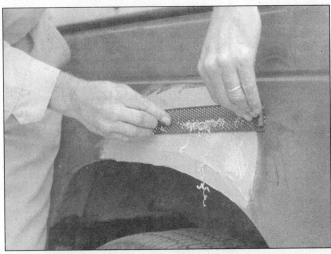

7   Let the filler harden until you can just dent it with your fingernail. Use a body file or Surform tool (shown here) to rough-shape the filler

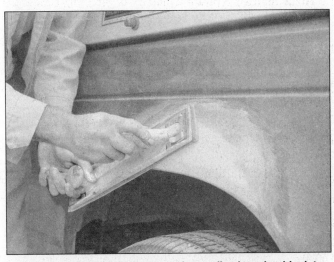

8   Use coarse-grit sandpaper and a sanding board or block to work the filler down until it's smooth and even. Work down to finer grits of sandpaper - always using a board or block - ending up with 360 or 400 grit

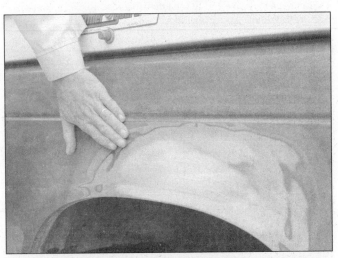

9   You shouldn't be able to feel any ridge at the transition from the filler to the bare metal or from the bare metal to the old paint. As soon as the repair is flat and uniform, remove the dust and mask off the adjacent panels or trim pieces

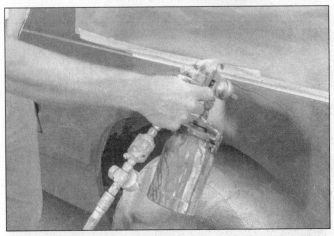

10   Apply several layers of primer to the area. Don't spray the primer on too heavy, so it sags or runs, and make sure each coat is dry before you spray on the next one. A professional-type spray gun is being used here, but aerosol spray primer is available inexpensively from auto parts stores

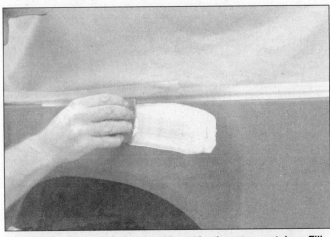

11   The primer will help reveal imperfections or scratches. Fill these with glazing compound. Follow the label instructions and sand it with 360 or 400-grit sandpaper until it's smooth. Repeat the glazing, sanding and respraying until the primer reveals a perfectly smooth surface

12   Finish sand the primer with very fine sandpaper (400 or 600-grit) to remove the primer overspray. Clean the area with water and allow it to dry. Use a tack rag to remove any dust, then apply the finish coat. Don't attempt to rub out or wax the repair area until the paint has dried completely (at least two weeks)

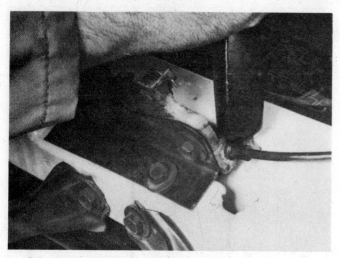

9.9   Use a screwdriver handle to seat the cable in the clip

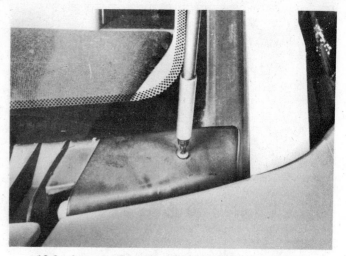

10.2   A special Torx bit will be required to remove the
cowl ventilator screws

5   Remove the two bolts and detach the latch. Installation is the
reverse of removal.
6   Fasten the string or wire to the new cable and pull it through into
the engine compartment.
7   Press the cable handle into place on the instrument panel until it
seats.

8   Seat the grommet and cable in the firewall.
9   Connect the cable end to the latch and seat the cable in the clip
(see illustration).

10   Cowl ventilator grille — removal and installation

Refer to illustration 10.2
1   Remove the windshield wiper arms (Chapter 12).
2   Remove the retaining screws with a Torx bit **(see illustration)**.
3   Lift the grille off.
4   To install the grille, place it in position and install the screws.
Tighten the screws securely.
5   Install the wiper arms.

11   Engine cover — removal and installation

Refer to illustrations 11.1a, 11.1b and 11.3
1   Working in the engine compartment, remove the engine cover
screws **(see illustrations)**.
2   Working in the passenger compartment, remove the instrument
panel lower extension (Section 30).
3   Disengage the support rods from the lower extension studs **(see
illustration)**.
4   Lift the two retaining latches and remove the engine cover.

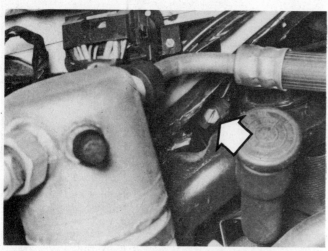

11.1a   Use a large screwdriver to unscrew the right side . . .

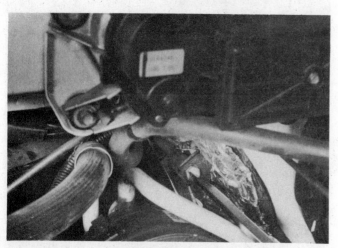

11.1b   . . . and left side engine cover screws in the
engine compartment

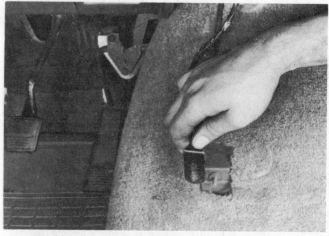

11.3   Detach the support rods from the studs

5   To install the engine cover, place it in position, tighten the screws in the engine compartment and engage the latches in the passenger compartment.
6   Install the support rods on the lower extension studs.
7   Install the instrument panel lower extension.

12   Fender — removal and installation

Refer to illustration 12.5

1   Remove the headlight bezel (Section 17).
2   Remove the front bumper (Section 18).
3   Remove the cowl ventilator grille (Section 10).
4   Remove the front wheelhouse panel (Section 16).
5   Remove the fender mounting bolts **(see illustration)**.
6   Lower the fender from the body.
7   To install the fender, place it in position and install the bolts.
8   The remainder of installation is the reverse of removal.

13   Radiator grille — removal and installation

Refer to illustration 13.2

1   Remove the headlight bezels (Section 17).
2   Remove the front grille mounting screws **(see illustration)**.
3   Remove the plastic splash panel under the bumper.
4   Remove the screws along the bottom edge of the grille and detach it from the vehicle.
5   Installation is the reverse of removal.

14   Front end panel — removal and installation

1   Remove the front bumper (Section 18).
2   Remove the radiator grille (Section 13).
3   Remove the front end panel mounting bolts and lower the panel from the vehicle **(see illustration 13.2)**.

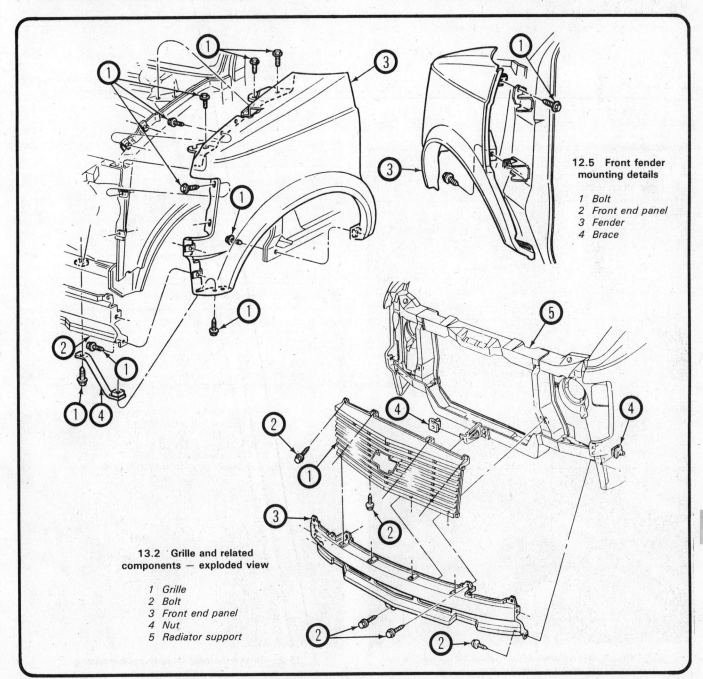

12.5 Front fender mounting details

1 *Bolt*
2 *Front end panel*
3 *Fender*
4 *Brace*

13.2 Grille and related components — exploded view

1 *Grille*
2 *Bolt*
3 *Front end panel*
4 *Nut*
5 *Radiator support*

11

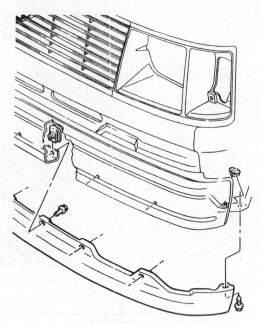

15.1   Front air deflector mounting details

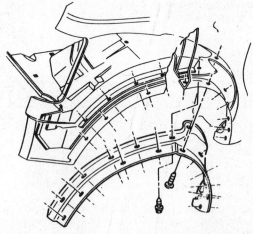

16.1   Front wheelhouse extension panel mounting details

4   To install the panel, place it in position and install the bolts. Tighten the bolts securely.
5   Install the grille and front bumper.

15   Front air deflector — removal and installation

Refer to illustration 15.1

1   Remove the air deflector-to-bumper and fender bolts (**see illustration**).
2   Detach the air deflector.
3   Installation is the reverse of removal.

16   Front wheelhouse panel extension — removal and installation

Refer to illustrations 16.1, 16.2a and 16.2b

1   Remove the panel extension mounting bolts (**see illustration**).
2   Release the retainers fastening the panel extension to the fender by prying out the center of each retainer with wire cutters (don't cut the center piece off, just pull it out) (**see illustration**). Once the center

has been pulled out, the retainer can be removed (**see illustration**).
3   Remove the panel extension from the fender.
4   To install the extension, place it in position and install the retainers. Once the extension and retainers are in place, press the center of each retainer in to lock them in place.
5   Install the bolts.

17   Headlight bezel — removal and installation

Refer to illustrations 17.1 and 17.2

1   Remove the four bezel retaining screws (**see illustration**). A special Torx screwdriver will be needed for this.
2   Rotate the bezel, disconnect the parking light and turn signal bulbs on the back side by turning the bulb holders a half turn and remove it from the vehicle (**see illustration**).
3   Installation is the reverse of removal.

18   Bumpers — removal and installation

Refer to illustrations 18.1a and 18.1b

1   Remove the brace-to-frame and the bracket-to-frame bolts (**see illustrations**).
2   Lift the bumper from the vehicle.
3   Installation is the reverse of removal. After installation tighten the brace-to-frame and bracket-to-frame bolts to the specified torque.

16.2a   Pry the center of the plastic retainer out with wire cutters — DO NOT cut it off!

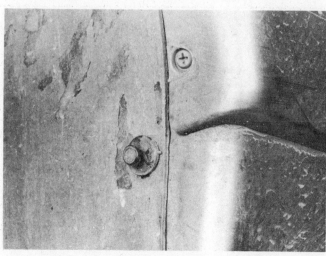

16.2b   With the center pulled out, the retainer can be removed

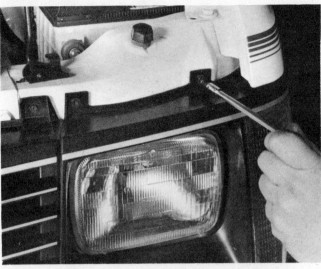

17.1 The Torx screws retaining the headlight bezel are accessible after raising the hood

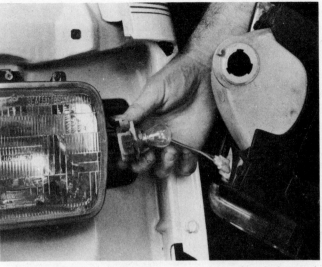

17.2 Rotate the bulb holders a half turn to detach them from the bezel

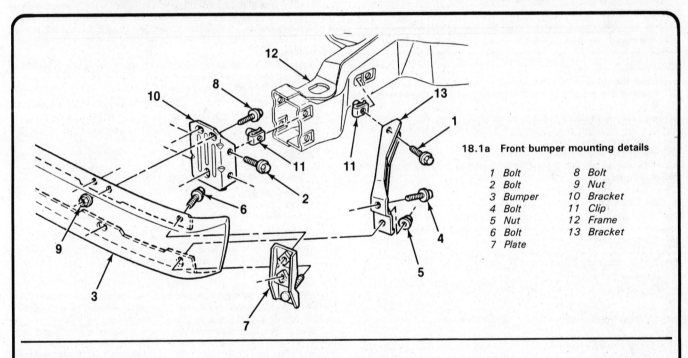

18.1a Front bumper mounting details

1	Bolt	8	Bolt
2	Bolt	9	Nut
3	Bumper	10	Bracket
4	Bolt	11	Clip
5	Nut	12	Frame
6	Bolt	13	Bracket
7	Plate		

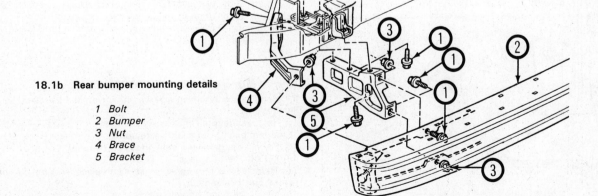

18.1b Rear bumper mounting details

1 Bolt
2 Bumper
3 Nut
4 Brace
5 Bracket

11

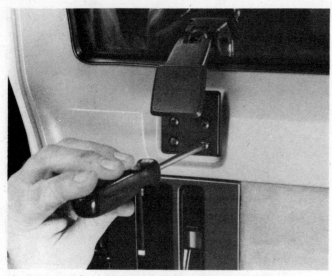

19.2   Use a Phillips screwdriver to remove the latch mounting screws

---

19   Swing-out window and latch — removal and installation

Refer to illustrations 19.2 and 19.3

1   Open the window.
2   Remove the window latch-to-body screws (**see illustration**).
3   While an assistant supports the window glass, remove the hinge screws (**see illustration**). Lift the window from the vehicle.
4   If a new window is being installed, transfer the latch and other hardware to the new glass.
5   Place the glass in position, have an assistant hold it in place and install the hinge screws. Install the latch and make sure the window closes securely.

---

20   Door trim panel — removal and installation

Front door

Refer to illustrations 20.2, 20.3, 20.4a, 20.4b and 20.6

1   Remove the armrest.
2   Pry off the door handle cover (**see illustration**).

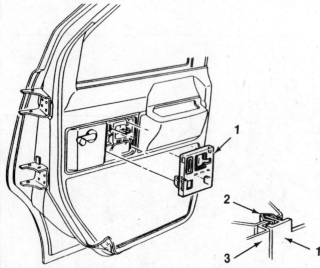

20.2   Front door handle details

1 Cover   2 Clip   3 Trim panel

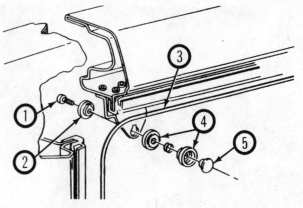

19.3   Window hinge details

1   Screw   4   Bushing
2   Retainer   5   Nut
3   Window

3   On manual window regulators, remove the window crank with tool no. J-9886 (**see illustration**). If the tool isn't available, press the door panel in and use a piece of bent wire to pull off the retaining spring.
4   Remove the four screws and then pry around the outer edge of the trim panel with a large screwdriver to disengage the retainers (**see illustrations**).
5   Rotate the trim panel up, pry it off the door frame at the window seal and remove it from the vehicle.

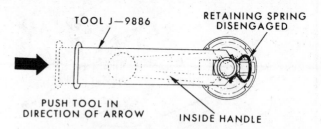

20.3   A special tool can be used to pull the clip off the manual regulator crank handle, but a hooked piece of wire works just as well

6   If access to the inner door is required, carefully peel away the watershield, taking care not to tear it (**see illustration**). The watershield can be reinstalled by pressing it back into place.
7   Prior to installation, remove any retainers from the door that didn't come out with the panel and reinstall them in the panel.
8   Insert the trim panel into the window seal and press the retainers into place until they're fully seated.
9   Install the armrest and door handle cover.
10   To install the window crank, first attach the clip to the handle and determine the position of the handle by comparing it to the one the opposite door. Press the handle onto the spindle until the retaining spring engages.

Side door

Refer to illustrations 20.11 and 20.13

11   Remove the retaining screws and lift off the handle cover (**see illustration**).
12   Remove the retaining screws and then pry around the outer edge of the trim panel with a large screwdriver to disengage the retainers.
13   Pry off the garnish molding (**see illustration**).
14   Lift off the trim panel.
15   To install the trim panel, press it into place, making sure the retainers are fully seated.
16   Install the handle cover and screws.
17   Place the garnish molding in position and press it in until the retainers engage.

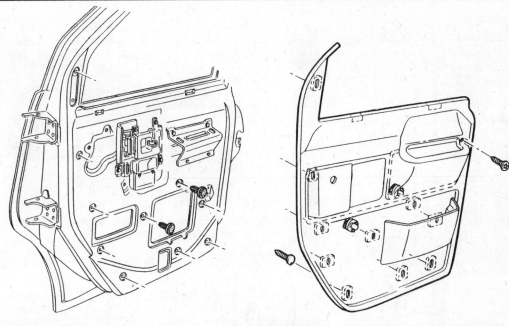

20.4a Front door trim panel mounting details

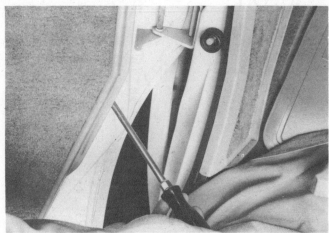

20.4b Insert a screwdriver behind the door panel and pry out very carefully to disengage the retainers

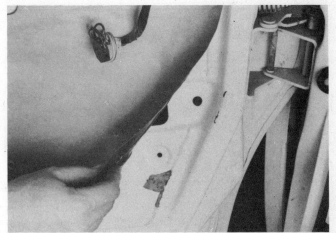

20.6 Peel the watershield back carefully — try not to tear it!

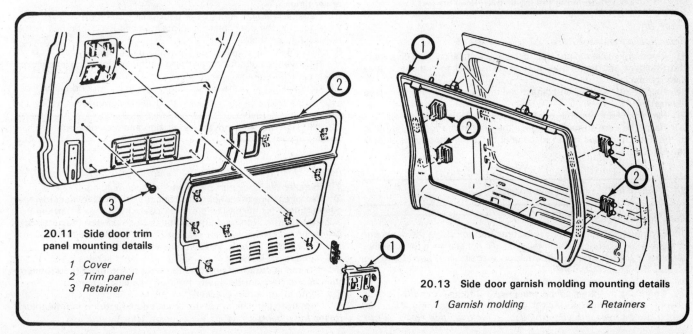

20.11 Side door trim panel mounting details

1 Cover
2 Trim panel
3 Retainer

20.13 Side door garnish molding mounting details

1 Garnish molding   2 Retainers

11

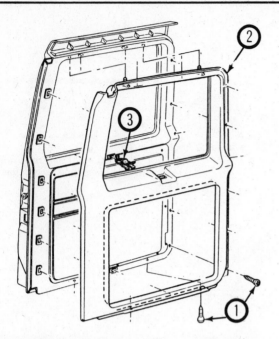

20.18a Rear door trim panel mounting details

1 Screw   2 Molding   3 Retainer

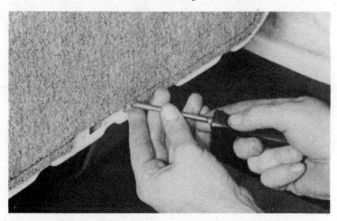

20.19 Remove the lower trim panel screws

Rear door

Refer to illustrations 20.18a, 20.18b and 20.19

18 Remove the screws, pry around the edges of the panel to disengage the retainers and lower the door garnish panel to remove it **(see illustrations)**.
19 Remove the screws and detach the trim panel from the door **(see illustration)**.
20 Place the trim panel in position and install the screws.
21 Raise the garnish panel, engage the pins at the top in the holes in the door and press it into place until the retainers engage. Install the screws.

---

21 Front door — removal and installation

Refer to illustration 21.4

1 Disconnect the negative cable at the battery. Place the cable out of the way so it cannot accidentally come in contact with the negative terminal of the battery, as this would once again allow power into the electrical system of the vehicle.
2 Unplug any wire harnesses.
3 Compress the hinge spring using tool J-28625-A or equivalent or cover the spring with heavy cloth before removal. **Warning:** *The door spring will be released when the door is removed and could fly out*

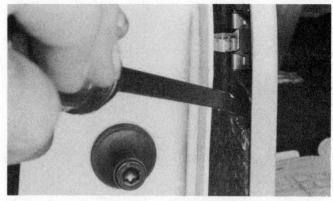

20.18b Pry the retainers out of the door very carefully with a screwdriver

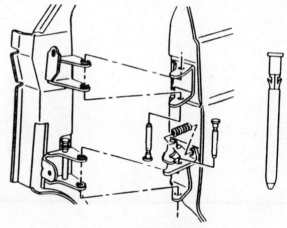

21.4 Door hinge details

of the door, causing personal injury, if it's not properly held in place.
4 Compress the clip on the lower hinge pin and remove the pin by pulling it out with locking pliers while tapping on the end with a soft-face hammer **(see illustration)**. The clip will ride up on the pin as it's removed and then fall out.
5 Insert a bolt into the lower hinge pin hole and then remove the upper hinge pin.
6 Remove the bolt and lift the door off.
7 To install the door, place it in position and install the bolt in the lower hinge pin hole.
8 Assemble the upper hinge pin using a new hinge pin clip.
9 Remove the bolt and install the lower hinge pin, using a new clip.
10 Install the spring.
11 Connect the wire harnesses and the battery ground cable.

---

22 Sliding door — removal, installation and adjustment

Removal

Refer to illustrations 22.2, 22.3a, 22.3b, 22.4, 22.5, 22.7 and 22.9

1 Remove the door trim panel and garnish molding.
2 Remove the right tail light lens (Chapter 12) and the rear stowage compartment for access to the track cover bolts **(see illustration)**.
3 Remove the bolts and lift off the track cover **(see illustrations)**.
4 Remove the upper roller bracket cover **(see illustration)**.
5 Outline the lower bracket bolt heads **(see illustration)**.
6 Remove the upper roller bracket Torx head screws.
7 With an assistant supporting the weight of the door, disconnect the latch cable from the lower bracket **(see illustration)**.
8 Remove the lower bracket.
9 With the help of an assistant, roll the door to the end of the track, rotate the roller out and lift the door off **(see illustration)**.

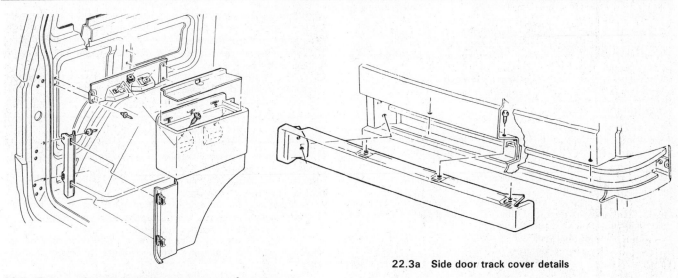

22.2   Remove the rear stowage compartment for access
to the sliding door cover bolts

22.3a   Side door track cover details

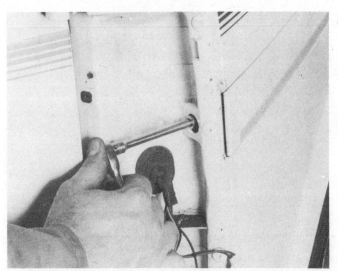

22.3b   Remove the rubber plug and use a ratchet and
socket extension to remove the rear track cover bolt

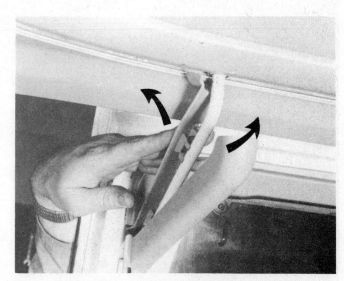

22.4   Remove the upper roller bracket covers by
unsnapping them in the direction shown (arrows)

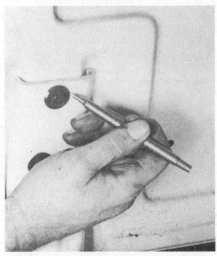

22.5   Mark the location of the lower
bracket bolts with a scribe or pencil

22.7   Use a small screwdriver to
disconnect the latch cable from the
lower bracket

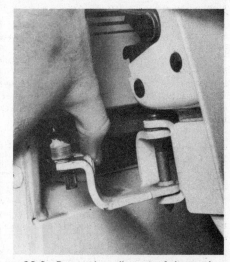

22.9   Rotate the roller out of the track
and lift the door off

11

Installation

10 To install the door, engage the roller with the track and move the door forward until the latch cable can be connected to the lower roller.
11 Install the lower roller bolts in the marked positions. Tighten the bolts securely.
12 Install the upper roller screws and the covers.

Adjustment

Refer to illustration 22.13

13 The door can be adjusted up-and-down and in-and-out slightly to provide an even fit in the door opening (**see illustration**).

Front edge up-and-down

14 Open the door part way and loosen the lower front catch and the roller track assembly bolts.
15 Move the front edge up-or-down and then tighten the bolts securely. Make sure the door is not moved beyond the point where the door alignment pins no longer engage.

Rear edge up-and-down

16 Loosen the roller track bolts.
17 Open the door and adjust the striker up-or-down. The roller track bolts must be loosened before any adjustment to the striker bolt is made.
18 Close the door and check the rear edge height.

19 If the height is correct, move the roller track up to meet the roller, tighten the bolts and recheck the height, adjusting as necessary.

Front and rear edge in-and-out

20 Loosen the rear latch striker bolt and move it in-or-out as required to achieve the proper gap.
21 Install the track cover, tail light lens, the rear stowage compartment and the side door garnish molding and trim panel.

---

23 Rear door — removal and installation

---

1 Disconnect the negative cable at the battery. Place the cable out of the way so it cannot accidentally come in contact with the negative terminal of the battery, as this would once again allow power into the electrical system of the vehicle.
2 On right side doors, remove the trim panel and unplug the electrical harnesses.
3 Remove the check strap.
4 With an assistant supporting the weight of the door, drive out the hinge pins with a hammer and pin punch. Detach the door from the vehicle.
5 Have an assistant hold the door in place, insert the hinge pins and drive them into place with a hammer.
6 Install all components that were removed.

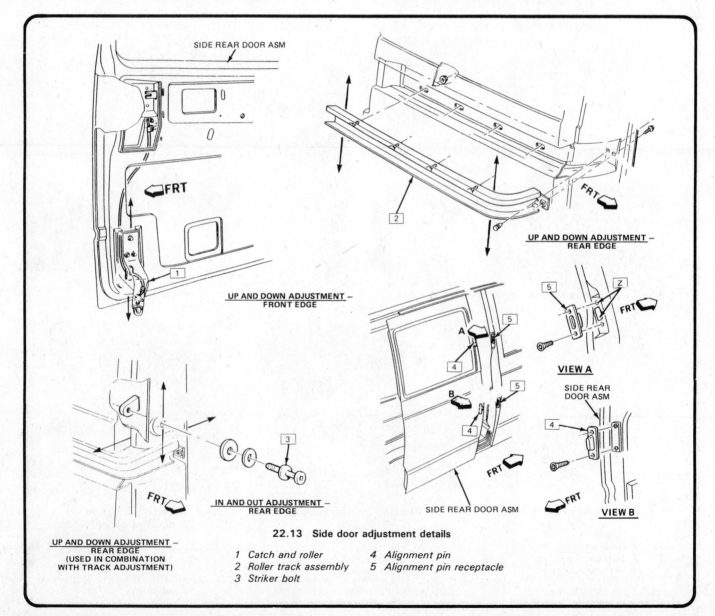

22.13 Side door adjustment details

1 Catch and roller	*4 Alignment pin*
2 Roller track assembly	*5 Alignment pin receptacle*
3 Striker bolt	

24 Door lock assembly — removal and installation

Front door

Refer to illustration 24.2

1   Remove the door trim panel and watershield (Section 20).
2   Disconnect the lock cylinder rods, remove the screws and detach the assembly from the door **(see illustration)**.
3   Installation is the reverse of removal.

Side door

Refer to illustration 24.5

4   Remove the door trim panel (Section 20).
5   Disconnect the outside handle and locking rods, remove the retaining screws and detach the lock from the door **(see illustration)**.
6   Installation is the reverse of removal.

Rear door

Refer to illustation 24.7

7   Remove the door trim panel (Section 20). Disconnect the locking and lock cylinder rods, remove the screws and detach the lock **(see illustration)**.
8   Installation is the reverse of removal.

25 Door lock striker — removal and installation

Refer to illustration 25.2

1   Mark the position of the striker bolt with a pencil.
2   Use a large Torx driver to unscrew the striker bolt **(see illustration)**.
3   To install the striker, reverse the removal procedure and line the bolt up with the marks made during removal. Tighten the bolt to the specified torque.

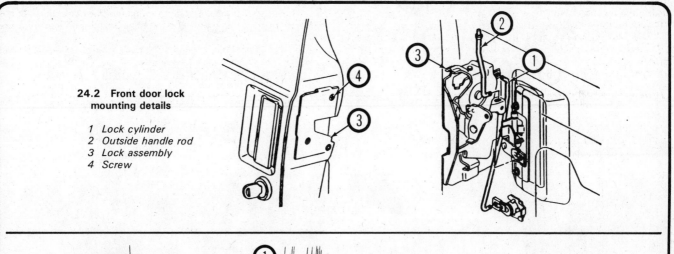

24.2 Front door lock mounting details

1 *Lock cylinder*
2 *Outside handle rod*
3 *Lock assembly*
4 *Screw*

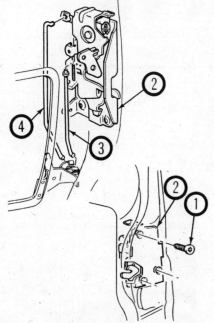

24.5 Side door lock mounting details

1 *Screw*
2 *Lock assembly*
3 *Outside handle rod*
4 *Lock cylinder rod*

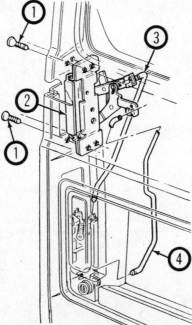

24.7 Rear door lock mounting details

1 *Screw*
2 *Lock assembly*
3 *Outside handle lock rod*
4 *Lock cylinder rod*

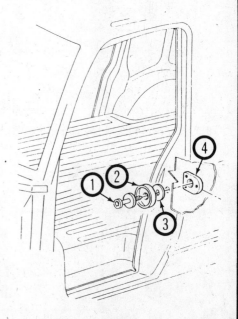

25.2 Typical door lock striker component layout

1 *Striker*   3 *Insulator*
2 *Spacer*   4 *Nut*

11

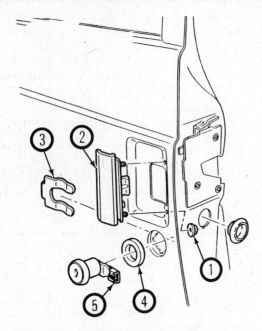

26.1   Front outside door handle mounting details

1 Nut	4 Gasket
2 Outside handle	5 Lock cylinder
3 Retainer	

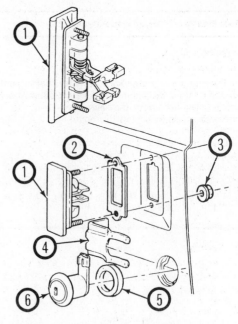

26.2   Side door outside handle mounting details

1 Outside handle	4 Retainer
2 Gasket	5 Gasket
3 Nut	6 Lock cylinder

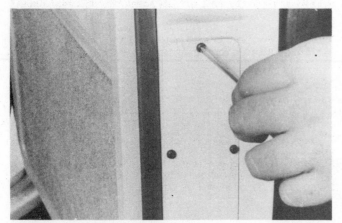

26.3   The rear door handle access cover is held in place by four screws

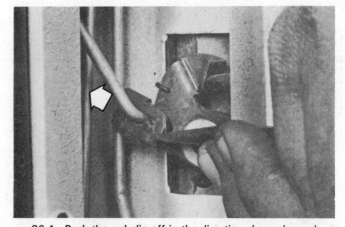

26.4   Push the rod clip off in the direction shown (arrow)

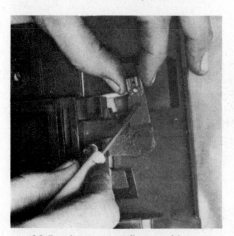

26.7a   Insert a small screwdriver through the hole in the clip to disconnect it from the rod

26.7b   Lift the assembly away from the door . . .

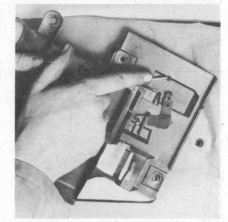

26.7c   . . . while guiding the rod out

26 Door handle — removal and installation

Outside handle

Refer to illustrations 26.1, 26.2, 26.3 and 26.4

1   On front doors, remove the door trim panel and watershield. Remove the door handle mounting nuts **(see illustration)**. Disconnect the lock rod clips and remove the handle from the door. Installation is the reverse of removal.

2   On the side door, remove the trim panel. Disconnect the lock rod clips, remove the mounting nuts and detach the handle from the door **(see illustration)**. Installation is the reverse of removal.

3   On rear doors, remove the access cover **(see illustration)**.

4   Push the clip off with a small screwdriver and disconnect the rods **(see illustration)**.

5   Remove the mounting nuts and detach the handle assembly from the door.

6   Installation is the reverse of removal.

Inside handle

Refer to illustrations 26.7a, 26.7b, 26.7c, 26.8, 26.9a and 26.9b

7   On front doors, remove the door trim panel and door handle mounting bolts. Disconnect the door handle lock rod clip by inserting a screwdriver through the hole in the handle arm **(see illustration)**. Disengage the rod and lower the door handle assembly from the door **(see illustrations)**. Installation is the reverse of removal.

8   On some models, the inside handle is riveted to the door panel. Drill out the center of the rivets with a 3/16-inch drill bit, disengage the lock rods and lift the handle from the door **(see illustration)**. Install the handle using 1/4-inch diameter by 1/2-inch long bolts, nuts and lock washers.

9   On the side door, remove the door trim panel. Disconnect the rod at the handle **(see illustration)**. Remove the mounting screws and detach the handle **(see illustration)**. Installation is the reverse of removal.

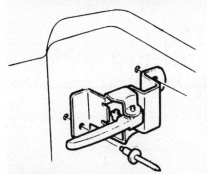

26.8   Some inside handles are riveted to the door panel

27 Front door window regulator — removal and installation

Removal

1   Disconnect the negative cable at the battery. Place the cable out of the way so it cannot accidentally come in contact with the negative terminal of the battery, as this would once again allow power into the electrical system of the vehicle.

2   Remove the door trim panel and watershield (Section 20).

3   Remove the armrest bracket.

4   Secure the window glass in the up position with strong adhesive tape fastened to the glass and wrapped over the frame.

5   Punch out the center of the rivets securing the window regulator to the door and drill out the rivets with a 3/16-inch drill bit.

6   Push the regulator into the door, move it forward and then to the rear to disconnect the arms from the glass and fold the arms together. Lift the regulator from the door through the access hole. On power window regulators unplug the electrical connector.

7   If the power regulator motor is being replaced, install a self-tapping sheet metal screw through the sector gear and backing plate in the provided hole, to lock it. **Warning:** *The regulator arms are under considerable tension from the counterbalance spring and could cause injury if the motor is removed from the regulator without first locking the sector gear in place.* Drill out the rivets and remove the motor from the regulator. Place the new motor in position and secure it with new rivets. Remove the metal screw and lubricate the gear teeth with multi-purpose grease.

Installation

8   Place the regulator in position in the door and connect the arm rollers to the sash and regulator rail.

9   Align the regulator holes with the holes in the door and secure it with 1/4-inch diameter by 1/2-inch long bolts with nuts and lock washers. On power regulators, plug in the electrical connector.

10   Install the armrest bracket, watershield and door trim panel.

11   Remove the tape from the glass and connect the battery.

28 Front door window glass — removal and installation

1   Remove the door trim panel and watershield (Section 20).

2   Remove the lower glass run channel and the other window sealing strip.

3   Remove the window regulator (Section 27).

4   Slide the glass up and out of the door to remove it.

5   Installation is the reverse of removal.

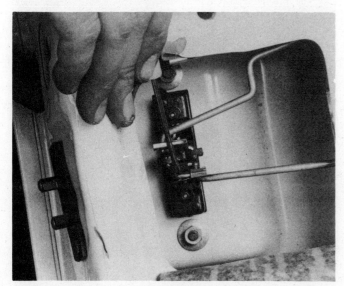

26.9a   Push the clip down with a small screwdriver and disengage the rod

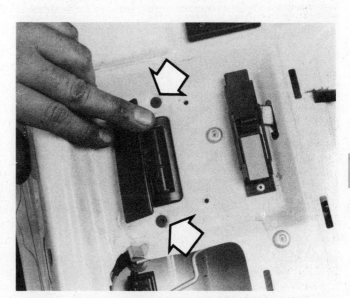

26.9b   Side door inside handle mounting screws (arrows)

11

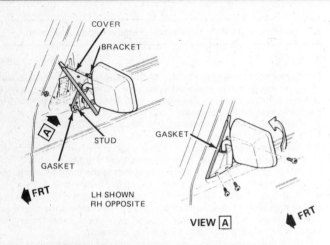

29.3a Base mirror mounting details

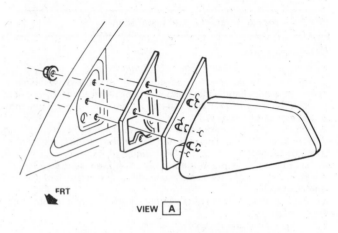

29.3b Standard mirror mounting details

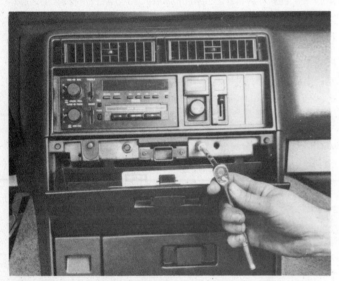

30.1 Remove the two extension bolts in the glove box

30.2 Use a Phillips screwdriver to remove the screws located in the vent openings

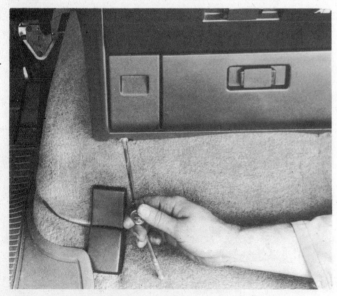

30.3 A socket and extension will make the job of removing the panel brace nuts easier

30.4 Rotate the panel extension down and unplug the electrical connectors

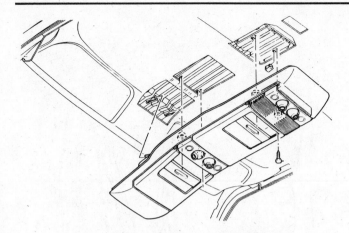

31.2 Roof console mounting details

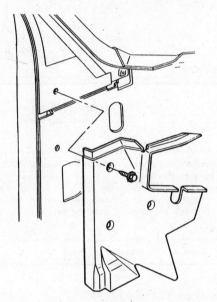

32.3 Front door hinge filler garnish molding
mounting details

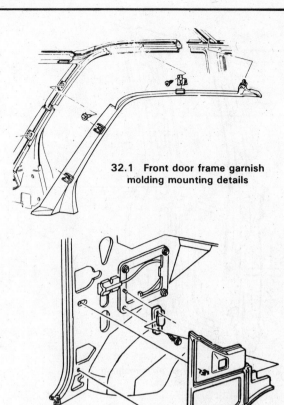

32.1 Front door frame garnish
molding mounting details

32.5 Cowl side vent cover
mounting details

29 Exterior mirror — removal and installation

Refer to illustrations 29.3a and 29.3b

1   Remove the door trim panel and peel back the watershield in the area of the mirror.
2   On power mirrors, unplug the electrical connector.
3   Remove the nuts or screws and detach the mirror (**see illustrations**).
4   Installation is the reverse of removal.

30 Instrument panel lower extension — removal and installation

Refer to illustrations 30.1, 30.2, 30.3 and 30.4

1   Open the glove box and remove the two extension mounting bolts (**see illustration**).
2   Remove the Phillips head screws located in the vent openings (**see illustration**).
3   Remove the two panel extension-to-brace rod nuts at the base of the extension (**see illustration**).
4   Rotate the panel extension away from the instrument panel, unplug the electrical connectors and remove the assembly from the vehicle.
5   To install the panel extension, connect the electrical connectors, position the panel extension and install the screws, nuts and bolts.

31 Roof console — removal and installation

Refer to illustration 31.2

1   Disconnect the negative cable at the battery. Place the cable out of the way so it cannot accidentally come in contact with the negative terminal of the battery, as this would once again allow power into the electrical system of the vehicle.
2   Remove the mounting bolts (**see illustration**).
3   Slide the roof console forward for access to the electrical harness. Unplug the electrical connector and lower the console from the vehicle.
4   To install the console, raise it into place, plug in the connector, insert the console into the slots in the roof and install the mounting bolts.

32 Interior trim panels — removal and installation

Refer to illustrations 32.1, 32.3, 32.5, 32.7a, 32.7b, 32.7c and 32.9

Front door garnish molding

1   Remove the mounting screw (some models), pry at the molding retainers to disengage the molding and remove it (**see illustration**).
2   To install the molding, press it into place until the retainers seat and install the screw.

Front door hinge pillar garnish molding

3   Remove the mounting screw and lift the molding off (**see illustration**).
4   Installation is the reverse of removal.

Cowl side vent cover

5   Remove the mounting screw, pry the cover retainer loose and remove the vent cover (**see illustration**).
6   Installation is the reverse of removal.

11

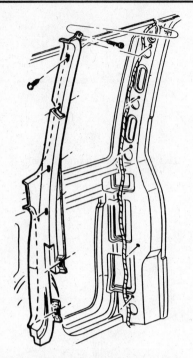

**32.7a   Sliding door lock pillar molding
mounting details**

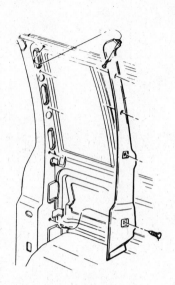

**32.7b   Sliding door lock pillar molding
mounting details**

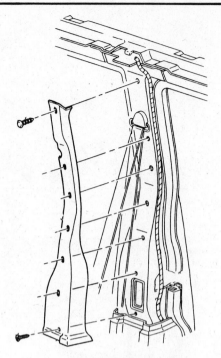

**32.7c   Sliding door pillar garnish
mounting details**

Sliding door pillar moldings
7   Remove the screws and detach the moldings **(see illustrations)**.
8   Installation is the reverse of removal.

Body side trim panels
9   Pry around the outer edge of the trim panel until the retainers are all detached **(see illustration)**.
10   Prior to installation make sure any retainers that were pulled from the panels during removal are reinstalled in the clips. Place the panel in position and press it into place until the retainers are seated.

---

33   Seats — removal and installation

Front seats
Refer to illustrations 33.1 and 33.2
1   Pry the seatbelt guide off **(see illustration)**.
2   Remove the four mounting nuts and lift the seat out **(see illustration)**.

Rear seats
Refer to illustration 33.4
3   Lift the lever and tilt the seatback forward.
4   Lift the latches in the rear seat legs and rotate the seat forward and out of the floor mounts **(see illustration)**.

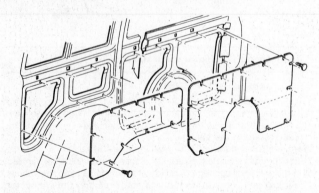

32.9   Body side trim panel mounting details

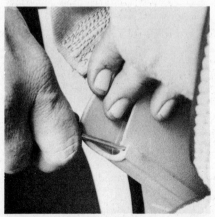

**33.1   Pry the seatbelt guide off with
a screwdriver**

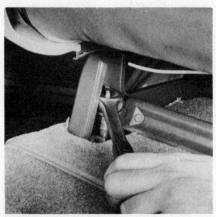

**33.2   Use a socket wrench to remove
the front seat mounting nuts**

**33.4   Hold the latch up and rotate the
rear seat forward**

Chapter 12   Chassis electrical system

Contents

Specifications

Bulb application

Bulb application	Number
Dome light	211-2
Indicator and warning lights (instrument panel)	168 or 194
Brake/tail lights	2057
Rear license plate light	194
Front parking/turn signal lights	2057
Headlights	
1985 through 1991	6014
1992 on	6052 or H6054
Side marker lights	194
Transmission control light	194
Back-up lights	1156
Heater/air conditioning indicator light	194

1   General information

The electrical system is a 12-volt, negative ground type. Power for the lights and all electrical accessories is supplied by a lead/acid-type battery which is charged by the alternator.

This Chapter covers repair and service procedures for the various electrical components not associated with the engine. Information on the battery, alternator, distributor and starter motor can be found in Chapter 5.

It should be noted that when portions of the electrical system are serviced, the negative battery cable should be disconnected from the battery to prevent electrical shorts and/or fires.
Caution: *If the vehicle is equipped with a Delco Loc II audio system (1992 and later models with a Compact Disc player), be sure the lockout feature is turned off before performing any procedure that requires disconnecting the battery (refer to your owner's manual for further information on this system).*

2   Electrical troubleshooting - general information

A typical electrical circuit consists of an electrical component, any switches, relays, motors, fuses, fusible links or circuit breakers related to that component and the wiring and connectors that link the component to both the battery and the chassis. To help you pinpoint an electrical circuit problem, wiring diagrams are included at the end of this book.

Before tackling any troublesome electrical circuit, first study the appropriate wiring diagrams to get a complete understanding of what makes up that individual circuit. Trouble spots, for instance, can often be narrowed down by noting if other components related to the circuit are operating properly. If several components or circuits fail at one time, chances are the problem is in a fuse or ground connection, because several circuits are often routed through the same fuse and ground connections.

Electrical problems usually stem from simple causes, such as loose or corroded connections, a blown fuse, a melted fusible link or a bad relay. Visually inspect the condition of all fuses, wires and connections in a problem circuit before troubleshooting it.

If testing instruments are going to be utilized, use the diagrams to plan ahead of time where you will make the necessary connections in order to accurately pinpoint the trouble spot.

The basic tools needed for electrical troubleshooting include a circuit tester or voltmeter (a 12-volt bulb with a set of test leads can also be used), a continuity tester, which includes a bulb, battery and set of test leads, and a jumper wire, preferably with a circuit breaker in-

12

corporated, which can be used to bypass electrical components. Before attempting to locate a problem with test instruments, use the wiring diagrams(s) to decide where to make the connections.

Voltage checks

Voltage checks should be performed if a circuit is not functioning properly. Connect one lead of a circuit tester to either the negative battery terminal or a known good ground. Connect the other lead to a connector in the circuit being tested, preferably nearest to the battery or fuse. If the bulb of the tester lights, voltage is present, which means that the part of the circuit between the connector and the battery is problem free. Continue checking the rest of the circuit in the same fashion. When you reach a point at which no voltage is present, the problem lies between that point and the last test point with voltage. Most of the time the problem can be traced to a loose connection. **Note:** *Keep in mind that some circuits receive voltage only when the ignition key is in the Accessory or Run position.*

Finding a short

One method of finding shorts in a circuit is to remove the fuse and connect a test light or voltmeter in its place to the fuse terminals. There should be no voltage present in the circuit. Move the wiring harness from side-to-side while watching the test light. If the bulb goes on, there is a short to ground somewhere in that area, probably where the insulation has rubbed through. The same test can be performed on each component in the circuit, even a switch.

Ground check

Perform a ground test to check whether a component is properly grounded. Disconnect the battery and connect one lead of a self-powered test light, known as a continuity tester, to a known good ground. Connect the other lead to the wire or ground connection being tested. If the bulb goes on, the ground is good. If the bulb does not go on, the ground is not good.

Continuity check

A continuity check is done to determine if there are any breaks in a circuit — if it is passing electricity properly. With the circuit off (no power in the circuit), a self-powered continuity tester can be used to check the circuit. Connect the test leads to both ends of the circuit (or to the "power" end and a good ground), and if the test light comes on the circuit is passing current properly. If the light doesn't come on, there is a break somewhere in the circuit. The same procedure can be used to test a switch, by connecting the continuity tester to the power in and power out sides of the switch. With the switch turned On, the test light should come on.

Finding an open circuit

When diagnosing for possible open circuits, it is often difficult to locate them by sight because oxidation or terminal misalignment are hidden by the connectors. Merely wiggling a connector on a sensor or in the wiring harness may correct the open circuit condition. Remember this when an open circuit is indicated when troubleshooting a circuit. Intermittent problems may also be caused by oxidized or loose connections.

Electrical troubleshooting is simple if you keep in mind that all electrical circuits are basically electricity running from the battery, through the wires, switches, relays, fuses and fusible links to each electrical component (light bulb, motor, etc.) and to ground, from which it is passed back to the battery. Any electrical problem is an interruption in the flow of electricity to and from the battery.

---

3   Fuses — general information

Refer to illustrations 3.1 and 3.3

The electrical circuits of the vehicle are protected by a combination of fuses, circuit breakers and fusible links. The fuse block is located under the instrument panel on the left side of the dashboard **(see illustration)**.

Each of the fuses is designed to protect a specific circuit, and the various circuits are identified on the fuse panel itself.

Miniaturized fuses are employed in the fuse block. These compact fuses, with blade terminal design, allow fingertip removal and replace-

3.1   The fuse block is located under the instrument panel to the left of the steering column

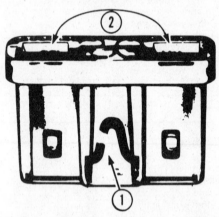

3.3   To test for a blown fuse, pull it out and inspect it for an open (1), then, with the circuit activated, use a test light across the terminals (2)

ment. If an electrical component fails, always check the fuse first. A blown fuse is easily identified through the clear plastic body. Visually inspect the element for evidence of damage **(see illustration)**. If a continuity check is called for, the blade terminal tips are exposed in the fuse body.

Be sure to replace blown fuses with the correct type. Fuses of different ratings are physically interchangeable, but only fuses of the proper rating should be used. Replacing a fuse with one of a higher or lower value than specified is not recommended. Each electrical circuit needs a specific amount of protection. The amperage value of each fuse is molded into the fuse body. **Caution:** *Never bypass a fuse with pieces of metal or foil. Serious damage to the electrical system could result.*

If the replacement fuse immediately fails, don't replace it again until the cause of the problem is isolated and corrected. In most cases, this will be a short circuit in the wiring caused by a broken or deteriorated wire.

---

4   Fusible links — general information

Some circuits are protected by fusible links. The links are used in circuits which are not ordinarily fused, such as the ignition circuit.

Although the fusible links appear to be a heavier gauge than the wire they are protecting, the appearance is due to the thick insulation. All fusible links are four wire gauges smaller than the wire they are designed to protect. The location of the fusible links on your particular vehicle may be determined by referring to the wiring diagrams at the end of this book.

Fusible links cannot be repaired, but a new link of the same size wire can be put in its place. The procedure is as follows:

a) Disconnect the negative cable from the battery.
b) Disconnect the fusible link from the wiring harness.
c) Cut the damaged fusible link out of the wiring just behind the connector.
d) Strip the insulation back approximately 1/2-inch.
e) Position the connector on the new fusible link and crimp it into place.
f) Use rosin core solder at each end of the new link to obtain a good solder joint.
g) Use plenty of electrical tape around the soldered joint. No wires should be exposed.
h) Connect the battery ground cable. Test the circuit for proper operation.

5   Circuit breakers — general information

Circuit breakers, which are located in the main fuse block, protect accessories such as power windows, power door locks and the rear window defogger.

The headlight wiring is also protected by a circuit breaker. An electrical overload in the system will cause the lights to go off and come on or, in some cases, to remain off. If this happens, check the headlight circuit immediately. The circuit breaker will function normally once the overload condition is corrected. Refer to the wiring diagrams at the end of this book for the location of the circuit breakers in your vehicle.

6   Turn signal and hazard flasher — replacement

1   Detach the cable from the negative terminal of the battery.

Turn signal flasher

Refer to illustration 6.3

2   The trim plate under the instrument panel must be removed to gain access to the flasher unit (Section 16).
3   Locate the turn signal flasher on the back of the hood release mount **(see illustration)**, remove it from the retaining clip and unplug it.
4   Installation is the reverse of removal.

Hazard flasher

5   Locate the hazard flasher above the fuse block, remove the bolt and unplug it.
6   Installation is the reverse of removal.

7   Multi-function switch lever — replacement

Refer to illustration 7.4

1   Detach the cable from the negative terminal of the battery.
2   Put the shift lever in Low and place the turn signal lever in the right turn position.
3   On tilt-column models, place the column in the Up position.
4   Locate the multi-function lever electrical connector **(see illustration)** and unplug it.

6.3   The turn signal flasher is mounted on the upper edge of the hood release mount (arrow)

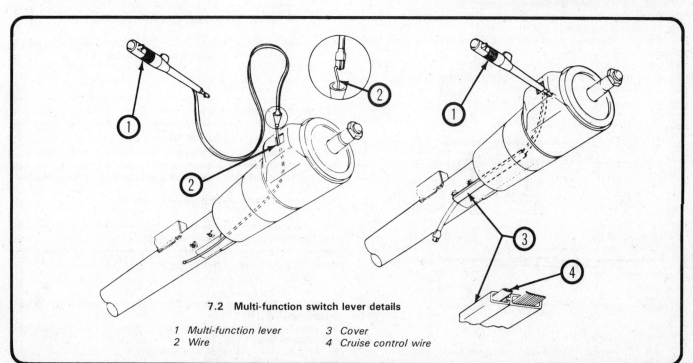

7.2   Multi-function switch lever details

1 *Multi-function lever*   3 *Cover*
2 *Wire*   4 *Cruise control wire*

12

5   Attach a length of wire to the pigtail to pull the pigtail back through during installation.
6   Pull the lever straight out of the steering column.
7   Pull the multi-function lever pigtail lead up through the steering column. Detach the wire from the pigtail lead and attach it to the lead of the new multi-function lever.
8   Carefully thread the new connector and lead back through the steering column.
9   Installation is the reverse of removal.

8   Ignition key lock cylinder — replacement

Refer to illustrations 8.4 and 8.12

1   Detach the cable from the negative terminal of the battery.
2   Remove the steering wheel (see Chapter 10).
3   Remove the column trim plate and pry off the lock plate cover.
4   Depress the shaft lock plate and remove the retaining clip **(see illustration)**. Remove the shaft lock plate.
5   Remove the the cancelling cam and the spring.
6   Remove the hazard flasher button.
7   Remove the screw and detach the signal switch arm.
8   Remove the three turn signal switch screws.
9   Pull the turn signal switch wire harness up through the steering column until there is sufficient slack to remove the turn signal switch.
10   Pull the turn signal switch out and set it aside.
11   Remove the key warning buzzer switch. The easiest way to get the buzzer switch out is to use a paper clip to pry it out. **Note:** *Don't lose the small retainer clip that holds the buzzer switch in place. The clip must be reinstalled in the same position.*
12   Remove the lock retaining screw **(see illustration)**.
13   Turn the ignition switch to the Run position and pull it out (see illustration 8.12).
14   Installation is the reverse of removal.

9   Ignition switch — replacement

Refer to illustration 9.5

1   Detach the cable from the negative terminal of the battery.
2   Place the ignition switch in the Lock position. If the key lock cylinder has been removed, pull the actuating rod up until a definite stop can be felt and then move down one detent.
3   Lower and support the steering column.
4   Remove the ignition switch retaining screws and lift the switch out of the steering column jacket.
5   Prior to installation, make sure the ignition switch is in the Lock position **(see illustration)**.
6   Connect the actuating rod to the switch.
7   Press the switch into position and install the screws.
8   Install the steering column bolts.

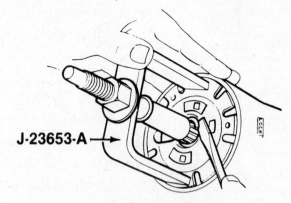

8.4   Depress the lock plate and pry out the retaining clip with a screwdriver

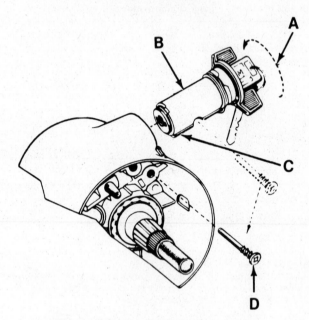

8.12   Ignition key lock removal details

A *Hold the lock cylinder sleeve and rotate the knob clockwise against the stop*
B *Lock cylinder assembly*
C *Locating key*
D *Lock retaining screw*

10   Headlight switch — replacement

Refer to illustrations 10.3a and 10.3b

1   Detach the cable from the negative terminal of the battery.
2   Remove the instrument cluster trim plate (Section 17).
3   Unplug the electrical connectors and remove the screws **(see illustrations)**.
4   Installation is the reverse of removal.

11   Headlight — removal and installation

Refer to illustrations 11.3a, 11.3b and 11.4

1   Detach the cable from the negative terminal of the battery.
2   Remove the headlight bezel (Chapter 11).
3   Remove the screws and detach the headlight retaining ring **(see illustrations)**.
4   Unplug the headlight electrical connector and remove the headlight **(see illustration)**.
5   Installation is the reverse of removal.
6   Adjust the headlights (Section 12).

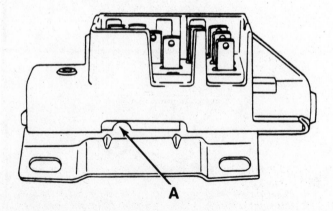

9.5   The ignition switch must be in the Lock position (A) before installation

10.3a Unplug the connectors from the headlight switch . . .

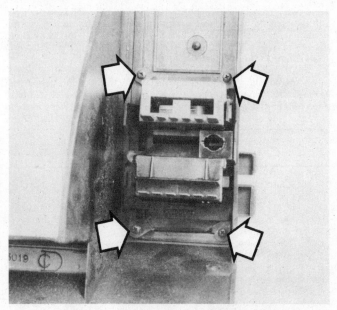

10.3b   . . . and remove the screws (arrows)

11.3a Remove only the headlight
retaining screws, not the
adjusting screws . . .

11.3b   . . . and lift off the
retaining ring

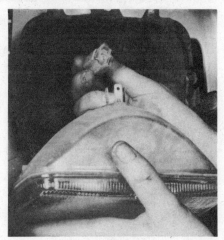

11.4 Pull the headlight out and unplug
the connector

12 Headlights — adjustment

Refer to illustration 12.2

1   It's important that the headlights be aimed correctly. If adjusted incorrectly they could blind an oncoming driver and cause a serious accident or seriously reduce your ability to see the road. The headlights should be checked for proper aim every 12 months and each time a new sealed beam headlight is installed or front end body work is performed.

2   Each headlight has two spring loaded adjusting screws, one on the top controlling up-and-down movement and one on the side controlling left-and-right movement **(see illustration)**. There are several methods of adjusting the headlights. The simplest method requires an empty wall 25 feet in front of the vehicle and a level floor.

3   Park the vehicle on a level floor 25 feet from the wall.

4   Position masking tape vertically on the wall in reference to the vehicle centerline and the centerlines of both headlights.

5   Position a horizontal tape line in reference to the centerline of all the headlights. **Note:** *It may be easier to position the tape on the wall with the vehicle parked only a few inches away.*

6   Adjustment should be made with the vehicle sitting level, the gas tank half-full and no unusually heavy load in the vehicle.

7   Starting with the Low beam adjustment, position the high intensity

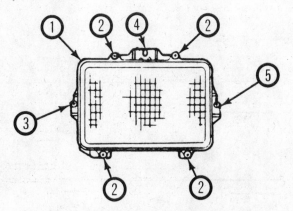

12.2 Headlight ring and adjustment screw locations

1 *Headlight retaining ring*
2 *Headlight retaining ring screws*
3 *Right headlight horizontal adjusting screw*
4 *Vertical adjusting screw*
5 *Left headlight horizontal adjusting screw*

12

zone two inches below the horizontal line and two inches to the right of the headlight vertical line. Adjustment is made by turning the top adjusting screw clockwise to raise the beam and counterclockwise to lower the beam. The adjusting screw on the side should be used in the same manner to move the beam left-or-right.

8   With the High beams on, the high intensity zone should be vertically centered with the exact center just below the horizontal line. **Note:** *It may not be possible to position the headlight aim exactly for both High and Low beams. If a compromise must be made, keep in mind that the Low beams are the most used and have the greatest effect on driver safety.*

13 Bulb replacement

1   Detach the cable from the negative terminal of the battery before attempting to replace any of the following bulbs.

Front turn signal/side marker lights

Refer to illustration 13.3

2   Remove the headlight bezel (refer to Chapter 11).
3   Turn the bulb holder counterclockwise and remove it from the turn signal lens assembly **(see illustration)**.
4   Turn the bulb counterclockwise and remove it from the bulb holder.
5   Installation is the reverse of removal.

Rear turn signal and back-up lights

Refer to illustrations 13.6a, 13.6b, 13.7, 13.8 and 13.9

6   Open the rear doors, remove the screws along the inner edge and rotate the tail light lens out of the tabs in the body **(see illustrations)**.
7   Rotate the bulb holders counterclockwise to remove them from the lens assembly **(see illustration)**.
8   Push the bulb in and turn it counterclockwise to remove it from the holder **(see illustration)**.

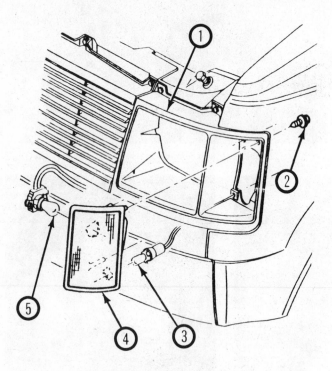

13.3   Front bulb component layout

1 *Headlight bezel*   4 *Light housing*
2 *Light housing screw*   5 *Park and turn signal light*
3 *Side marker light*

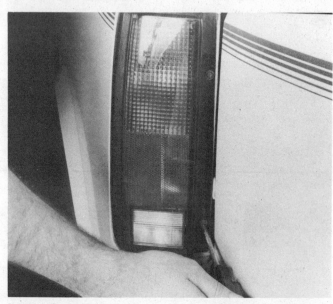

13.6a   Open the rear door, remove the taillight lens screws . . .

13.6b   . . . and rotate the lens out of the tabs in the body

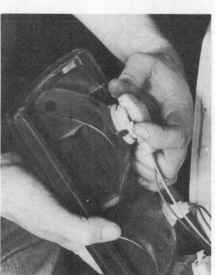

13.7   Turn the bulb holder counterclockwise and withdraw it from the lens assembly

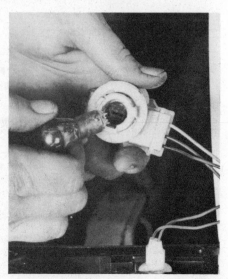

13.8   Push in and turn the bulb to remove it from the holder

9   Installation is the reverse of removal, taking care to align the lens tabs with the body tab recesses (**see illustration**).

License plate light
Refer to illustration 13.10
10   Remove the two bolts and lower the license plate light assembly (**see illustration**).
11   Pull the bulb from the light assembly and press a new one into place.

Dome light
Refer to illustrations 13.12a and 13.12b
12   Pry off the plastic dome light lens with a small screwdriver (**see illustrations**).
13   Pull the bulb straight out.
14   Installation is the reverse of removal.

Instrument cluster lights
Refer to illustrations 13.18, 13.19a, 13.19b, 13.19c and 13.19d
15   Remove the instrument cluster (Section 17).
16   Turn the instrument cluster upside down and lay it down on a clean work surface or shop rag.
17   Turn the bulb holder counterclockwise and pull it out of the back of the case.
18   Pull the bulb out of the bulb holder (**see illustration**).

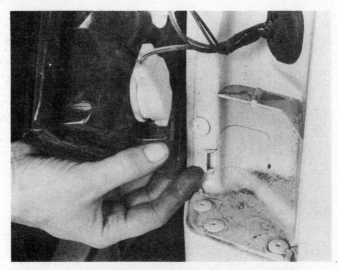

13.9   Fit the taillight lens into the tabs in the body and rotate it into position

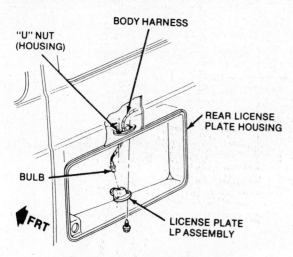

13.10   License plate light details

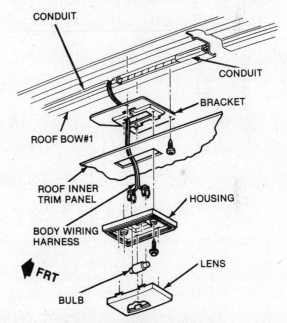

13.12a   Dome/reading light details

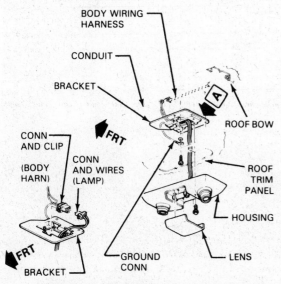

13.12b   Optional dome light components

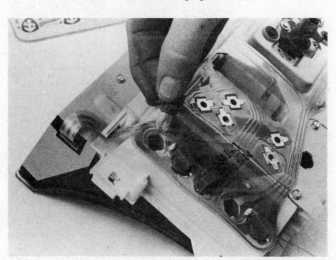

13.18   Turn the instrument cluster bulb then lift it out

12

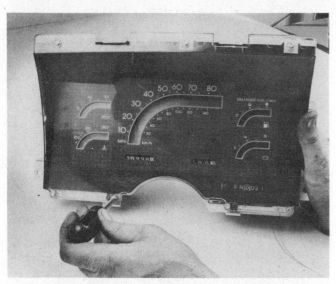

13.19a   Remove the cluster front case cover with a nut driver . . .

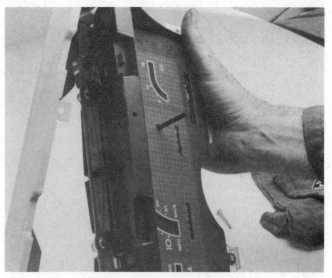

13.19b   . . . lift off the back cover . . .

19 To remove the upper bulbs, remove the case front and rear covers, unplug the circuit board and pull the bulbs straight out **(see illustrations)**.
20 Installation is the reverse of removal.

14   Radio and speakers — removal and installation

1   Detach the cable from the negative terminal of the battery prior to performing any of the following procedures.

Radio
Refer to illustration 14.3

2   Remove the instrument panel lower extension (Chapter 11).
3   Remove the radio mounting bolts **(see illustration)**.
4   Reach behind the radio and disconnect the antenna lead.
5   Pull the radio out of the dash and detach the wires.
6   Remove the radio.
7   Installation is the reverse of removal.

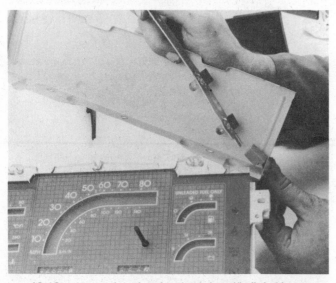

13.19c   . . . and unplug the circuit board/bulb holder

13.19d   The bulbs are replaced by pulling them straight out

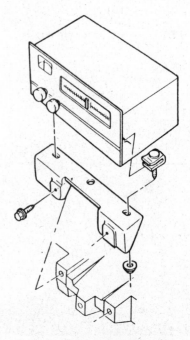

14.3   Radio mounting details

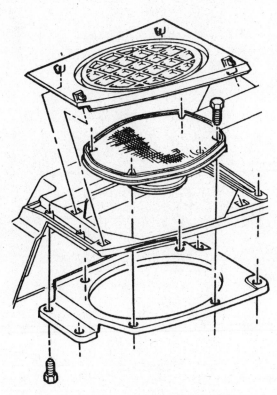

14.8   Dash-mounted speaker details

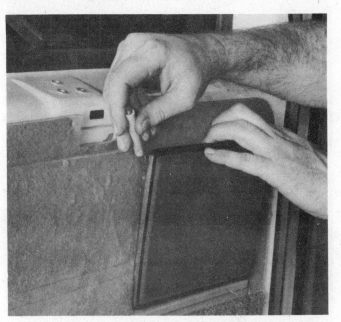

14.11a   Carefully pry the rear door speaker grille off with a small screwdriver . . .

Speakers

Refer to illustrations 14.8, 14.11a, 14.11b and 14.14

8   On dashboard speakers, pry the cover off with a screwdriver **(see illustration)**.
9   Remove the bolts and lift out the speaker.
10   Installation is the reverse of removal.
11   On rear door speakers, pry off the grille and remove the door trim panel **(see illustrations)**.
12   Remove the screws and lift out the speaker.
13   Installation is the reverse of removal.
14   To remove pillar-mounted speakers, pry off the grille for access to the speaker screws **(see illustration)**.
15   Remove the screws and lift out the speaker.
16   Installation is the reverse of removal.

15   Radio antenna — removal and installation

1   Unscrew the old antenna mast.
2   Install the new antenna and tighten it securely.

16   Instrument panel — removal and installation

Refer to illustration 16.5

1   Detach the negative cable from the battery.
2   Remove the instrument cluster (Section 17).
3   Remove the instrument panel lower extension (Chapter 11).
4   Remove the engine cover (Chapter 11).

14.11b   . . . and remove the door trim panel

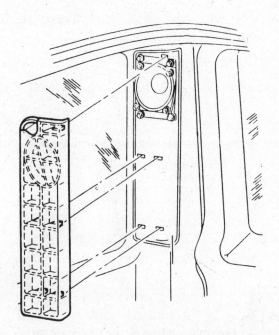

14.14   Pillar-mounted speaker details

12

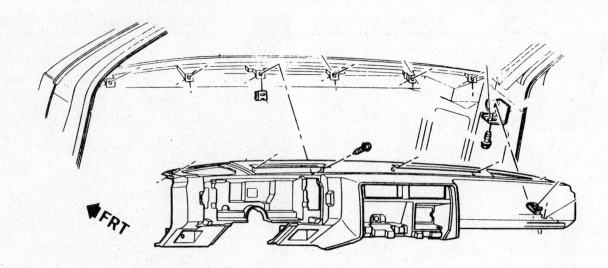

16.5 Instrument panel mounting details

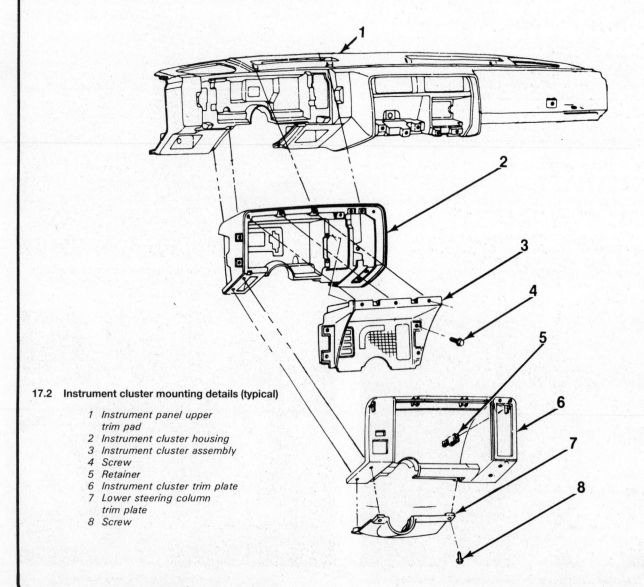

17.2 Instrument cluster mounting details (typical)

1 *Instrument panel upper
   trim pad*
2 *Instrument cluster housing*
3 *Instrument cluster assembly*
4 *Screw*
5 *Retainer*
6 *Instrument cluster trim plate*
7 *Lower steering column
   trim plate*
8 *Screw*

17.3a Pull the top edge of the cluster trim plate out
of the retainers . . .

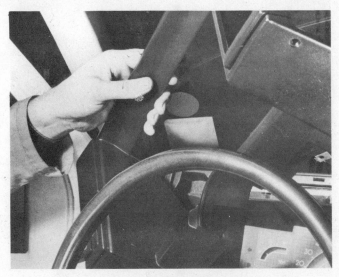

17.3b . . . and lift it up for access to the electrical
connectors

5   Remove the mounting bolts and lower the instrument panel (see
illustration).
6   Installation is the reverse of removal.

17 Instrument cluster — removal and installation

Refer to illustrations 17.2, 17.3a, 17.3b, 17.5, 17.7a and 17.7b
1   Detach the negative cable from the battery.
2   Remove the cluster trim plate and lower steering column cover (see
illustration).
3   Pull the upper panel cluster trim plate out of the retainers, detach
it from the cluster and unplug the electrical connectors (see illustrations).
4   Remove the instrument cluster mounting screws.
5   Reach behind the cluster and disconnect the speedometer cable
(see illustration).
6   Pull the cluster out and unplug the electrical connectors.
7   Remove the screw and detach the vehicle speed sensor from the
cluster (see illustrations).
8   Detach the cluster from the instrument panel.
9   Installation is the reverse of removal.

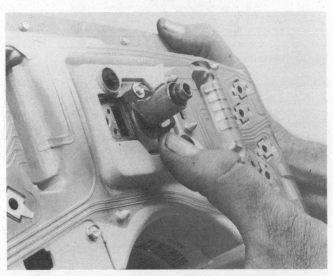

17.5 Press the clip toward the cluster with your thumb to
disconnect the speedometer cable (cluster and cable
removed for clarity)

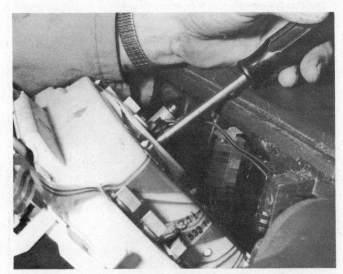

17.7a Use a nut driver to remove the VSS electrical
connector screw, . . .

17.7b . . . then unplug the VSS wire harness

12

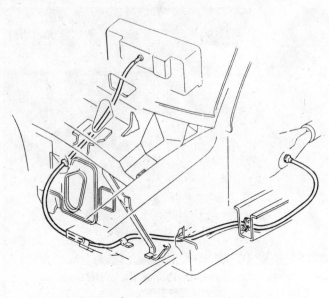

18.2   Speedometer cable routing details

18   Speedometer cable — replacement

Refer to illustration 18.2

1   Detach the negative cable from the battery.
2   Disconnect the speedometer cable at the transmission **(see illustration).**
3   Detach the cable from the fasteners in the engine compartment and pull it up enough to provide slack for disconnecting the cable from the speedometer.
4   Remove the instrument cluster screws and disconnect the speedometer cable from the back of the cluster.
5   Remove the cable from the vehicle.
6   Installation is the reverse of removal.

19   Windshield wiper arm — removal and installation

Refer to illustrations 19.1 and 19.2

1   Use a screwdriver to pry the release lever away from the windshield wiper arm. **(see illustration).**
2   Lift the wiper arm off, disconnect the washer fluid tube and remove the arm from the vehicle **(see illustration).**
3   Installation is the reverse of removal.

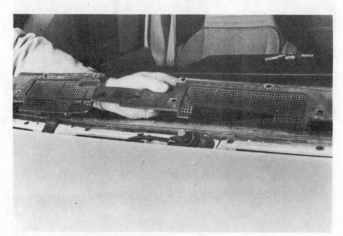

20.3   Remove the retainers and lift the grille out

19.1   Pry the lever away from the wiper arm to release it

19.2   Pull the washer fluid connector off the tube

20   Windshield wiper motor — removal and installation

Refer to illustrations 20.3 and 20.5

1   Remove the wiper arms (Section 19).
2   Remove the cowl ventilator grille (Chapter 11).
3   Remove the plastic wiper motor cavity grille **(see illustration).**
4   Remove the nut from the wiper motor and disconnect the wiper actuating arms.
5   Unplug the electrical connector, remove the mounting bolts and lift the wiper motor from the engine compartment **(see illustration).**
6   Installation is the reverse of removal.

20.5   Unplug the connector and remove the
wiper motor bolts

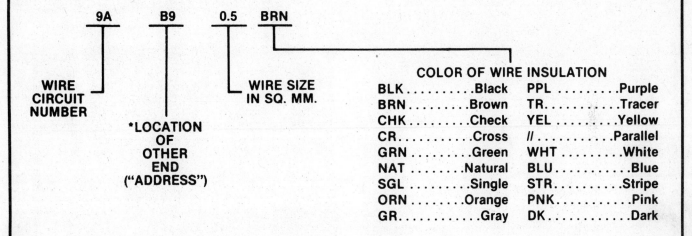

Wiring diagram color codes

WIRING DIAGRAMS
START ON NEXT PAGE

Typical front light and instrument panel wiring diagram (four-cylinder engine)

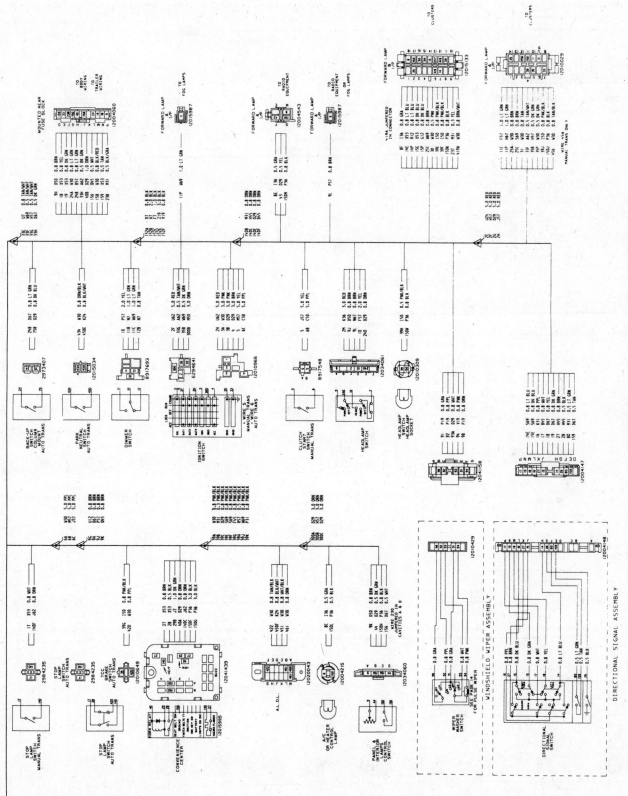

Typical front light and instrument panel wiring diagram (four-cylinder engine) (continued)

Typical front light and instrument panel wiring diagram (V6 engine)

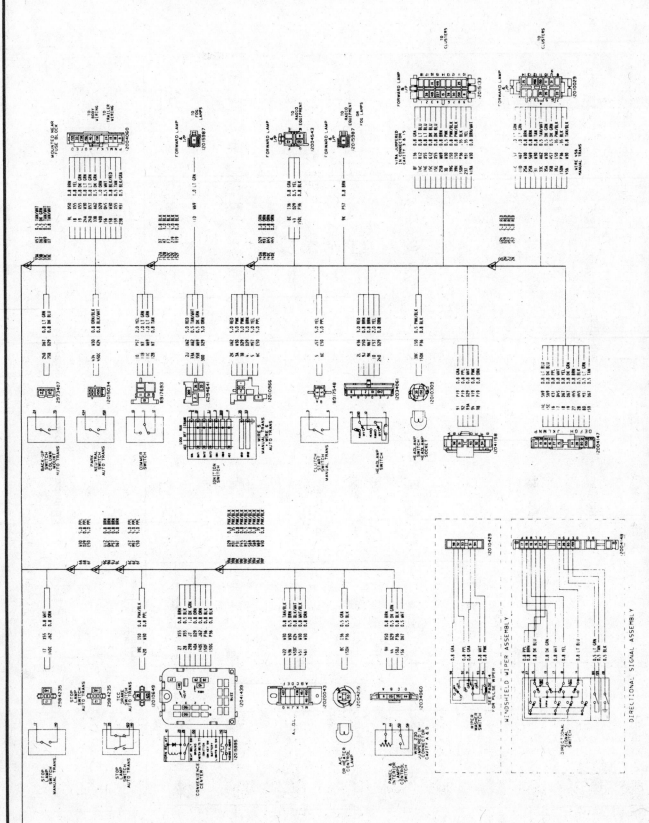

Typical front light and instrument panel wiring diagram (V6 engine) (continued)

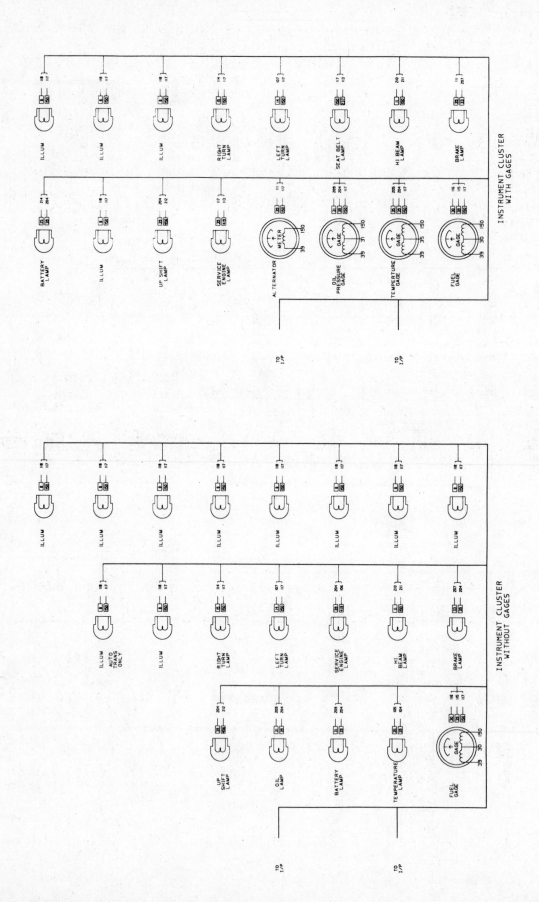

Typical instrument cluster wiring diagram

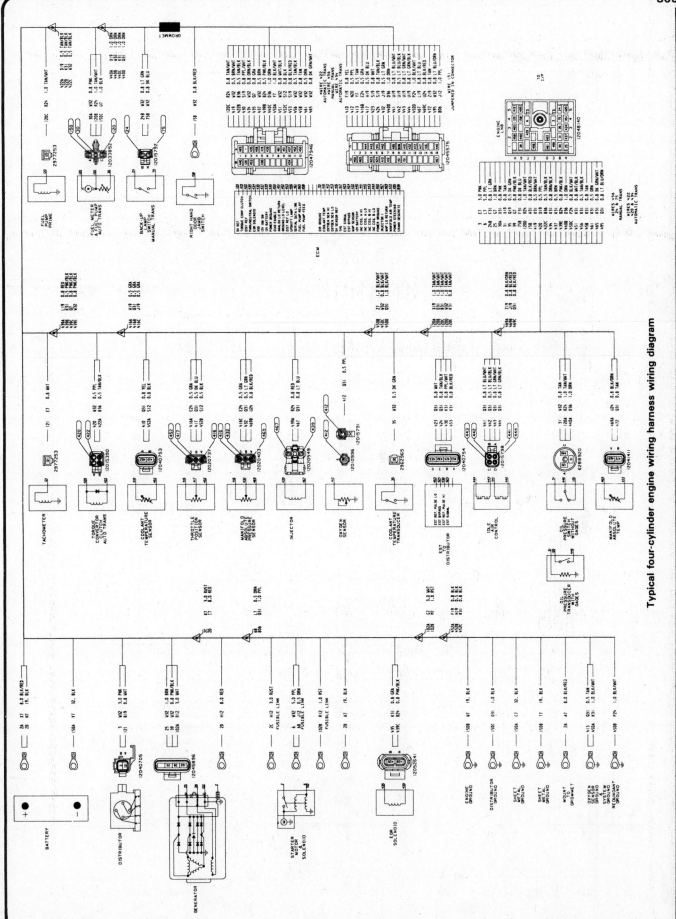

Typical four-cylinder engine wiring harness wiring diagram

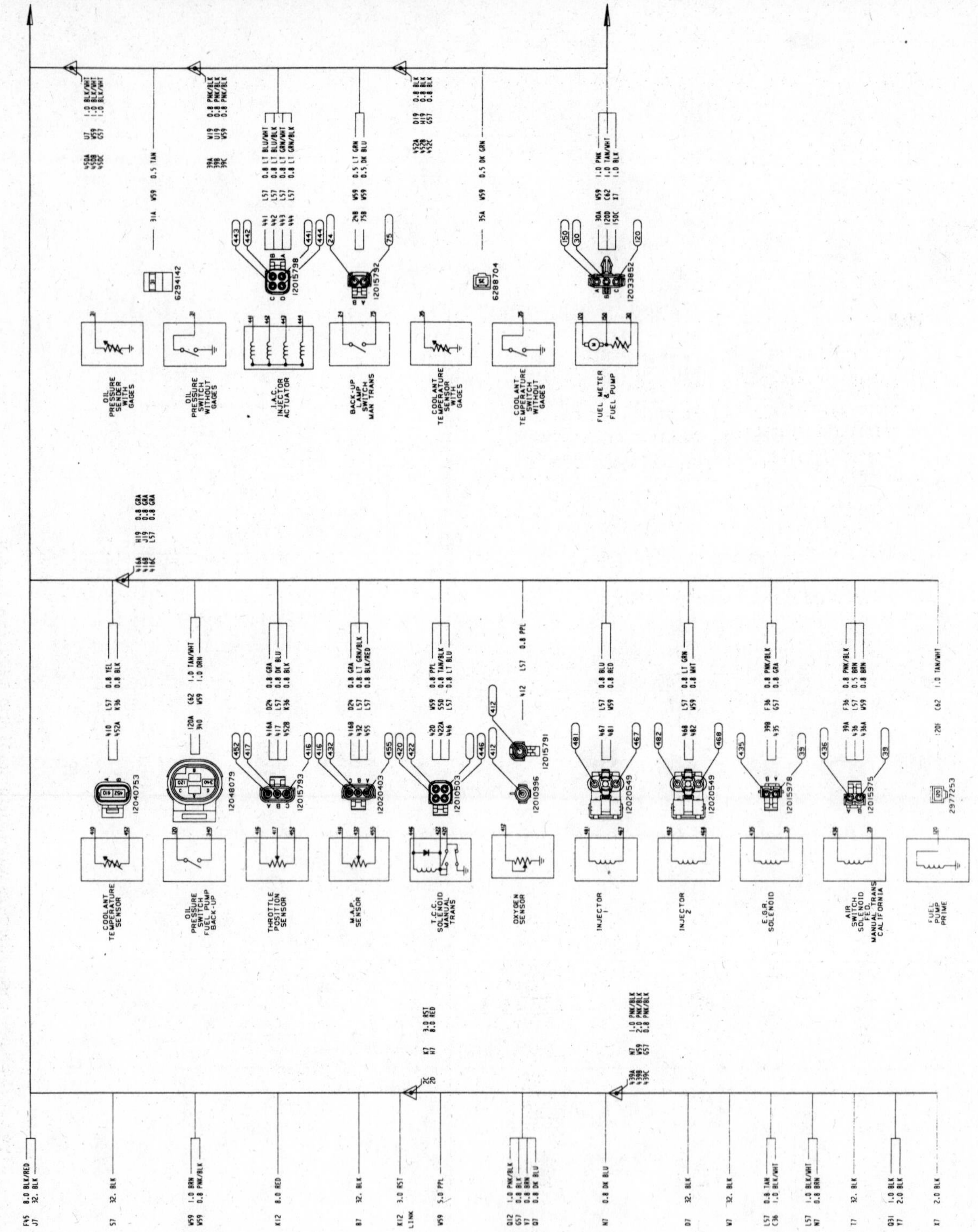

Typical V6 engine wiring harness wiring diagram (TBI models)

BATTERY

GENERATOR

STARTER MOTOR SOLENOID

E.S.C. HYBRID FUNCTION

E.S.C. SENSOR

SHEET METAL GROUND

SHEET METAL GROUND

GENERATOR BRACKET GROUND

LEFT HAND REAR CYLINDER HEAD GROUND

SHEET METAL GROUND REAR SILL AUTO TRANS

LEFT HAND CYLINDER GROUND

COOLANT TEMPERATURE SENSOR

OIL PRESSURE SWITCH FUEL PUMP BACK-UP

THROTTLE POSITION SENSOR

M.A.P. SENSOR

T.C.C. SOLENOID MANUAL TRANS

OXYGEN SENSOR

INJECTOR 1

INJECTOR 2

E.G.R. SOLENOID

AIR SWITCH SOLENOID MANUAL TRANS CALIFORNIA

FUEL PUMP PRIME

OIL PRESSURE SENDER WITH GAGES

OIL PRESSURE SWITCH WITHOUT GAGES

I.A.C. INJECTOR ACTUATOR

BACK-UP LAMP SWITCH MAN TRANS

COOLANT TEMPERATURE SENSOR WITH GAGES

COOLANT TEMPERATURE SWITCH WITHOUT GAGES

FUEL METER & FUEL PUMP

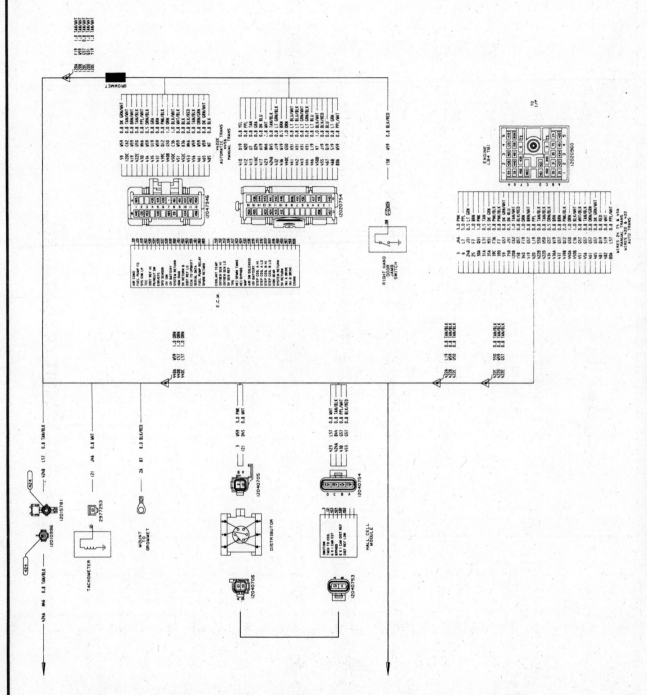

Typical V6 engine wiring harness wiring diagram (TBI models) (continued)

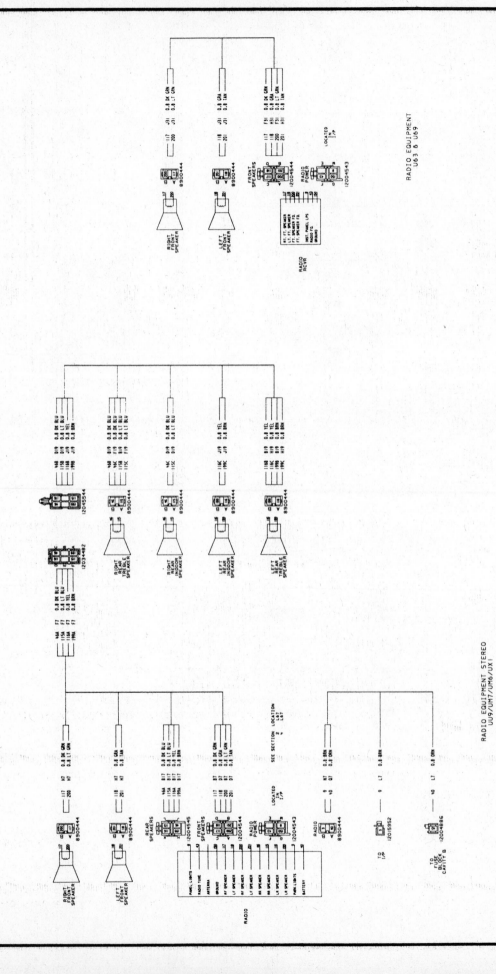

Typical radio and stereo equipment wiring diagram

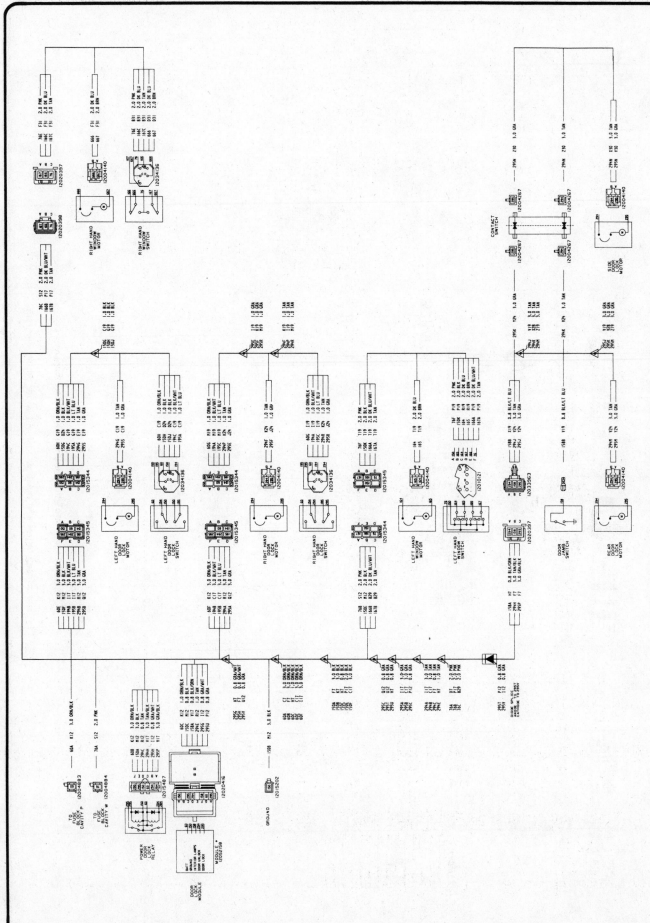

Typical power door lock and power window wiring diagram

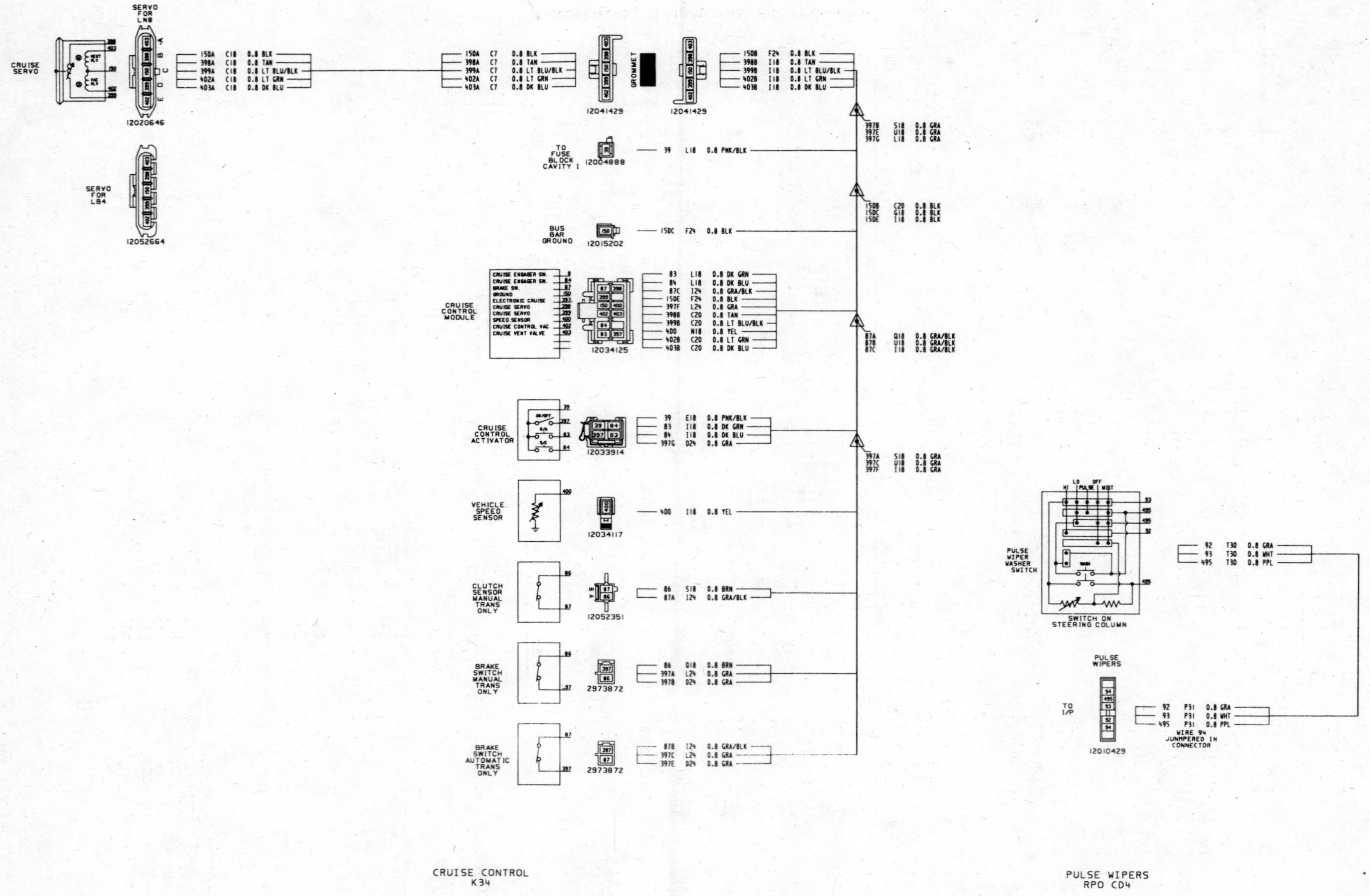

Typical cruise control and pulse windshield wiper wiring diagram

PULSE WIPERS
RPO CD4

CRUISE CONTROL
K34

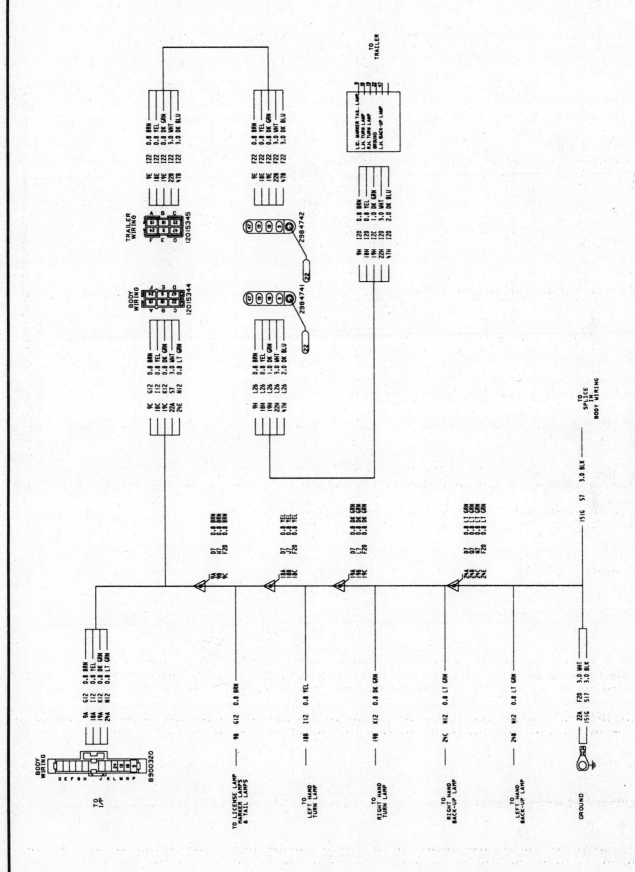

Typical trailer wiring harness wiring diagram

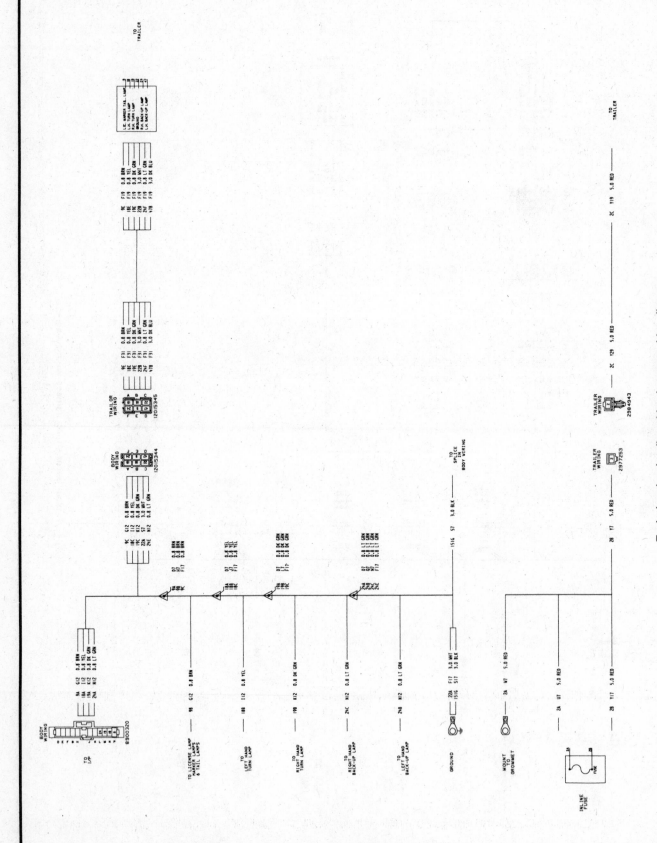

Typical optional trailer wiring harness wiring diagram

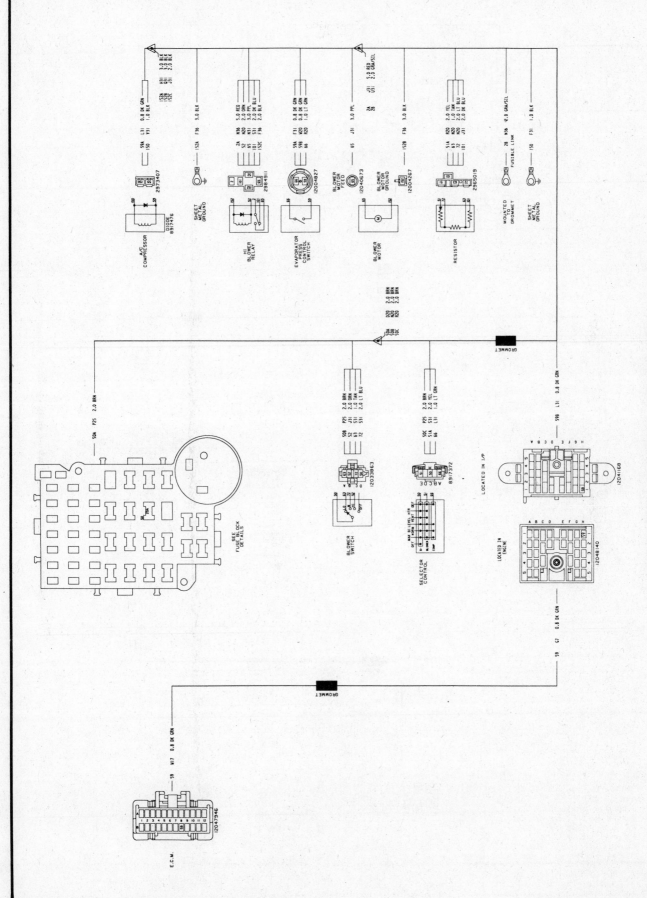

Typical air conditioning system wiring diagram (V6 models)

313

Typical air conditioning system wiring diagram (four-cylinder models)

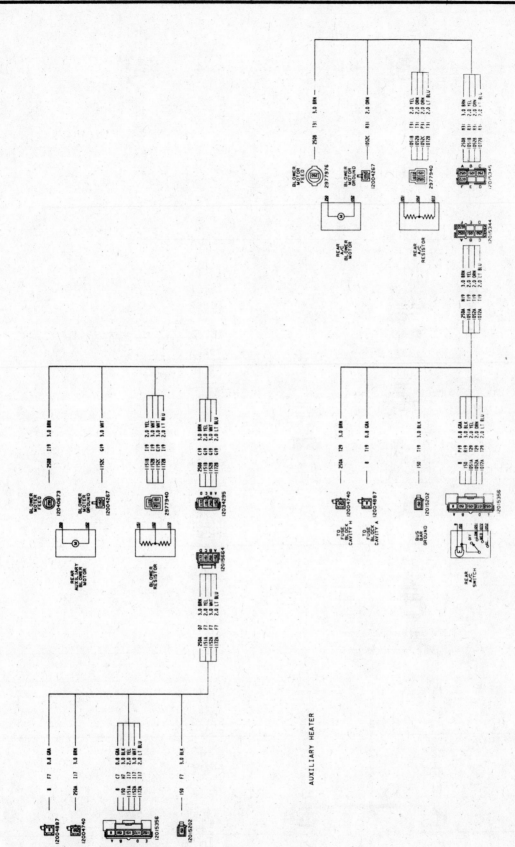

Typical rear air conditioning and auxiliary heater wiring diagram

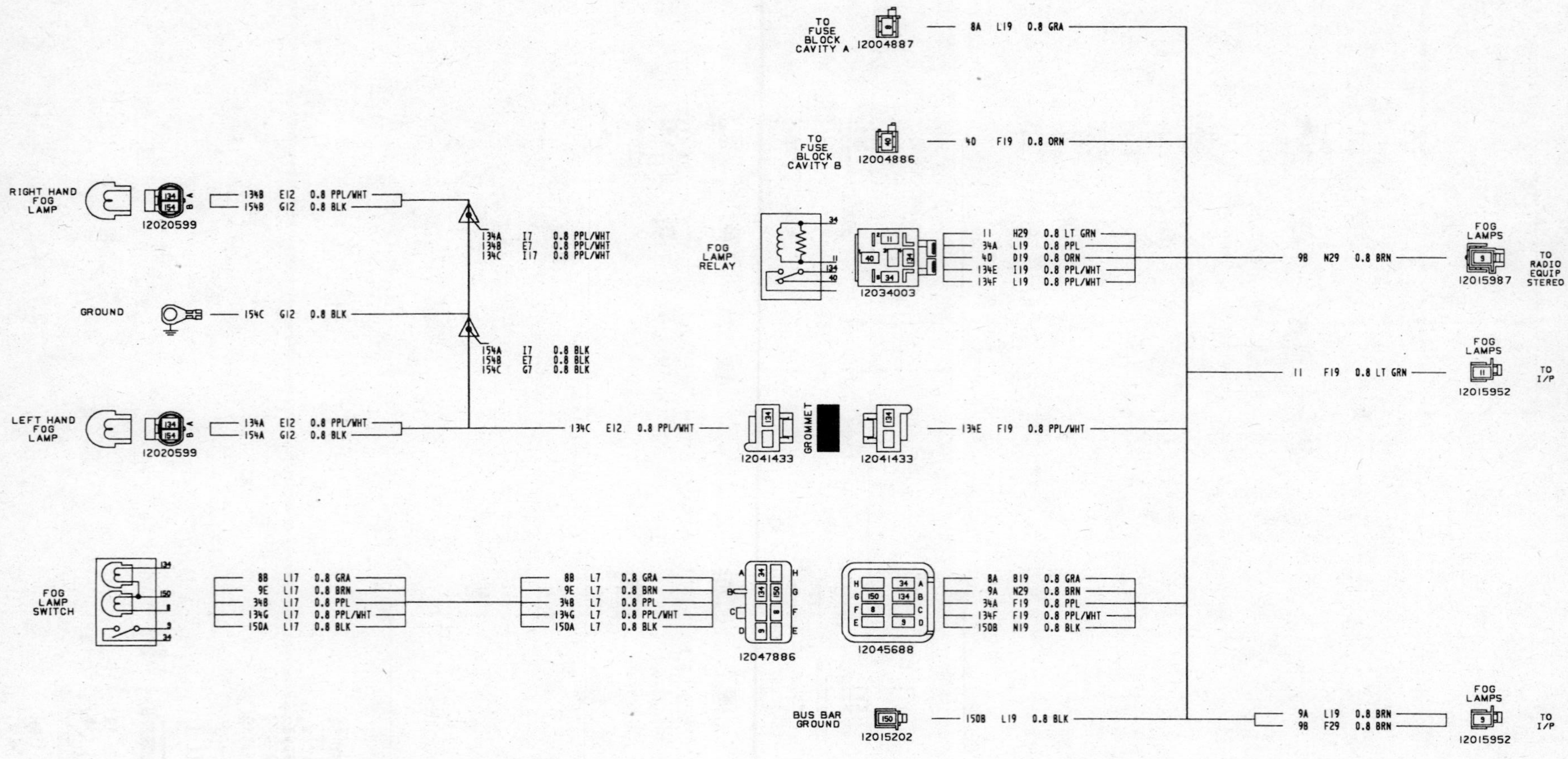

TO RADIO EQUIP STEREO

FOG LAMPS 12015987

FOG LAMPS 12015952 TO I/P

FOG LAMPS 12015952 TO I/P

9B N29 0.8 BRN

11 F19 0.8 LT GRN

9A L19 0.8 BRN
9B F29 0.8 BRN

8A L19 0.8 GRA

40 F19 0.8 ORN

11 H29 0.8 LT GRN
3VA L19 0.8 ORN
40 D19 0.8 ORN
13VE I19 0.8 PPL/WHT
13VF L19 0.8 PPL/WHT

13VE F19 0.8 PPL/WHT

8A B19 0.8 GRA
9A N29 0.8 BRN
3VA F19 0.8 PPL
13VF F19 0.8 PPL/WHT
150B N19 0.8 BLK

150B L19 0.8 BLK

TO FUSE BLOCK CAVITY A 12004887

TO FUSE BLOCK CAVITY B 12004886

12034003

12041433

GROMMET

12041433

12045688

BUS BAR GROUND 12015202

FOG LAMP RELAY

12047886

17 E12 0.8 PPL/WHT
E17 L17 0.8 PPL/WHT
17 L17 0.8 PPL/WHT

17 L17 0.8 BLK
15VB L17 0.8 BLK
G17 L17 0.8 BLK

13VC E12 0.8 PPL/WHT

8B L7 0.8 GRA
9E L7 0.8 BRN
3VB L7 0.8 PPL
13VC L7 0.8 PPL/WHT
150A L7 0.8 BLK

13VB
15VB
13VC

15VA
15VB
15VC

13VA E12 0.8 PPL/WHT
G12 0.8 BLK

15VC G12 0.8 BLK

13VA E12 0.8 PPL/WHT
G12 0.8 BLK

8B L17 0.8 GRA
9E L17 0.8 BRN
3VB L17 0.8 PPL
13VB L17 0.8 PPL/WHT
150A L17 0.8 BLK

RIGHT HAND FOG LAMP 12020599

GROUND

LEFT HAND FOG LAMP 12020599

FOG LAMP SWITCH

FOG LAMPS

Typical fog lamp wiring diagram

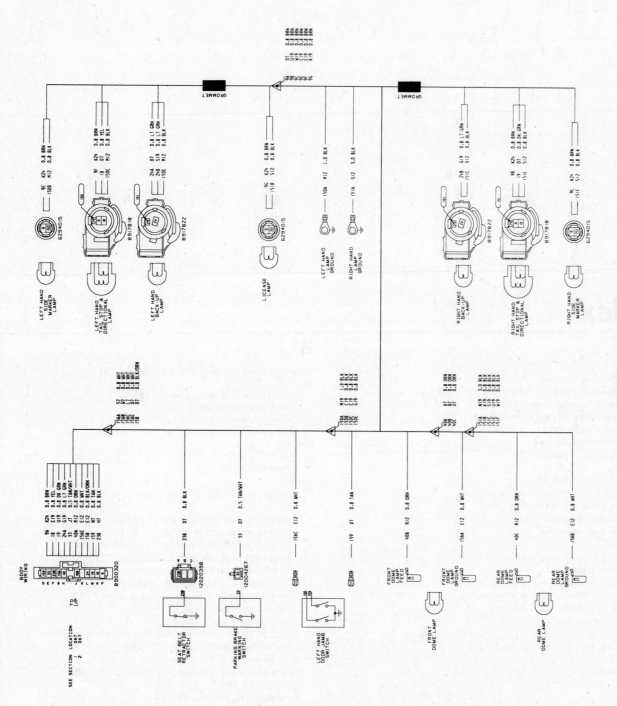

Typical rear light wiring diagram

Index

Haynes Automotive Manuals

NOTE: New manuals are added to this list on a periodic basis. If you do not see a listing for your vehicle, consult your local Haynes dealer for the latest product information.

ACURA
*1776   Integra '86 thru '89 & Legend '86 thru '90

AMC
        Jeep CJ - see JEEP (412)
694   Mid-size models, Concord, Hornet, Gremlin & Spirit '70 thru '83
934   (Renault) Alliance & Encore '83 thru '87

AUDI
615   4000 all models '80 thru '87
428   5000 all models '77 thru '83
1117   5000 all models '84 thru '88

AUSTIN-HEALEY
        Sprite - see MG Midget (265)

BMW
*2020   3/5 Series not including diesel or all-wheel drive models '82 thru '92
276   320i all 4 cyl models '75 thru '83
632   528i & 530i all models '75 thru '80
240   1500 thru 2002 except Turbo '59 thru '77

BUICK
        Century (front wheel drive) - see GM (829)
*1627   Buick, Oldsmobile & Pontiac Full-size (Front wheel drive) all models '85 thru '95
        Buick Electra, LeSabre and Park Avenue; Oldsmobile Delta 88 Royale, Ninety Eight and Regency; Pontiac Bonneville
1551   Buick Oldsmobile & Pontiac Full-size (Rear wheel drive)
        Buick Estate '70 thru '90, Electra '70 thru '84, LeSabre '70 thru '85, Limited '74 thru '79
        Oldsmobile Custom Cruiser '70 thru '90, Delta 88 '70 thru '85, Ninety-eight '70 thru '84
        Pontiac Bonneville '70 thru '81, Catalina '70 thru '81, Grandville '70 thru '75, Parisienne '83 thru '86
627   Mid-size Regal & Century all rear-drive models with V6, V8 and Turbo '74 thru '87
        Regal - see GENERAL MOTORS (1671)
        Riviera - see GENERAL MOTORS (38030)
        Skyhawk - see GENERAL MOTORS (766)
        Skylark '80 thru '85 - see GM (38020)
        Skylark '86 on - see GM (1420)
        Somerset - see GENERAL MOTORS (1420)

CADILLAC
*751   Cadillac Rear Wheel Drive all gasoline models '70 thru '93
        Cimarron - see GENERAL MOTORS (766)
        Eldorado - see GENERAL MOTORS (38030)
        Seville '80 thru '85 - see GM (38030)

CHEVROLET
*1477   Astro & GMC Safari Mini-vans '85 thru '93
554   Camaro V8 all models '70 thru '81
866   Camaro all models '82 thru '92
        Cavalier - see GENERAL MOTORS (766)
        Celebrity - see GENERAL MOTORS (829)
24017   Camaro & Firebird '93 thru '96
625   Chevelle, Malibu & El Camino all V6 & V8 models '69 thru '87
449   Chevette & Pontiac T1000 '76 thru '87
550   Citation all models '80 thru '85
*1628   Corsica/Beretta all models '87 thru '96
274   Corvette all V8 models '68 thru '82
*1336   Corvette all models '84 thru '91
1762   Chevrolet Engine Overhaul Manual
704   Full-size Sedans Caprice, Impala, Biscayne, Bel Air & Wagons '69 thru '90
        Lumina - see GENERAL MOTORS (1671)
        Lumina APV - see GENERAL MOTORS (2035)
319   Luv Pick-up all 2WD & 4WD '72 thru '82
626   Monte Carlo all models '70 thru '88

241   Nova all V8 models '69 thru '79
*1642   Nova and Geo Prizm all front wheel drive models, '85 thru '92
420   Pick-ups '67 thru '87 - Chevrolet & GMC, all V8 & in-line 6 cyl, 2WD & 4WD '67 thru '87; Suburbans, Blazers & Jimmys '67 thru '91
*1664   Pick-ups '88 thru '95 - Chevrolet & GMC, all full-size pick-ups, '88 thru '95; Blazer & Jimmy '92 thru '94; Suburban '92 thru '95; Tahoe & Yukon '95
831   S-10 & GMC S-15 Pick-ups '82 thru '93
*24071   S-10 & GMC S-15 Pick-ups '94 thru '96
*1727   Sprint & Geo Metro '85 thru '94
*345   Vans - Chevrolet & GMC, V8 & in-line 6 cylinder models '68 thru '96

CHRYSLER
25025   Chrysler Concorde, New Yorker & LHS, Dodge Intrepid, Eagle Vision, '93 thru '96
2114   Chrysler Engine Overhaul Manual
*2058   Full-size Front-Wheel Drive '88 thru '93
        K-Cars - see DODGE Aries (723)
        Laser - see DODGE Daytona (1140)
*1337   Chrysler & Plymouth Mid-size front wheel drive '82 thru '95
        Rear-wheel Drive - see Dodge (2098)

DATSUN
647   200SX all models '80 thru '83
228   B - 210 all models '73 thru '78
525   210 all models '79 thru '82
206   240Z, 260Z & 280Z Coupe '70 thru '78
563   280ZX Coupe & 2+2 '79 thru '83
        300ZX - see NISSAN (1137)
679   310 all models '78 thru '82
123   510 & PL521 Pick-up '68 thru '73
430   510 all models '78 thru '81
372   610 all models '72 thru '76
277   620 Series Pick-up all models '73 thru '79
        720 Series Pick-up - see NISSAN (771)
376   810/Maxima all gasoline models, '77 thru '84
        Pulsar - see NISSAN (876)
        Sentra - see NISSAN (982)
        Stanza - see NISSAN (981)

DODGE
        400 & 600 - see CHRYSLER Mid-size (1337)
*723   Aries & Plymouth Reliant '81 thru '89
1231   Caravan & Plymouth Voyager Mini-Vans all models '84 thru '95
699   Challenger/Plymouth Saporro '78 thru '83
        Challenger '67-'76 - see DODGE Dart (234)
610   Colt & Plymouth Champ (front wheel drive) all models '78 thru '87
*1668   Dakota Pick-ups all models '87 thru '96
234   Dart, Challenger/Plymouth Barracuda & Valiant 6 cyl models '67 thru '76
*1140   Daytona & Chrysler Laser '84 thru '89
        Intrepid - see CHRYSLER (25025)
*30034   Neon all models '94 thru '97
*545   Omni & Plymouth Horizon '78 thru '90
*912   Pick-ups all full-size models '74 thru '93
*30041   Pick-ups all full-size models '94 thru '96
*556   Ram 50/D50 Pick-ups & Raider and Plymouth Arrow Pick-ups '79 thru '93
2098   Dodge/Plymouth/Chrysler rear wheel drive '71 thru '89
*1726   Shadow & Plymouth Sundance '87 thru '94
*1779   Spirit & Plymouth Acclaim '89 thru '95
*349   Vans - Dodge & Plymouth V8 & 6 cyl models '71 thru '96

EAGLE
        Talon - see Mitsubishi Eclipse (2097)
        Vision - see CHRYSLER (25025)

FIAT
094   124 Sport Coupe & Spider '68 thru '78
273   X1/9 all models '74 thru '80

FORD
10355   Ford Automatic Trans. Overhaul
*1476   Aerostar Mini-vans all models '86 thru '96

268   Courier Pick-up all models '72 thru '82
2105   Crown Victoria & Mercury Grand Marquis '88 thru '96
1763   Ford Engine Overhaul Manual
789   Escort/Mercury Lynx all models '81 thru '90
*2046   Escort/Mercury Tracer '91 thru '96
*2021   Explorer & Mazda Navajo '91 thru '95
560   Fairmont & Mercury Zephyr '78 thru '83
334   Fiesta all models '77 thru '80
754   Ford & Mercury Full-size,
        Ford LTD & Mercury Marquis ('75 thru '82); Ford Custom 500, Country Squire, Crown Victoria & Mercury Colony Park ('75 thru '87); Ford LTD Crown Victoria & Mercury Gran Marquis ('83 thru '87)
359   Granada & Mercury Monarch all in-line, 6 cyl & V8 models '75 thru '80
773   Ford & Mercury Mid-size,
        Ford Thunderbird & Mercury Cougar ('75 thru '82); Ford LTD & Mercury Marquis ('83 thru '86); Ford Torino, Gran Torino, Elite, Ranchero pick-up, LTD II, Mercury Montego, Comet, XR-7 & Lincoln Versailles ('75 thru '86)
231   Mustang II 4 cyl, V6 & V8 models '74 thru '78
357   Mustang V8 all models '64-1/2 thru '73
*654   Mustang & Mercury Capri all models Mustang, '79 thru '93; Capri, '79 thru '86
*36051   Mustang all models '94 thru '97
788   Pick-ups & Bronco '73 thru '79
880   Pick-ups & Bronco '80 thru '96
649   Pinto & Mercury Bobcat '75 thru '80
1670   Probe all models '89 thru '92
*1026   Ranger/Bronco II gasoline models '83 thru '92
*36071   Ranger '93 thru '96 &
        Mazda Pick-ups '94 thru '96
*1421   Taurus & Mercury Sable '86 thru '95
*1418   Tempo & Mercury Topaz all gasoline models '84 thru '94
1338   Thunderbird/Mercury Cougar '83 thru '88
*1725   Thunderbird/Mercury Cougar '89 and '96
344   Vans all V8 Econoline models '69 thru '91
*2119   Vans full size '92-'95

GENERAL MOTORS
*10360   GM Automatic Transmission Overhaul
*829   Buick Century, Chevrolet Celebrity, Oldsmobile Cutlass Ciera & Pontiac 6000 all models '82 thru '96
*1671   Buick Regal, Chevrolet Lumina, Oldsmobile Cutlass Supreme & Pontiac Grand Prix front wheel drive models '88 thru '95
*766   Buick Skyhawk, Cadillac Cimarron, Chevrolet Cavalier, Oldsmobile Firenza & Pontiac J-2000 & Sunbird '82 thru '94
38020   Buick Skylark, Chevrolet Citation, Olds Omega, Pontiac Phoenix '80 thru '85
1420   Buick Skylark & Somerset, Oldsmobile Achieva & Calais and Pontiac Grand Am all models '85 thru '95
38030   Cadillac Eldorado '71 thru '85, Seville '80 thru '85, Oldsmobile Toronado '71 thru '85 & Buick Riviera '79 thru '85
*2035   Chevrolet Lumina APV, Olds Silhouette & Pontiac Trans Sport all models '90 thru '95
        General Motors Full-size
        Rear-wheel Drive - see BUICK (1551)

GEO
        Metro - see CHEVROLET Sprint (1727)
        Prizm - '85 thru '92 see CHEVY Nova (1642), '93 thru '96 see TOYOTA Corolla (1642)
*2039   Storm all models '90 thru '93
        Tracker - see SUZUKI Samurai (1626)

GMC
        Safari - see CHEVROLET ASTRO (1477)
        Vans & Pick-ups - see CHEVROLET (420, 831, 345, 1664 & 24071)

(Continued on other side)

---

* Listings shown with an asterisk (*) indicate model coverage as of this printing. These titles will be periodically updated to include later model years - consult your Haynes dealer for more information.

Haynes North America, Inc., 861 Lawrence Drive, Newbury Park, CA 91320 • (805) 498-6703

Haynes Automotive Manuals (continued)

NOTE: New manuals are added to this list on a periodic basis. If you do not see a listing for your vehicle, consult your local Haynes dealer for the latest product information.

HONDA

351	**Accord CVCC** all models '76 thru '83
1221	**Accord** all models '84 thru '89
2067	**Accord** all models '90 thru '93
42013	**Accord** all models '94 thru '95
160	**Civic 1200** all models '73 thru '79
633	**Civic 1300 & 1500 CVCC** '80 thru '83
297	**Civic 1500 CVCC** all models '75 thru '79
1227	**Civic** all models '84 thru '91
*2118	**Civic & del Sol** '92 thru '95
*601	**Prelude CVCC** all models '79 thru '89

HYUNDAI

*1552	**Excel** all models '86 thru '94

ISUZU

*1641	**Trooper & Pick-up,** all gasoline models Pick-up, '81 thru '93; Trooper, '84 thru '91
	Hombre - see *CHEVROLET S-10 (24071)*

JAGUAR

*242	**XJ6** all 6 cyl models '68 thru '86
*49011	**XJ6** all models '88 thru '94
*478	**XJ12 & XJS** all 12 cyl models '72 thru '85

JEEP

*1553	**Cherokee, Comanche & Wagoneer Limited** all models '84 thru '96
412	**CJ** all models '49 thru '86
50025	**Grand Cherokee** all models '93 thru '95
50029	**Grand Wagoneer & Pick-up** '72 thru '91 Grand Wagoneer '84 thru '91, Cherokee & Wagoneer '72 thru '83, Pick-up '72 thru '88
*1777	**Wrangler** all models '87 thru '95

LINCOLN

2117	**Rear Wheel Drive** all models '70 thru '96

MAZDA

648	**626** (rear wheel drive) all models '79 thru '82
*1082	**626/MX-6** (front wheel drive) '83 thru '91
370	**GLC Hatchback** (rear wheel drive) '77 thru '83
757	**GLC** (front wheel drive) '81 thru '85
*2047	**MPV** all models '89 thru '94
	Navajo - see Ford Explorer (2021)
267	**Pick-ups** '72 thru '93
	Pick-up '94 thru '96 - see Ford Ranger (36071)
460	**RX-7** all models '79 thru '85
*1419	**RX-7** all models '86 thru '91

MERCEDES-BENZ

*1643	**190 Series** four-cyl gas models, '84 thru '88
346	**230/250/280** 6 cyl sohc models '68 thru '72
983	**280 123 Series** gasoline models '77 thru '81
698	**350 & 450** all models '71 thru '80
697	**Diesel 123 Series** '76 thru '85

MERCURY

See FORD Listing

MG

111	**MGB** Roadster & GT Coupe '62 thru '80
265	**MG Midget, Austin Healey Sprite** '58 thru '80

MITSUBISHI

*1669	**Cordia, Tredia, Galant, Precis & Mirage** '83 thru '93
*2097	**Eclipse, Eagle Talon & Plymouth Laser** '90 thru '94
*2022	**Pick-up** '83 thru '96 & **Montero** '83 thru '93

NISSAN

1137	**300ZX** all models including Turbo '84 thru '89
*72015	**Altima** all models '93 thru '97
*1341	**Maxima** all models '85 thru '91
*771	**Pick-ups** '80 thru '96 **Pathfinder** '87 thru '95
876	**Pulsar** all models '83 thru '86
*982	**Sentra** all models '82 thru '94
*981	**Stanza** all models '82 thru '90

OLDSMOBILE

	Achieva - see *GENERAL MOTORS (1420)*
	Bravada - see *CHEVROLET S-10 (831)*
	Calais - see *GENERAL MOTORS (1420)*
	Custom Cruiser - see *BUICK RWD (1551)*
*658	**Cutlass V6 & V8** gas models '74 thru '88
	Cutlass Ciera - see *GENERAL MOTORS (829)*
	Cutlass Supreme - see *GM (1671)*
	Delta 88 - see *BUICK Full-size RWD (1551)*
	Delta 88 Brougham - see *BUICK Full-size FWD (1551), RWD (1627)*
	Delta 88 Royale - see *BUICK RWD (1551)*
	Firenza - see *GENERAL MOTORS (766)*
	Ninety-eight Regency - see *BUICK Full-size RWD (1551), FWD (1627)*
	Ninety-eight Regency Brougham - see *BUICK Full-size RWD (1551)*
	Omega - see *GENERAL MOTORS (38020)*
	Silhouette - see *GENERAL MOTORS (2035)*
	Toronado - see *GENERAL MOTORS (38030)*

PEUGEOT

663	**504** all diesel models '74 thru '83

PLYMOUTH

Laser - see *MITSUBISHI Eclipse (2097)*
For other PLYMOUTH titles, see DODGE.

PONTIAC

	T1000 - see *CHEVROLET Chevette (449)*
	J-2000 - see *GENERAL MOTORS (766)*
	6000 - see *GENERAL MOTORS (829)*
	Bonneville - see *Buick FWD (1627), RWD (1551)*
	Bonneville Brougham - see *Buick (1551)*
	Catalina - see *Buick Full-size (1551)*
1232	**Fiero** all models '84 thru '88
555	**Firebird** V8 models except Turbo '70 thru '81
867	**Firebird** all models '82 thru '92
	Firebird '93 thru '96 - see *CHEVY Camaro (24017)*
	Full-size Front Wheel Drive - see *BUICK, Oldsmobile, Pontiac Full-size FWD (1627)*
	Full-size Rear Wheel Drive - see *BUICK Oldsmobile, Pontiac Full-size RWD (1551)*
	Grand Am - see *GENERAL MOTORS (1420)*
	Grand Prix - see *GENERAL MOTORS (1671)*
	Grandville - see *BUICK Full-size (1551)*
	Parisienne - see *BUICK Full-size (1551)*
	Phoenix - see *GENERAL MOTORS (38020)*
	Sunbird - see *GENERAL MOTORS (766)*
	Trans Sport - see *GENERAL MOTORS (2035)*

PORSCHE

*264	**911** except Turbo & Carrera 4 '65 thru '89
239	**914** all 4 cyl models '69 thru '76
397	**924** all models including Turbo '76 thru '82
*1027	**944** all models including Turbo '83 thru '89

RENAULT

141	**5 Le Car** all models '76 thru '83
	Alliance & Encore - see *AMC (934)*

SAAB

247	**99** all models including Turbo '69 thru '80
*980	**900** all models including Turbo '79 thru '88

SATURN

2083	**Saturn** all models '91 thru '96

SUBARU

237	**1100, 1300, 1400 & 1600** '71 thru '79
*681	**1600 & 1800** 2WD & 4WD '80 thru '89

SUZUKI

*1626	**Samurai/Sidekick &Geo Tracker** '86 thru '96

TOYOTA

1023	**Camry** all models '83 thru '91
92006	**Camry** all models '92 thru '95
935	**Celica Rear Wheel Drive** '71 thru '85
*2038	**Celica Front Wheel Drive** '86 thru '93
1139	**Celica Supra** all models '79 thru '92
361	**Corolla** all models '75 thru '79
961	**Corolla** all rear wheel drive models '80 thru '87
1025	**Corolla** all front wheel drive models '84 thru '92
*92036	**Corolla & Geo Prizm** '93 thru '96
636	**Corolla Tercel** all models '80 thru '82
360	**Corona** all models '74 thru '82
532	**Cressida** all models '78 thru '82
313	**Land Cruiser** all models '68 thru '82
*1339	**MR2** all models '85 thru '87
304	**Pick-up** all models '69 thru '78
*656	**Pick-up** all models '79 thru '95
*2048	**Previa** all models '91 thru '95
2106	**Tercel** all models '87 thru '94

TRIUMPH

113	**Spitfire** all models '62 thru '81
322	**TR7** all models '75 thru '81

VW

159	**Beetle & Karmann Ghia** '54 thru '79
238	**Dasher** all gasoline models '74 thru '81
96019	**Golf & Jetta** all models '93 thru '97
*884	**Rabbit, Jetta, Scirocco, & Pick-up** gas models '74 thru '91 & Convertible '80 thru '92
451	**Rabbit, Jetta & Pick-up** diesel '77 thru '84
082	**Transporter 1600** all models '68 thru '79
226	**Transporter 1700, 1800 & 2000** '72 thru '79
084	**Type 3 1500 & 1600** all models '63 thru '73
1029	**Vanagon** all air-cooled models '80 thru '83

VOLVO

203	**120, 130 Series & 1800 Sports** '61 thru '73
129	**140 Series** all models '66 thru '74
*270	**240 Series** all models '76 thru '93
400	**260 Series** all models '75 thru '82
*1550	**740 & 760 Series** all models '82 thru '88

TECHBOOK MANUALS

2108	**Automotive Computer Codes**
1667	**Automotive Emissions Control Manual**
482	**Fuel Injection Manual, 1978 thru 1985**
2111	**Fuel Injection Manual, 1986 thru 1996**
2069	**Holley Carburetor Manual**
2068	**Rochester Carburetor Manual**
10240	**Weber/Zenith/Stromberg/SU Carburetors**
1762	**Chevrolet Engine Overhaul Manual**
2114	**Chrysler Engine Overhaul Manual**
1763	**Ford Engine Overhaul Manual**
1736	**GM and Ford Diesel Engine Repair Manual**
1666	**Small Engine Repair Manual**
10355	**Ford Automatic Transmission Overhaul**
10360	**GM Automatic Transmission Overhaul**
1479	**Automotive Body Repair & Painting**
2112	**Automotive Brake Manual**
2113	**Automotive Detailing Manual**
1654	**Automotive Eelectrical Manual**
1480	**Automotive Heating & Air Conditioning**
2109	**Automotive Reference Manual & Dictionary**
2107	**Automotive Tools Manual**
10440	**Used Car Buying Guide**
2110	**Welding Manual**
10450	**ATV Basics**

SPANISH MANUALS

98903	**Reparación de Carrocería & Pintura**
98905	**Códigos Automotrices de la Computadora**
98910	**Frenos Automotriz**
98915	**Inyección de Combustible 1986 al 1994**
99040	**Chevrolet & GMC Camionetas** '67 al '87 Incluye Suburban, Blazer & Jimmy '67 al '91
99041	**Chevrolet & GMC Camionetas** '88 al '95 Incluye Suburban '92 al '95, Blazer & Jimmy '92 al '94, Tahoe y Yukon '95
99042	**Chevrolet & GMC Camionetas Cerradas** '68 al '95
99055	**Dodge Caravan & Plymouth Voyager** '84 al '95
99075	**Ford Camionetas y Bronco** '80 al '94
99077	**Ford Camionetas Cerradas** '69 al '91
99083	**Ford Modelos de Tamaño Grande** '75 al '87
99088	**Ford Modelos de Tamaño Mediano** '75 al '86
99095	**GM Modelos de Tamaño Grande** '70 al '90
99118	**Nissan Sentra** '82 al '94
99125	**Toyota Camionetas y 4-Runner** '79 al '95

* Listings shown with an asterisk (*) indicate model coverage as of this printing. These titles will be periodically updated to include later model years - consult your Haynes dealer for more information.

Over 100 Haynes motorcycle manuals also available

5-97

Haynes North America, Inc., 861 Lawrence Drive, Newbury Park, CA 91320 • (805) 498-6703

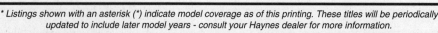